Section	VSTS Tools	Agile Practices
7: Implement Customer Testing	Generic Test Adapter	Real Customer Involvement (page 456)
8: Estimate, Prioritize and Plan	Task Management tools	Stories (page 513) Weekly Cycle (page 536) Quarterly Cycle (page 538) Slack (page 559)
9: Practice for Deployment	Logical Datacenter Designer Application Designer System Designer Deployment Designer	Daily Deployment (page 584) Incremental Deployment (page 590)
10: Provide and Reveal Value	Report Site Report Designer	Informative Workspace (page 673) Root-Cause Analysis (page 687)

Visual Studio Team System

Microsoft .NET Development Series

John Montgomery, *Series Advisor*
Don Box, *Series Advisor*
Martin Heller, *Series Editor*

The Microsoft .NET Development Series is supported and developed by the leaders and experts of Microsoft development technologies including Microsoft architects. The books in this series provide a core resource of information and understanding every developer needs in order to write effective applications and managed code. Learn from the leaders how to maximize your use of the .NET Framework and its programming languages.

Titles in the Series

Brad Abrams, *.NET Framework Standard Library Annotated Reference Volume 1: Base Class Library and Extended Numerics Library*, 0-321-15489-4

Brad Abrams and Tamara Abrams, *.NET Framework Standard Library Annotated Reference, Volume 2: Networking Library, Reflection Library, and XML Library*, 0-321-19445-4

Chris Anderson, *Essential Windows Presentation Foundation (WPF)*, 0-321-37447-9

Keith Ballinger, *.NET Web Services: Architecture and Implementation*, 0-321-11359-4

Bob Beauchemin and Dan Sullivan, *A Developer's Guide to SQL Server 2005*, 0-321-38218-8

Don Box with Chris Sells, *Essential .NET, Volume 1: The Common Language Runtime*, 0-201-73411-7

Keith Brown, *The .NET Developer's Guide to Windows Security*, 0-321-22835-9

Eric Carter and Eric Lippert, *Visual Studio Tools for Office: Using C# with Excel, Word, Outlook, and InfoPath*, 0-321-33488-4

Eric Carter and Eric Lippert, *Visual Studio Tools for Office: Using Visual Basic 2005 with Excel, Word, Outlook, and InfoPath*, 0-321-41175-7

Mahesh Chand, *Graphics Programming with GDI+*, 0-321-16077-0

Krzysztof Cwalina and Brad Abrams, *Framework Design Guidelines: Conventions, Idioms, and Patterns for Reusable .NET Libraries*, 0-321-24675-6

Len Fenster, *Effective Use of Microsoft Enterprise Library: Building Blocks for Creating Enterprise Applications and Services*, 0-321-33421-3

Sam Guckenheimer and Juan J. Perez, *Software Engineering with Microsoft Visual Studio Team System*, 0-321-27872-0

Anders Hejlsberg, Scott Wiltamuth, Peter Golde, *The C# Programming Language*, Second Edition, 0-321-33443-4

Alex Homer and Dave Sussman, *ASP.NET 2.0 Illustrated*, 0-321-41834-4

Joe Kaplan and Ryan Dunn, *The .NET Developer's Guide to Directory Services Programming*, 0-321-35017-0

Mark Michaelis, *Essential C# 2.0*, 0-321-15077-5

James S. Miller and Susann Ragsdale, *The Common Language Infrastructure Annotated Standard*, 0-321-15493-2

Christian Nagel, *Enterprise Services with the .NET Framework: Developing Distributed Business Solutions with .NET Enterprise Services*, 0-321-24673-X

Brian Noyes, *Data Binding with Windows Forms 2.0: Programming Smart Client Data Applications with .NET*, 0-321-26892-X

Brian Noyes, *Smart Client Deployment with ClickOnce: Deploying Windows Forms Applications with ClickOnce*, 0-321-19769-0

Fritz Onion with Keith Brown, *Essential ASP.NET 2.0*, 0-321-23770-6

Fritz Onion, *Essential ASP.NET with Examples in C#*, 0-201-76040-1

Fritz Onion, *Essential ASP.NET with Examples in Visual Basic .NET*, 0-201-76039-8

Ted Pattison and Dr. Joe Hummel, *Building Applications and Components with Visual Basic .NET*, 0-201-73495-8

Scott Roberts and Hagen Green, *Designing Forms for Microsoft Office InfoPath and Forms Services 2007*, 0-321-41059-9

Dr. Neil Roodyn, *eXtreme .NET: Introducing eXtreme Programming Techniques to .NET Developers*, 0-321-30363-6

Chris Sells and Michael Weinhardt, *Windows Forms 2.0 Programming*, 0-321-26796-6

Dharma Shukla and Bob Schmidt, *Essential Windows Workflow Foundation*, 0-321-39983-8

Guy Smith-Ferrier, *.NET Internationalization: The Developer's Guide to Building Global Windows and Web Applications*, 0-321-34138-4

Paul Vick, *The Visual Basic .NET Programming Language*, 0-321-16951-4

Damien Watkins, Mark Hammond, Brad Abrams, *Programming in the .NET Environment*, 0-201-77018-0

Shawn Wildermuth, *Pragmatic ADO.NET: Data Access for the Internet World*, 0-201-74568-2

Paul Yao and David Durant, *.NET Compact Framework Programming with C#*, 0-321-17403-8

Paul Yao and David Durant, *.NET Compact Framework Programming with Visual Basic .NET*, 0-321-17404-6

For more information go to www.awprofessional.com/msdotnetseries/

Visual Studio Team System

Better Software Development for Agile Teams

■ Will Stott
James Newkirk

♦ Addison-Wesley

Upper Saddle River, NJ • Boston • Indianapolis • San Francisco
New York • Toronto • Montreal • London • Munich • Paris • Madrid
Capetown • Sydney • Tokyo • Singapore • Mexico City

Many of the designations used by manufacturers and sellers to distinguish their products are claimed as trademarks. Where those designations appear in this book, and the publisher was aware of a trademark claim, the designations have been printed with initial capital letters or in all capitals.

The authors and publisher have taken care in the preparation of this book, but make no expressed or implied warranty of any kind and assume no responsibility for errors or omissions. No liability is assumed for incidental or consequential damages in connection with or arising out of the use of the information or programs contained herein.

The publisher offers excellent discounts on this book when ordered in quantity for bulk purchases or special sales, which may include electronic versions and/or custom covers and content particular to your business, training goals, marketing focus, and branding interests. For more information, please contact:

U.S. Corporate and Government Sales
(800) 382-3419
corpsales@pearsontechgroup.com

For sales outside the United States please contact:

International Sales
international@pearsoned.com

 This Book Is Safari Enabled

The Safari® Enabled icon on the cover of your favorite technology book means the book is available through Safari Bookshelf. When you buy this book, you get free access to the online edition for 45 days.

Safari Bookshelf is an electronic reference library that lets you easily search thousands of technical books, find code samples, download chapters, and access technical information whenever and wherever you need it.

To gain 45-day Safari Enabled access to this book:

• Go to http://www.www.awprofessional.com/safarienabled

• Complete the brief registration form

• Enter the coupon code 8THJ-6XJI-TPHH-RSI5-U9QW

If you have difficulty registering on Safari Bookshelf or accessing the online edition, please e-mail customer-service@safaribooksonline.com.

Visit us on the Web: www.awprofessional.com

Library of Congress Cataloging-in-Publication Data

Stott, Will.
    Visual studio team system : better software development for agile teams / Will Stott, James Newkirk.
        p. cm.
    Includes bibliographical references and index.
    ISBN 978-0-321-41850-0 (pbk. : alk. paper)
    1. Microsoft Visual studio. 2. Computer software—Development. 3. eXtreme programming. I. Newkirk, James. II. Title.

QA76.76.D47S775 2007
005.3—dc22

2007008442

ISBN 13: 978-0-321-41850-0
ISBN 10:   0-321-41850-6
Text printed in the United States on recycled paper at Courier in Stoughton, Massachusetts.
First printing, May 2007

For
Mark Newton Brearley
and
Beth Melanie Newkirk

Contents at a Glance

Preface xxvii
Acknowledgments xxxv
About the Authors xxxvii

Introduction: Broken Process 1

Section 1: Apply Sharp Tools and Values 9
1   Introduction to Visual Studio Team System   13
2   Agile Values   33
Review of Section 1: Sharp Tools and Values 45

Section 2: Introduce Agile Development 49
3   Overview of Agile Development   53
4   Forming an Agile Team   65
5   Team Foundation Process Frameworks   81
6   Improving Your Process Framework   107
Review of Section 2: Introduce Agile Development 119

Section 3: Use Version Control 123
7   Managing Change   127
8   Setting Up TFS Version Control   149
9   Using TFVC in Your Project   173
10 Policing Your Project with TFVC   191
Review of Section 3: Use Version Control 205

Section 4: Build and Integrate Often 209
11 Building and Integrating Software   213
12 Working with Team Foundation Build   229
Review of Section 4: Build and Integrate Often 255

Section 5: Practice Test-Driven Development 261
13 Introduction to TDD   265
14 Developing Your First Tests   283

15   Learning to Refactor   303
16   Code Coverage and Performance   325
17   Integrating TFP Code with a User Interface   339
Review of Section 5: Practice Test-Driven Development   351

Section 6: Explore by Modeling   357
18   Modeling with Agility   361
19   Creating Models   375
20   Using Models in an Agile Project   395
21   Modeling Solutions with Patterns   415
Review of Section 6: Explore by Modeling   433

Section 7: Implement Customer Testing   439
22   Involving Customers in Testing   443
23   Creating FIT Fixtures   459
24   Running FIT with Team Foundation Build   481
Review of Section 7: Implement Customer Testing   501

Section 8: Estimate, Prioritize, and Plan   507
25   Estimating and Prioritizing Stories   511
26   Agile Planning   527
27   Managing Agile Projects   545
Review of Section 8: Estimate, Prioritize, and Plan   571

Section 9: Practice for Deployment   577
28   Moving into Production   581
29   Developing Installation Programs   597
30   Deployment of Distributed Systems   625
Review of Section 9: Practice for Deployment   661

Section 10: Provide and Reveal Value   665
31   Producing Technical Reports   669
32   Generating Business Value   683
Review of Section 10: Provide and Reveal Value   693

Retrospective: Fixing the Process   697
Section 11: Appendixes   713
A   Setting Up VSTS for the Exercises   715
B   Software Project Environment for a Small Team   729
C   Agile Workspace   753

List of Exercises   763
List of Extreme Programming Practices   771
Glossary   773
Bibliography   789
Resources   797
Index   805

Contents

Preface   xxvii

Acknowledgments   xxxv

About the Authors   xxxvii

Introduction: Broken Process   1

Welcome to the OSPACS Team   1

Team Background   1

Current Organizational Structure and Personas   2

The Team's Road Map for Fixing Its Process   6

Section 1: Apply Sharp Tools and Values   9

Story from the Trenches   10

1 Introduction to Visual Studio Team System   13

The Purpose and Structure of VSTS   13

Elevator Pitch   14

Typical Organization of VSTS for a Small Team   14

Functional Components of VSTS   16

Client Parts of VSTS   17

Differentiation of VSTS Products   17

Visual Studio Professional   18

Team Explorer   20

VSTS Tools   22

Server Parts of VSTS　27
Team Foundation Server (TFS)　27
Project Portal and Report Sites　27
Team Foundation Build　29
Extending VSTS　30
Visual Studio Industry Partner Program　30
Visual Studio SDK　30

2　Agile Values　33
Tools and Values　33
Buy or Build?　34
Software Values and Traditions　35
The Agile Alliance　36
Extreme Programming (XP)　37
Communication　39
Feedback　40
Courage　41
Simplicity　42
Respect　43

Review of Section 1: Sharp Tools and Values　45
The Team's Impressions　45
Agile Values　46

Section 2: Introduce Agile Development　49
Story from the Trenches　50

3　Overview of Agile Development　53
What Is Different about an Agile Project?　53
No Separate Development Phases　54
Specifying Requirements with Customer Stories　55
Introduction to Extreme Programming　57
Software Project Life Cycle　58
Iterative and Incremental　58
Iteration and Release Cycles　59

Iterations Deliver Production-Quality Code   60

Project Closure   61

Isn't XP Just Hacking?   62

Why XP Doesn't Encourage Hacking   63

4 Forming an Agile Team   65

The Nature of Agile Teams   65

Working As a Design Team   66

Self-Organizing Teams   68

Team Size   68

Work That Doesn't Suit Agile Teams   69

Agile Team Structure   70

Customer Roles   70

Developer Roles   72

Associated Roles   75

Reorganizing the OSPACS Team   76

Identifying Customers and Developers   76

Rearranging the Office Space   78

5 Team Foundation Process Frameworks   81

Team Projects and Process Frameworks   81

Artifacts Generated When a Team Project Is Created   82

Creating an MSF for Agile Software Development Team Project   85

Deleting a Team Project   87

Giving Users Membership of Your Team Project Groups   88

Gaining Access to Your Team Project Services   89

Administering Your Team Project Security Settings   91

Administering Your TFS Security Settings   92

Connecting to a Team Project   93

Microsoft Solutions Framework (MSF) 4.0   95

Work Item   96

Role   97

Activity   97

Work Stream   97

Tracks and Governance Checkpoints   98

Frameworks for Specific Processes   100

    MSF for CMMI Process Improvement   100

    MSF for Agile Software Development   102

    MSF for XP   102

    Process Framework Comparison   103

6   Improving Your Process Framework   107

Providing a New Metric for an Existing Process Framework   107

    Adding a New Work Item Type   108

    Adding a New Query   109

Improving Your Process   110

    Process Template Structure   111

    Importing and Exporting Process Templates   112

    Changing Your Process Template   115

Review of Section 2: Introduce Agile Development   119

The Team's Impressions   120

Agile Values   121

Section 3: Use Version Control   123

Story from the Trenches   124

7   Managing Change   127

Sharing Information among Your Team   127

    Why You Shouldn't Keep Source Files in Shared Folders   128

    Keeping Source Files in a Repository   129

Using a Version Control System   133

    Security   133

    Frequent Integration   134

    Atomic Check-in   134

    Rolling Back Versions   134

    Storing Deltas   135

    Locking and Merging   136

    Labeling and Branching   138

    Software Configuration Management   142

VSTS Support for Version Control Tools   144

   Integration with Visual Studio   144

   TFVC Features   145

   TFS Support for Eclipse and Other Types of IDEs   147

8   Setting Up TFS Version Control   149

Structuring Your Team Project   149

   Production and Spike Folders   149

   Organization of Visual Studio Solutions, Projects, and Directories   151

   Deciding What to Put into Version Control   154

   Version Control for Team Documents   156

   Archiving Third-Party Libraries   158

Establishing the Initial Baseline for Your Project   160

   Adding Files and Directories to Version Control   160

   Check In and Label the Baseline   164

Other Set-Up Tasks   166

   Importing Source Files   166

   Team Project Version Control Options   167

   Visual Studio Source Control Options   168

   Setting Up Security   169

   Backup and Restore   170

9   Using TFVC in Your Project   173

Using TFVC When Coding   173

   Sample Programming Episode: Version Control   174

Common Version Control Tasks   177

   Using Workspaces   177

   Merging Changes   180

   Rolling Back to a Previous Version   183

   Creating a Branch   185

   Creating a Shelve   187

10   Policing Your Project with TFVC   191

Protecting Your Source Code   191

   Controlling Access to Individual Files and Folders   192

   Setting Check-in Constraints   193

Establishing Policies for Source Code   195
    Coding Standards   195
    Static Code Analysis   196
    Setting Static Code Analysis As a Check-in Policy   198
    Implementing New Coding Standards   200
    Updating Static Code Analysis Rules   201
    Overriding Check-in Policies   201

Review of Section 3: Use Version Control   205
The Team's Impressions   206
Agile Values   207

Section 4: Build and Integrate Often   209
Story from the Trenches   210

11 Building and Integrating Software   213
Software Construction   213
    Building and Integrating As a Team   214
    Automated Build Lab   214
    Software Integration and Test Environment   216
Automated Software Testing   217
    Smoke Tests   219
    Functional Tests   219
    Structural (Unit) Tests   220
    Quality of Service Tests   220
    Integration Testing   221
Build and Test Cycles   222
    Local Build   222
    Integration Build   225
    Daily Build   227

12 Working with Team Foundation Build   229
Welcome to Team Foundation Build   229
    Setting Up Team Foundation Build   230
    How Team Foundation Build Works   230
    The Role of MSBuild   231
    Making a Build Validation Test   233

Setting Team Build Permissions 235

Creating Team Build Types 237

Scheduling a Daily Build 239

Sample Programming Episode: Integration Build 240

Deleting Build Products 243

Build Management 245

Process Technician Role 245

Build Notification 246

Build Identification 247

Build Reports 248

Scaling Up Team Integration Builds 249

Incremental Builds 250

Optimizing Package Dependencies for Building 251

Review of Section 4: Build and Integrate Often 255

The Team's Impressions 256

Agile Values 258

Section 5: Practice Test-Driven Development 261

Story from the Trenches 262

13 Introduction to TDD 265

The Nature of Test-Driven Development 265

Settling into the Rhythm of Test-First Programming 265

Top Down versus Bottom Up 268

Simple Test-First Programming Exercises 269

Define the List of Tests 269

Set Up a Basic Test Harness 269

TFP Cycle for the First Test 271

TFP Cycle for the Second Test 273

Review of the Exercises 276

Getting Started with Test-First Programming 277

Applying TFP on Your Team 277

Creating a List of Tests 278

Finding Additional Tests 278

Refactoring 280

14 **Developing Your First Tests 283**

Creating Visual Studio Projects for TFP 283

How VSTS Supports Unit Testing 283

Setting Up Visual Studio Projects for Unit Testing 285

The Story behind the Tests 287

About the "Image Favorites" Story 288

Dividing the Story into Tasks 288

Create a Test List 289

Finding Your Initial Tests 289

Record the Test List 291

Organization of Your Test List Code 293

Shelving Your Test List Code 293

Implementing the Tests 294

Start with the Easiest Test 294

Fix a Failing Test and Refactor 296

Comments about the Refactoring 299

Do the Next Three Tests Yourself 300

15 **Learning to Refactor 303**

Doing Small Refactorings 303

Implement a Collection 304

Refactor the Test 306

Refactor the Production Code 308

Safely Changing Code Implementation 309

Comments about the Refactoring 312

Refactor As You Go 313

Implementing More of the Requirement 313

Refactoring Opportunities 316

Doing a Big Refactoring 318

Remove the Middle Man 318

Changing the Type of a Collection 319

Take a Break 322

16 **Code Coverage and Performance 325**

Code Coverage 325

How to Generate Code Coverage Information 326

Performance Analysis   331

 Sampling   332

 Instrumentation   332

 Example Performance Profiling Session   332

 Improving Your Library Code's Performance   335

 Improving System Performance   337

17 Integrating TFP Code with a User Interface   339

Implementing the User Interface   339

 Define the User Interface   340

 Create a Task List   341

 Implement the Windows Forms Application   342

 Aim to Create a Thin User Interface Layer   344

Simple Design   346

 Code Criteria for Simple Design   347

 Avoiding Big Design Up Front   348

Review of Section 5: Practice Test-Driven Development   351

The Team's Impressions   352

Agile Values   354

Reinforcement of Agile Practices   355

 Pair Programming   356

 Shared Code   356

 Single Code Base   356

 Ten Minute Build   356

 Continuous Integration   356

Section 6: Explore by Modeling   357

Story from the Trenches   358

18 Modeling with Agility   361

Introduction to Modeling   361

 Models and Process   362

Values, Principles, and Practices of Agile Modeling   363

 Values   363

 Principles   363

 Practices   364

Agile Modeling in Use   366

Group Modeling   367

Modeling in Pairs   370

Agile Model-Driven Development   372

19 **Creating Models**   375

Free-form Diagrams   375

UML Diagrams   377

Class Diagram Notation   377

Sequence Diagram Notation   382

Using Modeling Tools   385

Class Designer   385

Visio for Enterprise Architects   389

Top Ten Tips for Drawing Diagrams   391

20 **Using Models in an Agile Project**   395

Requirement Models   395

Domain Models and CRC Cards   396

User Interface Models   401

Use Case Models   403

Customer Stories   404

Architectural Models   405

The Architect's Role on an Agile Team   406

Creating a Skeletal Architectural Model   406

Evolving Your Architectural Model   408

System Metaphor   411

Implementation Models   411

Structural Models   412

Dynamic Models   413

21 **Modeling Solutions with Patterns**   415

What Is a Pattern?   415

Pattern Languages   416

Example: The Façade Pattern   417

Sources of Patterns   419

Using Patterns in an Agile Project   421
    Example: Evolving Legacy Code with the Façade Pattern   422
Implementation of Patterns and Models   424
    Design Patterns versus Components   425
    Reusable Components   425
Emergence of Domain-Specific Languages   426
    Use of DSL in Horizontal Market Applications   427
    The Language Workbench   427
    Software Factories   429

Review of Section 6: Explore by Modeling   433
The Team's Impressions   434
Agile Values   436

Section 7: Implement Customer Testing   439
Story from the Trenches   440

22 Involving Customers in Testing   443
Agile Customer Testing   443
    Testing throughout the Project   444
FIT: Framework for Integrated Test   445
    Overview   445
    Installing and Running FIT   447
    Test Organization   453
Storytest-Driven Development   454
    Costs and Benefits of STDD   455
    Role of Testers in STDD   457
    Relationship of Customer Testing to Your Release Process   457

23 Creating FIT Fixtures   459
Standard FIT Fixtures   459
    Column Fixtures: Testing Decisions in the Business Layer   460
    Row Fixtures: Testing Lists in the Data Layer   465
    Action Fixtures: Testing Workflow in the User Interface Layer   470
Custom FIT Fixtures   476
    Example of a Custom Fixture   476

24 Running FIT with Team Foundation Build 481

Performing Customer Tests in Your Build Lab 482

Wrapping FIT in a Generic Test 482

Running a Generic Test in Your Build Lab 485

Automated Customer Testing 487

Running Customer Tests in Team Foundation Build 487

Allowing Your Customers to Edit and Run Tests from Their PCs 489

Introducing Your Team to Customer Testing 491

Discussions around a Whiteboard 492

Putting the Information into a Table 493

Implementing the Fixtures for the Story 495

Using Sequences of Tables in Customer Tests 496

Top Ten Tips for Test Design 498

Review of Section 7: Implement Customer Testing 501

The Team's Impressions 502

Agile Values 504

Section 8: Estimate, Prioritize, and Plan 507

Story from the Trenches 508

25 Estimating and Prioritizing Stories 511

Working with Customer Stories 511

Overview 512

Generating Stories 514

Estimating 516

Sizing Stories 516

Absolute Values versus Relative Values for Estimation 517

Relative Estimate Scales 519

Task Points and Story Cost Estimation 519

Budgeting 521

Prioritizing 521

Value 522

Business Risk 522

Technical Risk 523

Removing Dependencies 524

26 **Agile Planning** 527

  The Nature of Plans 527

    Plans for Repeated Execution versus One-Time Plans 528

    Agile Planning 528

    Using Velocity to Measure Rate of Progress 529

  Planning at Every Time Scale 530

    Task Plan 531

    Iteration Plan 534

    Release Plan 536

  Controlling Plans 538

    Levers of Control 539

    Story Life Cycle 541

27 **Managing Agile Projects** 545

  Using Visual Studio Team System for Project Management 545

    Project Structure 546

    Work Item Types and Queries 547

    Documents 551

    Reports 554

  Example Agile Planning Life Cycle 556

    Start of Iteration 556

    Sample Programming Episode: Task Planning 560

    Between Programming Episodes 561

    Planning Customer Tests 562

    Completing a Story 563

    Completing a Bug Fix 563

    Daily Meetings 564

    End of the Iteration 565

    Release Planning 566

  Top Ten Tips for Managing Agile Projects 567

Review of Section 8: Estimate, Prioritize, and Plan 571

  The Team's Impressions 572

  Agile Values 574

Section 9: Practice for Deployment 577

Story from the Trenches 578

28 Moving into Production 581

Managing Deployment 581

The Release Process 582

Removing Bottlenecks 585

Handing Over the Release to a Deployment Team 586

Preparing for Deployment 587

The Installation Program 588

Deploying the First Iteration 589

Stubs and Scaffolding 591

Data Deployment 591

Monitoring the Production Environment 592

Logging 593

Creating a Support Web Site 594

29 Developing Installation Programs 597

Introduction to Windows Installer 597

Basic Concepts 598

Principles of Operation 600

Security 602

Creating an Installation Project with InstallShield 604

Using InstallShield with Visual Studio 604

Using the InstallShield IDE 605

Developing Installation Programs on an Agile Team 613

InstallShield Collaboration 614

Automating the Creation of Your Installation Program 619

ClickOnce Technology 620

Suitable Applications 620

Basic Concepts 621

Publishing and Deploying 622

30 Deployment of Distributed Systems 625

Distributed System Architecture 625

Distributed Components 626

Service-Oriented Architecture (SOA) 626

System Definition Model (SDM) 627

VSTS Distributed System Designers 628

Logical Datacenter Designer 629

Creating a Logical Model of a Datacenter 629

Endpoints and Servers in Your Toolbox 633

Properties, Settings, and Constraints 634

Importing Settings from Your Existing IIS 636

Application of LDD Models 637

Application Designer 638

Creating an AD Diagram 638

Defining Settings and Constraints 648

Application of AD Models 648

System Designer 649

Creating SD Diagrams 649

Defining Settings and Constraints 652

Application of SD Models 652

Deployment Designer 653

Creating a DD Diagram 653

Deployment Properties 655

Validating Deployment 656

Creating a Deployment Report 657

Application of DD Models 658

Review of Section 9: Practice for Deployment 661

The Team's Impressions 662

Agile Values 664

Section 10: Provide and Reveal Value   665

Story from the Trenches   666

31 Producing Technical Reports   669

Revealing Valuable Information   669

Standard Queries and Reports   670

Gathering and Presenting Information   672

Big Visible Charts   673

Extracting Data from Team Foundation Server   674

Introduction to the TFS Data Warehouse   675

Accessing Data in the TFS Relational Database   676

Creating a Custom Report from the TFS OLAP Database   677

32 Generating Business Value   683

Lean Thinking   683

Specifying Value   684

Identifying the Value Stream   684

Making Value Flow   685

Allowing the Customer to Pull Value   686

Seeking Perfection   686

Changing the Economics of Software Development   688

Value Generated by an Agile Project   689

Value Generated by a Waterfall Project   689

Linking Agile to Other Process Improvement Initiatives   690

Agile Development in the Context of Design for Six Sigma   691

Review of Section 10: Provide and Reveal Value   693

The Team's Impressions   693

Agile Values   695

Retrospective: Fixing the Process   697

About Retrospectives   697

Preparation   698

Creating a Plan   699

The OSPACS Team's Retrospective   700

Developing a Timeline   700

Other Exercises   704

Analysis of the Project Timeline   705

Structure of the Project   705

Things They Discovered   706

Has the OSPACS Team Fixed Its Process?   708

Is the OSPACS Team Extreme?   709

How the OSPACS Team Became Agile   710

Personal Agility   710

Appendixes   713

A   Setting Up VSTS for the Exercises   715

Set Up a Single Evaluation Server   717

Setting Up Team System VPC   717

Setting Up TFS Trial Edition   719

Set Up TFS and Team Suite on a Network   720

Hardware Overview   720

Team Foundation Server for Workgroups   720

Setting Up a Software Project Environment   721

Actions for All Set-Up Options   721

Software Installation   722

System Settings   723

Setting Up User Accounts and Security Groups   724

Identification of Machines and Users Named in the Exercises   726

B   Software Project Environment for a Small Team   729

Hardware Requirements   729

Computers   730

Other Equipment   732

Software Requirements   733

Software Tools to Buy and Install on the OSPACS Developer PCs   733

Software Products to Buy and Install on Server PCs   735

Software Supplied with Other Products   736

Open Source or Freely Available Software   738

Licensing Issues for a Five-Person Team   739

Primary Domain Controller   739

TFS (DevServer)   740

Developer PCs   743

Architect PC   745

Tester PC   746

BuildLab PC   747

Standby TFS   748

Multiprocessor PCs and Multicore Processors   749

Increasing Your Team beyond Five People   749

C   Agile Workspace   753

Basic Office Layout   753

Software Development Area   754

Kitchen Area   756

Hot-Desk Area   756

Library Area   758

Conference Room   758

Supplies and Equipment   759

Imposing the Team's Individuality   760

List of Exercises   763

List of Extreme Programming Practices   771

Glossary   773

Bibliography   789

Resources   797

Index   805

Preface

SCIENCE IS FOUNDED on the principle of creating experiments that give the same results each time they are performed. Unfortunately, a software development project isn't like a scientific experiment because the outcome is always different. Even teams that use the same tools and process will still produce different solutions to the same task, each unique in terms of code set, bugs, performance, and so forth. This variability arises because the results of software development depend upon individuals and their interactions as much as the process and tools they employ.

The idea that the outcome of a software project is largely dependent upon people and the way they work together caused Kent Beck to observe the habits of successful teams and then put them into a framework of values and practices, which he called Extreme Programming (XP). This provided an alternative to the decades-old notion that the only way to impose order upon software development was to apply expensive tools and a well-prescribed process. XP joined a number of similar lightweight approaches to software development, collectively known as Agile, which shared the common aim of satisfying customers through the early and continuous delivery of valuable software. Over the past five years, this Agile movement has grown to become a significant driver of change in our industry.

Agile seems to have successfully captured the middle ground of software development methodologies. Teams with too little process to guide them have found that embracing Agile allows them to make significant improvements in the outcome of their projects, without creating the sort of bloated bureaucracy they fear. Teams with too much process have found that adopting an Agile approach has made them much more productive and responsive, but without their projects descending into the sort of chaotic hacking they fear. Thousands of projects have been run along Agile lines. They haven't all succeeded, but this is to be expected because any worthwhile software project involves a degree of risk. However, plenty of these projects have produced spectacular results, and once people have tried Agile, they seldom want to return to their old ways of doing things. We suspect this is simply because most people find it, as we do, to be a more pleasurable and rewarding way to develop software.

> **■ NOTE**
>
> This book is primarily based on the values and practices of Extreme Programming as described in Kent Beck's book, *Extreme Programming Explained.*[1] We apply them in the context of a five-developer team using Microsoft's Visual Studio 2005 Team System.

Who Should Read This Book?

This is a book for people on real teams who are transitioning to Microsoft's Visual Studio Team System (VSTS), but who might not yet be ready to fully embrace a process such as MSF for Agile Software Development. It is written for people who want an easy way to gain value from the tools and at the same time lay the foundations for future process improvement. We envision our readers to include the following:

- **People new to software development**—Teaches you how to use VSTS and gives you the core skills you need in order to work effectively on an Agile team. There are few assumptions about your

---

1. [XPE2] Beck, Kent, with Cynthia Andres. *Extreme Programming Explained, Second Edition* (Addison-Wesley, 2005).

technical background, but some knowledge of using Visual Studio will help when completing the exercises.

- **Experienced developers**—Puts what you already know into the context of an Agile project and explains how to make good use of the new tools provided by VSTS. People who are encountering Microsoft technology for the first time should find the exercises and glossary particularly useful.

- **Architects**—Explains the new VSTS tools for software architects, but its real value lies in helping you to adapt your skills so that you can add value to an Agile team.

- **Testers**—Helps you understand the expanded role of testers on an Agile team and explains how to use the basic VSTS tools needed to test software in this new Software Project Environment.

- **Business analysts and customers**—Explains how an Agile approach can give your business a better return on investment. You'll also learn how an Agile team works to make sure you get the software you want, when you need it.

- **Project managers**—Describes how to transition your people onto a small Agile team so that they can deliver better-quality software, in less time and for less cost. In addition, you'll discover how VSTS gathers information about a project into one place to make the running of the project more transparent.

- **Software entrepreneurs**—Provides you with a road map for setting up a small, top-performing software team. It reveals the key technical and people issues you need to address through a series of anecdotes and comments gleaned from the decades we've spent working in the industry.

This book is not about process improvement applied from the top of an organization downward, it's about empowering teams to change things for themselves from the bottom up.

Tools Needed

In order to follow the exercises in this book, you will need access to an existing installation of VSTS or have the ability to install Visual Studio Team Suite in one of the following environments:

- Desktop PC able to host the Microsoft Virtual PC
- Single-server PC running Windows Server 2003 (SP2 or R2)
- Network comprising a server and several desktop PCs

You will be glad to hear that Visual Studio Team Suite is freely available from Microsoft's technical Web site[2] as a trial edition (full functionality, but expires after 180 days) as well as for purchase from your usual Microsoft reseller. In addition, MSDN subscribers can obtain Team System VPC, which is a "ready to run" virtual machine image of VSTS for use with the freely available Microsoft Virtual PC. Appendix A covers how to set up VSTS in all of these environments.

■ NOTE

Framework for Integrated Test (FIT) is required for Section 7, but it is freely available from the C2 Web site.[3] InstallShield and Installation Collaboration are needed for the exercises in Chapter 29, but free evaluation editions are available on the Macrovison Web site.[4]

Structure of the Book

The book's Introduction contains a story about a fictional software team called OSPACS that has a broken process; the team always delivers late, has high staff turnover, and is surprised to discover that its software is full of

---

2. Microsoft's Web site for Visual Studio Team System (http://msdn.microsoft.com/teamsystem).
3. Ward Cunningham's C2 Web site for FIT (http://fit.c2.com).
4. Macrovision's Web site for InstallShield (www.macrovision.com/downloads).

bugs and has gone three times over budget. The rest of the book is about how the team fixed these problems, but along the way we aim to give you insight into the use of VSTS and the meaning of better software development for a small Agile team.

The main body of the book is divided into ten sections, each concerned with a specific aspect of software development as practiced by Agile teams. These sections are ordered into a sequence that helps build up a team's proficiency in a step-by-step manner. For example, we don't present information about project planning until we've covered material such as testing and Team Build because clearly your team's plans will not be very reliable until you can dependably deliver quality software. However, with that said, each section is largely self-contained, so you can read them in any order that makes sense to you. Indeed, we expect this to happen as each reader will have different priorities for things they want to learn about.

Each section starts with a short story and ends with a review describing how the OSPACS team put the ideas into practice, the team's impressions about the material, and its relationship to a set of Agile values. In this way, we provide you with some light relief from the technical stuff while presenting another perspective on the subject matter that might help you apply it on your own team. Within each section, the chapters usually start by explaining some basic concepts and then put them in a practical context by giving you a series of exercises to follow using the tools provided by VSTS. You will also find sidebars in various chapters that summarize particular XP practices relevant to what is being discussed. In this way, theory and practice are put together into something that is hopefully reasonably entertaining and interesting to read.

■ NOTE

At the back of the book is information about relevant resources, a glossary, a bibliography, and a number of appendixes, as well as a list of the XP practices and a complete list of all the exercises.

Conventions

The XP practices listed on the inside cover are described in appropriate places throughout the book as sidebars which are given a different font and layout to distinguish them from the main body of the text. In addition to normal printing conventions, the following special conventions are also used in the book:

> **▪ TIP**
>
> Best practice or suggestion.

> **▪ WARNING**
>
> Issue that requires particular care or consideration.

> **▪ NOTE**
>
> Item of particular interest.

[XPE2]	Reference to an item in the bibliography.
File ∣ New ∣ Team Project	Shorthand for "select the menu item New from the File menu and then select its Team Project submenu item."
Right-click ∣ Delete	Shorthand for "choose Delete from the selected item's context menu."
… the Agile team	Words that are capitalized are used in a specific sense, so here we mean a team that shares the values of the *Agile* software movement.

> **■ NOTE**
>
> James Newkirk and Will Stott collaborated in the production of this book, but as Will did most of the writing, it's his voice you hear when you read something such as "I did so and so" or "We did this and that."

About the Book's Web Site

We have created a Web site for this book that contains most of the code created for the exercises, information about any errors in the text found after publication, and other supplementary material which we feel might be useful to readers:

www.BetterSoftwareDevelopment.org

We strongly encourage people to visit this site for the latest information about both VSTS and Agile software development. We would be delighted to receive feedback from readers and will try to respond to you as promptly as our other work commitments allow.

Acknowledgments

THE IDEA FOR THIS BOOK came from Sam Guckenheimer after Will Stott met him at a conference in Germany at the end of 2004. He has been hugely supportive of this project and we couldn't have done it without him. In addition, Joan Murray at Addison-Wesley has been a constant source of encouragement to us and handled a lot of administrative work so that we could get on with the writing. There are also many behind-the-scenes people at Addison-Wesley, including Audrey Doyle and Lara Wysong, whose professionalism and hard work in terms of getting the book from Word files to bookstore shelves need to be acknowledged, so thank you all.

The process of reviewing a manuscript is an essential part of the publishing process and adds considerably to the quality of the final work. Our formal reviewers have done an outstanding job of pointing out our mistakes and suggesting improvements, as well as telling us what needed to be pruned from the text. Therefore, we gratefully acknowledge the help of Scott Ambler, Raimond Brookman, Peter Himschoot, Jason Schmitt, and David Yak. In addition, we received many useful comments about the manuscript's first draft from George Bullock, Stuart Celarier, and Matt Ranlett. We also want to express our appreciation to Linda Rising for her comments about the Retrospective, as well as to Chris Page, Corey Ferengul, and Bob Corrigan at Macrovision for their input about InstallShield in Chapter 29. Though many people at Microsoft have helped us in various ways over the past two years, we must especially thank Bill Essary and Ajay Sudan for their comments about the licensing issues in Appendix B.

Will Stott would like to express his gratitude to James Newkirk, as well as to the people at Exoftware who encouraged him to write this book, especially Sean Hanly. He is also indebted to the many people he met through the London Extreme Tuesday group for their assistance and insights into the then-emerging field of Extreme Programming, particularly Tim Bacon, Peter Brown, Rachael Davies, Peter Lappo, Duncan Pierce, David Putman, and Karl Scotland. In addition, he thanks Chris Jones and Andy Ryan of University College London for providing the idea for the OSPACS project. Will also thanks his family and friends for their love and support, as well as the many other people he has met who have helped him in ways both large and small over the years. In particular he remembers the great inspiration provided by his physics teacher, the late Mr. Brown of Rossall School, and the practical help given during the writing of this book by Mark Brearley, Liz Hooper, Simon and Ann Battensby, Damain and Marnie Hopkins, and Lee Hyde and Anna Acland.

James Newkirk would like to thank Will Stott for his dedication to the project. The book simply would not have happened without Will. I would also like to acknowledge the support of my wife, Beth. Over the years, she has supported me through my various career moves and side projects. Thank you.

> **■ NOTE**
>
> We owe a huge debt to Kent Beck and others in the Agile community for promoting Extreme Programming, which forms the solid and well-proven foundation of our book.

About the Authors

Will Stott is a freelance consultant originally from the United Kingdom who now lives in Switzerland. He is an associate of Exoftware, a European company helping organizations to become more Agile in their software development practices. Will has worked with Microsoft technologies since the early days of MS-DOS and now specializes in C++ and C# development using Visual Studio. He has published a number of articles about Agile development and has spoken at various conferences in the United Kingdom and Europe.

James Newkirk is the product unit manager for CodePlex, Microsoft's community open source project hosting site. In this role, he is responsible for the site's strategic direction and product development. He is the coauthor of *Test Driven Development in Microsoft .NET* (Microsoft Press, 2004). Prior to joining Microsoft he coauthored "Enterprise Solution Patterns in .NET" (Microsoft patterns & practices) and *Extreme Programming in Practice* (Addison-Wesley, 2001). In between writing books and consulting on software projects, James led the development of NUnit V2.

◼ Introduction
Broken Process

I F YOUR PROCESS isn't broken, don't fix it! That is to say, if nobody wants to leave your team and it reliably delivers the best possible value to the business in the required time without any unexpected quality or cost issues, think carefully about adopting Visual Studio Team System (VSTS) or becoming an Agile team. This book is not written for people who already have a sound software development process, but rather for those who want to change their process because it is broken in some way.

Welcome to the OSPACS Team

The OSPACS team is entirely fictional and none of its members are intended to represent actual people. However, the team's problems are typical of those we've actually encountered over the past couple of decades while working for numerous organizations, and the characters are woven together from some of the individuals we've met during this time. Therefore, we have no reservations about treating the OSPACS team as though it were real.

Team Background
The OSPACS team is part of a small IT company in the healthcare business. Eighteen months ago it entered into a joint venture agreement with the Old Sainsbury (OS) Hospital for the development of a new Picture Archiving and Communication System[1] (PACS) intended to capture, store, and display digital images such as X-rays and ultrasound scans. The team released

---

1. Find out more about PACS at the AuntMinnie Web site (www.auntminnie.com).

the first version of this system to the hospital three months ago. However, it was not a great success, as the team had gone three times over its budget, delivered the product six months late, and then spent another two and a half months fixing its bugs.

The team's morale reached a low point a month ago, mainly because everyone was so exhausted after working weekends and late into the night to get the system into production. They then lost two key programmers to a competitor and rumors started circulating that more people were ready to follow them. However, we join the team as its outlook is starting to look a bit brighter, because it has been more than two weeks since the last serious bug was found and the system has finally gone "live" in the hospital's radiology department. Therefore, people are no longer working overtime and can start considering the next phase of the project, which is the development of a generic version of the system for deployment into other hospitals. Mike Hancock (CEO) recently showed his support for this new work by hiring a new senior programmer (Peter Powell) as well as agreeing that the team could upgrade its MSDN subscriptions to get Visual Studio Team Suite.

Current Organizational Structure and Personas

The OSPACS team is organized into a typical hierarchy so that its three programmers report to the project manager, who then reports to the CEO. The business analyst and test manager also report directly to the CEO, which effectively creates three separate departments: programming, test, and product development.

CEO: Mike Hancock

Mike is a serial entrepreneur who set up the company after selling his previous business to a large multinational. He spends most of his time driving the sales force and doesn't really understand why he can't manage the software team in the same way. However, Mike realizes that software people are very different from his salespeople, so he has learned to keep his distance from the OSPACS team.

"The team gives me a project plan that schedules its every task for the next three months, but a week later it's already out-of-date."

"These software people cost me a fortune, and I haven't a clue what they do all day."

Business Analyst/Sales: Sally Thompson

Sally worked as a business analyst for a major medical equipment manufacturer before she joined the company three years ago. The extensive knowledge she has about the business, combined with her skill at handling customers, means she has a joint business analyst and sales role reporting directly to Mike.

"If 80 percent of the value lies in 20 percent of the features, why do we bother developing 80 percent of our software?"

"Our project manager seems to spend most of the day hiding in his office, producing reports that nobody reads."

"The opportunities that arise have usually gone by the time we've developed the software."

Test Manager: Maggie Smith

Maggie was one of the original employees of the company and is good friends with its most senior programmer, Sarah Brown. However, this doesn't stop her from being very critical about the poor quality of the software landing on her desk from the development department.

"Sometimes when writing my tests, I just have to guess what the program is supposed to do. Sally needs to spend time helping me understand the customer requirement."

"Programmers don't seem to think that testing is part of their job description. There must be a better way of doing things."

"There's a cultural chasm between the development department and the test department."

Project Manager/Architect: Tom Stanton

Tom is the intellectual powerhouse of the company and knows a lot about different types of software engineering methodologies. However, so far this knowledge hasn't helped him create a successful team.

"People are very dissatisfied with their jobs, and poor tools don't help. I need to fix this problem fast, as we can't afford to lose anymore people."

"Rebuilding all the components takes us days, and then getting them to work together takes weeks of effort."

"I don't know why Sally produces all these long functional specifications, because none of the programmers reads them."

Senior Programmer: Sarah Brown

Sarah is the only programmer left from the original group that started OSPACS. Her software development skills are largely self-taught and she prefers writing code to producing elegant documents and Unified Modeling Language (UML) drawings. Without Sarah, there would be no system and no OSPACS team, so she is highly regarded by everyone, particularly Mike.

"Everyone works on his own separate components because people lock files out of SourceSafe for weeks at a time. The team just doesn't share a common code base."

"We always talk about restructuring the code for the next release, but when the time comes, there's always something else that takes priority."

"Deploying software into our client's environment is always a nightmare because we ship so infrequently that each time it feels like we've never done it before."

"The gap between us releasing each batch of code to testing just keeps on getting longer."

Senior Programmer: Peter Powell

Peter joined the team a couple of weeks ago. Before that, he spent five years working as a contractor for a variety of blue-chip companies. He has already established a reputation for being a bit of a geek who spends most of his time plugged into an iPod, writing code that no one else understands. Peter knows a bit about Extreme Programming (XP), though he has not yet put it into practice in a real project.

"The team needs to feel ownership of the process rather than feeling owned by it."

"When I look at the existing OSPACS code it's full of stuff that doesn't seem to have any real purpose. I'm not sure what's working code and what's still under construction."

"It seems to me that Visual Studio Team System, put into the wrong hands, could stop a project dead in its tracks."

Junior Programmer: Luke Harrison

Luke joined the company straight after graduating from college, where he earned a computer science degree. Initially he found it very difficult to relate his studies to what was happening in the company, but he has since come to realize that there's a difference between what happens in textbooks and what happens on a real team.

"Our installation program always works fine on my PC, but it often fails when we run it on our customer's machines."

"We spent months creating UML models for the first version of the product and then threw them away a week into coding. Our design work simply doesn't survive into implementation."

"We haven't really got a process—certainly not one that works."

The Team's Road Map for Fixing Its Process

Tom had first read about XP in the April 2004 edition of *MSDN Magazine*,[2] but at the time he put off introducing these ideas to the team because he was too busy. However, he now realizes that some drastic action is required, so transitioning the team to Agile development is now at the top of his agenda.

Last week Tom contacted some people from his local Agile community and persuaded them to explain their philosophy to the team during a few lunchtime sessions. The OSPACS team liked what it heard about Agile. However, the team decided to tackle its problems by taking a series of small evolutionary steps, because as well as developing the new generic version of its system, it also has to support the one installed in the Old Sainsbury Hospital. Therefore, following the advice given by one of the Agile experts it had met, the team identified its main problems as shown in Table I-1 and agreed to address these issues by undertaking the corresponding activities over the next six to nine months. In this way, the team hoped to build up its expertise and at the same time reinvent itself as an Agile team.

■ TIP

Contact your nearest Agile user group[3] to find people who might help your team make its transition to Agile. These groups usually attract people who are using some form of Agile process in their work and want to share this experience with others.

---

2. *MSDN Magazine* Web site (http://msdn.microsoft.com/msdnmag).
3. The Agile Alliance Web site lists user groups under Resources (www.agilealliance.com).

TABLE I-1: The OSPACS Team's Road Map

Team Building	
"People are very dissatisfied with their jobs, and poor tools don't help." "There's a cultural chasm between the development and the test departments."	Apply Sharp Tools and Values
"We haven't really got a process—certainly not one that works." "The team needs to feel ownership of the process rather than feeling owned by it."	Introduce Agile Development
Achieving a Consistent Level of Quality	
• "The team just doesn't share a common code base."	Use Version Control
• "Rebuilding all the components takes us days, and then getting them to work together takes weeks of effort." • "The gap between us releasing each batch of code to testing just keeps on getting longer."	Build and Integrate Often
• "Programmers don't seem to think that testing is part of their job description." • "Full of code that doesn't seem to have any real purpose."	Practice Test-Driven Development
• "Our design work simply doesn't survive into implementation."	Explore by Modeling
Satisfying Customer Requirements	
• "When writing my tests I just have to guess what the program is supposed to do." • "I don't know why Sally produces all these long functional specifications, because none of the programmers reads them."	Implement Customer Testing

Continues

TABLE I-1: *Continued*

Releasing Software on Time and on Budget	
• "The team gives me a project plan that schedules its every task for the next three months, but a week later it's already out-of-date."	Estimate, Prioritize, and Plan
• "We ship so infrequently that each time it feels like we've never done it before." • "Our installation program always works fine on my PC, but it often fails when run on our customer's machines."	Practice for Deployment
Delivering Business Value	
• "If 80 percent of the value lies in 20 percent of the features, why do we bother developing 80 percent of our software?" • "The opportunities that arise have usually gone by the time we've developed the software."	Provide and Reveal Value

■ WARNING

Do not expect any instant results from adopting Agile practices and tools such as Visual Studio Team System. It often takes a year (or even longer) for a team to get into the sweet spot of Agile development, though some of the benefits usually show up much sooner.

■ Section 1
Apply Sharp Tools and Values

T HE FIRST CHAPTER in this section introduces Visual Studio Team System (VSTS) and briefly reviews the tools it provides. However, it is important for you to realize that having a set of shiny new tools doesn't always lead to the development of better software. Therefore, the second chapter of this section presents some Agile values that may help you make good use of this product.

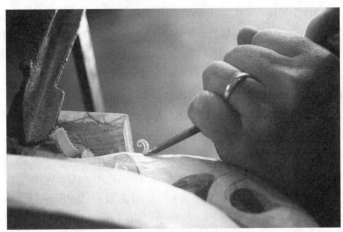

Photograph by Peter Buckley (Copyright Peter Buckley 2005).

A good craftsman doesn't blame his tools, because he selects them carefully, keeps them well maintained, and uses them properly. The people on your team also need to invest time acquiring good tools and learning how best to apply them.

Story from the Trenches

My first real job was working as a junior field engineer for an oil service company. It involved lowering instruments on the end of a cable 30,000 feet or so down a bore hole, to determine the exact depth of the well's oil bearing zones. Once this had been done, some high explosives were detonated at these depths to get oil to flow into the bore hole and thereby validate our measurements. The company was paid a huge amount of money to perform this service, and I was under a lot of pressure to come up with accurate answers in the shortest possible time.

I had a small team of people to help me, so I didn't have to do much manual work, but one of the tasks I was not allowed to delegate was connecting up the explosives. This involved attaching a detonator to the end of some primer cord that ran to the shaped charges in the gun. In order to get an efficient transfer of the detonator's explosive power, it was necessary to make a clean cut at the end of the primer cord so that it could be pushed into the detonator and sit flat against the fuse.

I had successfully fired hundreds of these perforating guns, until one day when I failed to make the cleanest of cuts through the primer cord because the blade of my knife was blunt. The problem only became apparent an hour later, after the shaped charges failed to detonate. It cost me three hours of rig time to retrieve the gun, make a repair, and then lower it down the bore hole again. This was not the first time my old knife had let me down, so I hurled it into the well-site mud in disgust, resolving to buy a new one as soon as I got back to town.

During the long journey back from the well site, I started to think about buying the new knife, and this made me consider the sort of tool my friend, Mark Barfield, used to cut primer cord. He was someone who always seemed to do things right. Mark wouldn't just buy a new tool; he would also learn how to use and maintain it properly. Then I started to realize that the root cause of my problems lay with me and my values rather than with the knife. The reason Mark succeeded more often than I did was not because he had better tools, but because his values were superior to mine. He put quality at the center of everything he did. I didn't need a new knife as much as a better set of values in my life, and this is something I'm still struggling to put into practice 25 years later.

Visual Studio Team System cannot help a team develop better software if its real problems are rooted in its values. For this reason, this book is as much about people as it is about technology.

▪ 1
Introduction to Visual Studio Team System

V ISUAL STUDIO TEAM SYSTEM (VSTS) is a huge product and we could fill this book simply explaining all its features and describing everything it contains. However, our intention is to show you how a small Agile team might use VSTS to help it develop better software, so we will concentrate on covering those parts of the product that help achieve this objective. We will not make any assumptions about your architecture or about what you're developing—Web site, stand-alone application, or whatever. Nevertheless, after reading this chapter, you should know enough about VSTS to discover the areas of the product that might help your team, and you should know whether those areas are covered in this book or elsewhere.

The Purpose and Structure of VSTS

The Microsoft technical Web site[1] contains a lot of information about VSTS, but for the benefit of anyone who hasn't already visited this site, we start with a quick review of the product, a look at the way a small team might use it, and a description of its main functional components.

---

1. MSDN: Microsoft Developer Network (http://msdn.microsoft.com).

Elevator Pitch

Geoffrey Moore[2] describes producing a vision about a product that can be recited to a prospective customer in the time taken for an elevator ride, so such a pitch about VSTS from a Microsoft staffer might go as follows:

Visual Studio Team System is for all the people working on a team developing Windows software; developers, testers, architects, and project managers. It provides them with a complete Software Project Environment so that their development process flows smoothly.

In the past, whenever a team started a project it had to assemble an assortment of different tools and then get them to work together: Visual Studio, NUnit, NANT, SourceSafe, and so on. VSTS now integrates everything a team needs into a common extensible environment that collects all project information in one place. It supports the entire software development life cycle, from analyzing requirements, through design, coding, build, and test, to actual deployment of your software products. Also, a process-enabling framework is built into VSTS, so you can start a wizard, select a process template, and then let VSTS set up everything you need to start your project: process guidance, source control, project management, reporting, bug tracking, project Web site, and so forth. Setting up a project in this way takes maybe an hour, and when you're done, you've got all the tools and infrastructure you need in order to work like a top-performing team.

That's the end of the sales talk. From now on we'll look at VSTS from the perspective of someone who needs to produce some commercial software in a working environment such as that shown in Figure 1-1. In fact, you could look at this book as a story about how the OSPACS team set up and operated this kind of Software Project Environment in order to reinvent itself as a small Agile team.

Typical Organization of VSTS for a Small Team

To help you put VSTS into some sort of physical context, Figure 1-1 illustrates the main components of VSTS as they might be set up in the OSPACS Software Project Environment.

---

2. Moore, Geoffrey. *Crossing the Chasm* (Harper Collins, 2002).

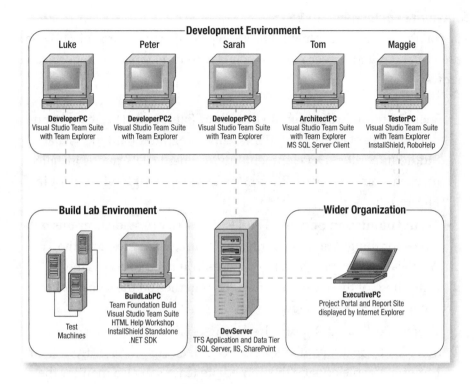

Figure 1-1: Structure of VSTS in a small-team Software Project Environment

> **■ NOTE**
>
> Appendix A describes the setup you need for the purposes of following the exercises in this book, and Appendix B specifies the typical hardware, software, and license requirements for a five-person team.

Although our book focuses on the scenario of a small team employing an Agile process such as Extreme Programming (XP), you should appreciate that VSTS is also capable of supporting large teams using a variety of Agile and formal methodologies, including MSF for Agile Software Development, MSF for CMMI Process Improvement, the Rational Unified Process (RUP), and Scrum. Indeed, the single-server configuration of VSTS shown in Figure 1-1 is likely to prove adequate for most teams unless they have many hundreds of users or are dispersed at multiple sites in different geographical locations.

Functional Components of VSTS

The collaborative environment that VSTS provides for your project is composed of client and server parts which can be functionally categorized as follows:

- **Visual Studio Professional with Team Explorer**—The Team Foundation Server (TFS) Client Tier is fully integrated with the Visual Studio Integrated Development Environment (IDE) and is installed on each team member's PC; see the Development Environment in Figure 1-1.

- **Team Foundation Server**—The TFS Data Tier provides various data stores for things such as your team's source code files, and the TFS Application Tier provides the services you need to access them. Typically, both of these tiers are installed together on the same server; see the DevServer in Figure 1-1.

- **Project Portal and Report Sites**—These TFS-hosted Web sites are accessed by team members from VSTS Team Explorer or from their browser. People outside the immediate team can also monitor the status and progress of the project from their browser, though licenses are required, as mentioned in Appendix B.

- **Team Foundation Build**—Components in the TFS Application Tier work in conjunction with Team Build to automatically build the team's software products from their shared source code stored on the TFS Data Tier. Normally you would install Team Build on a dedicated machine; see the BuildLabPC in Figure 1-1.

■ NOTE

The TFS Installation Guide[3] explains how to set up the Data and Application Tiers on different servers and then further distribute the Data Tier among a cluster of servers. It also describes how to cache the TFS on a proxy server so that teams can operate in remote locations.

---

3. TFS Installation Guide (http://go.microsoft.com/fwlink/?LinkId=40042).

Client Parts of VSTS

The client parts of VSTS are provided by Visual Studio Professional and Team Explorer, as well as by the various tools supplied with the particular product installed on your PC. However, before looking at these parts in detail, let's review the way Microsoft has divided VSTS into a set of products that can be sold to different sorts of people on a development team.

Differentiation of VSTS Products

In some cases, teams (such as OSPACS) will swallow the expense and install VSTS on all their PCs so that everyone gets Visual Studio Professional with Team Explorer, as well access to the complete set of VSTS tools. However, in other cases, teams will want to save money by just installing various combinations of the specific editions of VSTS on their PCs. In this way, each person gets Visual Studio Professional with Team Explorer as well as the following subset of VSTS tools according to their role on the team:

- **Visual Studio Team Edition for Developers**—Contains the common tools listed in Table 1-1, as well as the specific developer tools listed in Table 1-2. It is aimed at people who write code as well as structural (unit) tests.

- **Visual Studio Team Edition for Testers**—Contains the common tools listed in Table 1-1, as well as the specific tester tools listed in Table 1-3. It is aimed at people who write functional, Web, and load tests as well as people who manage the team's test suites.

- **Visual Studio Team Edition for Architects**—Contains the common tools listed in Table 1-1, as well as the specific developer tools listed in Table 1-4. It is aimed at people who want to model the deployment of a distributed Web-services-based system into a variety of different datacenters.

- **Visual Studio Team Edition for Database Professionals**—Contains tools useful to database developers. However, we decided against covering it in this book so that we could focus on the more general issues of software development.

■ NOTE

We recommend that Agile teams install Visual Studio Team Suite, if their budgets allow. Appendix B explains the licensing limitations faced by teams that decide to install just the different subsets of the Team System tools on their PCs.

Visual Studio Professional

Visual Studio Professional provides an IDE that allows you to edit files and create programs using the .NET language compilers and other tools supplied with the freely available .NET Software Development Kit (SDK).[4] This book's bibliography lists a number of excellent books covering the use of Visual Studio, so rather than describe it in detail here we'll just look at some of the principal window types you need to know about to follow the exercises in this book:

- **Main window**—Typically used to work with the file you have opened or created. Depending upon the type of file selected, different types of editing functions may be available to you.

- **Solution Explorer window**—A dockable window that displays your team's Visual Studio Solutions, Projects, and files in a treeview. Typically, a team would create one Visual Studio Solution for the product it is developing and then have separate Visual Studio Projects for each different assembly (.exe, .dll) it wants to build.

- **Class View**—A dockable window that displays the classes associated with each Visual Studio Project in your Visual Studio Solution. These classes are listed in a hierarchy to show their complete inheritance relationships. Selecting a particular class displays its properties, methods, and so on.

When Visual Studio 2005 with Team Explorer is put on your PC, a number of additional windows become available to you. The purpose of these

---

4. Microsoft's Web site for the .NET Framework (http://msdn.microsoft.com/netframework).

windows will become apparent as you complete the exercises, but the most important ones you need to know about are the following:

- **Team Explorer window**—This window is concerned with your Team Project (which you should not confuse with a Visual Studio Project) and contains information such as work items, documents, reports, and build results. We describe this window in more detail in the following section.

- **Source Control Explorer window**—This window lists the source files belonging to your team that have been added to TFS version control. We discuss this window further in Chapter 8.

- **Test View**—This window lists all the tests created for your team's project and allows you to execute one or more of them; see Exercise 14-3 in Chapter 14.

- **Test Manager window**—This window allows you to organize collections of tests into a hierarchy of test suites which can be executed to validate your Team Builds; see Exercise 12-1 in Chapter 12. However, this window is available only to people with Team Suite (or Team Edition for Testers).

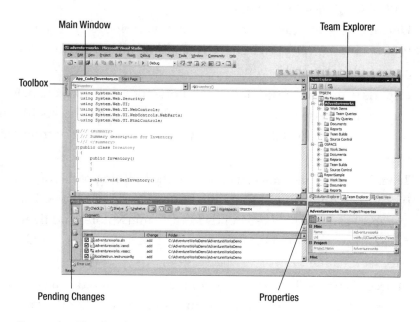

FIGURE 1-2: The Visual Studio IDE with Team Explorer

> **■ NOTE**
>
> You can pin dockable windows to a particular edge of the main window or detach and place them anywhere on your desktop. For example, in Figure 1-2, the Team Explorer window is pinned to the top right and other windows are pinned to the left and bottom.

Team Explorer

Visual Studio's Team Explorer window provides the main user interface of your TFS Client Tier and is composed of a treeview whose root item contains the name of the TFS to which you are connected, and whose first-level items correspond to the collection of Team Projects on this TFS to which you have membership rights. Looking at the Team View window in Figure 1-3 you get some idea of the sorts of things a Team Project is concerned with:

- **Work items**—You can break down the work necessary to complete your project into various items of work categorized into different types. You can then assign these individual work items (such as tasks and bugs) to people, schedule them, and track them to help control the project; see Chapter 27.
- **Documents**—You can store important project documents on the Project Portal (project Web site) to help disseminate information among the team and beyond.
- **Reports**—You can create standard reports for your project to help communicate issues and status among the team; see Chapter 31. You can run these reports directly from your Team Explorer or from the Report Site.
- **Team Builds**—The team can automate the building of its software products in different ways and on different build machines. Team members can initiate these builds from Team Explorer and then obtain the results from the corresponding Build Reports stored by TFS; see Chapter 12.
- **Source Control**—The team's source files can be stored in a version control system so that different team members can alter the same file in different ways without causing a conflict; see Chapter 7.

Most of the actual information about your team and its project is stored in a SQL Server database on the TFS Data Tier. The benefit of bringing all this data together in a single integrated system such as VSTS is that it allows you to automate many of the dull and laborious jobs associated with gathering management information and distributing it among the team. Therefore, rather than having to use separate spreadsheets, paper forms, and so forth, you can gather and distribute information directly from Visual Studio, often with no more than a click of your mouse button. This means teams can spend less time running a bureaucracy and more time analyzing and learning from the real-time information their project is generating.

> **■ NOTE**
>
> You create a Team Project to help organize a group of people who are developing software together, whereas you create a Visual Studio Project to organize a group of files for the purposes of building some form of executable (.exe, .dll, etc.).

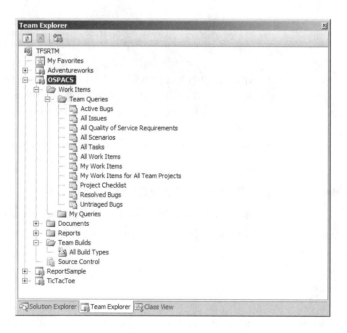

FIGURE 1-3: Team Explorer window (View | Team Explorer)

Although most of the time your Team Explorer window will be connected to your team's TFS, you can also continue working with Visual Studio while disconnected. For example, you might work at home for a few days and then reestablish your Team Explorer connection when you return to the office so that your PC is resynchronized with the work the rest of the team did while you were away. However, as you might expect, when disconnected from your TFS, the Team Explorer window will be empty and certain items in Visual Studio's Main menu will no longer appear.

VSTS Tools

Tables 1-1 through 1-4 describe the VSTS tools provided with the various Team Editions as of the end of 2006. However, you should confirm that this information is up-to-date by looking at the "Team System Editions Comparison" document available from the Production Information area of Microsoft's technical Web site for VSTS.[5]

Tools Provided with All VSTS Editions

Anyone who has any of the VSTS products installed on his PC will have access to the tools in Table 1-1.

> ■ **NOTE**
>
> People who have installed Team Suite will gain access to all the tools in Tables 1-1 through 1-4, as well as the tools provided by Team Edition for Database Professionals, which, as previously mentioned, we do not cover in this book.

Tools Provided with Visual Studio Developer Edition

People who have just installed Visual Studio Team Edition for Developers on their PCs will find the tools listed in Table 1-2 integrated with their Visual Studio IDE.

---

5. Microsoft's Web site for Visual Studio Team System (http://msdn.microsoft.com/teamsystem).

TABLE 1-1: Tools Available in All VSTS Editions

Tool	Description	References
Process Framework and Guidance	The content of your Team Explorer window provides a framework for your team's process that is determined by the template selected when the Team Project is created. People can also access a Web site that is created at the same time as their Team Project to obtain guidance about the software development process they are following.	Chapters 5, 6
Class Designer	Class Designer permits people to design and discuss the structure of programs using standard graphical representations.	Chapter 19
Visio and UML Modeling	Microsoft Office Visio for Enterprise Architects lets teams create a variety of technical diagrams for use cases, classes, database entity relationships, and so forth. It can also be used to perform round-trip engineering, generating code from Unified Modeling Language (UML) diagrams, and vice versa.	Chapter 19

TABLE 1-2: VSTS Tools for Developers

Tool	Description	References
Static Code Analysis	Select rules that you can apply to your source code (or assemblies) to produce a report about its conformance to project standards and good coding practice guidelines. Under the covers, this tool is actually FxCop for managed code and PREfast for unmanaged code (C/C++).	Chapter 10

Continues

TABLE 1-2: *Continued*

Tool	Description	References
Dynamic Code Analyzer (Performance Profiler)	You can sample or instrument your code to provide runtime information about thread states, call stacks, memory allocation, function execution times, and so on.	Chapter 16
Unit Test	Allows you to test the methods (and other parts) belonging to your classes with assertlike statements to check that they produce the expected results. It provides an alternative to the popular open source unit testing tool, NUnit.[6]	Chapters 14, 15
Code Coverage	Allows you to see which statements have and have not been executed during a test or debugging session.	Chapter 16

■ **NOTE**

You can still use NUnit with VSTS, and utilities exist for converting NUnit tests into VSTS unit tests. For further details, see Microsoft's Web site for Visual Studio Team System and the NUnit Web site.

Tools Provided with Visual Studio Tester Edition

People who have just installed Visual Studio Team Edition for Testers on their PCs will find the tools listed in Table 1-3 integrated with their Visual Studio IDE.

■ **NOTE**

Agile teams should try to combine the role of tester (and architect) with that of developer. However, a team that has opted to install the separate Team Editions rather than the Team Suite will find that its licenses restrict this sort of role assimilation; see Appendix B.

---

6. NUnit Web site (www.nunit.org).

TABLE 1-3: VSTS Tools for Testers

Tool	Description	References
Unit Test and Code Coverage	The same tools provided to software developers; refer to Table 1-2.	Chapters 14, 15
Test Case Management	Lets you organize individual tests by dragging them from the Test View window into a hierarchy of test suites (lists) displayed in a treeview. In this way, you can execute a set of related tests simply by running the required test suite.	Chapter 12
Generic Test Adapter	Allows you to wrap a third-party test program so that it can be run like a native Visual Studio test.	Chapter 24
Load Testing	Simulates users accessing a server during the execution of a test suite to measure its response under a variety of load conditions. Run the Team Test Load Agent on multiple PCs if you need to simulate a load that is beyond the limits of a single machine.	(not covered)
Web Test	Tests a Web application either by recording a user session or by creating a coded Web test using C# or Visual Basic. It is often used in conjunction with the Load Testing tool.	(not covered)
Manual Testing	Provides a mechanism for incorporating a manual script based on a Word document in a test and recording its results. This is used when it is impractical to create an automated test.	(not covered)
Ordered Test Adapter	Normally test cases are independent, so you can execute them in any order. However, certain test cases may be order-dependent, so this adapter allows you to specify the order of test cases in a test suite.	(not covered)

Tools Provided with Visual Studio Architect Edition

People who have just installed Visual Studio Team Edition for Architects on their PCs will find the tools listed in Table 1-4 integrated with their Visual Studio IDE.

TABLE 1-4: VSTS Tools for Architects

Tool	Description	References
Logical Datacenter Designer (LDD)	An architect works with operations staff to create a logical model of their datacenter using the LDD tool. This model captures the resources available in the datacenter as logical entities (rather than as physical devices) and includes security parameters, available ports, and datacenter policies relevant to deployment.	Chapter 30
Application Designer (AD)	An architect works with the developers on the team to create a model of the components they are developing using the AD tool. This model defines the constraints and interfaces for components which provide as well as consume Web services.	Chapter 30
System Designer (SD)	An architect uses the SD tool to model systems as units of deployment by aggregating the sort of applications defined in an AD model or by combining existing SD models. Therefore, armed with a collection of AD and SD models, an architect might satisfy a new business requirement simply by recombining existing applications into some form of new system.	Chapter 30
Deployment Designer (DD)	An architect uses the DD tool to model the deployment of a given set of components as defined by an SD model into a particular datacenter as defined by an LDD model. This DD model is first validated against the constraints in the SD (AD) model as well as those defined in the LDD model. It is then used to create a report that specifies the deployment requirements.	Chapter 30

> **■ NOTE**
>
> The tools that come with the Architect Edition really are useful only for teams that are developing Web services for deployment in distributed systems.

Server Parts of VSTS

The server parts of VSTS are provided by TFS. However, from a functional perspective, they can be subdivided into core data storage and application services, Web site services, and services that support the automated building of the team's software products.

Team Foundation Server (TFS)

TFS, as we have already discussed, is primarily concerned with storing data about your project and then providing this data as a service to the people and machines that need it. To connect Visual Studio to a particular Team Project you just specify the network address of the host TFS and then select the project from a list presented to you. The various TFS tiers then work together to manage all the connections, rights, and permissions as well as synchronizing the team's shared data to provide you with a view of the project on your PC that is consistent with the one provided to your fellow team members on their PCs. The exercises in Chapter 5 take you through the process of creating Team Projects and connecting to them.

> **■ NOTE**
>
> In many cases, an organization will have just one TFS hosting all its Team Projects. However, people working on an Agile team would not normally belong to more than one actual Team Project at a time.

Project Portal and Report Sites

The Project Portal is a Web site for your project, and anyone with the appropriate access rights (and license) can access it from anywhere, using nothing more than a browser. However, the Project Portal is primarily used by team members as a communication tool that provides them with a single place to find all the important information about their project. For example, in Figure 1-4, the OSPACS team's Project Portal has links to its latest build information and bug rates, as well as various announcements.

■ NOTE

The Project Portal is provided by SharePoint Services on the Application Tier of your project's TFS. Therefore, we suggest that you familiarize yourself with the basic operation of a SharePoint Web site by reading a book such as *Teach Yourself Microsoft SharePoint 2003 in 10 Minutes.*[7]

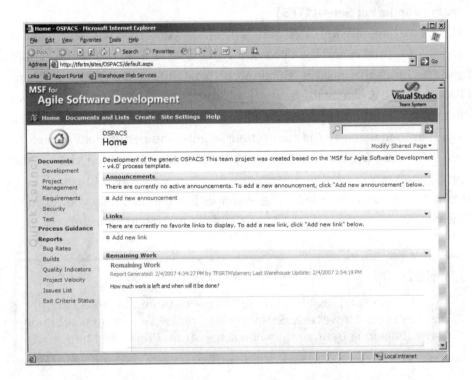

FIGURE 1-4: The OSPACS team's Project Portal (Team | Show Project Portal)

---

7. [TYSP] Spence, Noel. *Teach Yourself Microsoft SharePoint 2003 in 10 Minutes* (SAMS, 2004).

Your team's Report Site, like its Project Portal, is accessed using a browser, so it can be used to communicate information to team members as well as to people who are outside the team. It provides a collection of standard reports about your Team Project from data held in the SQL Server database on your TFS Data Tier. However, because this Report Site is actually provided by SQL Server Reporting Services, you can also use its Report Designer to create your own custom reports, as described in Chapter 31.

Team Foundation Build

Best practice suggests that teams sharing a common set of source files should regularly rebuild their programs on a separate build machine, such as the BuildLab PC in Figure 1-1. This separation of the development and build environments helps to ensure that a team's software can be built reliably and in a defined way, something we explore more thoroughly in Chapter 11.

Your team can build its software on a build machine in a number of different ways by defining different "Team Build types." So, for example, you might have one that just rebuilds any assemblies that depend on the source files that have changed, and another that rebuilds all assemblies and then runs a comprehensive set of tests to validate them. These Team Build types are listed in your Team Explorer window (refer to Figure 1-3), though they are actually XML files which are typically created by a wizard, as described in Exercise 12-3 in Chapter 12.

Under the covers, VSTS uses the same tools and source files to build the team's software on the build machine as it does on a developer's PCs. However, instead of the process being run locally by Visual Studio, it is run remotely by TFS, which stores the resultant build report in its Data Tier and puts the build products (.dll, .exe, etc.) into a specified "drop folder" on your network. The instructions that the build machine requires to rebuild your product are given to it by a part of the TFS called the Team Build Service, which in turn gets its instruction from the Team Build type definition created by your team. Collectively, the parts of VSTS concerned with executing this sort of team build are known as Team Foundation Build, and we explain their operation fully in Chapter 12.

> **■ NOTE**
>
> Your team can run multiple Team Builds at the same time and can have multiple build machines. In this way, people on your team can run Team Builds as often as they want, which is a key requirement for successful Agile development.

Extending VSTS

Although VSTS provides you with an array of built-in tools, it is also readily extendable, allowing you to add your own or third-party tools. Indeed, the development team at Microsoft has taken considerable care to provide interfaces and publish information with the aim of encouraging external organizations to integrate their products into VSTS, as well as allowing teams to customize VSTS for their own purposes.

Visual Studio Industry Partner Program

The Visual Studio Industry Partner (VSIP) program has signed up hundreds of companies to engage in this work, and the book's Web site provides details about some of the fruits of such partnerships. You can obtain details about VSIP and order a free DVD from the Visual Studio Extensibility Center area of the Microsoft technical Web site.[8]

> **■ NOTE**
>
> Far from reducing your choice of tools, it seems likely that VSTS will result in many more specialized tools becoming available to all members of the project team.

Visual Studio SDK

The Visual Studio SDK allows you to extend many aspects of Visual Studio as well as TFS. It is freely available from the Visual Studio Extensibility

---

8. Microsoft's Web site for Visual Studio (http://msdn.microsoft.com/vstudio).

Center area of the Microsoft technical Web site and contains tools, documentation, and plenty of sample code. Also, various open source utilities created for VSTS use this SDK on sites such as www.codeproject.com.

CONCLUSION

Now that we have presented the main components of VSTS, it's possible to describe them in terms of the main features they provide for a Software Project Environment; see Table 1-5. However, as we discuss in the next chapter, great tools on their own do not lead to better software development, for it is the values and practices of the people who use them that really matter.

TABLE 1-5: Feature Summary of VSTS

Area	Feature	Implemented by TFS +	References
Life cycle support	Process Guidance	Internet Information Services (IIS)	Chapter 15
• Requirement gathering	Creation of Scenario and Quality of Service (QoS) work item types	Visual Studio Team Explorer Word	Chapter 27
• Design	UML modeling, round-trip engineering	Visio, Class Designer	Chapter 19 Table 1-1
• Coding	IDE, unit testing, code coverage, code quality, and performance analysis	Visual Studio Developer Edition tools	Section 5 Table 1-2
• Building	Automated build	Team Foundation Build	Section 4
• Testing	Test management, unit testing, code coverage, load testing, manual testing, generic testing, Web site testing, ordered testing	Visual Studio Tester Edition tools	Sections 5, 7 Table 1-3

Continues

TABLE 1-5: *Continued*

Area	Feature	Implemented by TFS +	References
• Deployment	Architecting distributed systems for deployment using application, system, datacenter, and deployment modeling	Visual Studio Architect Edition tools	Chapter 30 Table 1-4
Project planning	Iteration definition, work item tracking/ scheduling/ prioritization	Visual Studio Team Explorer Excel and MS Project	Chapter 27
Quality assurance	Bug tracking, metric tracking	Visual Studio Team Explorer	Chapter 27
Change management	Source control	Visual Studio Team Explorer	Section 3
Document control	Document versioning and review	SharePoint Services	(not covered)
Security	Setting check-in policy and team access rights and security	Visual Studio Team Explorer	Chapter 5
Communication and feedback	Project Web site, reports, and queries	Visual Studio Team Explorer SharePoint Services, IIS, SQL Server Reporting Services	Chapter 31

■ **NOTE**

Scenario and QoS are work item types defined by MSF for Agile Software Development; see Chapter 5. They relate to the work needed to implement, respectively, functional and nonfunctional requirements.

2
Agile Values

O UR VALUES HELP establish the way we view the world and influence the principles we adopt when carrying out our actions. This chapter starts by looking at the relationship between people's tools and their values. It then presents the Agile Manifesto, which is a set of principles important to Agile teams. However, the bulk of the material is concerned with describing the core values of Extreme Programming (XP): communication, feedback, courage, simplicity, and respect. After reading this chapter, you should appreciate that although Visual Studio Team System (VSTS) can help your team tackle some of its technical issues, it is the way an Agile team addresses its people issues that really results in it delivering better software.

Tools and Values

Clearly, good tools are necessary for a team to do good work, but how does a team acquire its tools? In the next few pages, we investigate the differences between buying and building tools, which leads us to the issue of how the values and traditions of software developers might help them not only select the best tools, but also encourage better software development.

Buy or Build?

The business of finding good tools is basically a matter of buy or build. Buying means you are expecting someone else to develop and maintain the tool, and in this respect it is the total cost of ownership that really matters. For example, a free tool that takes everyone on a ten-person team six hours to assimilate can start to look expensive when compared with a $2,000 commercial tool that takes each team member only an hour to learn. However, you should also bear in mind that the most expensive tool in the shop isn't necessarily the best.

Building a tool means you take on the development and maintenance work yourself, which may be your only option for something innovative or particular to your project. However, you must think carefully before taking such a step, for those simple utilities that you aim to build in an afternoon sometimes end up occupying most of your spare time for months. You also need to be wary of creating an inferior copy of a tool which you could have bought and adapted for a fraction of the cost, particularly when you factor in ongoing maintenance.

Selecting tools, whether bought or built, is an activity on which every team needs to spend time. In the classic essay "Sharp Tools,"[1] Frederick Brooks suggests that each team should have a toolmaker responsible for keeping the team's tools sharp and communicating their use and value to the rest of the team. However, on an Agile team, it is usually more appropriate to share the role of toolmaker among the developers so that they all contribute to the identification, acquisition, development, and maintenance of their programming tools, whether bought or built.

> **■ NOTE**
>
> Although some discoveries about tools might require detailed explanation and formal training, most can be communicated among the team simply by virtue of people working together closely, such as when they practice pair programming, as described later in this chapter.

---

1. [MMM] Brooks, Frederick P. *The Mythical Man-Month* (Addison-Wesley, 1975).

Software Values and Traditions

Acquiring the right tools is just part of the picture, for the thing about tools is that they are effective only when kept sharp. Keeping a tool sharp involves learning how to use and maintain it. A good carpenter, for example, develops the skills needed to use, clean, and sharpen a chisel before ever attempting to cut a mortise into a block of wood. He spends time mastering these practices because having a sharp chisel allows him to produce sound joints. A good developer, likewise, needs to spend time learning to use and maintain the tools that allow him to produce great software. However, the willingness of people to undertake such efforts normally reflects their values. For example, why would someone who always used a hammer and nails to join wood bother to keep a chisel sharp, as clearly he has no regard for quality? Therefore, to develop better software we need to look further than just our tools; we must also consider our values and principles as well as the practices necessary to support them.

> ### ▪ NOTE
> Ancient craftsmen collaborating on grand projects were bound together by common values and practices, passed from master to apprentice over many generations. Without such traditions, they never could have produced their engineering masterpieces.

Unfortunately, today's software developers seem to have little in common with each other by way of common values and practices. Therefore, we often find ourselves working on teams full of tension caused by people with different values being forced to share tools and practices that they don't really care about. Not surprisingly, these sorts of teams seldom produce great work. For this reason, the Agile community is trying to promote new traditions for software development—sets of values and principles supported with sharp tools and backed up by certain practices.

The Agile Alliance

We can trace many of the principles that underpin Agile software development back to the ideas behind Lean Thinking as originally described in *Toyota Production System*.[2] These principles are stated in the "Manifesto for Agile Software Development,"[3] which was drafted at the formation of the Agile Alliance[4] in early 2001. We interpret them, in essence, as follows:

- **Customer collaboration**—Applying resources to finding out what customers really want and then devoting the entire project to meeting the needs and desires of these customers.

- **Working software**—The customer *defines* some tests, developers create software that can be *measured* against these tests, and *analysis* of the test results determines progress so that *improvement* can be made by generating new tests and better software. *Control* is provided by allowing the team to learn from each delivery of software.

- **Individuals and interactions**—Small groups of people with cross-functional skills work together to produce a piece of software that can be delivered to the business to give demonstrable value. The team is self-organizing, taking responsibility for things such as setting priorities and scheduling work.

- **Responding to change**—Waste and rework arising from changes in requirements or business priorities are minimized by delivering software through a succession of short iterations, each of which provides working software ready to pull into production should the business decide it provides sufficient value.

---

2. [TPS] Ohno, Taiichi. *Toyota Production System* (Productivity Press, 1988).
3. Agile Manifesto Web site (www.agilemanifesto.org).
4. Agile Alliance Web site (www.agilealliance.org).

> **▪▪ NOTE**
>
> Other people in your organization may find that these Agile principles closely correspond to what they are promoting in terms of Design for Six Sigma (DFSS),[5] an issue we discuss further at the end of Chapter 32.

The Agile Alliance is a nonprofit organization supporting people who want to take an Agile approach to software development. These approaches[6] include Agile Modeling, Scrum, Crystal, DSDM, and XP. Although each one subscribes to the same basic Agile principles, their specific values and practices differ, so you should select the Agile approach that seems most compatible with your team and the sort of work you do. However, in this book, you will find that the process of the OSPACS team corresponds most closely to XP.

Extreme Programming (XP)

XP is simply a collection of practices and values that Kent Beck[7] observed at work on good software development teams, but taken to their extremes and used in a coordinated way. One of these practices, Pair Programming, is described in the following sidebar. This takes the established practice of peer-reviewing work to the extreme by requiring that all your production code be reviewed continuously as you write it. We similarly will introduce the other practices to you chapter by chapter so as to present them in the context of the steps that you and your team are taking toward better software development.

> **▪▪ NOTE**
>
> Kent Beck originated Extreme Programming in the late 1990s, but he acknowledges contributions from people such as Ward Cunningham, Ron Jeffries, Martin Fowler, and Erich Gamma.

---

5. [DF6S] Chowdhury, Subir. *Design for Six Sigma* (Prentice Hall, 2003).
6. Roadmap to Agility (www.agilealliance.org/resources).
7. [XPE2] Beck, Kent, with Cynthia Andres. *Extreme Programming Explained, Second Edition* (Addison-Wesley, 2005).

Pair Programming Practice

Pair programming (pairing) is a buddy system requiring that all production code be written by two people sitting together at the same computer, sharing a single mouse, keyboard, and monitor. At any time, one person is focused on typing in the detail while the other is considering what his partner is doing in terms of the bigger picture, asking questions such as, Is this what the requirement means? Are we keeping to coding standards and team practices? Is there a simpler implementation? Partners change roles often, which helps keep the dialog going; sometimes you ask questions and sometimes you provide answers, either verbally or by just typing away.

People learn much faster when they work together and tend to develop better solutions, for as we know, two minds are often better than one. It is also harder for mistakes to persist when two people are constantly checking each other's work. What's more, the interaction of two people typically produces code that is easier to understand and maintain. Collaboration confers a clear advantage in these key areas of software development, so why do programmers still work alone? Usually it's simply a matter of personal habit or having mistaken beliefs about cost-effectiveness.

In order to implement pairing, you need enough people to rotate so that each developer can work with someone different at least a couple of times a day. This not only ensures that the "dialog" remains fresh and informative, but also that the knowledge becomes diffused throughout the team. Frequent swapping ensures that people get to know the entire code base rather than specializing in a particular part. It also means that tips and tricks get passed on quickly. Pairing doesn't mean you can never work alone to figure out some difficult problem or develop a quick prototype (spike), but it does mean that the information it generates can't just be pasted into production code; it must be added through a genuine pairing session.

Pair programming is demanding because you constantly have to focus on the task at hand and think hard to justify yourself to your partner; it's difficult to slack off or become distracted. You should expect to be as tired after six hours of pairing as you might be after 12 hours of working on your own. However, the economic advantages of pair programming are not realized just through the lines of code you both write. The real savings come over the entire software development life cycle, from the code you didn't write, the bugs you didn't insert, and the maintenance nightmares you avoided.

■ NOTE

Laurie Williams[8] (and others) describe how pair programming was adopted as a key Extreme Programming practice after Larry Constantine first observed it in 1995.

It is important to understand that XP is not just a list of practices from which you can pick and choose. The power of XP comes from all its practices being applied together in harmony, as all the practices are in some way related; not just to each other, but also to the supporting values of communication, feedback, courage, simplicity, and respect.

Communication

Many people involved in the development of software don't really value communication. In this book's Introduction, you encountered Peter Powell, a developer who spends most of his life sitting at a desk, plugged into an iPod and writing code that nobody else can understand. We also introduced you to Sally Thompson, a business analyst who occupies her time writing documents that nobody reads. In addition, you met Tom Stanton, a project manager who hides in his office producing reports packed with meaningless information. Perhaps these imaginary characters are larger than life, but you probably know people who share at least some of these traits. In order to collaborate, these sorts of people often replace real communication with a

---

8. Williams, Laurie, et al. "Strengthening the Case for Pair Programming" (*IEEE Software*, July/Aug. 2000).

bureaucracy based upon strict rules and process with the aim of making sure there's always someone else to blame when things go wrong.

Agile project teams value communication because they are more concerned with catching mistakes before they happen than they are apportioning blame after the event. It is better that developers engage in an ongoing dialog with their customer so that they deliver what is really needed rather than spending months negotiating a contract whose sole aim is to support some future litigation. The success of an Agile team depends not upon winning lawsuits, but upon satisfying the customer through early and continuous delivery of valuable software. The team recognizes that these objectives are better realized through individuals and their interactions than the application of process and tools, so it pays particular attention to the clear, timely, and correct transfer of information.

> **■ NOTE**
>
> Communication takes many different forms,[9] but it underpins everything the team does. Indeed, most XP practices are concerned with encouraging good communication in one way or another.

Feedback

Software development usually occurs in a rapidly changing world. The features that seemed so important to the business at the start of the project might be redundant six months later, the window of opportunity having closed. The technology that appears good today will doubtless be superseded next year by something even better. Agile teams embrace such change by applying **feedback**, periodic small adjustments to direction made on the basis of timely and accurate information about progress in a dynamic environment.

An Agile team values feedback because feedback permits the team to respond to change rather than having to follow some fixed plan. It helps the

---

9. Ambler, Scott. "Communication on Agile Software Projects" (www.agilemodeling.com/essays/communication.htm).

team keep its promise to deliver valuable software when it's needed. Agile teams can use feedback effectively because they have working software and tests available from the earliest stages of the project; the effects of change are quickly and accurately relayed to them. The other values and practices of an Agile team moderate this feedback so that the project doesn't descend into chaos as a consequence of the team trying to apply too many changes too quickly.

Feedback works on an Agile team not just at a macroscopic level in terms of controlling the project, but also at a microscopic level in relation to day-to-day activities. Therefore, it is as important for the team to gain feedback about a release as it is for a pair of developers to give each other feedback about a particular line of code.

Courage

Tom Demarco wrote "Projects with no real risks are losers. They are almost always devoid of benefit; that's why they weren't done years ago."[10] Few software projects have no risks, and for this reason, all the people involved need to show a degree of courage.

An Agile team values courage because courage shows that the team is taking the sort of technical and business risks that lead to worthwhile new software. However, such teams do not undertake these risks in a foolhardy fashion. The team will attempt to mitigate risks as far as possible. It might mitigate the risk of attempting to use a new technology, for example, by performing a mini project of fixed duration that investigates its feasibility (a spike). Other Agile values and practices also provide support when taking these necessary risks, so you share the burden (and the glory) as a team rather than as an individual.

Teams lacking courage tend to hesitate and lose the initiative, often deferring action until the opportunity has passed. Courageous teams balance the risks against the potential rewards, wait until the moment is right, and then commit themselves to a particular course of action with complete confidence in their ability to finish what they have set out to do.

---

10. [WWB] DeMarco, Tom, and Timothy Lister. *Waltzing with Bears* (Dorset House, 2003).

Simplicity

There is a danger of software teams using their advanced tools and technology to seek ever more complex solutions to a problem. From the outset, they are thinking in terms of a complex solution, so not surprisingly, that's what they produce. Valuing simplicity doesn't mean you can't take advantage of the latest tools and technology, but it does mean you must aim to move toward a simple solution and not away from it. This means continuing to improve the solution by making it simpler until you reach the point at which any further simplification degrades its functionality.

Simplicity is often an attribute of great designs, ones that are enduring and difficult to improve upon. A Lego brick, for example, has remained essentially unchanged for more than fifty years because no one has figured out a simpler design for building blocks that children can join together and pull apart (see Figure 2-1). Many other products share this same simplicity: paper clips, screw-top bottles, key rings. People have failed to improve these designs because they cannot be made simpler, and making them more complex doesn't make them any better.

FIGURE 2-1: Simplicity of classic Lego bricks

Agile teams value simplicity because it drives them to remove any unnecessary complexity and deters them from making compromises for some future need that might not materialize. They concentrate instead on producing only what is necessary for the present; the simplest thing that could possibly work. Thinking about simplicity helps an Agile team produce software that is immediately wanted, without wasted effort or materials. This is how the team gives its customers the best and most direct return on their investment.

Respect

Respect is about recognizing the contribution an individual can make in terms of his skills and talents. Without respect, it is difficult for us to collaborate. Why would we want to work with someone who offered no real value to us? However, we must be careful not to allow prejudice to influence this sense of value. Respect means recognizing the difference between people and capitalizing upon this diversity by working to our respective strengths and compensating for our various weaknesses. It isn't just a moral issue, for diversity also confers adaptability and many other benefits to the team.

An Agile team values respect because it helps the team work together more effectively in a changing environment. Practices such as Pair Programming and Real Customer Involvement (see Chapter 22) encourage respect to develop among members of the team by giving them the opportunity to work together. Respect requires a degree of trust and honesty among people, as you need to be able to speak your mind when necessary, without fear of reprisals. However, respect also means showing emotional maturity in terms of things such as being sensitive to other people's feelings and taking criticism constructively.

In some ways, *respect* is a catchall for the touchy-feely things that arise whenever people try to work together as a team. Although it can be embarrassing to discuss these issues because they include intensely personal things such as manners and social skills, this does not mean we can ignore them. A lack of respect, particularly self-respect, is often the root cause of team dysfunction.

CONCLUSION

Agile approaches to software development such as Extreme Programming (XP) provide a new tradition for people working together in teams; a set of values backed up by good tools and practices. The XP values of communication, feedback, courage, simplicity, and respect support each of its practices, which are all used in a coordinated way to achieve the aim of making valuable software available, economically, as it is needed.

> ■ NOTE
>
> We selected Extreme Programming as a basis for the OSPACS team's process because it's popular, so information about it is plentiful. However, you easily could adapt the material in this book for use with a different Agile approach, if that is what you want to do.

Review of Section 1
Sharp Tools and Values

THE OSPACS TEAM installed Team Foundation Server (TFS) on its new server machine and then updated each of its PCs by installing Visual Studio Team Suite. In addition to setting up its tools, the team also conducted a few training days to give team members a better understanding of Agile software development and to explore its values before creating its Team Project.

> **■ TIP**
>
> Teams usually achieve their intended objectives much quicker when they employ an experienced person (coach) to ensure that the various Agile values and practices are correctly interpreted and applied in a way which is appropriate to their own circumstances.

The Team's Impressions

The OSPACS team members responded favorably to the basic ideas of Agility, and some of the comments they made during their group discussion are given in the following sections. However, the consensus was that the introduction of Agile development was a good thing and would help them make better use of VSTS.

Project Manager/Architect: Tom

"The team members seem to appreciate the investment we are making in them in terms of the Agile training they're getting and the new tools we've bought. It's good to see some happy faces again."

Senior Programmer: Sarah

"VSTS is an impressive set of tools. I particularly like the way they are all integrated together and seem to generate a lot of information about the project automatically. I'm sure it's going to help us take a much more professional approach to our work."

Senior Programmer: Peter

"The emphasis on VSTS seems to be focused toward analyzing information rather than gathering it. I just hope we manage to put the analysis to good use in terms of actually improving the things we do."

"Everyone's fired up about Agile now. I just wonder whether it will be the same in six months."

Test Manager: Maggie

"I'm pleased the development department is taking such an interest in tools for testing. Perhaps this will help us to cooperate with each other a bit better."

Junior Programmer: Luke

"I hope VSTS means that I'll spend more time developing software and less time working as a clerk for Tom."

"I certainly agree that we need to improve our communication, as people seldom bother to tell me what's happening."

Agile Values

To clarify the way the terms *values, principles,* and *practices* are used, the OSPACS team members put the following quote on their wall:

> I'm a firm believer in simplicity and this value led me to the principle of minimalism which provides a basis for many of my actions, like the practice of keeping my office uncluttered. Simplicity also led me to the principle of taking small, baby steps which is why I follow the practice of Test-First Programming. [Anon]

Advances made in the field of software development are primarily concerned with making us more productive by introducing better practices, enhancing our tools, and improving the languages we use. Accordingly, change usually happens in a gradual and piecemeal fashion as people need time to assimilate ideas and learn new skills. For this reason, you can't expect a team to become Agile in a matter of weeks, or even months.

> ■ **NOTE**
>
> Great software is created by good people. However, people become good at software development because of the time and effort they put into their work. It's mostly a matter of nurture, not nature.

■ Section 2
Introduce Agile Development

A FTER COMPLETING THIS SECTION, you will be able to reorganize your team so that it can work in a more Agile way. You will have also set up the basic infrastructure you need to develop your software using Visual Studio Team System (VSTS).

We start this section by giving you an overview of Agile development with particular emphasis on Extreme Programming (XP), and we follow this with a chapter about the nature and structure of an Agile team. In Chapter 5, we review the standard process-enabling frameworks that come with VSTS and explain how they might be set up to support a software

Copyright Pro-Sport UK Ltd. 2006.

A rugby player's ability to exploit an opportunity quickly usually proves more important than his strength and size. Your team can likewise outperform much bigger and better-funded competitors simply by taking an Agile approach.

project. However, we recognize that these standard frameworks don't meet everyone's needs, so in Chapter 6, we describe how you can create a simple Agile process framework for your own team.

Story from the Trenches

A few years ago, I worked for a financial services company that was trying to jump on the Internet bandwagon by developing a cutting-edge Web site to sell its services. However, it had already failed to deliver this important product once, so it was now setting up a much bigger project to absolutely guarantee the successful delivery of its site.

On my first day, I was given a thick manual that introduced the company's methodology and was directed to a bookshelf containing the other five volumes of this mighty opus. It mapped out the activities that had to be performed by each type of worker on the team and then described in detail how these activities combined into workflows to generate each type of finished work product required of the project—its documents, models, tests, executable files, and so forth. Extensive checks and sign-offs were intended to catch defective workmanship at each stage, as the whole process depended upon everyone performing each task perfectly. After spending a short time skimming this material, I joined the rest of the team to start work on my prescribed activities.

The project team was organized into a strict hierarchy which pigeonholed everyone into a particular role. However, most people were managers of one sort or another, so there were relatively few people like me actually coding. I quickly discovered that the various people overseeing my work were much more interested in things such as coding standards than they were in seeing good code. Therefore, like my fellow programmers, I became highly proficient in manipulating the metrics used to measure my performance so that, on paper at least, it looked like we were doing a great job. Unfortunately, all this time spent keeping our managers happy meant that we had much less time to work on the product itself. Therefore, it took us much longer than planned to release even a demonstration version of the Web site.

Sadly, the business area funding our work didn't like what we had produced and requested a large number of changes which put the launch date back another six months. It soon became apparent that we were playing catch-up with a competitor's site, but clearly this was a game that we couldn't win, as our process was just too inflexible and the market was changing much more quickly than we could hope to respond. This project seemed doomed to fail for the same reason that the previous one failed—its development team was working more like people who were mechanically processing financial transactions than people who were creating innovative new software.

An organization's approach to software development often reflects the nature of its core business. However, in this section, we look at how Agile development confers significant advantages on teams that are prepared to break this mold.

■ 3
Overview of Agile Development

T HIS CHAPTER EXPLAINS why an Agile team doesn't have explicit phases of development, and how it delivers valuable software by encouraging direct dialog between the customer and developers. These ideas are then presented in terms of a software development life cycle that summarizes the self-governing activities of an Agile team during an Extreme Programming (XP) project. After completing the chapter, you should understand the basic nature of Agile development and therefore have a much better appreciation for the material presented in the rest of this book.

What Is Different about an Agile Project?

The thing that most surprises people when they first encounter an Agile project is the absence of traditional phases such as *design-code-test*. In a traditional project, these activities are performed separately over weeks or months, but in an Agile project, they are repeated many times each hour as part of test-driven development (TDD), as we will explain in Section 5. Another thing that surprises people is the Agile approach to *analysis*, which is done throughout the project by developing short stories rather than attempting to capture all requirements upfront and then putting them in large documents. In the next few pages, we'll explain why Agile teams approach software development in this way and perhaps encourage you to adopt these ideas on your own team.

No Separate Development Phases

The trouble with phased development processes such as Waterfall[1] is that teams typically spend many months working exclusively on each phase so that their feedback loops are too long. For example, only when the analysis is complete do they proceed to design, and only when the design is done do they move into the coding phase. Although exhaustive checks at the end of each phase attempt to validate the work, it is only during the *testing* phase that anyone actually knows whether the program meets its objectives. Therefore, the only real feedback about your work comes many months, even years, after it was completed. Waterfall treats software development like a production line, requiring perfection at each stage of the process. If there is any mistake or if the requirement changes during the process, the resulting software will not be correct. This may work when you're maintaining or adapting a mature software product, but not when you're developing new products in the face of changing or unknown requirements. In these sorts of circumstances, you need to increase the amount of feedback by drastically reducing the time between code creation and its validation.

■ **NOTE**

The Rational Unified Process (RUP) tries to improve feedback by repeatedly cycling through its core workflows,[2] but as these requirements, analysis, design, implementation, and test phases often last months, you still don't get enough feedback for Agile development.

---

1. Royce, Dr. Winston W. "Managing the Development of Large Software Systems" (*IEEE Proceedings*, Aug. 1970).
2. [UDP] Jacobson, Ivar, et al. *The Unified Software Development Process* (Addison-Wesley, 1999).

The emphasis on perfecting a design before it is put into code results from people's fear that cost of change will rise steeply as the project progresses. In a traditional Waterfall project, this fear is justified because the long feedback loop between design and test means that any mistakes will result in a significant amount of rework. However, as Scott Ambler[3] points out, in an Agile project, the feedback loop between design and test is very short, so mistakes can be corrected much more cheaply.

An Agile team eschews the whole idea of phases so that it can get valuable feedback continuously from the very start of the project by producing the only thing that really counts: working code. Indeed, by the end of the first week, many teams will have demonstrated running software to the customer with some feature that has business value. The price paid for this rapid delivery of working code is that the team doesn't produce thick documents or detailed models of the system. Instead, it just concentrates on writing the tests and code necessary to implement its customer's stories, as summarized on 6-by-4-inch index cards.

> ■ **NOTE**
>
> Agile teams still produce models and documents, but only when they add value. Therefore, later in the book, you will find us describing the sorts of models that may be useful to an Agile team (Section 6) and documents that can contain customer tests (Section 7).

Specifying Requirements with Customer Stories

A **customer story** (also known as a user story[4]) defines a feature of the software that has value to the business funding your project. It takes the form of some executable acceptance tests and a written memo that aims to

---

3. Ambler, Scott. "Examining the Agile Cost of Change Curve" (www.agilemodeling.com/essays/costOfChange.htm).

4. [USA] Cohn, Mike. *User Stories Applied* (Addison-Wesley, 2004).

summarize the various discussions about the feature that are held between a developer and someone representing the interests of the business—in other words, the customer. In this way, a story provides a specification for a particular requirement in terms of what Ron Jeffries[5] calls card, conversation, and confirmation:

- **Card**—The most important information about what a feature must do is captured as bullet points on an index card; see Figure 3-1. The intention is to remind people about the general issues rather than to write some legally binding contract.
- **Conversation**—The customer and developer must talk to each other if they are to really understand the requirement. The customer usually writes the card during this conversation.
- **Confirmation**—Executable acceptance tests are written as a formal specification of the feature and define it when it has been successfully implemented. These tests contain the actual details of the requirement; see Section 7.

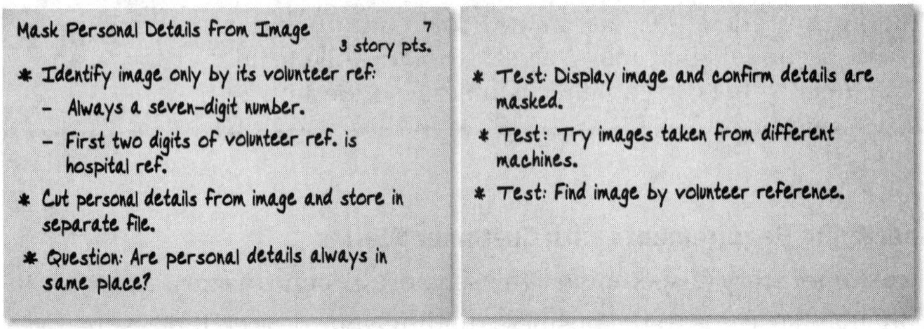

Mask Personal Details from Image   7
                                    3 story pts.
* Identify image only by its volunteer ref:
  - Always a seven-digit number.
  - First two digits of volunteer ref. is
    hospital ref.
* Cut personal details from image and store in
  separate file.
* Question: Are personal details always in
  same place?

* Test: Display image and confirm details are
  masked.
* Test: Try images taken from different
  machines.
* Test: Find image by volunteer reference.

FIGURE 3-1: Story from OSPACS project: front and reverse sides of 6-by-4-inch index card

---

5. Jeffries, Ron. "Essential XP: Card, Conversation, Confirmation" (www.xprogramming.com).

> **■. NOTE**
>
> Customer stories (or user stories) are not the same as the Use Cases described by Ivar Jacobson.[6] Although they both aim to do broadly similar things, Use Cases are more concerned with formally defining things, so they tend to encourage a more prescribed approach.

The customer owns the stories (what the software must do) and the developer owns the tasks necessary to implement them (how the software will work). At the beginning of the project, the customer will come up with a few initial stories, the ones that seem at the time to give the most value. More stories are generated as the project progresses. Sometimes stories will also be discarded as a consequence of changes to the business environment or due to the customer acquiring a better understanding of the requirement. This flexibility is the source of the Agile team's strength; it is able to respond to change. There is no need to identify all the requirements upfront, and the feedback given by working code allows the product to evolve in a way that is driven by fitness for purpose within the confines of a simple architecture.

In the next part of the chapter, you will see how customer stories are used in an XP project. However, they can also be used in a similar way by other types of Agile approaches, such as Scrum.

Introduction to Extreme Programming

Extreme Programming (XP) isn't actually a software methodology in the traditional sense because it avoids precisely defining the organization of a development project. Instead, it promotes values and practices that help people on a software team to do the right thing during the course of their work. Therefore, over the next few pages, we introduce XP by explaining

---

6. [UCA] Jacobson, Ivar, et al. *Object-Oriented Software Engineering* (Addison-Wesley, 1992).

how it is intended to help teams produce useful software over the life cycle of their projects.

> **■ NOTE**
>
> The nonprescriptive nature of XP encourages teams to mold their process around their project, for as Sam Guckenheimer[7] points out, "No one process fits all software projects, even within one organization."

Software Project Life Cycle

Software products start with an idea, but usually there is some reason why that idea can't be acted upon immediately. Typically, this is because implementing the idea would mean involving other people or otherwise spending money. However, if the idea is good enough and is sufficiently well promoted, someone might eventually put together a formal proposal, which is how a project starts in most organizations. Once the proposal has been accepted, a budget will be allocated to the project so that the proposal can be developed, and the work necessary to realize the idea begins. The project will then continue until there is no more money or enthusiasm to develop the idea further, at which point it ends; job done, product shipped, everyone is happy. The activities people perform between the start and end of a project are described in terms of a software development life cycle (SDLC).

Iterative and Incremental

An XP project is evolutionary; that is to say, it is *iterative* and *incremental*. This means its software is developed in a series of cycles which each deliver some working software (iteration) that builds upon what has gone before (incremental). One of the key aspects of XP is the way software is improved through small incremental changes made in short iterations that last weeks, not months.

---

7. [SETS] Guckenheimer, Sam, and Juan Perez. *Software Engineering with Microsoft Visual Studio Team System* (Addison-Wesley, 2006).

The SDLC of an XP project starts with a small team being assembled to implement a number of features which have some value to the people investing their time or money in the venture; in other words, the business. These features are described in terms of a collection of stories which are prioritized by the customer so that the ones with the greatest business value are done first, which is to say the development sequence is decided for business rather than technical reasons. Stories are sized at a few days' work, not more. Each developer then undertakes to implement one or more of these customer stories by splitting each one into its constituent tasks and estimating the total time it will take him to complete the work. The developers continue to undertake stories (according to the customer's priorities) until they are fully committed in terms of the time they have available and their estimates for the work they must do during an iteration.

> ■ **NOTE**
>
> We defer describing the planning of an Agile project until later in the book (Section 8), as we first want to tell you how your team can consistently deliver valuable software to its customer.

Iteration and Release Cycles

Life cycle diagrams typically illustrate the separate phases of development with a series of pictures, but as an Agile project doesn't have such distinct phases, it's more appropriate to show its life cycle as a series of timelines; see Figure 3-2.

The timeline at the bottom of the figure shows how an Agile team might implement a collection of stories during a weekly iteration cycle such that it releases some software to the business after the third week and then continues with its weekly cycle in subsequent weeks. Though we don't actually show the iterations after the fourth week, you can imagine that a release cycle would be formed by further releases of software occurring at the end of other iterations.

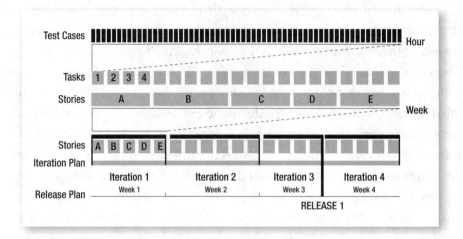

FIGURE 3-2: Agile software development life cycle: tasks, stories, iterations, and releases

During a weekly iteration, the developers work with each other on the coding tasks needed to implement their respective stories, as shown in Figure 3-2's middle timeline. Each task is completed in a "programming episode" lasting an hour or two, during which test-driven development (TDD; see Section 5) is performed so that dozens of structural (unit) test cases are created; this is shown by the thin vertical bars at the top of the figure. In this way, a customer story is implemented by decomposing it into a series of small tasks, each of which is divided into a series of small steps (tests) which individually take only ten minutes or so to complete.

> **■ NOTE**
>
> In Figure 3-2, the implementation of story A depends upon one pair of developers completing tasks 1 through 4. Therefore, other pairs may need to be concurrently implementing story B, C, D, or E so that by the end of the iteration, the team completes all five stories.

Iterations Deliver Production-Quality Code

Because the developers are writing production-quality code, even by the end of the first iteration the customer has a working product that supplies at least some of the features the business wants implemented. The customer knows these features work because they pass his acceptance tests, which he wrote during the iteration with the help of a developer; see Section 7. Therefore, this software could be shipped straight into the production environment and start giving some immediate payback, but it is more likely that the customer will decide to wait for a few more iterations so that he has something really useful before disrupting the business by giving it a new release. Accordingly, the second iteration will start and be run in the same way as the first, but new stories may be created and existing ones changed or discarded because the customer, having actually used the product, is now better aware of what is really needed. Slowly, iteration by iteration, the list of valuable features grows until the business representative on the team (customer) decides it is time to release the product into production. This is shown happening at the end of iteration 3, in Figure 3-2.

> **■ NOTE**
>
> On an Agile project, software is released into production much sooner than it would be on other types of projects. Therefore, the developers get better feedback from the business, which helps guide their future work.

Project Closure

The team continues with these iteration and release cycles until the supply of stories dries up, which usually happens when the business decides that it has received sufficient value from its investment. At this stage, the project ends and the life cycle is complete. The developers will then write a short document that will help anyone who might need to restart the project in the future, and finally will mothball the project so that they can move on to something more profitable.

> **■ WARNING**
>
> When mothballing the project, ensure that you keep copies of your tools as well as the source code so that you can restore your complete development environment, if required.

Isn't XP Just Hacking?

When Extreme Programming first started to become popular, some people claimed it encouraged hacking.[8] We use the word *hack* here in its original technological sense to describe an approach to software development that is likely to cause problems, such as the following:

- Development starts without considering the business needs or test requirements, so you start writing code without having a clear idea of what value it has to the business or how it can be validated. Nobody reads the specification document because it is too long, full of vague language, and out-of-date; it simply doesn't say what the software must do.

- The architecture is inappropriate for the product you're developing, or the design is flawed in some way, so you sit at the keyboard, writing code in the hope that if you write enough of it, sooner or later you will create something that can be released to the customer.

- Your code doesn't have any tests to validate that it works properly or that it correctly fulfills its purpose, so you spend days, weeks, even months using the debugger to make your software work without it mysteriously crashing or throwing up more defects.

> **■ WARNING**
>
> Hacking is particularly insidious when it's wrapped up in a cloak of bureaucracy that allows the team and the organization to continue living in denial. You can often hear them say, *"We can't be hacking; we've invested millions in our software process!"*

---

8. [QXP] McBreen, Pete. *Questioning Extreme Programming* (Addison-Wesley, 2003).

Why XP Doesn't Encourage Hacking

An XP team uses stories to make sure the developers understand what the software must do. The story card is just a reminder, for the real detail of the specification is contained in the *executable* customer tests (as well as the sorts of Agile models discussed in Section 6). These tests act like a specification language, except unlike formal methods, such as Z and SEDL, the customer actually writes them. Development does not start until the team has fully considered the business needs and test requirements.

The Agile team doesn't spend time producing a rich and complex architecture at a time when people can only make assumptions about what is needed; instead, it tries to defer applying such constraints until they are absolutely necessary, by which time the team may have a better idea of what is actually needed. For example, why decide to use SQL Server at the start of the project when later on you might discover that you need only a flat file? For this sort of reason, an Agile team doesn't do Big Design Up Front (BDUF[9]), and instead does the design continuously as the code develops using the practice of Test-Driven Development, guided by the sort of Agile models we discuss in Section 6. The architecture is appropriate for the product being developed and the code is backed up by tests that validate that it works properly.

It is hard for us to accept that XP might lead to hacking when teams fully apply its values and practices. XP is a very lightweight approach to software development, but this doesn't mean it isn't highly disciplined. The advantage of it being lightweight is that you can respond more quickly to change, which is an essential requirement for many projects being undertaken in today's business environment. An Agile team expects changes; it makes changes often and has the people, practices, and tools to do it effectively. This is why such teams can start creating working code from the very first iteration, without hacking.

---

9. Agile Community wiki. "Big Design Up Front" (http://xp.c2.com/BigDesignUpFront.html).

CONCLUSION

The iterative and incremental XP software development life cycle supports the delivery of valuable software by helping teams to

- Learn from the rapid feedback provided by their customers.
- Adopt a simple architecture before moving to a more complex one.
- Improve software through small incremental changes.
- Embrace change by becoming skilled at managing it.

XP is a lightweight process and therefore responds quickly to change, but it is also one that requires its team to show considerable discipline, because rather than relying on prescriptive procedures, the team must become self-organizing. In the next chapter, we will look at what it means to be self-organizing as well as how to form such teams.

> **■ NOTE**
>
> Although this book describes Extreme Programming as it might be practiced by a five-developer team in a small organization, as Kent Beck[10] reports, XP has also been successfully adopted by much bigger teams working for some of the world's largest companies.

---

10. [XPE2] Beck, Kent, with Cynthia Andres. *Extreme Programming Explained*, *Second Edition* (Addison-Wesley, 2005).

4
Forming an Agile Team

W E START BY identifying why Agile teams are needed and then look at the way they are organized in terms of the roles people play and their structure. This chapter also introduces two important practices for Agile teams: the Whole Team practice, which brings people together from different departments to work in the same organizational structure; and the Sit Together practice, which requires that the whole team work in a single open space. After reading this chapter, you should understand how to reorganize your team into an Agile team.

The Nature of Agile Teams

When people start developing software, they normally focus on learning a programming language and its interface to the operating system (the API). Within a few weeks, they will have produced their first useful program and may question why software development is reputedly so difficult. Indeed, software development isn't so difficult when you are writing small independent programs for your own use. However, the work starts to become far more complex once you move into the realm of producing larger programs for use by others, or which integrate with other programs and systems. Handling this sort of complexity is what makes software development so challenging, and it is why there are so many different ideas about the best way to do such work.

> **■ NOTE**
>
> The very teams we create to tackle software development that is too big for us to complete on our own, do themselves add significantly to the size and complexity of the work because of the need for people to coordinate their activities and interact with each other.

Working As a Design Team

You shouldn't look at developing software as a production activity, for the work isn't about following a set of plans that tell you how all the parts fit together. Instead, you must think of software development as a design activity which is concerned with creating the plans we need so that they can be fed into a machine that does the production work for us, automatically and with almost no cost. In other words, as Jim Reeves[1] says, the hard work of software development is concerned with producing designs expressed as source code from which executable files can then be effortlessly generated, copied, and distributed.

> **■ NOTE**
>
> Innovations such as Domain-Specific Languages (DSLs; see Chapter 21) may make it possible for people to generate source code from higher-level design documents, but they don't change the fact that software development is fundamentally about design, not production.

Design activities are about the effective generation of valuable information, so, as Donald Reinertsen[2] points out, the more people you have generating this information, the more time they need to spend interacting to ensure that it is put to good use. For this reason, people who work on large teams must spend a lot of their time simply interacting with each other, typically through e-mails, weekly meetings, and so forth. People who work on small Agile teams value this interaction just as much, but they do it far more efficiently because fewer people are involved, and being organized on a

---

1. Reeves, Jack. "What is Software Design?" (Publications, www.bleading-edge.com).

cross-functional basis (see the sidebar, Whole Team Practice) means less formal communication is needed. Accordingly, they can spend more time interacting in pairs to produce the sort of information that really matters: working code.

Whole Team Practice

The Whole Team practice brings people with different expertise together so that they can work as a cross-functional team. In other words, people on the team don't work for the Software Department or the Testing Department or even the Marketing Department; everyone works for the project and shares its objectives.

Organizing a project team on a cross-functional basis has two main advantages. First, the team can respond to events quickly because decision making happens at the team level rather than being referred back to different departmental management teams. Second, productivity is improved due to flexible working practices, so people are expected to work where they are needed and not just in their primary area of expertise, such as testing or coding. However, cross-functional teams also have some potential drawbacks, such as breaking up the centers of excellence in an organization and making it harder for the same code to be reused in different projects.

Small organizations seldom have any difficulty adopting the Whole Team practice, as it usually reflects the way they already work; the management structure is usually very flat and everyone does whatever it takes to make the project succeed. However, when you're working in a large organization, this practice can be more difficult to implement because it usually involves dismantling hierarchies and changing people's reporting lines. Therefore, in the short term, at least, you might need to make certain compromises. For example, if developers are required to work on more than one project at once, insist that the Whole Team practice is applied to just one project which is then given absolute priority over all other commitments.

Continues

---

2. [MTDF] Reinertsen, Donald. *Managing the Design Factory* (Simon and Schuster, 1997).

The need for people to work outside their primary area of expertise can be challenging, but it can also be rewarding. For example, a tester and a programmer can expand their areas of expertise considerably, simply by pair programming together. This is not to say that you can't bring an expert onto the team to supply a particular skill. However, when you do so, the expert must be required to pass on his skills and then leave. In this way, the team becomes self-supporting and its staff turn into the sort of people Scott Ambler[3] describes as *generalizing specialists.*

Self-Organizing Teams

An Agile team needs to be self-organizing in the sense that it should make most of the decisions about how the work will be done. Therefore, although the team still needs advice from senior and more experienced people, it does not need micromanaging in terms of day-to-day matters such as writing software, creating stories, or scheduling work. This means an Agile team is relatively autonomous, which allows it to become more responsive to changes in its own environment, or in the business it serves.

■ NOTE

The rapid feedback that members of an Agile team obtain makes them acutely aware of quality problems and areas of their process that are causing them problems. For this reason, they should have responsibility for making their own process improvements.

Team Size

Agile teams are small, which usually means they are composed of fewer than 18 people. However, on teams with fewer than four developers, the practice of Pair Programming (see Chapter 2) becomes difficult. Therefore,

---

3. Ambler, Scott. "Generalizing Specialists" (www.agilemodeling.com/essays).

our OSPACS team (see Introduction) is within the bounds of a normal Agile team size and has plenty of room to expand, as its membership could be doubled without too much difficulty. Indeed, James Atherton[4] suggests the optimum size for group interaction is between eight and 12 people, so adding a few more developers would actually be beneficial in this case. However, you should be aware that an Agile team would typically handle any increases in the size and complexity of the software it is developing, not by adding people to the team, but by limiting the scope of its work and by finding ways to split it with other teams.

> **▪ TIP**
>
> Don't divide a large team into a collection of subteams; instead, create separate Agile teams which each work on different parts of the product connected only by agreed interfaces.

Work That Doesn't Suit Agile Teams

It makes sense to set up a small, self-organizing team to undertake design activities such as developing a new software product in the face of changing or unknown requirements. However, not every team faces such challenges, so there can be good technical reasons for organizing software teams more like production lines with a suitably rigorous process. For example:

- When the work is mechanical and involves making a series of small, well-understood adaptations to existing code
- When the team is producing safety-critical software to control something such as a nuclear power station, and therefore needs to follow a particular formal method

In addition to these technical reasons, there are also various sociological grounds for teams not organizing themselves along Agile lines, but typ-

---

4. Atherton, James. "Group size" (www.dmu.ac.uk/~jamesa/teaching/group_size.htm).

ically they boil down to the simple matter of people's unwillingness to change. It is pointless trying to become Agile when most of the people on your team are firmly against the idea. Likewise, attempting to become Agile is futile when your manager or other powerful people in your organization will not allow the changes needed for you to introduce Agile values into your team, or implement its practices.

Agile Team Structure

There are two fixed functions on an Agile team: customer and developer. The customer gets to say what the software must do, whereas the developer says how it will work. This separation of responsibilities is essential whenever software is being developed for others. The person creating the software knows all about the technicalities of building programs, but ultimately doesn't have to use it. The person commissioning the software knows all about what is required, but doesn't have to build it. In the next few pages, we will examine how these two primary roles relate to the plethora of roles you will find on a traditional team, as well as look at the roles of people who are not actually full-time members of an Agile team, but are involved with it from time to time.

> **■ WARNING**
>
> Unless you are writing software for your own use, you should never attempt to take on the customer role. Customers, likewise, should not adopt the developer role unless they are writing their own programs.

Customer Roles

A customer is considered a full member of the project team and so should be located in the same workspace; see the Sit Together practice sidebar. He (or she) is the business representative on the team and so has responsibility for creating and validating software requirements (see Section 7), as well as setting the order in which they should be implemented (see Section 8).

The customer must be readily available to the developers for clarifying what the software must do from the perspective of the following roles:

- **Product manager**—Concerned with the development of the long-term product plan. His industry experience and client contact allow him to observe and understand what the user needs rather than just what she asks for.

- **Business analyst**—Understands the flow of information in the business and how it relates to the various systems. The business analyst has a very technical understanding of the requirement and what the solution must provide.

- **Purchaser**—Wants to get features that add the most value to the end user's work for the least cost, but is also concerned about support issues and the future plans for the product.

- **End user**—Interested in features that in the short term will enhance and facilitate her own particular work. End users have detailed knowledge of the business (or problem domain) and usually have experience using similar products.

- **Interaction designer**—Concerned with meeting the goals of the various types of people who will use the product, and giving them a pleasant and consistent user experience. Such a person knows the psychology of human relationships with software and has personal contact with the sorts of people who will be using the product.

- **Support staff (installer, trainer, help desk)**—Want to make the product easy to support in the end user's environment.

- **Technical writer**—Concerned with developing a product that is properly described by its documentation; the user manuals, online help, installation instructions, and sales and marketing material. This person collates information from many sources, so he often understands better than anyone what the product should do.

Although in some cases just one person may be seconded to the team as "the customer," it is usually difficult to find a single person with real-life experience in all of these functions who is also available to sit with the team on a full-time basis. Therefore, you might consider having a collection of people who take turns at being the team's customer. This gives each stakeholder an opportunity to represent his views. However, when you have a collection of customers you must take care to ensure that they interact properly and speak with the same voice, therefore forming a proper "customer group."

> **■ NOTE**
>
> Customers will usually need to perform work that is not related to the project while sitting in the team's workspace, so it is important to ensure that their space requirements are met, as discussed in Appendix C.

Developer Roles

Developers typically work exclusively for the project and work as members of a cross-functional team to perform whatever technical work is necessary for implementing the customer's requirements. They sit together and often swap seamlessly among the following roles:

- **Programmer**—Responsible for writing the structural (unit) tests and code needed to implement customer-requested features as well as providing estimates for this work and breaking it down into tasks.
- **Tester**—Works for the team's customer, helping with the creation of functional tests to prove that the requested features have been properly implemented.
- **Process technician**—Ensures that the development infrastructure is properly assembled and kept in good order. She implements source control and arranges for the automation of tasks such as the project build, system backups, and so forth.
- **Architect**—Evolves the system as it grows so as to provide better support for the functionality it contains. This person is concerned

with maintaining the conceptual integrity of the system and providing a suitable framework to support the software written by programmers.

- **Tracker**—Records the information that the team needs to keep on target and improve its process. He is responsible for gathering the metrics that the team has decided are important and publishing this information in an appropriate way.

- **Mentor**—Uses her experience to guide other team members, assisting them with their professional development as well as helping them to learn and improve their skills.

> **■. NOTE**
>
> The Whole Team practice requires developers to work on just one project at a time. However, if you are forced to work on two projects simultaneously, Tom DeMarco[5] suggests you should allow at least six hours per week for the time wasted switching between them.

Sit Together Practice

The practice of sitting together means that the team works in an open space that is large enough to accommodate everybody. The team is not sitting together when people are working in their own offices or even when some of their desks are separated by 5-foot-high partitions; everyone on the team needs to be visible to everyone else.

Sitting together is about fostering the sort of good team communication that underpins successful software development projects. This communication is not just about technical matters; it needs to work on a social level as well. When you can see someone isn't busy, you might invite her to join you for coffee, whereas if you have to pop your head over her partition, you

Continues

---

5. [SLAK] DeMarco, Tom. *Slack* (Broadway Books, 2002).

might not bother; it could seem a bit intrusive. Drinking coffee with someone is one of those activities that helps build the sort of personal network which is crucial to getting things done in most organizations. It is also an opportunity to find out about those small details that become so important when you're dealing with other people on the team. This sort of communication just doesn't happen when the team is sitting apart.

When the team sits together you get a better sense of what's going on. You can look around and immediately see who's busy and who might be available for a pairing session. You can also overhear snippets of information, perhaps about problems with the latest Team Build or issues about version control file conflicts. Most of the time people are barely conscious of the volume of information they are absorbing just by sharing a common space. This is information that would otherwise need to be explicitly communicated by reports, e-mail, formal meetings, video conferences, and so forth. Sitting together is usually the simplest and cheapest way for a team to communicate.

Persuading people to move out of their private spaces and into a common space isn't always easy. There may also be practical considerations to overcome, such as gaining an official sanction to change the office floor plan; see Appendix C. At first you might try holding a whole-team meeting early each morning so that people can start to experience the benefit of a more open style of communication. This might in turn encourage people to stay after the meeting and work together for a short time in small groups. You could also try moving a few of the partitions in the office on a trial basis to open up the space. However, people will always need some form of personal area, so make sure this is provided. Once the team starts to accept that sitting together is making them more successful, the technicalities tend to be quickly resolved. Given the will, it is usually not difficult to find a way to apply this practice.

Associated Roles

The team also needs support from people who are required for only short periods during the project. Such people are not full members of the team, but will work with them as the need arises to perform the following roles:

- **Project manager**—An Agile team is self-organizing, so rather than managing the work, this person manages the people on the team; facilitating communication, hiring people, resolving problems, and so forth. The project manager is also responsible for maintaining the formal reporting lines between the team and the rest of the organization.

- **Coach**—Helps the team to follow Agile practices and, when necessary, adapt them to the needs of the project. She takes a high-level view of the team and seeks ways in which it can improve.

- **Executive**—The business sponsor of the project who provides the budget and expects a good return on this investment. The executive sustains the political will inside the organization to keep the project going and helps remove obstacles in its way.

- **Enterprise architect**—Responsible for ensuring that the various teams in an organization produce solutions that result in an overall convergence of systems and technology.

- **Applications, infrastructure architect**—An applications architect applies enterprise architecture in terms of creating application solutions from components, services, and so forth. An infrastructure architect, meanwhile, helps deploy such solutions to an organization's servers, services, and so on.

- **Consultant, trainer**—Provide short-term assistance to the project in terms of skills or knowledge that can be transferred to people on the team; see comments in the Whole Team practice sidebar earlier.

- **Support role**—People on the team who support employees in terms of their human resources (HR), secretarial, and other similar needs.

> **■. NOTE**
>
> People undertaking these associated roles would usually be expected to perform several roles and possibly work on a number of different teams.

Reorganizing the OSPACS Team

In the book's Introduction, you met some of the people who work for a small company in the healthcare business run by CEO, Mike Hancock. The company had set up the OSPACS team and organized it into the product development department (Sally), the test department (Maggie), and the programming department (Sarah, Peter, and Luke, who all reported to Tom). In this section, we will explain the steps this team took to reorganize itself along Agile lines so that you might appreciate how to do something similar on your own team.

Identifying Customers and Developers

To reorganize themselves along Agile lines, the different departments were merged together so that everyone became full members of the new Agile OSPACS team, which was organized as follows:

- **Customer**—Sally becomes the team's customer because she has a good perspective of what the product must do due to her business analyst skills and contact with the company's clients at a business level. Mike has agreed to cover for Sally when she is away from the office.

- **Developers**—Tom and Maggie join Peter, Sarah, and Luke to become the people who decide how the product must work. Tom retains his architect role, but he agrees to undertake development tasks. Maggie expands her testing remit to include helping Sally produce her customer tests (see Section 7) and will also attend a training course in C# so that she can get involved in pair programming.

- **Project manager**—Michael becomes responsible for managing the people on the OSPACS team, so he helps them resolve high-level issues and personnel matters. He will monitor their progress regularly and provide input to them as their business sponsor, but otherwise he is content to let them work with a minimum of management interference.

It takes time and effort to build a group of people into an effective Agile team, but it is these sorts of teams that have the potential to perform well above other teams in an organization. Therefore, you should pay heed to the Team Continuity practice, as the sum value of such teams is greater than its individual parts.

Team Continuity Practice

Team continuity is the practice of keeping effective teams together rather than splitting them apart at the end of a project. It is a case of recognizing that good social interaction among people plays as much a part in the team's success as the knowledge and skills provided by the team's individual members.

Team continuity is important because it helps retain those traditions, often not formally stated or even acknowledged, which are fundamental to the group's success. When too many people leave the team in a short period, these traditions may be easily lost, for the team can just forget to do the small things that help make its members productive and content. It also takes time for trust and respect to be established among people, so frequently moving them between projects doesn't allow time for cohesive groups to form; the teams simply never gel. Some degree of staff movement is inevitable, indeed even healthy, as it helps to spread knowledge and skills. However, excessive staff turnover is often a sign that the team's process is broken, so something needs to be fixed.

Team continuity is not difficult to apply when the team is successful, as managers are usually reluctant to change a winning formula. It also helps

Continues

when people are happy and therefore do not want to leave the team. However, when your team does change, you must ensure that newcomers are properly introduced to its customs and practices and that the people who leave are suitably thanked and remembered for the contributions they have made. Such rituals foster team spirit, which ultimately is what the Team Continuity practice is all about.

Rearranging the Office Space

The new OSPACS team structure was initiated by the need to implement the Whole Team practice so that everyone worked for the project and shared its objectives. However, like most Extreme Programming (XP) practices, applying one practice has limited value if it is not supported by others. Therefore, we suggest that once you've introduced the Whole Team practice to your team, you should exercise your power to self-organize by rearranging the furniture to create a space large enough to implement the Sit Together practice. In this way, you can start looking like an Agile team at least in terms of your physical organization.

> **■. NOTE**
>
> Appendix C shows the new layout of the OSPACS team's workspace which helped team members to implement the Whole Team and Sit Together practices. You can discover what the OSPACS team thought about this reorganization by reading the Section Review after Chapter 6.

CONCLUSION

Typically an Agile team has fewer than 18 full members organized such that one person (or customer group) has the customer role and the rest share the various developer roles—programmer, tester, architect, and so on:

- **Customer**—Develops stories with developers, prioritizes them, and then writes their functional tests. He also plans releases to pull software into the production environment. Most of the customer's time is spent nailing down requirements by writing tests.

- **Developer**—Develops stories with the customer, estimates them, and then takes responsibility for their delivery using test-driven development (TDD); test, code, refactor. Most of a developer's time is spent doing TDD.

There is a clear division of responsibility on an Agile team between customers who get to say what the software must do and developers who say how it will work. Accordingly, power is balanced in a project according to people's respective areas of expertise, which helps build respect and trust between the different factions and thus creates a more cohesive team.

■ WARNING

Do not allow someone to become a customer unless he has direct relevant experience working in one (or more) of the customer roles. Particularly avoid having someone with a software development background as your customer.

■ 5

Team Foundation Process Frameworks

A FTER READING THIS CHAPTER, you will be able to create your own Team Project using a process template and understand why you might want to adapt it for your team, as described in the next chapter. We also explain how the process-enabling framework provided by Visual Studio Team System (VSTS) allows your team to structure its work, and we briefly review a number of different process templates that you might consider using.

Team Projects and Process Frameworks

You can configure VSTS for use with a variety of software development processes just by selecting an appropriate template during the creation of your Team Project. In addition to the template for the two standard methodologies shipped with VSTS, you can obtain others from third parties or by adapting them from existing templates exported from Team Foundation Server (TFS). In this way, TFS can support multiple Team Projects, each set up for a different type of software development process.

> **■ NOTE**
>
> An Agile team is an autonomous group of people who are collaborating on the development of some software and who share a common schedule. Each team of this nature in your organization should have its own Team Project.

Artifacts Generated When a Team Project Is Created

During the creation of a Team Project, various artifacts (files, database records, etc.) are generated and stored in your TFS Data Tier, either by the SQL Server database or by SharePoint Services. The types of artifacts created for your Team Project depend upon the process template selected, but they usually fall into a similar set of categories. In the following sections, we describe the artifacts generated by an MSF for Agile Software Development process template.

Project Structure

A single project area and a collection of three iterations are initially created for your Team Project. However, you can add more iterations as your project proceeds using the Visual Studio Areas and Iterations dialog box (Team | Team Project Settings | Areas and Iterations); see Chapter 27. You can also add more project areas if you have subteams that share the same development timetable as the rest of the team, but we do not recommended you do so because this conflicts with the idea of having autonomous Agile teams; see Chapter 4.

Users, Groups, and Permissions

A number of Windows security groups are created for your Team Project, such as Project Administrators, Contributors, Readers, and Build Services. These groups are administered using the Visual Studio Project Security dialog box (Team | Team Project Settings | Security), as described later in this chapter.

Work Products

A set of documents are generated for your Team Project from the default Word, Excel, and MS Project files contained in its process template. They include things such as your team's Project Vision and its Development Project Plan. You can locate these documents in the Documents folder of your Team Project, as displayed in Visual Studio's Team Explorer window (View | Team Explorer).

Work Items and Queries

An initial collection of tasks are generated which detail the work required to complete the setup of your project. You can assign these tasks to members of your team as well as to the iterations in your project structure. A set of standard queries are also created in your Team Project's Work Items folder to provide information about these tasks as well as other types of work items.

Reports and Report Site

Dozens of standard reports are created to provide people with information about your Team Project from the data stored in its TFS; see Chapter 31. Anyone with the necessary rights (and license) can access these reports from the report Web site generated for your Team Project by SQL Server Report Services (Team | Show Report Site). However, team members usually access them from the Reports folder in their Team Explorer window.

Source Control Folder

A root folder is created in the TFS version control system for your team's source code; see step 6 of Exercise 5-1. You can access this folder from the Visual Studio Source Control Explorer window (View | Other Windows | Source Control Explorer), as described in Chapter 8.

Project Portal

A Web site is generated for your Team Project from the static files in its process template as well as from the live data in its TFS. This project Web site is hosted by Internet Information Services (IIS), so anyone with the necessary rights (and license) can obtain information about your project simply by entering the project's URL into his browser. However, team members usually open this site from the menu in their Visual Studio Integrated Development Environment (IDE) (Team | Show Project Portal).

Process Guidance

Your team can get advice about how to follow the specific process that applies to its Team Project from a Web site hosted by TFS; see Figure 5-1. The team can access this Web site from the home page of its Project Portal, or directly from Visual Studio (Help | Team Project Process Guidance).

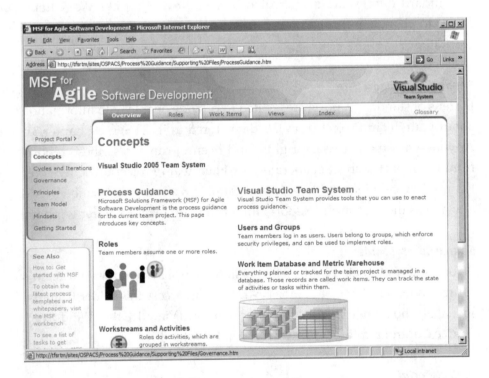

FIGURE 5-1: The MSF for Agile Software Development Process Guidance site

> **■ NOTE**
>
> You can access the Team Project's Process Guidance from Visual Studio (Help | Team Project Progress Guidance), from the home page of the MSF Agile Project Portal, or directly from the Process Guidance folder in Visual Studio's Team Explorer window.

Creating an MSF for Agile Software Development Team Project

Traditional teams often spend the first few days of a project doing little more than setting up security groups and installing various tools so that people can work together properly. VSTS helps your team get started much more quickly by providing a wizard so that you can perform these sorts of administrative tasks in a matter of minutes. Exercise 5-1 takes you through this process.

> **■ NOTE**
>
> "File | New | Team Project" is our way of saying "choose the *New* menu item from Visual Studio's *File* menu and then select its *Team Project* submenu item." We use this syntax in exercises throughout the book.

EXERCISE 5-1: Creating a Team Project

After completing the following exercise, you will have created the OSPACS Team Project on the machine that hosts your TFS—for example, DevServer in Figure 1-1 in Chapter 1.

1. Log on to the DeveloperPC as Tom (Team Foundation Administrator) and start Visual Studio; see Appendix A for details about this PC and Tom's security groups.

2. Select File | New | Team Project to open the Team Project Wizard. Connect to your TFS, if prompted, as described in step 2 of Exercise 5-7.

3. Enter "OSPACS" as the name of your Team Project; click Next.

4. Select MSF for Agile Software Development as your process template (see Figure 5-2); click Next.

5. Accept the suggested title for the Team Project Portal (make sure you note its URL); click Next.

6. Select "Create an empty source control folder"; click Next.

7. Click Finish to create your Team Project. Wait several minutes for this action to complete and then click Close to complete the wizard.

8. Check that this new OSPACS Team Project appears in your Team Explorer window (View | Team Explorer) below the name of the machine that hosts your TFS.

9. Finally, log off, as you have completed this exercise.

■. WARNING

Select your process template carefully when creating a Team Project because you cannot change it later. You can, however, make minor changes such as adding new work item types, queries, and reports, as described in Chapter 6 and Chapter 31.

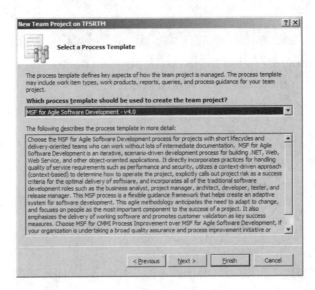

FIGURE 5-2: Using the Team Project Wizard to select a process template (File | New | Team Project)

Deleting a Team Project

You would not normally delete a Team Project unless you wanted to clear up some space on your TFS after you have backed up and closed the project. However, you may want to delete some of the Team Projects you have created while experimenting with different types of process templates, so Exercise 5-2 explains how to do this using the tfsdeleteproject utility, which you must execute from the command line.

EXERCISE 5-2: Deleting a Team Project

This exercise permanently deletes the OSPACS Team Project from the DevServer TFS so that you lose all its data, including the source files in its version control system. If you take this action, you should repeat Exercise 5-1 afterward so that you can complete the other exercises in this book.

1. Log on to DevServer (TFS) as Tom (Team Foundation Administrator); see Appendix A for details about this PC and Tom's security groups.

2. Search for the tfsdeleteproject.exe file and confirm that it is located in a directory that is part of your PATH environmental variable (see Appendix A).

3. Open a command prompt window and type the following:

```
TFSDELETEPROJECT /server:DevServer OSPACS
```

4. Close the command prompt and then log off.

> **TIP**
>
> Before deleting a Team Project, review the advice about backing up and restoring TFS provided in its Administrators Guide.[1]

---

1. TFS Administrators Guide (http://go.microsoft.com/fwlink/?LinkID=52459).

Giving Users Membership of Your Team Project Groups

Before members of your team can access the Team Project you created in Exercise 5-1, you need to make them members of the appropriate security groups. A number of groups are automatically created for each Team Project and members of your team should be given membership of the group that is most appropriate for their needs. In the case of the OSPACS Team Project, the following groups were created:

- [OSPACS]\Project Administrators—People who administer the project; Tom
- [OSPACS]\Contributors—People who generate information for the project; all
- [OSPACS]\Readers—People who just want to view project information

Although you can make people's domain user accounts members of these groups using the various dialog boxes provided by Visual Studio (Team | Team Foundation Project | Groups), it is often more convenient to make them members of a particular Windows security group and then add this security group to the appropriate project group using the TFSSECURITY command-line tool, as described in Exercise 5-3.

> ■ NOTE
>
> Before starting Exercise 5-3, you need to create the OSPACSDevs security group and add to its list of members the domain user accounts of the various developers on the OSPACS team (in other words, Tom, Maggie, Sarah, Peter, and Luke).

EXERCISE 5-3: Making a User into a Team Project Contributor

In this exercise, you will add the OSPACSDevs Windows security groups to the Contributors security group for the OSPACS Team Project. After you do this, the members of OSPACSDevs will be able to connect to the OSPACS Team Project; see Exercise 5-7.

1. Log on to DevServer (TFS) as Tom (OSPACS Project Administrator).

2. Open a command prompt window and type the following to list all the groups associated with OSPACS:

```
TFSSECURITY /server:DevServer /g [OSPACS]
```

3. Type the following to make the OSPACSDevs security group in the Signaustr domain a member of the [OSPACS]\Contributors group:

```
TFSSECURITY /server:DevServer /g+ "[OSPACS]\Contributors" n:Signaustr\OSPACSDevs
```

4. Repeat the preceding step to grant the other Windows security groups defined in Appendix A access to their corresponding groups in the OSPACS Team Project.

5. Log off.

■ **TIP**

It is good practice to grant rights to a security group rather than to individual team members' user accounts. In this way, when people join or leave your project, you need to add (or remove) people from just one security group, such as OSPACSDevs.

Gaining Access to Your Team Project Services

In addition to granting people membership of specific Team Project groups (for example, Contributors), you must also grant them the necessary rights so that they can access the Windows SharePoint Service that runs their Team Project's Web site as well as the SQL Reporting Service that provides their Team Project's Report Site.

At present, only Tom has access to the OSPACS Project Portal and its Report Site because he created their associated Team Project. However, after completing the following exercise, all members of the OSPACSDevs Windows security group will have access to these sites.

1. Log on to the DeveloperPC as Tom (OSPACS Project Administrator) and start Visual Studio.

2. Connect to the OSPACS Team Project (see Exercise 5-7), open its Project Portal (Team | Show Project Portal), and then add the OSPACSDevs security group to the list of users who can access the site, as follows:

   a. Click Site Settings in the top menu bar of the site's home page.

   b. Click the Manage Users link in the Site Settings page, and from this page, click the Add Users button to access a series of pages that allow you to add users to the site.

   c. Enter "OSPACSDevs" in the Users text box and select Contributor from the Site Groups list in the "step 1 and 2" page; click Next to continue.

   d. Enter the e-mail address assigned to OSPACSDevs (if any) in the "Email address" text box and enter something into the Message text box in the "step 3 and 4" page; click the Finish button to complete the operation.

3. Close the Project Portal Web site.

4. Open the OSPACS Team Project's Report Site (Team | Show Report Site). Add the OSPACSDevs security group to the list of users who can access the site, as follows:

   a. Open the site's home page; click the "home" item in the menu at the top right of the page.

   b. Click the Properties tab at the top of the home page and then click the New Role Assignment button in the menu bar to open the New Role Assignment page.

   c. Type "\OSPACSDevs" (remember the forward slash) into the "Group or user name" text box and select the rights you want to grant: Browser, My Reports, Publisher, and Report Builder. Click OK to close the page and grant OSPACSDevs access to the site.

5. Close the Report Site and log off.

■ NOTE

In the initial version of VSTS, you need to repeat Exercise 5-4 each time you create a new Team Project, but this may change in subsequent versions of the product.

Administering Your Team Project Security Settings

The project administrator (or Team Foundation administrators) can fine-tune the rights of particular security groups (or users) for a specific Team Project. You might, for example, want to allow some of the people on your team to administer a Team Build. Exercise 5-5 shows how you can grant such permissions.

After completing the following exercise, all members of the OSPACS Contributors group will have the rights they need to administer a Team Build.

1. Log on to the DeveloperPC as Tom (OSPACS Project Administrator), start Visual Studio, and connect to the OSPACS Team Project as you did in the preceding exercise.

2. Open the Project Security dialog box (Team | Team Project Settings | Security) and select the OSPACS\Contributors security group before adding a checkmark to the Administer a Build box in the list at the bottom of the dialog box. Apply your changes by clicking OK.

3. Log off.

■ NOTE

You can administer security group membership for the users in your domain directly from Visual Studio (Team | Team Project Settings | Group Membership), but it is often more convenient to use the TFS command-line tools you used in Exercise 5-3.

Administering Your TFS Security Settings

The Team Foundation administrators can fine-tune the rights of particular security groups (or users) for all the Team Projects hosted by your TFS. You might, for example, allow people to create new Team Projects; see Exercise 5-6.

The following exercise grants the right to create a Workspace to all the people who can access your TFS.

1. Log on to the DeveloperPC as Tom (OSPACS Project Administrator), start Visual Studio, and connect to the OSPACS Team Project as you did in the previous exercise.

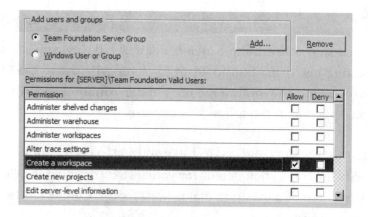

FIGURE 5-3: Part of the Global Security dialog box (Team | Team Foundation Server Settings | Security)

2. Open the Global Security dialog box (Team | Team Foundation Server Settings | Security), select the SERVER\Team Foundation Valid Users security group (at the top of the dialog box), and then add a checkmark to the Create a Workspace box (see Figure 5-3).

3. Click OK to close the dialog box and apply your changes.

4. Log off.

■. NOTE

Any user who is a member of the Team Foundation Administrators security group for a particular TFS automatically has the right to connect his Visual Studio Team Explorer to all of its Team Projects.

Connecting to a Team Project

The person who creates a Team Project (Exercise 5-1) will usually send an e-mail to the people he has added to its security groups (Exercise 5-3), inviting them to connect their Visual Studio Team Explorer to it. It is a good idea to include in such e-mail general information about the Team Project as well as some basic instructions to get people started; see Exercise 5-7.

EXERCISE 5-7: Connecting to Your Team Project

This exercise shows how Luke, a member of the OSPACS team, starts work by connecting his Visual Studio Team Explorer window to the OSPACS Team Project. Anyone who is a member of the Windows security groups defined in Appendix A can follow this exercise.

1. Log on to the DeveloperPC as Luke and start Visual Studio.
2. Specify the connection details for your TFS by opening the Connect to Team Foundation Server dialog box (Tools | Connect to Team Foundation Server):
   a. Click the Servers button to open the Add/Remove Team Foundation Server dialog box and then click its Add button to open the Add Team Foundation Server dialog box.
   b. Into the Add Team Foundation Server dialog box, enter "DevServer" as the name of your server, "8080" as its port number, and "HTTP" as its protocol. Appendix A specifies this machine; your server may have different details.
   c. Close both dialog boxes.
3. All the available Team Projects hosted by your TFS are now listed in the Connect to Team Foundation Server dialog box. Select the OSPACS Team Project and click OK. The OSPACS project will now appear in your Team Explorer window; see Figure 1-3 in Chapter 1.
4. Log off.

Visual Studio stores your TFS connection settings and Team Project selection so that you do not need to repeat this exercise each time you start work. However, remember to make sure the *correct* Team Project item is selected in your Team Explorer window so that actions applied from the Visual Studio menu bar can operate on it.

Microsoft Solutions Framework (MSF) 4.0

Microsoft Solutions Framework version 4.0 is a metamodel defined on the Microsoft technical Web site[2] that allows you to build software development process models. MSF for Agile Software Development and MSF for CMMI Process Improvement are just two of the process models that have been built using MSF 4.0. In object terms, you can think of a Team Project as having a process framework that is an instance of MSF 4.0 whose properties are set by the MSF for Agile Software Development process template. Figure 5-4 shows this MSF 4.0 metamodel together with its main elements, and although most of this material is not really relevant to an Agile team, reading about it may help you understand how process templates relate to the various functions and facilities of VSTS.

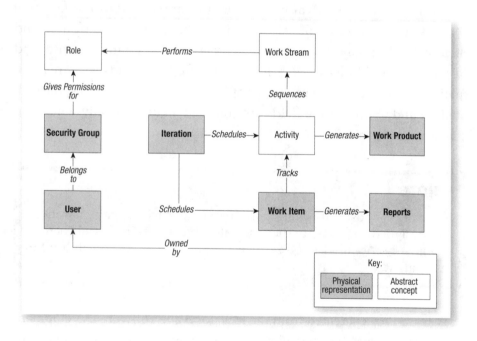

FIGURE 5-4: MSF 4.0 metamodel (diagram inspired by Richard Hundhausen[3])

2. Microsoft Web site for MSF (www.microsoft.com/technet/itsolutions/msf).
3. [VSTS] Hundhausen, Richard. *Working with Visual Studio 2005 Team System* (Microsoft, 2005).

> **■ NOTE**
>
> Role, Work Stream, and Activity have no physical representation in VSTS, so they cannot be associated with actual data in your TFS, like work items can. Therefore, some process models include them, and others do not.

Work Item

Work items are the record types in a Team Project that help you gather the information you need to monitor its health as well as to discover who did what, when, and why. This data is stored in the TFS database and provides the basic metrics from which your team's reports are generated.

Specific team members can schedule, track, and own work items. They have certain general fields as well as ones that are specific to a certain type of work item. For example, all work items have Title, Description, and State fields, but only Bug work items have Priority, Found in Build, and Resolved in Build fields. Work items may also have fields that are automatically updated as a consequence of your actions. For example, the Created By and Created Date fields are completed automatically when you create a work item.

> **■ NOTE**
>
> Some of the most important work item fields are the State, Iteration, and Assigned To fields, for they indicate whether the item is still active, when is it scheduled to be resolved, and who has responsibility for resolving it.

A Team Project created from the MSF for Agile Software Development process framework has the following types of work items: Bug, Quality of Service (QoS), Risk, Scenario, and Task. During the course of such a project, you can add additional work item types, or edit existing ones (see Chapter 6). However, you cannot delete one of these work item types (or the corresponding work item records) because this may violate your auditing requirements and alter the meaning of some reports based on historical data.

Role

Members of your team act in certain roles depending on the activities they are performing. For example, when someone is performing a "writing code for a development task" activity, he or she is acting in a developer role. Team projects with different process frameworks may have a different collection of roles and activities. However, there is no physical manifestation of a role in VSTS beyond what you can read on your Process Guidance Web site.

> **■ NOTE**
>
> Thinking about someone's roles helps you decide the permissions that should be granted to him, as each role in a project has an associated set of activities (see the Work Stream section, later in this chapter) that each require particular rights and permissions.

Activity

An activity is something a team member does when acting in a particular role. For example, one of the activities performed by a developer in a Team Project with the MSF for Agile Software Development framework is "writing code for a development task." However, different types of processes usually have different types of activities.

Activities are defined in the Process Guidance in terms of work streams. Activities create work products such as source code, project documents, and so forth in the satisfaction of a particular work item assigned to a team member (user). However, like roles, there is no physical manifestation of an activity in VSTS beyond what you can read on your Process Guidance Web site.

Work Stream

A work stream is a sequence of activities performed by a role for a given software development process, and it typically involves processing some form of work product. Work streams have entry (optional) and exit criteria that define when they may be started and when they are complete. For example, your Team Project may define the Capture Project Vision work stream which has no entry criteria, but lists the activities someone in the business analyst role must complete to achieve the exit criteria—in other words, write a vision statement (such as the "elevator pitch" in Chapter 1) and publish the user personas on the team's Project Portal.

A work stream, again, has no physical manifestation in VSTS. It is no more than a suggestion for the order of activities that need to be performed in order to satisfy a work item assigned to someone acting in a particular role. The Index page of the Process Guidance Web site lists the work streams in your Team Project and the roles that should perform this type of work.

> **■ NOTE**
>
> "Personas" are intended to help you visualize the sort of people who might use the system your team is developing, so they serve a similar purpose to the descriptions we gave about the OSPACS team members in the Introduction.

Tracks and Governance Checkpoints

MSF 4.0 intends that during its various iterations, your project will progress through a number of phases which it terms **tracks.** A checkpoint must be satisfied before a track can be started; this provides a governance mechanism to stop a project that will not ultimately deliver value before too much time and money are spent on it. For example, if your Team Project has the MSF for Agile Software Development process framework, you might encounter the sorts of tracks and governance checkpoints that are shown in Table 5-1.

TABLE 5-1: Tracks and Governance Checkpoints in an MSF for Agile Software Development Process

Track	Main Activities	Checkpoints
Envision	Form the team and create a vision statement to provide the team with a common vision of the project's scope and what it will accomplish over a given time scale. During this phase, the team sets up the project and may create some prototypes to investigate the technology.	–Confirm that the project has realistic goals and a viable plan to achieve them. –Create test and deployment strategy. –Development environment is proven.
Plan	Create the functional specification, risk management plan, and master project plan/schedule. The work is identified and estimated.	–Documents are reviewed and accepted. –Key prototypes are demonstrated.
Develop	The solution is built and the infrastructure is developed to support it. Test cases are produced to validate the solution.	–Operational software is delivered that satisfies the functional specification.
Stabilize	The solution is fully tested, bugs are removed, and it is prepared for release.	–Master copy of the product is delivered with documentation and installation program. –Test results show product is ready for deployment.
Deploy	The solution is moved into the business environment and any problems that might arise are resolved with patches, and so on.	–Customer assesses the product and signs for its acceptance. –Training and support are arranged.

■ NOTE

Table 5-1 provides just a summary of the activities and checkpoints that you might expect to find on a team that had adopted the MSF for Agile Software Development process.

Tracks and governance checkpoints, like many other elements of MSF, have no physical representation in VSTS. They are just suggestions for giving a series of iterations some special focus in the hope that upon their completion, certain physical evidence (code, models, etc.) will be delivered which helps the project pass a governance checkpoint, thereby gaining management support for the team to continue into the next track. Clearly, different types of software development processes will have different tracks and checkpoints.

Frameworks for Specific Processes

So far, we have talked about MSF 4.0 in the context of MSF for Agile Software Development. However, the real power of MSF 4.0 is that it allows you to define a process framework for almost any type of modern software development process. Therefore, let's now review the process templates supplied with VSTS, together with a template available from this book's Web site, to help you find a starting point for the sort of process framework most suited to your project and team.

> **■ NOTE**
>
> Although this book is written for a small team following an Agile process such as Extreme Programming (XP), much of the information can also be applied to larger teams that are following other types of software development processes.

MSF for CMMI Process Improvement

MSF for CMMI Process Improvement (MSF for CMMI) is supplied with VSTS, so you do not need to install this process template on your TFS; it's already there.

The Software Engineering Institute's (SEI) Capability Maturity Model Integration (CMMI[4]) provides five levels at which an organization's

---

4. Carnegie Mellon. "What is CMMI?" (www.sei.cmu.edu/cmmi/general/general.html).

process maturity can be measured, and it is often used to guide process improvement across a project or an entire organization. CMMI was originally produced to allow the U.S. Department of Defense to assess its contractors, but this certification is now highly regarded by many people (but not by all) as a mark of excellence.

In theory, you can select MSF for CMMI when creating your Team Project and then simply follow the Process Guidance to become ready for level three certification while having a clear way to reach level five. However, in practice, your team will have to do a lot more than just follow a set of instructions in order to achieve CMMI certification *and* produce great software. You can get some idea of the amount of work involved in using the MSF for CMMI framework by reading its Process Guidance and looking at the documents it creates in your Team Project's document folder. This development process, as you might imagine, is completely prescribed and there is almost no scope for variation, which makes it an unattractive option for a team that wants a design process; see the section Working As a Design Team, in Chapter 4.

> ### ■ NOTE
>
> A prescriptive process seeks to identify the sequence of activities required to transform a work product from one state into another and then describe each activity in such detail that there is little possibility for error or variation occurring.

If you are working for a defense contractor or are involved with safety-critical projects, your team may have no option but to obtain CMMI certification, in which case MSF for CMMI could be a good choice. However, teams working on other types of projects might want to look for alternative frameworks. Given the amount of management expected for people using the MSF for CMMI framework, it is difficult to see how its use could be justified in a small or even medium-size team.

MSF for Agile Software Development

MSF for Agile Software Development (MSF for Agile) is also supplied with VSTS, so you do not need to install this process template on your TFS.

The development process for MSF for Agile is not as completely pre-scribed as MSF for CMMI, but neither is it a completely elective process such as MSF for XP. The approach that MSF for Agile takes to risk and proj-ect management is explicit, as there are particular activities to be performed which are comprehensively described in its Process Guidance. It also has a dozen or so prescribed workflows and requires the representation of at least five given roles on your team. However, such structure may be appro-priate on some Agile teams, so you should give it serious consideration when you are selecting a template for your Team Project.

MSF for XP

MSF for XP is available from this book's Web site (or from www.msf4xp.org), and instructions for importing its process template into your TFS are given in Chapter 6. It is maintained as an open source project and operates under a BSD license, so essentially you can freely use and modify it, but at your own risk.

MSF for XP was produced for this book, so it is specifically aimed at very small teams that want a process framework to support the values and prac-tices of Extreme Programming. It is actually a cut-down version of MSF for Agile and provides a suitable starting point for a team that wants to start with a simple process framework to which it can then add complexity as it discovers the need for it.

XP approaches software development as an elective process and pro-vides little specific guidance about what you should do beyond proposing some practices and values that the team should adopt. That is to say, it's the team that decides whether a particular practice should be adopted, though some risk is always associated with not doing any XP practice. A team doing XP is expected to be self-organizing, so its project management is implicit; the team itself decides what needs to be done. Likewise, the cus-tomer and developers are expected to know best how to handle the risks associated with their project, so risk management is also implicit. In terms of governance, the team reveals value to the business at the end of each iteration, and when this stops flowing, the project is terminated. For this reason, we do not provide explicit checkpoints for the business to decide whether it is worth the team continuing its work.

MSF for XP is not very suitable for teams that require a formal management structure. It also lacks the explicit traceability and audit capabilities required for certain types of software projects, such as the development of safety-critical systems. However, for small teams working on projects that do not have such restrictions, MSF for XP may provide a highly effective process framework that allows them to deliver valuable software, even when the requirements are not fully known or understood at the start of the project.

Process Framework Comparison

The selection of your team's process framework is an important decision because it cannot be changed after you have selected the corresponding template during the creation of your Team Project; see step 4 of Exercise 5-1. Therefore, we suggest you study Table 5-2 carefully to confirm that you have made the most appropriate choice for your team and its project before creating a Team Project which you intend to use for real work.

TABLE 5-2: Process Comparison: MSF for CMMI, MSF for Agile, MSF for XP

	MSF for CMMI	MSF for Agile	MSF for XP
Process compatibility	Rational Unified Process (RUP) and similar	vRUP, Microsoft	Extreme Programming, Agile Model-Driven Development
Typical team size	50+	12+	4–18
Team type	Managed	Managed or self-organizing	Self-organizing
Project structure	Iterative with phases	Iterative with phases	Iterative, no phases

Continues

TABLE 5-2: *Continued*

	MSF for CMMI	MSF for Agile	MSF for XP
Governance	Envision, Plan, Build, Stabilize, Deploy, Governance, Operational Management	Envision, Plan, Build, Stabilize, Deploy	Implicit
Mandatory roles	[Same roles as MSF for Agile] + Auditor, Sponsor, and various managers and specialists	Business Analyst, Project Manager, Architect, Developer, Tester, Release Manager	Developer, Customer
Response to change	Slow; requirements fixed at start of project, and altered only by Change Review Board. Full audit trial.	Medium; requirements mostly identified at start of project. Managers authorize change. Audit trail available.	Fast; requirements identified as the project proceeds. Customer authorizes change. Audit trial possible.
Nonfunctional requirements (QoS)	Nonfunctional requirements specification document	Security, performance, and user experience issues are separately identified.	Handled during the exploration of a story by developer and customer
Risk management	Explicit	Explicit	Implicit
Project management	Explicit	Explicit	Implicit
Mandatory documents	Many	Few	None, but optional Vision Statement, Project Plan, and Check List documents
Work items (metrics)	Issue, Requirement, Review, Change Request, Risk, Bug, Task	Scenario, QoS, Risk, Bug, Task	Bug, Task, Story
Reports	Many	Many	Few
Process Guidance	Highly detailed and prescriptive	Detailed and may be prescriptive	Conceptual and elective

> **■ NOTE**
>
> A team type that is "managed" has no responsibility for deciding how or when its work should be done. Its activities are controlled by someone in a supervisory role, so by definition it cannot be self-organizing in the way we discussed in the preceding chapter.

CONCLUSION

This chapter introduced the concept of VSTS having a process-enabling framework that can be configured by the process template selected when you create your Team Project. In this way, VSTS can support teams that are following a wide variety of different software development processes, including MSF and CMMI. However, it also opens up the possibly of a team improving its process by exporting the process template from TFS at the end of a project, modifying it, and then importing it back into TFS for use with the next project; see Chapter 6. Therefore, with VSTS, you can make the process fit the specific needs of your project and team, rather than vice versa.

> **■ NOTE**
>
> VSTS Team Projects are organizational units for a group of people who share the same source code files and have a common development timetable. Visual Studio Projects (and Solutions) are organizational units for the programs developed by such a team.

6

Improving Your Process Framework

THIS CHAPTER PRESENTS two different ways in which you can improve the TFS process framework your team uses. First, we describe how you can add another work item type to an existing process framework to provide a new metric. Then, we explain how to export your current process framework to a process template so that it can be changed and then imported back into Team Foundation Server (TFS), ready for the team's next project. After reading this chapter, you will know how to adapt a process framework to fit better with your team and its work.

Providing a New Metric for an Existing Process Framework

The improvements you can make to a process framework once you've used it to create your Team Project are strictly limited. Indeed, the only thing you can really do is define some additional metrics so that you can monitor your progress in new ways. This is simply a matter of adding new work item types and then providing corresponding queries (or reports) to display the information that has been gathered.

Adding a New Work Item Type

A team will often decide to gather information about some new metric which suddenly seems important to the team. The OSPACS team, for example, became aware that it was spending much of its time changing the user interface, and it decided to add a new type of work item to help team members discover exactly how much effort was going into this type of work. Exercise 6-1 details the steps the team took to achieve this objective.

> **■ NOTE**
>
> Before starting the following exercises, check that the witexport.exe and witimport.exe programs have been installed in a directory of DevServer (TFS) that is included in its PATH environment variable; see Appendix A.

EXERCISE 6-1: Adding a New Work Item Type to a Team Project

The following exercise creates a new work item type called GuiTask for the OSPACS Team Project which you created in Exercise 5-1 in Chapter 5.

1. Log on to DevServer as Tom (OSPACS Project Administrator); see Appendix A for details about this PC and Tom's security groups.

2. Open a command prompt window and enter the following command, where /f defines the output file to be created, /t is the name of your TFS, /p is the name of your project, and /n is the name of the work item type:

```
witexport /f c:\Tom\GuiTask.xml /t DevServer /p OSPACS /n "Bug"
```

3. Edit the GuiTask.xml file and create your new work item type by changing the name attribute of WORKITEMTYPE from "Bug" to "GuiTask", and then perform a Find and Replace to replace "Bug" with "GuiTask" in the rest of the file. Save your work.

4. At the command prompt, enter the following command, where /f defines the input file containing the new work item type, /t is the name of your TFS, and /p is the name of your project:

```
witimport /f c:\Tom\GuiTask.xml /t DevServer /p OSPACS
```

5. Log off.

> **■ NOTE**
>
> The book's Web site contains information about Process Template Editors that allow you to add new work item types and perform similar template customization without having to edit the XML directly.

Adding a New Query

There is not much point in gathering information about a new metric unless you have the means to display it. Therefore, we explain in Exercise 6-2 how you might create a new query to list all the new GuiTask work items that the OSPACS team has generated on a form in Visual Studio's main window.

EXERCISE 6-2: Adding a New Query to a Team Project

This exercise creates a query called All GuiTasks and then creates a GuiTask work item so that you can run your new query to check that everything works correctly.

1. Log on to the DeveloperPC as Tom, start Visual Studio, and then connect to the OSPACS Team Project, as described in Exercise 5-7 in Chapter 5.

2. Add a GuiTask work item to the OSPACS project (Team | Add New Work Item | GuiTask), and then enter as much information about it as you feel is appropriate.

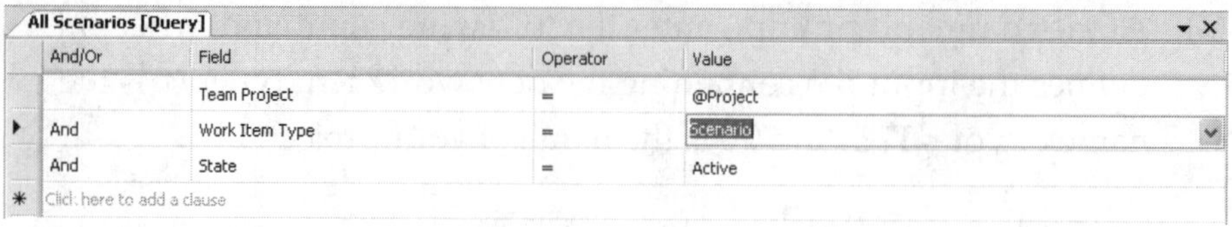

	And/Or	Field	Operator	Value
		Team Project	=	@Project
▶	And	Work Item Type	=	Scenario
	And	State	=	Active
✱	Click here to add a clause			

All Scenarios [Query]   ▾ X

FIGURE 6-1: Editing a query (Right-click I View Query)

3. Open your Team Explorer window and locate the All Scenarios query in your Team Queries folder. Open this query for editing (Right-click I View Query) so that you can set the value of its Work Item Type field to GuiTask; see Figure 6-1.

4. Save this adapted query as "All GuiTasks" (File I Save As) and use the controls in the Save Query As dialog box to specify it as a Team Query for the OSPACS Team Project.

5. Run the query (Right-click I View Results) and confirm that it displays the GuiTask work item created in step 2.

6. Log off.

■ NOTE

You can only add new work item types to your Team Project because editing or deleting existing work item types (or work item records) in the middle of a project might change the meaning of certain historic data used in your reports and queries.

Improving Your Process

Any substantial improvement to the team's process framework is expected to happen at the end of the project, when the experience is reviewed and the lessons learned are carried forward to the next project. This review often takes the form of a retrospective that typically comprises potentially days of discussions for the team (and managers) led by an experienced moderator at an offsite location. The resulting changes to your team's process will probably require some alterations to the process template it uses to create new Team Projects, which is what the rest of this chapter is about.

> **NOTE**
>
> The various process templates available to your team are stored in the TFS database. However, you can export this information as a set of XML files which you can then modify before importing them back into TFS in order to update the template.

Process Template Structure

The large collection of XML files and directories that are created when you export a process framework to a process template can initially appear intimidating. However, the key file you need to understand is ProcessTemplate.xml, which you can find in the template's root directory. This file is essentially a list of plug-ins, each with an identifier, a description, and a reference to another XML file. The following plug-ins are defined in the template belonging to MSF for Agile Software Development (a.k.a. MSF for Agile):

- **Classification**—The Classification.xml file defines the Team Project life cycle, which, in the case of MSF for Agile, is just a list of iterations. You can add or remove life cycle items as the project proceeds using the Areas and Iterations dialog box (Team | Team Project Settings), so there is usually no need to alter this file.

- **Groups**—When a Team Project is created the TFS Project Administrator group is created automatically. However, the GroupsAndPermissions.xml file defines some additional TFS groups, such as Reader and Contributor, together with their various permissions. Again, there is usually no need to alter this file because these groups and their associated permissions can be administered from the Team menu after the project has been created; see the section Administering Your Team Foundation Server Security Settings, in Chapter 5.

- **Reporting**—The ReportsTasks.xml file defines the reports in the Reports Site created for your Team Project. However, as you can add additional reports to this site using SQL Server's Report Designer (see Exercise 31-2 in Chapter 31), there is no need to change this file.

- **VersionControl**—The source files, documents, and other items created by your team. All this material is held securely on the TFS's version control database in a repository folder belonging to your Team Project. The VersionControl.xml file contains the settings and permissions necessary to access this repository, but as you can alter most of these settings after the Team Project has been created (see Section 3), there is seldom any reason to change this file.

- **WorkItemTracking**—All work that needs to be tracked in a project is described by appropriate work items. The following work item types are defined for MSF for Agile at the beginning of its WorkItems.xml file: Bug, Task, Quality of Service (QoS), Scenario, and Risk. These work items types are each defined by an additional XML file stored in the TypeDefinitions folder. WorkItems.xml also contains a list of queries appropriate to the types of work items in the project as well as an initial list of tasks for the project.

- **Portal**—The Web site created to help the team run the project is provided by Windows SharePoint Services (WSS) and contains the initial list of document libraries, folders, and files defined by the WssTasks.xml file. Most of this material is concerned with Process Guidance.

Importing and Exporting Process Templates

You can export and import the process templates stored in your TFS database from corresponding sets of directories and XML files on your hard disk using the Process Template Manager shown in Figure 6-2.

EXERCISE 6-3: Exporting a Process Template to Your Hard Disk As XML

After completing this exercise, you will have created on your local hard disk the collection of XML files that define the MSF for Agile process template.

1. Log on to the DeveloperPC as Tom (Team Foundation Administrator), start Visual Studio, and then connect to the OSPACS Team Project.

2. Open the Process Template Manager dialog box (Team | Team Foundation Server Settings | Process Template Manager):

   a. Select MSF for Agile Software Development from the list of process templates.

   b. Click Download to open a dialog box that allows you to select the directory for storing your template files. Create the directory C:\Tom\BSDAgile, and then select it.

   c. Click Save to close this directory selection dialog box and export the MSF for Agile process template as a collection of XML files into c:\Tom\BSDAgile.

3. Close the Process Template Manager dialog box and log off.

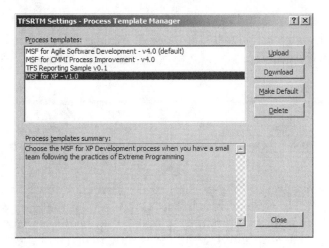

FIGURE 6-2: Process Template Manager (Team | Team Foundation Server Settings)

EXERCISE 6-4: Importing a Process Template from Your Hard Disk

In this exercise, you will alter the name of the process template exported in the preceding exercise and then import its collection of XML files back into your TFS before creating a new Team Project using this modified template.

1. Log on to the DeveloperPC as Tom (Team Foundation Administrator), as described in the previous exercise.

2. Use a text editor (Notepad) to open the file ProcessTemplate.xml within the directory containing the downloaded process template, and then alter the "name" and "description" elements, which are in the "metadata" section at the top of the file, so that they are unique in respect to any other templates stored in your TFS.

3. Open the Process Template Manager dialog box (Team | Team Foundation Server Settings | Process Template Manager):

    a. Click the Upload button to open a dialog box that allows you to select the folder containing your template's ProcessTemplate.xml file.

    b. Click the Upload button in this folder selection dialog box to copy the template into your TFS database.

    c. Close the dialog box.

4. Create a new Team Project (see Exercise 5-1 in Chapter 5), selecting the template you have just imported. After you have finished, confirm that it appears in your Team Explorer window as expected.

5. Log off.

■ TIP

It may seem strange to import a process template immediately after exporting it. However, errors in the XML files that make up a process template can be difficult to find, so make modifications in small steps and check that your template still works after each modification.

Changing Your Process Template

In this section, we describe the general procedure for altering your process template, but the nature of the changes will depend upon what you are seeking to do. In this case, the OSPACS team is adapting the MSF for Agile process template to make it more suitable for its use.

■ **NOTE**

The fact that most changes to the process can only be applied when you create a new Team Project limits your ability to make improvements as the project progresses. Accordingly, teams that rely completely on VSTS for process management may find this restriction a serious impediment to them working in a truly Agile way.

EXERCISE 6-5: Changing Work Item Types in Your Process Template

After completing the following exercise, you will have removed the QoS and Risk work item types from the MSF for Agile process template and renamed its Scenario work item type to "Story". You will also have removed the initial list of tasks created to help teams set up a Team Project of this type.

1. Log on to the DeveloperPC containing the exported process template directories and XML files created in Exercise 6-3.
2. Edit WorkItems.xml in the WorkItem Tracking directory so that you can remove any unnecessary set-up tasks by deleting the corresponding WI sections in the WORKITEMS section. Tip: Search for WI sections whose value for the field name System.Title begins with "Setup:".
3. Delete the QoS and Risk work item types in the WORKITEMTYPES section at the top of the WorkItems.xml file.

4. Add the new work item type, Story, by renaming the Scenario.xml work item type to "Story.xml", and then save your changes to WorkItems.xml.

5. Rename the file TypeDefinitions\Scenario.xml to "Story.xml", and then edit this file so that you can replace all occurrences of "scenario" with "story". Save your changes.

6. Re-create the OSPACS Team Project from this modified process template by deleting the existing Team Project (see Exercise 5-2 in Chapter 5) and then repeating Exercise 6-4, as well as Exercises 5-1, 5-3, 5-4, and 5-5 in Chapter 5. You should also add the GuiTask work item and query to your new OSPACS Team Project by repeating Exercises 6-1 and 6-2.

7. Log off, as you have finished the exercises in this chapter.

■ TIP

Yet again, we emphasize the need to make changes to your process template in a series of small steps. You should validate the template after each change by importing it back into TFS and using it to create a new Team Project.

CONCLUSION

Process improvement is the goal of any good software team, but in the case of an Agile team, this usually results in less process, not more. You can see this effect happening in Exercise 6-5, which shows how the OSPACS team adapted the MSF for Agile process template to create the first version of the MSF for XP template by removing various work items. In contrast, teams that have a prescriptive process tend to add things to their process rather than remove them, for every problem usually results in more process being added to avoid its reoccurrence. This difference goes to the very heart of what it means to be an Agile team, because by giving people responsibility for organizing their own work, you empower them to use their judgment and expertise rather attempting to identify their actions for every possible contingency.

> **■ TIP**
>
> Do not burden your team with unnecessary bureaucracy by adopting a process that is too sophisticated for the work you are doing. Start with a very simple process and then adapt it over the years with the goal of making it simpler still.

Review of Section 2
Introduce Agile Development

THE OSPACS TEAM undertook the following activities in an effort to create a process that was suitable for itself and its work:

- **Forming into an Agile team**—The OSPACS team restructured itself into a cross-functional OSPACS team that was located in the same room.
- **Learning about Agile**—An expert Extreme Programming (XP) practitioner helped the team understand what it means to have an Agile approach to software development.
- **Using the Visual Studio Team System (VSTS) process framework**—The team experimented by creating various types of process frameworks and assessed its strengths and weaknesses.
- **Creating its own process framework**—The team adapted the MSF for Agile template to fit better with the needs of the team and its project.

Appendix C shows how the OSPACS team supported its new organizational structure by removing the old partitions which had separated the offices of Sally, Tom, and Maggie from the area where the rest of the team worked. In addition, the team put the poster shown in Table S2-1 on its notice board in order to clarify its roles on this new Agile team.

TABLE S2-1: The OSPACS Team's New Organizational Structure

Role	Primary Responsibility	People
Customer	Says what the software must do and verifies that these requirements are met by creating suitable tests	Sally
Developers	Say how the software will be implemented, which means they must write the code and prove it works	Luke, Peter, Sarah, Tom, Maggie
Project Manager	Supports the project and provides its interface with the rest of the organization	Mike

> **▪ NOTE**
>
> People on Agile teams do not specialize in particular tasks or follow the prescriptive procedures of a production line; they simply apply themselves to whatever tasks are necessary for the delivery of valuable software.

The Team's Impressions

The team realized that its new process would not be perfect at the beginning. However, the process framework the team had created would at least allow the team members to make better use of VSTS during the next part of their project.

Project Manager: Mike

"I agreed to take on the project manager role only when Tom assured me that I would not need to spend hours gathering information and preparing reports."

Customer: Sally

"We should give this Agile idea a chance. I certainly like the idea of the team working on the features that the business can sell rather than just the stuff the techies want."

Developer: Maggie

"In the past, the time we took to create a release was determined by how quickly I could complete my testing. Now that everyone can get involved in this work, we should be able to eliminate this bottleneck."

Developer: Tom

"I was really impressed by how little time it took me to create a Team Project and set up all the team's tools and infrastructure."

Developer: Sarah

"Becoming self-organizing does mean proving ourselves worthy of being allowed to take responsibility for organizing our own work. We need to show that this results in a better job, done faster, and with fewer resources."

Developer: Peter

"Adapting the MSF for Agile process template helped us feel that we actually owned the process. We just didn't need a lot of the stuff it provided."

Developer: Luke

"Anything is going to be better than the 'no process' situation we had before."

Agile Values

The work the team did in applying the Whole Team and Sitting Together practices helped foster the following values.

Communication

Working together as a whole team promotes communication, as does the practice of Sitting Together. This is necessary because a design team needs to interact much more freely than other types of teams.

Feedback

Decision making now happens within the team, which shortens the feedback loop and therefore should make teams more responsive to change.

Courage

The cross-functional nature of an Agile team encourages people to work in a spirit of mutual cooperation. This generates courage because people realize they are not working alone and can share their responsibilities.

Simplicity

One of the strengths of an Agile team is the simple way in which it manages its own work, so you must take care that introducing a tool such as VSTS doesn't compromise this virtue by introducing layers of needless bureaucracy. The fact that you can e-mail the whole team each time you alter some code doesn't mean that you should!

Respect

Making the customer a part of the team makes business and development people work together, and this generates respect because they each gain an understanding of their respective importance to the success of the project.

◼ Section 3
Use Version Control

VERSION CONTROL IS a fundamental prerequisite for any sort of safe development in a team-based environment. Chapter 7 introduces the fundamental concepts of version control in terms of how it helps us manage changes to a shared code base. The next chapter explains how you might set up version control for your project using the Team Foundation Version Control (TFVC) tool, and this is followed by Chapter 9, which explains how it is used. Finally, Chapter 10 suggests ways in which you can police the use of version control, for without a few rules, your team cannot hope to manage its code effectively.

Photograph by Darren McCollester (Copyright Getty Images, 2004).

Version control acts a bit like a traffic cop. It controls the way files are moved in and out of the team's repository.

> **■ NOTE**
>
> Is it better to use term *version control* or *source control?* Clearly, the team developing VSTS at Microsoft went through the same dilemma, as you will find both terms used in the product. We decided to use the term *version control* in this book because it reflects the fact that you can put more things under version control than just your source files.

Story from the Trenches

Unfortunately for the software industry, the millennium bug was a problem that was all too easy for people to understand; after midnight December 31, 1999, the year would need to be represented by four digits, not just the usual two. The required change seemed so trivial and the cost so huge that questions were asked as to whether the millennium bug wasn't masking a more fundamental problem in the way computer systems were built and maintained.

Early in 1998, I visited a well-known investment bank in London to discuss joining its millennium bug task force. The interview started with a brief presentation from the senior manager who was heading up the task force. He told me all about the bank's proud history and the part its systems played in the smooth running of the financial world. However, his initial confidence evaporated as soon as we started to discuss the millennium bug issue. I was given a printout showing the Y2K readiness of the bank's various systems, and it was evident that it was in a mess. In order to fix the millennium bug, the bank would need to rebuild its systems, but the list showed that some systems didn't have any source code, while others had source code versions that didn't match the versions in production. This was why the manager was so worried.

Many organizations around the world had the same problem; they were simply unable to rebuild all of their production systems. Most of these systems hadn't been touched for years because the need for them to change had long since ceased to justify the cost of keeping their development teams together. The project's source code files were often on old tapes and floppy disks scattered around in cabinets and at the back of people's desks. Nobody really knew what versions of what files would actually re-create the system. Typically, the code changes themselves were trivial. What took the time was building a new version of the production code, and in many cases, this proved impossible. Therefore, entirely new systems had to be built which significantly increased the scope and cost of the work. In this way, our industry learned the hard way that proper version control wasn't just about controlling changes to a file during its development; it was also about safeguarding these valuable assets over their entire lifetime.

Most of what is written about version control relates to the way it allows a single code base to be shared among a team. However, as the preceding story illustrates, version control has an equally important role in ensuring that you can always rebuild your project from its source code.

■ 7
Managing Change

THIS CHAPTER EXPLAINS the basic concept of version control and introduces the essential terminology you must know when using tools designed to help you manage and control a shared set of project files. Therefore, all readers, regardless of their background, should be able to understand the purpose of the features provided by the Team Foundation Version Control (TFVC) system that are summarized at the end of the chapter. In subsequent chapters, we will build upon this information to explain how a small Agile team can make good use of the TFVC tool when implementing version control for its project.

Sharing Information among Your Team

A software team generates lots of information, but only a small fraction of it will eventually become part of the product it is developing. This is because design is a process of discovery, and frequently you find out how to do something only by generating information about how not to do it.[1] Consequently, we often find ourselves *refactoring* code several times before arriving at an acceptable solution; each time revising one or more code files. And it isn't just our source code files that change; bug reports, schedules,

---

1. [MTDF] Reinertsen, Donald. *Managing the Design Factory* (Simon & Schuster, 1997), Chapter 4.

specifications, and all manner of other documents undergo a similar series of revisions as the project progresses.

Why You Shouldn't Keep Source Files in Shared Folders

Any software project involving more than just a few files maintained by one person needs to consider change management, particularly in respect to the project's source code; otherwise, project files tend to end up in a shared network folder (directory), which leads to the following sorts of problems:

- **Fixing bugs**—You spend all day changing a source file to fix a bug and then copy it into the shared directory ready for the overnight build. However, the next day your code changes don't appear in the product because someone else changed the same file and copied it into the shared directory after you did.

- **Controlling change**—Anybody with access to the shared directory can add new files, change existing ones, or even delete them; there's no record of who did what and why. One moment your project builds without error, but the next it is broken and all you know is that someone recently changed a few files.

- **Distributing consistent changes to the team**—A change in one file often depends upon a change in another; for example, adding a text box to MyForm changes both MyForm.cs and MyForm.resx. However, in a shared directory, there's no mechanism to tie these changes together, so a developer might not update both files; consequently, the rest of the team gets only part of the change.

- **Making backups**—There is no point in backing up a set of source files unless they are consistent and can be used to rebuild the software without any errors: You need to create backups that work. Unfortunately, in a shared directory, there's no guarantee of this.

- **Rolling back**—When a bug is discovered you might want to return the project to a working state by restoring the shared directory from a backup, thus rolling back the changes that caused the problem. However, if you have to roll back several days to find a backup that works, you lose a lot of code.

In software development, version control is a big issue because you are potentially managing changes made by many people across hundreds of files, all of which are intrinsically interrelated. You cannot approach this task in the same way you might share a Word document among a group of reviewers. You need to have proper procedures supported by an appropriate version control tool.

> **■ NOTE**
>
> Effective version control does not result from putting an expensive tool on your team's desktops. It results from the team understanding why version control is important and then working in a way that makes good use of such a tool.

Keeping Source Files in a Repository

A version control tool provides your team with a central repository to keep its project files safe and to manage the changes made to them. You can think of a repository as being like a special sort of filesystem which can be accessed using only your version control tool. For example, the Team Project Wizard uses TFVC to make a root folder (see step 6 of Exercise 5-1, in Chapter 5), and your team then uses the TFVC tools to fill this root folder with the files and directories it wants to share. In small projects, your team might have just one such directory and a few source files, but in large projects, there may be dozens of different directories and hundreds of files to control.

The repository will normally reside on a server that is accessible to all members of the project team. The version control tool's "checkout" function copies all the project's files from this repository to a directory on your PC that becomes your workspace (also known as the working folder or working copy). Subsequently, you use the version control tool's "get latest version" function to resynchronize this collection of files with the repository, thereby keeping your workspace up-to-date with the changes that fellow team members made to the project files. Conversely, when you want to make the changes in your workspace directory available to the rest of the team, the tool's "check-in" function will upload into the repository your new (or changed) files and directories. You don't have to remember which files you've altered in your workspace directory because the version control tool will typically track the changes you've made and apply them to the repository as a single *changeset* to ensure their consistency; see Exercise 8-3 in Chapter 8.

Although a version control tool often has a large number of other functions, most of the time you will simply cycle through the following sequence (see Luke's actions in Figure 7-1):

- Update your workspace from the repository; *get latest version*.
- Edit, build, and test these files on your computer.
- Put the files back into the repository to share your work; *check-in*.

■ NOTE

The preceding terminology applies to TFVC, but other version control tools often have different names for these functions. For example, the Subversion[2] tool uses "Update" instead of "get latest version" and "Commit" in place of "check-in".

A version control tool allows you to add a set of files to a project folder in your repository and then apply a sequence of changesets to them. Every time a changeset is applied to the repository, the files it contains are stamped with a unique number. In this way, the task of software development becomes little more than applying a series of discrete changes to progress the team's shared code (and tests) from one version to another.

---

2. Subversion Web site (http://subversion.tigris.org).

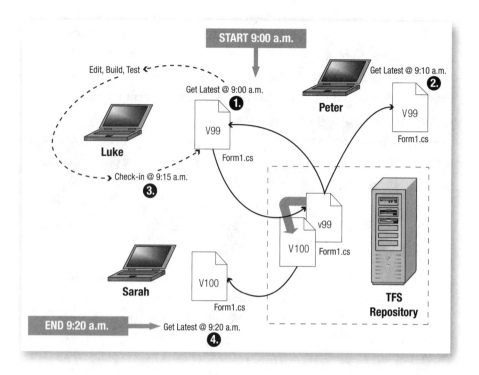

FIGURE 7-1: Version control tools helping a team of people to share a file

Shared Code Practice

Shared code means the system's source code doesn't belong to individuals; it belongs to the team. There are no off-limits areas in the code base, so everyone is able, and indeed expected, to make improvements whenever the opportunity arises.

On a team using the Shared Code practice, there's no finger-wagging about who wrote a bad bit of code; it's just quickly rewritten to make it better. In this way, the quality of the entire code base is allowed to continuously improve. It's a case of tidying up as you go, rather than letting the code base get into such a state that months need to be scheduled for doing little else but working through a long list of essential renovations. The Shared Code practice helps distribute knowledge about code throughout

Continues

the team. It naturally widens the scope of what people have worked on and so avoids **black holes,** areas of code that are the sole preserve of one or two individuals. The Shared Code practice is about learning to play nicely. It is a key differentiator between a group of individuals employed on a project and a team working together.

A first step toward implementing the Shared Code practice is doing pair programming, as all production code is then written by two people, not just one, which helps break down the habit of people owning the code they write. However, before extending the Shared Code practice to the point of allowing anyone to change any code at any time, you need to put in place various other practices and conventions:

- Put all source code files under proper version control because this provides the essential mechanism that allows team members to share a common set of files and reverse any individual changes that later prove problematic.

- Implement the Continuous Integration practice so that any conflicts between the changes made by different people are quickly identified and fixed; see Chapter 12.

- Use test-driven development (TDD) to help you safely make your changes by providing a comprehensive set of tests to find any unexpected side effects which might break the program; see Section 5.

- Adopt a common set of coding standards to make the coding style consistent. This avoids situations such as when two people repeatedly change the same code because they can't agree on the common placement of curly brackets; see Scott Ambler's essay, "Coding Guidelines."[3]

You know when you've implemented the Shared Code practice properly because there is a sense of collective responsibility for the team delivering quality code that works.

---

3. Scott Ambler's Coding Guidelines (www.ambysoft.com/essays/codingGuidelines.html).

> **▪▪ NOTE**
>
> Chapter 10 describes how the TFVC helps enforce a team's coding standards by requiring people to verify their source code files with the VSTS Static Code Analysis tool before checking them into the repository.

Using a Version Control System

Many different types of version control systems are available to developers. You may have already encountered products such as Microsoft's Source-Safe and open source projects such as CVS[4] and Subversion. Most version control systems have a common feature set and differ primarily in areas such as price, reliability, and ease of use. Therefore, let's review the ways in which a version control system is commonly used before looking at the specific features of TFS version control.

Security

The central repository is controlled so that only authorized users can access the files it holds. Usually, each user's access is limited to areas of the repository that contain the files related to their projects. For example, the Team Project created in Exercise 5-1 in Chapter 5 made a folder called $/OSPACS in the TFS version control repository, and only people who have been made members of the OSPACS team can access it. All files in the OSPACS project added to version control are put into this folder, or one of its subfolders.

> **▪▪ NOTE**
>
> You can implement security using a security service provided by the version control system itself or by using the security mechanisms of the underlying operating system.

---

4. CVS documentation (http://sourceforge.net/docs/E04/).

Frequent Integration

Efficient use of version control depends upon everyone agreeing that they will check in only working code. This means you must always test the software on your own PC before checking in your changes. When everyone follows this rule, anyone can check out the project files at any time and get a collection of files on her PC that she can build into a working product. Inevitably, though, someone will check in files that haven't passed all the tests, so the latest set of files in the repository will contain errors. Therefore, it is good practice to have a central machine that automatically updates, rebuilds, and tests the team's software regularly throughout the day. This allows you to quickly detect such errors and fix them before they propagate to the working copies on everyone's machine.

> **■ NOTE**
>
> Agile teams often perform **continuous integration,** which means that a central build machine (BuildLab PC) rebuilds the team's software after each check-in. In this way, each developer's changes are verified almost as soon as they have been made; see Chapter 11.

Atomic Check-in

When a **changeset** (a collection of files) is checked into the repository, it is important that the operation is atomic; either all the files in the changeset are checked into the repository or none of them is checked in. This is because changes in one source file often depend on changes to another; therefore, a collection of changes must be made consistently. Otherwise, you might not be able to rebuild the products.

Rolling Back Versions

When a problem is detected in the contents of the repository, the version control tool makes it very easy to restore the file collection to some previous working state. This is because the repository records each changeset that is applied so that you can undo the changes simply by rolling back a sequence of changesets. Each time a changeset is applied, a new version number (sometimes called a revision number) is created for the repository; therefore, rolling back simply returns each file to its state at a previous version.

The repository never deletes a changeset, so the version control tool allows you to roll back the workspace on your PC from, say, version 100 (with the error) to version 99 (without the error). You might then reimplement the feature correctly, test it, and check in the changes to create version 101. In this way, anyone can subsequently investigate this error simply by checking out these versions and comparing them. The error is contained in the difference between the files at versions 100 and 101; see Figure 7-2.

Storing Deltas

Although you can store any type of file in your project's repository folder, version control tools are usually optimized for handling standard text files. This means that when you check in a source code file, the tool will find the lines that have actually changed and then record them in what is known as a **delta.** Conversely, when you check in an image file (JPEG) the entire file must be recorded because the same tool is unable to determine the pixels you have changed. It is clearly more efficient to store changes to source files as deltas because seldom do you alter more than a few lines in your code at a time. Storing changes in this way also allows you to use certain special features of your version control tool, such as diff or merge, as we will discuss next.

■ **NOTE**

Deltas allow a changeset to become simply a list of files and the contents of the lines that have changed in each of them. In this way, your team can apply thousands of changesets without consuming huge amounts of storage.

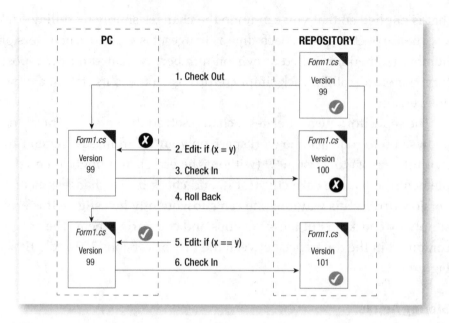

FIGURE 7-2: Version control tools rolling back a file to a working state

Locking and Merging

On a team, there is always the potential for conflict when more than one person works on the same file at the same time. To help resolve such problems, locks are applied to the files held under version control to ensure that write access to them is suitably controlled. There are basically two approaches to locking files: single-checkout and multiple-checkout.

In the **single-checkout approach** (also known as strict locking), the lock is applied when the file is checked out, so once you've altered a file in your workspace, it effectively becomes a read-only file in everyone else's workspace. Different version control tools achieve this goal in different ways, but the idea is the same: the first person to change the file applies a lock that is released only when it is checked back into the repository. Single-checkout can waste a lot of time when different people frequently change the same file, because they will each have to wait for it to be checked in before they can make their alterations.

The other approach to locking files under version control is the **multiple-checkout approach** (also known as optimistic locking). It prevents you from checking in a file when the version in the repository is later than the version last copied into your workspace—in other words, the version of the file that you altered and are now attempting to check in. You can resolve this problem simply by updating your workspace to get the latest changes to the file from the repository, reimplementing your changes, and then again trying to check in the file. Multiple-checkout means that many people can edit the same file at the same time, and this can significantly speed up the pace of development. However, it comes at the cost of having to merge your changes with those made by anyone else who checked in the file before you. Fortunately, when you update your workspace, the version control tool is smart enough to notice whether you've changed a file that it is attempting to update, and rather than just overwriting it with the latest version from the repository, it will prompt you to merge the two files together (and even volunteer to do the job for you).

> **▪ TIP**
>
> Work on just one project at a time and keep all its files in a single work-space directory on your PC. Regularly update this workspace and promptly check your changes back into the repository to minimize file conflicts with other team members.

Multiple-checkout usually works well in practice because people tend to work on their own tasks, so usually they need to change different parts of the file. For example, if Luke and Sarah had updated their workspaces at the same time and now both were editing version 99 of the file app.cs, Luke might alter line 55 to fix a bug in the app.print method while Sarah might change line 86 to correct a problem in the app.backup method. In such circumstances, the changes are totally independent, so after Luke checks in his changes to create version 100, Sarah can update her workspace and then let the version control tool automatically merge this new version of app.cs with the one in her workspace. Effectively, this adds Luke's changes at line 55 to Sarah's changes at line 86. After creating this merged app.cs, Sarah would then build the software on her own PC and run the unit tests (see Section 5) to assure herself that all was well before checking the file into the repository to create version 101. If anyone wanted to know what Luke and Sarah had done to fix these separate bugs, he could use a tool such as diff to compare version 99 of app.cs with version 101; see Figure 7-3.

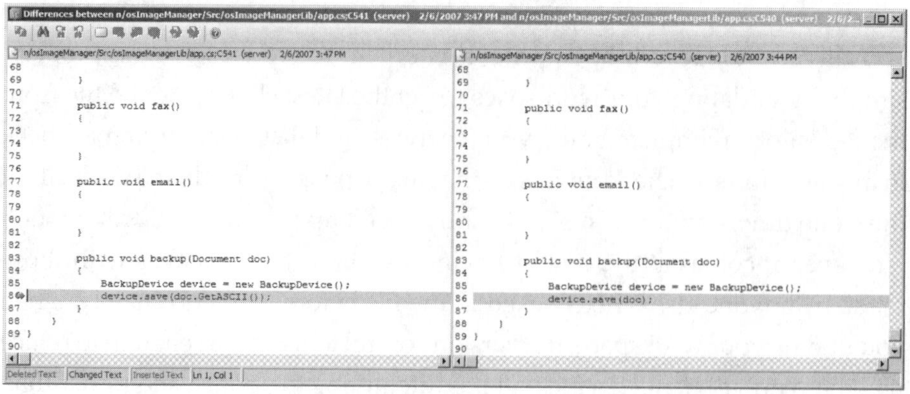

FIGURE 7-3: Visual Studio version control diff tool (File I Source Control I Compare)

Multiple-checkout is very effective when you have a version control tool with these diff and merge features for the types of files you're attempting to manage; usually text files containing version code. It is less effective when you're using files that are not supported by the tool's diff and merge features, such as image (JPEG) files, for example. For this reason, VSTS allows you to select the type of locking used for each type of file in your project (Team I Team Foundation Server Settings I Version Control File Types) as well as select different types of merge and diff tools for them.

Labeling and Branching

Version numbers allow the version control tool to identify your changesets so that, when necessary, you can roll back the changes made to your project files and restore them to some previous state. However, sometimes the collection of project files reaches a particularly noteworthy state, such as when you can build them into a product which may be released to the business. Although you might remember these significant version numbers, it is better to use the version control tool to "label" the contents of the repository at such points in your project. You might, for example, label the latest versions of all the files in your team's repository as "Release 1.0.3". This would allow you to roll back to this state in the future by specifying the label name rather than trying to recall the correct version number of the individual files.

▪ TIP

Use the file AssemblyInfo.cs to link the version labels in your repository to the executable files you deploy. This file is automatically generated when you create a Visual Studio Project, and it defines the
assembly's file version number in a form such as "1.0.0.0."

Most version control tools support a feature to allow the creation of separate lines of development called **branches** (see Figure 7-4). Essentially, this
allows you to make a separate copy of your repository so that you can
develop the code base in more than one direction at the same time. For example, most of your team might be working with the "main" branch (trunk)
while a smaller group works with the "Release 1.0.3" branch to fix some bugs
in your last release. However, working with multiple branches of development can be challenging, so we suggest that you consider the alternatives (see
the Single Code Base Practice sidebar) before creating a branch; often you
will find that creating a label is a simpler way to achieve the same objective.

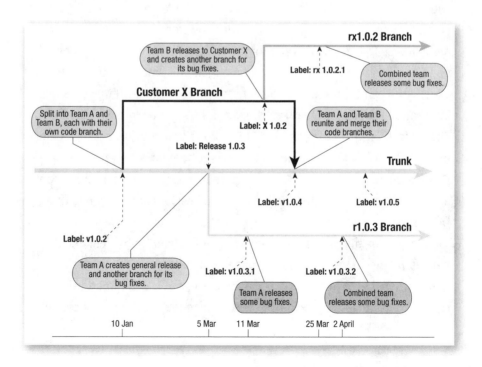

FIGURE 7-4: Timeline showing the creation of labels and different code branches

> ## ■ WARNING
>
> The management of your team's source code becomes more complex once you start creating additional branches, so you need to take particular care to follow a consistent system of labeling; otherwise, it can be difficult to keep it under proper control.

Single Code Base Practice

The Single Code Base practice means that VSTS version control manages just one main line of development for your Team Project, so all shared code (and test) files relate to a single representation of the system under development. Therefore, you avoid creating different sets of files (i.e., branches) for particular customers, special releases, and so forth.

Code duplication is an evil that most developers spend a considerable amount of time trying to eradicate; refactoring (Chapter 15) is concerned with eliminating duplication, and so are many design patterns. It seems crazy, therefore, to undo all this good work by creating a parallel development branch that duplicates your entire code base. Multiple lines of development mean that once you've fixed a bug in one branch, you have to do exactly the same work in another branch. Each branch will have its own integration problems (Chapter 11), so one fix soon becomes many fixes. The difficulties of keeping these multiple code branches synchronized are exceeded only by the problems of merging them back together at some point in the future. Most people who have ever worked for any significant amount of time with multiple code branches will tell you the same thing: Don't do it; find another way!

Implementing the Single Code Base practice is a matter of seeking alternatives whenever you're tempted to create a code branch. If you've inherited a product with more than one code branch, you need to address the reasons they arose so that you can find ways to reunite them; if necessary, do this one branch at a time. Let's look at some of the common reasons people cite for creating a code branch and the alternatives they might have:

- **Release branch**—Development continues in the main branch while a small team prepares the code in a release branch for customer deployment. Alternative: Make the product ready for release at the end of each iteration (see Chapter 11).

- **Branch for each customer**—There are separate development branches to customize the product for each customer. Alternative: Make code execution depend upon certain configuration settings.

- **New-product development**—One team continues to maintain the existing product while another works on the next-generation product. Alternative: Split the code base according to certain well-defined interfaces so that both teams can work on their own set of independent components for both the new and the old product.

It's not always a bad idea to make a code branch. For example, you might want to create a temporary branch to try out an idea or to do some major refactoring. This allows you to keep your work safe in the VSTS repository and perhaps even make it available to a few other members of the team. However, your temporary branch should not contain shared code in the sense of the Shared Code practice; you might need to discard this code if the cost of its maintenance becomes too high or if its reunion with the main code line seems too difficult. There are other justifiable reasons for creating a separate code branch, but you must always carefully consider the alternatives before taking such a step, particularly if the branch might have a long life.

■ NOTE

The TFVC tool supports the idea of people creating temporary code branches with its "shelve" feature, which we describe in Chapter 9.

Software Configuration Management

In order to properly establish and maintain the integrity of your project's software products throughout their development life cycle, you need to look further than just managing your source code. You need to consider everything that makes your software products what they are: the setup of your development environment, the bug reports and feature requests (stories), the third-party libraries, and so forth. All these things play a part in driving your project forward, so you need to include them in your change management strategy.

■ NOTE

Our story about the millennium bug at the beginning of this section illustrated the cost of failing to manage the configuration of your software properly.

One of the ways you can implement a change management strategy is to introduce some form of Software Configuration Management (SCM). Essentially, this involves establishing a baseline to define the current configuration of your project and then managing all subsequent changes to this baseline until you establish a new baseline, at which point you repeat the process. In this way, the entire history of your project can be traced simply by looking at a series of baselines and the changes that made them happen. It is a matter of extending the concept of a changeset to include not just the source code, but also all the things that cause your project to progress.

There is considerable interest in SCM because it gives people detailed information about the progress of a project. This information helps the team understand what is happening so that it can better control the project. A report, for example, might show that the number of outstanding bug reports increased significantly between one baseline and the next; information that might prompt an investigation so that the underlying cause can be identified and resolved. Some projects, particularly those with formal auditing and traceability requirements, put you in the realm of sophisticated SCM practices. However, for other types of projects, you might be able to implement SCM effectively enough for your needs just by taking the following steps:

- **Uniquely identify items**—Establish the current configuration by identifying all the things you need in order to make your software products in some form of list that will form the baseline. Your source code, for example, may be identified by a label, your tools and third-party libraries can be identified by their product versions, and so forth. A Word document (BuildNotes.doc) might be a good way to keep such a list, and when the file is added to your repository, its version number effectively defines the baseline.

- **Review items before baselining**—Set up a procedure so that items are reviewed before they are baselined. You might require, for example, that all source code files pass their unit tests before they are checked into the repository. You might also require a colleague to peer review your work before checking it into the repository; see the Pair Programming practice in Chapter 2. Such reviews ensure the quality of the software product at each baseline.

- **Implement change control**—Set up a mechanism so that all changes to the project are made according to an agreed protocol. You can achieve this simply by ensuring that everyone on the team uses the version control tool to make her changes to the project. VSTS can then be configured to police these procedures as well as the review process; see Chapter 10. This may avoid the need for you to set up a formal Change Review Board.

- **Secure storage in a repository**—The source code, tests, bug reports, stories, build notes, project files, and so forth need to be kept safe and secure. The repository provided by TFS version control has a facility to audit and control user access, so it is ideal for this purpose.

Although SCM can bring significant benefits in terms of better controlling and understanding your project, also be aware that it can encourage just the sort of heavy reliance on software process that an Agile project is seeking to avoid. It is easy to get carried away and create a bloated bureaucracy of change requests, sign-offs, and endless documentation. Therefore,

Agile teams should seek guidance from sources such as Berczuk and Appleton[5] and then focus on those aspects of SCM that actually help them produce better software.

> **■ WARNING**
>
> It is almost impossible to retrospectively apply SCM. Therefore, talk with your customer about change management at the start of every project, decide on a suitable strategy, and then take expert advice as needed.

VSTS Support for Version Control Tools

Now that we have dealt with the basic concepts of version control, we can sensibly describe the support that VSTS provides for version control in terms of the way different tools can be integrated with your Integrated Development Environment (IDE), the features of the new TFVC tool, and support for teams that are not using Visual Studio. In this way, you should get some idea of the options that are available to your team when managing and controlling the changes to its project files.

Integration with Visual Studio

The integration between your version control tool and Visual Studio is achieved using various published interfaces.[6] Therefore, vendors other than Microsoft can provide version control tools that offer a high degree of integration with your IDE simply by developing a standard plug-in component. Indeed, the TFVC tool is integrated with Visual Studio in exactly this way, as is Microsoft's original version control tool, SourceSafe.[7] Therefore, it is

---

5. [SCM] Berczuk, Stephen P., with Brad Appleton. *Software Configuration Management Patterns* (Addison-Wesley, 2003).
6. Microsoft publishes details of these SCCI and Visual Studio Industry Partner (VSIP) interfaces to its technology partners.
7. Microsoft Web site for Visual SourceSafe 2005 (http://msdn.microsoft.com/vstudio/products).

quite feasible for your team to use a version control tool other than TFVC with VSTS.

> **▪. NOTE**
>
> The Visual Studio Options dialog box (Tools | Options) allows you to select other types of Source Control plug-ins.

TFVC Features

Team Foundation Version Control is an entirely new version control system that uses a SQL Server database as its file store rather than relying on the specialized directory structures found in products such as Microsoft's SourceSafe and Subversion. TFVC also provides close integration not just with the Visual Studio Client Tier, but also with the rest of VSTS by using the Version Control Service in the TFS Application Tier; see Figure 12-1 in Chapter 12.

TFVC is an enterprise-level product which Microsoft claims has been successfully used on a number of large projects to support hundreds of developers. However, we feel it will serve small Agile teams (or even one-developer projects) as well. In terms of the material we have covered in this chapter, the various TFVC features can be summarized as follows:

- **Project Repository**—A central place where valuable project information can be deposited for safekeeping. TFVS implements atomic check-in and can restrict access to this repository to particular people. However, you must establish your own procedures for backing up and restoring its data; see the TFS Administrators Guide.[8]
- **Undo**—Each time a file is altered and checked into the repository, a new revision is created and its changes are stored away. This means you can use the TFVC diff tool to review how the contents of a particular file have changed revision by revision. It also allows you to

---

8. TFS Administrators Guide (http://go.microsoft.com/fwlink/?LinkID=52459).

undo these changes when required by rolling back to a specific revision; see Exercise 9-4 in Chapter 9.

- **Lock and Merge**—TFVS supports both single- and multiple-checkout, so you can work efficiently with other members of the team and manage any conflicts that arise when more than one developer attempts to work on the same file; see Chapter 9.

- **Version labeling**—Apply a label to a snapshot of the project files at their latest revision in order to associate them all with common events, such as a specific Team Build. You can subsequently check out this particular version of the project files, effectively allowing you to roll back the state of the project, as described earlier. However, such labels are also not applied to other TFS information stores, such as the Work Item database.

- **Branching**—TFVS allows you to create multiple branches of your code base and gives you a tool to help merge them together again. This book does not discuss branching in any great detail because it conflicts with the Single Code Base practice.

- **Shelving**—You can put all the files in your current workspace onto a virtual "shelve" in the Team Project's repository folder so that you can check out another file collection into your workspace and work on something else for a while; see Chapter 9. Shelves support those interruptions that inevitably occur during development by providing a secure way to save work that has not yet been built and integrated.

- **Check-in policy/notes/links to work items and builds**—These features may allow you to implement SCM by ensuring that source code is reviewed and tested before being checked into the repository and then linked to a specific build. They also give your project facilities for auditing and traceability so that you can discover who made what changes, when, and why.

- **Remote access**—Teams that are geographically separated can gain remote access to shared code stored in the TFVC repository by installing a proxy server to make best use of their network connections.

We hope this list helps you compare TFVC with any other version control tools you may be considering. However, before deciding to use something different, you should investigate the sort of integration the tool offers with other parts of TFS, for it is the close integration of tools that really differentiates Visual Studio Team System as a product.

> ### ■■ NOTE
>
> The contents of your Team Project's Documents folder are managed by Windows SharePoint Services, which has an entirely separate version control system, so any label applied to the contents of your TFVC repository will not be applied to these files.

TFS Support for Eclipse and Other Types of IDEs

Some teams may decide to use TFVC for their Team Project repository, but they may not want to use Visual Studio to access it. TFVC makes it possible to develop such a client by providing the necessary interfaces. Indeed, a number of vendors have already created such products. For example, SourceGear[9] has developed Teamprise, which is a suite of client applications that access the source control and item tracking features of TFS from the Eclipse[10] IDE as well as from platforms such as Linux and Mac OS X.

CONCLUSION

Over the years, we've encountered a frightening number of teams that are developing software without any form of version control and an even larger number of teams that are using it as just a backup and restore mechanism for their source files. Let us be clear about this: Until your team is using version control properly, you simply cannot work in an Agile way.

---

9. SourceGear: access to TFS from Eclipse (www.teamprise.com).
10. Eclipse: open source IDE supported by IBM (www.eclipse.org).

This is why we discuss version control so early in the book. It is the first step your team needs to take toward better software development, for it allows your team to control the changes made to a common set of source files as well as to manage the configuration of its software. The following chapters in this section of the book explain how the TFVC tool can help your team safely take this step.

■8
Setting Up TFS Version Control

THIS CHAPTER EXPLAINS how to set up an initial collection of files and directories for your Team Project to provide a consistent structure into which subsequent Visual Studio Projects and Solutions can be stored. We introduce the Code and Test practice so that you can understand which files you need to store in this structure, and we discuss the various ways in which you can handle the archiving of third-party libraries. The chapter concludes with some advice about importing source files and backing up your repository as well as administering its settings and security.

Structuring Your Team Project

The Team Foundation Version Control (TFVC) system is set up during the installation of Team Foundation Server (TFS) and its associated tools are installed on your desktop with Visual Studio Team Suite (or the separate Editions). Therefore, most of the work involved in setting up version control for your project is concerned with organizing your TFVC repository so that everyone on the team can find things easily.

Production and Spike Folders

In Visual Studio Team System (VSTS), all root folders in the TFVC repository must belong to a Team Project that reflects the fact that the primary level of organization for material in the repository is the project team. Teams are free to organize their part of the repository as they see fit within this root folder, but we suggest you start by creating a division between the material your team intends to deliver to the business and any nonproduction code or tests that it might develop from time to time.

■. TIP

Apply the simple rule that only code developed according to the team's production standards and practices goes in the Production folder hierarchy; everything else goes in the Spike folder.

EXERCISE 8-1: Creating Folders in Your Repository

The following exercise creates two folders called Production and Spike immediately below the $/OSPACS repository root folder.

1. Log on to DeveloperPC2 as Peter (OSPACS Contributor), start Visual Studio, and then connect to the OSPACS Team Project, as described in Exercise 5-7 in Chapter 5; see Appendix A for details about this PC and Peter's security groups.

2. Open the Source Control Explorer (View | Other Windows), select the $/OSPACS root folder created in Exercise 5-1 in Chapter 5, and choose Get Latest Version from its context menu.

3. The Browse for Folder dialog box opens because you have not yet defined a workspace directory on DeveloperPC2. Therefore, create the directories c:\Peter\OSPACS for the workspace with the Make New Folder button and then click OK to close the dialog box and complete the Get Latest Version operation.

4. Select the $/OSPACS root folder in your Source Control Explorer and create two new folders for $/OSPACS, named "Production"

and "Spike", by choosing New Folder from the Source Control menu (File | Source Control | New Folder).

5. Synchronize the repository with your workspace by repeating step 2 so that the Production and Spike directories are created in c:\Peter\OSPACS.

Agile teams often use the term *spike* when describing the prototyping work people do to explore some aspect of their project. Normally a developer would store such code in a personal shelveset (see Exercise 9-6 in Chapter 9) until it was no longer required, at which point it would be discarded. However, we suggest you create a standard repository folder called Spike in the root folder of your Team Project in order to emphasize the fact that no code found in this folder can be used for production purposes. Defining this folder at the start of your project will help ensure that this policy is upheld.

> **WARNING**
>
> The software produced during a spike should never be simply pasted into production code. Instead, it must be completely rewritten using production standards and practices agreed on by your team (e.g., Pair Programming, Test-First Programming, etc.).

Organization of Visual Studio Solutions, Projects, and Directories

A Team Project is typically concerned with the development of software in one or more Visual Studio Solutions, each of which contains a separate collection of Visual Studio Projects. Your team should agree on a standard directory structure in which to store these Solutions and Projects, as this encourages people to place files correctly which then makes it easier for others to find them. For example, the OSPACS team has two Visual Studio Solutions: one for its image management product osImageManager, and another for its Web site product ospacsWeb. Therefore, the team might decide to arrange the files and directories it is going to create for the osImageManager Solution into the following structure within the $/OSPACS/Production folder in its repository:

- **osImageManager**—Contains the Visual Studio Solution files that the team needs to share:
  - **Db**—Contains database scripts to rebuild the product's database, run queries, and so forth
  - **Documents**—Contains team documents such as Release Notes that need to be added to TFVC version control rather than put into a SharePoint Document Library
  - **Help**—Contains the files needed to create the product's help file (*.chm)
  - **Install**—Contains the files needed to create the application's installation program
  - **Libs**—Contains third-party libraries used by the application
  - **Src**—Root for the various Visual Studio Projects that belong to the Solution and so may be built together (Build | Build Solution):
    - **osImageManagerApp**—Windows Forms app; the startup project that provides the graphical user interface
    - **osImageManagerLib**—Class library containing most of the code
    - **osImageManagerUT**—Test Project containing unit tests for the osImageManagerLib class library (see Chapter 12 and Section 5)
    - **osImageManagerCT**—Test Project containing generic tests for the osImageManagerFIT class library (see Chapter 24)
    - **osImageManagerFIT**—Class library containing the Framework for Integrated Test (FIT) acceptance tests for osImageManager (see Chapter 22)
  - **Utils**—Miscellaneous scripts, batch files, and information needed for development

> **■ TIP**
>
> Consider creating an additional Visual Studio Solution only if you have more than one collection of Visual Studio Projects that you want to build as a unit. Projects that will be built together belong in the same Solution.

EXERCISE 8-2: Adding a Visual Studio Solution into a Directory Structure

In this exercise, you will make some directories for Peter in DeveloperPC2 and then create a blank Visual Studio Solution called osImageManager in such a way that its files become mapped between Peter's workspace directory and a corresponding folder in the repository.

1. Use Windows Explorer (or something similar) to create the directories shown in Figure 8-1 in Peter's directory in DeveloperPC2. In each directory, create the file index.txt so that you can document the directory's purpose.

2. Create a blank Visual Studio Solution for the osImageManager product:

   a. Select File | New | Project from the menu bar to open the New Project dialog box.

   b. Select Visual Studio Solutions in the Other Project Types node, and then select Blank Solution.

   c. Name the Solution "osImageManager" and click the Browse button to select the c:\Peter\OSPACS\Production directory created in step 4 of Exercise 8-1. Check the box labeled Add to Source Control and then click OK.

   d. When the Add Solution to Source Control dialog box appears, select the Production folder you created in Exercise 8-1, but leave osImageManager as the solution folder name. Click OK to add your blank Visual Studio Solution to version control.

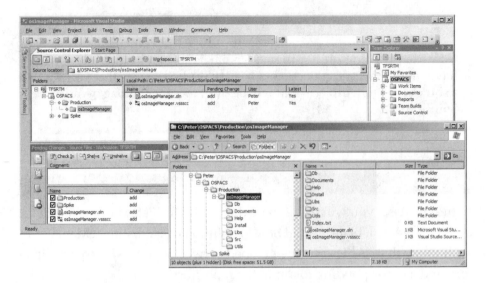

FIGURE 8-1: Mapping workspace directories to repository folders

---

■ WARNING

Remember to put into version control not just the source code files used to build the software product, but also files needed to create its associated utilities and tools, as well as scripts used for things such as data migration and database definitions.

Deciding What to Put into Version Control

Once you have added a Visual Studio Solution or Project to version control, most of the decisions about what to store are handled for you. When you create a new class, for example, Visual Studio will automatically add its associated file to version control. However, files in your workspace that you wouldn't normally want to share with the rest of the team are automatically excluded from this process; for example, your personal Integrated Development Environment (IDE) settings file (.suo), executables (.exe, .dll), and the various build by-products.

> ## ■ TIP
>
> Use the Add to Source Control dialog box (File | Source Control | Add to Source Control) to change the types of files excluded from version control. Effectively, this edits the "hint" files belonging to your Solution (.vssscc) or Project (.vspscc).

Deciding what to put into version control and what to leave out is a matter of some debate among developers. On the one hand, there is the argument often made on large teams that every file needed by the project, including all the development tools, should be put in version control. On the other hand, there is the Agile practice of the Code and Tests practice.

Code and Tests Practice

Agile project teams concentrate on generating the things that drive development forward; in other words, the executable tests that say "what" must be done and the source code that says "how" these requirements are satisfied. The Code and Tests practice treats such test and source code files as the primary artifacts of your project and, when possible, uses them to generate other files and documents automatically as they are needed. In this way, you avoid unnecessary information cluttering up your repository; information that serves only to confuse people and provide a potential source of error.

Development projects tend to generate paperwork; often, the bigger the project, the more paper generated. The Code and Tests practice is an antidote to the bureaucracy that often arises when you attempt to drive a project with documents. The problem is that software development is a process of discovery, so documents quickly become out-of-date as requirements change, models improve, plans change, and so on. Therefore, as the project progresses, you spend more and more time maintaining documents, leaving less time for important stuff such as producing code and tests. The Code and Tests practice addresses this problem by reducing the project's dependence on documents that need to be maintained.

Continues

Implementing the Code and Tests practice requires you to look carefully at everything your project generates in order to determine which of these things actually adds value to the customer. Code and test files are clearly important because without them, you couldn't deliver the product to your customer. But what about a Class diagram? Would the customer notice if you didn't have a Class diagram in your repository? What documents could you remove from the repository because they are redundant once the associated code and test files have been produced? What documents could be removed because they can simply be reverse-engineered from your primary artifacts? Working in this way, little by little you remove the excess baggage that slows down the flow of value to your customer and wastes your resources by making you perform needless maintenance.

■ **NOTE**

The Code and Tests practice does not stop you from creating documents and models when they are needed, but it does require you to discard them after they have served their purpose.

Version Control for Team Documents

The documents associated with your Team Project, such as its vision statement, are typically located in your Project Portal; see the list in Team Explorer's Documents folder. In this way, people can produce, edit, and review this sort of material from their browser using just Windows Share-Point Services (WSS) and the Microsoft Office applications.

■ **TIP**

Use WSS version control to help your team share the documents stored in its Project Portal by selecting an individual document in a Document Library page and then clicking Check Out (or Check In) from the associated drop-down list box.

Unfortunately, the documents in WSS are not actually stored in the TFVC repository, though this may change in some future release. Therefore, using your Project Portal for the purpose of controlling changes to team documents means you end up managing two completely independent version control systems. Accordingly, you cannot baseline all your project artifacts simply by applying a label to the TFVC repository because it will not be applied to the documents in your team's WSS file store. In fact, WSS doesn't even support the concept of applying a label across the contents of its file store, so you must perform such actions manually for each file (in other words, check the file out and then give your label as a comment when checking it in again). For these reasons, we suggest that you put project artifacts into a SharePoint Document Library only when they are needed by people who do not have Team Explorer; you should put everything else into the appropriate folders of your Visual Studio Solutions so that they can be stored by TFVC under proper version control.

An Agile team should not create a large number of team documents, but there are some documents that are deliverable parts of the product or otherwise are integral to its construction. Therefore, you might consider putting the following sorts of documents into your Visual Studio Solution's Documents folder:

- **License**—You should never distribute any software without defining some form of license that secures your intellectual property rights and states your liabilities in respect to the work. The license file is just as much a part of the deliverables as an executable file is.
- **Release notes**—When installing your software, people usually want to know something about it; for example, its target environment, limitations, new features, and so forth. It is good practice to put release notes into a readme.txt file in the root of your program's install directory.
- **Vision statement**—This explains the purpose of your program, what it comprises, who might use it, and the benefits that it brings. It's a good idea to provide an external link to this type of document

from the product's help system, installation program, or download Web page.

- **Build notes**—You should keep an up-to-date list of the tools and settings in your development environment, paying particular attention to details such as version numbers and license terms; see the Software Configuration Management section in Chapter 7. Putting such a file into your TFVC repository allows you to apply a label that links the documentation of your development environment to a specific version of the code.

■. TIP

You can link labels applied to TFVC to the documents stored in WSS by creating a file in your Visual Studio Solution's Documents folder into which you can manually enter the names and version history of all the files stored in your team's Project Portal.

Archiving Third-Party Libraries

Even the simplest .NET program needs the libraries that come with the Common Language Runtime (CLR), and therefore the issue of managing third-party libraries is something that every team needs to address. Broadly, your options are as follows:

- **Install the library separately from your product**—Let the third party manage the issue of installing its libraries in your various software environments, as well as the tasks of development, build, test, production, and so on. In this case, you simply need to add a section to your build notes explaining where to obtain the third-party library and its installation instructions. You also need to make installing the library a prerequisite in your product's release notes, much like the operating system, and so on. It is usually better to keep these types of third-party libraries on disks or network drives rather than attempting to store them in your version control system.

- **Install the library with your product**—Add the library's redistributables (.exe, .dll, .msi, .msm) to your product's installation program, but let the third-party vendor take responsibility for building them. You should add a section to your build notes describing the library; its provenance, version, names and locations of its redistributable files, and so on. You may also need to add a section to your release notes describing its license terms, copyright notices, and so forth. We advise adding these sorts of libraries to your version control system by putting them in the Solution's lib directory. In this way, you can always rebuild a particular version of your product and be sure that the correct versions of the third-party libraries are included in its installation program.

- **Build the library separately from your product**—You take responsibility for building the third-party redistributables from their source files, but this is done in a separate Team Project. You then add the redistributables to your product's installation program (as described earlier). In effect, you're taking on the role of the library developer or passing on this work to another team in your organization. This approach works well if the adaptation of the third-party library follows a different release cycle than that of your own Team Project.

- **Integrate the library with your product**—Put the source files of the third-party library into a Visual Studio Project (or Solution) associated with your Team Project so that it has the same release cycle as your other code. You should consider this approach only if you're going to make extensive adaptations to the third-party code throughout your product's life cycle, because managing third-party libraries in this way often makes it difficult to resynchronize your version of the library's code with any periodic updates and patches supplied by the vendor.

> **▪ NOTE**
>
> Using third-party libraries (.dll) in a Windows environment can be challenging due to the difficulties of managing different versions of the same library when they are shared by different applications; the notorious DLL Hell described by Don Box.[1]

Establishing the Initial Baseline for Your Project

At the start of a project, you should create the initial set of directories and projects your team needs to begin its first iteration. In the case of the OSPACS team, this involves making the standard set of directories discussed earlier and then adding into this structure a couple of new Visual Studio Projects: one for the user interface code and another to act as the main class library. After checking this work into the repository, the team will apply a label to the repository in order to baseline the initial state of its project.

Adding Files and Directories to Version Control

When you create a Visual Studio Solution (or Project) you can automatically add the files and directories that are created to version control just by setting a checkbox; see step 2c of Exercise 8-2. However, you can also manually add specific files and directories to the folders in your TFVC repository.

EXERCISE 8-3: Adding Existing Files and Directories to Version Control

This exercise adds the directories and files you created in Exercise 8-2 into corresponding folders in your team repository. It also creates a Documents folder in your Visual Studio Solution and populates it with the files in your repository Documents folder so that you can access them from your IDE in the same way as your team's source files.

---

1. [ECOM] Box, Don. *Essential COM* (Addison-Wesley, 1998).

1. Open the Source Control Explorer (View | Other Windows) and select the osImageManager folder, which you will find in the $\OSPACS\Production folder; see Figure 8-1.

2. Open the Add to Source Control dialog box (File | Source Control | Add to Source Control) and then add the Documents directory (created in step 1 of Exercise 8-2) to your repository by taking the following steps:

   a. Click its Add Folder button to open another dialog box called Browser for Folder so that you can find and select the Documents directory. Close the Browser dialog box.

   b. Click OK to close the Add to Source Control dialog box and add the Documents directory as well as its contents (index.txt) to version control.

3. Repeat the preceding step to add into the OSPACS repository the other directories which you created in your workspace to define the team's standard directory structure; see Figure 8-2.

4. Create a Documents folder for your Visual Studio Solution by taking the following steps:

   a. Open your Solution Explorer window (View | Solution Explorer).

   b. Select the root item in this window (osImageManager); right-click to open its context menu and then select Add | New Solution Folder (i.e., Right-click | Add | New Solution Folder).

5. Add the contents of your workspace Documents directory (created in step 2) to the Documents folder for your Visual Studio Solution (created in step 4) as follows:

   a. Open the Add Existing Item dialog box by selecting the Documents folder and choosing Add | Existing Item from its context menu (Right-click | Add | Existing Item).

   b. Use this dialog box to select the file Index.txt in your workspace's Document directory, and then add it to the corresponding Visual Studio folder by clicking OK.

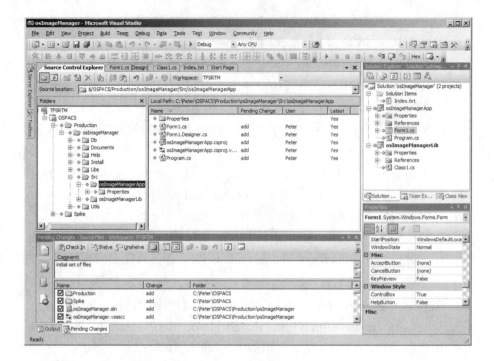

FIGURE 8-2: Source Control Explorer (View | Other Windows)

> **■. WARNING**
>
> You cannot put an empty directory into the TFVC repository, so we suggest you create the file index.txt in each folder in your project's directory structure to overcome this limitation. This file also serves to document the purpose of each directory.

When you create files and directories using Visual Studio, you do not usually have to add them manually to your TFVC repository, because the changes you make in your workspace are being monitored and a change-set is created for you in your Pending Changes window; see Figure 8-3. Exercise 8-4 shows how this works.

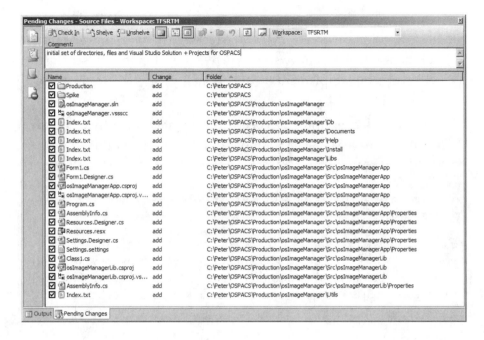

FIGURE 8-3: Pending Changes window (View | Other Windows)

EXERCISE 8-4: Adding a Visual Studio Project into a Directory Structure

This exercise continues from Exercise 8-3 and creates a Visual Studio Project in your workspace, which results in a collection of files being added to the Pending Changes window.

1. Create a new Visual C# Windows Application project by opening the New Project dialog box (File | New | Project) after selecting the appropriate template, so you can:

    a. Name your new project "osImageManagerApp".

    b. Set its location as the Src directory in Peter's workspace (created in Exercise 8-2).

    c. Select Add to Solution from the drop-down list so that it will be added to your existing Visual Studio Solution. Click OK to complete this task.

2. Repeat the preceding step, but this time, add a Visual C# class library project called "osImageManagerLib" to the osImageManager Solution so that you have somewhere to develop the classes that will eventually implement the functionality for your product; see Chapter 14.

3. Confirm that everything has been implemented correctly by building the osImageManager Solution (Build | Build Solution).

■ WARNING

Once you have checked in your changes, the files and directories in your workspace will be copied into the TFVC repository and will become available to other people on your team, so you must always make sure your software works before clicking the Check In button.

Check In and Label the Baseline

After you have created your project's initial directory structure, it is a good idea to check it into the repository and apply a label that identifies it as your initial baseline. This procedure should then be repeated as the project reaches each milestone or significant moment in its history. In particular, you must ensure that your project is labeled in this way at the end of each iteration.

EXERCISE 8-5: Checking In Pending Changes and Creating a Baseline Label

This exercise continues from Exercise 8-4 by checking in all the changes you have made in this chapter and applying a suitable label.

1. Open the Pending Changes window (View | Other Windows) and enter a suitable comment before clicking the Check In button to add your new solution, its projects, and the directories you have created into the repository within the $\OSPACS\Production folder.

2. Apply a label to this version of the OSPACS software by taking the following steps:

   a. Open the Choose Item Version dialog box by selecting $/OSPACS in the Source Control Explorer and choosing Apply Label from its context menu (Right-click | Apply Label).

   b. Select OSPACS, "all files," and "latest version" in this dialog box before clicking OK to open the Apply Label dialog box; see Figure 8-4.

   c. Type a suitable label and comment into the Apply Label dialog box before clicking OK to close it, and apply your label to repository items you have selected.

3. Log off, as you have now finished all the exercises in this chapter.

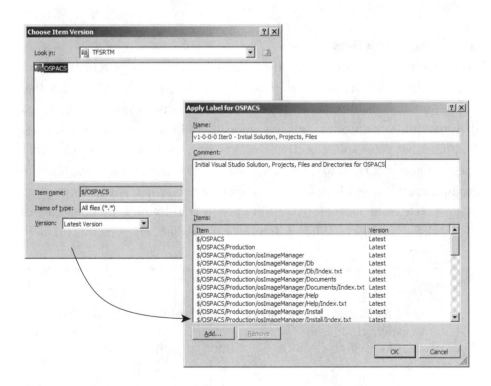

FIGURE 8-4: Apply Label dialog box (File | Source Control | Label)

> **■ TIP**
>
> The OSPACS team labels always start with the version information taken from the project's AssemblyInfo.cs file, but with the periods replaced with dashes. Establish a similar convention on your own team so that its labels can be linked to executable file versions.

Other Set-Up Tasks

After your team has set up the initial Visual Studio Solutions, Project, and directories it needs, there are usually a number of other issues to address before work begins, such as importing existing software into the project, setting up options and security, and defining a process to back up (and restore) your Team Foundation Server.

Importing Source Files

The basic task of adding some existing files into your team's version control folders is not difficult; see Exercise 8-3. However, you need to take care that all information relating to any previous version control system is removed before adding the files to the TFVC repository. In some instances, this just requires that you avoid selecting certain directories and files, but in other cases, you might need to remove various elements from the Visual Studio Solution and Project files (.sln, .csproj). Fortunately, when you are importing source code from SourceSafe, a utility program automatically takes care of this task for you; see the Microsoft technical Web site[2] for more information.

> **■ NOTE**
>
> Unbinding a Visual Studio Solution or Project from TFS version control automatically removes any version control content from the files and directories in your workspace (File | Source Control | Change Source Control).

---

2. Search for "Migrating from Visual SourceSafe" at http://msdn.microsoft.com/teamsystem.

Team Project Version Control Options

The team's collective version (source) control settings are concerned with their check-in policies and the way certain types of files are handled in terms of allowing multiple checkouts and associating them with particular tools to facilitate the merging of changes made by different people to the same file; see Exercise 9-3 in Chapter 9. These settings are defined from the following dialog boxes:

- **Source Control Settings**—To open this dialog box, select Team Project Settings | Source Control from the context menu of the selected Team Project in your Team Explorer window. This allows you to enable or disable multiple-checkout at a team level, but we suggest you keep the default setting, which is enabled. In addition, you will use this dialog box to set your team's "check-in policies" (and notes), as described in Chapter 10.

- **Source Control File Types**—To open this dialog box, select Team Foundation Server Settings | Source Control File Types from the context menu of the machine hosting your TFS in your Team Explorer window. This allows you to enable or disable file-merging and multiple-checkout for specified types of files in all the Team Projects hosted by your TFS that have multiple-checkout enabled at a team level.

Source file types, such as .cs, .cpp, .js, and .aspx, have multiple-checkout and merging enabled by default, so the standard VSTS tools are used to merge (or compare) them. However, you may define other tools to perform these sorts of operations on other types of files. For example, your team might create a utility that compares two files containing data in a special binary representation developed for its project, and want to ensure that it is used whenever someone attempts to compare files of this type from the Source Control Explorer (Right-click | Compare). In such a case, you would use the Source Control File Types dialog to enable file-merging and multiple-checkout for these types of files and then set up your Visual Studio Configure User Tools dialog (Tools | Options) so that the utility would be used to compare files with this particular file extension; see Figure 8-5.

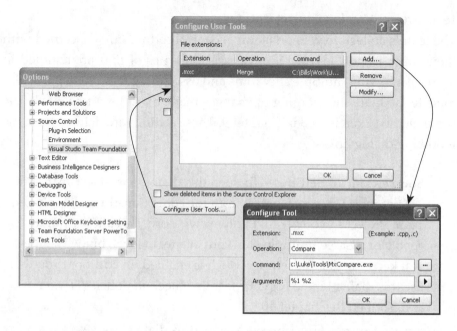

FIGURE 8-5: Specifying a custom utility to compare files of a special type (Tools | Options)

> **▪ NOTE**
>
> All the source code files in your Team Project are set for multiple-checkout and merging by default because this promotes the Shared Code practice and encourages people to improve the code they encounter, as we describe when we cover refactoring in Chapter 15.

Visual Studio Source Control Options

Individual team members can control certain aspects of their version (source) control system's behavior by changing settings in the Source Control section of Visual Studio's Options dialog box (Tools | Options). However, we recommend the following:

- **Plug-in selection**—Visual Studio Team Foundation Server
- **Visual Studio Team Foundation Server:**
  - **Use Proxy Server**—Set when accessing your TFS remotely or when scaling VSTS for hundreds of users

- **Show Deleted Items in Source Control Explorer**—No
- **Configure User Tools**—Set tools to use when merging or comparing specific types of files as explained earlier; see Figure 8-5
- **Environment**—Team Foundation:
  - **Get Everything when a Solution or Project is opened**—No
  - **Check in Everything when a Solution or Project is closed**—No
  - **Display silent checkout command in menus**—No
  - **Keep items checked out when checking in**—No
  - **Checked-in Items, Saving**—Check out automatically
  - **Checked-in Items, Editing**—Check out automatically
  - **Allow checked-in items to be edited**—No

■ TIP

Implement a common set of standards on your team for these Visual Studio Environment Options in order to facilitate the sharing of PCs during pair programming.

Setting Up Security

You can set the access permissions for a specific folder or file selected in the Source Control Explorer window from the Securities page of its Properties dialog box (Right-click | Properties). In this way, you can restrict operations such as the check-out and labeling of certain folders and files to particular Windows (Domain) users or security groups; see Figure 8-6. However, the default settings do not usually need to be adjusted because they give the members of your team appropriate rights to use the facilities of the TFVC tools in respect to everything in the Team Project's root folder and below.

For example, developers on the OSPACS team can check files in and out of any folder in the $\OSPACS hierarchy because they are members of [OSPACS]\Contributors, but only Tom can undo another user's changes because he is also a member of [OSPACS]\Project Administrators. We will deal with other ways to safeguard the source code in your TFVC repository when we describe how to police version control in Chapter 10.

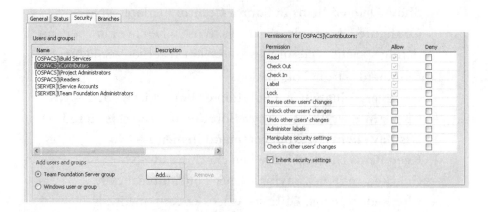

FIGURE 8-6: Security properties for a folder in your repository (Right-click | Properties)

> ### ■. NOTE
>
> Appendix A describes how to make your team members of security groups that will gain them access to the facilities of Visual Studio Team System they need during the course of their work.

Backup and Restore

One significant advantage of VSTS is that individual developers do not need to be overly concerned with backing up their PCs, as all their work is safely stored on the Team Foundation Server. If the hard disk fails on a PC, getting back to work is just a matter of buying a new computer, reinstalling Team Explorer and Visual Studio, and then connecting to the team's Foundation Server—a few hours of lost time at a maximum. However, if the hard disk fails on the server hosting your team's TFS, this may be more serious because it means that the entire team may be affected. Therefore, an effective backup and restore policy for your TFS is clearly essential.

The backup and restore policy in larger organizations may be complicated if it is decided that teams, Agile or otherwise, should have different Team Projects but share the same TFS. This is because the current version of TFS does not allow Team Projects to be backed up and restored independently, so rolling TFS back to the last backup will lose not just one, but many teams' work. Teams working in this sort of environment should take particular care to frequently apply labels to their folders in the TFVC repository (see Exercise 8-5) so that they can roll back using version control, as rolling back the entire TFS by restoring its database is unlikely to be an option. Indeed, even teams that have their own TFS should consider "backup and restore" as a procedure that is only for emergency use.

> ### ■. WARNING
>
> There no point in backing up your TFS unless you are also prepared to check that it can be fully restored from its backup data. Ideally, you should regularly perform this task on a spare computer, as we discuss in Appendix B.

CONCLUSION

A software product is usually generated from information held in many different files, and its development advances as these files are changed. Therefore, you can view software development as simply moving the project between a series of states, each defined by the content in a set of files at a particular moment in time. In this chapter, we examined the general composition of such snapshots by defining a standard directory structure in which to store project artifacts such as source files and important team documents. We also explained how to populate this directory structure with the sort of Visual Studio Solutions and Projects your team might need at the beginning of a project, and we described various other set-up tasks that should be undertaken at this time, such as selecting options to configure the way your team uses TFVC, setting up security, as well as implementing a backup and restore procedure.

> ### ■. NOTE
>
> In an Agile project, version control setup is usually performed during a period termed **Iteration Zero.** During this time, the team tries to ensure that its environment is properly prepared before starting the real work of developing valuable software.

■ 9
Using TFVC in Your Project

T HIS CHAPTER EXPLAINS how to perform some of the most common version control tasks using Team Foundation Version Control (TFVC). We start by taking you step by step through the use of TFVC during the sort of programming episode most developers repeat over and over again throughout a project. We then take you through a number of other tasks you will probably need to perform at some stage during your project, such as resolving the conflicts that arise when several developers make changes to the same file and rolling back your source code to a previous version. Therefore, by the time you have completed the exercises in this chapter, you should be well on the road to being able to use TFVC in a real project.

> ■ TIP
>
> Create a Visual Studio Solution containing a number of Projects in the Spike folder of your team's repository (see Chapter 8) so that people can build up their skills and confidence with TFVC in an environment where they can make mistakes without consequence.

Using TFVC When Coding

Whether it is your first day as a member of the team or your last, each time you implement some code, you will find yourself repeating the same sequence of steps. You need to update your workspace with the latest version of the code from the Team Foundation Server (TFS) repository, make a set of changes to this code, build and test the code on your own PC, and then check in the changeset to create a new version of the software in the TFS repository. In the next few pages, we will walk you through this sequence and show how you might use the TFVC version control tool when you are actually writing code.

Sample Programming Episode: Version Control

You should perform this sort of programming episode using test-driven development (TDD) in conjunction with the team's Build and Test environment, as described in the next two sections of the book.

EXERCISE 9-1: Using Version Control to Share Code Changes among Your Team

The first part of this exercise creates a workspace for Luke on the DeveloperPC and populates it with the latest versions of the Visual Studio Solution, Projects, and directories created by Peter in Exercises 8-2 through 8-5 in Chapter 8.

1. Log on to the DeveloperPC as Luke (OSPACS Contributor), start Visual Studio, and then connect to the OSPACS Team Project, as described in Exercise 5-7 in Chapter 5; see Appendix A for details about this PC and Luke's security groups.

2. If this is the first time you have performed this exercise, use Windows Explorer (or something similar) to create the directory c:\Luke\OSPACS, which will be used as Luke's workspace on the DeveloperPC.

3. Open the Source Control Explorer (View | Other Windows), select the $/OSPACS folder, and then choose Get Latest Version from its context menu (Right-click | Get Latest Version).

4. If this is the first time you have performed this exercise, the Browse for Folder dialog box opens automatically and prompts you to select a local directory for the workspace that in the future will be mapped to the $\OSPACS folder. In this case, select the directory you created in step 2.

Now that the contents of the repository's $\OSPACS folder have been copied into Luke's workspace in the DeveloperPC, you are ready for the next stage of the exercise, which requires you to make some changes to these files.

5. Load the osImageManager Solution into your Visual Studio Integrated Development Environment (IDE) by using the Open Project dialog box (File | Open | Project/Solution) to open the osImageManager.sln file in Luke's workspace. This populates your Solution Explorer window (View | Solution Explorer).

6. Alter the title of the osImageManagerApp Project's main form by editing its Text property. The easiest way to make such a change is by taking the following steps:

    a. Open the main form of the osImageManagerApp Project in the Designer Editor by doubling-clicking the file Form1.cs in your Solution Explorer's treeview; see Figure 9-1.

    b. Use the Properties window (View | Properties Window) to change the Text property of this form from Form1 to osImageManagerApp. This alters the files Form1.cs, Form1.Designer.cs, and Form1.resx.

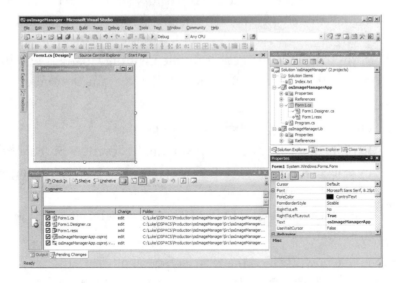

FIGURE 9-1: Changing the Text property of Form1.cs with Visual Studio

> **▪ NOTE**
>
> Visual Studio detects any alterations you make to the files in your workspace and lists them in the Pending Changes window. This list ultimately forms the changeset that you will apply to the repository; see step 9 of this exercise.

You must now check that your changes do what they are intended to do and have not somehow broken the program. Therefore, the next part of the exercise rebuilds the Solution and runs a quick test.

7. Start the application from the Debug menu (Debug | Start without Debugging) so that Visual Studio will automatically incorporate your changes by rebuilding the program before executing it.

8. Check that you have successfully renamed the window title of osImageManagerApp from "Form1" to "osImageManagerApp" by looking at its main form, which is displayed on your desktop.

Finally, you are ready to share your changes (see step 6b) with the rest of the team by checking them into the repository so that the final part of the exercise creates this changeset.

9. Perform the following actions in the Pending Changes window (View | Other Windows), which is shown at the bottom of Figure 9-1:

    a. Enter a suitable comment for your changeset.

    b. Explore other ways in which you might describe this changeset by selecting items in the Tool Strip attached to the Pending Changes window.

    c. Copy the changeset into the TFS repository by clicking the Check In button.

10. You have now finished the exercise, so log off.

> **■ TIP**
>
> You'll find it much easier to work with version control if you perform your work by taking a series of small steps. This will allow you to regularly update your workspace and check in your changes as soon as they pass your tests.

Common Version Control Tasks

In addition to your day-to-day use of version control during programming episodes, you will sometimes need to perform other tasks, such as creating a new workspace, merging the changes made by others with the changes you have made to a file, rolling back a version, and creating a branch (or shelve) from your team's main code base. The rest of this chapter explains how to carry out such tasks.

Using Workspaces

The Team Project files and folders in the repository are copied into your workspace when you get the latest version of its files. This workspace maps a set of directories on your own PC to a corresponding set of folders in the TFVC repository; see Figure 8-1 in Chapter 8.

Typically, the root directory of your workspace is mapped to the root folder of your Team Project in the repository, so when you select this root folder and ask for the latest version, a complete copy of your team's files and folders is put in your workspace. However, you should be aware that if you select a folder in the repository that is lower in the hierarchy, only its contents are copied into your workspace; parent directories are created as needed, but they are not populated. For example, if you map $\OSPACS to the new workspace c:\work\OSPACS and ask for the latest version of the osImageManager repository folder, the Production and osImageManager directories will be created within this workspace and the osImageManager directory will be populated, as will its various subdirectories. However, your workspace will not contain any sibling repository folders, such as ospacsWeb, nor will it contain any files or other folders present in $\OSPACS (the parent folder).

> **■ TIP**
>
> Avoid creating multiple workspaces by mapping the root of your workspace to the root of your Team Project folder so that when different parts of the code base are checked out, they automatically will be put into an existing directory structure.

Most of the time you don't need to worry about workspaces too much, as you will be prompted to create one when there is not an existing mapping between a repository folder and a directory on your hard disk; see step 4 of Exercise 9-1. However, sometimes you may need to create more than one workspace for the same person. For example, Luke might need to work on two different branches at the same time, or want different workspaces for different parts of the product (such as osImageManager and ospacs-Web). In such cases, Exercise 9-2 explains how you might create additional workspaces using the Add Workspace dialog box.

> **■ WARNING**
>
> In the case of multiple workspaces owned by the same person, different directories on a PC cannot be mapped to the same folder in the TFVC repository. Similarly, different folders in the repository cannot be mapped to the same directory on the PC.

EXERCISE 9-2: Creating an Additional Workspace

This exercise creates an additional workspace for Luke so that he can separate his production and experimental (spikes) work into two separate areas in the DeveloperPC.

1. Log on to the DeveloperPC as Luke (OSPACS Contributor), start Visual Studio, and then connect to the OSPACS Team Project as you did before.

2. Use Windows Explorer (or something similar) to create the c:\Test\Spikes directory for the new workspace.

3. Open the Workspaces dialog box (File | Source Control | Workspaces) and then click Add to open the Add Workspaces dialog box; see Figure 9-2:

   a. Enter "Spikes" as the name of the workspace and give it a suitable comment.

   b. Click on the various columns in the bottom row of the "Working folders" list to define your new workspace. You should set its Status as Active, the Source Control Folder as $/OSPACS/Spikes, and the Local Folder as c:\Test\Spikes.

   c. Click OK to create this Spikes workspace.

4. Close the dialog box and log off.

▪ NOTE

When adding or editing a workspace you can set the status of a Working Folder to "cloaked." This means that the folder is invisible to certain TFVC tools, so, for example, the local folder will not be updated when you apply the Get Latest command to its parent.

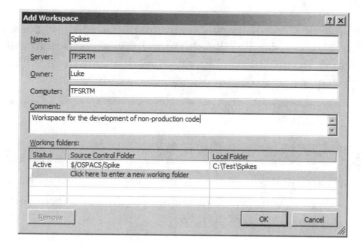

FIGURE 9-2: Add Workspace dialog box (File | Source Control | Workspaces)

The workspaces that are available to you are displayed in a drop-down list at the top of the Source Control window; see Figure 8-1 in Chapter 8. This window actually displays the contents of the repository with the contents of the selected workspace layered on top of it. Therefore, a folder in the repository that is not mapped to a workspace is shown grayed, and when selected, just its repository contents are displayed in the right pane. But when a mapped repository folder is selected its repository contents are overlaid with the contents of the workspace together with status information, such as whether it is up-to-date with respect to the current contents of the repository; latest is "yes."

Merging Changes

When a file is set for multiple-checkout more than one person can change it at the same time. However, after the first person checks the file back into the repository, everyone else must merge their copy of the file with the latest version from the repository before being allowed to check in their changes. Let's see how this works by repeating our programming episode, but this time with two developers: Sarah, who sets the BackColor property in the main form; and Luke, who alters its window title.

■. **NOTE**

A team member's workspace usually maps a repository folder to a local directory on his own PC, therefore physically isolating it from other people's workspaces. However, even when people share the same PC their workspaces should still be considered private.

EXERCISE 9-3: Merging Changes Made by Two Developers to the Same File

In the first part of the exercise, Sarah gets the latest version of the osImageManager Solution with the changes to the main form window title made by Luke in step 6b of Exercise 9-1.

1. Log on to the DeveloperPC3 as Sarah (OSPACS Contributor), start Visual Studio, and then connect to the OSPACS Team Project, as

described in Exercise 5-7 in Chapter 5; see Appendix A for details about this PC and Sarah's security groups.

2. Repeat steps 2, 3, and 4 of Exercise 9-1, but specify the workspace so that the latest version of the osImageManager Solution is put in c:\Sarah\OSPACS.

3. Log off from the DeveloperPC3.

The next part of the exercise sees Luke making some additional changes to the main form of osImageManagerApp using the same version of files that Sarah got from the repository, and then checking them back into the repository to create another version of these files.

4. Log on to the DeveloperPC as Luke, start Visual Studio, and connect to the OSPACS Team Project.

5. Repeat step 3 of Exercise 9-1 so that you have updated Luke's workspace with the latest version of the osImageManager Solution, just to make sure it is the same version as what Sarah copied into her workspace.

6. Open the osImageManager Visual Studio Solution in Luke's workspace and change the main form (Form1) title by editing its Text property; see steps 5 and 6 of Exercise 9-1. This changes the Form1 files in Luke's workspace.

7. Build and test the osImageManager Solution in Luke's workspace and then check in the changeset by clicking the Check In button in the Pending Changes window; see steps 7, 8, and 9 of Exercise 9-1.

8. Log off from the DeveloperPC.

In the last part of the exercise, Sarah makes some changes to the files in her workspace and then merges these changes with the latest version of the files in the repository before checking them back into the repository to create a new version containing both sets of alterations.

9. Log on to the Developer3 as Sarah, start Visual Studio, and once more connect to the OSPACS Team Project.

10. Open the osImageManager Visual Studio Solution in Sarah's workspace and change the main form (Form1) title by editing its

BackColor property in a similar way to step 6 of Exercise 9-1. This changes the Form1 file in Sarah's workspace.

> **■ NOTE**
>
> The VSTS Merge tool handles check-in conflicts by default, but you can specify a different tool to handle the merging of your files by changing the Configure User Tools settings for Source Control; see Figure 8-5 in Chapter 8.

11. Build and test the Solution in Sarah's workspace and then check in the changeset by clicking the Check In button in the Pending Changes window. However, this time the check in will not succeed and the Resolve Conflicts dialog appears.

12. The Resolve Conflicts dialog indicates that the copy of Form1.designer.cs in Sarah's workspace is older than the current version in the repository, checked in by Luke in step 7. Take the following steps:

   a. There is only one file conflict to resolve, so Form1.designer.cs is the only item listed in the Resolve Conflicts dialog. Select this file and click the Resolve button to open another dialog which suggests some ways of resolving the conflict. Select "Merge changes in merge tool" and then click OK to open the Merge tool.

   b. The Merge tool displays the difference between the file in Sarah's workspace and the one stored in the repository; see Figure 9-3. You decide what action to take by altering the code in the bottom window. In this case, the two changes do no conflict, so click OK to let the Merge tool combine them in the file located in Sarah's workspace and save the file changes.

   c. The Resolve Conflicts dialog contains no additional conflicts, so click Close.

13. You should now be able to check in the changeset in Sarah's workspace as its copy of Form1.designer.cs originates from the latest version in the repository. Therefore, click the Check In button in the Pending Changes window.

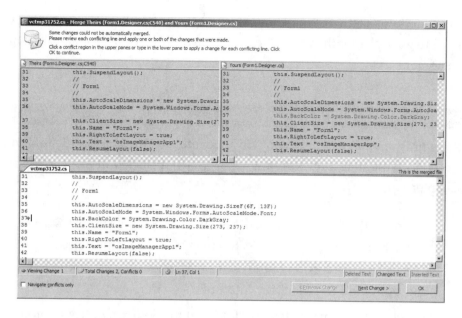

FIGURE 9-3: Resolving conflicts with the VSTS Merge tool

14. Follow the same steps given in step 2 of Exercise 8-5, in Chapter 8, to label this latest version of osImageManager in the repository as "v1-0-0-0 Iter0 - Set title and background".

15. You have now finished the exercise, so log off.

TIP

Graphics files are usually set for "strict locking" because it would be difficult to merge the changes that arise when different people edit the picture. Accordingly, restrict the check-out rights of such files to just the people who will actually maintain them.

Rolling Back to a Previous Version

One of the big gains you get with implementing version control is the ability to go back and rebuild the product as it existed at any point in its development history. Sometimes you just want to go back a few hours to return the code to its last working state. However, on other occasions you may need to go back months to rebuild a version of the product for a particular customer.

After finishing this exercise, you will have returned the OSPACS Team Project code to the state that existed when it was first labeled in Exercise 8-5 in Chapter 8.

1. Log on to the DeveloperPC as Luke (OSPACS Contributor), start Visual Studio, and then connect to the OSPACS Team Project.

2. Copy a specific version of the osImageManager Visual Studio Solution from the TFS repository into Luke's workspace:

   a. Select the osImageManager folder in the Source Control Explorer and select the Get Specific Version context menu (Right-click | Get Specific Version) to open the Get dialog box.

   b. Select Label in the By drop-down list box and click the "…" button to open the Find Label dialog box.

   c. Click Find and select the label you created in Exercise 8-5, in Chapter 8, for the initial baseline. Click Close to return to the Get dialog box.

   d. The Get dialog box's label box now contains the initial baseline label and the Get button is enabled. Select Get to close the dialog and update Luke's workspace.

3. Open the osImageManager Solution (File | Open | Project Solution) and rebuild it (Build | Build Solution) to check that you have successfully re-created this initial baseline. When you run osImageManagerApp, Form1 should appear as the window title of its main form.

4. You have now finished the exercise, so log off.

> **■ NOTE**
>
> Labeling your Team Project at significant milestones makes it easier to identify versions that you might want to subsequently restore. Make sure you apply the label to the root folder ($/OSPACS) so that it applies to everything in your Team Project.

Creating a Branch

Sometimes you may need to roll back to a previous version without changing the latest version of the source files in your repository. For example, you might need to apply a quick bug fix to v1.2 of your product while the rest of the team continues working on the release of v1.4. In such circumstances, you don't want to roll back the entire code base because this means the team will then need to reimplement all its work from v1.2 to v.1.4. Some of the options you might consider include the following:

- **Creating a code branch for the bug fix and releasing it to the customer**—You create two separate code bases: the v1.2 branch and the main (trunk) branch. You fix the bug in the v1.2 branch and then generate a bug-fix release for the customer from this code base. This is often your best tactical solution.

- **Creating a local build and releasing it to the customer**—You roll back to v1.2 just in your own workspace, fix the bug, and then generate a bug-fix release for the customer from the files in your local directory. However, you save these changes in the repository by creating a shelve called "1.2.1," as described in Exercise 9-6.

- **Fixing the problem for the next scheduled release to the customer**—You roll back to v1.2 in your own workspace just to identify the problem, and then apply these changes to the latest version of the code base so that it will be corrected in the next scheduled release. This is the more Agile solution, as we explained in the Single Code Base practice; see Chapter 7.

The most appropriate option depends upon the nature of your Team Project and the sort of bug you're dealing with. If you're developing custom software for a business unit that's losing thousands of dollars per hour because of a simple bug in one line of code, it might not be appropriate to go through the process of creating a code branch or asking your customer to wait for the next scheduled release. However, releasing software to customers that hasn't been through an agreed build, test, and release process might be an unacceptable practice for a team developing control software for a nuclear power station. Ultimately, such decisions need to be driven by business need.

EXERCISE 9-5: Creating a Code Branch

The following exercise creates the branch osImageManager-v1.2 from osImageManager to give your team two entirely separate code bases for its development work.

1. Log on as Luke (Team Foundation Contributor) to the DeveloperPC, start Visual Studio, and then connect to the OSPACS Team Project, as described in Exercise 5-7 in Chapter 5.

2. Open the Source Control Explorer (View | Other Windows), select the osImageManager folder in $/OSPACS/Production, and then choose Branch from its context menu (Right-click | Branch) to open the Branch dialog box; see Figure 9-4.

3. Replace "-branch" at the end of the proposed Target name with "-v1.2" and click OK to create this branch in Luke's workspace.

4. Edit the AssemblyInfo.cs files in each of the Solution's Visual Studio Projects so that the AssemblyVersion attribute is 1.2.0.0 in order to link the version number of the executables to the version label in the repository you set in step 3.

5. Check the branch into the repository by clicking the Check In button in your Pending Changes window, though you may want to provide a suitable comment before you do so. This creates a new folder in the $/OSPACS/Production folder called osImageManager-v1.2.

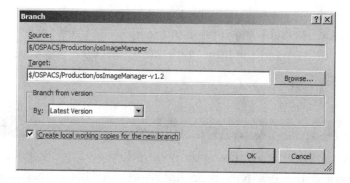

FIGURE 9-4: Branch dialog box (File I Source Control I Branch)

6. Label this latest version of osImageManager in the repository as "v1-2-0-0 Iter0 - Branched from trunk" by following the same steps as those given in step 2 of Exercise 8-5.

7. You have now finished the exercise, so log off.

> **■ NOTE**
>
> Agile teams tend to avoid creating code branches unless they are absolutely necessary. However, if you must create a branch, try to keep its lifetime as short as possible to reduce the amount of work needed to merge it back into the main branch.

Creating a Shelve

You should consider creating a shelve whenever you want more than one copy of the code base for your own personal use. It gives you a way of storing your work in the repository without it being integrated with the rest of the team's work, so it is ideal for those situations in which you need to save the code in your workspace without following the team's normal check-in policies; see Chapter 10. This might happen, for example, after a telephone call from a client who needs a bug fix so urgently that you don't have enough time to finish what you were working on. In this sort of situation, you would simply save your current workspace as a "shelveset" and then replace its contents with the version of the files you need in order to fix the bug. Once you've fixed the bug, you can restore your shelveset and continue with your work.

EXERCISE 9-6: Saving and Restoring a Shelveset

In the first part of this exercise, you will update your workspace with the latest version of the files in the repository and then change the window title text to alter a few files before saving them as a shelveset.

1. Log on as Luke (Team Foundation Contributor) to the DeveloperPC, start Visual Studio, and then connect to the OSPACS Team Project.

2. Open the Source Control Explorer (View | Other Windows), select the $/OSPACS folder, and then choose Get Latest Version from its context menu so that you can then load the osImageManager Visual Studio Solution by opening the osImageManager.sln file in Luke's workspace (File | Open | Project/Solution).

3. Repeat step 6 in Exercise 9-1 to alter the window title text of the osImageManagerApp main form to MyShelve, thereby causing a few files to be added to your Pending Changes window.

4. Click the Shelve button in the Pending Changes window to open the Shelve dialog box (see Figure 9-5). Enter a suitable name and comment for your shelveset and remove the check from the "Preserve pending changes locally" box before clicking the Shelve button to create this shelveset for Luke in the repository.

5. Repeat step 2 to restore your workspace with the latest version in the repository, and then repeat step 6 in Exercise 9-1 to alter the window title text of the osImageManagerApp main form to "Bug Fix".

6. Test your changes by building and running the osImageManager-App application (Debug | Start without Debugging) and then save your changes to the repository by clicking the Check In button in the Pending Changes window.

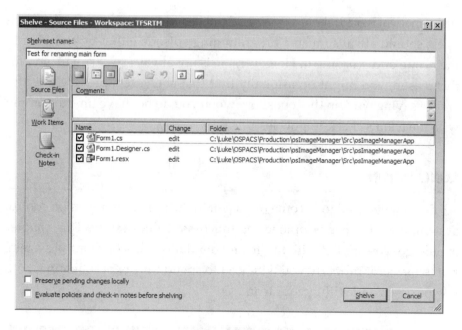

FIGURE 9-5: Shelve dialog box (File | Source Control | Shelve Pending Changes)

7. Restore your shelveset by clicking the Unshelve button in the Pending Changes window to open the Unshelve dialog box. Select the shelve whose name you defined in step 4 and click the Unshelve button to copy it back into your workspace. Confirm that the window title text of the osImageManagerApp main form is MyShelve.

8. Undo the changes that are now present in your workspace by selecting the files in your Pending Changes window and choosing Undo from their context menu (Right-click | Undo). When prompted to "undo checkout and discard changes," click Yes.

9. Log off, as you have now finished the exercises in this chapter.

■ **WARNING**

Shelvesets create the same sorts of problems as branches in terms of generating duplicates of your code base and, therefore, should be used with care; see the Single Code Base practice in Chapter 7.

In an ideal world, shelvesets would not be required because Agile developers should always finish a programming episode either by checking in their code or discarding it. However, life is not always so clear-cut, and for this reason, you might occasionally find that shelvesets provide a useful way of saving work in the repository when you do not have time to comply with the team's check-in policies.

CONCLUSION

All developers need to become proficient in the use of their version control system, and this needs practice as much as it does study. This chapter should get you started with the Team Foundation Version Control system, but to master it properly you will need to spend time experimenting, both on your own and within your team.

> ■ **WARNING**
>
> Do not allow your team to share a common set of source files until it has mastered the basics of using version control; otherwise, your project will almost certainly descend into total chaos.

10
Policing Your Project with TFVC

THIS CHAPTER DESCRIBES how Team Foundation Version Control (TFVC) helps your team protect its source code by introducing policies for things such as restricting access to particular files, allowing single- or multiple-checkout, and enforcing the validation of a source code file against project-defined coding standards before permitting it to be checked into the repository. Our objective is to help you introduce sensible policies for policing your own project that will help your team members work together more effectively.

Protecting Your Source Code

Source code is almost always the primary product of the design, and therefore it must be protected above all the other artifacts your team generates. To help you implement this protection, let's first see how TFVC allows you to set the access rights for particular files and folders. We will then look at the core material of this chapter, which is setting check-in policies so that you can police your project's coding standards.

> **■. NOTE**
>
> Innovations such as Domain-Specific Languages (DSLs; see Chapter 21) may change the role of source code files in the future, but at present, most programs are generated from instructions written by people in a general programming language, such as C# or Visual Basic.

Controlling Access to Individual Files and Folders

The Windows filesystem allows you to control access to a file or directory by a set of domain users or security groups. Therefore, you can ensure that Michael has full access to a file such as Salaries.xls, while Tom is only able to read the file by selecting it with Windows Explorer and then setting the appropriate security properties (Right-click | Properties | Security). TFVC allows you to control access to the files and folders in your team's repository in much the same way, except that you use Source Control Explorer to set their security properties, as described in Exercise 10-1.

EXERCISE 10-1: Making a File Check Out Only for Project Administrators

In this exercise, you will set the security permissions for a file stored in the TFVC repository so that it can be read by any team member, but cannot be checked out for editing by anyone except Tom, the project administrator.

1. Log on to the DeveloperPC as Tom (OSPACS Team Project Administrator), start Visual Studio, and then connect to the OSPACS Team Project, as described in Exercise 5-7 in Chapter 5; see Appendix A for details about this PC and Tom's security groups.

2. Open the Source Control Explorer (Views | Other Windows | Source Control Explorer) and repeat steps 2, 3, and 4 of Exercise 9-1, but specify your workspace so that the latest version of $\OSPACS is put into c:\Tom\OSPACS.

3. Create a bitmap file (File | New | File) and save it in your workspace as Logo.bmp within osImageManager's Documents directory. Add this bitmap file to the corresponding Documents folder in your

repository by using the Add to Source Control dialog box, as described in step 2 of Exercise 8-3, in Chapter 8, and then clicking the Check In button in the Pending Changes window.

4. Use the Source Control Explorer window to select Logo.bmp and open its Property dialog box (Right-click | Properties). Select the Security tab and then set its permissions so that only OSPACS project administrators are allowed to check out this file.

5. Close the Properties dialog box and log off, as you have finished this exercise.

■ TIP

Normally, you grant all developers read and write access to your project's source code files; see the Shared Code practice in Chapter 7. However, it can make sense to restrict access to a file such as Logo.bmp if it contains a graphic, such as a company logo, that must not be altered.

Setting Check-in Constraints

The Source Control Settings dialog box allows you to add constraints that are applied whenever members of the team check in their code; see Figure 10-1. The simplest constraint to apply is Check-in Notes, which allows you to define one or more categories of notes that must be completed before you can check in your changeset. We recommend that you remove the default categories and just add "Programming Pair Name" for the name of the person with whom the developer produced the code.

The other type of constraint is Check-in Policy, which has three predefined categories:

- **Code analysis**—Check-in is allowed only for changesets that produce a clean build which includes static code analysis. Therefore, you may fail this policy if your changes don't comply with the team's coding standards; see Exercise 10-3.

- **Testing policy**—You must have successfully run the build product resulting from your changeset against one or more tests, as defined by a Visual Studio Tests Metadata file (*.vsmdi). This might mean that failing to pass all unit tests would result in your failing this policy; see Sections 5 and 7.

- **Work items**—The changeset needs to be associated with one or more work items. Essentially, this means that you must select at least one of the work items listed in the Pending Changes window.

Team members can override these check-in policies, but when they do so, they must give a reason. This means that you could, for example, check in changes that didn't comply with the team's coding standards with respect to globalization rules in order to release an urgent fix.

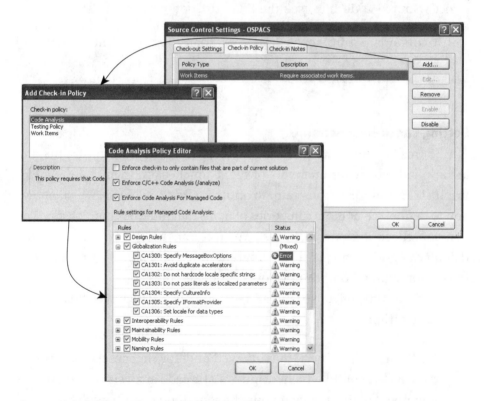

FIGURE 10-1: Setting code analysis check-in policy

> ### ■ WARNING
>
> Take care when setting a code analysis policy to generate an error rather than a warning, because once this policy has been migrated to your Visual Studio Solution, it cannot be reset upon subsequent migrations; see the section Updating Static Code Analysis Rules later in this chapter.

Establishing Policies for Source Code

In order to maintain a consistent level of quality, certain policies should be applied whenever the developers on your team are producing code that is intended for eventual use in the production (business) environment. Visual Studio Team System (VSTS) allows you to enforce such policies by checking that all source code files are compliant before checking them into the repository.

Coding Standards

Working on a team that has adopted the Shared Code practice means that everyone must agree about things, such as the placement of the opening brace for a block of code. Should it be on a new line or at the end of the preceding statement? Without such coding standards, your code base can quickly become a confused mess of different coding styles. Scott Ambler[1] gives some good advice for Agile teams about such issues in his essay, "Coding Style Guidelines."

> ### ■ TIP
>
> Apply a common standard for code formatting by exporting your text editor settings from Visual Studio into a file (Tools | Import and Export Settings) which you put into the repository so that the rest of your team can copy it into their workspaces and then import it.

---

1. Ambler, Scott. "Coding Style Guidelines" (www.ambysoft.com/essays/codingGuidelines.html).

Static Code Analysis

The effective implementation of coding standards depends upon reaching a consensus about the need for the rules and then policing their application. This is where the VSTS Static Code Analysis tool comes into play. It is actually a version of FxCop and is supplied with more than one hundred fifty standard rules that Microsoft considers important in areas such as globalization, security, and so forth. You can add your own custom FxCop rules, though this is not officially supported and does involve some programming.[2] In this way, when you enable Code Analysis for a Visual Studio Project, your code is inspected against these rules each time you perform a build, and the results are displayed in the Error List window (View | Error List), as described in Exercise 10-2.

■ TIP

Before developing your own custom FxCop rules, check that the rules you want are not already available on the Internet. However, remember to distribute any DLLs containing such rules to all the PCs on which your team performs static code analysis.

EXERCISE 10-2: Using Static Code Analysis on Your Own PC

This exercise applies static code analysis to the Visual Studio Project you created in Exercise 8-4 in Chapter 8.

1. Log on to the DeveloperPC as Luke (OSPACS Contributor), start Visual Studio, and then connect to the OSPACS Team Project, as described in Exercise 5-7 in Chapter 5.

2. Update Luke's workspace with the latest version of the files in the repository and open the osImageManager Visual Studio Solution, as described in steps 3 and 5 of Exercise 9-1, in Chapter 9.

---

2. Robbins, John. "Bugslayer" (*MSDN Magazine*, Sept. 2004, http://msdn.microsoft.com/msdnmag).

3. Open the osImageManagerApp Project Properties window by selecting osImageManagerApp in your Solution Explorer and then selecting osImageManagerApp Properties from Visual Studio's Project menu (Project | Properties).

4. Select the Code Analysis tab in the Project Properties window and then set the checkbox labeled Enable Code Analysis. Investigate the rules that will be applied to your code by expanding the rule categories in the lower part of the page.

5. Rebuild the osImageManager Solution (Build | Build Solution) and review the warnings that appear in your Error List window (View | Error List); see Figure 10-2.

   a. Obtain further information about a specific warning in your Error List window by selecting it and then pressing F1.

   b. Open the source code file at the statement that has caused a warning by double-clicking the item in your Error List window.

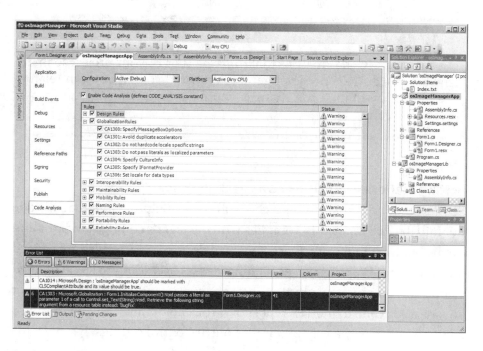

FIGURE 10-2: Error List window (View | Error List)

6. Fix the warnings listed in the Error List window or suppress them (Right-click | Suppress Message) and then rebuild your Solution (Build | Build Solution). Note that any suppressed warnings are listed in the project file GlobalSuppressions.cs.

7. Check your changes into the repository using the Pending Changes window (View | Other Windows), as described in step 9 of Exercise 9-1; see the warning at the end of this exercise.

8. Log off, as you have completed this exercise.

■ WARNING

The changes made to your Visual Studio Project Properties are stored in files that are normally under version control. Therefore, after you check your changes into the repository, they will be propagated to other people's PCs when they next do a "get latest version."

■ TIP

Use the Static Code Analysis tool from the start of your project so that the list of warnings does not get too long, and so that you can relate them directly to the code changes you have made during your programming episode.

Setting Static Code Analysis As a Check-in Policy

Setting static code analysis as a check-in policy helps ensure that all code put into the TFS repository complies with the team's coding standards and can be built without error. Once you have decided which rules are needed for your Team Project, such as naming classes according to some defined standard, you must ensure that they are consistently applied whenever anyone adds code to the TFS repository. You can do this easily by setting a check-in policy in the Team Project's Source Control settings.

EXERCISE 10-3: Setting a Static Code Analysis Check-in Policy

This exercise sets some static code analysis rules that people must test their source code files against before checking them into the repository.

1. Log on to the DeveloperPC as Tom (OSPACS Team Project Administrator), start Visual Studio, and then connect to the OSPACS Team Project, as described in Exercise 5-7 in Chapter 5.

2. Open the Source Control Settings dialog box for OSPACS (Team | Team Project Settings | Source Control):

   a. Select the Check-in Policy tab and click the Add button to open the Add Check-in Policy dialog box.

   b. Select Code Analysis and then click OK to open the Code Analysis Policy Editor dialog box. Expand the list of Naming Rules and then double-click in the Status column of code policy CA1724 so that a violation of this rule generates an Error rather than a Warning.

   c. Click OK to close the dialog box and return to the Source Control Settings dialog box.

3. Click OK to close the Source Control Settings dialog box. Your policies will be applied from now on when anyone adds code to the TFS repository.

4. Update Tom's workspace with the latest version of the files in the repository and open the osImageManager Visual Studio Solution, as described in steps 3 and 5 of Exercise 9-1, in Chapter 9.

5. Migrate the Team Project's code analysis policy settings to all the projects in your Visual Studio Solution by selecting osImageManager as the root item in the Solution Explorer window and applying Migrate Code Analysis Policy Settings to Solution from its context menu. This causes all your Visual Studio Project files to be checked out.

6. Rebuild your Visual Studio Solution (Build | Build Solution) and correct any Code Analysis errors that are detected.

7. Check your changes into the repository using the Pending Changes window (View | Other Windows), as described in step 9 of Exercise 9-1 in Chapter 9.

8. You have now finished this exercise, so log off.

After you have completed Exercise 10-3, any team member who subsequently updates his workspace will find that code analysis has been enabled for each of his Visual Studio projects and that the team's various rules have been selected. This means that code analysis will be run each time the team members rebuild the code on their PCs. Therefore, complying with the new check-in policy simply requires people to obtain a clean build before checking in their code changes.

Implementing New Coding Standards

Applying coding standards retrospectively to a code base of any size can involve a significant amount of reworking, and as Scott Ambler says, "It's generally a bad idea to change the rules partway through a project." Therefore, whenever possible, decide on the standards that will apply to the team at the start of a project, before any code has been written. It's a good idea to hold a workshop before attempting to implement new coding standards so that your team can identify which of the standard code analysis (FxCop) rules should apply to the project and discover whether any additional rules need to be developed. In particular, you should try to do the following:

- Eliminate as many unnecessary rules as possible; for example, if your product will never by used by non-English-speaking users, you might want to ignore all the globalization rules.

- Use this opportunity to educate the team about the rationale of the rules that it has selected and show some code examples of each problem as well as its resolution.

The objective is to achieve a consensus among the team about coding standards so that people see them as being generally beneficial rather than oppressive.

Updating Static Code Analysis Rules

You should be aware that the migration of the Team Project's code analysis policy settings to the Visual Studio Solution is an additive operation. That is to say, if a particular rule has not previously been set for the Solution, it will be applied during any subsequent code analysis once you migrate your Team Project Policy settings with the new rule selected. However, this rule will not be reset if someone later migrates his Team Project Policy settings with it unselected. You should also bear in mind that the rules for the check-in policy are uniformly applied to all code being checked into the repository, so you cannot apply different check-in policies to different Visual Studio Projects or Solutions. This is a limitation that may be lifted in some future release of VSTS.

> ### ▪ WARNING
>
> Any local alterations you make to your code analysis rules that result in them becoming more restrictive than the agreed policies may be unintentionally propagated to the rest of your team if you subsequently check in the changes to your project files.

Overriding Check-in Policies

Once your team has decided to implement a static code analysis check-in policy, you should perform static code analysis on the contents of any changeset before checking it into the repository. If you fail to do this, a dialog box appears prompting you to abort the check-in or explain why you haven't complied with the check-in policy; see Figure 10-3. Sometimes there may be good reason for you to ignore a check-in policy, but mostly developers will not want to go on record as needlessly flouting team standards.

EXERCISE 10-4: Overriding a Static Code Analysis Check-in Policy

This exercise explains how you can ignore a check-in policy and still check your code into the repository, but this event will be recorded, so your reasons for doing so may be investigated.

1. Log on to the DeveloperPC as Luke (OSPACS Contributor), start Visual Studio, and then connect to the OSPACS Team Project, as described in Exercise 5-7 in Chapter 5.

2. Update Luke's workspace with the latest version of the OSPACS files from the repository, and open the osImageManager Visual Studio Solution; see steps 3 and 5 of Exercise 9-1, in Chapter 9. This will include the new code analysis policy settings you made in Exercise 10-3.

3. Rename the osImageManagerLib file from "Class1.cs" to "osImageManagerLib.cs" and, when prompted, click Yes to rename the references to this code element. Effectively, this renames the class in a way that violates the code analysis rules CA1724.

4. Rebuild the osImageManager Solution (Build | Build Solution). The build will fail because you have violated the preceding code analysis rules.

5. Check your changes into the repository using the Pending Changes window (View | Other Windows), as described in step 9 of Exercise 9-1, in Chapter 9. However, because you have not fixed the code analysis warnings, the Policy Failure dialog box appears (see Figure 10-3). Therefore:

    a. Enter a suitable comment in the Policy Failure dialog box.

    b. Click OK to acknowledge that you have checked in some code that doesn't comply with the team's coding standards.

6. You have now finished this exercise, so log off.

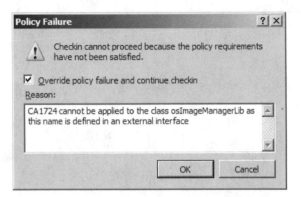

FIGURE 10-3: Policy Failure message during check-in

> ■ **NOTE**
>
> We leave it as an exercise for the reader to make sure that the workspaces of Tom, Peter, Sarah, and Luke all contain the latest version of the code which can be built without generating errors when static code analysis is applied.

CONCLUSION

Policing access to the repository allows your team to implement quality assurance for its code base by restricting access to its files and folders as well as by setting constraints for checking them out and checking them back into the repository. This ensures that everyone is able to share code effectively, and helps maintain the quality of common source code files by policing the team's coding standards.

> ■ **NOTE**
>
> Good coding standards do not just improve the quality of your team's shared code base; they also have an educational role by steering people away from coding pitfalls and thereby encouraging them to write code like expert programmers.

Review of Section 3
Use Version Control

THE THIRD SECTION of the OSPACS team's road map to better software development addresses the problems it was having sharing code with each other. Using version control properly was the first step the team took toward improving the basic quality of its software development. The following were among the activities the team completed:

- **Managed change**—The team decided to have just one main line of development for its new OSPACS system rather than having a different branch for each client, as it had originally conceived. Accordingly, the team introduced the Single Code Base practice for its OSPACS Team Project.

- **Organized its repository**—The team partitioned the $/OSPACS folder it created in the repository for the Team Project into a Production folder and a Spike folder. The team then created a standard directory structure for its new code in the Production folder.

- **Migrated its legacy code base to Team Foundation Version Control (TFVC)**—The team migrated the code from its legacy Picture Archiving and Communication System (PACS) into the Spike folder. It then created a new branch for its legacy code, called Sandpit, so that it had a separate code base to use when practicing with the TFVC tools.

- **Created a skeletal Visual Studio Solution**—The team created an initial collection of Visual Studio Projects in the Production folder from which to start the development of its new system.

- **Learned to use TFVC**—The team became proficient in using its new version control system by using the Sandpit branch of the legacy code base in its Spike folder to conduct sample programming episodes during which it merged files, created shelvesets, and rolled back changes.

- **Introduced coding standards**—Nobody really wanted any coding standards, but the team realized that they were a necessary part of working together effectively. After conducting a coding standards workshop, the team introduced a common format for Production code layout and created a set of rules against which source code files could be automatically validated before they were checked into the repository.

■ TIP

Get into the routine of putting proper version control in place at the start of *every* project to avoid running into difficulties later when the problems have become much bigger and there is usually less time to fix them.

The Team's Impressions

The team was happy that at last it was starting to use some of the new Visual Studio Team System (VSTS) tools. It was very impressed with the facilities of TFVC, as it seemed so much better than the Visual SourceSafe tool the team had been using previously. However, the team also took care to understand how this tool might help team members to work in an Agile way.

Developer: Luke

"It is clear that part of the problem was that people didn't really know much about version control, or even how to use the tool properly."

Developer: Sarah

"I'm the first to admit that version control wasn't my strong point. However, I'm much more comfortable with these ideas now that we've spent time playing with TFVC in our Sandpit."

Developer: Tom

"Demonstrating the version-by-version development of our code will help us to defend any future intellectual property action taken by our venture partner."

Developer: Sarah

"We started by introducing a very simple set of rules against which we could check our code before checking it into the repository. However, within three months, we plan to have a much stricter set of rules and most of our legacy code validated."

Developer: Peter

"Before we can really implement the Shared Code practice, we are going to have to improve the quality of our code significantly. The coding standards put in place are a start, but we also need to implement thorough unit testing."

Agile Values

The team agreed to implement the following practices: Shared Code, Single Code Base, and Code and Tests. The team hoped this would help team members in the following ways.

Communication

The Shared Code practice allows people to communicate at the code level across the whole project. There are no black holes that are the sole preserve of one or two people. This allows knowledge to spread throughout the team and allows people to learn from each other.

By concentrating on code and tests rather than pieces of paper and e-mails, the team improves communication about the things that matter. It also reduces the danger of people filling the repository with documents that are redundant and out-of-date.

Having a single code base means the team needs to communicate about only one code branch, not many.

Feedback

The Shared Code practice allows people to learn from the changes other people have made to their code. It also allows them to discover mistakes more quickly because it drives the team to implement other practices such as Continuous Integration, Pair Programming, and so on.

Courage

People are more confident about undertaking challenging work because other people on the team have access to the code and will improve it, if required. There's no finger wagging.

The version control tools act like a safety net, allowing you to roll back the changes in your workspace.

Simplicity

The Single Code Base practice reduces duplication that often accumulates in different code branches. There is only one code base for the team to learn.

Whenever possible, documents are automatically generated from the code and tests, and this helps the team focus on producing artifacts that have real value to the customer, thereby removing unnecessary bureaucracy.

Respect

The Shared Code practice allows junior members of the team to improve the work of more senior people and therefore gain their respect. It also encourages teamwork by making people "play nicely" together and take collective responsibility for their work.

■ Section 4
Build and Integrate Often

B UILDING AND INTEGRATING need to be part of your team's every-day activities because putting together the parts of your software is not something that you want to leave until the end of the project. Chapter 11 introduces the basic ideas of creating an environment to centralize this work and validating the resulting software with different types of tests. It also makes the case for automating these actions so that they can be performed regularly, reliably, and consistently. Chapter 12 explains how to put the theory into practice using Team Foundation Build, which allows your team to progress its work toward final deployment in the business

Photograph by Simon Lewis (Copyright Science Photo Library 2006).

You can see progress taking place during the construction of a house, but in software development you must rely on regularly checking the results of the team's Integration Build. This is the heartbeat of your project.

environment by creating frequent versions of its software in an automated production line.

Story from the Trenches

Many years ago I joined a team producing engine management software for a large automobile manufacturer. Our job was to produce the software needed to control the injection of gas into the various cylinders of an engine and then precisely time the sparks to give good performance over a wide range of operating conditions. The company had dozens of different engine configurations all supported by a code base containing hundreds of thousands of lines of assembly code. There were about thirty people on the team and we developed our software on a VAX cluster. The huge size of this computer contrasted starkly with the size of our target machine, which was a box about the size of this book.

I spent the first few weeks shadowing a more experienced member of the team, but thereafter I was given my own task to complete. As I recall, it was something to do with retarding or advancing the spark to make the catalytic converter operate more efficiently. The VAX development environment provided version control and all the other tools we needed. However, it was slow work because of the time needed to build the binary file and load it into the simulator for testing. Typically, our edit-build-test cycle took four or five hours, so consequently we each worked with our own branch of the code base to avoid extending this cycle any further. It took me several months to complete my task, but fortunately I finished in time for the code to be included in the team's next software integration phase.

The integration process was very complex because it involved merging together the changes made by dozens of programmers in their individual branches of the code base. This was a task made more difficult because the code was completely monolithic, and therefore the effect of each change was not limited to a particular area of the program. For example, I could write a value into the spark timing variable to make the catalytic converter operate more efficiently and then find that it was overwritten by someone attempting to improve the engine's power output. The more changes we attempted to integrate at the same time, the more complex these sorts of interactions became.

We spent three months trying to integrate the team's work and produce a single branch of the code base that would pass all the necessary tests. Eventually, though, we succeeded in integrating only two people's work into the same code branch, and this became the basis of our next release. Everyone else's work, mine included, was added to the growing mountain of code pending integration which had been left over from previous releases. During my entire time working with this team, I contributed less than a dozen lines of code to any actual release of the software, but I didn't feel too bad because some people worked on the team for two years without contributing a single line.

The fundamental problem this company had was the slowness of the build process which encouraged the team to work independently and therefore postpone integration. I've experienced this problem in numerous organizations, but seldom was it as evident as it was in this case. In the next two chapters, we explain how to set up your project for the frequent building and integration of everyone's work to make sure this sort of thing doesn't happen to you.

11

Building and Integrating Software

THIS CHAPTER DESCRIBES how teams go about assembling their software. We introduce the idea of a Build Lab and explain the way it automates the various tasks required to generate a version of software. We also consider the different types of software testing performed during this build process and then finally walk you through a typical programming episode to put these procedures into a realistic context. After completing this chapter, you will know enough about the basics of building and integrating software to understand the purpose of Team Foundation Build, whose setup and use are described in the next chapter.

Software Construction

Transforming source code into a set of binary files (.exe, .dll) is a mechanical process which most people learn to automate within the first few weeks of their programming career. For example, you might run your compiler from some form of batch file to save you the bother of typing out the commands each time the program needs rebuilding. Automating such a task helps make it reliable so that you can be confident that the executable binary files will accurately reflect the changes you've made to your source files. It also makes the operation consistent so that running your batch file twice generates exactly the same program.

> ■ **NOTE**
>
> Whether you're working on your own or as part of a team, the ability to perform reliable and consistent software builds is an essential prerequisite for any sort of serious software development.

Building and Integrating As a Team

When you're developing software as a team, the process of assembling programs is particularly demanding because you must consider applying the changes made by several people to the same set of source files. This is the problem that software integration must solve by testing the software as a system rather than as just a set of separate classes and components. It is work that needs to be automated so that it can be regularly, reliably, and consistently completed just like the build itself. Therefore, when working with others you can no longer simply run a script on your PC and then perform a few manual tests. Instead, you need to start thinking about creating an automated facility that builds and tests the team's shared code base in a common environment. For this reason, teams typically create some form of "automated build lab" that performs such work for them.

Automated Build Lab

The Build Lab is an environment which allows your team to automate the building and integration of its work in a reliable as well as consistent way. Accordingly, your Build Lab should operate according to a prescribed process, just like a factory except its raw materials are source files and its finished products are programs.

> ■ **NOTE**
>
> Building and integrating software requires a *production process* to minimize the variation in its results. This contrasts with the sort of *design process* needed during analysis, design, and coding which promotes variance so as to yield useful information.

The term *Build Lab* reflects the fact that it provides a separate environment from both the development environment in which you create source files and the production environment where the programs are actually employed; see Figure 11-1. However, keep in mind that although the Build Lab and development environments are separate, they usually exist in the same physical place, unlike the final production environment which is typically located outside the team's workspace. You will want to control the movement of software among these various software environments with a set of formal procedures to help ensure that only a fully tested and properly audited system ends up being used for business purposes.

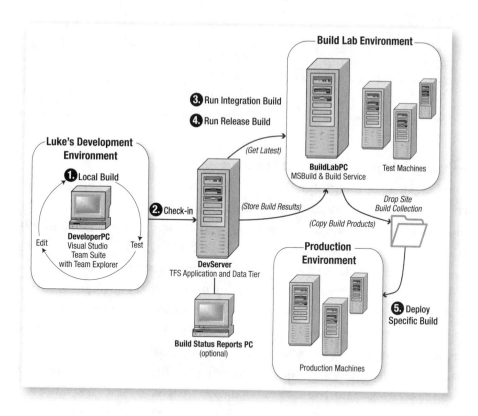

FIGURE 11-1: Flow of software from its origination to final use

It is not difficult to see how the idea of having a set of instructions (or a script) to automatically assemble the software on your development PC can be extended in a Build Lab to include tasks such as getting the latest source files into the Build Lab's workspace, running tests, and copying the build products to some form of public "drop folder" on your network. However, a Build Lab needs to run these instructions not just at the click of a button (on demand), but at scheduled times and in response to events such as the detection of a change to a source file in your version control system (continuous integration). In this way, you can start automating the entire process of constructing and testing the integration of the source code changes made by different members of your team.

> **■ NOTE**
>
> The types of automated structural (unit) and functional tests needed to prove your build products are described in Sections 5 and 7 of this book. You can also find details of other types of tests to perform on the products of your builds later in this chapter.

Software Integration and Test Environment

The first stage of integration is done when different developers add their changes to the team's version control system; see Chapter 7. However, the real work of integration involves verifying that these changes result in software that works together as required. Therefore, in addition to providing a software construction environment, your Build Lab must also provide a suitable operating environment for your tests so that they can be run as realistically as possible. Ideally this test environment would exactly mirror the production environment into which the software will ultimately be deployed. However, in practice, teams usually just provide some sort of emulation of the production environment within their Build Lab, though in some cases a separate Test Lab may be used instead.

The deployment of software into a production environment becomes an increasingly complex matter as we start to build larger distributed systems, rather than client-server solutions and stand-alone applications. This means that your Build Lab (and to a lesser degree your development environment) must undertake more work to provide the necessary data, services, machine configurations, and so on needed for the proper testing of the team's build products; see the section Making a Build Validation Test in Chapter 12. Accordingly, in addition to automating the building and testing of your team's software, you should consider automating the maintenance of your Build Lab's test environment so that you can quickly restore it to a standard state before starting your tests.

▪ TIP

It is particularly useful to emulate[1] your production environment in the Build Lab by using Microsoft's Virtual PC[2] product, because when you need to restore the operating system or a database to a known state, you can simply reload the virtual image.

Automated Software Testing

The time taken to resolve incompatibilities in our code rises steeply with the numbers which exist at any one time because the number of permutations rises factorially. Therefore, it makes sense to address such problems as they arise rather than letting them accumulate. For this reason, you must reduce the time delay between someone making a change to the code base and receiving confirmation of its success, because the longer this feedback takes, the greater the opportunity for incompatible changes to accumulate in the code base.

On an Agile team, the rule is simple: Regularly check in small changes with business value and verify that they work within ten minutes, or back them out. In this way, the software is kept in a working state almost all of the time, which reduces the overall time the team spends addressing software integration issues. However, in order to apply this policy, your Build Lab needs to automate a substantial part of its software testing so that at the click of a button, a new version of the product can be rapidly generated and

---

1. Waldon, Ben. "Program Customized Testing Environments" (*MSDN Magazine,* Aug. 2004 http://msdn.microsoft.com/msdnmag).
2. Microsoft Virtual PC Web site (www.microsoft.com/windows/virtualpc).

validated. For this reason, Agile teams work to streamline the integration and testing of their work so that they can complete it in less time than it takes to drink a cup of coffee; see the upcoming sidebar, Ten Minute Build Practice.

■ TIP

You shouldn't seek to automate your testing entirely, because manual testing often reveals obvious problems (sanity checks) and introduces a degree of variance which allows you to discover new bugs.

Ten Minute Build Practice

The Ten Minute Build practice means that less than ten minutes after someone puts his changes into the repository, the latest version of the team's software has been rebuilt and its integration tests run.

The Ten Minute Build practice makes integration into a low-overhead task that can be done each time you take a break from the Test-First Programming practice. Ten minutes is time enough to get a cup of coffee and reflect upon what you've done with your programming partner. If you take a break for longer than ten minutes, you'll get sidetracked on some other issue. However, break for less than ten minutes and there's not enough time to have a decent conversation. The Ten Minute Build practice ties together the need for periodic breaks, taking small steps and regular integration. It also gives you some time to think.

Automation is the key to implementing the Ten Minute Build practice. You need to be able to kick off the build before you go for a break and then come back ten minutes later to check the result. Fortunately, Team Foundation Build allows you to completely automate your build and test process so that at the start of your project, it is usually not difficult to rebuild everything and then run all the tests within ten minutes. Of course, this does mean that you must monitor the time needed to complete such a build and take steps to speed things up when the size of your code base starts to make it difficult for you to achieve this target. For example, you might need to implement incremental builds, as described in Chapter 12.

Smoke Tests

When testing a new build of software, you need to find out quickly whether it is worth spending more time and effort progressing it toward possible release into the production environment. People often use the term *Smoke Test*[3] to describe this sort of testing, the idea being to rapidly detect any fires in the code by looking for the telltale signs of smoke. You need to run new tests to confirm that the changes made to your software produce the desired new behavior, but more important, you also need to run your old tests to check that these changes don't impair any existing behavior; this is called **regression testing.**

Without automated software testing, a Smoke Test might simply involve running the program for 15 minutes so that you can check that you can perform a basic set of operations without encountering any obvious bugs. However, when automated tests are used, the amount of testing that you can perform during a quick Smoke Test rises considerably because it becomes quite feasible to run hundreds of regression tests to check the new version of the program in terms of both its structure and its function. Therefore, by using the automated part of your Smoke Test to weed out obvious problematic builds, you can concentrate more of your efforts performing the manual part and thereby find the subtler problems which often exist in the remainder.

> ▪ **NOTE**
>
> Regression testing helps you detect bugs that your code changes create indirectly, by running all the old functional and structural (unit) tests for parts of the code you have not changed, in addition to the new tests for the code you have changed.

Functional Tests

Functional testing is often called *black-box testing*[4] because it treats the software under test as a system inside a sealed box which has a given state and

---

3. McConnell, Steve. "Daily Build and Smoke Test" (*IEEE Software*, Vol. 13, No. 4, 1996).

produces particular outputs in response to certain inputs. Functional testing in its most general sense involves validating what the software does, but we shall defer explaining the specifics of its implementation until we cover customer tests in Section 7.

Functional tests are useful from an integration point of view because they usually test the program (or system) from end to end, verifying that each separately developed element does what it is meant to do and thus forms part of a cohesive whole. The problem with a functional test is that when it fails you usually have no indication to help you identify the code or data that is causing the problem. In terms of the black-box analogy, all you know is that the output of the box is just not what was predicted for the given set of inputs.

Structural (Unit) Tests

Structural testing allows us to look inside the sealed box that represents your software during functional testing so that we can write tests for the various parts of this code working in isolation. For example, we might write a structural test to check the operation of a particular function or an individual method of a class. Structural testing is generally concerned with validating how software works, which is why it is sometimes called *white* or *glass box* testing. However, it is most commonly termed *unit* testing to emphasize the fact that you are testing separate pieces of code in isolation. We will show you how to write structural tests (also known as Programmer's Tests) when we cover test-driven development (TDD) in Section 5.

Structural testing is a bottom-up approach. It relies on the idea of rigorously testing the individual parts of a program to ensure that when they are put together they will all work correctly. When a structural test fails you usually have a good indication of the exact line of code or data value that is causing the problem, but it is often difficult to relate that information to some reported failure of the system as a whole.

Quality of Service Tests

In addition to tests that validate software against its functional requirements, you must also test it against nonfunctional requirements such as

---

4. [BBT] Beizer, Boris. *Black-Box Testing* (John Wiley & Sons, 1995).

security, performance, and so forth. Microsoft refers to such nonfunctional requirements as Quality of Service (QoS) items. Typically you implement QoS testing by running functional tests to exercise the software and then measure things such as its performance under high-transaction volumes (loading testing), or its response when system resources such as memory are in short supply (stress testing).

You might perform QoS testing during integration if there was a particular nonfunctional requirement that the team was trying to satisfy. For example, you might be striving to reach a target of 50 transactions per second (TPS) and therefore want to reject at the Smoke Test stage any build that was unable to achieve at least 45 TPS. However, it is more usual to make QoS testing part of any final system testing which must be completed before the software is judged ready for release into the production environment; see Chapter 28.

Integration Testing

An Agile team validates each version of software produced by its Build Lab by performing integration testing which includes a regression test of most, if not all, of the automated structural and functional tests that have been developed for the project. It combines tests that functionally go from one end of the system to the other with tests developed to prove its structural integrity. This sort of orthogonal testing can be very effective at finding the incompatibilities that inevitably result when different people work on a common code base, but of course, it is highly dependent on having a collection of tests that adequately cover both code and features; we address this matter in Sections 5 and 7.

> **▪ NOTE**
>
> You may also need to add further structural or functional tests for the specific purpose of testing the interfaces between the software that is being integrated. Robert Binder's book,[5] *Testing Object-Oriented Systems*, provides excellent advice in this area.

---

5. [TOOS] Binder, Robert. *Testing Object-Oriented Systems* (Addison-Wesley, 2000).

Build and Test Cycles

Figure 11-1 (earlier) shows the flow of software from its origination in the development environment to its final use in the production environment. This flow results from the repetition of activities which can be described in terms of various build (and test) cycles that drive the iterative and incremental nature of Agile software development. Let's now see what these activities involve by following the building and integrating of software during a typical 24 hours with the OSPACS team we described in the Introduction.

Local Build

Luke has assumed responsibility for implementing the "Mask Personal Details from Image" story; see Figure 3-1 in Chapter 3. He has broken down the story into a number of tasks, one of which involves reading the patient identifier field (volunteer ref) from a DICOM-formatted file so that he can create a record for its image data in the OSPACS database. This task should take him a couple of hours to complete, and he will perform it while pair programming with Sarah, his teammate, in what we term a **programming episode.**

Luke and Sarah get the latest version of the OSPACS code base into Luke's workspace (see Exercise 9-1 in Chapter 9) so that they can do test-driven development (TDD) by repeatedly cycling through the following sequence:

1. Write a structural (unit) test.
2. Write the code to make the test pass.
3. Improve the code by removing duplication, and clarifying and simplifying it.

We will cover the technicalities of TDD in Section 5, but for now, just understand that Luke and Sarah are building and testing a few classes every few minutes using the Visual Studio Integrated Development Environment (IDE). Although these classes are part of the OSPACS system, only the files that have been altered need compiling, so it doesn't take more than a few seconds to build and test each change. This encourages Luke and Sarah to stay focused on the programming task at hand and to solve the problem by taking a succession of small steps. Working in this way, it takes them a couple of hours to write the tests and code needed to implement the programming task and check their changeset into the repository.

TDD requires intensive concentration, so you need to take regular breaks. Therefore, Luke and Sarah end their programming episode by initiating an Integration Build and then going for coffee to talk through what they have just achieved. They are confident that the changes they have made in their development environment are ready to be promoted to the Build Lab environment because they have done the following:

- Peer-reviewed their work through the Pair Programming practice
- Built their software in the development environment without incurring any errors from the compiler or warnings from the team's static code analysis rules
- Passed the unit tests they had developed and recorded the lines of code that were executed (code coverage) to make sure they adequately exercised their new code
- Regression-tested their work against all the unit and customer tests that were passing before they started the programming episode to check that they hadn't inadvertently broken anything

> **■ NOTE**
>
> You may find that certain customer tests fail in your development environment simply because you do not have access to the same sort of data and services set up to emulate the production environment in the Build Lab.

Continuous Integration Practice

The Continuous Integration practice requires your software to be rebuilt from the team's shared code base whenever you check in any changes to the repository.

During a programming episode, you will first update your workspace with the latest source code from the TFS repository and then implement some changes which you will build and test on your own PC before finally checking the resulting changeset into the repository. The Continuous Integration practice requires that these programming episodes take little more than an hour or so and conclude with the ten-minute (integration) build which constructs and tests the latest version of the software in the repository, therefore demonstrating the successful integration of the changeset.

The rationale often given for delaying integration is that developers take less time to integrate their work when it is batched up and done together as a distinct phase or task. However, there is ample evidence to suggest that the longer you postpone integrating people's work, the longer and more complex the job becomes. It is now customary for teams to integrate their work as a task at the end of each day (Daily Build), but if you lower the overhead associated with integration even further, there is no reason why it can't be done even more frequently. This is precisely what the Ten Minute Build practice provides: the ability to automate integration so that it can be done during the coffee break that takes place after each developer completes a programming episode.

Some Agile teams use tools such as CruiseControl.NET to implement continuous integration so that a Team Build is automatically kicked off each time a changeset is checked into the repository. This is certainly very cool, but it can make you feel a bit remote from the integration process. Personally, we like the idea of manually starting a ten-minute build before going for coffee and then checking the results upon our return. We value these breaks because they give us time to think and stop us burning out on test-first programming. In this respect, we view continuous integration as being more a case of frequent rather than instantaneous integration.

> ### ■ TIP
>
> Rather than updating your workspace from the latest version of files in the repository, you might instead update it from the version used to create the most recent Integration Build which has been judged successful.

Integration Build

The Integration Build and Test cycle repeats at the conclusion of each successful programming episode and ensures that changes to the code base are safely shared among the team. It is performed by running a sort of script in the Build Lab that checks out the latest version of the code base (including its tests) into a working directory where it is rebuilt and tested over a short period; see the sidebar, Ten Minute Build Practice, earlier in this chapter. All this happens in a well-defined way because the Build Lab is a standardized environment, unlike the development PCs belonging to Luke and the other developers. A report is generated upon completion of an Integration Build and Test that details any errors or warnings found.

> ### ■ NOTE
>
> Controlling the configuration of a developer's PC is usually difficult because these machines will frequently have new libraries, tools, and so forth installed on them, which sometimes results in a developer using the wrong version during a local build.

Luke checks the results of his Integration Build after returning from coffee, and fortunately there are no problems, so he doesn't need to back out his changes (see Exercise 9-4 in Chapter 9). Luke knows that although the work Sarah and he did in the development environment may have helped eradicate many of the problems that arise when people share source files, it is only in the Build Lab that the subtler issues are identified. Accordingly, he now feels more confident that anyone updating his workspace to get the version of code from the repository corresponding to this build will receive a collection of files that can be assembled into a fully functioning version of the software. This is due to the following:

- The Build Lab provides the gold standard for building the team's software, so a successful build in this environment means that any build problems subsequently encountered in someone else's development environment probably result from incompatibilities on her PC; for example, out-of-date libraries, incorrect compiler settings, and so forth.

- The testing of the programs generated in the Build Lab is more complete because it emulates the production environment more closely than in Luke's development environment. The tests are also performed in a more controlled way with the Build Lab being reset to a known state before the tests are started; for example, databases are rebuilt, Web services restarted, and so on.

- In Luke's development environment, the testing was primarily focused on running structural (unit) tests. However, in the Build Lab more functional tests are run that exercise processes from one end to the other. The success of these tests is a better indication that different areas of the code base work together properly.

- The changes made during Luke's programming episode (including tests) have been combined with changes made in other areas of the code base by people who have also completed a programming episode over the past few hours. The success of the Integration Build and Test indicates that the software still interoperates correctly after all these changes.

■ WARNING

Roll back your changeset from the repository immediately if you discover that it contains an error (or other issue) because the longer it remains there, the more likely it is that other developers will copy the problem into their workspaces when they get the latest version of the files.

Had it been necessary for Luke to back out his changeset because it failed the integration Build Validation Test (BVT), he might have decided to ask Sarah if she could help him resolve the problem by continuing their programming episode. Alternatively, he might have chosen to defer the matter by repeating the entire programming task at some future date, possibly with another developer. Whatever approach is taken, the Ten Minute Build practice allows Luke to back out a troublesome changeset within ten minutes of it being checked in, which significantly helps to retain the integrity of the OSPACS code base.

Daily Build

Each day after the OSPACS team has left the office, the Daily Build (and test) is run as a scheduled job in the Build Lab. This provides a regular synchronization point for the project that gathers together in one build all the changes made during the previous day's programming episodes. It is a complete rebuild of the system and should generate everything needed to deploy the system in the production environment, including installation programs, help files, and so forth. The programs created by the build are subjected to all the available automated tests, and the next morning, the person given responsibility for maintaining this Daily Build (the process technician) will perform additional manual testing needed to complete the Smoke Test and any other forms of testing[6] that may be judged necessary.

Performing a Daily Build means that at any time, the OSPACS team is able to deploy everything it has done apart from what has been achieved in the current day. However, in practice, the team's software will actually be deployed into the production environment only at the end of certain iterations every few months or so; see Section 8. In this way, the team regularly practices for deployment, and consequently, when it really happens, it just needs to follow a well-polished procedure. Deployment itself is a very simple task on the OSPACS team at this early stage of the project because it just requires that the team grant access rights to folders containing the appropriate Daily Build so that its installation program can be downloaded when someone clicks on the appropriate link in the company's public Web site.

---

6. Ambler, Scott. "The Full Life Cycle Object-Oriented Testing (FLOOT) Method" (www.ambysoft.com/essays/floot.html).

Typically, the team will know when the results of an iteration are scheduled to be deployed into the production environment, and therefore will put particular emphasis in that iteration to performing more intensive system testing. The products of any Daily Build may potentially be deployed, though inevitably most are not, either because they fail at some stage during the testing performed as they progress through the team's formal release process, or simply because they do not offer enough value to the business to warrant the cost of their deployment in terms of training, changing business processes, and so forth.

> **■ NOTE**
>
> Some organizations adopt the less than Agile approach of never releasing software into the production environment without it first passing through a separate team responsible for conducting further tests which typically may take days, weeks, or even months.

CONCLUSION

Building and integrating your team's software is a production process that you need to automate so that it can be performed regularly, reliably, and consistently. This is the purpose of a Build Lab. It allows the team to create a production line that moves software from its various development environments into a single area where it can be built and tested before being progressed into the production environment. The automated software testing that is carried out in a Build Lab dramatically reduces the cost of this software integration work, thereby making it an activity that can be repeated many times each day. A team that is able to regularly build and integrate its work improves the value delivered to the business because overall, the team spends less time putting its work together and can also reveal its worth much earlier in the project.

12
Working with Team Foundation Build

This chapter explains the practicalities of building and integrating your team's software in the way we described in the preceding chapter. We will introduce you to Team Foundation Build and show how you can use it to automate the process of building and testing the source files stored in your team's repository. You will also learn how to perform incremental builds and optimize the dependencies between your code libraries so that you can scale up Team Build for larger code bases. The aim of the chapter is to help your team regularly create versions of its software and use the information generated to progress its work toward eventual deployment in the production environment.

Welcome to Team Foundation Build

The Team Foundation Build that comes with Team Foundation Server (TFS) provides everything you need to set up your own public Build Lab. The underlying engine performing the various build tasks is MSBuild, with the associated source control, reporting facilities, and Web services being provided by TFS. Put together in the framework of Team Foundation Build, you've got the functionality you need to implement the sort of integration and build process discussed in Chapter 11.

Setting Up Team Foundation Build

Although you can install Team Foundation Build (TFB) on the machine hosting your TFS or on a Client Tier PC, we strongly recommend that you run it on a machine used exclusively as your Build Lab, such as the Build-LabPC shown in Figure 1-1 in Chapter 1. You have plenty of flexibility in terms of the physical machine used for this purpose, because typically TFB does not demand either a very fast processor or large amounts of RAM. The TFS Installation Manual[1] gives full details about the TFB minimum hardware requirements and its installation procedure. However, there are two things that you should keep in mind: First, TFB must be explicitly installed on a PC because it is not installed with TFS or Visual Studio Team Suite. Second, you should have Visual Studio Team Suite installed on the same machine as your TFB so that you can run a full range of automated VSTS tests as part of your build process: unit tests, code coverage, static code analysis, generic tests, and so forth.

How Team Foundation Build Works

A Team Build is started when a command is passed from the TFS Client Tier to the Team Foundation Build Web Service running on the Application Tier; see step 1 in Figure 12-1. This Build Web Service coordinates the execution of the build steps executed by MSBuild by communicating with the Build Service running on the Build machine (steps 2 through 4). The results of running the Team Build are then passed back to this Build Web Service for storage in the Team Foundation Build Store, the database responsible for maintaining a record of each Team Build performed by your team (steps 5 and 6). When your Team Build completes, all its products (.dll, .exe, and .msi files) are stored in a subfolder of the "build drop folder" which is named after the build type, the date, and its sequence number; for example, MyBuildType_20061128.3.

---

1. TFS Installation Guide (http://go.microsoft.com/fwlink/?LinkId=40042).

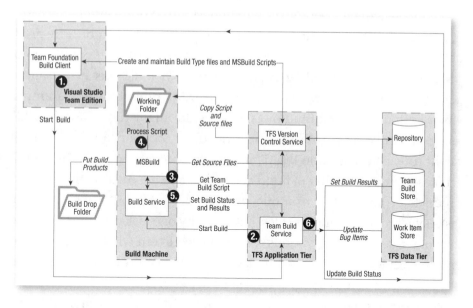

FIGURE 12-1: Components of Visual Studio Team System (VSTS) associated with Team Foundation Build

Fortunately, when you run a Team Build you don't need to worry about any of the preceding technical details; you simply select the type of build you want to run from Visual Studio's Build Team Project dialog box and then click its Build button. Alternatively, you can schedule the running of a Team Build at a particular time of day (or night), as we explain in Exercise 12-4.

The Role of MSBuild

MSBuild allows you to automate the various tasks required to build your software. Although it usually integrates with hosts such as Visual Studio 2005, you can also run MSBuild directly from the command line, so you don't absolutely need to install Visual Studio Team Suite in your Build Lab. However, we don't recommend this choice, because as we mentioned earlier, it prevents you from running the VSTS automated tests as part of your build process.

People who have used NAnt will find MSBuild quite familiar because both tools use XML to define the steps needed to build your software product. However, as you might expect, each tool required a different form of XML. You can use MSBuild to perform all types of builds because its input parameter simply requires a reference to an XML project file. For example, when hosted by Visual Studio 2005, MSBuild might run a "local build" using myApp.csproj, and when run remotely on your build machine it might run an "Integration Build" using teamIntegration.proj. These project files contain a number of build tasks related to the construction of build products or targets (for example, an assembly). MSBuild executes such tasks synchronously and the files generated by one task can form the input to another, so by setting various conditions to govern whether a particular task is executed, you can exercise a great deal of control over the creation of your software, its testing, and even its deployment.

Most of the time you don't need to edit the XML in your MSBuild project files directly because Visual Studio does the job for you. For example, if you add a class to a project or change the build configuration, your project file is automatically updated. However, you can edit the project file itself should the need arise, but bear in mind that although it forms a type of script, it does not support many of the features you might associate with a proper scripting language such as JavaScript. Therefore, if you want to add some special control logic to your build, you should extend MSBuild with a custom .NET library; see the book's Web site for details.

> **■ NOTE**
>
> Visual Studio 2005 replaces the traditional NMAKE[2] build tool with MSBuild so that whenever you press F6 (or apply Build | Build Solution, and so on) you are actually using the same tool to build your programs as your team uses in its Build Lab.

---

2. NMAKE is Microsoft's adaptation of MAKE, a build tool originating from UNIX and C.

Making a Build Validation Test

A Build Validation Test (BVT) serves to validate the products of a build and is typically run as a build task at the end of a Team Build. It is basically a list of the tests people have created to prove the software in some way. For example, after writing a unit test to check some aspect of the code in your development environment, you might check in the test and then add it to a BVT to ensure that the same test was subsequently executed whenever the Integration Build was run in your Build Lab environment.

■. TIP

Change the number and type of default tests created for your Test Projects by changing the settings in your Visual Studio Options dialog box: Tools | Options | Test Tools, Test Project.

In order to create a BVT you need to have some tests. Therefore, you should start by creating a Visual Studio C# Test Project which, by default, has two initial tests: a unit test called TestMethod1 and a manual test called ManualTest1. Exercise 12-1 takes you step by step through this procedure.

EXERCISE 12-1: Creating a Build Validation Test

In this exercise, you will create the osImageManagerUT Visual Studio C# Test Project and then add its TestMethod1 unit test to a Test List you make in your Test Manager window. This Test List forms your BVT.

1. Log on as Luke (OSPACS Contributor) to the DeveloperPC, start Visual Studio, and then connect to the OSPACS Team Project, as described in Exercise 5-7 in Chapter 5; see Appendix A for details about this PC and Luke's security groups.

2. Make sure Luke's workspace is up-to-date by opening the Source Control Explorer (View | Other Windows), selecting the $/OSPACS folder, and then choosing Get Latest Version from its context menu (Right-click | Get Latest Version).

3. Load the osImageManager Visual Studio Solution by opening the osImageManager.sln file in Luke's workspace (File | Open | Project/Solution).

4. Create a new Visual Studio Project called osImageManagerUT; open the New Project dialog box (File | New | Project) and select Test Project from the Visual C# project types. Use the dialog box to add this project to the osImageManager Solution and select a suitable directory in Luke's workspace for its source files (for example, osImageManager\src).

5. Open the Test Manager window (Test | Windows) and create a new Test List for your BVT by opening its Create New Test List dialog box, typing "IntegrationBVT" as the test list name, and then clicking OK. You open this dialog box by selecting Lists of Tests and then choosing New Test List from its context menu (Right-click | New Test List).

6. Add a unit test to your new Test List by dragging the osImageManagerUT test named TestMethod1 from the Test View window (Test | Windows) onto IntegrationBVT in the left pane of the Test Manager window. To make sure this test is run as part of the integration test, click the selection box next to IntegrationBVT in the right pane of the Test Manager window.

7. Check that your IntegrationBVT test runs without error by clicking the Run Checked Tests button in the toolbar at the top of the Test Manager window; see Figure 12-2. The results appear in the Test Results window.

8. Check-in your changes into the TFS repository for OSPACS by opening the Pending Changes window (View | Other Windows) and clicking its Check In button; see Figure 8-2 in Chapter 8.

9. This exercise is now complete, so log off.

■ TIP

Install Visual Studio Team Suite on all the team's PCs so that people can add the tests they create to the IntegrationBVT Test List after they have successfully run them in their own development environment and checked them into the repository.

Run Checked Tests

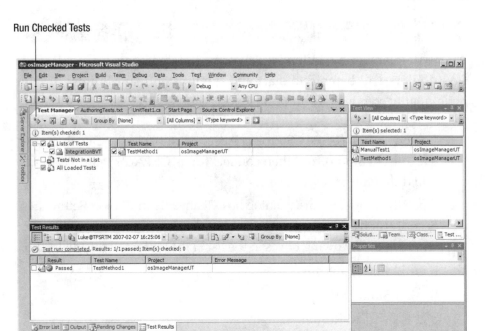

FIGURE 12-2: Running a BVT in your Test Lab environment

Setting Team Build Permissions

Three security groups were formed when the OSPACS Team Project was created in Exercise 5-1 in Chapter 5: [OSPACS]\Administrators, [OSPACS]\Readers, and [OSPACS]\Contributors. The default permissions of [OSPACS]\Contributors allow the developers on your team to use whatever facilities of VSTS they need to do most parts of their job. However, in order for developers to create and run Team Foundation Builds, they need the additional permissions granted in Exercise 12-2.

■ NOTE

Create the OSPACSDevs security group for the developers on your team so that you can grant them the permissions they need for using the various facilities of VSTS simply by making OSPACSDevs a member of [OSPACS]\Contributors.

EXERCISE 12-2: Allowing Developers to Create and Run Team Builds

After completing the following exercise, all members of [OSPACS]\
Contributors will be able to start and administer Team Builds, provide
build quality comments, and publish test results.

1. Log on as Tom (OSPACS Project Administrator) to the DeveloperPC,
   start Visual Studio, and then connect to the OSPACS Team Project as
   you did in the previous exercise.

2. Open the Project Security dialog box (Team | Team Project Settings |
   Security) and select the OSPACS\Contributors security group before
   checking the following boxes in the list at the bottom of this dialog box:

   a. Administer a Build

   b. Edit Build Quality

   c. Publish Test Results

   d. Start a Build

   e. View Project Level Information (already checked)

3. Apply your changes and close the dialog box by clicking its Close
   button.

4. Create the directories c:\TeamBuild\Drops\OSPACS and
   c:\TeamBuild\Builds. Make the Drops directory a shared directory
   of the same name with the following permissions:

   a. Read permissions for members of OSPACSDevs

   b. Write permissions for the Team Build Service account specified
      during the installation of Team Foundation Build on your
      BuildLabPC

5. You have completed this exercise, so log off.

■ TIP

You can share a directory on your PC and set its permissions using
Windows Explorer by choosing Sharing and Security from its context
menu (right-click). If this menu item does not appear, try logging on as
the original owner, for example, "darren".

Creating Team Build Types

Each Team Build a team performs is an instance of a particular build type as defined by an MSBuild project file. You can create this project file by running the Team Build Type Wizard, as described in Exercise 12-3, and therefore define such things as the following:

- A list of Visual Studio Solutions that will be built
- A build configuration such as "release" or "debug" and the target platform
- The name of the build machine and the location of the build drop folder
- A list of any Build Validation Tests to be executed and whether static code analysis should be performed

---

■ **TIP**

Create a collection of Team Build types, each with different settings and Build Validation Tests, so that your team can perform builds to satisfy particular objectives. For example, create one for fast Integration Builds and another for more thorough Daily Builds.

EXERCISE 12-3: Creating a Team Build Type for Integration

In this exercise, you will create the osImageManagerIntegration Team Build type with a Release configuration for the osImageManager Visual Studio Solution. Builds of this type will be validated by the IntegrationBVT and the build products will be copied into subdirectories of the \\DevServer\Drops\OSPACS shared directory.

1. Log on as Luke (OSPACS Contributor) to the BuildLabPC, start Visual Studio, and then connect to the OSPACS Team Project, as described in Exercise 5-7 in Chapter 5.

2. Create a new Team Build type by completing the appropriate wizard (Build | New Team Build Type):

   a. Enter "osImageManagerIntegration" as the name of the new Team Build type and give a description of its purpose before clicking Next.

   b. Select the osImageManager Solution as the Visual Studio Solution to build. If you want to build more than one solution, use the arrow buttons at the side of the list of Solutions to set their build order. Click Next to continue.

   c. Select the Release configuration as the "type of configuration" to use during the build. In this way, all Visual Studio Projects will be built according to the release settings in their corresponding *.vsproj files. Click Next to continue.

   d. Enter the build machine name as "BuildLabPC", the build directory as "c:\TeamBuild\Builds", and the drop location as "\\DevServer\Drops\OSPACS". Click Next to continue.

   e. Select Run Test, and from the test metadata file, select the IntegrationBVT Test List created in Exercise 12-1. You should also select Perform Code Analysis before clicking Next to continue.

   f. Check the summary of your selections, and then click Finish to create a directory containing the various files that define your new Team Build type. The wizard will also check all these items into the TFS repository for you.

3. This exercise is complete, so log off.

■ NOTE

You can share a directory on your PC and set its permissions using Windows Explorer by choosing Sharing and Security from its context menu (right-click). If this menu item does not appear, try logging on as the original owner; for example, "darren".

Scheduling a Daily Build

A Daily Build provides a regular synchronization point for all the changes the team has made during a single day. It is usually performed after everyone has left the office, so it needs to be a scheduled task which you can perform from the command prompt, as we describe next.

EXERCISE 12-4: Scheduling a Daily Team Build

This exercise runs a Team Build from the command prompt and then sets up a Windows scheduled task to repeat this action each weekday at 10:00 p.m.

1. Log on as Luke (OSPACS Contributor) to the BuildLabPC, start Visual Studio, and then connect to the OSPACS Team Project, as described in Exercise 5-7 in Chapter 5.

2. Open an MS-DOS command prompt and execute a Team Build by typing:

```
TFSBuild Start BuildLabPC OSPACS osImageManagerIntegration
```

The progress of the build will be displayed, and after a few minutes, the build should successfully complete. You can obtain more information about TFSBuild by issuing the command with just the parameters: Start /?.

3. Allow your Daily Build to be started automatically at a given time of day by starting the Window Scheduled Task Wizard (Control Panel | Scheduled Tasks | Add Scheduled Task) and making the following choices:

   a. Select Command Prompt as the program you want to schedule.

   b. Enter "OSPACS Daily Build" as the name of the task, and set it to be performed daily.

   c. Enter "10:00 p.m." as the start time of the task, and set it to be performed on weekdays from the current date.

    d. Enter Luke's username and password so that the task will be performed with his rights and permissions.

    e. Click Finish to add the task to the BuildLabPC's list of scheduled tasks. You can subsequently edit the settings for this task from the Control Panel | Scheduled Tasks menu and thereby set the necessary command-line parameters in the Task Run edit box.

4. You have finished the exercise, so log off.

■. NOTE

We have specified that the OSPACS team's Daily Build should use the Team Build type created in Exercise 12-3 for its Integration Build. However, as work progresses, you will need to create specialized Team Build types for these different sorts of builds.

Sample Programming Episode: Integration Build

To give you some practice completing the sorts of Team Builds you need to perform in your day-to-day work, let's now walk through the programming episode we described in Chapter 11.

■. NOTE

A programming episode typically involves completing a discrete chunk of work, such as fixing a bug or implementing some distinct part of a story. It concludes after you check your changeset into the repository and successfully perform an Integration Build.

EXERCISE 12-5: Programming Episode Walkthrough and Integration Build

In the first part of this exercise, you will make a small alteration to the Visual Studio Project created in Exercise 8-4 in Chapter 8, and then validate it with the test you created in Exercise 12-1.

1. Log on as Luke (OSPACS Contributor) to the DeveloperPC, start Visual Studio, and then connect to the OSPACS Team Project, as described in Exercise 5-7 in Chapter 5.

2. Make sure Luke's workspace is up-to-date by opening the Source Control Explorer (View | Other Windows), selecting the $/OSPACS folder, and then choosing Get Latest Version from its context menu (Right-click | Get Latest Version).

3. Load the osImageManager Visual Studio Solution by opening the osImageManager.sln file in Luke's workspace (File | Open | Project/Solution) and then change the title of the osImageManagerApp main form by opening Form1.cs from the Solution Explorer and editing its Text property (View | Properties Window), as you did in Exercise 9-1 in Chapter 9.

4. Validate the change in your development environment by performing a local build and then running your automated tests as follows:

   a. Press F6 to build the solution (Build | Build Solution).

   b. Select the TestMethod1 test in your Test View window (Test | Windows) and select Run Selection from its context menu (Right-click | Run Selection).

   c. Open the Test Results window (Test | Windows) to see the results of the test.

   Next you will associate the changeset you have just created with a work item and then check it into the repository.

5. Open the Pending Changes window (View | Other Windows) and then select Work Items from its left toolbar so you can select the All Work Items query and thus list all the work items for the OSPACS Team Project.

6. Place a checkmark against the GUITask (created in Exercise 6-2 in Chapter 6) and set its Check in Actions as Resolve; then click the Check In button to put your changeset into the repository.

   The final part of the exercise performs a Team Build to integrate these changes with the team's shared code base and then sets the status of the build to inform other team members that it successfully validates the work item associated with the changeset.

7. Open the OSPACS Build dialog (Build | Build Team Project OSPACS), select the Build Type as osImageManagerIntegration (created in Exercise 12-3), and then click the Build button.

8. The Team Build Report window opens in Visual Studio (see Figure 12-3) to show the progress of the build on the BuildLabPC, though you can close this window at any time without interrupting your Team Build.

9. After the Team Build completes, expand the items at the bottom of the Team Build Report window to confirm that it includes the changeset and its associated work item; see steps 3 and 6.

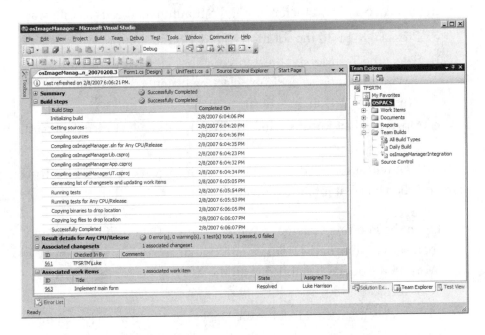

FIGURE 12-3: Team Build Report window

10. Specify the quality of the Integration Build you have just performed by changing its Build Quality to Integration OK, as follows:

   a. Display the list of Team Builds of this type that have been performed by using Team Explorer to select osImageManagerIntegration in the OSPACS Team Builds folder and then choose Open from its context menu.

   b. Add a new build quality value for the OSPACS project by selecting any item in the build list's Build Quality column and then choosing <Edit...> from its drop-down list to open the Edit Build Quality dialog box.

   c. Add a new build quality value by clicking the dialog's New button and typing "Integration OK" into the dialog box that appears. Click the Close button to save this new value and close the dialog box.

   d. Apply the Integration OK value to the build you have just performed by selecting it from the list of builds and then selecting the appropriate value from the drop-down list in the Build Quality column. You should save this change by selecting another column in the list.

11. This exercise is complete, so log off.

> **■ NOTE**
>
> Your team needs to agree to immediately back out from the TFS repository any changeset that causes the Integration Build to fail, but this should rarely happen because the changes made will have been thoroughly tested in your development environment beforehand.

Deleting Build Products

Most teams will be content to let their build products accumulate in the Build Store and Drop Site folders because lack of storage space should not be a significant concern. However, sometimes the need arises to perform a bit of housekeeping, so we explain in Exercise 12-6 how you can delete the build products from the drop site and remove all information about the build from your Build Store database.

EXERCISE 12-6: Deleting Build Products

After you have completed this exercise, you will have deleted all the products of the Team Build performed in Exercise 12-5—that is, its build report in TFS as well as the executable files in its "drop" directory in your BuildLabPC.

1. Log on as Luke (OSPACS Contributor) to the DeveloperPC, start Visual Studio, and then connect to the OSPACS Team Project, as described in Exercise 5-7 in Chapter 5.

2. Identify the name of the Team Build you want to delete from the list of Team Builds that have been performed. You can display this list by double-clicking the osImageManagerIntegration item in Team Explorer's Team Builds folder.

3. Open the command prompt and enter the following command, where the final parameter is the name of the Team Build identified in step 2:

```
TFSBuild Delete BuildLabPC OSPACS osImageManagerIntegration_20060228.3
```

Confirm this action by pressing the y key and wait for the process to complete before closing the command prompt.

4. Log off, as this exercise is complete.

■ NOTE

In order to complete Exercise 12-6 successfully, you need to have permission to administer builds for the OSPACS Team Project, permissions that were granted to [OSPACS]\Contributors in Exercise 12-2.

Build Management

Over the course of a project, the output from perhaps thousands of builds accumulates into a complete archive of your team's build history. However, like any archive, it can quickly lose its value useless you manage it properly. In this part of the chapter, we will discuss a number of ways in which your team might make better use of the information generated by performing Team Builds.

Process Technician Role

Giving the job of process technician (build coordinator) to a team member makes someone ultimately responsible for ensuring that Team Builds are properly executed and managed. Typically, the role is performed by developers in rotation so as to encourage knowledge about the job to become distributed throughout the team. This is a practice which also fosters cooperation, as each developer knows that sooner or later he will undertake the role, so it is in everyone's interest to make the job easy.

At the start of the project, it is the process technician who will create the initial Team Builds and help establish check-in policies (see Exercise 10-3 in Chapter 10) or manual procedures to make certain that the teams agreed practices and policies are met. However, as the project proceeds, the job becomes more a matter of running the daily Smoke Test, keeping the build and test environment in good working order, and maintaining the Team Build types. The process technician might, for example, have to implement an Incremental Build in order to maintain the team's target, running its Integration Build within ten minutes, or delete a series of Integration Builds because they no longer serve any purpose.

> **TIP**
>
> During your turn as the process technician, try to make some lasting improvement in the way your team builds its software. For example, create a new type of build report or restructure a library to make Incremental Builds more efficient.

Build Notification

Team Builds are like a heartbeat in that a regular series of successful builds gives a fair indication that your project is in good health. Everyone on the team can easily monitor this heartbeat by setting up a Project Alert so that an e-mail is sent to each team member when a Team Build completes or its status (build quality) changes.

> **TIP**
>
> Create a Project Alert by selecting one of the standard alerts from the Project Alerts dialog box (Team | Project Alerts) and then entering an appropriate e-mail address or distribution list.

The problem with setting up alerts using the Project Alerts dialog box is that you can quickly become inundated with e-mails telling you a build has completed, something that might happen a dozen or so times a day on a small team and much more often on a larger team. This can be especially irritating if you have also arranged to receive a Systems Management Server (SMS) message on your mobile telephone whenever you get an e-mail from your Team Foundation Server (TFS). What you really want is an e-mail when a Team Build fails, rather than when it completes. This might be particularly important if you were the current process technician and needed to be called in the middle of the night if the Daily Build failed. In this sort of situation, you might want to use the BisSubscribe command-line tool, as shown in Listing 12-1.

LISTING 12-1: Receiving Project Alerts Only When a Team Build Fails[3]

```
BisSubscribe.exe /eventType BuildCompletionEvent
/address <email address>
/deliveryType EmailHtml
/server <server name>
/filter "TeamProject='<Team Project>' AND CompletionStatus='FAILED'"
/userid <your id>
```

---

3. The solution in Listing 12-1 was suggested on the MSDN VSTS Forum by M.N. Kishore.

> ## ■ NOTE
>
> Replace the contents of the angle brackets in Listing 12-1 with details relevant to your own project and enter them all on the same line from the command prompt. The parameters are shown on different lines in the listing only for reasons of space and clarity.

Build Identification

The output of a Team Build is identified by a unique build name formed by the Build Type name, the date it was performed, and an incremental build number for that date. This build name appears both on the list of build records created when you run a build report (see Figure 12-3) and as the name of the folder containing the build products in the "drop site." Therefore, it is not difficult to find a particular set of build products given their date and sequence number. However, you often need to run some form of query to discover this information. For example, you might run a query to find a particular work item so that you can then determine the build name in which it was resolved; see Figure 12-4.

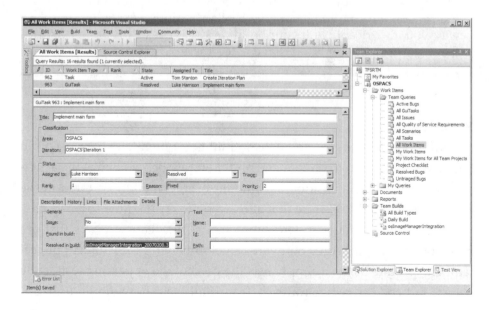

Figure 12-4: Work item's "Resolved in build" details

> ■ **NOTE**
>
> Associating a work item with a changeset in the Pending Changes window (View | Other Windows) and setting its State to Resolved will result in its "Resolved in build" details being automatically updated the next time you run a Team Build.

Build identification is particularly important when you are attempting to resolve a bug because you will often need to identify the exact configuration of the software in which the bug was found so that you can re-create it in your development environment. Given the build name, it is usually not difficult to find the changeset from its build report (see Figure 12-3) and then check out this version of the software into your workspace; see Exercise 9-4 in Chapter 9. However, when the software has been deployed outside the Build Lab environment, it can be difficult to correctly identify this build name because it is not automatically written into the executable files.

> ■ **TIP**
>
> Make it part of your release process to associate the build name with the version information belonging to your various assemblies. In this way, you inextricably link your build product files (.exe and .dll) with the name of the Team Build that created them.

Build Reports

The information gathered about Team Builds is potentially very useful in terms of helping you to understand and therefore better control the activities of your team. A considerable amount of information is stored in the Team Foundation Build store that allows you to create quite sophisticated reports. However, the standard build report for Team Projects that are based on the MSF for Agile Software Development (or MSF for XP) project template is quite basic. It simply lists the percentage of passing tests, code churn, and code coverage for each Team Build, as shown in Figure 12-5.

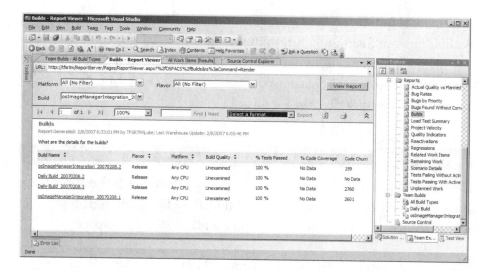

FIGURE 12-5: Build report details

■ NOTE

Display the VSTS standard build report in Visual Studio's main window by double-clicking the appropriate item in your Team Explorer's Reports folder. Alternatively, display it in your browser using the links in your team's Report Site (Team | Show Report Site).

The standard build report provides some useful quality metrics, but they might be better displayed in a chart regularly printed out on a large sheet of paper and then pinned to your office walls. Your challenge as an Agile team is always to pull the data out of the computer and make it accessible, rather than hiding it inside a report that nobody reads.

Scaling Up Team Integration Builds

So far, we've just considered the case of setting up a new Team Project with a small code base when your problem is making the Integration Build take long enough to give people a decent break between programming episodes. However, as your project progresses, the code base grows in size and starts to take longer to build. Therefore, sooner or later you encounter the issue of being able to complete your Integration Build within ten minutes.

Incremental Builds

Scaling up your Team Integration Builds to handle larger code bases usually means building only what has changed rather than trying to rebuild everything, and for this reason you may want to create the incremental Team Build type described in Exercise 12-7.

EXERCISE 12-7: Creating an Incremental Team Build Type

The TFSBuild.proj file belonging to the osImageManagerIntegration Team Build is edited here so that it will rebuild only the parts of the product whose source files have changed in the BuildLabPC's workspace.

1. Log on as Luke (OSPACS Contributor) to the DeveloperPC, start Visual Studio, and then connect to the OSPACS Team Project, as described in Exercise 5-7 in Chapter 5.

2. Perform Team Build for osImageManagerIntegration to create an up-to-date set of build products; see step 7 of Exercise 12-5.

3. Check out the TFSBuild.proj file belonging to the osImageManagerIntegration Team Build by selecting it in your Source Control Explorer window (View | Other Windows) and choosing Check Out for Edit from its context menu.

4. Use Visual Studio's XML editor to open the TFSBuild.proj file which is now in Luke's workspace (File | Open) so that you can add to the bottom of its PropertyGroup section the lines shown in Listing 12-2. This will cause the file to be added to your Pending Changes window (View | Other Windows).

5. Use the Pending Changes window to check in the changeset you have just created by entering a suitable comment and then clicking its Check In button.

6. Perform another osImageManagerIntegration Team Build (repeat step 2), and upon completion, review the BuildLog.txt file to confirm that you have not built the files that remained unchanged—in other words, that you are now building incrementally.

LISTING 12-2: Settings for Performing an Incremental Team Build[4]

```
<PropertyGroup>
<SkipClean>true</SkipClean>
<SkipInitializeWorkspace>true</SkipInitializeWorkspace>
<ForceGet>false</ForceGet>
</PropertyGroup>
```

Optimizing Package Dependencies for Building

In a project with a large code base which is organized into many separate class libraries, the time taken to run a Team Build may be significantly reduced if you have to rebuild only the parts of your software that have changed. For example, rather than rebuilding all 50 class libraries, you might need to rebuild only one. Therefore, altering your Integration Team Build type so that it builds incrementally may be an effective way of upholding the Ten Minute Build practice for a team that has such a code base. However, you can easily lose these gains if many of the team's changes involve a library upon which all the other libraries depend, such as the Maths library in Figure 12-6.

Consider the package hierarchy shown in Figure 12-6, where the arrows show dependencies arising from a class in one library "using" a class in another: Is it better to move the Calc class into the ImageHandlerAuto library or keep it in the Maths library? Your decision may be influenced by a number of factors, but if you expect the Calc class to change frequently, keeping it in the Maths library might not be such a good idea because each single alteration will necessitate a rebuild of all the libraries. In contrast, alterations to a class contained within the ImageHandlerAuto library will require only its own library to be rebuilt because no other libraries are dependent upon it.

---

4. The solution in Listing 12-2 was obtained from Nagaraju Palla's Web log.

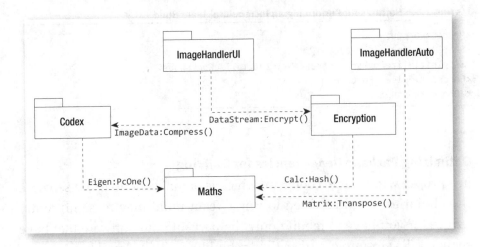

FIGURE 12-6: Package diagram showing dependences between code libraries

It is not always easy to decide which classes should go into which libraries, because you must balance the need to build your software against the need to maintain your architectural design. One of the reasons it is so difficult to perform architectural design upfront is that information about the volatility of a particular class becomes evident only when you start to develop the code. Referring again to Figure 12-6, it is likely that someone decided to put the Calc class in the Maths library well before it became evident that this class would often need alteration. The Agile approach of letting the package structure evolve as the project progresses (bottom-up) confers significant advantages over fixing such matters at an early stage in the project when thoughts are usually focused solely on functional decomposition (top-down). It is a fact of life that requirements will change; the issue, therefore, becomes one of deciding which parts of the code will flex. Big projects that put this flexibility into packages which are inherently difficult to change tend to pay a big price in terms of the time it takes them to build their code.

> ▪ **NOTE**
>
> Typically, you will have all night to run a Daily Build, so there is no need to build your libraries incrementally. However, failing to give proper consideration to the dependencies in your libraries may also make it pointless to attempt an incremental Integration (ten-minute) Build.

CONCLUSION

During the course of your project, your team might create thousands of builds, but only very few will ever be released into the production environment. The tools provided with Visual Studio Team System help you to manage all of these builds so that you can then select the ones that offer the best value to your business in terms of features, quality, and timeliness. In this chapter, you have gained the knowledge and basic skills you need to put these tools to good use. Therefore, you should be able to reliably and consistently release your software, which provides a solid foundation for other areas of improvement.

Review of Section 4
Build and Integrate Often

THE OSPACS TEAM wanted to introduce a process that would regularly, reliably, and consistently move its software from its development environment into production. Providing effective version control had helped the team take the first steps toward this objective by allowing it to combine the changes made by different developers to the same source files. However, the team now wanted to implement the rest of the process by centrally building and integrating its code so that it could be tested in an environment that more closely emulated its production environment. This required the team to undertake the following activities:

- **Set up the build environment**—Visual Studio Team Suite, Team Foundation Build, and InstallShield Standalone were installed on the team's build machine; see the BuildLabPC in Figure 1-1 in Chapter 1. In addition, the team set up a Virtual PC to emulate the production environment and created a Build Validation Test (BVT) so that it might validate the products of its Team Builds.

- **Perform the Ten Minute Build Practice**—The team built the Integration Team Build type along with its associated working directories and drop folders. It took a matter of minutes for the team to run the Team Build because at this stage of the project, there was very little code and few tests to process. Nevertheless, the team was now able to perform Integration Builds after each programming episode, so it had the infrastructure it required to implement the Continuous Integration practice. The team saw this as a major milestone.

- **Perform the Daily Build**—The team created the Daily Team Build type with additional build steps to create an Installation Program using the InstallShield Standalone command-line tool and then ran it. The team also set up a scheduled task on the Team Foundation Server to run this Team Build at 10:00 p.m. each weekday so that it would get into the habit of performing a Daily Build. But the team was aware that a lot of hard work was ahead in terms of improving this Daily Build to meet the demands of its project as it progressed.

- **Perform Team Builds**—All the team's developers went through a number of programming episodes to create a skeletal OSPACS system that they could flesh out with real functionality once they had mastered test-driven development. This helped the team get a feel for the process it had created which would eventually move its software from its development environment into production.

■ NOTE

The OSPACS team created a simple installation program which was built as part of its Daily Build so that it could address deployment issues from the start of the project. See Chapter 29 for information about creating this installation program.

The Team's Impressions

The usual objective of the project's first iteration is the delivery of a thin vertical slice of the system, some small piece of functionality that goes from its input all the way through to its output. This skeletal collection of libraries and classes is fleshed out in subsequent iterations as additional functionality is implemented. In this way, the features of the system are incrementally delivered iteration by iteration. The comments of the teams as they built the infrastructure required to integrate and build this skeletal system are given in the following sections.

Developer: Tom

"The time taken for the team to produce any form of software release kept on increasing because the more we deferred integration, the longer the task became. We didn't notice this effect so much at the start of the project, but when the code base grew, so did our problems. I didn't need much convincing that regular integration was a good thing."

"The decision to deploy a build must be driven by business need rather than IT time scales. Therefore, a build will be deployed into the production environment only when its potential value to the business is greater than the cost of its deployment."

Developer: Sarah

"Now that I've seen what we can do, our old approach to building and testing the system seems so inadequate. It involved little more than pressing F6 in Visual Studio and then running the program in a debugger to exercise a few of its key features. It's not surprising that we found it so difficult to integrate our work."

"This new Build Lab makes sure our test data stays separate from the live data in our production environment."

"Writing an installation program is easy at this stage of the project, but I know from bitter experience that it gets much harder as time goes by."

Developer: Peter

"The key to making this work is to convince everyone to run all of the unit tests and most of the functional tests from his development environment so that he can be confident that the Integration Build will succeed before checking in a changeset."

"Viewing a successful check-in as evidence of successful integration is like taking a clean compile as a reason to suppose that your code is working. Integration can be judged successful only when you have rebuilt and tested the software in the build and test environment."

"You must test as part of integration; if you're not testing, you're not integrating."

Developer: Luke

"My usual response to Maggie complaining about a bug in my code was 'but it works on my machine!' I can see now that my PC didn't really match the production server, so it's not surprising that the program behaved differently in the two environments."

Agile Values

Although the team isn't yet ready to attempt the sorts of Agile iterations we discussed in Chapter 3, it has managed to create a skeleton for the OSPACS system and put together the infrastructure needed for to start working in this way. This allowed the team to implement the Ten Minute Build practice and the Continuous Integration practice, which helped the team develop its Agile values as follows.

Communication

The Ten Minute Build practice encourages developers to take time for coffee and discuss informally what they have done. Other developers who are standing in the kitchen often get involved in such conversation, which helps to spread ideas and knowledge throughout the team.

Practicing continuous integration means that the whole team regularly resynchronizes its work, so changes are communicated to everyone swiftly.

Feedback

The Integration Build is like the project heartbeat because it repeatedly signals that the project is progressing. It validates that the team is producing working code, and when a small problem does arise, it can be fixed before it becomes a large problem which is difficult to solve.

Courage

Integration is performed in small, simple steps so that any problems are quickly apparent. This means the team does not have to worry about having to perform complex "big-bang" integration at some future date.

Simplicity

Automated Team Builds performed in the BuildLabPC are reliable and consistent, which means people tend to blame themselves rather than their tools.

Respect

The team members gain respect for each other by regularly integrating their work, because when someone does check in some code that causes the Integration Build to fail, it serves as a reminder that they are all mutually dependent.

■ Section 5
Practice Test-Driven Development

T EST-DRIVEN DEVELOPMENT (TDD) is the mechanism that underpins an Agile team's ability to deliver valuable and high-quality code in a reliable fashion. This section is all about TDD. It starts in Chapter 13 with an introduction to the basic concepts of TDD in preparation for Chapters 14 and 15, which guide you through a complete working example using the tools provided by Visual Studio Team System (VSTS). Chapter 16 wraps up this example by showing you how you can use the tests you have developed to check performance and produce code coverage information. Finally, we conclude Section 5 with Chapter 17, which proposes how you

Photograph by Camerique (Copyright Getty Images 1935).

Each test performed by an Agile team acts like a small experiment which proves the software and helps the design evolve.

might integrate your TDD code with a user interface generated by the Windows Forms Designer in order to create a complete application.

Story from the Trenches

I had always felt a bit inadequate working as a programmer because my degree was in electronic engineering and not computer science. Therefore, I jumped at the chance to work for two of the software industry's biggest players, which were collaborating on the development of a new operating system. I hoped that this experience might help me better understand how software should be produced.

The development team contained hundreds of people split into dozens of small groups at sites located across two continents However, what struck me more than the size of the team was the caliber of its staff, for everyone seemed very smart and clearly knew a lot about software development. Consequently, I listened to our group leader with particular care as she explained to us the importance of performing rigorous analysis and design before contemplating writing even a single line of code. We were assured that the coding stage would take no time at all once we got the design right. Therefore, our group set to work aiming to create the perfect design for the graphics printing module which was the component of the operating system we were charged with developing.

For the next four months, we worked on the design of this graphics printing module and in the process generated copious amounts of documentation, models, and diagrams which described every aspect of our design. We then spent weeks collectively walking through this design on paper trying to foresee every problem and coming up with increasingly complex solutions. Our design was next subjected to an in-depth review involving some of the most senior people on the project, but after a number of revisions, we finally got the go-ahead to start writing the code. Everything went well for the first few weeks and we made good progress, just as our group leader had predicted. The few minor glitches in the design that did appear were quickly papered over and we resolved to address them properly once we had delivered the first release.

After about a month of coding, we came to realize that all these minor problems were beginning to have a significant impact on the design. Take the simple matter of a poorly named function, for example. When we started coding we could have changed the name quite easily, but we didn't because this would have involved changing the design document and going through the whole sign-off process again. Therefore, after a month of coding, this inappropriately named function came to be invoked in hundreds of places throughout our code base, therefore making any future attempt to change its name so much harder. Poor names made our code more difficult to understand, which in turn caused bugs. However, badly named functions were the least of our worries, because the design was starting to unravel in more serious ways as well. There were unexpected data dependencies, holes in the functionality, and numerous other issues which necessitated tactical coding solutions, causing the design and the code to diverge.

We wanted to use our experience of coding this module over the past month to revisit the design. However, we had committed ourselves to producing a perfect design upfront, so the process denied us this opportunity. Our group struggled with the flawed design over the next month, and eventually we managed to produce a release of the graphics printing module which managed to pass system testing. However, nobody was particular proud of the achievement, because given all our effort to design the software correctly, we had still managed to produce something that looked like a big ball of mud. These sorts of problems were not isolated to our group, and it was soon apparent to me that even some of the best people in the industry were having trouble following this upfront design process. Clearly there had to be a better way to design software.

█ 13
Introduction to TDD

I N THIS CHAPTER, we introduce the concept of writing tests much earlier in the development process so that they drive not just the validation
of our software, but also its specification, analysis, and design; hence the
term *test-driven development (TDD)*. We cover the basic principles of TDD to
describe what it involves and walk you through a few cycles of the Test-
First Programming practice to illustrate just how easily you can adopt this
approach to software development.

The Nature of Test-Driven Development

Programmer tests are similar to unit tests in traditional software testing in
that they focus on the structure of the software and are written from the
programmer's point of view. However, these tests have a greater purpose
than simply checking our code; they also form a scaffold that supports its
development. Therefore, writing programmer tests forms an integral part
of the software development process. It is not just a task that might be performed at the end if there is enough time.

Settling into the Rhythm of Test-First Programming

Programmer tests act like scaffolding because they are written before the
code is implemented. This avoids the programmer's judgment about what

to test being clouded by the code he has written. However, more important, it discourages him from writing code that isn't necessary to satisfy the test. Because programmer tests play a role in analysis and design as well as during coding and testing, you cannot separate these activities into distinct phases of the project, as you might when following the sort of Waterfall process or Rational Unified Process (RUP) we discussed in Chapter 3. Instead, for the duration of the programming episode, you repeat the simple rhythm of

1. Writing a failing test

2. Writing just enough code to make all the tests pass

3. Refactoring to improve the code by removing duplication, making it simpler and easier to maintain

---

■ NOTE

In this book, we use the term *test-first programming (TFP)*[1] to describe the practice of cycling through the steps of testing, coding, and refactoring. We use the term *test-driven development (TDD)*[2] to describe the bigger picture of developing software using this practice.

Test-First Programming Practice

Test-first programming (TFP) requires you to let your coding activities be driven by two simple rules:

- Never develop new code unless you have a failing automated test.

- Eliminate duplication.

The first of these rules requires you to write code only after writing one or more tests to reveal the defect it must fix. The second rule drives you to

---

1. [XPE2] Beck, Kent, with Cynthia Andres. *Extreme Programming Explained, Second Edition* (Addison-Wesley, 2005), p. 50.
2. [TDDE] Beck, Kent. *Test-Driven Development by Example* (Addison-Wesley, 2003), p. 203.

improve your code once it passes its tests because, as Kent Beck[3] says, duplication is a symptom of the dependencies which seriously inhibit our ability to change our code in a simple and easy way.

TFP makes teams more effective because they develop new code only when there is a tangible requirement—in other words, a failing test. This test begins as a way to specify the work and ends up checking that it has been completed correctly. Working in this way encourages you to do only what you need to do to meet the specification, and to stop once you've met the objective. Therefore, your code, being free of unnecessary embellishment, is quicker to write and quicker to test. Furthermore, the passing of tests unambiguously marks progress, so there is less risk of people wasting time on work that has no purpose. TFP also removes the need for teams to produce a perfect upfront design because it allows them to work from the bottom up to evolve a design which is both simple and easy to adapt if their requirements change or they discover a better way to do things.

In order to implement TFP, developers need to have access to tools that allow them to write and execute tests quickly enough so that the natural flow of their everyday work is not disturbed. In this respect, NUnit[4] has proven to be so successful that Microsoft seems to have based the unit testing tools for Visual Studio Team System (VSTS) around the same concept. However, regardless of which tool you use, the basic pattern of the Test-First Programming practice is the same. First, you create a test that initially fails when run, as indicated by a red icon in the VSTS Test Results window or by a red bar in NUnit. Second, you write just enough code to get all your tests to pass so that the icon or bar goes green. Finally, you refactor your code to improve its structure without changing its purpose, thereby keeping the icon (or bar) green. This cycle repeats as you write another test to specify something else that needs implementing. Piece by piece, you add functionality to your program, always keeping it in a working state and refactoring when necessary to let the design converge into the desired solution.

---

3. [TDDE] Beck, Kent. *Test-Driven Development by Example* (Addison-Wesley, 2003), p. 8.
4. NUnit is supported at www.nunit.org.

> **■ NOTE**
>
> Agile teams should create all their production code using the Test-First Programming practice. Otherwise, the code will become difficult to adapt as their requirements change.

Top Down versus Bottom Up

The traditional top-down approach to software development requires that you decompose a problem into a number of parts so that you can design solutions for each part before you begin building and testing them. It's a case of "design everything, code everything, and then test everything." In contrast, the bottom-up approach, which TFP takes, builds up the system by specifying one part, getting it to work, and then addressing the next part, letting the refactoring step converge the design into a solution. It's a case of "test a bit, code a bit, and then design a bit."

The bottom-up approach of TFP probably goes against everything you've ever been taught about good software development practice. However, the advantage of this approach is that it's much more responsive to change than the top-down approach is. When you're building things using TFP, a change to the requirements doesn't matter so much because you can evolve your working software through a series of small changes to make your design converge to a different solution. This means you don't have to throw away your work and return to the drawing board, as you do when requirements change in a top-down approach.

Unfortunately, the flexibility of a bottom-up approach comes at a cost, because after each small change, you need to check that the software still works. However, as you will see in this section of the book, with efficient tools and the right process, all this extra testing is no longer the impediment it once was to teams working in a bottom-up fashion.

Simple Test-First Programming Exercises

The following exercise aims to convince you that there is nothing fundamentally difficult about the TFP approach. It contains the sort of code that you might write when you're learning to program in C# and doesn't require the use of any special tools. However, it is obviously much easier to practice TFP with the VSTS tools.

Define the List of Tests

In Exercise 13-1, we will help you implement the part of a story that is concerned with calculating the number of bytes needed to store an image (e.g., an X-ray) given its length and width. The exercise starts with you having defined the follow list of tests:

- Size is 6 units when length is 3 units and width is 2 units; a typical case.
- Size is 0 units when length is 0 units and width is 0 units; a boundary case.

> ## ■ NOTE
>
> You would normally expect to produce a list of perhaps a dozen or so tests at the start of a proper programming episode; see Table 14-1 in Chapter 14. However, the two tests in the preceding list are sufficient for our purposes in this short exercise.

Set Up a Basic Test Harness

A team's testing efforts need the support of some form of test harness which provides a convenient way to run the test adapters (also known as *test drivers*) and other tools needed for the reliable and consistent execution of their various test suites. The implementation of a test harness can range from the sort of simple program shown in Listing 13-1 to a completely integrated system such as that provided by Visual Studio Team System; see Chapter 14.

> **■ NOTE**
>
> In this book, we use Robert Binder's[5] description of a "test case" as a set of inputs, execution conditions, and expected results developed for a particular objective. We also use the term *test suite* to describe a collection of one or more such test cases which are run together.

EXERCISE 13-1: Implementing a Simple Test Harness

1. Log on as Luke and start Visual Studio. You will not need to connect with Team Foundation Server (TFS) for the purposes of this exercise.

2. Create a new Visual Studio Project for a Console application called TestHarness (see Listing 13-1). Make a directory for the Solution, but locate its files on your local hard drive outside of Luke's workspace (File | New | Project, Visual C#, Windows Console Application).

LISTING 13-1: Test Harness

```
namespace TestHarness
{
    class Program             //Test Harness
    {
        static void Main (string[] args)
        {
            TestDrivers.ImageTest test = new TestDrivers.ImageTest();
            test.Run();
        }
    }
}
```

---

5. [TOOS] Binder, Robert. *Testing Object-Oriented Systems* (Addison-Wesley, 2000).

3. Create the new namespace, `TestDrivers`, at the bottom of the Program.cs file. Add into this namespace the test adapter class, `ImageTest`, together with a method called `Run`:

```
namespace TestDrivers
{
    class ImageTest      //Test Adapter
    {
        public void Run() {}
    }
}
```

4. Add the statements shown in Listing 13-1 to create a `Main` static method in the `Program` class so that your test adapter will be invoked when the program is executed.

5. Finally, build and run the application to confirm that all is well by selecting Debug | Start Debugging.

Your test adapter invokes the implementation under test (IUT) and typically has responsibility for providing test input, controlling test execution, and reporting test results. In this case, we have put everything in one file that contains two classes, such that the `ImageTest` class serves as a test adapter for the `Image` class, which is the IUT we will develop in Exercise 13-2.

TFP Cycle for the First Test

Let's now complete a simple TFP cycle by writing a test, writing enough code to make the test pass, and completing a small refactoring. You should note that the tests are implemented using `Assert` statements which, as you are probably aware, throw an exception when their first parameter is passed a false value, but do nothing when this parameter is set as true.

■ TIP

When using an `Assert` statement in your own code, remember to use an identifying text label as its message parameter. Otherwise, it can be hard to determine the one that fired, particularly if you have multiple `Assert` statements in the same block of code.

1. Add the `Assert` statement to the `Run()` method of `ImageTest`, your test adapter class:

```
public void Run()
{                       //Test Case
    System.Diagnostics.Debug.Assert(pic.Area(3,2) == 6);
}
```

2. So that you can build the program, add the `Image` class to the `Ospacs` namespace at the bottom of Program.cs and implement the `Area` method so that it returns 0. You will also need to add an `Image` instance variable to `ImageTest` and initialize it in the constructor (see Listing 13-2).

LISTING 13-2: Test Adapter and Implementation under Test

```
namespace TestDrivers
{
    class ImageTest            //Test Adapter
    {
        private Ospacs.Image pic;
        public ImageTest() { pic = new Ospacs.Image();        }
         public void Run()
        {                       //Test Case
            System.Diagnostics.Debug.Assert(pic.Area(3,2) == 6);
        }
    }
}

namespace Ospacs
{
    class Image                //Implementation Under Test
    {
        public int Area (int length, int width) { return 0; }
    }
}
```

3. Build and run the application to confirm that the program asserts because `Image.Area()` doesn't return the value 6 when the test is executed (Debug | Start Debugging).

The failing test proves that the `Assert` statement is executed, and when we fix the code, it gives us confidence that our changes have corrected the problem. It is important to get into the habit of creating a failing test because you will not always be working with such simple code.

EXERCISE 13-3: Fixing the Code to Pass the Test

1. Do the simplest thing to make the test pass by hardcoding 6 as the return value of `Image.Area()`:

```
class Image        //Implementation under test
{
    public int Area (int length, int width) { return 6; }
}
```

2. Build and run the application to confirm that the program no longer asserts because `Image.Area()` now returns the value 6 when the test is executed (Debug | Start Debugging).

After fixing the code to pass a test, you should consider the option of refactoring. However, it is not always necessary to alter the code. Therefore, when there is nothing obvious to do, as in this case, you should proceed to the next test.

TFP Cycle for the Second Test

The second test checks the boundary condition to ensure that the area is 0 when the length and width are 0.

EXERCISE 13-4: Writing Another Failing Test

1. Add an additional `Assert` statement to the `Run` method of the `Test` adapter class, `ImageTest`:

```
public void Run()
{
    System.Diagnostics.Debug.Assert(pic.Area(3,2) == 6);
    System.Diagnostics.Debug.Assert(pic.Area(0,0) == 0);
}
```

2. Build and run the application to confirm that the program asserts
    because `Image.Area()` doesn't return the value 0 when the second
    test is executed (Debug | Start Debugging).

EXERCISE 13-5: Fixing the Code Again

1. Make `Image.Area()` return the product of its parameters so that it
    will pass both tests:

    ```
    class Image           //Implementation under test
    {
       public int Area (int length, int width)
       {
          return length * width;
       }
    }
    ```

2. Build and run the application to confirm that the program no longer
    asserts because `Image.Area()` now returns the correct value for both
    tests (Debug | Start Debugging).

EXERCISE 13-6: Refactoring (To Make the Code Easier to Maintain)

1. Move the parameters for length and width to the `Image` constructor
    so that the data required for the Area calculation can be stored in the
    object responsible for performing this action instead of being held in
    the various objects invoking the method; see the boldface code in
    Listing 13-3.

    LISTING 13-3 : Refactored Test Harness, Test Adapter, and IUT Source Code

    ```
    namespace TestHarness
    {
       class Program           //Test Harness
       {
    ```

```csharp
        static void Main (string[] args)
        {
            TestDrivers.ImageTest test = new TestDrivers.ImageTest();
            test.Run();
        }
    }
}


namespace TestDrivers
{
    class ImageTest          //Test adapter
    {
        private Ospacs.Image picSix;
        private Ospacs.Image picZero;

        public ImageTest()
        {
            picSix = new Ospacs.Image(3,2);
            picZero = new Ospacs.Image(0,0);
        }
        public void Run()
        {
            System.Diagnostics.Debug.Assert(picSix.Area() == 6,"Test 6");
            System.Diagnostics.Debug.Assert(picZero.Area() == 0, "Test 0");
        }
    }
}
namespace Ospacs             //Production Code
{
    class Image             //Implementation under test
    {
        private int length;
        private int width;

        public Image (int len, int wd)
        {
            length = len;
            width = wd;
        }
        public int Area (int length, int width)
        {
            return length * width;
        }
    }
}
```

2. Build and run the program to confirm that it still passes its tests (Debug | Start Debugging).

3. This exercise is complete, so log off.

Avoid changing both the IUT and the Test Case code at the same time by refactoring in small steps. For example, add the new `Area` method (without any parameters) and check that the original tests pass. Then, change the tests to use the new method signature and remove the old `Area` method (with parameters). In this case, the refactoring is quite simple; you will be thankful for this advice when you start doing more extensive refactoring.

Review of the Exercises

The exercises in this chapter demonstrate that even a complete novice can use TFP to produce useful software. However, this technique didn't dumb down the job of developing software; on the contrary, it encouraged you to work like an expert by

- Forcing you to consider the purpose of the code before you wrote it; your tests specified software and later validated it.

- Promoting simple design by eliminating unnecessary code and complexity; you didn't write any software without a supporting test, and you refactored your work to make it easier to maintain (see Exercise 13-6).

- Producing software that you can easily and safely adapt as the system grows; your tests allowed you to improve the structure of the code without changing its purpose.

TFP didn't require you to create a perfect design upfront. Instead, you allowed the code to slowly evolve and correct itself. For example, the mistake we encouraged you to make by failing to recognize that length and width should be stored in the `Image` object was soon identified and corrected. In fact, this refactoring was the only part of TFP that needed any real thought, because even through using this basic test harness and driver, you required very little effort to write the tests, develop the code, and then perform the unit testing.

> **NOTE**
>
> When developing code for use in a production environment, you must do TFP and pair programming at the same time, because the discussions you have with your partner about tests and refactoring opportunities are what actually lead to better software.

Getting Started with Test-First Programming

TFP is something you must learn through practice, which is why this section of the book has so many exercises for you to follow. However, to help you understand their relevance, we conclude this chapter by explaining the applicability of TFP to your team as well as the basic concepts of creating a list of tests, finding more tests, and refactoring.

Applying TFP on Your Team

You can use TFP to develop almost any sort of procedural code for which you can find (or make) the necessary test tools, harnesses, and drivers. Almost anyone can master the basic technique of TFP within a few hours. However, you can practice it for a lifetime and still discover something new about TDD each time you use it. This means that the whole team can contribute to the development of production code, not just a few experts, thereby enabling the Whole Team practice.

> **NOTE**
>
> TFP does not lend itself to the sort of declarative programming that involves dropping components on a form and then setting their properties and events (for example, the creation of Windows Forms). However, we suggest how you can handle this type of code in Chapter 17.

Creating a List of Tests

The starting point for TFP is a list of tests which you and your programming partner produce during the first 15 to 30 minutes of a programming episode. You make this list by analyzing the task in hand using traditional top-down problem decomposition, brainstorming, or other techniques. During this process, you might meet with the customer to make sure you understand the requirement, or perhaps you may do a bit of Agile modeling to help you explore the design; see Section 6. After you have created a list of tests, you should start with the one that seems the easiest to address, and when you have completed it, you should attempt the next most obvious test on your list. Continue to apply TFP in this manner until all your tests pass and no further tests can be identified; at this point, the task is complete.

> **■ NOTE**
>
> Identification of the tasks needed to implement a customer story starts during iteration planning (see Section 8), but often continues as the iteration progresses.

The secret of TFP is to keep moving forward by writing simple tests and equally simple code. When you become stuck and don't know what to do next, just choose the next simplest thing. You should expect to identify additional tests as you and your programming partner work through the test list, using your judgment to decide whether you should write such tests immediately or add them to your list for later implementation. Experience will help you write more discriminating and meaningful tests. It will also help you write simpler code and make better refactorings. However, you should not use lack of experience as an excuse for not doing TFP, because it's hard to make a truly catastrophic mistake when you apply TFP properly. It should always be possible to refactor your work at a later date or just undo your changes using version control.

Finding Additional Tests

The Image class shown in Listing 13-3 is far from complete, because clearly we need to write more tests, and this will drive additional extensions of the class. For example, the introduction of tests containing negative values for length or width would require additional code for error handling. Without much thought, you could probably identify half a dozen additional tests, but would that be enough? To give you some idea of the number of tests that you could develop, consider the classic problem posed by Glen Myers:[6]

> Three integer values representing the lengths of each side of a triangle are read from an input dialog so that your program can determine whether you have specified a scalene, isosceles or equilateral triangle. What test cases do you need to write in order to prove adequately that the program works correctly?

Myers' challenge concerns a program that is not much more complex than the one we have been developing in this chapter, yet he manages to identify 24 test cases. Robert Binder[7] later extends this list to 64 test cases by addressing the object-oriented aspects of the program Myers did not consider when he originally stated the problem in 1979. Therefore, it is not so much a case of considering how many tests to write, but of knowing what tests to write and when to stop. In this respect, people who have a strong background in testing have a distinct advantage because their knowledge and skill will help them quickly find meaningful tests.

If you are not fortunate enough to have an expert tester on your team, this book's bibliography contains references to a number of books that may help you write better tests; *The Art of Software Testing* [AST] is particularly recommended. However, the key thing to remember is that there is no point in writing tests that don't tell you anything, so you need to concentrate on writing tests that yield important information. In the case of TFP, this means writing a test that gives you information about some flaw or omission in your code; in other words, a failing test. For this reason, stop writing tests for a task when you can no longer start a TFP cycle with a failing test, because this typically means that your existing tests cover all the necessary code paths and it's time for you to move on.

---

6. [AST] Myers, Glenford J., et al. *The Art of Software Testing* (John Wiley & Sons, 2004 edition).
7. [TOOS] Binder, Robert. *Testing Object-Oriented Systems* (Addison-Wesley, 2000).

> **■ TIP**
>
> Make sure any testing experts on your team become as much involved in TFP as people who come from a programming background. Use pair programming to spread this expertise throughout the team.

Refactoring

Martin Fowler[8] describes refactoring as improving the structure and design of the code without changing its functionality. You should think of refactoring as the ongoing maintenance of your software.

The motto you must apply to refactoring is "Clean as you go!" This means that if you see a mess, you should clean it up. It does not mean that you should accumulate messes and then at some point come back and fix all of them. It also does not mean that you should refashion as you go. There is a definite distinction between the two; don't be tempted to add features as you refactor the code. Think of writing software as an experiment. If you change too many things at once, you will not know which one caused the problem. Therefore, if you hold the functionality constant, make small changes to the code, and run the tests, you will know immediately whether the change you made has altered your expectations.

The decisions you make during refactoring are usually a matter of personal choice combined with a certain amount of judgment and experience. In Exercise 13-6, for example, the decision to change the `Image` constructor was driven by the realization that length and width needed to be stored in the `Image` object and not passed as parameters to its `Area` method. We chose to address the problem immediately and to refactor, but there is also some justification for deferring this work until the need to refactor becomes more compelling. Ultimately, successful refactoring is not about the rights and wrongs of such decisions; it is about managing to evolve the software safely without compromising your ability to respond to future changes.

The best way to improve your refactoring skills is to spend a lot of time pairing with good programmers who understand the nature of TDD.

---

8. [RIDEC] Fowler, Martin, et al. *Refactoring* (Addison-Wesley, 1999).

However, you will gain more from such opportunities if you already appreciate the main concepts of object-oriented programming as presented in books such as *The Object Primer* [OP3] and have acquired some insight into the way refactoring decisions are made; see Chapters 14, 15, and 16 in this book, as well as books such as *Test-Driven Development in Microsoft .NET* [TTDM] and *Extreme Programming Adventures in C#* [XPAC].

> **■ TIP**
>
> You will find it helpful to learn some of the standard refactoring patterns found in books such as Martin Fowler's *Refactoring: Improving the Design of Existing Code* [RIDEC], William Wake's *Refactoring Workbook* [RWB], and Joshua Kerievsky's *Refactoring to Patterns* [R2P].

CONCLUSION

In this chapter, we introduced you to test-driven development and explained in some detail the practice of Test-First Programming. You saw how this simple yet powerful technique allows the whole team to engage in the development of production code. However, the tools we used in this chapter are very primitive and are not really suitable for use in a real-life project. Therefore, in the next few chapters, we will take you through a sequence of additional exercises which show you how to develop test adapters and production code as components in their own assemblies so that you can use the test harness and tools provided by Visual Studio Team System. In this way, you will learn how you might use this powerful technique to develop all of your project's production-quality procedural code.

> **■ TIP**
>
> Make the running of your tests into a stress reliever by ensuring that you can execute them in so little time that you can repeat this action whenever you fear your changes have somehow broken the program; transform testing from a burden into a good thing.

■14
Developing Your First Tests

THIS CHAPTER STARTS by showing you how to set up the Visual Studio Projects you need for test-first programming (TFP) and then describes "Image Favorites," which is the story you will implement in this section of the book. After creating an initial list of tests for this story, we spend the rest of the chapter implementing the first two of these tests with the goal of showing you how easy it is to implement the Test-First Programming practice using the tools provided by Visual Studio Team System (VSTS).

Creating Visual Studio Projects for TFP

The primitive test environment you created in the preceding chapter was useful for demonstrating the basic concepts of TFP, but it really is not suitable for doing any proper work. Therefore, let's examine the way VSTS supports unit (structural) testing, and then we'll create a set of Visual Studio Projects to support the exercises in the remainder of Section 5, which show how you would practice TFP in a real project.

How VSTS Supports Unit Testing

When you perform unit testing with VSTS, you still have the same essential parts that were present in the small console application we developed in Chapter 13. However, instead of just three classes contained in a single file, they are separated into different components, as shown in Figure 14-1. Consequently, when testing with VSTS the following are still present:

- **Test harness (runner)**—A convenient way to run test adapters and other tools needed for the reliable and consistent execution of a collection of test cases
- **Test adapter (driver, fixture)**—Controls test method execution, sends the results back to the test harness, and performs test initialization as well as cleanup
- **Test method (case)**—Sets up the implementation under test (IUT) objects, invokes their methods, and tests the return values to provide the results of the test case
- **IUT**—The software being developed for eventual deployment in the production environment

This arrangement requires that the various classes and methods that form your test adapters and test cases be decorated with certain attributes so that the VSTS test harness can find them; see Figure 14-1. It also means that your test code needs to be contained in an assembly which has been created from a Visual Studio Test Project, thereby forcing the separation of your test and production code.

Locating the test and production code in separate assemblies inside the test environment conflicts with the object-oriented concept of information hiding, because it means the production code in your IUT assembly must be accessible to the test adapter classes located in your test driver assembly. However, we are happy to recommend this approach because it does have the advantage of allowing you to deploy your IUT assembly directly into the production environment without you having to rebuild it in order to remove any test code.

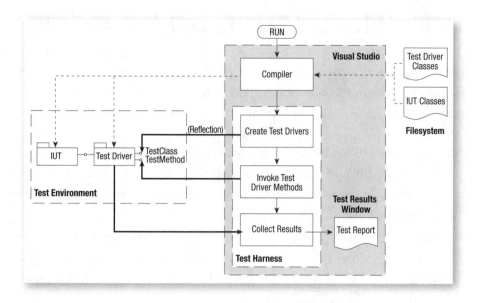

FIGURE 14-1: Visual Studio test harness and unit test process

> **■ NOTE**
>
> Booch's classic book,[1] *Object-Oriented Analysis and Design,* explains information hiding. You can find out more about making production code accessible to test adapter classes by reading about Friend Assemblies in C# *Programmers Reference.*[2]

Setting Up Visual Studio Projects for Unit Testing

In order to run unit tests in the VSTS environment, you must create a Visual Studio Test Project and then add it to the Solution containing the Visual Studio Projects you want to test.

---

1. Booch, Grady. *Object-Oriented Analysis and Design, Second Edition* (Benjamin Cummings, 1994).
2. Microsoft. *C# Programmers Reference* (http://msdn.microsoft.com).

EXERCISE 14-1: Creating Visual Studio Projects for Tests and Production Code

This exercise creates a Visual Studio C# Test Project for your test environment called LocalFavoritesTest and a C# Class Library Project for your production environment called LocalFavorites. It then adds them to the osImageManager Solution you created in Exercise 8-2 in Chapter 8.

1. Log on as Luke (OSPACS Contributor) to the DeveloperPC, start Visual Studio, and then connect to the OSPACS Team Project, as described in Exercise 5-7 in Chapter 5; see Appendix A for details about this PC and Luke's security groups.

2. Make sure Luke's workspace is up-to-date by opening the Source Control Explorer (View | Other Windows), selecting the $/OSPACS folder, and then choosing Get Latest Version from its context menu (Right-click | Get Latest Version).

3. Load the osImageManager Visual Studio Solution by opening the osImageManager.sln file in Luke's workspace (File | Open | Project/Solution).

4. Create a new Visual Studio C# Test Project for your test adapters, called LocalFavoritesTest, by opening the New Project dialog box (File | New | Project) so that you can do the following:

   a. Select Test Project from the Visual C# project types.

   b. Add this project to the osImageHandler Solution.

   c. Select a suitable directory in Luke's workspace for its source files (e.g., osImageHandler\src).

5. Delete any unit tests and manual tests created by default in your new Test Project by opening the LocalFavoritesTest folder in the Solution Explorer, selecting the files, and then choosing Delete from its context menu (Right-click | Delete).

6. Create a new Visual Studio C# Class Library Project for your production code, called LocalFavorites, by following the instructions given in step 4, but this time select a Class Library Project. You

should also delete any default classes created for this Class Library Project in the same way you deleted the default test files in step 5.

7. Build the osImageHandler Visual Studio Solution to check that you've correctly created these projects so that they can be rebuilt without errors (Build | Build Solution).

8. Put your work in a version control shelve so that you can always return to this point in the future; click the Shelve button in the Pending Changes window (View | Other Windows); see Exercise 9-6 in Chapter 9.

> **■ NOTE**
>
> It is not strictly necessary to integrate the LocalFavorites and LocalFavoritesTest projects with the OSPACS Team Project, but not doing so means you lose the benefits of working with VSTS (e.g., version control, work item tracking, etc.).

The Story behind the Tests

TFP is typically initiated by someone's need to implement a story (see Chapter 3), so to put the following exercises into context let's quickly review the "Image Favorites" story and divide it into the two programming episodes that will occupy us for the rest of Section 5.

> **■ NOTE**
>
> The complete implementation of the "Image Favorites" story is provided as an independent Visual Studio Solution on the book's Web site.

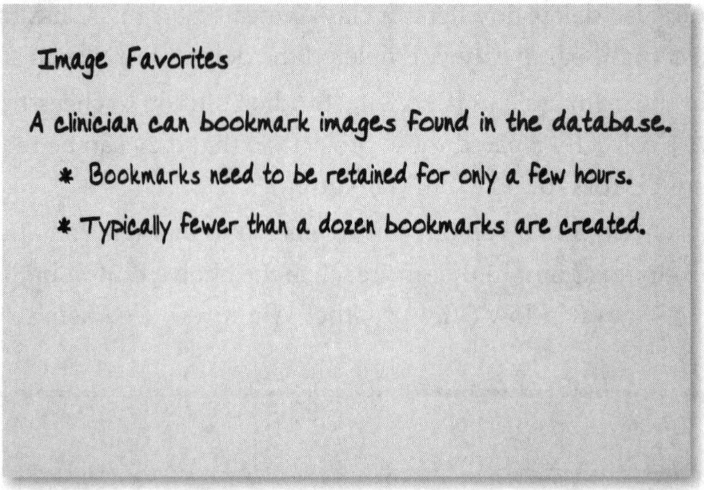

Image Favorites

A clinician can bookmark images found in the database.
* Bookmarks need to be retained for only a few hours.
* Typically fewer than a dozen bookmarks are created.

FIGURE 14-2: "Image Favorites" customer story

About the "Image Favorites" Story

Clinicians prepare for a conference about a patient by reviewing all the available images and selecting the ones that are particularly significant. This process is termed *bookmarking,* and OSPACS will support this activity by implementing the "Image Favorites" story shown in Figure 14-2. The customer isn't interested in having any sort of facility for organizing Favorite items, nor is it a requirement that individual clinicians have these items restored when they log on to different machines. Therefore, an apt metaphor for the "Image Favorites" story is the "favorites" facility in Internet Explorer. However, instead of being used to bookmark particular Web page addresses, it will be used for bookmarking references in the OSPACS database to specific patient images, such as X-rays, ultrasounds, and so forth.

Dividing the Story into Tasks

The story we need to deliver is mostly about implementing a collection of Favorite items, each of which is just a text label and a reference to an image in the database. Accordingly, it seems reasonable to split the work into two tasks which can be completed in separate programming episodes:

- Implement the Favorite items functionality which is similar to that required for almost any type of collection, namely Create, Retrieve, Update, and Delete (CRUD).

- Invoke this functionality from some user interface code generated by the Visual Studio visual editor.

We do not recommend using TFP to generate code that is produced declaratively using the visual editor, wizards, and other Visual Studio tools. Therefore, the exercises in this chapter (as well as those in Chapters 15 and 16) will focus on this first task. However, in Chapter 17, we will address the second task by suggesting how you might integrate your work with a Windows Forms application.

> **NOTE**
>
> The implementation of the "Image Favorites" story represents the sort of task that a pair of developers on your team might be able to complete within two programming episodes, each lasting about a couple of hours.

Create a Test List

The secret of getting ahead is getting started. The secret of getting started is breaking your complex overwhelming tasks into small manageable tasks, and then starting on the first one. —Mark Twain

Finding Your Initial Tests

Let's now create an initial test list for our programming task by thinking about what we are trying to accomplish and how certain tests might show progress toward this goal. We will assume all tests execute independently of each other, so data and state don't persist between tests; the collection of Favorites is therefore always created fresh at the start of each test (see Table 14-1).

TABLE 14-1: Initial Test List for Favorites

1. Count == 0
2. Add(Favorite), Count == 1
3. Add(Favorite), Remove(Favorite), Count == 0
4. Add(Favorite1), Add(Favorite2), Count == 2
5. Add(Favorite1), Add(Favorite2), Remove(Favorite1), Count == 1
6. Add(Favorite1), Add(Favorite2), call Clear(), Count == 0
7. Add(Favorite), Remove(Favorite) should return true
8. Add(Favorite), Contains(Favorite) should return true
9. Remove(Favorite) that is not in the collection, should return false
10. Contains(Favorite) that is not in the collection, should return false
11. Add 3 x Favorite items call GetEnumerator and verify that the 3 Favorites are enumerated
12. Add(Favorite1), Add(Favorite2), Find(Favorite1.Label) should return Favorite1
13. Add a Favorite with a null label, expect ArgumentNullException
14. Add a Favorite with a null URI, expect ArgumentNullException
15. Add a Favorite, add another with the same label, expect ArgumentException

Looking at the test list we seem to have hit most of the areas associated with the task that we expect to complete during our first programming episode. A number of tests focus on making sure the count is correct when we add and remove favorites. Also, a number of tests focus on the contents of the collection and whether we can retrieve the favorites from the collection. There are bound to be other tests, but for now the list is sufficient. If we discover the need to add or subtract tests during development, we can easily change the list.

Our idea was to be able to complete this list of tests and the associated code implementation in a single programming episode which lasts about a couple of hours. Now that you and your partner have spent some time thinking about the problem and its potential solutions, make sure you don't need to split the task again in order to achieve this objective. You don't want to make tasks too big, because you want to get and give feedback as quickly as possible. If your task is estimated to take a week, you might not know until the end of the iteration that it's not going to be completed on time, but if the task is meant to take half a day, you should discover much sooner that it is running behind schedule and therefore be able to take appropriate action to mitigate the impact of the problem.

> **⬛ TIP**
>
> You certainly want to be able to finish a programming episode without you and your partner having to stay in the office until midnight; see our discussion of the Energized Work practice in Chapter 15. Therefore, make sure your targets are realistic.

Record the Test List

There are a number of ways to record your test list. You could simply write it down on an index card or other suitable piece of paper kept by your desk. This allows you to cross off each test as you complete it, which provides a convenient visual reminder of the work you've done and the work that still remains. Clearly this is very simple and helps keep you focused on the task at hand. However, it has the drawback of making the list difficult to change. A better solution is to create your test list as code, which we will do in Exercise 14-2.

EXERCISE 14-2: Implementing a Test List

This exercise continues from Exercise 14-1 by creating a test method for each test case in Listing 14-1 within a new `FavoritesTests` class. These test methods simply act as placeholders for the tests you will implement in future exercises.

1. Create a new C# test class called `FavoritesTests` in the LocalFavoritesTests project by selecting the project in the Solution Explorer window and choosing Add New Test | Unit Test from its Project context menu.

2. Edit the name of the `TestMethod1` method in the class you just created to make it more meaningful, and add an `Assert.Inconclusive` statement, as shown in Listing 14-1.

LISTING 14-1: Creating a Test List

```
using System;
using Microsoft.VisualStudio.QualityTools.UnitTesting.Framework;
[TestClass]
public class FavoritesTests
{
    [TestMethod]
    public void EmptyFavoritesCountShouldBeZero()
    {
        Assert.Inconclusive("Test List: Count == 0, Not Implemeneted");
    }
}
```

3. Copy the entire method together with its `TestMethod` attribute and then paste additional methods into the `FavoritesTests` class, one for each test on your list. Change their names and the comment in the `Assert` statement to something appropriate.

4. Build the project on your own PC to check that you've done the job properly (Build | FavoritesTests).

5. Add your work to a version control shelve so that you can always return to this point in the future by clicking the Shelve button in the Pending Changes window (View | Other Windows); see Exercise 9-5 in Chapter 9.

> **■ TIP**
>
> We do not recommend that you create a work item for each test on your test list because it should take less than five minutes to complete a test run and there seems little value in tracking the team's work at this sort of granularity.

Organization of Your Test List Code

There are a few things you should notice about the code in Listing 14-1. First, a `using` directive appears at the top of the file to declare the namespace for the Visual Studio unit testing framework. Second, the `[TestClass]` attribute marks the class as containing test methods, therefore informing your VSTS test tool (the test harness) that this class must be treated as a test adapter. Third, each individual test method (test case) must be marked with the `[TestMethod]` attribute to ensure that the VSTS test tool invokes it during a test run. Finally, the name of the test method doesn't have to follow any particular syntax, so it is made as descriptive as possible in an attempt to be self-documenting.

You should note that naming a method appropriately and descriptively pays dividends later when you encounter a test failure because its name immediately gives you a clue as to what has gone wrong. For example, the method name in Listing 14-1 makes it clear that you are testing that the count is 0 when the `Favorites` object is empty, as it is when first created. The names of your other test methods should be similarly informative, as should the comments in their `Assert` statements.

Shelving Your Test List Code

All the tests you have created are listed in the Test View window (Test | Windows), and if you selected and ran them, they would simply be reported in the Test Results window as being "inconclusive." This typically signifies that the test has not yet been implemented. Therefore, as you would not normally want to share any file with other members of your team until all the associated unit tests have passed, it makes sense to keep everything safe in your own personal shelve in the repository (see Exercise 9-6 in Chapter 9) rather than checking your changes into the main branch of your team's code base.

Implementing the Tests

Now that we've created a test list, we'll start implementing it. However, we are not going to describe the implementation of all the tests because that could get boring; programming is not a spectator sport. We're just going to implement ones that describe interesting aspects of the solution or ones that assist in the understanding of the test tool.

Start with the Easiest Test

Let's start with the simplest test, EmptyFavoritesCountShouldBeZero, which also happens to be the first on our list. What could be simpler than checking that a newly created Favorites object has no initial collection of Favorite items? You should write the test without regard to what is already implemented, or in this case, what is not implemented, because the compiler is very happy to tell you whether what you are asking for has been defined.

EXERCISE 14-3: Implementing the First Test

In this exercise, you will replace the placeholder statement in your first test with some functional code, and in so doing drive the creation of the production code Favorites class and the implementation of its Count property.

1. Replace the Assert statement in the EmptyFavoritesCountShouldBeZero method and type the following test. This creates an instance of the Favorites class and asserts that the value returned from its Count property is 0. It also states that we are using the LocalFavorites namespace:

```
using LocalFavorites;
[TestMethod]
public void EmptyFavoritesCountShouldBeZero()
{
    Favorites favorites = new Favorites();
    Assert.AreEqual(0, favorites.Count);
}
```

2. Build the project (Build | FavoritesTests). This will produce an error because we haven't created the `Favorites` class, so it cannot be found.

3. Add a new C# class called `Favorites` by selecting the LocalFavorites project in the Solution Explorer window and then selecting Project | Add Class | Class. Edit the Favorites.cs file and type "public" immediately before the word *class*.

4. Add a reference for the `LocalFavorites` assembly to your LocalFavoritesTests project by following these steps:

   a. Open the Add Reference dialog box by selecting the LocalFavoritesTest project in the Solution Explorer window and choosing Add Reference from its context menu (Right-click | Add Reference).

   b. Select LocalFavorites from the Project page of the Add Reference dialog box and then click OK to close the dialog box and add the reference.

5. Rebuild the solution (Build | Build Solution). You will still see an error because the `Favorites` class doesn't have a definition for `Count`, so implement it in the simplest way possible, as shown here:

```
Namespace LocalFavorites
{
    public class Favorites
    {
        public int Count { get {return 0;}}
    }
}
```

6. Again, rebuild the solution (Build | Build Solution) so that finally you get a clean build and can run the test.

7. Run the test by selecting EmptyFavoritesCountShouldBeZero in the Test View window (Test | Windows) and then clicking the Run Section button (top left). Observe the results in the Test Results window (Test | Windows); you should see results similar to Figure 14-3.

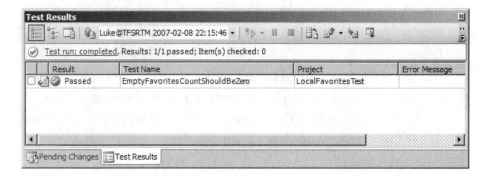

Figure 14-3: Test Results window

This first test is clearly as simple as we can make it. There is no need to worry about how naïve it may seem. We have many more tests to implement and the additional tests will add the information we need to come up with a better implementation. We could speculate on an implementation, but we encourage you not to do that. Let the additional tests and the code itself tell you what the implementation should look like.

Fix a Failing Test and Refactor

Let's now address the next four simplest tests on our list. They add and remove various `Favorite` items from the `Favorites` object to verify that the `Count` property always returns the correct value. In the process, we'll create a new class that doesn't have any tests and check out a new feature in Visual Studio 2005 that allows you to automatically generate methods that are declared, but not implemented.

> ### ■ NOTE
>
> OSPACS defines the URI format of db://xxxxxxx for identifying an image in its database, where x is a digit between zero and nine and the seven-digit number is formed by combining the patient identifier with the image sequence number.

This final exercise in the chapter implements an additional test that just adds something to a Favorites object and then confirms that its Count is one rather than zero. In order to provide this *something* we have to create a new class called Favorite, which contains the label and URI of a particular image.

1. Implement the AddFavoriteCountIsOne test in FavoritesTests.cs by replacing the test's Assert statement with the following code:

```
[TestMethod]
public void EmptyFavoritesCountIsOne()
{
    Favorites favorites = new Favorites();
    favorites.Add(new Favorite("Label",
                        new Uri("db://0000101")));
    Assert.AreEqual(1, favorites.Count);
}
```

2. Add a new C# class called Favorite to the LocalFavorites project (see step 3 of Exercise 14-3). Make the class public, but otherwise keep the code generated by Visual Studio.

3. Implement the Add method for Favorites using a new feature in Visual Studio 2005 that allows you to generate methods that are not implemented:

   a. Click on the word *Add* in AddFavoriteCountIsOne and then hold your mouse over the small bar that appears under the letter *A* to reveal a smart tag with a menu item to generate the missing code.

   b. Click this menu item so that the following code is automatically added to Favorites.cs:

   ```
   public void Add(Favorite favorite)
   {
       throw new Exception(
               "The method or operation is not implemented.");
   }
   ```

4. Build the project (Build | Build Solution). This produces an error because the new `Favorite` class requires two parameters for its constructor. Implement the required constructor (Listing 14-2) and rebuild; this time it should succeed.

LISTING 14-2: Favorite Class Implementation

```
public class Favorite
{
    private string label;
    private Uri     uri;

    public Favorite(string label, Uri uri)
    {
        this.label = label;
        this.uri = uri;
    }
    public string Label { get { return label; }}
    public Uri     Uri { get { return uri; }}
}
```

5. Run the test by selecting it in the Test View window and then clicking the Run Section button. The Test Results window will show that the test failed, and if you double-click the corresponding red icon a window will open giving you further details. In this case, the `Add` method threw an exception because it wasn't implemented.

6. Do the simplest thing to get the test to pass: Replace the `Exception` statement in `Favorites.Add()` with a statement that increments the count instance variable. You will also have to add this variable to the class and change the `Count` property to return its value, as shown in Listing 14-3.

LISTING 14-3: Favorites Class Implementation

```
public class Favorites
{
    private int count;

    public int  Count { get { return count; }}
    public void Add(Favorite favorite){ count++; }
}
```

7. Rerun all the tests you have implemented so far by selecting them in the Test View window and clicking the Run Section button; they should pass. You will notice that whenever you run the tests the project is automatically rebuilt.

8. We have now reached the refactoring step, when duplication is banished and the code is made simpler, more flexible, and easier to understand. However, each time you make a change, you should rerun all the tests to check that you haven't accidentally broken anything.

9. Add your work to a version control shelve so that you can always return to this point in the future. Click the Shelve button in the Pending Changes window (View | Other Windows); see Exercise 9-6 in Chapter 9.

10. Log off, as you have finished the exercises in this chapter.

Comments about the Refactoring

Refactoring your code can be the most challenging part of TFP, but often there is not much to do, as was the case here. Looking at the Favorites class, it made sense to introduce a variable to manage the number of Favorite objects and return its value in the Count property; otherwise, we could not have made both our tests pass. We must accept that the implementation of the Favorites class is still quite rudimentary and will require adaptation as we complete the test list. However, it is hard to think of a simpler or more flexible solution that meets the needs of our current two tests. There is no duplication and the code is easy to understand; see Listing 14-3. What more could we ask for? Let's just postpone thinking about how we are going to store and access Favorite items until we implement a test that needs this functionality.

Turning our attention to the Favorite class, how might we refactor that? Review Listing 14-2 and you'll see there is nothing to do. Should we write some tests for this class? Again, there is nothing to do; we recommend that you do not write tests for a class when the compiler is able to catch more or less everything that could go wrong. In this case, the only obvious source of error arises in the constructor where values might not be properly assigned to member variables, but as this isn't something that often trips us up, we don't test for it. However, if the Favorite class became a base class, you might want to create some additional tests to check that it was properly initiated by any derived class. Alternatively, if people on your team often forget to initialize an object properly, by all means create some tests.

We'll come back to refactoring in the next chapter, but for now, just get into the habit of reviewing the code with your pairing partner after you've succeeded in making it pass all its tests. You should always select and run all the tests in your Test View window after refactoring just to make sure that none of your changes has any unexpected impacts on the existing code. Indeed, it is advisable to do this whenever you have made any change to the code.

> **■ NOTE**
>
> You should write tests only for your own team's code, not for code generated by Visual Studio or code in a third-party library. However, occasionally you may put tests around the interfaces of such libraries to detect changes in behavior when a new version is installed.

Do the Next Three Tests Yourself

We've now completed the implementation of AddFavoriteCountIsOne, so we need to start on the next simplest test on our list. However, we'll leave the completion of the next three tests as an exercise for the reader:

- AddRemoveFavoriteCountIsZero
- AddTwoFavoritesCountIsTwo
- AddTwoFavoritesRemoveFavoriteCountIsOne

These tests are very similar to the one we just implemented, and they require only the addition of a Remove method in Favorites to decrement the Count variable in the Favorites class.

CONCLUSION

If you've been following our instructions, you have implemented five tests and written the production code necessary to manage the count of `Favorite` items in the `Favorites` object. Let's reflect on what else you've done:

- You wrote tests before the production code and therefore implemented just the classes and methods that were absolutely necessary to pass the tests. There was no redundant functionality or unnecessary complexity.

- The tests you've implemented should make you confident about making any future changes to the way you manage the count of Favorite items. Your tests will always tell you whether the `Count` property is working correctly, even if you completely change the way it is implemented.

- Writing tests forced you to think about the way others may use your code; code that you find difficult to test is usually also difficult to use.

- You wrote the code by taking a succession of very small steps that didn't require you to be an expert C# programmer or know much about Visual Studio. You didn't need to use the Debugger or any complex tools, and you got the code working quickly before thinking about how you could improve it.

- You've spent less than an hour writing five tests, but you're a significant way through the task. The tests prove that you've made progress and that your code works. You don't need to give your boss any reassuring messages; just tell him to run your tests!

- Anyone who wants to know how your code works has a number of examples to follow. The tests document the code, and to check that it's up-to-date you simply run the tests; there's no static document that needs to be kept up-to-date.

We've now covered the basics of test-first programming, so let's dig a bit deeper in the next chapter and learn some more about refactoring.

15
Learning to Refactor

I N THE PRECEDING CHAPTER, you implemented the first part of the "Image Favorites" story and along the way learned how to use the new unit testing facilities of Visual Studio 2005 to perform test-first programming (TFP). This chapter is more concerned with the refactoring required as you implement more of the "Image Favorites" story and, therefore, find yourself wanting to improve the structure and design of your code without changing its functionality. We will start by making refactorings that cause such improvements to happen in a small way, but by the end of the chapter, you will have learned how to make refactorings that result in a significant enhancement of your code.

Doing Small Refactorings

The secret of refactoring is to make your changes through a series of small, safe steps. Therefore, you need to gain experience in making small refactorings before you can string them together to achieve some big change in your code. However, you don't need to worry about making mistakes as you are learning to take these small steps, because your programmer tests should detect any problems, and you can always roll back the changes you have made by restoring your workspace to some previous version of the code base; see Exercise 9-4 in Chapter 9.

Implement a Collection

We start by addressing AddTwoFavoritesClearCountIsZero, which is the sixth test on our list; see Table 14-1 in Chapter 14. This test involves adding two Favorite items, invoking Clear, and then checking that Count is 0, as shown in Listing 15-1. Accordingly, we need to introduce a Clear method for the Favorites class. This brings us to a point where it seems to make sense to have the Favorites class implement the ICollection<Favorite> interface, for we will shortly need some mechanism to store Favorite items in Favorites.

EXERCISE 15-1: Implementing the ICollection Interface

1. Log on as Luke (Team Foundation Contributor) to the DeveloperPC, start Visual Studio, and then connect to the OSPACS Team Project, as described in Exercise 5-7 in Chapter 5.

2. Make sure Luke's workspace is up to date and then load the osImageManager Visual Studio Solution by opening the osImageManager.sln file (File | Open | Project/Solution) so that you can continue from the work you did in Chapter 14.

3. Implement the AddTwoFavoritesClearCountIsZero test in FavoritesTests.cs by replacing the test's Assert statement with the code shown in Listing 15-1.

LISTING 15-1: Test for Clear

```
[TestMethod]
public void AddTwoFavoritesClearCountIsZero()
{
    Favorites favorites = new Favorites();
    favorites.Add(new Favorite("X-Ray of left humerus",
                            new Uri("db://0000102")));
    favorites.Add(new Favorite("X-Ray of right humerus ",
                            new Uri("db://0000103")));
    favorites.Clear();
    Assert.AreEqual(0, favorites.Count);
}
```

4. Implement the `Clear` method by adding the following line of code to the `Favorites` class:

```
public void Clear() { count = 0; }
```

5. `ICollection` is part of the new Generic collections provided in .NET 2.0, so you also need to add a `using` statement at the top of the Favorites.cs file:

```
using System.Collections.Generic;
```

6. Change the definition of the `Favorites` class to state that it implements the `ICollection` interface by editing Favorites.cs as follows:

```
public class Favorites : ICollection<Favorite>
```

7. You can make the `Favorites` class implement all the methods required by the interface by taking the following steps:

   a. Click on the word *ICollection* and then move your mouse pointer over the bar that appears under the letter *I* in order to reveal its smart tag menu.

   b. Click the "Implement interface ICollection<Favorite>" item so that Visual Studio will automatically add the required code to the class; see the warning at the end of this exercise.

8. Remove the automatically added method, called `Remove`, and change your existing implementation of `Remove` so that it returns true and therefore conforms to the interface:

```
public bool Remove(Favorite favorite)
{
    count--;
    return true;
}
```

9. Trigger the rebuilding of the Solution by rerunning all the tests you have implemented so far; select them in the Test View window and click the Run Section button. All the tests should pass (or be inconclusive) so that you can start refactoring.

> **■ WARNING**
>
> Don't select the smart tag menu item that "Explicitly" implements the interface in step 8, because this will add all the methods required for the interface, including ones that you have already defined, such as Add and Count.

Refactor the Test

You may notice by looking at the tests in FavoritesTests.cs that a Favorites object is created in every test method. Although the duplication occurs in the test code, it still is bothersome, so let's use the [TestInitialize] attribute to move this declaration code to one place. The resulting code after the change is shown in Listing 15-2. This is an example of the Set Up Refactoring pattern described in the book *Test-Driven Development in Microsoft .NET*[1] and it moves common initialization code into one place in a test adapter class.

LISTING 15-2: Example of a Set-Up Refactoring

```
[TestClass]
public class FavoritesTests
{
    private Favorites favorites;
    private Favorite armLeft;
    private Favorite armRight;
    private Favorite legRight;


    [TestInitialize]
    public void BeforeTest()
    {
        favorites = new Favorites();
        armLeft = new Favorite("X-Ray of left humerus",
                            new Uri("db://0000102"));
        armRight = new Favorite("X-Ray of right humerus ",
                            new Uri("db://0000103"));
```

---

1. [TDDM] Newkirk, James W., and Alexei A. Vorontsov. *Test-Driven Development in Microsoft .NET* (Microsoft, 2004).

```
        legRight = new Favorite("X-Ray of right fibia",
                                 new Uri("db://0000105"));
    }

    [TestMethod]
    public void EmptyFavoritesCountShouldBeZero()
    {
        Assert.AreEqual(0, favorites.Count);
    }
                        // The rest of the tests
}
```

■ **NOTE**

In a test class, a method marked with the [TestInitialize] attribute will be executed by the test harness prior to the execution of each test. The [TestCleanup] attribute causes a method to be executed after the execution of each test.

EXERCISE 15-2: Implementing the SetUp Refactoring Pattern

1. Implement the BeforeTest method in FavoritesTests.cs and remove the declaration of Favorites from each method. You can also remove the duplication that each test has with the creation of the Favorite objects armLeft and armRight; see Listing 15-2.

2. Trigger the rebuilding of the Visual Studio Solution by rerunning all the tests as before. All the tests should pass because you have not changed the functionality of the code, just removed some unnecessary duplication.

3. Add your work to a version control shelve so that you can return to this point in the future. Click the Shelve button in the Pending Changes window (View | Other Windows); see Exercise 9-5 in Chapter 9.

Refactor the Production Code

Now let's see if any refactoring is required in the production code file Favorites.cs. You will recall that we changed the declaration of the Remove method because the ICollection<Favorite> interface wanted this method to return a "bool." The documentation[2] for this interface says that Remove will return true if a Favorite item is successfully removed from the collection. Therefore, rather than refactoring the code, let's add a test to verify that the return value of Remove is true if the Favorite item is removed.

EXERCISE 15-3: Adding a New Test: AddRemoveReturnsTrue

1. Implement AddRemoveReturnsTrue in FavoritesTests.cs, as shown in Listing 15-3, and change the Favorites class method, Remove, in Favorites.cs so that it returns true.

   LISTING 15-3: Making the Code Clearer by Adding a Test

   ```
   [TestMethod]
   public void AddRemoveReturnsTrue()
   {
       favorites.Add(armLeft);
       Assert.IsTrue(favorites.Remove(armLeft));
   }
   ```

2. Rerun all the tests (as before) to trigger the rebuilding of the Solution. Again, all the tests should pass because you have simply made the code clearer by adding a test rather than changing its functionality.

3. Add your work to a version control shelve by clicking the Shelve button in the Pending Changes window (View | Other Windows); see Exercise 9-5 in Chapter 9.

The last bit of cleanup we need to perform before moving on is to update our test list. Implementing the interface brought in a couple of functions, such as IsReadOnly and CopyTo, which we did not take into

---

2. C# Language reference, ICollection (http://msdn.microsoft.com).

account in the test list. So let's add the following three tests to Table 14-1 in Chapter 14:

- **RemoveFromEmptyCollectionReturnsFalse**—This test will call Remove for an empty Favorites collection, which should return false.
- **IsReadOnlyShouldBeFalse**—This test will call IsReadOnly on the Favorites collection, which will always return false.
- **Add3FavoritesCopyTo**—This test will add three Favorite objects to a collection, call CopyTo, and then verify that the array has the three Favorite objects.

We now have 18 tests in our test list of which we have eight tests implemented and passing. In the next section, we'll implement some additional tests and, in the process, learn a bit more about using the Test Results window.

Safely Changing Code Implementation

The AddFavoriteContainsReturnTrue test is interesting because it makes us turn our attention to storing Favorite objects in some form of collection implemented by our Favorites class. The test shown in Listing 15-4 adds a Favorite object to the Favorites object and then confirms that it has been correctly stored by invoking the Contains method, as defined by the ICollection interface.

EXERCISE 15-4: Storing Favorite Items in a Collection

1. Implement the AddFavoriteContainsReturnTrue test in FavoritesTests.cs by replacing the test's Assert statement with the code shown in Listing 15-4.

   LISTING 15-4: Making the Code Clearer by Adding a Test

   ```
   [TestMethod]
   public void AddFavoriteContainsReturnTrue()
   {
       favorites.Add(armLeft);
       Assert.IsTrue(favorites.Contains(armLeft));
   }
   ```

2. Rebuild the Solution and rerun all your tests by selecting them in the Test View window and then clicking the Run Section button. The new test should fail because the Contains method has not been implemented, as shown in Figure 15-1.

After you run a set of tests, the results are displayed in your Test Results window. Unfortunately, though, this window displays all test results, even the successful ones, so it doesn't give you an immediate indication about whether the test run passed or failed; the equivalent of the NUnit[3] green bar. You can overcome this limitation to some degree by changing the order in which the Test Results window displays its results so that the failures are listed first.

> **■ TIP**
>
> To group the test results by their outcome, select Result Value from the Group By drop-down list in the window's toolbar; see Figure 15-1. This produces a much more useful report because you don't need to scroll down to discover which tests failed.

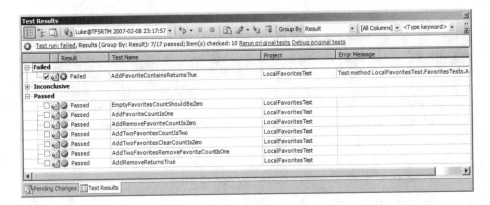

FIGURE 15-1: Tests grouped by result in the Test Results window (Test | Windows)

---

3. NUnit is the original programmer test tool for .NET development (www.nunit.org).

EXERCISE 15-5: Implementing a Linked List

Let's now get the failing test to pass. This requires us to implement some form of storage mechanism.

1. Create a LinkedList to store your Favorite items by changing the code in Favorites.cs, as shown in Listing 15-5.

LISTING 15-5: Using a Linked List for the Favorites Collection

```csharp
public class Favorites : ICollection<Favorite>
{
    private LinkedList<Favorite> favorites =
                            new LinkedList<Favorite>();

    public int Count
    {
        get { return favorites.Count; }
    }

    public void Add(Favorite favorite)
    {
        favorites.AddLast(favorite);
    }

    public bool Remove(Favorite favorite)
    {
        return favorites.Remove(favorite);
    }

    public void Clear()
    {
        favorites.Clear();
    }

    public bool Contains(Favorite favorite)
    {
        return favorites.Contains(favorite);
    }

    // ...
}
```

2. Rerun all the tests to trigger the rebuilding of the Solution. This time the test should pass, signaling that we can start refactoring again.

3. Add your work to a version control shelve by clicking the Shelve button in the Pending Changes window (View | Other Windows); see Exercise 9-5 in Chapter 9.

You can gain a sense of when some refactoring is needed from indications of bad code, which are termed *smells* and are catalogued in books such as Martin Fowler's *Refactoring*.[4] It is often said that sometimes you choose to ignore a smell and it goes away; other times the longer you leave the smell, the worse it becomes. When you can stand a smell no longer it is time to refactor it away.

Comments about the Refactoring

There isn't anything obvious to refactor in Listing 15-5, but we need to keep an eye on the Favorites class because it seems to be somewhat redundant now that we're using the LinkedList<Favorite> collection. Let's not do anything right now, but wait until we've implemented some more tests to see if there is a continuing justification for having a separate class rather than just using the LinkedList directly. Don't get too hung up on these sorts of decisions, for it is often better to have code that represents the requirements than it is to go for a totally minimal solution.

You might want to pause and reflect on what we've just done here. The original implementation of Favorites was based on maintaining the simple integer property, Count. However, in a single stroke we've completely replaced it with the much more complex LinkedListCollection. We made this fairly significant change to the Favorites class in total safety because we had a half dozen or so tests to check that we didn't break any existing behavior. The ability of TFP to keep the cost of changes low in this way is the reason that we can defer making significant architectural decisions until we know more about the problem we're solving, as we discuss later in this chapter when we consider simple design.

---

4. [RIDEC] Fowler, Martin, et al. *Refactoring* (Addison-Wesley, 1999).

> **TIP**
>
> Although you should be seeking to have a simple design, this doesn't necessarily mean expressing the code in the minimum number of lines. Sometimes it is better to use a few more statements so that you can express an idea simply and clearly.

Refactor As You Go

Refactoring is performed each time you get a new test to pass, for two main reasons: First, you want to think more deeply about the test and code you've written while the issues are still fresh in your mind; and second, you want to make changes to code that already works. Therefore, to gain more experience in refactoring, you simply need to write some more tests.

Implementing More of the Requirement

In the preceding section, we entrusted most of the work being performed by `Favorites` to its `LinkedList` member variable. One of the consequences of this change was that its `Remove` method no longer has a hardcoded return value, but instead uses the return value of the object to which it entrusted the task; this `LinkedList` variable. We can use this same technique to implement a number of the remaining tests.

EXERCISE 15-6: Removing Items from an Empty Collection

1. Implement the RemoveFromEmptyCollectionReturnsFalse test in FavoritesTests.cs by replacing the test's `Assert` statement with the code shown in Listing 15-6.

   LISTING 15-6: Removing Items from an Empty Collection That Fails

   ```
   [TestMethod]
   public void RemoveFromEmptyCollectionReturnsFalse()
   {
       Assert.IsFalse(favorites.Remove(armLeft));
   }
   ```

2. Rebuild the Solution and rerun your tests by selecting them in the Test View window and then clicking the Run Section button, as

you have done before. All the tests should pass or be declared inconclusive.

3. There is nothing to refactor here, so add your work to a version control shelve; click the Shelve button in the Pending Changes window.

The following tests are also quite simple to implement; therefore, you should gain experience in TFP by doing them yourself. When you have implemented these tests, you should have 14 passing tests:

- **Add(Favorite), Remove(Favorite), Contains(Favorite)**—Should return false.
- **Contains(Favorite) that is not in the collection**—Should return false.
- **Add(Favorite1), Add(Favorite2), Add(Favorte3) and copy collection to an array**—May suggest additional tests, such as passing a null collection.
- **Add(Favorite1), Add(Favorite2), Add(Favorte3), call GetEnumerator, verify that the three Favorites are enumerated**—Should return true.
- **IsReadOnly()**—`LinkedList<T>` does not define `IsReadOnly`, so implement it by just returning false.

All of these tests and their resultant implementations may convince you that we don't need a separate `Favorites` class because we can use the `LinkedList<Favorite>` class directly; a "smell" known as the (redundant) middle man. However, you do not want to take this refactoring step just yet because the next few tests might reveal some new information. Therefore, let's leave refactoring for the moment and continue with the implementation of our solution by implementing a test to find a `Favorite` in our collection using its label, which is something that the customer thought would provide useful business value.

■ TIP

You don't always need to change code during refactoring because sometimes it is better to wait rather than act, particularly if there is a chance that a refactoring done now might need to be reversed later. You get better at making these sorts of judgment calls with experience.

1. Add a new test method that contains the code shown in Listing 15-7.

LISTING 15-7: Finding a Favorite Using Its Label

```
[TestMethod]
public void AddTwoFavoritesFindByLabel()
{
    favorites.Add(armLeft);
    favorites.Add(armRight);
                        //note: indexing not yet implemented
    Assert.AreEqual(armLeft.Uri,
                favorites[armLeft.Label]);
    Assert.AreEqual(armRight.Uri,
                favorites[armRight.Label]);
}
```

2. When you compile, an error is reported which will remind you that you need to implement indexing for Favorites, so add the code in Listing 15-8 to the Favorites class. Run your tests from the Test View window to rebuild the Solution and display the result. This new test should pass.

LISTING 15-8: Implement Index for Favorites

```
public Uri this[String label]
{
    get
    {
        foreach (Favorite item in favorites)
        {
            if (item.Label.Equals(label))
                    return item.Uri;
        }
        return null;
    }
}
```

3. It is now time to refactor, but again you might want to spend more time thinking than actually making code changes. Add your work to a version control shelve by clicking the Shelve button in the Pending Changes window.

Refactoring Opportunities

Several possible refactorings jump out at us here. Because we have to access the Favorite objects by their labels, we could store them in a Dictionary instead of a LinkedList, but can we justify this change right now? There is also the ongoing question of the purpose of our Favorites class; do we really need it? Although implementing the preceding test has spawned some code that does more than just entrust its work to the LinkedList<Favorite> class, there is still no strong justification for keeping Favorites because we could get a similar result by using the Find method on LinkedList<Favorite>.

The next test is AddFavoriteNullLabel, which says that you should get an error when you try to add a Favorite with a null label to the Favorites collection; see Listing 15-9. It is debatable as to whether it is better to detect and handle such an error in the Favorite constructor or wait until you attempt to add an invalid Favorite item to the Favorites collection; we chose the latter, but the test could equally have driven us to implement the former.

■ NOTE

We are putting our thought processes down on paper, and this might make us seem unsure or indecisive. However, this reflects the fact that there are seldom any absolute rights or wrongs when refactoring, and you often find yourself simply exploring matters with more tests.

EXERCISE 15-8: Testing for an ArgumentNullException

1. In the FavoritesTests.cs file, replace the Assert statement of the AddFavoriteNullLabel test with the code shown in Listing 15-9 and rerun your tests. This new test will fail because we haven't implemented any parameter checking in the Add method of the Favorites class.

LISTING 15-9: Implement Index for Favorites

```
[TestMethod]
[ExpectedException(typeof(ArgumentNullException))]
public void AddFavoriteNullLabel()
{
    Favorite favorite = new Favorite(null, armLeft.Uri);
    favorites.Add(favorite);
}
```

NOTE

The [ExpectedException] attribute defines the expected exception. Therefore, the test in Listing 15-9 will pass only when the execution of its code results in the generation of an ArgumentNullException.

2. Insert into the Add method the parameter check, as shown here, and again rerun the test; this time it should pass, so let's start refactoring.

```
if (favorite.Label == null)
    throw new ArgumentNullException("Label cannot be null");
```

3. Looking at the implementation of the Add method, it is clear that we need to do some more parameter checking for the AddFavoriteNull-Uriand AddFavoriteAddAnotherSameLabel tests, so we should implement the code shown in Listing 15-10.

LISTING 15-10: Parameter Checking in Add

```
public void Add(Favorite favorite)
{
    if (favorite.Label == null)
        throw new ArgumentNullException("Label cannot be null");
    if (favorite.Uri == null)
        throw new ArgumentNullException("Uri cannot be null");
    if (this[favorite.Label] != null)
        throw new ArgumentException("Duplicate Label");

    favorites.AddLast(favorite);
}
```

You should now write tests for adding a `Favorite` with a null URI and adding two `Favorites` with the same label to exercise the new parameter code you have just implemented.

4. When we rerun the tests, all 18 are now passing and we have no inconclusive results. However, we haven't finished yet, as there is still some more refactoring to do. Therefore, add your work to a version control shelve; click the Shelve button in the Pending Changes window before starting the next exercise.

■ TIP

Refactoring, like any worthwhile experiment, can go wrong. Therefore, before embarking upon any significant refactoring, save your work in a version control shelve in case you decide to abandon it part way through and need to back out your changes; see Exercise 9-4 in Chapter 9.

Doing a Big Refactoring

Although all the tests in our test list are now passing, there are a couple of issues we still need to resolve. First, for some time we've been questioning the need for the `Favorites` class because it seems to entrust most of its work to `LinkedList<Favorite>`. Second, there is the matter of whether we should use a `Dictionary` or a `LinkedList` to store our `Favorite` objects.

Remove the Middle Man

Remove the Middle Man is a refactoring pattern described by Martin Fowler[5] that applies to a class that is doing too much simple delegation. Therefore, we have to ask ourselves whether the `Favorites` class is a candidate for such a refactoring because it clearly delegates its responsibility for maintaining the collection of `Favorite` items to `LinkedList<Favorite>`.

---

5. [RIDEC] Fowler, Martin, et al. *Refactoring* (Addison-Wesley, 1999).

Upon reflection, we would probably remove the Favorites class at this stage if its sole responsibility was to maintain the collection of Favorite-Items. However, now that we have implemented all of the tests, it becomes clear that the Favorites class has another responsibility, for as you can see from Listing 15-10, its Add method provides an important parameter-checking function. For this reason, we will leave the Favorites class as it stands.

> **■ NOTE**
>
> You don't always need to change the code when refactoring. Sometimes it is better to spend time considering potential code changes and then to do nothing, as we did in this case. Perhaps we should define this as the "Do Nothing" refactoring pattern!

Changing the Type of a Collection

When it comes to deciding whether to change the implementation of our Favorite item collection from a LinkedList to a Dictionary, there is a clear case for refactoring because it would allow us to access Favorite objects directly by their Label properties rather than forcing us to iterate through the entire collection, looking for a match; see Listing 15-8. However, this is a rather big refactoring because it means changing practically every method in the Favorites class to use a Dictionary<string, Favorite> collection in place of a LinkedList<Favorite>. We must ask ourselves, is it worth the effort?

In this case, we will implement the refactoring because it makes the code easier to understand and maintain. We might have reached this conclusion sooner if we had done some modeling earlier, but we could also argue that writing some better tests would have led us to this decision more quickly as well. However, the approach we took is certainly not wrong because it identified the problem and created the tests that now allow us to correct the situation easily. Indeed, we should be feeling quite satisfied that we have explored a number of options for implementing our collection and we have actually arrived at a good solution in a reasonable amount of time.

1. Replace the code in Favorites.cs with that shown in Listing 15-11.

2. Rerun the tests by selecting them in the Test View window and then clicking the Run Section button, as you have done many times before. All the tests should pass, as you have not changed the functionality of the code, just its implementation.

3. Add all the tests you have developed to the Integration Build Validation Test created in Exercise 12-1 in Chapter 12 so that they can be run whenever anyone performs the osImageManagerIntegation Team Build.

4. Add your work to a version control shelve by clicking the Shelve button in the Pending Changes window. However, you should be aware that the tests added to IntegrationBVT in the previous step will not be run as part of the Integration Team Build until your changes are actually checked in.

5. You have now finished the exercises in this chapter, so log off.

We have now completed the test list which we initially expressed in Table 14-1 in Chapter 14, and have since expanded to 18 tests; see Figure 15-2. However, we have not quite finished the programming episode because we need to demonstrate that our code is properly tested and performs well, matters we will cover in Chapter 16.

LISTING 15-11: Favorites Class after Refactoring

```
using System.Collections.Generic;
public class Favorites : ICollection<Favorite>
{
    private Dictionary<string, Favorite> favoriteDictionary =
                            new Dictionary<string, Favorite>();
    public int  Count {get { return favoriteDictionary.Count; }}
    public bool IsReadOnly { get { return false; }}
```

```csharp
    public void Add(Favorite favorite)
    {
        if (favorite.Label == null)
            throw new ArgumentNullException("Label cannot be null");
        if (favorite.Uri == null)
            throw new ArgumentNullException("Uri cannot be null");
        if (Contains(favorite))
            throw new ArgumentException("Duplicate Label");
        favoriteDictionary.Add(favorite.Label, favorite);
    }
    public bool Remove(Favorite favorite)
    {
        return favoriteDictionary.Remove(favorite.Label);
    }
    public void Clear()
    {
        favoriteDictionary.Clear();
    }
    public bool Contains(Favorite favorite)
    {
        return favoriteDictionary.ContainsKey(favorite.Label);
    }
    public void CopyTo(Favorite[] array, int arrayIndex)
    {
        favoriteDictionary.Values.CopyTo(array, arrayIndex);
        return;
    }
    public Uri this[string label]
    {
        get
        {
            Favorite favorite = favoriteDictionary[label];
            return  (favorite == null) ? null : favorite.Uri;
        }
    }
    public IEnumerator<Favorite> GetEnumerator()
    {
        return favoriteDictionary.Values.GetEnumerator();
    }
    public System.Collections.IEnumerator
        System.Collections.IEnumerable.GetEnumerator()
    {
        return favoriteDictionary.Values.GetEnumerator();
    }
}
```

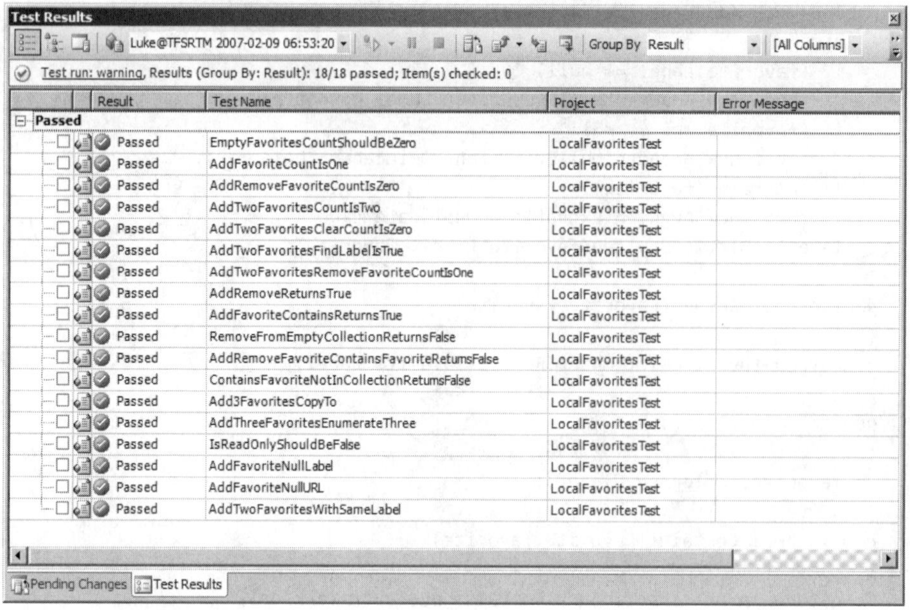

FIGURE 15-2: The test list containing 18 passing tests

Take a Break

The path you have followed to arrive at this point may appear to be somewhat convoluted and tortuous, but in practice, without the need to read the exercises, it would probably take you less than an hour to implement these 18 tests. With that said, TFP is very tiring work, so make sure you take regular breaks. Indeed, it is recommended that you limit the duration of your programming episodes to one or two hours and attempt only three or four in a day. Only in this way will you be able to apply the Energized Work practice.

You should aim to complete any refactoring within a few hours and finish by checking in your code so that it can be tested and integrated with the team's common code base; see Exercise 12-5 in Chapter 12. Therefore, you should break up big refactorings into a series of small steps which are individually no more difficult than the ones you have completed in this chapter. In this way, you should be able to complete a major refactoring without needing to undertake any marathon programming sessions which disrupt your ability to work in a sustainable way.

Energized Work Practice

The Energized Work practice helps the team avoid any long-term decline in its productivity by ensuring that people get the frequency, quality, and duration of breaks they need in order to recover fully from their work. It's about each individual achieving a satisfactory balance between work, rest, and play over the various cycles of his life: daily, weekly, and yearly.

People have different capacities for sustaining work, but at some stage all need some time to recover; otherwise they will not be able to work at the same pace as before. It makes no sense to perform test-driven development continuously all morning if it means you and your partner are unable to work effectively in the afternoon. In the same way, it is counterproductive to work all night completing a task at the end of one iteration when it results in a loss of contribution during the first few days of the next iteration. An Agile team recognizes that a smooth flow of work over months and years gets more done than occasional spurts of high-intensity activity over a few days or weeks.

Implementing the Energized Work practice is not just a case of insisting that everyone works from 9:00 a.m. to 5:00 p.m. and takes an hour for lunch. It calls for you to address various complex cultural and social issues. For example, developers usually like to work hard and tend to measure this effort in terms of the time they spend at their desks. This is because elapsed time is easy to calculate and has strong psychological associations with effort and reward. Therefore, introducing the Energized Work practice means you must convince such people to swap this cherished metric of individual office hours with one that better reflects their productivity as a group. In this way, people start getting the rest and play they need because it leads to an improvement in something they now care about: a metric-based productivity rather than elapsed time.

Continues

When it comes to adopting the Energized Work practice, each team will have its own set of issues to identify and overcome. You should not expect this process to happen in a few weeks, and you must also accept that from time to time, an urgent deadline will still require people to undertake heroic amounts of overtime. However, the point about energized work is that you try to make such events the exception rather than the rule so that most of the time the team operates at a pace it can sustain over the lifetime of the project and beyond.

CONCLUSION

Test-driven development means you don't have to start with a perfect design, but instead evolve the design to meet your needs. This evolution is driven by refactoring, but it is possible only because your tests give you a safety net which encourages you to make changes in the implementation. Everyone is obliged to refactor whenever they encounter any code that needs attention. You refactor code to remove duplication, and make it simpler, easier to understand, and more flexible while taking care not to change its functionality—a case of cleaning up, not remodeling. In this way, the design of the team's software improves over time, making it easier to work with, not harder, as the project progresses.

16
Code Coverage and Performance

THIS CHAPTER EXPLORES some activities related to test-first programming (TFP) by finishing the programming episode we started in Chapter 14 with some exercises that reveal the adequacy of your unit testing as well as the presence of any unexpected performance bottlenecks. After finishing this chapter, you should be able to use the Visual Studio tools to identify any parts of your code that are not exercised by unit tests and understand how to improve the code's performance using the Dynamic Code Analyzer.

Code Coverage

The exercises in Chapters 14 and 15 showed you how to implement part of a story called "Image Favorites" using the Test-First Programming practice. This involved creating an initial list of tests which drove the development of a class library for your production code, called LocalFavorites, and a corresponding library for your tests, called LocalFavoritesTest. If you were following the exercises, by the end of Chapter 15 you should have succeeded in passing 18 tests and have confidence in your software's capability to manage a collection of bookmarks for images in the OSPACS database.

You may be confident that your code works, but how do you convince other people that it works? How can you be sure that every important part of the team's software is covered by tests when they are run from the Test View window? The Visual Studio Team System (VSTS) integrated Code Coverage tool provides answers to such questions.

How to Generate Code Coverage Information

The Code Coverage tool allows you to record each line of code executed during a test run so that you can subsequently identify those areas of the code base which haven't been exercised by a test. Exercise 16-1 shows how it works for the Visual Studio Solution you created by following the exercises in Chapters 14 and 15.

EXERCISE 16-1: Generating Code Coverage Information

In this exercise, you will create coverage information to identify the statements in your code that are executed when you perform the programmer (unit) tests for the favorites.dll file developed in the previous chapters.

1. Log on as Luke, start Visual Studio, and connect to the OSPACS Team Project. Open the osImageHandler.sln solution file (File | Open | Project/Solution) so that you can continue from your previous work in Chapter 15.

2. Select the localtestrun.testrunconfig item in your Solution Explorer window's Solution Items folder and double-click it to open the dialog box shown in Figure 16-1.

3. Select Code Coverage from the list displayed in the left pane of the dialog box, and then select the name of the assembly you would like to instrument; in this case, choose the LocalFavorites.dll file that appears in the Favorites directory. Close the dialog box and save your changes when prompted.

4. Rerun your tests by selecting them in the Test View window and clicking the Run Selection button. After the tests have completed, information about the code that has been executed is displayed in the Code Coverage Results window (Test | Windows | Code Coverage Results); see Figure 16-2.

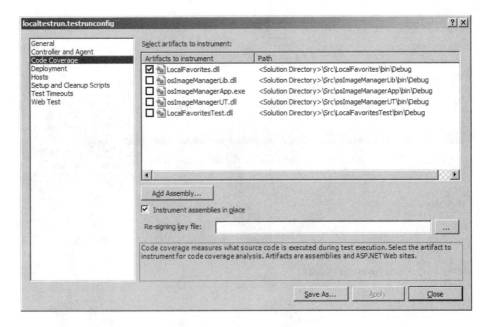

FIGURE 16-1: Code coverage configuration

▪ TIP

Don't instrument assemblies containing the unit tests because you need to know which statements in your production code have been executed, not which statements were executed in the test.

```
public Uri this[String label]
{
    get
    {
        Favorite favorite = favoriteDictionary[label];
        return (favorite == null) ? null : favorite.Uri;
    }
}
```

FIGURE 16-2: Code not covered by tests in Favorites.cs

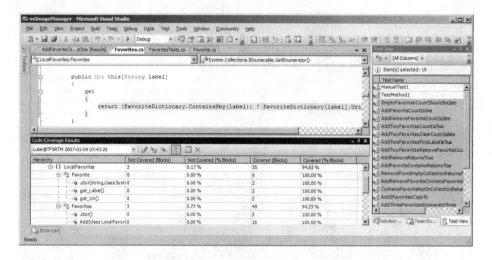

FIGURE 16-3: Code coverage results

Looking at the results in Figure 16-3, we can see that even our little example did not get 100 percent code coverage. We got to only 93.10 percent. Where did we miss some code? Drilling down into the hierarchy displayed in the left column of the Code Coverage Results window, we can follow the items with the largest percentage of uncovered code down to individual methods.

5. Open the hierarchy in the Code Coverage Results window to locate the index property in the Favorites class which is not well covered by tests. Double-click on this line to open the corresponding source file, Favorites.cs, at the position this property is implemented.

6. The red highlighted code in Favorites.cs shows the lines that were not executed during the test. It seems we didn't write a test for the case when we attempted to find a Favorite for a label that doesn't exist in the collection; see Figure 16-2.

7. Write a test to make sure the statement is exercised by adding the code in Listing 16-1 to FavoritesTests.cs.

LISTING 16-1: Test for Null When Label Not Found

```
[TestMethod]
public void FavoritesIndexerLabelNotContainedInCollection()
{
    Assert.IsNull(favorites["Unknown"]);
}
```

8. Rerun the tests to build the Solution and confirm that everything now works. Unfortunately, all is not well because `Dictionary` throws an exception saying that the key wasn't present. Fix the problem in Favorites.cs by swapping the statements in the `get` block with the following code:

```
get
{
    return (favoriteDictionary.ContainsKey(label)) ?
                        favoriteDictionary[label].Uri : null;
}
```

9. When you rerun the tests they should all pass. If you hadn't checked your code coverage, you might not have caught this potential bug so quickly.

10. Add your work to a version control shelve so that you can mark the changes; click the Shelve button in the Pending Changes window.

11. You have now finished the exercise, so log off.

■ **NOTE**

When James Newkirk originally developed these exercises, he realized that he had forgotten to test for a label that didn't exist only after obtaining code coverage information. This illustrates the importance of including code coverage in your testing.

Following the Test-First Programming practice has allowed you to get high code coverage, very close to 100 percent. However, sometimes you may fall out of the practice and implement something without tests. This might happen when you are working with an external system that prevents you from writing tests for all of the conditions. It could also happen when you've done a large refactoring and have added code which is not covered by tests. Running the Code Coverage tool will inform you of such holes and give you the opportunity to provide more tests (if appropriate) before proclaiming your task complete.

You should also keep in mind that it is not difficult to get complete code coverage by following examples in books such as this one, but in practice, 100 percent coverage is very difficult to achieve and often you should not even try to achieve it. Remember that code coverage is not a universal panacea, and people must look at coverage data in context. In particular, you need to question whether the data is telling you something that's important (as in the preceding example) or whether it is telling you something that you can safely ignore. You must also beware of people who simply focus on achieving the metric rather than truly advancing the state of the software. For example, what is the point of getting 100 percent code coverage for code that has no business value, or for code that has serious quality issues such as resource leaks, missing functionality, and so forth? In our opinion, a goal of 100 percent code coverage is not realistic or desirable in a commercial project of any significant size, as you would be better off putting this effort into areas that yield actual business value.

> **■ TIP**
>
> Divide your system in functional components and then set coverage targets based on factors such as their relative risk and importance. For example, you might aim for an average coverage of 80 percent, but raise the bar to 90 percent in some components and lower it to 70 percent in others.

Performance Analysis

The Dynamic Code Analyzer tool provided with Visual Studio Team System helps you obtain information about the operation of your program that may help you identify problems such as performance bottlenecks. It does this in two different ways:

- **Sampling**—Your program is periodically interrupted so that performance data can be collected about all the code currently executing. You can also trigger such sampling by employing on-chip performance counters for certain events such as page faults, register access, or process and thread operations.

- **Instrumentation**—Small pieces of code called *probes* are inserted into the entry and exit points of selected methods, which results in performance data being collected about them each time they are executed.

This performance data is gathered during an analysis session when your program is run by the Code Analyzer tool. The data is used to create reports so that you can determine things such as the most frequently called functions, memory allocation, and so forth; see Figure 16-4.

Launch button

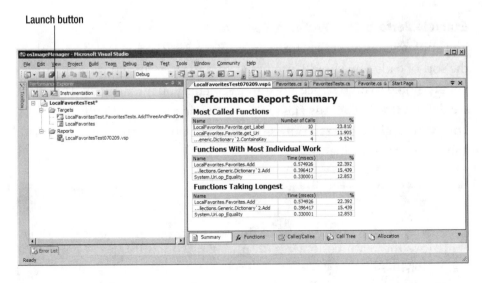

FIGURE 16-4: Performance analysis report

Sampling

The advantage of sampling is that it has very little impact on the normal execution of your program, so the results more accurately reflect the actual performance you will encounter in a production environment. It also gives you an overall picture of your program's performance and therefore will typically be used to guide subsequent gathering of data for specific parts of the code with instrumentation. The disadvantage of sampling is that the performance data snapshot is not guaranteed to be taken at the right moment, so it can fail to gather all the information you need to fully understand the problem.

Instrumentation

Instrumenting your code for performance analysis has the advantage that you can hone in on a precise area of code and therefore find the root cause of the problem. It yields much more data and the results are much more consistent than the hit-and-miss approach of sampling. However, the drawback of instrumentation is that it alters the code you are trying to measure and, therefore, increases the amount of experimental error. You also need to remove the instrumentation from the code before you release it into the production environment, so you might spend a lot of time tuning a program with performance probes only to discover that it becomes detuned again once you remove them.

Example Performance Profiling Session

The implementation of the "Image Favorites" story is not a good example of the sort of code you should attempt to optimize because it is unlikely that your customer would notice any improvements you might make. Therefore, we will use the Favorites class in the following exercise to illustrate only how you might analyze your code and will not concern ourselves with enhancing its performance.

> ■ **TIP**
>
> Let your customer drive any efforts to improve performance. Try to identify the features that need optimizing, quantify the amount of improvement they each require, and then deliver these improvements incrementally.

This exercise instruments a new test which you will add to the LocalFavoritesTests Visual Studio Project created in Exercise 14-2 in Chapter 14.

1. Log on as Luke, start Visual Studio, and connect to the OSPACS Team Project. Open the osImageHandler.sln solution file (File | Open | Project/Solution) and continue from your previous work in Chapter 15 (or Exercise 16-1).

2. Write a new test in FavoritesTests.cs to reflect how the code in LocalFavorites might be used to implement a feature needed by a clinician. Add three favorites and then find one; see Listing 16-2.

LISTING 16-2: Performance Test

```
[TestMethod]
public void AddThreeAndFindOne()
{
    Favorites.Add(armLeft);
    Favorites.Add(armRight);
    Favorites.Add(legRight);
    Assert.AreEqual(armRight.Uri, favorites[armRight.Label]);
}
```

3. Run the test by selecting AddThreeAndFindOne in the Test View window and then choosing Run Selection from its context menu (Right-click | Run Selection). Observe the execution of the test in your Test Results window.

4. Create a Performance Session for this test using the Performance Wizard by selecting AddThreeAndFindOne in the Test Results window and then choosing Create Performance Session from its context menu.

5. Use the Performance Wizard to specify Instrumentation Profiling and then click Finish. This opens the Performance Explorer window where you can see the newly created LocalFavoritesTest as an item in its treeview.

6. Run the test from the Dynamic Code Analyzer tool by clicking the Launch button in the Performance Explorer toolbar. This automatically starts the profiler, executes the test, and generates a series of reports from the profile data.

7. Change the properties of the Performance Session to suit your requirements by selecting the LocalFavoritesTest item in the Performance Explorer window and then choosing Properties from its context menu (Right-click | Properties). See Figure 16-5.

8. Rerun the test using the Dynamic Code Analyzer and inspect the reports it generates.

9. Check in your changes following the procedures agreed upon by your team (see Chapter 10) and then run the osImageManagerIntegration Team Build to ensure they are correctly integrated into the team's code base.

10. Log off, as you have finished the exercises in this chapter.

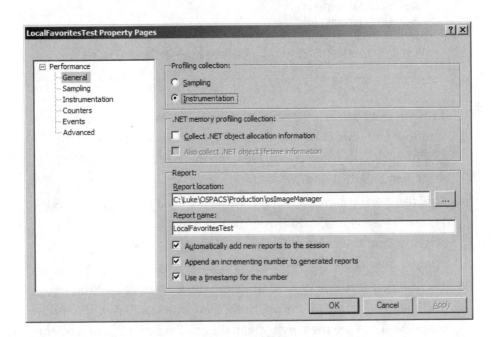

FIGURE 16-5: Performance session property pages

Creating a Build Configuration for Performance Analysis

Minimize the differences between the program you release and the program you analyze by creating a special build configuration for performance-based testing. Base this configuration on your release settings, but then include symbolic information for your class libraries so that your reports contain proper class names and other symbolic information. This can be achieved as follows:

- Open the Configuration Manager dialog box from the Build menu so that you can create a new configuration by selecting New from its Active Solution Configuration drop-down list.

- Select the Visual Studio Project for the class library in your Solution Explorer window and open its Properties window: Project | Favorites Properties). Click the Advanced button in the Build page to open a dialog box from which you can set the output debug information as "full."

After you have created your new Build Configuration, select it as the Active Solution Configuration in the Configuration Manager dialog box, and then rebuild your Visual Studio Solution (Build | Build Solution) before conducting another performance profile session.

Improving Your Library Code's Performance

The reports that the Dynamic Code Analyzer tool generates help you identify areas of your code that suffer from poor performance so that you can start trying to eliminate them. Typically, this involves rewriting the code so that you can execute it in a more efficient way. It's a job much like refactoring because it requires you to improve your code without changing its functionality. However, after optimizing your code, it may not always be easier to understand and maintain.

> ■ **TIP**
>
> You might need to avoid (or undo) a refactoring in order to optimize your code for performance. When this happens, you should add some comments to the code to explain what you've done, and why.

The Test-First Programming practice supports your optimization activities by providing a set of tests which allow you to experiment and make significant changes to your code in relative safety. You can often achieve the performance you need simply by doing something such as moving a single statement out of a loop so that it is invoked once rather than many times; see Listing 16-3. The Dynamic Code Analyzer helps you identify that statement and your tests to make sure that any change you make doesn't then break the existing behavior.

LISTING 16-3: Code with Potential for Performance Improvement

```
public string GetListing
{
    string outputText = "My Favorites: ";
    IEnumerator<Favorite> myEnum = GetEnumerator();
    while (myEnum.MoveNext())
    {
        outputText += myEnum.Current.ToString();
        outputText  = formatListing(outputText);
    }
    return outputText;
}
```

■ NOTE

In Listing 16-3, moving the invocation of formatListing to the return statement may significantly improve the performance of GetListing because the string will be formatted only once instead of in the loop each time a favorite item is added.

You should attempt to improve performance by making a series of small steps so that you can measure the gain you achieve after each one and use this feedback to guide further work. This helps you avoid wasting time on unproductive activities so that you can concentrate on doing the things that actually create results. For example, you might be tempted to try hand-optimizing the statements in a section of code to improve on the work your compiler has already performed. However, by taking small steps, you will quickly learn that performance isn't usually improved by removing whitespace, writing terse code, or even switching to a different .NET language.

> **■. NOTE**
>
> The biggest gains usually come from changing the design of a method rather than from hand-optimizing its statements. Indeed, certain hand optimizations can prevent the compiler from performing much better optimizations of its own and, therefore, can actually reduce performance.

Improving System Performance

Improving the performance of your code libraries can achieve only so much because often the big problems lie at a system level. It is a case of finding and then eliminating such issues as unnecessary calls across the network, inefficient resource allocation, and so forth. To resolve these sorts of problems you usually need a detailed knowledge of the operating system design as well as a good understanding of the various server products in your system. Therefore, improving system performance is not a job that an average developer is qualified to tackle. However, you can gain some insight into the causes of your problems by using the Dynamic Code Analyzer tool in sampling mode to find the general areas that are suffering from poor performance. The information yielded by such an investigation may then help you to identify the sort of expertise you need to employ.

> **■. NOTE**
>
> You can attach a performance session to other types of programs besides those used when running unit tests, allowing you to analyze the performance of your program in various sorts of situations; see the Visual Studio Team System Help Topics.

CONCLUSION

Code coverage and performance analysis are both ways of objectively measuring the quality of the job done during test-first programming. However, you must be careful that the effort you spend on these activities provides value to the customer. In a real-life situation, it is seldom possible to cover 100 percent of your code with unit tests, so you must balance the cost of further improving your coverage against the customer benefits that this brings in terms of reliability. Likewise, you must balance the time taken to improve the execution time of your software against the benefits that this faster code gives to the customer.

■ 17

Integrating TFP Code with a User Interface

T HE PREVIOUS THREE chapters described the way in which test-first programming (TFP) allows you to implement most of the "Image Favorites" story in a class library called Favorites. In this chapter, we suggest how you might finish this story by integrating this class library with a suitable user interface to provide a complete Windows Forms application. We also review how TFP makes design something that you do all the time instead of a specific phase you do at the start of a project.

Implementing the User Interface

At the beginning of Chapter 14, we divided the "Image Favorites" story into two programming episodes. The subsequent exercises guided you through the first of these episodes: implementing the functionality that allows a clinician to create a collection of favorite images. Therefore, you should now be ready to address the second episode, which requires you to invoke this functionality from user interface code generated by the Visual Studio editor. In order to do this, you need to model the user interface, create a task list, and then implement the application.

Define the User Interface

We suggest you start developing the user interface (UI) by modeling its layout and behavior with your customer; see Chapter 20. Accordingly, you might decide that the simplest form of UI for the "Image Favorites" story requires just three static menu items so that a clinician can display, add, and discard Favorite items, as well as a dialog box in which he can specify the label and database reference of a new Favorite item. Figure 17-1 shows how this might look in a Windows Forms application.

> **■ TIP**
>
> Use the Visual Studio Forms Designer to create quick prototypes of your forms with your customer when discussing the user interface. In this way, the user interface may evolve into something that better meets your user's needs and expectations.

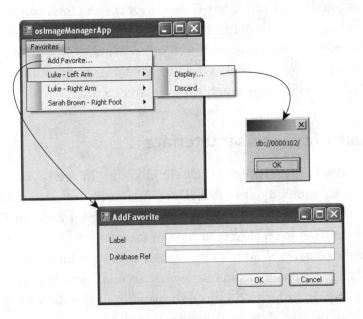

FIGURE 17-1: User interface for the "Image Favorites" story

Create a Task List

Most of the work associated with constructing a UI involves declarative programming activities such as dragging items onto a form, setting their properties, and creating handlers for the various events they need to process. For this reason, developers tend not to drive the development of the user interface by writing tests. Therefore, instead of creating a list of tests (as you did in Chapter 14), we suggest you simply make a list of the main tasks you need to complete in order to assemble the UI. For example, to create the UI shown in Figure 17-1 for the "Image Favorites" story, you might summarize the following tasks on an index card:

1. Provide osImageHandlerApp with a reference to LocalFavorites.dll.
2. Create a dialog box called Add Favorite for labeling a new Favorite item.
3. Create an item in the application's main menu bar for Favorites and create a submenu item for Add Favorite.
4. Create an event handler for the Add Favorite menu item that will open the dialog box and then use the information supplied by the user to create a new Favorite item which can be added to the collection.
5. Create an event handler for the Delete menu item which removes the associated Favorite from the collection.
6. Create an event handler for the Display menu item which displays the URI value associated with the favorite item.
7. Populate the Favorites menu with submenu items from the Favorites collection. Each item will require an additional two submenus for the display and delete functions, as well as connections to appropriate event handlers.

■. TIP

Write your task list on a 6-by-4 index card and stick it to your monitor so that you can cross off each item as you complete it. This helps you to keep track of how much work you still need to complete as you progress through your programming episode.

Implement the Windows Forms Application

Implementation of this second task requires only basic Windows Forms programming skills,[1] so we leave it as an exercise for the reader. However, to get you started, Exercise 17-1 shows you how to implement the event handler for the Add Favorite menu item; see the fourth item in the preceding list.

EXERCISE 17-1: Providing a User Interface for LocalFavorites

In this exercise, you will add a menu strip with a number of menu items to the Windows Forms application you developed in Exercise 8-4 in Chapter 8 so that you can link them with appropriate event handlers to your code in Form1.cs. You will then create a dialog box so that a user can specify the information needed to create a new Favorite item and then dynamically add it to this menu.

1. Log on as Luke, start Visual Studio, and connect to the OSPACS Team Project. Open the osImageHandler.sln solution file (File | Open | Project/Solution) and continue from your previous work in Chapter 16.

2. In the osImageHandlerApp project, add a reference to the LocalFavorites class library; see step 4 of Exercise 14-3, in Chapter 14.

3. Open the application's main form in Design View by double-clicking the Form1.cs item and choosing Designer from the View menu. Next, drag a MenuStrip item from the Visual Studio toolbox (View | Toolbox) and drop it onto the form to create a main menu for your application.

4. Add the Favorites menu item by typing "Favorites" into the MenuStrip control, and then add a submenu by typing "Add..." into the box that appears below this new Favorites menu item.

5. Add an event handler for the Add submenu item by first clicking the Favorites menu item and then double-clicking the Add submenu; a

---

1. [PWF] Petzold, Charles. *Programming Microsoft Windows Forms* (Microsoft Press, 2006).

skeletal method will automatically be created and the editor will switch to Code View (View | Code) so that you can implement the handler. Type the code in Listing 17-1 into this method.

LISTING 17-1: Adding an Item to the Favorites Collection

```
private void toolStripMenu_AddFavorite(object sender, EventArgs e)
    {
        AddFavoriteDlg dlg = new AddFavoriteDlg();
            if (dlg.ShowDialog() == DialogResult.OK)
                favorites.Add(new Favorite(dlg.Label, new Uri(dlg.Uri)));
    }
```

6. Implement AddFavoriteDlg by adding a Windows Form to the osImageHandlerApp project and then dragging and dropping the necessary controls onto it from the toolbox.

7. Add a private instance variable for Favorites to the Form1 class and instantiate it in the class constructor to provide "favorites."

8. Build the Solution (Build | Build Solution) and then run the application (Debug | Start without Debugging) so that you can confirm that a form appears with a Favorites menu containing the Add... item, which opens the AddFavoriteDlg dialog box when clicked.

9. Check in your changes following the procedures agreed by your team (see Chapter 10) and then run the osImageManagerIntegration Team Build to ensure that they are correctly integrated into the team's code base.

10. Log off, as you have completed the exercises in this chapter.

> **NOTE**
>
> The Form1.cs file (Listing 17-2) contains the part of the class edited in Code View, and the Form1.Designer.cs file contains the part of the class edited in Designer View; see Figure 17-2. However, you can download the entire solution from the book's Web site.

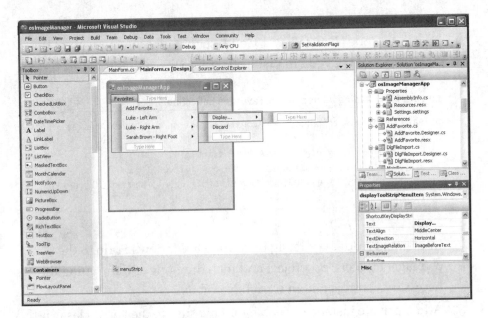

FIGURE 17-2: Visual Studio Forms Designer

Aim to Create a Thin User Interface Layer

When producing user interface code, you should adopt the strategy of keeping the user interface layer as thin as possible. For example, looking at the Windows Forms code in Listing 17-2, you can see that most methods are only two or three lines long and defer any complex processing to the Favorites class we developed using TFP in the preceding chapters. In fact, it could be argued that the PopulateFavoritesMenu method in Listing 17-2 is too complex to sit in the user interface layer and should have been moved to a class library so that it could be developed with the necessary unit tests, but we leave this as an exercise for the reader.

During the development of your user interface, it is really a case of trusting the Visual Studio editors and the Forms framework to do their jobs properly so that you can connect the resultant code to the fully unit-tested library classes with a minimum number of intermediary statements. Clearly, the simpler you can make this connecting code, the less chance there is that it will contain an error.

> ■ **WARNING**
>
> Take care to test the user interface because it is very easy to acciden-
> tally alter the properties of elements in a Window Form or incorrectly
> bind them to your code. However, it is notoriously difficult to auto-
> mate such tests, so you may need to perform manual testing instead.

LISTING 17-2: Implementation of the User Interface in the Partial Class Form1.cs

```
using LocalFavorites;
public partial class Form1 : Form
{
    private Favorites favorites;

    public MainForm()
    {
        favorites = new Favorites();
        InitializeComponent();
    }
    private void favoritesMenu_DropDownOpened(object sender, EventArgs e)
    {
        PopulateFavoritesMenu();
    }
    private void toolStripMenu_AddFavorite(object sender, EventArgs e)
    {
        AddFavoriteDlg dlg = new AddFavoriteDlg();
        if (dlg.ShowDialog() == DialogResult.OK)
            favorites.Add(new Favorite(dlg.Label, new Uri(dlg.Uri)));
    }
    private void toolStripMenu_DisplayFavorite(object sender,EventArgs e)
    {
        ToolStripDropDownItem item = sender as ToolStripDropDownItem;
        if (item != null)
            MessageBox.Show(favorites[item.OwnerItem.Text].ToString());
    }
    private void toolStripMenu_DeleteFavorite(object sender, EventArgs e)
    {
        ToolStripDropDownItem item = sender as ToolStripDropDownItem;
        if (item != null)            //you must implement Favorites.Find()
            favorites.Remove(favorites.Find(item.OwnerItem.Text));
    }
```

```
private void PopulateFavoritesMenu()
{
    favoritesToolStripMenuItem.DropDownItems.Clear();

    ToolStripItem[] FavItems = new ToolStripItem[favorites.Count+1];
    FavItems[0] = new ToolStripMenuItem("Add...", null,
                    new System.EventHandler(toolStripMenu_AddFavorite));
    int cnt = 1;
    IEnumerator<Favorite> myEnum = favorites.GetEnumerator();
    while (myEnum.MoveNext())
    {
        ToolStripMenuItem item = new
        ToolStripMenuItem(myEnum.Current.Label);
        item.DropDownItems.Add("display image", null,
        toolStripMenu_DisplayFavorite);
        item.DropDownItems.Add("delete favorite", null,
                    toolStripMenu_DeleteFavorite);
        FavItems[cnt++] = item;
    }
    favoritesToolStripMenuItem.DropDownItems.AddRange(FavItems);
}
}
```

> **■ NOTE**
>
> You do not need to write unit tests for third-party software unless
> your team is treating such code as its own or needs to isolate problems
> by covering the interfaces with tests to detect any changes in their
> behavior.

Simple Design

Some people will doubtless be surprised that we embarked on implementing the "Image Favorites" story without first producing any sort of formal
design. However, we question whether such effort would have resulted in
us creating a better solution than the one we have produced. Therefore, let's
complete this chapter by taking a brief look at how we have arrived at this
simple, yet adequate, design without needing a big investment in upfront
design work.

> **■ NOTE**
>
> We have actually spent a great deal of time thinking about the design and how it could be improved. It's just that we interspersed this work with writing tests and code, so perhaps it wasn't very visible.

Code Criteria for Simple Design

Simple design is about stopping the build-up of unnecessary complexity in code. It requires you to improve the product by making it simpler until you reach the point at which further simplification results in loss of value. Unnecessary complexity impedes change and, left unaddressed, this will eventually bring a project to its knees. Each refactoring step is an opportunity to simplify the design which you need to exploit by evaluating the code against the following minimum set of criteria, shown in priority order:

- **The code should be appropriate for your audience**—It provides an example of how you think people should write code in the context of the given problem. There shouldn't be too many examples of bad code, otherwise people may lose confidence in the overall solution.

- **The code must pass all the tests**—If the code does not pass the tests, stop. Fix the code and then continue the evaluation.

- **The code must communicate the design intent**—As Jack Reeves says,[2] the only real blueprint for software is the source code itself. It needs to express all the things you had in mind when you were designing the program and must communicate to other people how the implementation works.

- **The code should contain the smallest number of classes**—Your code should satisfy the first three criteria and do it in the smallest number of classes.

- **The code should contain the smallest number of methods**—Last but not least, the code should have the smallest number of methods.

---

2. Reeves, Jack. *What is Software Design?* (Publications, www.bleading-edge.com).

In 1657, Blaise Pascal said something that embodies the intent of simple design: "I have made this letter longer than usual because I lack the time to make it shorter." The implication is that it is quicker to create superfluous material than it is to consider how you might reduce something to its bare essentials. This is certainly true of software, which often accumulates unnecessary complexity because it's more difficult to take steps to prevent complexity from being added to the code than removing it afterward.

Avoiding Big Design Up Front

Simple design means there is no need for you to perform Big Design Up Front (BDUF) because the tests validate the operation of the code at the lowest level, which permits you to make in relative safety any large refactorings that might later become necessary. Accordingly, you can defer making decisions until you have a better understanding of the problem, which avoids the need for you to add complexity at the start of the project just in case it is needed. Therefore, you might well question when the right time would be to address such issues.

In the words of Kent Beck, "You should design your software at the last responsible moment."[3] When is the last responsible moment? It really depends on your project and the situation. If you are designing a Web site that has 10 million page views and 400,000 unique visitors per month, you should not wait until the software is finished to think about the scalability of your solution. However, if you're designing a program that provides access to people's favorite Web sites, you may be able to defer a decision about exactly how to store the data until late in the project.

> **■ NOTE**
>
> Most stories are more complex than the "Image Favorites" story, so it can be beneficial for teams to spend more time exploring the design than we have. Therefore, in Section 6, we describe the sort of Agile modeling that might help you in such situations.

---

3. [XPE2] Beck, Kent, with Cynthia Andres. *Extreme Programming Explained, Second Edition* (Addison-Wesley, 2005).

CONCLUSION

Test-first programming is a very good way to produce class libraries such as LocalFavorites, but it's difficult to practice when you are not writing procedural code—for example, when you are creating a user interface with the Visual Studio Designer tool. Therefore, in this chapter, we showed how you can address this problem by moving most of your user interface logic into a class library, thereby leaving only a thin veneer of untested code which has been primarily generated by your Visual Studio tools. In this way, you can automate the testing of the parts of your interface that involve complex processing and leave the manipulation of its user interface elements to manual testing, or to a specialist UI test tool.

> **■ WARNING**
>
> When a form is open in the Visual Studio Designer, it is easy to change a property unintentionally. Therefore, we suggest you open forms only when absolutely necessary and conduct a thorough test of the user interface before checking in any change to a form source file.

Review of Section 5
Practice Test-Driven Development

THE TEAM WANTED to master test-driven development (TDD) so that everyone on the team could help write the new code required for the OSPACS Team Project instead of having to rely on just the expert programmers on the team. The team members also hoped that the quality of their software would improve by making sure that structural (unit) testing was an integral part of the process rather something that could be dropped whenever time was short. They undertook the following activities to implement the Test-First Programming practice as a first step toward making the whole development approach test-driven:

- **Created Visual Studio Test Projects**—They permitted the structural testing of the team's class libraries. In this way, each new class library would have a corresponding test library for its structural test adapters.

- **Added tests to the Build Validation Test (BVT)**—Developers were made responsible for adding all new tests created during their programming episodes to the list of tests run during build validation testing; see Chapter 12. In this way, they could run these programmer tests (and coverage) in the Build Lab using the command-line tools.

- **Enforced coding practices and policy**—They agreed that all new production code should be developed using TFP and pair programming. The team decided to enforce this decision, creating a check-in policy that required the unit testing of its changesets prior to them being checked into the repository; see Chapter 10.

- **Replaced legacy code**—They decided to replace their legacy code class by class whenever there was a need to change any part of it so that eventually, the entire code base would be rewritten using TFP. However, in the meantime, the team would try to manage the risk of having code not covered by tests by isolating the legacy code in separate class libraries and covering the important (or troublesome) interfaces with unit tests.

> **■ NOTE**
>
> The term *programmer tests* is preferred to *unit tests* when talking about the sort of structural tests written during TFP. This helps emphasize the fact that these tests aim to help programmers write the code rather than validate their work after the event.

The Team's Impressions

The team was intrigued by the idea of test-first programming because it was such a radical departure from the way it had developed code in the past. However, it was clear that this idea worked and would help the team write much higher-quality code. Here are their comments as they started to apply this practice.

Developer: Tom

"Tests give us a safety net for making changes. I feel confident about refactoring because any mistake will be picked up by our tests."

"It looks like, test by test, the software will evolve into a solution formed from solid code that we can prove works as intended. This programmer testing and refactoring clearly support the development of high-quality software."

"The lack of tests for the legacy code is something we are going to have to watch. Everyone will need to take great care when altering this code."

Developer: Maggie

"I'm a bit worried about actually developing some code, but it will be OK if I'm pair programming with someone such as Peter or Sarah. I might even teach them a thing or two about testing!"

"Making unit testing a nonoptional part of the development process will make a huge difference to the quality of our code. I'm delighted by the idea of test-driven development."

Developer: Peter

"TDD is about applying a series of simple solutions to small problems and letting the design emerge from the bottom up rather than the top down."

"We will need to keep the execution time of our tests short so that it doesn't disturb the natural rhythm of red/green/refactor."

"Writing a test causes me to think from the outset about how my code might be used by other people. What's difficult to test will probably be difficult to use."

"The information provided by the Dynamic Code Analyzer tool gives me a different perspective on the code. I can see how it actually operates in terms of objects and their method calls, memory allocation, etc."

Developer: Sarah

"TDD changes our paradigm of software development in much the same way as other significant advances such as object-oriented languages and managed code. It's going to give our company a big competitive advantage."

"Tests give me early feedback about my code because I am using classes, interfaces, and so forth at the same time as I'm implementing them. Making my code easy to test helps me create code that is easy to stick together (cohesive) while also being less dependent on other parts of the code base (loosely coupled)."

"I like the idea of using code coverage to reveal any serious holes in our testing rather than aiming for an arbitrary score such as 90 percent. We should spend our time testing what's important, not writing tests that will never generate any useful information."

Developer: Luke

"Test-first programming is a great way to learn a new language or technology, particularly when combined with pair programming. It helps alleviate my fear of writing some code that messes up the system for everyone else."

"Creating a list of tests is simply a matter of breaking down a task into a number of subtasks and then thinking about what sort of test might prove they had been successfully implemented. It's no different from the problem decomposition we did during ninth grade science classes."

"Anytime you run into problems, just use version control to go back to code that passed all its tests and try again, but this time taking smaller steps."

"The simplest refactoring involves renaming something so that it is more meaningful to people. For example, rather than using a cryptic code such as 'dwParam' to represent a variable, use a name such as 'FuelLitersInTank' instead."

> **■ WARNING**
>
> Hungarian notation such as "dwParam" makes sense when programming in languages such as C that don't express type information, but it is completely redundant in object-oriented languages such as C#.

Agile Values

The team has passed a critical milestone in adopting the Test-First programming practice, not just in terms of being able to develop software as a team, but also in terms of the reinforcement it gives to Agile values.

Communication

A number of points in TFP reinforce the value of communication. For example, when brainstorming a test list, developers learn to talk through ideas with their pair programming partner. They also learn to write code that communicates their design intent so that others can understand what was done, and why, after they move on to different tasks.

Feedback

TFP is mostly about providing feedback sooner rather than later. In particular, code evolves through the feedback provided by running software and passing tests. However, feedback is given in other ways, such as when a complex task is broken up into smaller ones, allowing people to better understand its nature and therefore adjust their estimates, consider alternatives, and so forth.

Courage

The ability to perform effective regression testing using the tests developed during TFP gives the team courage to undertake large refactorings of the code base. The Energized Work practice addresses the fear people have that the project will take an unacceptable toll on their health and personal life by ensuring that they get the rest they need so that they can work at a sustainable pace.

Simplicity

One of the core values embodied by TFP is simplicity. The goal for the team's code is best stated as "Everything should be made as simple as possible, but not simpler." By focusing on the requirements that are known and not speculating on future unstated requirements, the team achieves a design that best suits the given requirements. However, this is no shortcut, for simplicity is usually more difficult to achieve and may take people much longer.

Respect

The improvements developers are expected to make to each other's code help remove the ego from their programming activities and, therefore, foster a climate of mutual cooperation.

Reinforcement of Agile Practices

At this stage of the OSPACS road map, the team was starting to understand how the various Agile practices reinforced each other, for clearly the

Test-First Programming practice didn't operate in isolation, but worked with other practices in the following ways.

Pair Programming

Working with someone else helps you break down tasks and brainstorm the test list. It is also better to apply the experience and knowledge of two people when refactoring than just one; you should try to learn from each other.

Shared Code

You have an obligation to refactor whenever you believe it is necessary to do so. This applies to any code you encounter. Therefore, you must have implemented the Shared Code practice to start the Test-First Programming practice. However, version control needs to be in place before you start the Test-First Programming practice because refactorings can go wrong, leaving you with a pile of broken code and tests which can be fixed only by rolling back the changes from your workspace.

Single Code Base

When there are multiple code branches (see Chapter 7), you may need to retrofit the same refactoring in more than one place, which creates the very duplication that TDD is trying to eradicate. For this reason, it is usually much better to develop the production code in a single main branch.

Ten Minute Build

Part of the build process involves running all programmer (and customer) tests. You need to keep the process short so that it can be performed frequently, so make sure that your programmer tests execute quickly.

Continuous Integration

The longer you leave integration, the more likely problems will arise when you try to assemble everybody's work. Continuous integration gives you better feedback on your test-first programming, which helps stop small problems from becoming much bigger and more difficult to solve.

Section 6
Explore by Modeling

THIS SECTION EXPLAINS how models and patterns help you improve the quality of your team's software. We start in Chapter 18 by presenting the values, principles, and practices of Agile Modeling (AM) and then describe how such modeling fits into your development process. We follow this with a brief introduction, in Chapter 19, on creating the sorts of diagrams that will cover most of your modeling needs so that in Chapter 20 we can bring these two preceding chapters together by presenting a variety of approaches to Requirement, Architectural, and Implementation Modeling in an Agile project. Finally, Section 6 concludes with Chapter 21, which

Photograph by Daniel Mordzinski/AFP (Copyright Getty Images 1993).

Simple blackboard models helped Watson and Crick deduce the structure of DNA. Why should you need anything more complex to explore the composition of your software?

explains how various forms of patterns allow you to produce better software by leveraging the work of experts.

Story from the Trenches

A confocal microscope is essentially like a normal light microscope, except that instead of viewing the image through an eyepiece, you see it displayed on a monitor as a series of optical slices which are created by scanning the specimen at different depths with a laser. Biologists find this tool very useful for obtaining high-resolution images and 3D reconstructions at the tens to hundreds of micrometers scale.

Some years ago I worked on a small team, developing software to control the scanning and display of images from a confocal microscope. The code was written in C++ and it was quite mature in the sense that we were working on something like version 8.1. There had been a high turnover of staff on the team, so all the original developers had long since been replaced by new people, including a succession of software contractors like myself. Our job was to implement a number of new features and fix some of the bugs so that we could periodically release a new version of the software.

I spent the first morning of my contract exploring the project's numerous artifacts, and during this time I encountered an impressive number of Unified Modeling Language (UML) diagrams that had been created to model the software. However, upon closer inspection, it became clear that they had all been created by the same person within a few weeks of each other. In fact, they appeared suspiciously like the work of someone who had just completed a training course and wanted to practice drawing every conceivable type of UML diagram with her new set of CASE tools. A teammate later confirmed these suspicions, but told me that we couldn't discard the diagrams because they were the work of the person who was now the company's chief technical officer. I gathered from what he said that the team was rather skeptical about the value of modeling and preferred to design while typing code at the keyboard.

Not surprisingly, a closer examination of the code base revealed that it was a pastiche of different ideas, styles, and designs which had amalgamated over the years into the software equivalent of a big ball of mud. In fairness to the team, it was no different from the code in most of the mature systems I had encountered over the years. However, I remember feeling that the situation could have been improved considerably if the team had taken a more suitable approach to modeling. The idea of summarizing key collections of classes in a graphical form was sound; it was just the way the UML diagrams had been used that was poor. Unfortunately, at the time, I couldn't suggest a better approach to modeling, so like everyone else, I ignored these diagrams and got on with my coding.

Many developers are not very enthusiastic about software modeling. Often this is because they have had bad experiences struggling to produce UML diagrams with CASE tools that ultimately proved to have little value. In this section of the book, we present an Agile approach to modeling which will help you deal with the growth of your software and therefore prevent it from maturing into the sort of mess that typically characterizes old code.

18
Modeling with Agility

THIS CHAPTER INTRODUCES Agile Modeling, which is an approach to modeling that is more about helping teams to model effectively than prescribing the sorts of models they should produce. It is defined by a number of values, principles, and practices which we present at the start of the chapter, before explaining how members of an Agile team can apply them when they engage in modeling activities, either as a group or while pair programming. The chapter concludes by describing how such modeling fits into the iterative life cycle of an Agile team through a process called Agile Model-Driven Development (AMDD).

Introduction to Modeling

We produce models to help us understand things. However, the models themselves capture only a small amount of the information we generate during the modeling process. Anyone who has participated in a group modeling session will appreciate how little information ends up on the actual diagram. Ultimately, all the discussions, the disagreements, and hopefully those rare moments of insight may be summarized by no more than a few boxes joined together by some lines on a whiteboard. The value here clearly lies in the modeling and not in the model.

When we start to view a model as something that facilitates modeling, its appearance becomes less important to us. Indeed, we can form a model from almost anything; a simple system drawing on the back of an envelope, a collection of text in a document, a free-form illustration on a flip chart, or even a series of detailed diagrams produced by a sophisticated CASE tool. The content of a model should concern us, not its presentation.

> **■ NOTE**
>
> When it comes to sharing our model with others, we obviously need to adopt some rules in terms of the way we display it. Therefore, in Chapter 19, we present a brief overview of some conventions that will help you communicate better when drawing your models.

Models and Process

The sort of modeling you need to do depends on the sort of software development process you follow. People who adopt a formal process may feel uncomfortable writing code, unless they have a prescribed set of models to guide them and they willingly devote a significant amount of time to this activity. Conversely, people who are not following any sort of real process may want to go straight to coding, and therefore, they spend almost no time producing models. An Agile team needs to take a path between these two extreme positions.

> **■ NOTE**
>
> It is very difficult to develop anything but trivial software without doing some sort of modeling. Most teams create models, even if it is just a case of drawing some diagrams on paper napkins while drinking a few Jolt Colas at a local bar.

Values, Principles, and Practices of Agile Modeling

Scott Ambler defined an approach to modeling for Agile teams that he calls Agile Modeling.[1] It is influenced by the ideas of Extreme Programming (XP), and therefore, it complements the information you'll find elsewhere in this book. Agile Modeling is a collection of values, principles, and practices that help your team realize value from its modeling work.

> **■ NOTE**
>
> Agile Modeling is not a complete software process. Instead, it is intended to enhance the modeling activities for a variety of different types of host processes, including XP, the Rational Unified Process (RUP), and the Microsoft Solutions Framework (MSF).

Values

Agile Modeling shares the XP values of communication, simplicity, feedback, and courage, as discussed in Chapter 2. However, in place of "respect" it promotes the value of "humility." There doesn't appear to be much difference between the words *respect* and *humility* in the sense in which they are used in Extreme Programming and Agile Modeling. However, humility seems to go further than just valuing the importance of other people's contributions. It implies that we must also expect others to be more knowledgeable about certain aspects of the work than we are, and that others should have a willingness to learn from them.

Principles

There are 11 core principles of Agile Modeling, five of which are based on Agile concepts that should already be familiar to you: Rapid Feedback, Assume Simplicity, Embrace Change, Software Is the Primary Goal (working

---

1. Agile Modeling Web site (www.agilemodeling.com).

software, that is), and Incremental Change. However, the other six core principles require some additional explanation beyond just their names:

- **Model with a Purpose**—Produce a model only when you can identify who will use it and how it will help him or her.

- **Multiple Models**—Create different models so that the same issue can be viewed from various perspectives.

- **Travel Light**—Provide just enough information to meet your objectives, and keep only those models that continue to serve a purpose.

- **Enabling the Next Effort**—You must aim to solve today's problems in the simplest way, but not at the expense of losing your ability to respond to additional changes in the future.

- **Quality Work**—Your customer probably doesn't need a perfect job, but good enough doesn't excuse poor workmanship.

- **Maximize Stakeholder Investment**—Modeling must be justified in terms of giving the people who are paying for the work the best return on their investment.

In addition to these core principles, Agile Modeling also identifies two supplementary principles that reinforce them. One is largely self-explanatory: Open and Honest Communication. The other states that Content Is More Important than Representation, which basically means that it's not the accuracy of the drawing that counts, but the value of the information the drawing contains.

Practices

The principles of Agile Modeling give rise to 13 core practices which are concerned with the actions you take during a modeling session. Again, we address the ideas behind some of these practices in other sections of this book—Model with Others (similar to Pair Programming), Model in Small Increments (similar to Incremental Design), Collective Ownership (the same rationale as Shared Code), and Create Simple Content (similar to Simple Design). Here is a summary of the remaining nine core practices:

- **Apply the Right Artifacts**—All models have different strengths and weaknesses, so let purpose decide the type of model you create. For example, if you want to model the dynamic behavior of the objects in your program, create a sequence diagram, not a class diagram.

- **Create Several Models in Parallel**—Don't expect one model to reveal everything; address the same problem in different ways and then switch among these various types of models to gain different perspectives. (See the Apply the Right Artifacts bullet point.)

- **Iterate to Another Artifact**—The point of modeling is the generation of information, so when this stops, try switching your attention to another type of model in the hope that the flow of information will resume. (See the Create Several Models in Parallel bullet point.)

- **Depict Models Simply**—Don't clutter diagrams with unnecessary details. The fact that the standard notation allows you to represent all the methods and attributes of a class doesn't mean that your Class diagram must include all this information.

- **Use the Simplest Tools**—The principle of content being more important than representation leads us to prefer a meaningful drawing on a whiteboard over a less useful diagram produced by a UML-conforming CASE tool.

- **Prove It with Code**—Regularly check that you can actually implement the various models you are developing; prove that they are valid abstractions of the real world.

- **Single Source of Information**—Information should be stored in just one place, so keep only one model of a particular concept, even if the final model is actually your code. (See the core principle on traveling light, earlier in this chapter.)

- **Display Models Publicly**—Models should uphold the Open and Honest Communication principle by conveying information rather than hiding it. Therefore, make the artifacts from a modeling session immediately available to the rest of the team, and to your project stakeholders.

- **Active Stakeholder Involvement**—Like the XP practice of Real Customer Involvement, all the people who have a stake in your project should be involved in creating models that at least help them to understand what the system must do.

In addition to these core practices, there are five supplementary practices which can we put into three groups. First, the Apply Modeling Standards and Formalize Contract Models practices are concerned with providing information after the process of modeling has finished. They counterbalance the tendency for value to lie only in the modeling rather than in the model by addressing the need for a model to speak to people beyond just those who created it; in other words, the principle of Open and Honest Communication. For example, you might model the organization of your system's data layer as an Entity Relationship (ER) diagram so that the company's database administrator can understand it.

Second, the practice of Apply Patterns Gently encourages you to use modeling to explore the problem space, identify and analyze the requirements, and investigate design alternatives before attempting to apply a pattern (see Chapter 21). Third, the practices of Update Only When It Hurts and Discard Temporary Models help you to implement the principle of traveling light. They recognize the fact that most of the models you produce are not formalized contract models which must be kept up-to-date and retained. Often you will create a model by reusing some existing pattern, sketch it on a whiteboard, and then leave it for a few days before erasing it. These sorts of models act simply to jog your memory and don't need to be updated unless they start to cause misunderstandings.

Agile Modeling in Use

The five values, eleven core principles, six supplementary principles, thirteen core practices, and eight supplementary practices of Agile Modeling are a lot to digest. Therefore, when introducing Agile Modeling to a team, Scott Ambler recommends that you start with the principles and practices that will improve communication, keep things simple, and encourage people to model in an iterative and incremental way. In this way, Agile Modeling can be seen as complementing the values and practices of Extreme Programming and just requires the team to embrace modeling as a part of its work, both as a group and as individual programming pairs.

Group Modeling

Group modeling happens when the entire team gets together around a whiteboard or conference table and starts to discuss the system under development. It is one way to implement the Model with Others practice, and it usually generates lots of useful information because people's assumptions are challenged and alternative viewpoints are considered. Typically, more value is generated from this sort of collaborative thinking when you have a diverse group, so make sure you involve project stakeholders as well as developers in this activity. We cannot overstate the importance of soliciting contributions from people who really understand the nature of the business which will ultimately benefit from the project.

The presence of nontechnical people in a group modeling session also helps prevent unnecessary detail and arcane UML notation from sneaking into your models, thereby encouraging the Depict Models Simply practice. This is where simple tools such as whiteboards come into their own, because anyone can grab a pen and sketch out an idea without necessarily having any in-depth knowledge of CASE tools or standard modeling notation. In this respect, whiteboards democratize modeling by encouraging a more informal style that puts the emphasis on producing meaningful content rather than pretty diagrams.

> ### ■ TIP
>
> The number and type of project stakeholders will vary according to the objectives of the modeling session, but you must ensure that someone acts as the customer so that developers do not end up guessing what the business wants.

Group modeling can occur at any time during the lifetime of a project, but in particular, it should take place during the first few weeks to provide the team with an opportunity to explore the problem space as well as to develop the following initial requirements and architectural models for the system:

- **Requirement models**—Allow customers and developers to explore the system together so that they can gain a better insight into what it must do. In addition, they play an important role in helping customers to identify and prioritize their initial stories.
- **Architectural models**—Stimulate the production of something such as the System metaphor described in Chapter 20, or even just a whiteboard drawing.

When developing these initial models, it is important to realize that the value lies in the activity, not necessarily in the resulting model. Therefore, travel light during the session by creating just the material you really need in order to move forward, and at the end of the session, be prepared to discard temporary models that no longer serve any purpose.

■ TIP

Allow your team to photograph the whiteboard (or flip chart) with a digital camera so that they can store the images on the Project Web site. People may be more willing to implement the practice of discarding temporary models when they realize that these images are never actually accessed.

A group modeling session (see Figure 18-1) may last for a few hours or even an entire day, but it should certainly not take weeks. You should model in small increments, aiming to provide only as much detail as you can prove in your code over the next iteration. You must keep the larger picture abstract so that you can defer actual design decisions to the last responsible moment. In this regard, a metaphor can prove to be a helpful representation of an architectural model. Such a metaphor will develop as the project progresses and needs to be complemented by other types of architecture models created in parallel. Similarly, you should use multiple models to express requirements so that you can see the same issue from different perspectives, with each one contributing in some way to the overall level of understanding. You must aim to evolve these models over the lifetime of the project by regularly engaging in group modeling sessions.

▪. TIP

Don't fool yourself into believing that you can create a single model that will remain unchanged and drive the entire development effort throughout your project. Agile Modeling seeks to move your team away from this sort of Big Design Up Front (BDUF) thinking.

FIGURE 18-1: Group modeling session around a whiteboard

Modeling in Pairs

Modeling in pairs happens during a programming episode when two developers create some form of model in an attempt to discover new tests or better understand the nature of their task. It implements the Modeling with Others practice. Although such models more likely contain implementation details rather than plain abstractions, they should not take long to produce—a matter of minutes, not hours. For example, two developers might spend a few minutes sketching a fragment of their class hierarchy to help them find a new base class which would simplify their code; see Figure 18-2.

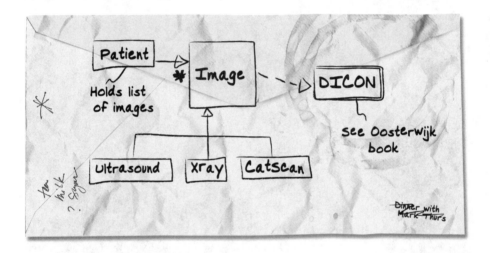

FIGURE 18-2: Model sketched on the back of an envelope

■ NOTE

Use the Visual Studio Team System (VSTS) Class Designer (Chapter 19) while modeling in pairs if you find this quicker and more convenient than sketching on paper. However, when using such tools, keep in mind the need to *depict models simply, travel light,* and *discard temporary models.*

There is no prescribed time to model during a programming episode, nor is there a particular type of model that you should produce. It is a case of spending a few minutes modeling when it seems productive to do so and generating the sort of model that looks most likely to generate the information you need. This type of group modeling works best when both developers are familiar with a number of different model types, because you will often want to create several models in parallel so that you can iterate to another artifact (diagram) during a programming episode. Clearly, if your programming partner doesn't really understand the nature of these models, there is no point producing them. Therefore, you must ensure that everyone on your team is familiar with basic modeling techniques (see Chapter 20), particularly as models developed during pairing tend to include additional notation for expressing implementation details.

> ■ **TIP**
>
> Not everyone likes to think visually, so consider using lists and tables rather than diagrams if they help you communicate better. Good models don't necessarily need to be graphical; personas, acceptance tests, and even design patterns[2] are all valid types of models.

You can quickly prove with code the models you produce during pair programming because you developed them in conjunction with Test-First Programming (TFP); it's a case of model a bit, then code and test a lot. Sometimes you create a model simply to suggest some tests, and therefore you may discard it almost immediately, but on other occasions you may retain the model over several programming episodes and numerous revisions, each one revealing some additional detail and taking you closer to your goal. Therefore, it can be appropriate to consider modeling in terms of the Incremental Design practice proposed by XP (see the following sidebar), particularly when the results are used to evolve the team's requirement and architectural models.

---

2. [DP] Gamma, Erick, Richard Helm, et al. *Design Patterns* (Addison-Wesley, 1994).

Incremental Design Practice

The Incremental Design practice makes design an everyday activity, so you perform it in small steps which you immediately validate by coding and testing. It makes the consequences of your decisions immediately apparent and therefore forces the person who is creating the design to take responsibility for its implementation.

Big Design Up Front (BDUF) is the antithesis of incremental design, as it advocates completing the entire design before starting any form of implementation work and therefore decouples design from coding. Most teams find that perfecting the design upfront is very difficult. In fact, we've never worked with anyone able to produce a design that didn't subsequently need modification once coding had begun. The advantage of taking an incremental approach is that it encourages you to go back and improve your design using the knowledge you've gained during its implementation. It results in the production of a design that proves itself capable of responding to change. This means you can defer certain decisions and then use the experience of coding to guide you toward a better solution a little further down the line.

Refactoring captures the very essence of the Incremental Design practice, for it results in your design being improved through a succession of small steps, each of which is validated against a growing collection of tests. You are providing just enough design to solve today's problems without making tomorrow's problems any worse.

Agile Model-Driven Development

Agile Model-Driven Development (AMDD) is the term Scott Ambler used to describe his version of model-driven development, for it provides an alternative to the sort of extensive upfront modeling required by approaches such as the Object Management Group's Model-Driven Architecture (MDA).[3] Figure 18-3 summarizes AMDD by showing the relationship between the requirement and architectural models that are produced

---

3. The Object Management Group provides details of MDA on its Web site: www.omg.org/mda.

through group modeling and the detailed modeling performed during pair programming.

AMDD requires initial requirement and architectural models to be produced when the project is being set up; this is the part of the project that is often called *iteration zero*. The requirement model helps your team identify what the customer wants the system to do, and the architectural model aims to define just enough of the infrastructure to support the team's immediate coding needs; Chapter 20 provides examples of these types of models. AMDD intends that these initial models will be improved in subsequent iterations as a consequence of the experience gained during detailed modeling and actual implementation.

Detailed modeling happens frequently during the iterations that follow iteration zero, as we described earlier; see the section Modeling in Pairs. AMDD doesn't insist that any particular types of models be produced during this activity, just ones that are appropriate. The objective is to model the detail rather than to create a detailed model, so these models should not take very long to develop and will often be quickly discarded. AMDD allows you the option of performing periodic reviews to validate the various models, but it is preferable to perform such validation by following the Prove It with Code practice.

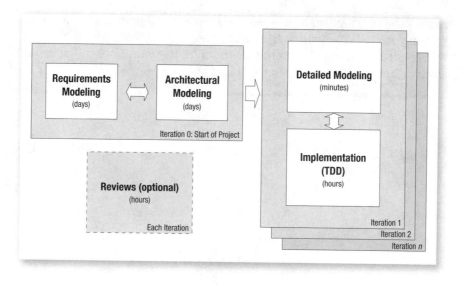

FIGURE 18-3: Activities during Agile Model-Driven Development

> **■ TIP**
>
> We recommend that you introduce AMDD into your project simply by initiating group modeling and modeling in pairs, as described earlier. These activities complement the values and practices of Extreme Programming and can add significant value to your work.

CONCLUSION

Agile Modeling is more about helping teams to model effectively than prescribing the sort of models they should produce. It gives you a framework of values, principles, and practices that help your team gain better value from its modeling activities. You don't need to implement every Agile Modeling practice or embrace all its principles at once. Indeed, you should modify Agile Modeling to suit the nature of your project, team members, and organization. However, you do need to make group modeling and modeling in pairs a part of your team's development process; otherwise, you are not really performing Agile Model-Driven Development.

> **■ TIP**
>
> Expect the production of models to generate and communicate ideas within your team as well as to explore their implementation. However, we repeat once more the point that much of the value lies in the modeling rather than within the model itself.

■ 19
Creating Models

W E WROTE THIS CHAPTER for people who have been put off modeling by the perception that it involves creating a multitude of diagrams which must each conform rigidly to some cryptic standard. Accordingly, we start by encouraging you to sketch out your ideas as free-form drawings which pay scant attention to formal conventions. We then introduce a minimal subset of the Unified Modeling Language (UML) by describing two types of diagrams that cover most of your modeling needs: the Class diagram and the Sequence diagram. After reviewing some tools that might help you create such diagrams, we conclude the chapter with a set of tips for producing better model diagrams.

Free-form Diagrams

Models that are represented by free-form diagrams do not have to comply with any standard form of notation, so you can draw them without requiring any special training. Typically, you would sketch these diagrams on a whiteboard during the sort of group modeling session we described in Chapter 18. Such drawings usually contain just a few rectangular boxes joined by various lines, because the detail here lies in the discussion, not in the diagram; see Figure 19-1.

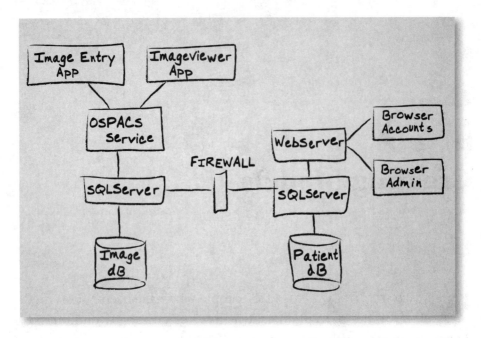

FIGURE 19-1: Free-form diagram of the OSPACS system

The main advantage of a free-form diagram is that it allows you to concentrate on communicating ideas without being constrained by notation. Therefore, you will often find that a single free-form diagram can not only take the place of numerous formal diagrams, but also better capture the key concepts being modeled. However, this lack of formality comes at a price, because a free-form diagram does not always properly represent all the critical details which can make it unintelligible to people who did not take part in the modeling session. For this reason, various types of formal notation have been developed, the most significant of which is UML.

■ TIP

The vast majority of models an Agile team produces will involve the production of free-form diagrams, so make sure you can draw them quickly without using a rule or stencil.

UML Diagrams

Unified Modeling Language[1] is a standard graphical notation for describing and designing software systems that is controlled by the Object Management Group.[2] The first version of the standard was introduced in 1997 and unified the notation used in a number of software development methods, including the Booch, Object Modeling Technique (OMT), and Objectory methods; the forerunners of the Rational Unified Process (RUP). However, UML is applicable to most forms of object-oriented processes because it makes no assumptions about the actual way it is used, which is a facet that has allowed it to quickly become the lingua franca of the object-oriented software modeling world.

Martin Fowler makes the point[3] that people tend to use UML in three ways: for sketching, for creating blueprints, or as a programming language. When people use it to create blueprints or as a programming language, the models must be complete enough so that coding becomes a task which can be respectively semi-automated or fully automated. However, in this book, we use UML just for sketching, particularly in terms of creating the sort of Class diagrams and Sequence diagrams described in this chapter, as well as the Package diagram and Deployment diagram depicted in Figure 12-6 (in Chapter 12) and Figure 30-6 (in Chapter 30), respectively. Therefore, we attempt to describe only the parts of the notation that are most likely to be used during Agile Modeling and refer you to other sources for complete coverage of the subject; see the Bibliography.

Class Diagram Notation

The UML Class diagram is probably the most common type of UML diagram you will need to draw. You use it to model the static structure of an object-oriented program by showing the nature and organization of the

---

1. You can freely download the full specification from www.uml.org.
2. Object Management Group is a not-for-profit industry consortium; www.omg.org.
3. [UMLD] Fowler, Martin. *UML Distilled* (Addison-Wesley, 2004).

classes from which it is composed. People often use Class diagrams to help them explore the problem domain during Requirement Modeling, but you might also create a Class diagram during test-driven development (TDD) because it can help you identify tests or possible refactorings. Indeed, the sort of Class diagram you might produce during detailed modeling is shown in Figure 19-2 and contains the following key elements:

- **Class box**—This box often contains just the name of the class, though it can also be divided into ordered sections containing lists of things such as field (property) and method names qualified with the symbols shown in Table 19-1. It is rare, though, for such documentation to be complete unless the diagram will be used to automatically generate the implementation files.

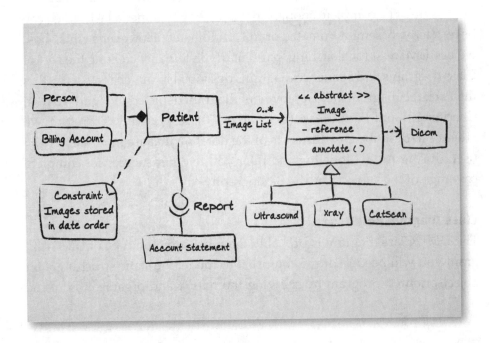

FIGURE 19-2: UML Class diagram

- **Relationships**—When a class has a property which is another class rather than a simple field such as an integer, a line is drawn connecting the two class boxes to show the type of relationships between them, which may be one of the following:
  - **Association**—Models the collaboration between classes, typically resulting from an object of one type having some form of reference to an object of another type. By default, associations are assumed to be bidirectional; however, in Figure 19-2, the Patient class knows about the Image class but the Image class doesn't know about the Patient class, so the relationship is shown by the arrowhead to indicate that it is directed. A Patient object can also have an association with zero to many Image objects, as shown by the "0..*" multiplicity indicator; see Table 19-1 for a full list.
  - **Inheritance**—Models the specialization that exists between a set of similar classes. For example, in Figure 19-2, the UltraSound class is like an Image class, but it is specialized to handle the particular aspects of images that concern only ultrasound pictures. Inheritance is shown by a triangle that has its apex next to the base class, which is the more general class from which the more specialized classes are derived.
  - **Composition**—Models the relationship in which an instance of one class contains an instance of another, which it owns exclusively. In Figure 19-2, we deduce that a Patient object has a Person object as well as a BillingAccount object contained within it. They are not references that might be shared with other objects, so when the Patient object dies, its composite objects die as well. Composition is shown by a solid diamond on the side of the relationship that represents the owning class.
  - **Dependencies**—Model reliance between classes such that a change to one class might necessitate a change to the other. For example, the Annotate method of the Image class contains a parameter of type Dicom, so Image is dependent upon the Dicom class, as shown by the dotted line.

- **Stereotypes**—Extend the use of a modeling element in a particular way. For example, in Figure 19-2, the Image class has the <> stereotype to show that you can create objects only from its derived classes. You can indicate stereotypes using text surrounded by angle brackets, as well as visually with special symbols (see the Interfaces entry, next in this list) or through the use of different fonts. An abstract class, for example, is often shown in an italic font.

- **Interfaces**—Models a cohesive set of behaviors for a class to provide. For example, in Figure 19-1, the Patient class provides the Report interface which allows it to be connected to any class that requires such an interface in order for it to work. The provision of an interface by a class is indicated by the lollipop symbol, or by a dependency to a class box stereotyped as an interface. The requirement for a class to be provided with an interface is indicated by the socket symbol; see AccountStatement in Figure 19-2.

- **Notes**—You can add miscellaneous information about the model in a note which can be attached to the element to which it refers. The note may contain some form of structured language, but often free-form text is used, as in Figure 19-2, which details a constraint for an Image collection held by a Patient object. UML provides a modeling element specifically for constraints, but they are often better expressed, as here, as notes in plain language.

■ NOTE

Multiplicity indicators may appear in requirement models and detailed models. However, visibility symbols should be used only in detailed models because they are related to coding decisions.

■ NOTE

The immediate benefit of learning UML is that you are able to communicate with others using diagrams that contain a standard notation. This makes it much easier to explain models to people who didn't attend the modeling session.

TABLE 19-1: Visibility Symbols and Multiplicity Indicators for Class Diagrams

Visibility Symbols		Multiplicity Indicators	
+	Accessible from all objects (default); public	1	One object only (default)
#	Accessible only from objects of the same type or derived from that type; protected	n	A specific number of n objects (e.g., 5)
~	Accessible only from objects in the same program; internal	*	Many objects
-	Accessible only from objects of the same type; private	0..1	Zero or one object
		0..*	Zero or more objects
		0..n	Between zero and n objects
		1..*	One or more objects
		1..n	Between one and n objects
		n..*	Between n and many objects
		m..n	A minimum of m objects and a maximum of n objects

■ CLASS BOX DETAILS

Various custom sections can follow the property and method sections in a class box, allowing you to document other key information such as the list of exceptions thrown by the class. You can also show the types of methods and properties, but it is necessary to provide this information only if the type is some form of constraint. For example, you might want to show explicitly that a value in your class was a 32-bit integer because it's corresponding to the value in a particular database field.

> ## ■ₗ MORE ABOUT RELATIONSHIPS
>
> It is worth knowing the following additional information about relationships among classes. First, you can model an association as a class during Requirement Modeling, but you cannot actually implement the concept in C# or in any other .NET language because you cannot create pointer data types (unlike in C and C++). Therefore, you will need to evolve your association into a normal class during Detailed Modeling. Second, aggregation is indicated by an open diamond and expresses a relationship that is similar to composition, but without the idea of ownership. Therefore, it is not much different from a simple association, though it is often used to indicate that the classes should be developed together.

Sequence Diagram Notation

Sequence diagrams are useful when modeling the *dynamic behavior* of the objects in your program. Normally, they show objects that participate in a particular scenario. For example, Figure 19-3 shows the objects involved in implementing the "Acquire Image" story, and by reading the diagram from top to bottom, you can see how they collaborate to achieve the required behavior. People usually draw Sequence diagrams during Implementation Modeling, but they can also be useful during Requirement Modeling when you want to capture interactions among objects in the domain model; see Chapter 20.

> ## ■ₗ NOTE
>
> A **scenario** is a sequence of steps that describe a particular interaction between a user and the system. A collection of related scenarios forms a **use case**, which provides an alternative to a customer story when it comes to describing a system's requirements.

The boxes at the top of a Sequence diagram are typically objects; instances of the classes identified in your Class diagrams. The vertical dotted lines emanating from them are called **lifelines,** and when they are active they become tall, thin rectangles called **activation blocks,** which you would draw just as a thick line on a whiteboard. Method calls between these objects are more properly called **messages** and are shown by various arrows arranged from top to bottom in the diagram to reflect their order of execution.

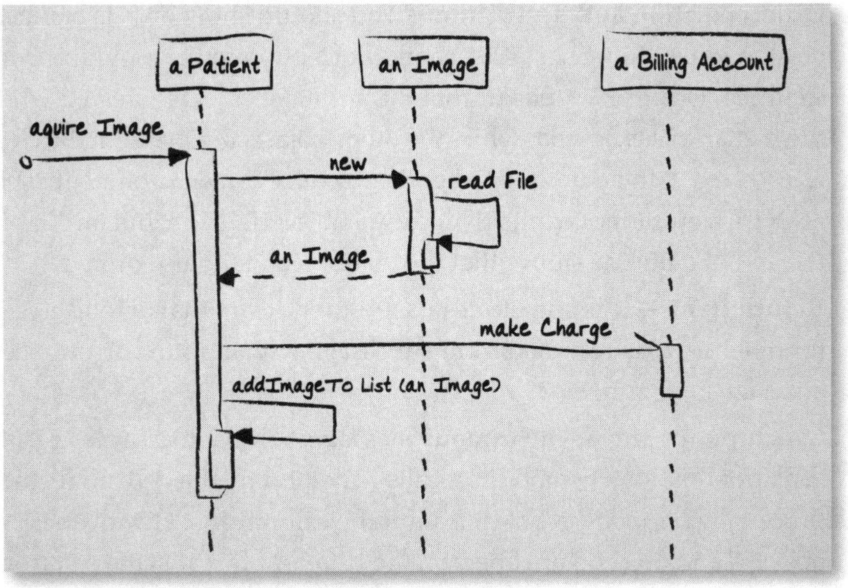

FIGURE 19-3: UML Sequence diagram

You should have no difficulty determining from Figure 19-3 that the scenario is initiated when the acquireImage method of the aPatient object is
invoked, which causes the anImage object to be created (new). The anImage
object reads a file with a call to its own readFile method and is then returned
to aPatient, which invokes the makeCharge method of the BillingAccount
object before adding anImage to the list of images it keeps with a call to
addImageToList. The notation in Figure 19-3 also contains the following
noteworthy aspects:

- **Found message**—The message that starts the scenario, acquireImage,
  has a solid dot at its origin to indicate that it comes from an unde-
  fined source.
- **Naming**—You name an object by putting "a" or "an" before its associated class name; for example, an instance of the Patient class is
  called aPatient. You can also adopt the syntax of "name:class," as
  in WillStott:Patient. The message name usually corresponds to the
  name of the method being invoked in the activated object and may
  include parameters; see addImageToList(anImage), in Figure 19-3.

- **Object creation and destruction**—You should show objects being created when doing so adds useful information to the diagram. For example, Figure 19-3 tells us that the anImage object is created when the scenario is executed, while the other objects are presumed to already exist. In an automated garbage-collection environment such as .NET, you cannot explicitly indicate object deletion, but an X at the end of a lifeline shows that the object is no longer required.

- **Return items**—It is sometimes useful to indicate that an object (or other item) is returned from a message with a dotted arrow; see anImage, in Figure 19-3.

- **Synchronous and asynchronous messages**—Most messages are synchronous, so when object A calls a method in object B, no further processing happens in object A until the call returns. However, if object A and object B are operating in different threads, the call from object A doesn't necessarily need to wait for the call to return before continuing with its processing, so the message can be synchronous or asynchronous. A synchronous message is indicated by a solid arrowhead, whereas an asynchronous message is usually shown with a half-stick arrowhead; see makeCharge(), in Figure 19-3. However, UML version 2.0 doesn't make this distinction.

- **Self-calls**—A message that an object sends to itself is indicated by an arrow that reverses back upon itself and creates a subactivation block. This might happen when an object invokes one of its own methods; see readFile() and addImageToList(), in Figure 19-3.

UML version 2.0 defines some additional notation for Sequence diagrams, but we will not describe them because they are unlikely to be useful in terms of helping you to communicate your ideas during Agile Modeling sessions. Sequence diagrams are a great way to show how objects collaborate during the execution of your program to implement a scenario. However, beware of adding too much detail to these diagrams as it is easy to convert what was originally an informative drawing into something that looks like a circuit diagram for the Starship Enterprise.

> ### ■ TIP
>
> If you want to show loops, conditionals, and other forms of program logic, forget about putting ULM notation such as interaction frames, iteration markers, and guards into Sequence diagrams, and express your ideas as code instead.

Using Modeling Tools

A whiteboard, a flip chart, or even the back of an envelope are all highly effective modeling tools when people need to explore ideas together as a group. Such tools encourage the sort of participation which is simply not possible when everyone is huddled around a monitor struggling to operate a complex CASE tool. You must remember that Agile Modeling is more about producing good ideas than delivering neat diagrams. Therefore, before adopting any new tool, you need to assess the advantages it gives you over simpler alternatives. For this reason, we will compare the Class Designer and Visio tools provided with Visual Studio Team System (VSTS) against the humble whiteboard and leave you to decide which tool is more appropriate for your team's needs.

Class Designer

Class Designer is a part of Visual Studio 2005 and therefore is available with every edition of VSTS (see Figure 19-4). It provides you with a visual editor for your source files as an alternative to the usual text editor you open when you double-click a file in Solution Explorer. Class Designer renders a set of source files as a collection of graphical objects which look similar to a UML Class diagram. It allows you to edit a class's source code in the context of the other classes in your Visual Studio project, which helps keep you aware of the relationships and hierarchies that exist between them.

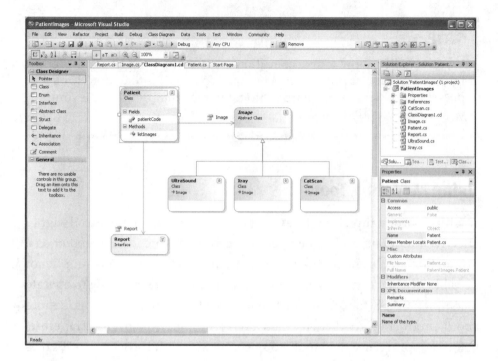

FIGURE 19-4: Class Designer

> **■ NOTE**
>
> Class Designer is a step toward emerging technologies such as Language Workbenches, which allow us to project the construction of a program in different ways, not just as individual files containing language statements rendered in a text editor; see Chapter 21.

Because Class Designer is directly editing your source files, any changes you make will be reflected in any other sort of editor that is providing views of the same files. To illustrate this point, in Exercise 19-1 we will add a member variable to the source file of a class using a text editor, and then observe the diagram in Class Designer as it is updated. We will then make a change to this source file from Class Designer and watch the corresponding update in the text editor.

EXERCISE 19-1: Editing a Source File Using Class Designer and Text Editor

1. Log on as Luke and start Visual Studio. You will not need to connect with Team Foundation Server for the purposes of this exercise.

2. Create a new Visual Studio Project for a class library called PatientImages. Make a directory for the solution, but do not locate its files in Luke's workspace or add them to version control; select File | New | Project (Visual C#, Windows Class Library).

3. Open the file Class1.cs, which is in the Class Library you have just created; double-click the file in Solution Explorer.

4. Use Class Designer to open all the source files in the PatientImages project; select the project in Solution Explorer (Right-click | View Class Diagram).

5. Use Class Designer to rename the `Class1` class in Class1.cs by selecting the name in the diagram and typing "Patient". Click on the text editor view of this same file and check that the class name has been updated.

6. Add a private integer member variable, called `patientCode`, to the `Patient` class using the text editor in the normal way. Click on the Class Designer view of this class and then click the Show button in the top right of the Patient class box to reveal the new member variable you have just added.

7. Add a method called `listImages` to the `Patient` class using the Class Designer view by selecting its class box and then right-clicking and selecting Add | Method. Type the name "listImages" into the class box and press Enter to complete the job. Click on the text editor view of the file and observe that the method is correctly displayed.

8. Experiment with adding new classes to the Class Designer view by dragging them from the toolbox (View | Toolbox) and providing appropriate names for the classes and their files. Try to implement the Class diagram shown in Figure 19-1 to explore this new way of creating and editing source files.

9. Log off, as you have completed this exercise.

> **■ NOTE**
>
> Object Test Bench is a tool provided with Visual Studio 2005 that allows you to test the methods in a class without having to create some form of test application. However, the current version of the tool has a reputation for not been entirely stable.

You should understand that Class Designer does not attempt to draw UML-compliant diagrams; it is primarily a source file editor. However, you can use Class Designer for modeling and even to test the execution of the resultant class methods using the Object Test Bench tool. With that said, unless you intend to use the classes created by Class Designer for your implementation, it doesn't seem to have any significant advantage over using a whiteboard. In terms of a tool for modeling, Class Designer also has certain disadvantages when compared to a whiteboard:

- It supports only a small subset of the UML-like Class diagram notation. It is particularly restricted in terms of the relationships it can express between classes.
- It is not very convenient for group modeling, which is true of any PC-based tool.
- It requires you to create a Visual Studio Project for the implementation files it creates, which makes it cumbersome when used for modeling in pairs with TDD.
- It doesn't naturally suggest tests, and it puts you very close to the implementation at a time when you may want to take a higher-level view.

Although in its present form Class Designer doesn't fit well with Agile Modeling and TDD, you shouldn't dismiss it because it provides you with a very convenient way to create classes for your project, and it gives you a view of their structure at absolutely no cost in terms of maintaining diagrams and so forth.

> **■ NOTE**
>
> Class Designer reads and displays the same physical file as your text editor, but it renders the information as graphics rather than text. Therefore, there is no conversion of diagrams to source code and vice versa (in other words, the round-trip engineering typically performed by CASE tools).

Visio for Enterprise Architects

Visio for Enterprise Architects is a specialized version of the Visio application that forms part of the Microsoft Office suite, and it is available from Microsoft as a stand-alone product as well as being included in the MSDN Universal Subscription. The product is supplied with stencils for a wide variety of different drawing types, including those used for UML and database work. It also allows you to generate appropriate source files from a Class diagram (i.e., forward engineering).

You should have no difficulty using Visio to generate a Class diagram such as the one in Figure 19-5, as its user interface is consistent with other applications in the Microsoft Office suite. Mostly, it is a case of dragging drawing elements such as class boxes from the toolbox and then dropping them onto the drawing surface so that you can specify their properties and then establish relationships between them using additional elements from the toolbox.

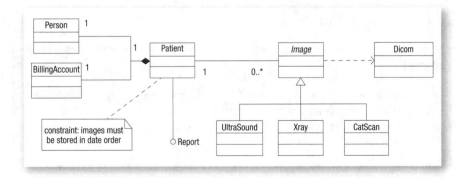

Figure 19-5: Class diagram produced using Visio for Enterprise Architects

Visio allows you to create neat diagrams which you can export to a wide variety of graphics formats. Therefore, it makes sense to use this sort of tool when generating formal documentation for your project, because unlike Class Designer, it can produce proper UML diagrams, and unlike a photograph of a whiteboard, these diagrams can be edited. Visio can also generate source files and Data Definition Language (DDL) scripts from its diagrams, which helps you transition between the model and its implementation. However, it is primarily just a drawing package, so you should not equate it with more sophisticated CASE tools, such as Rational Rose.[4] Visio as a modeling tool suffers from the following drawbacks:

- It is not very convenient for group modeling, unless you have a large wall-mounted screen and a team that is comfortable using the product.
- The supplied stencils tend to push you toward creating a particular type of diagram, which can unnecessarily constrain the creation of a free-form diagram.
- Unnecessary details are sometime needed in a diagram to satisfy the tool; for example, you must name the ends of certain binary associations.

However, in our opinion, Visio's redeeming feature is its capability to generate the scripts you need to create a database. For example, you might use Visio to create a Database Model diagram for the data structures in your system, and then generate a schema as a DDL script which you can then run with your database management system (DBMS) to create the required database.

> **■ NOTE**
>
> Visio also allows you to generate a Database Model diagram from an existing database, so when you use it in conjunction with its database script-generating facilities, you can perform round-trip engineering on your database.

---

4. IBM: Rational Rose Web site (www.ibm.com/software/rational).

Top Ten Tips for Drawing Diagrams

Whether you decide to use a whiteboard, Class Designer, Visio, or some other form of drawing tool, the following tips will help you produce diagrams that better serve your modeling needs:

1. **Respect the Agile Modeling values, principles, and practices given in Chapter 18**—In particular, consider the content of a diagram over its presentation, travel light, update the diagram only when it hurts not to do so, use the simplest tools, and depict your models simply.

2. **Use a sensible subset of UML**—Opt for common sorts of drawing elements and supply a legend for any symbols that your audience might not understand.

3. **Use names consistently**—Make sure names are spelled correctly and are used consistently in different diagrams. Adopt the sort of naming convention we discuss in Chapter 20.

4. **Specifically show omissions**—Indicate incomplete areas of your diagrams with question marks to make it clear that the information is required, but not yet supplied.

5. **Limit the detail**—Do not put too many drawing elements in one diagram, and show only those attributes and methods that add value to the model. When necessary, split large diagrams into a general overview and a number of smaller diagrams containing specific details.

6. **Use big sheets of paper**—Do not start drawing a diagram on a piece of paper (or whiteboard) that is too small because you will undoubtedly produce something that is difficult to read.

7. **Create a pleasing visual effect**—Use plenty of white space and use horizontal or vertical lines rather than diagonals or curves. Arrange boxes symmetrically and join them by lines that terminate in the middle of their boundaries rather than at a corner. Also, pay attention to the placement of labels and the fonts they use.

8. **Beware of crossed lines or lines that are too close together**—Reorganize the elements in your drawing to minimize the need for lines to cross over each other or appear to follow long paths; your diagrams should not look like wiring or circuit diagrams.

9. **Make the diagram read from left to right and top to bottom—** In most Western cultures, this is the way people instinctively read material, but adapt this tip if your audience is from a culture that reads material differently.

10. **Use visual clues—**Color helps emphasize relationships among the various elements of a drawing; similarly, the size or line thickness of a drawing element is usually used as an indication of its importance.

■. NOTE

Many of these tips are suggested in Scott Ambler's[5] excellent little book on UML, which we strongly suggest you read, along with Martin Fowler's book, *UML Distilled*.

CONCLUSION

In this chapter, we attempted to balance the need for you to create drawings that other people can understand against the need to free people from overzealous application of standards such as UML. Standards play an important part in fostering communication among the people on your team and beyond, but remember that the value of a diagram is determined by its content more than its representation.

People who are reading this chapter with little or no previous experience in software modeling should take heart from the fact that they don't need to know every aspect of the UML standard to start producing good models. We concentrated on covering only the essential information you need to start participating in your team's Agile Modeling activities: Class diagrams to express your program's static structure and Sequence diagrams to show

---

5. [EUML] Ambler, Scott. *Elements of UML 2.0 Style* (Cambridge University Press, 2005).

its dynamic behavior. In the next chapter, we will show you how to put such drawings to use in creating the types of models that often prove useful in Agile projects.

■. TIP

You should try to develop your knowledge about different model types so that you have a wide range of artifacts to apply should Class or Sequence diagrams prove inadequate for your needs.

■ 20
Using Models in an Agile Project

T EAMS THAT HAVE adopted the sort of Agile approach to modeling described in Chapter 18 will find that their models fall into one of the following three categories:

- **Requirement models**—Help the team understand the nature of the problem and identify what the software must do
- **Architectural models**—Provide the team with a high-level view of the system design typically showing how its components will be organized, implemented, and deployed
- **Implementation models**—Supply detailed information that suggests developer (unit) tests as well as possible refactorings for test-driven development (TDD)

After reading this chapter, you will understand the nature of these types of models and have some examples of them so that you can realize such models in the context of your own project.

Requirement Models

Developers usually produce requirement models during group modeling sessions in order to help them gather and analyze their customer's requirements. This work starts at the beginning of the project and continues as new requirements arise throughout the life of the project. Typically, a team will explore the requirements for the system it is developing by producing a domain model and a model of the user interface in addition to modeling the functional requirements as stories and possibly even use cases.

Domain Models and CRC Cards

Domain models allow you to explore the business problem and therefore identify the fundamental types of objects for the required system, as well as the essential relationships that exist among them. For example, a domain model might reveal that OSPACS needed an Image and a Patient class. In some cases, such Domain classes end up becoming implemented in code, and in other cases, they may evolve into completely different classes as a result of your team's detailed design efforts. Therefore, you should realize that the domain model is not concerned with implementation issues; it is concerned only with analysis of the requirement.

You can perform Domain Modeling in a number of ways,[1] but an approach that is particularly suitable for an Agile team involves CRC cards. CRC is an acronym for Class, Responsibilities, and Collaborations. It refers to the way in which you can divide an index card to show this information; see Figure 20-1. The technique was first published in a paper[2] by Ward Cunningham and Kent Beck, but was later popularized by Rebecca Wirfs-Brock in her classic book,[3] *Designing Object-Oriented Software* (though *Object Design* is a more up-to-date book[4] on the subject). She built on the basic idea of CRC by suggesting that people should write on index cards the following parts of speech which the customer uses to express what the system must do, its inputs, and its responses:

---

1. [TOP] Ambler, Scott. *The Object Primer* (Cambridge University Press, 2004), Chapter 8.
2. Beck, Kent, and Ward Cunningham. "A Laboratory for Teaching Object-Oriented Thinking." OOPSLA '89 Conference Proceedings (http://c2.com/doc/oopsla89/paper.html).
3. [DOOS] Wirfs-Brock, Rebecca, et al. *Designing Object-Oriented Software* (Prentice-Hall, 1990).
4. [OD] Wirfs-Brock, Rebecca, and Alan McKean. *Object Design* (Addison-Wesley, 2003).

- **Nouns**—Write each significant noun phrase at the top of a separate index card. Pay particular attention to proper nouns that name abstractions and which can be given a clear statement of purpose. You should also look for nouns that model physical objects and interfaces to other systems, as well as nouns that form categories for other nouns.

- **Verbs**—Add any significant verb phrase to the left column of the index card that is most clearly associated with the action it describes. You should also add to the same column a name for any sort of information that is related to the action. For example, if you had the verb *Save* on a card named "Image," you might put *Date* in the left column after learning that the date the image was saved had to be maintained.

■ NOTE

Wirfs-Brock envisioned that these nouns and verbs could initially be identified by highlighting them in the requirement specification document. However, you can identify them just as easily during a conversation with a customer.

Classes and Responsibilities

The initial objective of using CRC cards during a Domain Modeling session is to create a stack of index cards (nouns) representing candidates for the *classes* in your system with information in the left column of each card (verbs) detailing the specific *responsibilities* of the particular class—in other words, the knowledge every object of that type needed to maintain and actions it could perform. Figure 20-1 shows an example of a CRC card.

■ NOTE

The responsibilities of a class represent only the publicly available services it provides. During Domain Modeling, you do not need to consider anything it must "do" or "know" internally in order to fulfill these responsibilities.

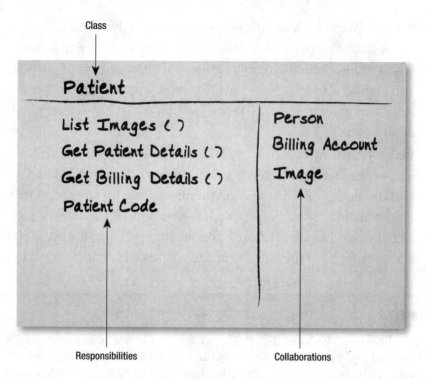

FIGURE 20-1: Example CRC card

Given a stack of such CRC cards, you can then identify additional classes and responsibilities by laying them out on a table so that everyone can see them and move them around. In this way, the cards provide a focus for the group modeling session and stimulate discussion, which in some cases may lead to classes being discarded as irrelevant and in other cases may cause responsibilities to be moved from one card to another. The intention is to keep behavior with related information, redistribute intelligence evenly throughout the system, and split larger general responsibilities into smaller specific ones, perhaps divided across several classes. During this process, people will naturally move some of the cards together on the table because they seem related somehow. This sort of grouping provides an initial structure for your classes and encourages discussions about how a class might fulfill its responsibilities.

Collaborations

In some instances, the responsibilities of a class will be satisfied internally, but in other cases, it may be more convenient to fulfill a particular responsibility through collaboration with services which other classes provide. Such collaboration creates dependencies among certain classes that should be listed in the column on the right-hand side of the card that needs the service. The search for collaborations will result in more discussion and cause additional changes to the cards on the table as more responsibilities are found, split up, or just moved from one class to another. Collaborations help you further structure the classes in your system because they identify groups of classes that need to work with each other and therefore identify potential subsystems, as well as roles for classes such as client and server.

You should not spend more than a few hours doing CRC modeling, and during this time you should aim to keep the discussion at a high level so that you retain the interest of nontechnical participants. Domain Modeling is certainly not an opportunity for developers to engage in detailed discussions about the design or about the merits of particular object-oriented concepts. However, at the end of the modeling session, you should have walked through the whole system and have a consistent model for the classes that your customer considers to be important. You should produce this model as a set of CRC cards which you lay out on a table; see Figure 20-2. In this way, you produce an initial structure for your classes that you can then express in the sort of Class diagram we previously discussed. Formally such a diagram is called an **Analysis Class diagram** to differentiate it from the detailed Class diagrams you might produce during your Implementation Modeling.

■ NOTE

The real benefit of using CRC cards is that they encourage people to explore alternatives, because they can pick up physical cards and move them around during the course of a discussion without incurring the overhead of redrawing.

FIGURE 20-2: CRC cards used for Domain Modeling

Naming Conventions

An important reason to draw Analysis Class diagrams is to help you find appropriate names for your classes that correspond to how they fit into the overall structure of the system. Choosing a good name is important because it improves communication and reduces the need for other forms of documentation by providing a clue about what the class does and how it is used. Part of selecting a good name is having some form of convention to make sure your names are consistent with each other. We took the following suggestions from *The Elements of UML 2.0 Style.*[5] It also includes suggestions for naming attributes and methods.

- Base class names on common terminology from the business or technical domain so that everyone can understand the class's purpose—for example, Account, Dicom.

---

5. [EUML] Ambler, Scott. *The Elements of UML 2.0 Style* (Cambridge University Press, 2005).

- Change names to make them appropriate for your audience. For example, the requirement model should present names in a customer-friendly way, such as First Name, whereas a detailed model can use more technical representation, such as firstName.

- Use complete singular nouns for class names; so, use Account instead of names such as Accounts and Acnt.

- Use complete names and capitalize the first letter of each noninitial word for methods and attributes—for example, verifyPatientAccount(), patientSex.

- Start method names with a strong verb, so use printImage() rather than imagePrint().

- Name attributes with nouns from the business domain—for example, patientCode.

> **■ NOTE**
>
> It is often difficult to find the best name for a class, even with the help of a Class diagram. Therefore, during refactoring you may often find yourself renaming a class by changing the code as well as any models you have kept.

User Interface Models

Modeling the user interface requirement with your customer complements the work you do when modeling the domain, so it is a good idea to develop such models together. In this way, when ideas for the domain model stop coming, you can switch to the user interface model and vice versa. You will also find that thinking about one model may stimulate some ideas for the other, thereby helping the team to develop a more complete picture of the system it is building.

It is important to avoid making assumptions about the eventual implementation when you are modeling the user interface requirements. The idea is to identify that someone using the system will require a certain report containing a given collection of data, or a particular screen with certain buttons, input fields, and so forth. At this stage, you are not concerned with matters such as whether the screen will be formed by a window, an HTML page, or even an old character-based terminal. Therefore, you should avoid using any prototyping tools that might inadvertently steer you toward a specific technology. As suggested by Constantine and Lockwood,[6] the best way to create a technologically neutral user interface model is to use sheets of paper for things such as screens and reports, and to use sticky notes for the elements they contain, such as buttons and lists. You can then produce a diagram such as the one shown in Figure 20-3 to highlight how a user might navigate among the various screens, and thereby start to develop a basic architecture for your user interfaces as well as stimulate ideas about the sorts of user stories you might need to support them.

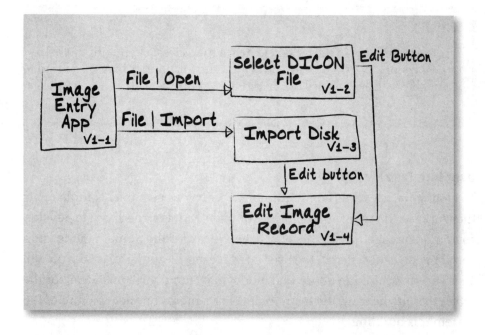

FIGURE 20-3: User interface flow diagram

---

6. Constantine and Lockwood, Ltd. "Rapid Abstract Prototyping" (1999) (www.foruse.com).

> ## ■ TIP
>
> You should name each sheet of paper or sticky note that corresponds to some type of user interface element so that it reflects its purpose. In addition, create an identifier such as S-101 so that you can reference the same user interface element in different diagrams without having to write out its full name.

Use Case Models

You construct a use case from a collection of scenarios relating to a particular form of interaction between a user and the system; for instance, saving a medical image into the database. You start by listing in a text file the main success scenario, or the steps that most users will take to produce the desired outcome during this type of interaction. The remaining scenarios are then documented as variations of this main success scenario, called *extensions.* Typically, a collection of use cases are put in a Use Case diagram as this can provide a useful summary of your system's requirements; see Figure 20-4.

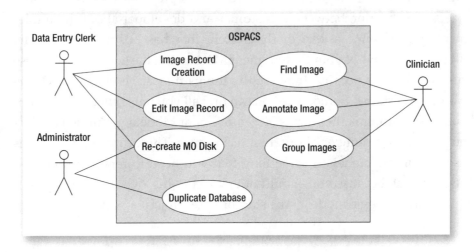

Figure 20-4: Requirements summarized in a Use Case diagram

> **▪ NOTE**
>
> Nontechnical people usually find Use Case diagrams easy to under-
> stand, and customers in particular tend to like them because they can
> express their requirements in terms of a specific type of person (actor)
> using the system to achieve a particular objective (use case).

The idea of modeling requirements with use cases was pioneered by
Ivar Jacobson[7] in 1986, but the approach can also be applied to Agile Projects; see books such as Alistair Cockburn's[8] *Crystal Clear*. However, there
is no direct equivalent between a use case and a customer story, so XP teams
tend to use them simply as a mechanism for simulating discussion between
developers and the customer about new stories. With that said, you might
also want to create a Use Case diagram such as Figure 20-4 in order to provide an overview of your system in terms of its main features and the people who will use them. You could then include such a diagram at the
beginning of user manuals and help files as an introduction to the system
for both technical and nontechnical people.

Customer Stories

We introduced the customer story cards in Chapter 3 as a way to summarize a conversation between a customer and developer about the implementation of some aspect of the system that has business value. The
ultimate objective of your Requirement Modeling is the generation of these
customer stories because they are the things that drive your project forward; see Section 8. Sometimes you can find all your customer stories without going through other forms of Requirement Modeling, but usually it is
helpful to try a number of different techniques. This searching for stories
using multiple models is something that you need to repeat throughout
your project, because you should not expect to discover them all by producing just a single model at the start of your project.

---

7. [OOSE] Jacobson, Ivar. *Object-Oriented Software Engineering* (Addison-Wesley, 1992).
8. [XC] Cockburn, Alistair. *Crystal Clear* (Addison-Wesley, 2005).

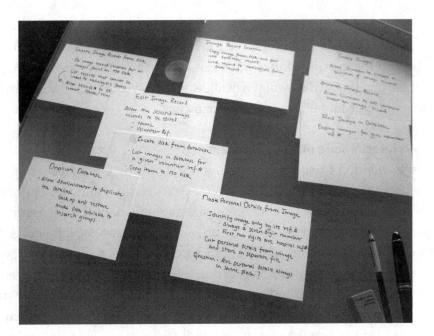

FIGURE 20-5: Customer stories on a desk

▪■ NOTE

Laying out customer stories on a desk, similar to the way you lay out
CRC cards, helps you spot inconsistencies and gaps in your functional requirements (see Figure 20-5). It also allows you to group
related requirements and thereby provide the beginning of the system architecture.

Architectural Models

Architectural models are often just extensions of the models developed for
exploring the requirements—for example, a glossary provides the vocabulary for the system's architecture, domain models identify the key classes,
and your user interface model and customer stories provide a high-level
view of what the system must do. This is appropriate because one of the
key purposes of architecture is to provide a link between requirement and

design. In this respect, you can consider an architectural model simply as a statement of the high-level design for your system. It explains the rationale behind the organization of your classes and suggests how you might put them together in a way that will allow them to be successfully deployed and used in the target business environment.

The Architect's Role on an Agile Team

Agile teams don't usually have a role for a full-time architect. Instead, developers are expected to make architectural decisions and are supported by people acting in the customer role who might manage the datacenter or otherwise have responsibility for IT architecture within the larger organization. Therefore, you must include such people in the sort of group modeling sessions described in Chapter 18. Typically, they will help the team develop initial architectural models during iteration zero, when the primary objective is to establish enough architecture for coding to commence. However, throughout the project, they will also be expected to help evolve the more important of these models so that the changes which inevitably arise during software development can be properly accommodated.

> **■ TIP**
>
> People with the title "architect" on their business card should have many years of experience backed up with detailed knowledge about the technology used by their organization. They must also demonstrate an ability to apply this expertise by spending a considerable amount of time writing code with their teams.

Creating a Skeletal Architectural Model

When describing simple design in Chapter 15, we explained that an Agile team tries to defer design decisions until the last possible moment because it is usually better to wait until you have more information about a problem before committing yourself to a particular solution. Applying the same logic, you should also avoid making too many architectural commitments at the start of the project, because at this time, you know the least about the system you are developing. Therefore, your initial architectural model should be as simple as possible, typically just enough for the purposes of deploying the code you are going to write in the first iteration.

> **■ NOTE**
>
> In most projects, we must accept that some architectural decisions will have already been made. For example, your client might want to use some existing IT infrastructure, so there is no point delaying your commitment to providing a compatible architecture.

Normally, an Agile team will be very conservative about the functionality it is committing to provide in the first iteration. In part, this is because nobody really knows how much work your team can achieve during an iteration, so it makes sense to accept only a few customer stories. However, the main reason for being cautious is the need for your team to be able to deploy a system that provides a thin vertical slice that goes from one end of the system to the other. This forms the basic skeleton which subsequent iterations will flesh out with the functionality described by appropriate customer stories.

The free-form diagram shown in Figure 20-6 is one way to model the architecture of such a skeletal system, because it can show the essential layers that must be implemented in the thin vertical slice. In this case, there is a user interface layer, a business layer, and a data layer. Therefore, by implementing a very small number of classes in each layer, you can deploy a system that goes from acquiring data from a user to storing it in the database. It doesn't matter that the only functionality you have provided is something such as storing a patient's name; what matters is that you've got your thin vertical slice. A free-form diagram is very suitable for exploring this sort of initial architecture because you can put into it all the information you need to start implementing the code and then deploy it later. When the system starts to become more complex, you might consider splitting this general diagram into the more specific ones we will describe in the next section.

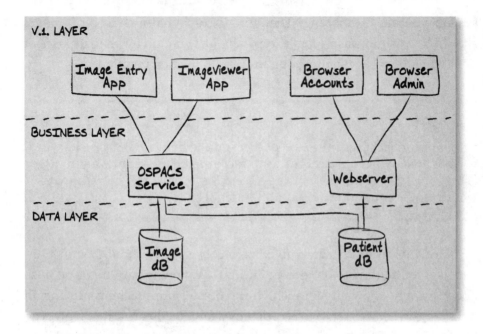

FIGURE 20-6: Free-form system layer diagram

■ NOTE

Teams creating Web services for deployment in distributed systems may create their skeletal architectural model using the Application Designer tool, which can also generate an initial set of Visual Studio Projects complete with the interfaces you need; see Chapter 30.

Evolving Your Architectural Model

Once you have created a thin vertical slice of the system, your initial architectural model will need to evolve during subsequent iterations to help your team construct a system that is robust in the face of change, a system that the team can scale and adapt to meet the anticipated needs of the business over a period of time. You should take care to establish a mechanism for handling changes which might impact the system in the future, even if it is a matter of just capturing such potential causes of change in some form of personal project notebook.

Although you should keep your focus on providing only enough architecture to support the stories which are currently being developed, it is inevitable that you will need to create additional models in order for you to explore specific aspects of the system under construction. Therefore, you should acquaint yourself with the following types of models so that you can follow the Agile Modeling practice of applying the right artifact:

- **Class Package diagrams**—Help you split up a large collection of classes by organizing them into appropriate assemblies for deployment as well as development; see Figure 12-6 in Chapter 12 and the associated text. Historically, package diagrams were used to model the relationships between Java classes so that they could be put into appropriate packages, but it is also appropriate to use them with .NET and other languages.

- **Component diagrams**—Define interfaces and ports as well as the associated underlying classes for modeling deployable units of code produced by third parties or other teams in your organization. You may also use these diagrams when a large project is split among a number of subteams to model the contracts among the various components they are developing. Essentially, these are diagrams similar to the one in Figure 19-1 in Chapter 19, except they have a rectangular boundary containing small squares for the interaction points (ports) between the classes in the component and those in its external environment.

- **Network diagrams**—Allow you to model the hardware that will support the various parts of your system. Typically, these diagrams show things such as the desktop PC upon which the application is installed, the server that hosts your database, and the firewalls that protect the connections between these machines; see Figure 20-7.

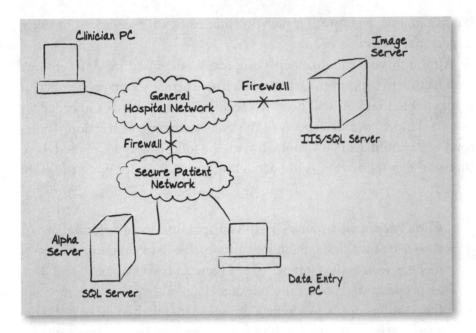

FIGURE 20-7: Free-form Network diagram

The evolution of the architectural models must take into account events going on outside the project as well as those happening within it. In particular, the project's architecture should attempt to converge with the architecture evolving in other projects so that the organization as a whole moves toward an environment in which the sharing of resources and reuse of code is an accepted part of the development culture. People who consider themselves "architects" should play an important part in ensuring that this sort of enterprise-level architecture is eventually achieved by helping the various project teams to reach some form of consensus about such matters.

> ■ NOTE
>
> Models produced by the various tools in Visual Studio Team System for Architects may also help your Architectural Modeling efforts, particularly in respect to Web service deployment; see Chapter 30.

System Metaphor

The development of a system metaphor was intended to address the need for an architectural model in Extreme Programming (XP). It was hoped that teams could easily create a suitable metaphor for their systems that would act like the picture on a jigsaw puzzle and therefore guide the placement of the pieces to form a coherent whole. However, the creation of an appropriate metaphor is not always easy, so the value of this modeling technique is often questioned.

It is true that a poor metaphor is usually worse than having no metaphor at all, but when you are able to discover some story or image that manages to capture the essence of what your system is all about, it is certainly worth pursing the idea of the XP system metaphor. Use of a shopping cart as a metaphor for a Web site payment system, for example, provides a very powerful vision of the system that everyone involved in the project can easily understand. It suggests that you need a mechanism which allows a shopper to move things from the shelves into the shopping cart, a means of adding up their cost, and then finally a way to pay for them. With the help of the shopping cart metaphor and this one short sentence, you have the basis of your initial architecture, so after creating a simple free-form diagram such as the one in Figure 20-6, you may have sufficient technical detail to start work on the initial implementation.

> **■ TIP**
>
> If you can't find a suitable metaphor, create a collage of apt pictures on the wall of your project room so that you can subsequently relate them to customer stories as well as to the technical parts of the system.

Implementation Models

Implementation models are normally created by two developers who are working together (pair programming) during a programming episode, and they serve to help the developers discover new tests or better understand the nature of their task. Often the models are simple free-form sketches similar to the one shown in Figure 18-2 in Chapter 18, and they take only a few minutes to create and will not be kept after the end of the programming episode. However, such sketches are typically based on more formal types of models, such as those we introduce in the following section.

> ■ **NOTE**
>
> Familiarity with different types of models allows you to apply the Agile Modeling practices of Create Several Models in Parallel and Iterate to Another Artifact, which often result in the generation of more useful information; see Chapter 18.

Structural Models

Static structural models help you understand the organization of the classes and data in your system. Here are the most common types of this class of model:

- **Class diagram**—Use this type of diagram to show the classes in your system, the relationships that exist between them, and (optionally) their important methods and properties. It is one of the essential types of diagrams that you need to be able to draw and understand. See Chapter 19 for a more detailed explanation.

- **Object diagram**—This sort of diagram often clarifies a Class diagram by showing how the classes might be used. It uses a notation similar to that used in a Class diagram, except class boxes name the specific object (e.g., WillStott:Person) and assign values to any relevant fields (e.g., city = Montreux).

- **Component diagram**—There is little difference between a Component diagram and a Class diagram, except that you represent a component as a class box stereotyped with either a symbol or the text "<<component>>", and the links between the boxes represent connections to their public interfaces. This sort of diagram is useful when you need to show the division of your system into components.

- **Package diagram**—Technically, a package diagram can take any Unified Modeling Language (UML) construct and group its elements together into a simple high-level representation. However, it is typically used to group classes into namespaces or libraries; see Figure 12-6 in Chapter 12. Therefore, it is often useful for identifying components for deployment.

- **Logical Data Model (LDM) diagram**—This sort of diagram can be drawn using the same notation as Class diagrams, but instead of helping you to model your classes it lets you explore your system's data structures so that you can identify the entity types and attributes required for your database.

> **■. NOTE**
>
> Although UML doesn't specifically support diagrams for modeling the data in your system, a wide range of templates for drawing database diagrams are provided with Visio for Enterprise Architects.

Dynamic Models

Dynamic models are concerned with representing your system in terms of the runtime behavior of its classes and their collaborations. You can express such models using the following types of drawings:

- **Sequence diagram**—Illustrates how a scenario is implemented in terms of the objects involved and the messages that pass between them. It is good for showing how classes are used, but poor at expressing program logic. We explain Sequence diagrams in Chapter 19, as they are one of the essential types of diagrams that you need to be able to draw and understand.

- **State (machine) diagram**—This type of diagram describes how something moves among different states as it is used. For example, an X-ray machine object starts in the ready state, moves to the busy state when an image is acquired, and then returns to the ready state.

Such diagrams allow you to model the way an object responds to multiple scenarios, but they are most often used for specialist purposes such as the development of real-time systems or for objects with complex state behavior.

- **Activity diagram**—This diagram looks like a traditional flowchart and serves a similar purpose in terms of displaying things such as business logic and workflows. Although by adding "fork" and "join" elements you can use these diagrams to model forms of parallel processing, we suggest you keep your Activity diagrams simple and use them just to confirm the business behavior your customer needs.

> **■ NOTE**
>
> You can discover more about these types of implementation models by reading the UML books listed in the Bibliography. However, you will probably learn much more by pairing with someone who has experience using them.

CONCLUSION

Although many traditional approaches to software modeling are decidedly un-Agile, this should not discourage you from adopting the sort of Agile Model-Driven Development (AMDD) we described in Chapter 18. Accordingly, we have introduced a wide range of Requirement, Architectural, and Implementation Modeling techniques so that you can apply AMDD during your group modeling sessions as well as when you are modeling in pairs.

You should now recognize that you can practice these techniques without having to learn extensive amounts of specialist modeling notation. Indeed, you should be able to produce all the models you need by combining the material in this chapter with the information about creating UML Class and Sequence diagrams provided in the preceding chapter. In an Agile Project, modeling allows you to achieve your goals better, faster, and cheaper, a theme we explore further in the next chapter, when we tell you how to apply patterns to your work.

■ 21
Modeling Solutions with Patterns

THIS CHAPTER EXPLAINS how various forms of patterns allow you to reuse ideas in different contexts so that you don't need to implement every solution from scratch. We start by introducing you to a common software engineering pattern called the Façade and show you how you might use it to gradually introduce test-driven development (TDD) into a project that has a lot of existing code without supporting programmer tests. We then look at the way reusable components and Domain-Specific Languages (DSLs) help people describe and assemble the sorts of things they want to build without having to write masses of low-level code.

What Is a Pattern?

Martin Fowler defines a pattern as "an idea that has been useful in one practical context and will probably be useful in others."[1] In this sense, a pattern can include almost anything capable of expressing an idea, ranging from a handy fragment of code to an abstract model of a software system. However, it is equally reasonable to define a software pattern in terms of a mechanism for cataloging proven designs to create some form of language that will help people describe and build their programs. Indeed, this is what software engineers usually mean when they talk about software patterns.

---

1. [AP] Fowler, Martin. *Analysis Patterns* (Addison-Wesley, 1997), p. xv.

Pattern Languages

One of the first papers about pattern languages[2] was presented by Kent Beck and Ward Cunningham at the Object-Oriented Programming, Systems, Languages, and Applications (OOPSLA) conference in 1987. This paper made a connection between the way software might be designed and the work of architect Christopher Alexander, who had created a language[3] for the building and planning of towns, houses, gardens, and rooms. Alexander expressed his language as a collection of patterns which provided an extensible vocabulary allowing people to describe in a cohesive and harmonious way the things they wanted to build. Beck and Cunningham realized that the identification of corresponding patterns in software programs might provide developers with similar benefits, so they wrote their paper to promote these ideas.

Pattern languages gained widespread recognition after the so-called "gang of four" (Gamma, Helm, Johnson, and Vlissides) published their seminal book, *Design Patterns*,[4] in 1994. This book provided software developers with a type of language for describing their designs and gave them guidance about their implementation. Therefore, instead of spending hours walking someone through the specifics of your code or model, you could explain the nature of your design in a few minutes just by discussing the patterns you had implemented. Furthermore, these patterns allowed you to work like an expert because each pattern explained the situations in which it should be used, its association with related patterns, the trade-offs of applying the pattern, and implementation details including sample code.

Armed with *Design Patterns*, you no longer had to implement every solution from the ground up because you could reuse the book's high-quality, proven designs in your project as you needed them. The success of *Design Patterns* spawned many other books which followed the same basic formula of providing a collection of patterns, each documented in some common format that would typically include the information shown in Table 21-1.

---

2. Beck, Kent, and Ward Cunningham. "Using Pattern Languages for Object-Oriented Programs" (OOPSLA, 1987).

3. Alexander, Christopher, et al. *A Pattern Language* (Oxford University Press, 1977).

4. [DP] Gamma, Erich, et al. *Design Patterns* (Addison-Wesley, 1995).

TABLE 21-1: Common Information Provided about a Design Pattern

Section	Content
Name	By naming patterns, you create a vocabulary for discussing design issues.
Description	The problems the pattern addresses and the solution it supplies. This often takes the form of a short statement of the pattern's intent, followed by a scenario describing its use in the real world. Alternative names for the pattern may also be listed.
Structure of solution	The classes that participate in the design pattern are represented by suitable Unified Modeling Language (UML) diagrams. The collaborations and responsibilities of these classes are also described.
Context	Explains the situations in which you can apply the pattern as well as the consequences of the pattern's use in terms of the trade-offs involved.
Implementation	Provides sample code to show how you might implement the pattern as well as describes pitfalls, hints, and language-specific issues of which you should be aware. Known uses of the pattern may also be detailed.
Related patterns	Other patterns which are closely associated with the pattern, along with suggestions for the circumstances in which you should use them.

Example: The Façade Pattern

In order to illustrate how a pattern works, here is an abbreviated form of the Façade pattern cataloged in *Design Patterns*. Later in the chapter, we will describe how you can apply this pattern to a legacy system so that you can gradually replace the old code with code produced by TDD.

- **Name**—Façade.
- **Description**—Allows access to a subsystem through a single unified interface rather than via multiple internal classes. For

example, to store an image of a patient, you might currently have to invoke methods in four different objects, but by introducing a Façade, you might be able to complete this operation by invoking just one method in the single object responsible for implementing the interface.

- **Structure of solution**—Figure 21-1 shows the classes that participate in the Façade. The client classes collaborate with the Façade class, which then collaborates with the various internal classes of the subsystem to provide the required behavior.

- **Context**—Use a Façade when you want to decouple a subsystem from its clients so that you can gradually replace it, or when you need to provide a simple interface to a complex subsystem. However, you should note that although a Façade makes a subsystem easier to use, it may also make the subsystem less general-purpose.

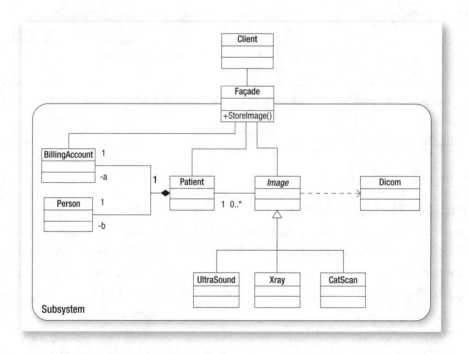

FIGURE 21-1: Structure of the Façade pattern

- **.NET implementation**—Move the classes in the subsystem into their own class library and then change their accessibility to "internal" so that you can provide your Façade class as the only public interface to the library. The following code illustrates the Façade interface method for storing an image of a patient:

```
public class ImageHandler
{
    public void StoreImage( string PatientID, Image image)
    {
        Patient patient = new Patient(PatientID);
        image.Store(patient, DateTime.now);
        patient.DebitAccount(image.Cost);
    }
}
```

- **Related patterns**—The Façade pattern is sometimes confused with the Adapter pattern. You should use the Adapter pattern when you want to adapt an existing interface on a single object, and the Façade pattern when you want to provide a new interface for an entire subsystem.

■ TIP

Don't be satisfied with just reading about a pattern; apply it, explore its use in different situations, and discuss your experiences with other people. Extend your knowledge by collecting notes about each pattern you encounter, and create your own catalog for any new patterns you find.

Sources of Patterns

You can find patterns presented in a format similar to the one used in *Design Patterns* in many books covering a wide range of software development issues, including the following:

- **Analysis**—Captures the knowledge of experts from the business. For example, Martin Fowler's book,[5] *Analysis Patterns*, contains patterns that represent common constructions in business modeling,

---

5. [AP] Fowler, Martin. *Analysis Patterns* (Addison-Wesley, 1997).

such as conversion ratios and accounting systems, as well as models that relate to the construction of complete systems.

- **Design**—Catalogs of reusable object-oriented software concepts produced by experienced developers. Most of the books in this field tend to provide additional insight into *Design Patterns,* and in this respect, *Design Patterns Explained*[6] does a particularly fine job.

- **Refactoring**—A list of procedures for removing duplication from your code, simplifying it, or making the code easier to understand and maintain. Such patterns help you to perform refactoring like an expert, and you can find them in books such as Martin Fowler's *Refactoring*[7] and Joshua Kerievsky's *Refactoring to Patterns.*[8]

In addition to patterns presented in a formal way, there are various other representations for things that have proven to be useful in one context but may be applied in others:

- **Code fragments**—Smaller, language-specific patterns are often called *idioms* because collectively they lack the connections necessary to form a true pattern language. However, they remain an important source of information which you can find in books such as Allen Jones's *C# Programmer's Cookbook,* as well as in the .NET electronic documentation. You should also investigate the "Code Snippet" facilities of Visual Studio 2005, as they provide a convenient way to both manage small, standard blocks of code and add them to your programs.

- **Frameworks**—A collection of classes that provide a general structure for your programs. For example, the C++ Microsoft Framework Classes (MFCs) implemented a number of common design patterns, most notably the Observer pattern, which provides a model-view-controller for user interfaces.

---

6. [DPE] Shalloway, Alan, and James Trott. *Design Patterns Explained* (Addison-Wesley, 2002).
7. [RIDEC] Fowler, Martin. *Refactoring* (Addison-Wesley, 2000).
8. [R2P] Kerievsky, Joshua. *Refactoring to Patterns* (Addison-Wesley, 2005).

- **Template projects**—Visual Studio 2005 allows you to create a template project or an item template from the content of an existing project (File | Export Template). Project templates will appear in your New Project dialog box, whereas Item templates appear in the Add New Item dialog box (Project | Add New Item).

- **Reusable application blocks**—These are collections of code which blur the distinction between a pattern and a component. They are part of the Enterprise Library for .NET v2.0 produced by the people in Microsoft's Patterns and Practices group.[9] The current implementations focus on providing nonfunctional requirements such as logging, exception handling, and security, as well as architectural mechanisms such as data access and caching.

■ NOTE

Our intention here is just to give you some idea of the range of patterns that are available. A list of additional sources for patterns which might prove useful to you is given on the book's Web site.

Using Patterns in an Agile Project

Patterns provide you with a powerful way to exploit the experience gained by other people, and this clearly supports the key Agile objective of providing good value to your customer. However, you should be aware that patterns don't always lead to better solutions, because sometimes developers introduce them where they aren't needed and therefore produce excessively complex solutions to what are essentially simple problems, a condition known as being **pattern-happy.** More than anything else, the need to address this issue characterizes the way patterns are used in an Agile project.

The Agile antidote for being pattern-happy is to introduce design-related patterns during refactoring, and to do so only when you can justify them in terms of making the program simpler or easier to understand.

---

9. Microsoft: Patterns and Practices Initiative (http://msdn.microsoft.com/practices).

Therefore, you might implement a Façade pattern to simplify access to a subsystem after it has been built, but not to address upfront concerns that it may prove difficult to use. This approach to pattern usage is called *apply patterns gently* and promotes the value of simplicity as well as the practice of Incremental Design, as explained in Chapter 18, in the section Agile Modeling in Use.

Example: Evolving Legacy Code with the Façade Pattern

Background: You want to introduce test-driven development into a project with lots of existing code that lacks the sort of programmer (unit) tests described in Section 5. In the long term, you will rewrite all this legacy code so that it is test-driven, but in the short term, you need to continue delivering valuable software to the business.

The use of design type patterns in an Agile project starts with the realization that you have a problem with your code, so the time to consider such issues is during refactoring. Therefore, let's suppose you have just passed a test for part of the new class you're writing to implement an element of some initial customer story. Consequently, you are now reviewing with your programming partner the method which was developed to pass the test. Essentially, this method passes much of the actual work to other classes in the legacy code, and therefore makes your new class act like a client of the existing system. However, it is apparent that anyone working with this class in the future will need to have extensive knowledge of the legacy code. This means that the new members of your team must spend a lot of time acquiring knowledge that will become redundant once the legacy code has been rewritten. For this reason, you consider refactoring the code to make it simpler and easier for them to maintain.

> ■ **NOTE**
>
> You often can identify problems in your code by looking for certain telltale signs of trouble known as **bad smells in code,** a term originally used by Kent Beck and Martin Fowler in the book *Refactoring*[10] to describe their pattern catalog of such issues.

---

10. [RIDEC] Fowler, Martin. *Refactoring* (Addison-Wesley, 2000).

It appears unlikely that the problem you are facing is unique to your project, so you consult the collection of design patterns in the team's library in the hope that you will find a good solution. In the structural section of *Design Patterns*, you find the Façade pattern, which seems appropriate, so you look for further information about it from other sources. After a bit of research, you discover that implementing a Façade will not only provide a simple interface for your new class to use, but also allow you to achieve your aim of slowly evolving the system so that the legacy code is rewritten in a test-driven way. Joshua Kerievsky[11] identifies the process in terms of a series of steps which you adapt for your purposes:

1. **Divide the legacy system into subsystems**—This is easy to achieve if the classes are loosely coupled and cohesive, but unfortunately, your legacy code is poorly structured, so you will have to move it into one large class library with its own Visual Studio project.

2. **Write Façades for one of the subsystems**—You identify the collection of legacy classes that might form a subsystem for the client class you are refactoring. You will need to create a class to act as a Façade for this subsystem, as described earlier in the chapter. This Façade class will be developed in a test-driven way and put into a new class library, again with a separate Visual Studio project.

3. **Refactor the client class to use the Façade**—You change the implementation of your method so that it uses the Façade class rather than the classes in the legacy code. Your client class is already in a separate class library and has associated programmer tests, so you will be able to rerun them to confirm that all these changes haven't altered the existing behavior.

4. **Rewrite the subsystem used by your client class**—You will reimplement the subsystem in the class library containing the Façade class using TDD. Again, rerunning your tests will give you confidence that your changes haven't broken anything.

---

11. [R2P] Kerievsky, Joshua. *Refactoring to Patterns* (Addison-Wesley, 2005).

5. **Refactor the Façade to use the new subsystem**—The implementation of the Façade will be changed so that it no longer uses the large class library containing the legacy code. The tests for the client class will confirm that the new subsystem behaves in the same way as the legacy code.

6. **Repeat the process**—Implement the next new subsystem and Façade so that the system will gradually evolve until you are able to discard the old legacy code library after having replaced it with new classes developed using TDD.

Potentially you have identified a huge refactoring that will involve the whole team and probably take several months to complete. However, because you must complete your programming episode within a couple of hours, you take just a small first step and create a simple Façade class which you can use to refactor the method whose test you have just passed. This gives you an example of the sort of refactoring the team needs to undertake and therefore helps make the case for the team agreeing to the much larger refactoring effort at its next morning meeting.

> **■ NOTE**
>
> You should refactor in a series of small, safe steps. You will find that the patterns identified in Martin Fowler's book, *Refactoring*, will help you break down big refactoring into a series of such moves.

Implementation of Patterns and Models

According to the definition we gave at the beginning of this chapter, you can consider many things to be patterns, from an abstract idea described in a book to a very specific concept expressed in executable code. Indeed, we have stretched the definition further than some people might like by describing Microsoft's reusable application blocks as forms of patterns.

Design Patterns versus Components

The point about a software pattern is that there has to be some form of practical application, and there is always a trade-off between the ease of such implementation and its generality. For example, the .NET calendar control provides us with a pattern for selecting dates which we can reuse simply by dropping the calendar control onto a form and declaring its properties. However, the calendar control is a pattern that you can use only in .NET programs. Conversely, you can implement the Façade pattern in almost any sort of object-oriented program, but you need to hand-code it each time you use it. We are now going to blur the boundaries between patterns, components, and language so that we can look at various ways in which we can leverage the expertise of others to provide real solutions to our problems.

Reusable Components

The early promise of object-oriented development to deliver significant code reuse within organizations has largely failed to materialize. People on the same team may reuse a class through mechanisms such as aggregation or inheritance, but in practical terms, for the class to be more widely reused it must be formally released in some form of library or component; this is known as the Reuse-Release Equivalence Principle.[12] Unfortunately, the challenge of a team making its libraries available to the wider organization has proven to be significant, and the sort of vibrant market of component producers and consumers predicted by advocates of component-based development[13] has so far failed to materialize. Therefore, the sorts of components you are most likely to use in your programs today are produced by third parties and comprise things such as grid controls, which can be sold into large horizontal markets.

12. [ASD] Martin, Robert. *Agile Software Development* (Prentice Hall, 2003).
13. Allen, Paul, and Stuart Frost. *Component-Based Development for Enterprise Systems* (SIGS Books, 1998).

> ■ **NOTE**
>
> Selling in a horizontal market means you produce a general product (such as a word processor) that appeals to different classes of customers, whereas selling in a vertical market requires you to produce a highly customized product for a certain class of customer.

The challenge you face when attempting to make your team's libraries available as resources within your organization is to make their use as easy as placing something such as a calendar control on a Windows Form, but also providing the high level of sophistication typically required for reuse in a vertical market application. For example, you could hardly configure a component that calculates the yields of exotic financial instruments in the same way that you might use a drop-down list to set the date format of a calendar control. To address these sorts of challenges there is currently considerable interest in the use of models and languages to help construct systems from such specialized components.

Emergence of Domain-Specific Languages

Pattern languages are concerned with helping people describe and assemble the sorts of things they want to build (or rebuild). At present, most software pattern languages are aimed at developers and concentrate on aspects of systems that are not specific to a particular market segment. For example, you might find a Façade design pattern in a capital markets trading system, but you also might find it in a healthcare product such as OSPACS. However, people are now starting to consider whether pattern languages might also be created which would allow domain experts (customers) to describe and assemble systems for a specific vertical market. One way in which this ambition might be achieved is through the development of Domain-Specific Languages (DSLs).

Use of DSL in Horizontal Market Applications

At present, it is more common to find DSLs in software tools marketed horizontally. For example:

- **Structured Query Language (SQL)**—Allows data experts to query a database using terms that are familiar to them, such as *tables, joins,* and *views*
- **HyperText Markup Language (HTML)**—Permits graphic design experts to render information on Web pages using terms such as *bold, font,* and *heading*
- **MATLAB**—Enables engineers and mathematicians to produce programs expressed in the symbolic language of algebra and differential calculus

Historically, the huge amount of effort required to create a DSL has restricted their appeal to large horizontal markets where the development costs can be more easily recouped from high sales volumes. However, the availability of tools which can be described as being forms of a "language workbench" promise to bring DSLs into more specific vertical markets as well.

> **■ NOTE**
>
> You might create a DSL to allow someone to define the rules for trading certain types of exotic financial instruments. Such a language would appeal only to people working in a small vertical segment of the financial services marketplace.

The Language Workbench

The commercial viability of creating and using a DSL is about to be changed by the advent of a new class of tools which Martin Fowler calls *language workbenches.*[14] It is predicted that these tools will form part of an Integrated Development Environment (IDE) and facilitate the creation and use of DSLs in the production of your software systems. However, in order to realize this aim, you must move away from developing software by editing text files containing computer language statements and start working with projections created from the abstract form of your program generated by the compiler.

> **■. NOTE**
>
> The Visual Studio Team System (VSTS) Class Designer described in Chapter 19 shows how mainstream IDEs are starting to provide language workbench facilities. It allows you to manipulate the classes in your program using an editor that provides a projection of them in a Class diagram.

A language workbench promises to provide separate representations of a program based on its transitory abstract form created by the compiler. Therefore, when you open a program in an editor, your language workbench will first read the storage representation previously stored on your hard disk and then use a suitable compiler to regenerate the abstract form before representing it as an appropriate projection in your editor's window. You will then work with this projection and the compiler to make your changes to the underlying abstract form before producing from it the final executable representation (IL code) for use by your customer.

On the surface, this might not be much different from loading a C# source file into a text editor, adding a new property to a class, and then building a new executable. However, you should realize that beneath the covers, the editor isn't rendering the contents of a source file, but instead is giving you a projection of your program as a set of C# language statements in a window. You can, of course, have multiple projections of your program, so you might open one type of editor to work on its classes rep-

---

14. Fowler, Martin. "Language Workbenches: The Killer-App for Domain Specific Languages?" (www.martinfowler.com).

resented in a Class diagram, and open another one when you want them shown as a treeview.

The great advantage of a language workbench is that it allows you to work at the level of the abstract program rather than at the level of the instructions used in its construction. This makes it much easier to work in an integrated fashion with a collection of different languages, and hopefully will encourage the exploitation of DSL in various vertical markets.

> **■ NOTE**
>
> Section 9 explores the tools provided with Visual Studio Team Edition for Architects that were produced using Microsoft's DSL tools[15] in order to help operations staff deploy your systems into their datacenters.

Software Factories

The term *software factory* is historically associated with attempts to transform software development into a sort of production-line activity. However, the book *Software Factories*[16] applies the term in a way which is more compatible with the values and practices of an Agile team. This more enlightened view of a software factory promotes the idea of creating software product lines from reusable components whose properties and behavior are set by a DSL to accommodate variants from some standard system or application. To many companies the possibility of creating such a software factory is appealing for the following reasons:

- **DSLs**—Models and patterns can be mined as well as created so that domain knowledge can be represented in the DSL and then directly applied to the solutions being developed.
- **Reusable components and frameworks**—These greatly reduce the amount of new code that needs to be written in order to deliver a

---

15. Microsoft's DSL tools are supplied as a technology preview with the Visual Studio 2005 Software Development Kit (SDK).

16. Greenfield, Jack, et al. *Software Factories* (Wiley Publishing, 2004).

solution. In many cases, the variations between different implementations can be expressed entirely in the DSL.

- **Automation**—Many of the repetitive tasks needed to produce the variations in the company's products can be handled by an appropriate DSL and associated tools. This particularly applies to issues such as deployment, testing, and documentation.
- **Software product lines**—By developing core assets such as DSLs, reusable components, and automation, a company can create integrated environments that support the rapid development and maintenance of variants of standard products to meet the specific needs of a particular market segment.
- **Agility**—Working with DSLs promotes closer communication with the business, rapid development gives earlier feedback, the creation of software product lines gives people the safety they need to be courageous, and thinking in terms of components makes for simplicity in design.

This brief introduction should give you sufficient information to decide whether Microsoft's DSL tools and software factory approach are worth investigating further. However, remember that not everyone needs to develop and maintain variants of a standard product, so it might not be appropriate for your organization to set up a software factory.

CONCLUSION

A pattern language allows you to talk about design by creating a vocabulary describing a connected set of predefined solutions whose properties and relationships provide the syntax which controls the way you can bring them together. Clearly such languages can capture expert knowledge, but currently most of what we record is development knowledge, not domain knowledge.

It is hoped that new technologies such as language workbenches will make it much easier to create DSLs that can express these domain patterns. This would allow domain experts to become much more closely involved in the development of vertical market applications, leading to a fundamental shift in the nature of software development for some teams. They would no longer be concerned with supplying the solution, but rather would build the tools needed to support a DSL that would empower businesspeople to provide the software solutions to their own problems.

> **■ NOTE**
>
> Developers already have access to the sophisticated tools and languages they need to build highly advanced systems. Therefore, future advances in technology will probably focus on helping the business play a more direct part in providing the solutions to their problems.

Review of Section 6
Explore by Modeling

THE OSPACS TEAM whose road map to Agility we presented in the Introduction now has a much better appreciation of how exploring problems with models will allow team members to achieve their aim of delivering software with a consistent level of quality. They undertook the following actions to improve the way modeling was done on the team:

- **Model drawing**—Every person on the team was expected to learn the basic notation for drawing Class diagrams and Sequence diagrams so that they could communicate better. They practiced producing these sorts of diagrams both freehand and with the use of tools such as Class Designer and Visio.

- **Free-form drawing**—The team accepted that every drawing didn't need to conform to Unified Modeling Language (UML) standards, enabling people to freely express their thoughts without being inhibited by notation.

- **Group modeling**—The team bought a large whiteboard on a frame with wheels so that they could perform group modeling during their regular technical meetings. They also bought a digital camera so that they could make a record of any drawing and then store it on the Project Web site.

- **Modeling in pairs**—Pads of paper and pencils were put next to people's computers to encourage them to draw during pair programming sessions.

- **Brown-bag pattern sessions**—Once a week the developers on the team decided to hold a technical session in a meeting room during their lunch hour, with sandwiches supplied in brown bags. During this time, they planned to address one type of design pattern so that week by week, they would collectively discover more about patterns by looking at examples of their use and engaging in discussions about them.

The Team's Impressions

The team was surprised that it could do so much modeling without using any electronic tools. However, it was also clear to team members that future generations of the Visual Studio Team System (VSTS) modeling tools would fundamentally change the way people approached software development.

Developer: Tom

"Walking through a design is no substitute for observing working software. Models by their nature are not complete representations of the real world, and as it is often remarked, you can't crash a flow diagram!"

"Models allow people to explore ideas without incurring the cost of implementing the product in final form. It makes sense to spend a lot of time doing this when the product is a spaceship, but not necessarily when it's a computer program."

"People are entitled to have their own values, and it seems wrong to insist that one value is compatible with Extreme Programming (XP) or Agile Modeling while another is not. What is important is that the interplay of values at work on a team supports team members' activities and makes them successful."

Developer: Luke

"I now realize that simple is best when it comes to UML diagrams. There's no need to worry about most of the notation because you only really need to know about basic forms of Class and Sequence diagrams."

"The five values, thirteen principles, and eighteen practices of Agile Modeling are a lot to digest, so I've pinned a list of them to the kitchen wall to remind us."

Developer: Sarah

"I'm very self-conscious about drawing UML diagrams in public because I don't really know the notation. This tends to make me avoid modeling altogether."

"I'm not really a visual thinker. I much prefer expressing things in text, tables, and lists, which I guess explains why I like coding so much."

"When you're designing software, it often takes less time to model the idea in code than it does to create a diagram."

Customer: Sally

"I always felt so stupid when developers showed me UML diagrams because they were usually full of little boxes, lines, and funny symbols, which frankly I didn't understand. However, I'm actually looking forward to using them now that Tom has taken the time to explain to me the simple ones I need to know about."

Developer: Peter

"Modeling tools produce really neat diagrams which you can put in your documentation, but when it comes to group modeling, give me a whiteboard every time."

"A diagram showing a class hierarchy might help you understand the structure of a program, but without being involved in the production of the model, you wouldn't necessarily know why the classes are arranged in this way."

"The sections of XML config files relating to Microsoft's reusable application blocks are a bit like a Domain-Specific Language because they allow deployment experts to program the way your program handles exceptions, security, logging, and so forth."

Agile Values

The OSPACS team thought that Agile Modeling fit very well with the values and practices of Extreme Programming (XP), so by adopting this approach they hoped it would help them develop their values in the following ways.

Communication

Modeling facilitates discussion; models don't. The practices of Modeling with Others and Producing Multiple Models help people see a problem from different perspectives; the practices of Storing Information in One Place and Displaying Models Publicly encourage the team to develop the design together.

Feedback

Proving it with code means the team validates its designs almost immediately with code and tests. The team can then go back and improve the design using the knowledge gained during implementation.

Courage

Implementing the design incrementally results in people taking more risks because they don't have to wait months to discover whether their ideas worked out.

Simplicity

Agile Modeling encourages the team to travel light, depict models simply, and discard temporary models, which stops people from becoming bogged down with superfluous information. People are constantly reminded to look for the simplest and most elegant solution by using only the simplest tools and providing just enough design to solve today's problems without making tomorrow's any worse.

Respect

Active stakeholder involvement helps the customer appreciate the skill and dedication of the developers; likewise, the developers see the contribution their customer is making to the product. The team also became more aware that due to group modeling, great suggestions came from the most unlikely of people, and this helped people realize that everyone on the team had a contribution to make.

◼ Section 7
Implement Customer Testing

T HIS SECTION EXPLAINS how customer testing can provide the details you need to fully understand the requirements of the software you're developing, and can supply the information necessary to improve both the product and your process throughout the project. We will take you step by step through the process of setting up a Visual Studio Team System (VSTS) generic test so that you can use a tool often used in Agile projects for customer testing: Framework for Integrated Test (FIT). We explain how various FIT fixtures allow your customer to test the part of the system he can see (user interface), the information he wants to store (data layer), and the

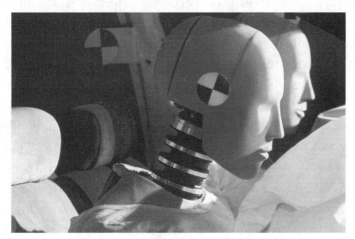

Photograph by Wayne Eastep (Copyright Getty Images).

Customer tests confirm that a feature works properly so that there are no nasty accidents after the software goes into production.

business rules he requires implementing (business layer). By the end of this section, you should be able to implement customer testing in your own project and understand how the team can use the information it generates to create better software.

Story from the Trenches

The problem with waiting for public transportation in a city is that you never know when it's going to arrive. Heavy traffic, diversions, and the occasional vehicle breakdown conspire to make bus timetables inherently unreliable. To tackle this problem many city authorities have invested in technology that provides a digital sign at each bus stop announcing when the next bus is due. A few years ago I worked for a small start-up company that was supplying this sort of public transportation information system.

I joined the company when it was about to roll out a system to its first client, the transit authority of a medium-size city. On my first day, I spent a few hours reading some thick documents that specified the client requirements and described the tests that needed to be satisfied during the commissioning of the system—the user acceptance tests (UATs). Unfortunately, these documents were full of vague language and glossed over the detail, so they didn't really help me understand what the system was intended to do. When I talked to my manager about them, he smiled and told me that the technical content had largely been removed during months of negotiation with lawyers. However, he seemed confident that the client would accept whatever we delivered because they had little knowledge of the technology and needed the system installed in a hurry.

Over the next week, I spent most of my time with David, a senior developer, watching him test the system. He favored a structural approach to testing, involving the use of debuggers, unit tests, and trace logs to check that the data was correctly moving around the system and didn't crash the program. This type of testing relied on an understanding of the way the software was constructed to validate its operation; for example, we could confirm things such as "method 'X' with parameters '1, 2, 3' returns value

'A'." Working in this way, we checked the individual parts of the code, but it was hard to test the system as a whole because analyzing the detailed information our structural tests generated took too long when more than a few methods were involved. Therefore, we produced little evidence that the system actually satisfied its main requirement: predicting bus arrival times at each sign according to the current vehicle locations. Nevertheless, by the end of the week, our manager was satisfied that we had done enough to justify releasing the system, so the following week we arrived at the client's site to start the UAT.

The manager's assumption that our client knew very little about software proved to be correct. However, their expert understanding of the way buses were operated allowed them to produce an impressive collection of tests for the messages which had to be displayed at each sign as the buses traveled along their routes—the detail that was missing from the UAT document. They viewed the system as just a black box to which particular outputs were expected in response to certain inputs, and therefore avoided all the complexity that was inherent in our structural testing. This functional approach to testing allowed our client to exercise the system in ways that we had simply not considered during structural testing. When the system started to fail the client's functional tests, it became obvious that we really hadn't grasped how their business worked; the system just didn't do what they wanted.

Over the next few months, we worked closely with our client to fix the problems their functional tests identified. In the process, we learned a lot about the way a bus company operates, and this resulted in some big changes to our system and the way we tested it. However, eventually we were able to pass the UAT, so the company got paid for the system, though not with the amount of profit everyone had anticipated.

The point about this story is that relying solely on structural tests and excluding the business from your testing until the final stages of a project is very risky. Therefore, in the next three chapters, we consider how you should drive the delivery of useful software from the start with functional tests written by the "customer."

■ 22
Involving Customers in Testing

A<small>FTER READING THIS CHAPTER</small>, you will be aware of the benefits that arise from involving customers in the functional testing of your software. You will also have installed and used Framework for Integrated Test (FIT), an open source product that allows customers to specify their software by writing acceptance tests in a Word (HTML) document for execution against the code being developed. The chapter concludes by describing storytest-driven development (STDD), which is a way to let customers drive a software project by writing tests that define the features of each story they want implemented.

Agile Customer Testing

It is a developer's job to decide how the software will work, and it is the customer's job to know what the software must do. The main objective of unit testing is to find defects in the code by checking how it works using structural tests; see Section 5. The main aim of customer testing is to confirm that the software meets the needs of the business by checking what it does using functional tests, called customer acceptance tests (or just customer tests).

> ### ■ NOTE
>
> Functional tests treat the system like a sealed (black) box[1] which generates certain outputs in response to particular inputs. Structural tests, on the other hand, require you to look inside the sealed box so that you can test some aspect of the way the code inside works.

Testing throughout the Project

In most traditional projects, functional testing happens only at the end of the project. Conversely, in Agile projects, this sort of testing is performed throughout the project, which has a number of advantages:

- It provides a reliable measure of progress because the passing of customer tests is an unambiguous way of validating that the project is continuing to deliver functionality valued by the business.

- Developers can learn from the problems revealed by early customer testing and apply this knowledge in subsequent iterations. This encourages high-quality work and helps keep the bug count low throughout the project.

- It confirms that changes to the code do not break existing functionality. This encourages developers to be bold when refactoring or implementing new requirements because there is an additional layer of testing to catch bugs.

- It immediately tells developers when they have satisfied a requirement. The story is deemed complete when it passes all its customer tests, and this helps keep the code simple by avoiding the accumulation of unnecessary features.

- It encourages customers to explore the requirement by writing and running tests. This ensures frequent feedback and communication between developers and customers, which is particularly important for projects that start with unknown or vague requirements.

---

1. [BBT] Beizer, Boris. *Black-Box Testing* (John Wiley & Sons, 1995).

However, performing customer testing throughout the project means you must automate the tests so that you can run them at little cost. It also means you must make it easy for customers to write these tests using the business (domain) language they understand and tools that are familiar to them, such as Word and Excel. Fortunately, an open source tool, called FIT, helps teams meets these needs.

FIT: Framework for Integrated Test

Framework for Integrated Test (FIT) is an open source tool developed by Ward Cunningham, inventor of the wiki and one of the founders of the Agile movement. It is often used for customer testing in Agile projects because it provides a simple, yet effective, tool that customers can learn quickly. You can obtain a copy of FIT for .NET development from Ward's Web site,[2] though Java, Python, Perl, Smalltalk, C++, and Ruby are also supported.

Overview

FIT allows customers to write their tests in the form of HTML tables in a text document file. This file forms the input for the FIT test harness program which parses the document and matches each table to a particular type of object called a *test fixture*. FIT then invokes methods in this test fixture object according to the information found in the table. For example, in Figure 22-1, the fixture object is an instance of the `osImageManagerFIT.DICOMFileValidation` class and the first four columns of the table form the input values for its `IsValid()` method, whose expected return value is shown in the last column.

> **■ NOTE**
>
> The output file has exactly the same form as the input document, except that the result column is rendered in a color that indicates whether the test passed (green), failed (red), or was not processed (gray), or whether the fixture was not found (yellow).

---

2. Ward Cunningham's FIT Web site (http://fit.c2.com).

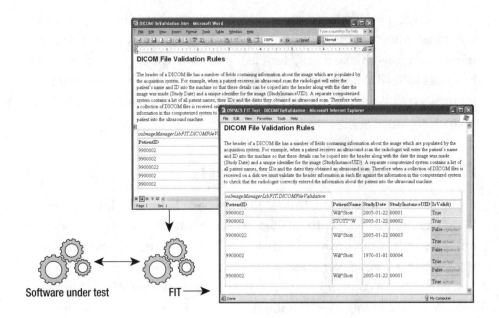

FIGURE 22-1: FIT executing a test contained in a Word document

Essentially, FIT allows your customer to write a functional specification in Word containing tests that can be executed directly from the document. Information that is not in a table is ignored and the results are shown in the same form as the original document, so there is no excuse for your customer not understanding them. Therefore, to write and execute a functional test your customer just needs to create a document such as the one shown in Figure 22-1 (or Table 23-1 in Chapter 23), save it to an agreed-upon location on your network, start a batch file to run the test, and then open the results file in Internet Explorer.

In order to give your customer this sort of ownership of his tests, the team's developers need to provide some supporting infrastructure, but as you will see, it is very easy to install and run FIT in a development or test environment. The only significant work is related to developing the fixtures that provide the link between FIT and the software under test, a topic we cover in Chapter 23. However, to give you an idea of what this involves, the code for the fixture used in Figure 22-1 is shown in Listing 22-1.

LISTING 22-1: Column Fixture for Supporting the Tests Shown in Figure 22-1

```
using System;
using fit;         //The FIT library (ColumnFixture)
using osImageManagerLib;      //Your software under test
namespace osImageManagerFIT    //Your FIT Fixture namespace
{
    public class DICOMFileValidation : ColumnFixture
    {
        public string PatientID;
        public string PatientName;
        public string StudyDate;
        public string StudyInstanceUID;

        public bool IsValid()
        {
                //TODO: call validation method in software under test
            return true;
        }
    }
}
```

> **■ NOTE**
>
> FIT's test fixtures execute directly against classes in your class library, so it could be argued that they are a form of structural (unit) testing. However, from the perspective of the person writing the tests (customer), they are undoubtedly viewed as functional tests.

You will note that the fixture's class name appears in the top left of the table in the customer's test document; see Figure 22-1. The public instance variables correspond to its first four column headings and the IsValid() method corresponds to the heading of the final result column. Typically, the language of the business domain is used to name the fixture, its methods, and public instance variables, so customers do not have to type arcane names into their test documents.

Installing and Running FIT

In the next two chapters, we describe how to set up and execute customer tests using FIT in the Visual Studio Team System (VSTS) environment.

However, we suggest that you start by installing and running FIT in a simple Visual Studio Solution so that you can gain some experience before attempting to use it in a larger project.

■ NOTE

The version of FIT used for the exercises in this book is contained in the fit-dotnet-1.1.zip file, which you can find on the DownloadNow page of http://fit.c2.com.

EXERCISE 22-1: Installing FIT on a Developer PC

In this exercise, you will simply install FIT on your PC and confirm that it is operating correctly by running one of the tests supplied as part of the package.

1. Log on as Luke to a DeveloperPC and download the FIT ZIP file for .NET, from http://fit.c2.com/wiki.cgi?DownloadNow. Extract the files into a suitable installation directory, such as c:\FIT; see the warning at the end of this exercise.

2. Open a command prompt, navigate to your FIT installation directory, and check that FIT is working by typing the following in order to run the supplied arithmetic.html tests:

```
runfile source/examples/arithmetic.html MyResults.html .
```

If you remember to type the final dot, RunFile should respond by giving you the number of tests it executed: right (37), wrong (10), ignored (0), and exceptions (2). You should then open MyResults.html and check the result of each test for yourself.

3. Log off.

> **■ WARNING**
>
> Windows XP blocks files that have arrived on your computer from e-mail or downloads as a security measure. To unblock an executable file in the FIT directory, select the file, open its Properties dialog box, and then click "unblock" on the General page.

RunFile Command-Line Parameters

RunFile is a test runner that will execute FIT tests according to the following input parameters supplied to it:

- **Input-file**—Path and name of the HTML input file (save Word docs as HTML).
- **Output-file**—Path and name of the result file.
- **Fixture-dir**—Path of the directory containing your fixture DLL. It serves a similar purpose to Java's CLASSPATH and allows you to specify multiple directories by separating their pathnames with semicolons.

> **■ NOTE**
>
> Most of the FIT files you need you can find in the top-level directory of the FIT installation directory, but the product's source code is provided in case you need to rebuild the libraries or the test runners.

EXERCISE 22-2: Setting Up FIT for Customer Testing on a Developer PC

After completing the following exercise, you will have created a bit of software to test and a simple Column fixture to link it to your test document. You will also have set up all the files you need to run this test on a development PC.

1. Log on to the DeveloperPC as Luke (OSPACS Contributor), start Visual Studio, and then connect to the OSPACS Team Project, as described in Exercise 5-7 in Chapter 5; see Appendix A for a specification of this PC and details of Luke's security groups.

2. Update Luke's workspace with the latest version of the files in the repository and open the osImageManager Visual Studio Solution, as described in steps 3 and 5 of Exercise 9-1, in Chapter 9. This Solution contains the osImageManagerLib Visual Studio Project you created in Exercise 8-4 in Chapter 8.

3. Delete any default classes in osImageManagerLib and add a new class, called `DICOMFile`, by selecting osImageManagerLib in Solution Explorer and choosing Add Class from the Visual Studio Project menu (Project | Add Class).

4. Create another Visual Studio Project for a C# class library, named osImageManagerFIT, and add this project to your osImageManager Solution in the same way you created and added osImageManagerLib in Exercise 8-4 in Chapter 8.

5. Delete any default classes that might exist in osImageManagerFIT and add the new class, `DICOMFileValidation`, in the same way you did in step 3. Type the code in Listing 22-1 into this new class.

6. Create a batch file to run your FIT tests by taking the following steps:

   a. Create a new text file (File | New | File), which will then open in your editor.

   b. Type the following two commands into the file, not forgetting the final dot!

   ```
   del fit.dll
   runfile ValidateImageFile.htm VIFResults.htm c:\FIT;.
   ```

   c. Save your file as RunFIT.cmd in the same directory as your `DICOMFileValidation` class.

7. Add RunFIT.cmd to your osImageManagerFIT Visual Studio Project and set its properties so that it will be copied to the output directory:

   a. Select osImageManagerFIT in your Solution Explorer and choose Add and then Existing Item from its context menu. This opens the File Browser dialog box.

b. Select your RunFIT.cmd file in the File Browser dialog box and then click OK to add it to your Visual Studio Project.

c. Select RunFIT.cmd in your Solution Explorer and use the Properties window to set its "Copy output to Directory" property to "Copy if newer".

8. Add references to FIT.dll and osImageManagerLib.dll as explained in step 4 of Exercise 14-3, in Chapter 14, though you will need to use the browse page of the Add Reference dialog to select the FIT.dll file in the c:\FIT directory.

■ WARNING

You must only add references to the FIT.dll file in the c:\FIT directory, and then ensure that this particular library file is loaded by runFile.exe when you run your tests by deleting the copy in your project's output directory; see the first command in RunFIT.cmd.

EXERCISE 22-3: Running Customer Tests on Your Developer PC

The aim of this exercise is to create a document containing some functional tests and to run them against the software under test using the fixture you developed in Exercise 22-2.

1. Create your test document by taking the following steps:

a. Create a new HTML file (File | New | File, HTML page) which will then open in your editor; see Figure 22-2.

b. Add the table as shown in Figure 22-2.

c. Save your test document as ValidateImageFile.htm in the same directory as your `DICOMFileValidation` class.

d. Add your test document to the osImageManagerFIT Visual Studio Project and set its properties so that it will also be copied to the output directory; see step 7c of Exercise 22-2.

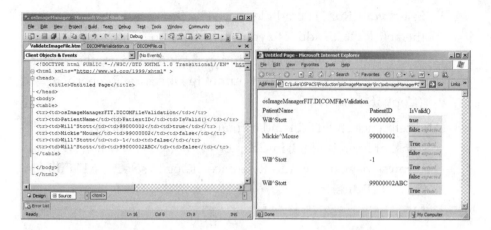

FIGURE 22-2: Test document in HTML markup form

2. Rebuild the osImageManager solution (Build | Build Solution) to copy the files needed to run your customer tests into the output directory of osImageManagerFIT.

3. Open Windows Explorer and select RunFIT.cmd, which is now in the osImageManagerFIT output directory. Double-click this batch file in order to run it and thus create VIFResults.htm.

4. Open VIFResults.htm and check that it looks like the output file shown in Figure 22-2.

5. Add your work to a version control shelve by clicking the Shelve button in the Pending Changes window. You should not check in your work because the test you have created cannot yet be run automatically by your integration Team Build.

6. Log off, as you have finished all the exercises in this chapter.

Now that you've successfully installed FIT and created a Visual Studio Solution that demonstrates how it is used, there is no reason why you can't implement this sort of customer testing in any small project. It's just a matter of granting your customer access to a directory containing the output directory files so that he can edit and run these tests without your assistance. Using FIT in a bigger project requires a little more thought, as you will see in Chapter 24, when we consider how to do customer testing with FIT in a Team System project, but you'll be relieved to discover that the basic concepts remain the same.

> **■ WARNING**
>
> Customers must keep a separate copy of their test documents safe in another directory because the contents of a Visual Studio Project's output directory (e.g., bin/Debug) may be overwritten or deleted.

Test Organization

In Exercise 22-3, you executed your customer test by running a batch file that passed an appropriate set of parameters to RunFile.exe in order to run the test. RunFile.exe is a small program supplied with FIT that acts as a test runner (i.e., a program, like a test harness, that supports the execution of tests). It is convenient to execute this program from a batch file so that you can run all the tests in your development environment just by double-clicking the RunFIT.cmd file; see Listing 22-2.

LISTING 22-2: RunFIT.cmd Running a Collection of Test Cases Using FIT's Test Runner

```
del fit.dll
runfile ValidateImageFile.htm VIFResults.htm c:\FIT;.
runfile PatientNameValidation.htm PNVResults.htm c:\FIT;.
runfile ImageList.htm ILResults.htm c:\FIT;.
runfile ImageListOrdered.htm ILOResults.htm c:\FIT;.
runfile ImportFile.htm IFResults.htm c:\FIT;.
runfile ImportFileImageList.htm IFILResults.htm c:\FIT;.
```

> **■ NOTE**
>
> The third parameter of runFile contains a list of directory paths separated by semicolons. These directories contain the various assemblies needed by your tests and should include those in the c:\FIT directory as well as those in your project's output directory, the current directory denoted by the "dot".

When it comes to running your collection of customer tests as a test suite, there other more sophisticated mechanisms than the sort of simple batch file we just described, including the following:

- **FitNesse**[3]—A wiki-based Integrated Development Environment (IDE) for FIT that allows you to create, run, and manage your customer tests as a collection of Web pages.
- **WinFITRunner**[4]—Permits customers to write their tests in Excel spreadsheets which are then managed and run by WinFITRunner.
- **Visual Studio Team System Test Lists**—Allows you to use the VSTS tools to manage a collection of generic tests, each invoking RunFile for a specific test document. Team Build also can run these test lists; see Chapter 24.

It is a good idea to review the way your team organizes its tests on a regular basis because a large collection of test documents can quickly become unwieldy without proper attention to its management.

Storytest-Driven Development

Giving customers the ability to write and run their own tests usually changes the way a software project is run. This provides the benefits we already identified concerning functional testing throughout the project, and it can result in the business taking a more active role in driving the project through storytest-driven development (STDD).

In Chapter 3, you learned that Agile teams create stories to represent their customer's requirements. Although this is helpful in a number of ways, the lack of precise information about a story can make it difficult to know when the implementation has managed to satisfy the customer's expectations, so there is a risk that developers will provide more of the feature than is strictly required. STDD manages this problem by requiring that storytests

---

3. FitNesse Web site (www.fitnesse.org).
4. Stott, Will. "Get Your Customers Involved in the Testing Process" (*MSDN Magazine*, Feb. 2005; http://msdn.microsoft.com/msdnmag).

(customer tests) be available before the developers start working on a story, and deems their work complete when all the storytests pass. In this way, the business, through the customer, assumes much of the responsibility for delivery of useful features within the available development time.

> **■ NOTE**
>
> Without a mechanism such as storytests, the business has little chance of successfully managing a project because it has no accurate means of measuring progress and therefore must rely on reports from developers about work that is "almost completed."

Costs and Benefits of STDD

The benefit of STDD to developers is that they are freed from having to decide "what" the customer wants and therefore can concentrate on "how" to implement the requirements in the simplest possible way. Any temptation for developers to gold-plate the requirement with superfluous functionality is avoided by insisting that only enough code is written to pass the storytest; something that can be monitored by measuring code coverage when the storytests are run. The cost of STDD to developers arises from the need to support the storytests, which in the case of FIT means developing additional code for the fixtures.

The advantage of STDD to the business is that it allows them more control of the project so that they can better manage the associated risks, because typically risk management is something the business is good at doing. However, this benefit comes at the cost of the customer having a much closer involvement with the project and the creation of tests.

> **■ NOTE**
>
> Chapter 24 explains how you might use FIT to support storytest-driven development in a Team Project such as the one you created for OSPACS in Exercise 5-1 in Chapter 5.

Real Customer Involvement Practice

The practice of involving a real customer requires that the voices of the people who will use the software (or who have a stake in its use) are properly heard by making them a part of the team. It puts the people with the requirement in direct contact with the people responsible for satisfying their needs: the developers.

Many benefits are associated with having real customers talking directly to the people who are developing the software. However, one of the main justifications for this practice is avoiding the addition of features that provide little or no value to the business. When a developer and a customer discuss a feature face to face, it quickly becomes obvious whether the feature is really required. For example, a customer who is unable to provide a developer with any proper acceptance criteria for a feature obviously has no real idea how it might be used, usually a sure sign of a redundant feature.

Making a real customer part of the team is difficult when the role is not being shared, because businesspeople are usually not available to sit with the rest of the team for months at a time. Therefore, it is more realistic to make a real customer part of a customer team (see Chapter 4) because this ensures that someone is always available to the developers and provides the added benefit that more than one customer voice is heard. You might also consider letting developers visit the users of the software in their work environment so that they can experience firsthand the issues such people face. However, this type of exercise is no substitute for ongoing involvement between developers and their customer.

■ NOTE

Until a real customer is able to demonstrate that there is a pressing need for a feature, it remains useless and any effort expended on its development is wasted.

Role of Testers in STDD

Team members who have testing experience usually spend a lot of their time helping customers write good tests. However, they may also take part in the Pair Programming practice described in Chapter 2, as their knowledge and skill in developing tests is equally as valuable during TDD as a programmer's ability to write code. Therefore, if your team is fortunate enough to have someone with testing experience, encourage them to coach not just customers but also developers so that everyone starts writing better tests.

> **■ WARNING**
>
> Coaching does not mean writing tests for the customer. It is important that the customer write his own tests, because otherwise there is a danger that he might not understand them and accept a story which doesn't really meet the business need.

Relationship of Customer Testing to Your Release Process

FIT allows you to automate the process of running customer tests, not just in your development environment, as we described in this chapter, but also in your Build Lab, because typically you would run FIT tests as part of your Team Build; see Chapter 24. In this way, automated customer acceptance testing is performed during your team's Integration Builds as well as during its Daily Builds. Therefore, you should be confident that software that has passed such tests does what the customer wants and thus meets the needs of the business. However, this doesn't necessarily mean that the software is ready to be used in the business environment, for as we discuss in Chapter 28, most teams will follow some form of prescribed release process to further prove the software before taking this step. The ultimate aim of this release process is to ensure that the software provides the anticipated benefit to the business without any unexpected side effects, such as losing data or trashing your users' hard disks.

The business must learn to balance the benefits of any new software against the risk that its testing has failed to detect some potential side effect which could cause significant damage. In this respect, the sort of customer testing that lies at the heart of STDD may prove persuasive, particularly when combined with the programmer tests and coverage information described in Section 5. However, you should bear in mind that the main purpose of customer testing is to support STDD, thereby enabling an approach to user acceptance testing that continues throughout a project rather than one that happens only at the end. Therefore, you should make the business aware that customer acceptance testing is not intended to provide the only form of testing required before your team deploys its software.

> **■ NOTE**
>
> It is difficult to give specific advice about the steps you need to take during a release process because that depends so much on the nature of your team and its project. However, Sam Guckenheimer's book[5] about VSTS gives some good advice in this regard.

CONCLUSION

FIT allows customers to develop tests in their own language and therefore build a model of the system that they can understand. Their tests should be focused on validating that the software meets its business requirements so that it does what the customer wants. Putting the responsibility for creating and running such functional tests in the hands of the customer permits the business to better track and understand the project's risks as the software evolves from iteration to iteration. This allows the team to fix problems as they arise and to learn from them so that both the product and the process improve as the project progresses.

> **■ NOTE**
>
> The transparency of STDD builds trust between technical people and businesspeople, allowing them to leverage their respective strengths and skills so as to deliver the best possible return on investment.

---

5. [SETS] Guckenheimer, Sam, and Juan Perez. *Software Engineering with Microsoft Visual Studio Team System* (Addison-Wesley, 2006).

■ 23
Creating FIT Fixtures

T HIS CHAPTER INTRODUCES the standard Framework for Integrated
Test (FIT) fixtures for supporting tables that allow customers to create
tests for their business rules (column fixture), for the information stored by
the system (row fixture), and for the workflow of their user interface (action
fixture). We describe each fixture in turn and provide an example of their
use in a project. The chapter then concludes by describing how to create a
custom fixture so that your customer's tests can be made to look more like
the actual things they test.

Standard FIT Fixtures

You will recall from Chapter 22 that FIT connects your customer's executable test documents to the associated "software under test" through a
collection of simple objects, called *fixtures,* created by the developers on
your team; see Listing 22-1 in Chapter 22. These fixtures can be considered
Adapters (see the *Design Patterns* book[1]) and you usually derive them from
one of the three standard classes provided by FIT.dll: `ColumnFixture`,
`RowFixture`, or `ActionFixture`.

Each standard fixture class supports a particular type of table that is
useful for customer testing. These tables correspond to the three layers of

---

1. [DP] Gamma, Erich, et al. *Design Patterns* (Addison-Wesley, 1994).

architecture commonly found in today's software: the business layer, the data layer, and the user interface layer. Therefore, the customer can create a test model of the system in terms of the parts she can see (user interface layer), the business rules she can define (business layer), and the information she needs to store (data layer). It doesn't matter whether these layers map to the actual implementation because your fixtures provide an adapter which can handle the abstraction. What is important is that the customer can write tests for a model of the system that she understands, so let's now take a closer look at these three tables in terms of the way customers use them to write their tests and the sort of code needed to support them.

> **■ TIP**
>
> Present your customers with examples of the three types of tables which standard FIT fixture classes support, and then let them decide which sort of table is most appropriate for the type of test they want to perform.

Column Fixtures: Testing Decisions in the Business Layer

A column fixture table is intended to test the system's business logic. The table forms a test case and the rows (after the first two rows) are its test scenarios. These sorts of tables have the same general form as Table 23-1, which shows the expected results of validating the contents of a DICOM file's patient name field against names given by the corresponding patient record.

The first row of the table references the FIT fixture developed to support the test case. The next row of the table contains the headers for subsequent rows which map each column to the name of a particular method or input field in the fixture object. Each subsequent row contains input and output data for a test scenario which FIT will read by going from the left column to the right column in the same sequence as the header row. Customers rather than developers should name the fixture, its input fields, and its result methods so that the tests are expressed in the language of the business. The only restrictions you must apply, as for all FIT fixtures, are that result column names need to end with a set of parentheses, and names must resolve to .NET tokens (i.e., they cannot contain white spaces, keywords, operators, directives, or various special symbols).

TABLE 23-1: Sample Column Fixture Table

osImageManagerFIT.PatientNameValidation			
DICOM_PatientName	Db_Surname	Db_FirstNames	IsValid()
William^Stott	Stott	William	true
Stott^William	Stott	William	true
STOTT^WILLIAM	Stott	William	true
Stott^Will	Stott	William	false
William^Scott	Stott	William	false

> **■ NOTE**
>
> The PatientNameValidation fixture referenced in Table 23-1 takes strings as data types for its input fields and gives its results as a Boolean. However, you can also develop fixtures that use different data types, such as integers or fit.ScientificDouble.

EXERCISE 23-1: Using a Column Fixture in a Customer Test

In the following exercise, you will re-create Table 23-1 inside a test document and then add some business layer code to osImageManagerLib and a ColumnFixture to osImageManagerFIT. You will complete the exercise by running these tests in your development environment.

1. Log on to the DeveloperPC as Luke (OSPACS Contributor), start Visual Studio, and then connect to the OSPACS Team Project, as described in Exercise 5-7 in Chapter 5; see Appendix A for a specification of this PC and details of Luke's security groups.

2. Open the osImageManager Visual Studio Solution, as described in step 5 of Exercise 9-1, in Chapter 9. This Solution contains the Visual Studio Projects osImageManagerLib and osImageManagerFIT,

which you created in Exercise 8-4 (in Chapter 8) and Exercise 22-2 (in Chapter 22), respectively.

3. Create an HTML file for your test document (File | New | File, HTML page) and add the table shown in Table 23-1 by typing the appropriate <TABLE>, <TR>, and <TD> tags as well the associated values. Save this file as PatientNameValidation.htm in the same directory as the osImageManagerFIT source code files.

4. Add PatientNameValidation.htm to the osImageManagerFIT Project and then set its properties so that this test document will be copied to the output directory; see step 7c of Exercise 22-2, in Chapter 22.

5. Add a new class, called `PatientName`, to osImageManagerLib so that you can implement your business layer code as follows:

   a. Select the project in Solution Explorer and select Add Class from Visual Studio's Project menu (Project | Add Class).

   b. Type the code given in Listing 23-1 into this new class.

■ NOTE

osImageManagerLib is destined for your production environment, so you should implement your code changes using test-driven development (TDD); see Section 5. However, we have not described this work due to space limitations.

LISTING 23-1: Implementation of PatientName.Validate in the OSPACS Business Layer

```
using System;
namespace osImageManagerLib
{
    public class PatientName
    {
        public static bool Validate(string fullName, string surname,
                          string firstNames)
        {
            bool rc = false;
            string dicomName = fullName.ToUpper();
            if (   (dicomName.IndexOf(surname.ToUpper()) > -1)
```

```
                && (dicomName.IndexOf(firstNames.ToUpper()) > -1))
            rc = true;
        return rc;
        }
    }
}
```

6. Add the new class, `PatientNameValidation`, to osImageManagerFIT by following the same procedure described in step 5. Type into this class the code given in Listing 23-2 to provide a suitable fixture for your test document.

LISTING 23-2: Implementation of the PatientNameValidation Column Fixture

```csharp
using System;
using osImageManagerLib;
using fit;
namespace osImageManagerFIT
{
    public class PatientNameValidation : ColumnFixture
    {
        public string DICOM_PatientName;
        public string Db_Surname;
        public string Db_FirstNames;

        public bool IsValid()
        {
            return PatientName.Validate(DICOM_PatientName, Db_Surname,
                                Db_FirstNames);
        }
    }
}
```

7. Add the following command to the bottom of the RunFIT.cmd batch file created in Exercise 22-2 in Chapter 22, remembering to save the file (File | Save) after typing the final dot:

```
runFile PatientNameValidation.htm PNVResults.htm c:\FIT;.
```

8. Rebuild the osImageManager solution (Build | Build Solution) to copy into the output directory the files needed to run your customer tests.

9. Run the RunFIT.cmd batch file (double-click it) in the output directory to create PNVResults.htm and then open it so that you can confirm that all your customer tests have passed.

10. Add your changes to a version control Shelve by clicking the Shelve button in the Pending Changes window (View | Other Windows) and then log off, as you have finished this exercise.

Figure 23-1 shows the sort of customer test you have developed in the preceding exercise embedded in the specification document for a real system. You should also consider adding your customer test tables to a formal specification of the software written in a Word document (and then saved as an HTML file), because in this way, your specification not only describes the requirement, but also validates it.

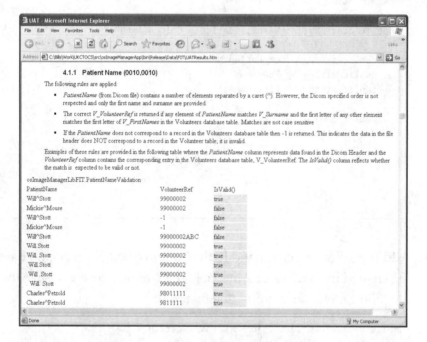

FIGURE 23-1: Specification document for a real system[2] displaying the actual results of a customer test

---

2. The document shown in Figure 23-1 is reproduced with kind permission of the Institute of Women's Health, University College London.

> **▪ NOTE**
>
> After you have set up the sort of Build Validation Test (BVT) described in Chapter 24, your customer tests will automatically run in the Integration and Test environment whenever anyone performs an Integration Team Build.

Row Fixtures: Testing Lists in the Data Layer

A row fixture table is intended to support tests for the information a customer wants the system to store; this is usually some form of list held in the table's data layer. These sorts of tables have the same general form as Table 23-2, which shows a list of patients and their corresponding image data.

The first row of the table references the FIT fixture developed to support the tests in the table. The second row contains headers for subsequent rows which map each column to the name of a field provided by the system's ImageList data set. Subsequent rows contain the values of these fields for each record the customer expects to find in the system. In Table 23-2, the customer expects just three image records to be stored in the system without any consideration about their order. When the test is run, a "missing" error will be raised if any of these records cannot be found, and a "surplus" error will be raised if extra records appear. Errors will also be raised if the values of these records are not correct.

TABLE 23-2: Sample Row Fixture Table

osImageManagerFIT.*ImageList*			
Surname	FirstNames	SOPInstanceUID	ImageDate
Newkirk	James	999-1-1	06-07-2006
Stott	William	999-0-1	07-02-2006
Stott	William	999-0-2	07-15-2006

> **■ NOTE**
>
> Specify the order of the records by adding a column to the table containing the sort order and then creating a corresponding field in the `ImageAdapter` class whose value is incremented for each record returned by the data layer; see the `Order` variable in Listing 23-4.

EXERCISE 23-2: Using a Row Fixture in a Customer Test

The following exercise repeats Exercise 23-1, except that you will re-create Table 23-2 inside your test document and add to your class library projects some data layer code in osImageManagerLib and a row fixture in osImageManagerFIT.

1. Repeat the first two steps of Exercise 23-1 so that you have logged on to the DeveloperPC as Luke and opened the osImageManager Visual Studio Solution.

2. Create an HTML file for your test document (File | New | File, HTML page) and then add the table shown in Table 23-2. Save this file as ImageList.htm in the same directory as the source code files of osImageManagerFIT and then add the file to the project, setting its properties so that it will be copied to the output directory; see step 7c of Exercise 22-2, in Chapter 22.

3. Add the new class, `Image`, to osImageManagerLib in the same way you did in step 5 of the preceding exercise, and type into this new class the code in Listing 23-3 in order to implement some data layer code.

LISTING 23-3: Implementation of the OSPACS Data Layer

```
using System;
using System.Collections.Generic;
namespace osImageManagerLib
{
```

```csharp
public class Image
{
    private string patientLastName;
    private string patientFirstNames;
    private string imageID;
    private DateTime acquiredDate;

    public Image(string lastName, string firstNames, string ImageID,
                DateTime date)
    {
        patientLastName = lastName;
        patientFirstNames = firstNames;
        imageID = ImageID;
        acquiredDate = date;
    }
    public string PatientLastName {get { return patientLastName; } }
    public string PatientFirstNames {get { return patientFirstNames; }}
    public string ImageID { get { return imageID; } }
    public DateTime AcquiredDate { get { return acquiredDate; } }
}

public class Data
{
    private static Data data = null;
    private List<Image> images;
    private Data() { }
    static Data()
    {
        data = new Data();
        Data.Instance.images = new List<Image>();
                        //hardcode the record entries for now
        Data.Instance.images.Add(new Image("Stott", "William",
                        "999-0-1", new DateTime(2006,7,2)));
        Data.Instance.images.Add(new Image("Stott", "William",
                        "999-0-2", new DateTime(2006,7,15)));
        Data.Instance.images.Add(new Image("Newkirk", "James",
                        "999-1-1", new DateTime(2006,6,7)));
    }
    static public Data Instance { get { return data; } }
    public List<Image> Images { get { return images; } }
}
}
```

> **■ NOTE**
>
> Initially, just to get the test to pass, we created the `Data` class, as shown in Listing 23-3, which is actually implemented as a Singleton pattern (see the *Design Patterns* book[3]). However, you would normally replace it with a class that better serves the needs of your system to store and retrieve image information.

4. Add the new class, `ImageAdapter`, to osImageManagerFIT in the same way you did before. Type into this class the code in Listing 23-4 to provide the fields for the ImageList data set as required by Table 23-2.

LISTING 23-4 : Implementation of ImageAdapter to Provide the ImageList Properties

```
using System;
using osImageManagerLib;

namespace osImageManagerFIT
{
    public class ImageAdapter
    {
        private static int order = 1;            //support for ordered lists

        public string Surname;
        public string FirstNames;
        public string SOPInstanceUID;
        public string ImageDate;
        public int Order;                        //support for ordered lists

        public ImageAdapter(Image image)
        {
            Surname = image.PatientLastName;
            FirstNames = image.PatientFirstNames;
            SOPInstanceUID = image.ImageID;
            ImageDate = image.AcquiredDate.ToString("MM-dd-yyyy");
            Order = order++;                     //support for ordered lists
        }
    }
}
```

---

3. [DP] Gamma, Erich, et al. *Design Patterns* (Addison-Wesley, 1995).

> **■ NOTE**
>
> The order and Order variables in Listing 23-4 are not required for the test in Table 23-2. However, if you wanted to confirm that the system was returning rows in a specific order, they would support an Order column in your table containing ascending integer values.

5. Add the new class, `ImageList`, to osImageManagerFIT in the same way as before. Type into this class the code in Listing 23-5 to provide a suitable fixture for your test document. In most cases, you just need to override the query and `getTargetClass` methods of the RowFixture base class.

LISTING 23-5 : Implementation of the RowFixture ImageList

```
using System;
using System.Collections.Generic;
using osImageManagerLib;
using fit;
namespace osImageManagerFIT
{
    public class ImageList : RowFixture
    {
        public override Type getTargetClass()
        {
            return typeof(ImageAdapter);
        }

        public override object[] query()
        {
            ImageAdapter[] rc = null;

            List<Image> imageList = Data.Instance.Images;
            rc = new ImageAdapter[imageList.Count];
            for (int index = 0; index < imageList.Count; index++)
                rc[index] = new ImageAdapter(imageList[index]);
            return rc;
        }
    }
}
```

6. Edit the RunFIT.cmd batch file in the same way you did in step 7 of Exercise 23-1. Add the following command to the bottom of the batch file, not forgetting the final dot, and then save your changes (File | Save):

```
runFile ImageList.htm ILResults.htm c:\FIT;.
```

7. Rebuild the osImageManager solution (Build | Build Solution) to copy into the output directory the files needed to run your customer tests.

8. Run the RunFIT.cmd batch file (double-click it) to create ILResults.htm and confirm that all the tests pass.

9. Add your changes to a version control Shelve by clicking the Shelve button in the Pending Changes window (View | Other Windows), and then log off.

■ NOTE

In a real project, you would use test-driven development (TDD) to develop the Image and Data data layer classes so that you could be certain that your code was structurally sound before attempting to start functional testing.

Action Fixtures: Testing Workflow in the User Interface Layer

An action fixture table is intended to test the sequence of actions a user will follow when completing some task. Typically, such tests mimic the entering of text, pressing of buttons, and checking of output fields that occur when someone is completing a dialog box or other part of the user interface. These sorts of tables have the same general form as Table 23-3, which shows the steps a customer would take when adding an image from a DICOM file to OSPACS.

TABLE 23-3: Sample Action Fixture Table

fit.ActionFixture		
start	osImageManagerFIT.ImportImageDialog	
enter	Filename	C:\999-1-1.dicom
press	Import	
check	ImageID	999-1-1
check	ImageDate	06-07-2006
check	PatientName	James^Newkirk

> **■ NOTE**
>
> Action fixtures test the functions of a user interface, not its operation. Therefore, as part of your release process, you may need to perform additional testing to test the setup of things such as the data binding to the form, its control behavior and properties, event activation, and so forth.

The top row of an action fixture table defines the standard Action Fixture class which supports the commands listed in Table 23-4, though you can define additional commands by deriving your own action fixture from this class. The following rows declare the sequence of actions this class performs, with the left column defining the action and subsequent columns containing its arguments. Therefore, in Table 23-3, the first command (start) is equivalent to a user opening the system's Import Image dialog box. The second command mimics someone entering a filename into a text box, the third command is equivalent to clicking the Import button, and the final three commands check that ImageID, ImageDate, and PatientName have been read correctly from the header as a result of importing the file c:\999-1-1.dicom.

> ### ■ NOTE
>
> FIT processes sequences of tables in a test document in the order they appear, so your document might start with an action fixture table that imports a number of images and then have a row fixture table which confirms that they have been stored correctly in the system.

EXERCISE 23-3: Using an Action Fixture in a Customer Test

The following exercise repeats Exercise 23-1, except that you will re-create Table 23-3 inside your test document and add to your class library projects some user interface code in osImageManagerLib, and an action fixture in osImageManagerFIT.

1. Repeat the first two steps in Exercise 23-1 so that you have logged on to the DeveloperPC as Luke and opened the osImageManager Visual Studio Solution.

2. Create an HTML file for your test document (File | New | File, HTML page) and add the table shown in Table 23-3. Save this file as ImportFile.htm in the same directory as the source code files of osImageManagerFIT, and then add the file to the project, settings its properties so that it will be copied to the output directory; see step 7c of Exercise 22-2, in Chapter 22.

3. Add the new class, ImportDlgUI, to osImageManagerLib by selecting the project in Solution Explorer and select Add Class from Visual Studio's Project menu. Type the code in Listing 23-6 into this new class to implement some user interface layer code.

> ### ■ TIP
>
> Make the user interface code in your Windows Forms classes as simple as possible by putting any additional processing logic in a class library, as suggested in Chapter 17. In this way, the part of the user interface that you can't test with FIT is kept small.

LISTING 23-6: User Interface Layer Code to Support the Import Image Dialog

```csharp
using System;
using System.Collections.Generic;

namespace osImageManagerLib
{
    public class ImportDlgUI
    {
        private string imageRef;
        private DateTime imageCreated;
        private string firstNames;
        private string surname;

        public bool ImportFile(string fileName)
        {            //Todo: implement code to read actual dicom file header
            imageRef = "999-1-1";
            imageCreated = new DateTime(2006,7,6);
            firstNames = "James";
            surname = "Newkirk";
                //save image item in data layer; see Exercise 23-2
            Data.Instance.Images.Add(new Image(surname, firstNames,
                            imageRef, imageCreated));
            return true;
        }
        public string ImageRef { get {return imageRef;}}
        public string ImageCreated
        {
            get { return imageCreated.ToString("MM-dd-yyyy"); }
        }
        public string ImageName
        {
            get { return firstNames + "^" + surname;}
        }
    }
}
```

> **■ NOTE**
>
> ImportDlgUI.ImportFile creates an Image object which is saved in the data layer using the Data class created in Exercise 23-2. You may use this feature later with a test that first imports an image and then confirms that it has been correctly stored in the system.

4. Add the new class, `ImportImageDialog`, to your osImageManagerFIT project in the same way as before. Type the code in Listing 23-7 into this class to support the commands in Table 23-4.

LISTING 23-7: Implementation of the ActionFixture ImportImageDialog

```
using System;
using osImageManagerLib;
using fit;

namespace osImageManagerFIT
{
    public class ImportImageDialog : ActionFixture
    {
        private string filename;
        private string imageID;
        private string imageDate;
        private string patientName;

        public void Import()
        {
            ImportDlgUI ui = new ImportDlgUI();
            ui.ImportFile(filename);
            imageID = ui.ImageRef;
            imageDate = ui.ImageCreated;
            patientName = ui.ImageName;
        }

        public void Filename(string pathfilename)
        {
            filename = pathfilename;
        }
        public string ImageID() { return imageID; }
        public string ImageDate() { return imageDate; }
        public string PatientName() { return patientName; }
    }
}
```

5. Edit the RunFIT.cmd batch file to add the following command (not forgetting the final dot) and then save your changes (File | Save):

```
runFile ImportFile.htm IFResults.htm c:\FIT;.
```

6. Rebuild the osImageManager solution (Build | Build Solution) to copy into the output directory the files needed to run your customer tests.

7. Run the RunFIT.cmd batch file (double-click it) to create IFResults.htm and then open it to confirm that all your tests pass.

8. Add your changes to a version control Shelve by clicking the Shelve button in the Pending Changes window (View | Other Windows) and then log off, as you have finished the exercises in this chapter.

> **■ NOTE**
>
> In your own project, use the Visual Studio Design Editor to create the dialog box and defer all processing to the part of the user interface layer code you developed using TDD (e.g., `ImportDlgUI`) so that the Windows Form code is thin enough not to need unit testing; see Listing 23-8.

LISTING 23-8: Invoking User Interface Layer Code from the Windows Form

```
using System.Windows.Forms;
using osImageManagerLib;

namespace osImageManagerApp
{
    public partial class DlgFileImport : Form
    {
        public DlgFileImport()
        {
            InitializeComponent();
        }

        private void buttonImport_Click(object sender, EventArgs e)
        {   //only the following three lines were written by a programmer
            //so thereís not much to unit test in this class
            ImportDlgUI ui = new ImportDlgUI();
            if (ui.ImportFile(textBoxFileName.Text))
                this.Close();
        }
    }
}
```

TABLE 23-4: Standard fit.ActionFixture Commands and Their Arguments

Command	Argument List	Equivalent Pseudocode
start	myFixture	ShowDialog (new myFixture)
enter	methodA, value1	myFixture.methodA(value1)
press	doSomething	myFixture.doSomething()
check	methodB, result1	Assert (myFixture.methodB() == result1)

> **■ NOTE**
>
> You should derive the name of the action fixture from the title of the dialog box your customer expects to open when using the actual application. Likewise, the names of the command arguments correspond to the labels of user interface components found in this dialog box.

Custom FIT Fixtures

The standard row, column, and action fixtures are sufficient for the customer testing needs of most projects. However, you can also develop custom fixtures so that tables look like certain forms in your problem domain. For example, Figure 23-2 shows a type of data entry form which radiologists would use when storing an ultrasound scan image in the OSPACS system. In this way, the customer's tests can look more like the feature in the system that the tests are testing.

Example of a Custom Fixture

In order to create a test with a table that looks more like a real form than the sorts of tables you have developed in the previous exercises, you need to write a customer fixture such as the one shown in Listing 23-9. This fixture is derived from the TableFixture class, which is available for download from this book's Web site. Essentially, it creates an instance of the production code you want to test (e.g., UltraScanForm), and then invokes its methods to check that the data in the test table is valid by reading the values at specific locations (i.e., row, column).

For example, in order to validate that the Patient Ref corresponds to the Last Name in Figure 23-2, the fixture reads the values in cells 1,3 and 2,3 and passes them to its Check method, which invokes the right or wrong TableFixture method, depending on whether the values in the test match those that UltraScanForm expects. The right or wrong method then arranges for the result of the test to be displayed in the test document at runtime.

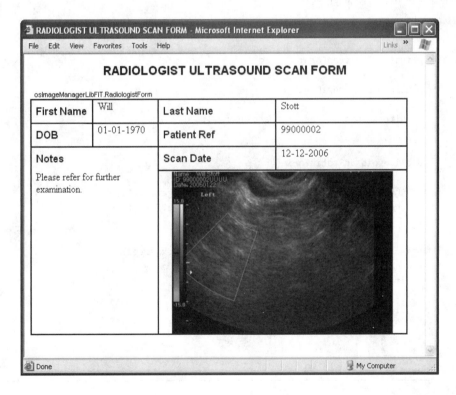

FIGURE 23-2: Custom fixture allowing close emulation of a real form during testing

In order to perform further customization of the FIT fixture, you will need to become familiar with the source code supplied with the FIT download. In this respect, we recommend you read the excellent book about FIT, written by Rick Mugridge and Ward Cunningham,[4] which contains a good explanation about customizing fixtures, though the examples are given in Java. Indeed, the idea for the preceding custom fixture as well as various other matters in Section 7 came from this source.

LISTING 23-9: Deriving a Custom Fixture from the TableFixture Class

```
using System;
using bsdFITLib;               //contains TableFixture class
using osImageManagerLib;       //contains ultrascanForm class
using fit;

namespace osImageManagerFIT
{
    public class ImportImageDialog : TableFixture
    {
        private ultrascanForm;

        public ImportImageDialog()
        {
            ultrascanForm = new ultrascanForm();
        }

        public void doStaticTable()
        {
            Check (1,3, ultrascanForm.GetPatientName(getText(2, 3)));
            Check (2,3, ultrascanForm.GetPatientRef(getText(1, 3)));
        }

        private void Check(int row, int col, String expected)
        {
            if (expected.Equals(getText(row, col)))
                right (row, col);
            else
                wrong (row, col);
        }
    }
}
```

---

4. [FIT] Mugridge, Rick, and Ward Cunningham. *Fit for Developing Software* (Prentice Hall, 2005).

> **▪▪ NOTE**
>
> The `TableFixture` class originates from a class of the same name in FitNesse,[5] but it has been rewritten in C# and is available for download from the book's Web site as the class library called `bsdFITLib`.

CONCLUSION

It is essential that your customers understand the importance of becoming involved in the team's testing in order to get the functionality they want from the system being developed. FIT encourages such involvement by helping customers develop a model of the system through their tests in terms of the parts they can see (user interface), the business rules they define, and the information they need to store or retrieve. Although these tests are developed in collaboration with the rest of the team, they are owned by the customers and expressed in their own language. This raises the profile of testing on the team, making it into something that is perceived as driving the project forward rather than dragging it backward.

> **▪▪ NOTE**
>
> Teams that are fortunate enough to have people with testing experience have a significant advantage because they have the resources on hand to coach their customers in the art of writing effective tests, which is often the most challenging aspect of introducing STDD to a team.

---

5. FitNesse Web site (http://fitnesse.org).

■ 24
Running FIT with Team Foundation Build

T HIS CHAPTER IS concerned with running Framework for Integrated Test (FIT) customer tests in your project test and integration environment (Build Lab) as part of a Team Foundation Build (TFB). It explains how you can wrap such tests in the generic test types provided by Visual Studio Team System (VSTS) and then execute them automatically from MSTest as Build Validation Tests (BVTs). In this way, you can run all your customer tests whenever you perform a Team Build. The chapter then walks through the development of a customer test from its inception on a whiteboard to its successful execution in a Team Build, before concluding with a list of ten test design tips.

> **■ NOTE**
>
> In order to follow the exercises in this chapter, you need access to a PC that has Visual Studio Team Suite or Team Edition for Testers installed, because otherwise you cannot create generic tests; see Appendix B for a discussion about these license issues.

Performing Customer Tests in Your Build Lab

In the preceding chapter, we described how you could use FIT to run customer tests in your development environment to confirm that your implementation of a story satisfied the functional requirements of the business. However, before a story is deemed complete, you must perform an Integration Build and Test so that you can confirm that your code changes do not conflict with changes that other members of the team have made. Therefore, your customers will want to run their functional tests in the Build Lab environment because this gives them assurance that the story still works when fully integrated into the code base. You can give your customers this facility by making their tests run as part of the Team Build and providing access to the results from the Project Portal.

> **■ NOTE**
>
> Running customer tests in your development environment is sometimes difficult because you may lack all the resources and data you need. However, your Build Lab should be much closer to the production environment, so such problems will arise less often.

Wrapping FIT in a Generic Test

Visual Studio permits you to create, manage, and run a number of standard tests such as unit tests, load tests, Web tests, and so forth. However, it also permits you to work with other forms of tests in a similar way by putting them into a generic test wrapper. The only requirements for wrapping a test in this way are that the test runner or harness can be run from the command line and that it returns a value of either true or false, depending upon whether the tests passed or failed. The FIT test tester, runFile.exe, meets these requirements, so we can wrap it into a generic test which we can then manage and run using Team System tools.

> **■ NOTE**
>
> Technically, a **test runner** is an independent program (.exe) whereas a **test harness** is a collection that objects need to support the execution of a test. However, in practice, the two terms are mostly used interchangeably.

EXERCISE 24-1: Setting Up FIT for Customer Testing in Your Build Lab

This exercise deploys to your Build Lab a generic test that wraps the FIT test runner so that you can run the osImageManager customer tests in your Integration Build and Test environment.

1. Log on to the DeveloperPC as Luke (OSPACS Contributor), start Visual Studio, and then connect to the OSPACS Team Project, as described in Exercise 5-7 in Chapter 5; see Appendix A for a specification of this PC and details of Luke's security groups.

2. Open the osImageManager Visual Studio Solution, as described in step 5 of Exercise 9-1, in Chapter 9. This Solution contains the osImageManagerUT and osImageManagerFIT Visual Studio Projects, which we created in Exercise 12-1 (in Chapter 12) and Exercise 22-2 (in Chapter 22), respectively.

3. Add a new class for your generic test to osImageManagerUT, and call it ValidateDICOMFile, by following these steps:

   a. Select the project in Solution Explorer, and then choose Add and New Test from its context menu to open the Add New Test dialog box (Right-click | Add | New Test).

   b. Select the Generic Test template from the Add New Test dialog box and name your test ValidateDICOMFile.GenericTest.

4. Ensure that ValidateDICOMFile.GenericTest will be included in your build products by setting its Copy to Output Directory property to "Copy if newer"; see step 7c of Exercise 22-2, in Chapter 22.

5. Set the test runner for ValidateDICOMFile.GenericTest by entering the following into the form displayed in your Visual Studio Editor; see Figure 24-1:

   a. Program: c:\FIT\runFile.exe

   b. Working directory: (leave blank)

   c. Run Settings (runFile's command-line arguments):

   ```
   "%TestDeploymentDir%\ValidateImageFile.htm"
   "%TestDeploymentDir%\VIFResult.htm" "%TestDeploymentDir%"
   ```

   Set the additional files you need to deploy for the test by clicking the form's Add button and then selecting the following files from your osImageManager Solution directory:

   ```
   Src\osImageManagerFIT\ValidateImageFile.htm
   Src\osImageManagerFIT\bin\Release\osImageManagerLib.dll
   Src\osImageManagerFIT\bin\Release\osImageManagerFIT.dll
   ```

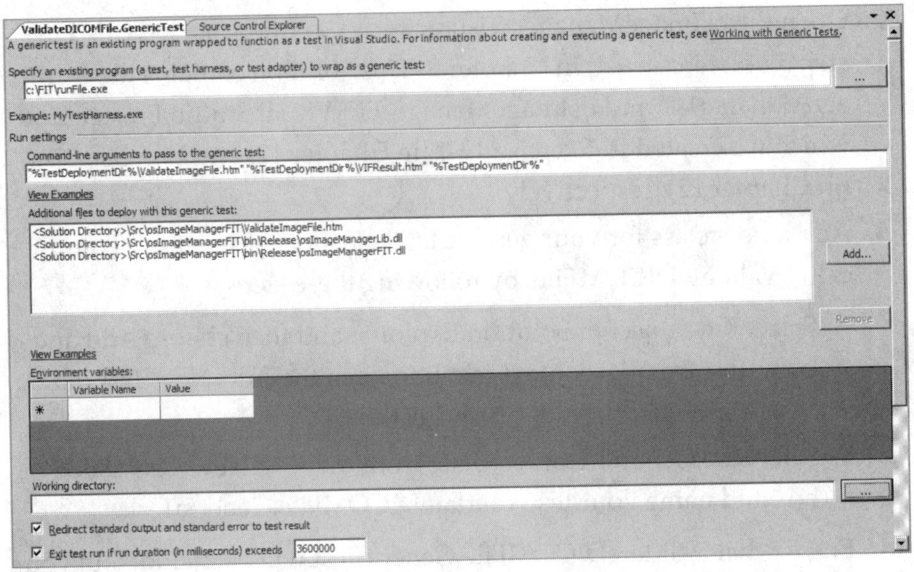

FIGURE 24-1: Creating a generic test for FIT

6. Implement `DICOMFileValidation.IsValid()` in Listing 22-1 so that all your customer tests pass when run in your Development environment. Therefore, you should be able to rebuild the osImageManager Solution (Build | Build Solution) and then execute RunFIT.cmd without any test failing.

7. Check in your changes, as described in step 9 of Exercise 9-1 in Chapter 9, and then log off, as you have finished this exercise.

■ WARNING

When performing the build in Exercise 24-1, you will not actually run the generic test, so before checking in your changes, you should run your customer tests in the development environment, as described in Exercise 22-3 in Chapter 22.

Running a Generic Test in Your Build Lab

The generic test created in Exercise 24-1 allows you to run the customer tests which you prepared in Chapter 22 in your Build Lab (Test PC). Therefore, you can now perform customer testing in both your development and test environments.

■ NOTE

Each time you run the osImageManagerIntegration Team Build Type created in Exercise 12-3 in Chapter 12, its build products will be copied into a directory created specifically for them in your BuildLabPC's c:\TeamBuild\Drops\OSPACS directory. This is termed the latest build directory.

After completing the following exercise, you will have successfully run the generic test prepared in Exercise 24-1 from the command line using MSTest.

1. Log on to the DeveloperPC as Luke (OSPACS Contributor), start Visual Studio, and then connect to the OSPACS Team Project, as you did in Exercise 24-1.

2. Perform a Team Build of osImageManagerIntegration (Build | Team Build). This deploys the customer tests, the associated test fixture, the generic test wrapper, and the rest of the build products to the "release" subdirectory of the latest build directory in the Build-LabPC, but it does not yet automatically run the generic test.

3. Open Windows Explorer so that you can confirm that Team Build has successfully deployed the following into the release subdirectory of your latest build directory:

   a. Your software under test: osImageManagerLib.dll

   b. Your FIT fixture: osImageManagerFit.dll

   c. Your generic test: ValidateDICOMFile.GenericTest

4. Open the Command Prompt and navigate to the location of the "release" subdirectory where ValidateDICOMFile.GenericTest can be found. Type the following and wait for your customer tests to execute:

   ```
   mstest /testcontainer:ValidateDICOMFile.GenericTest
   ```

5. Check that the VIFResult.htm file has been created in the "out" sub-directory of the directory created for your test's results. Open this file in your browser and confirm that all of its tests have passed.

6. Log off, as you have finished this exercise.

> ■ **NOTE**
>
> Each time you execute MSTest, as described in Exercise 24-2, a new directory is created for its results. This can be found in the TestResults directory of your latest build directory's "release" subdirectory.

Automated Customer Testing

The ability to automatically run all your customer tests as part of your Team Build in the same way as your unit tests should give you considerable confidence that your code changes have been properly integrated into the code base because you are orthogonally testing from both a structural and a functional perspective. It also gives your customer the opportunity to judge what progress the team is making in terms of satisfying the business requirements because upon the completion of each Team Build, the results of his customer tests are available from the project Web site.

Running Customer Tests in Team Foundation Build

All the team's customer tests and unit tests should be run each time someone integrates his work in the Build environment to confirm that the changes are successful. Therefore, you need to add the sort of generic test developed in Exercise 24-2 to your osImageManagerIntegration Team Build, as described in Exercise 24-3.

EXERCISE 24-3: Running Customer Tests As Part of a Team Build

After completing this exercise, you will add a Build Validation Test (BVT) to your Team Build so that you can run your customer tests as part of the team's code integration process.

1. Log on as Luke (OSPACS Contributor) to the DeveloperPC, start Visual Studio, and open the osImageManager solution, as explained in Exercise 24-1.

2. Create a new Visual Studio Test Project for your customer tests in the same way you created one for your unit tests in Exercise 12-1 in Chapter 12, except this time do the following:

   a. Name the project osImageManagerCT.

   b. Delete the default tests, ManualTest1.htm and UnitTest1.cs. Also take this opportunity to delete from osImageManagerUT the generic test you created in Exercise 24-1.

   c. Recreate ValidateDICOMFile.GenericTest by repeating steps 3, 4, and 5 of Exercise 24-1, but this time add your test to osImageManagerCT. Then add a new test list to this Visual Studio Project, called CustomerBVT; see steps 5 and 6 of Exercise 12-1, in Chapter 12.

d. Create similar generic tests for the other customer tests you have developed and add them to your CustomerBVT test list.

e. Make sure these tests are run as part of the integration test by clicking the selection box next to CustomerBVT in the right pane of the Test Manager window.

3. Add CustomerBVT to your osImageManagerIntegration Team Build by editing its Build Type Definition file as follows:

a. Open the osImageManagerIntegration TFSBuild.proj file for editing, as described in steps 3 and 4 of Exercise 12-7, in Chapter 12.

b. Edit the <MetaDataFile> section at the bottom of the file to include your CustomerBVT test list:

```
<TestList>IntegrationBVT;CustomerBVT</TestList>
```

4. Check in your changes, as described in step 9 of Exercise 9-1, in Chapter 9.

5. Run the osImageManagerIntegration Team Build (Build | Team Build Project) and confirm that your customer tests have been executed by opening the corresponding Build Report as follows:

a. Use Team Explorer to open the Team Builds folder for your Team Project.

b. Double-click the osImageManagerIntegration item to open a list of builds from which you can view individual results.

6. Log off, as you have finished the exercises in this chapter.

> **■ NOTE**
> Visual Studio displays a summary of your Team Build results, as shown in Figure 24-2. However, you should also check the actual FIT result file in the "out" subdirectory of the TestResults subdirectory of your latest build directory.

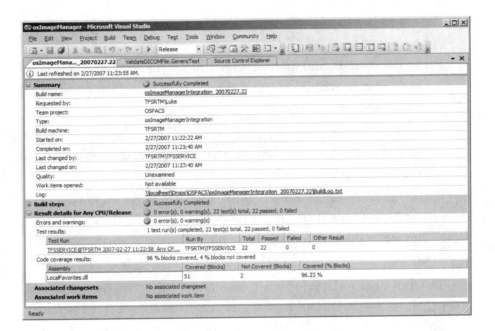

FIGURE 24-2: The results of the tests run by a Team Build

Allowing Your Customers to Edit and Run Tests from Their PCs

Customers will generally not appreciate having to learn how to use Visual Studio Team Test in order to perform their testing. Therefore, you must provide a simple way for your customer to edit her test document, run the tests it contains during an Integration Build, and then review the results. There are a couple of ways you can provide such a facility:

- **E-mail**—Ask the customer to send her test document to one of the developers as an e-mail attachment. The developer will then check the test document into the repository, run a Team Build, and then return the resulting FIT output file to the customer in another e-mail.

- **Remote access to Team Foundation Server (TFS)**—Allow the customer to use a freely available program such as PsExec[1] so that she

---

1. PsExec v1.73 (www.microsoft.com/technet/sysinternals/utilities/psexec.mspx).

can remotely run a set of scripts (see Listing 24-1) on the Team Foundation Server from her PC. In this way, she might

- Use the Team Foundation Version Control (TFVC) command-line tool (TF.exe) to check out her test document from the repository onto a workspace on her PC

- Edit the test document in her workspace

- Use the TFVC command-line tool to check her test document back into the repository

- Use the Team Build command-line tool (TFSBuild.exe) to start a Test Build that puts the build products (including the FIT output file) into a shared drop folder on the TFS

- View in her browser the FIT output file in the shared drop folder

• **Test dashboard**—Develop some form of utility, such as the one shown in Figure 24-3, so that your customer can perform the preceding actions from her own PC. We will put on the book's Web site details about any utilities of this nature that are bought to our attention.

■ NOTE

If you followed the instructions in Appendix A, you should be able to find TFSBuild.exe and TF.exe in the directory added to your PC's path environment variable.

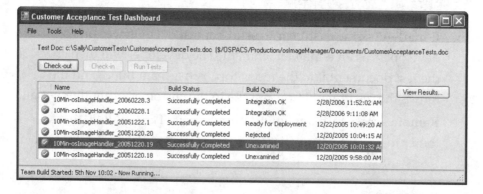

FIGURE 24-3: Mockup of a customer acceptance dashboard

According to the current "Microsoft Visual Studio 2005 Team System Licensing White Paper,"[2] your VSTS license allows nonlicensed users to access the operating system and server software "solely for the purpose of user acceptance testing." It is possible that the sort of customer acceptance testing we have proposed here meets this criterion, so you would not need to buy a license for each member of your customer group. However, as mentioned in Appendix B, we advise that you obtain proper legal advice on such issues.

LISTING 24-1: Script to Run a Customer Test Suite from the Command Line

```
tf get :: get latest version files from repository document folder
tf checkout *.*   :: allow customer to edit files
tf checkin /comment:"added name test" /noprompt
tfsbuild start DevServer OSPACS osImageManagerIntegration
```

■ NOTE

Listing 24-1 assumes that you have previously created a workspace for your customer that is mapped to your Documents folder in the repository.

Introducing Your Team to Customer Testing

After setting up your Build Lab so that customer tests can be run automatically as part of a Team Build and experimenting with the three basic types of FIT tables described in the previous chapter, you are ready to introduce customer testing to your team. You should start by implementing a simple customer test for a particular aspect of a story that is currently under development; some type of business rule is ideal. Once people experience the benefits of customer testing, it is usually not difficult to expand the practice so that all new stories start with the production of a storytest, as we proposed in Chapter 22.

2. "Microsoft Visual Studio 2005 Team System Licensing White Paper" (http://go.microsoft.com/fwlink/?LinkId=55164), Nov. 2005.

> **■ NOTE**
>
> Teams become test-infected when people start viewing test creation as a good thing that helps them deliver better software more quickly and less expensively.

Discussions around a Whiteboard

A customer test usually originates from a discussion around a whiteboard (or flip chart) about some feature of a story that is scheduled for completion before the end of the current iteration. The customer will be involved in this discussion, as will the developers who are charged with implementing the story. It is also helpful if someone with testing experience is present as well.

The customer should be encouraged to describe the feature by providing examples of how it will work, starting with the normal case and then expanding the discussion to include all exceptions. For example, when developing the Patient Name Validation business rule described in the previous chapter, the whiteboard might look like Figure 24-4. The developers and people with testing experience should then suggest additional tests in order to explore the requirement more fully. During the ensuing conversations, the real requirement will slowly start to be revealed as all parties consider additional test scenarios. We suggest that you do the following:

- Keep the discussion focused on the creation of customer tests rather than attempting to identify any form of technical solution.
- Attempt to capture any underlying business algorithm or rules.
- Focus on functional issues; for example, you could discuss the content of a dialog box, but not its layout.
- Make notes during these discussions in some form of personal project notebook,[3] but give as much space to capturing design issues as to planning and tracking your work.

---

3. [PSP] Humphrey, Watts. *Introduction to the Personal Software Process* (Addison-Wesley, 1997).

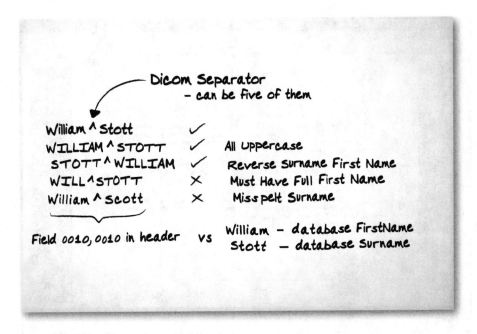

FIGURE 24-4: Early development of the Patient Name Validation business rule

■ TIP

It is not unusual for discussions about these tests to expose gaps in your customer's knowledge about the requirement, so adjourn the meeting if necessary to allow time for your customer to discuss the tests with colleagues.

Putting the Information into a Table

When the customer has finished creating the tests on the whiteboard(s), the tests need to be put into a table that the FIT can read. Normally, this requires the customer to create a set of tables in a Word document (see Figure 24-5), but other tools may be used instead; all that matters is that the customer is comfortable using the tool and the document can be saved as an HTML file.

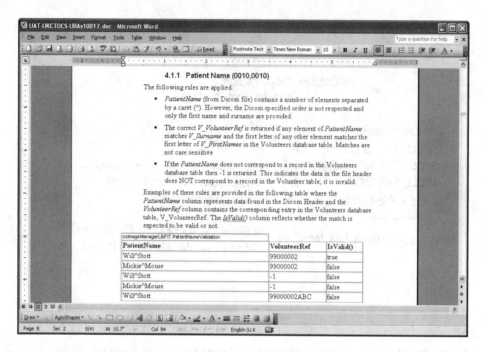

FIGURE 24-5: Word document with customer test (used with kind permission of UCL)

> **■ NOTE**
>
> Most of the customers we have observed put their tests in tabular form without any prompting from us or other developers. It seems that Excel spreadsheets or Word tables are the way businesspeople naturally present this sort of information.

You should show your customer examples of the standard tables for column, row, and action fixtures and let her decide which one is more appropriate for her needs without necessarily explaining the intended use of each table. However, you should explain the basic format of each table and ask the customer to decide on the names of the columns and fixtures, and add the namespaces later. It is important that the customer takes responsibility for creating the table rather than delegating the task to a developer (or tester) because this helps establish her ownership of the resultant tests. You should also take this opportunity to demonstrate the way in which such documents can be managed and where results of tests can be found after a Team Build, as we discussed previously.

> ■ **TIP**
>
> If your customer uses Microsoft Word to create her test document, make sure she saves it as an HTML file before checking it into the repository. Alternatively, create an Office Automation task so that it can be done as a custom build step prior to executing your BVT.

Implementing the Fixtures for the Story

After the customer has saved her tests in a shared network directory accessible from your Build Lab (TestPC), you should review them and add any additional information that might be required for successful execution, a fixture namespace, for example. Developers must then implement the fixtures named in each table, as described in Exercises 23-1, 23-2, and 23-3 in Chapter 23. At this stage, you do not need to implement the code for the story under development (software under test). However, tests that are not fully implemented should fail (red) when executed so that the customer is kept aware of what features are incomplete.

When you are satisfied that the customer tests are running correctly as part of each Team Build, you can start work implementing the associated story using test-driven development (TDD) within a normal programming episode. Eventually, you will know that you've completed the story because all its associated customer tests will pass during the Integration Team Build performed after you check in your code changes. Your customer will also know you've completed the story because when she looks at the results of the latest team build, all her customer tests will now pass.

> ■ **NOTE**
>
> The standard row, column, and action fixtures are sufficient for the needs of customer testing in most projects. However, you can develop custom fixtures (see Chapter 23) so that a table can be made to look like a particular form in your problem domain (see Figure 23-2).

Using Sequences of Tables in Customer Tests

Some customer tests are best expressed in independent tables, but others require the execution of tests in a sequence of tables. For example, if the customer wanted to write a test that first added some images to the system and then confirmed that they had been correctly stored, this would involve creating several related tables such as those shown in Figure 24-6. You will recall that FIT allows you to add any number of tables to a test document and will execute them in order, going from the top to the bottom of the file.

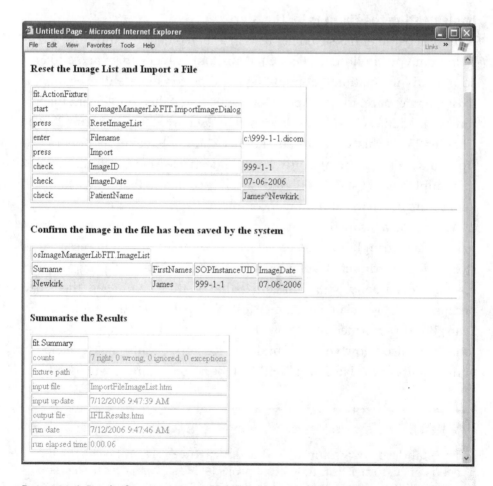

FIGURE 24-6: Results from a customer test document containing a sequence of tables

> **⯊ NOTE**
>
> At the bottom of Figure 24-2 is an FIT Summary Table that conveniently summarizes the results of the tests in the document. To include this information in your test documents, just add a table with one row and one column containing fit.Summary.

When running a test that involves a sequence of tables, you will usually find you need to perform some form of setup to put the system into a certain state as well as to communicate changes in this state among the tests in different tables. In Figure 24-6, the first command in the first table is labeled `ResetImageList` and this removes any images already stored in the system by invoking the method shown in Listing 24-2. You will also notice that the `Instance` static variable provides a convenient way to pass information around. You should develop similar ways of controlling the state of your system to ensure the successful execution of your customer tests.

LISTING 24-2: ImportImageDialog ResetImageList Method

```
public void ResetImageList()
{
    Data.Instance.Images.Clear();
}
```

> **⯊ NOTE**
>
> In general, you will test a feature of the system by creating a sequence of tables in the same document. However, you should always ensure that test documents can be run independently of any other and in any order.

Top Ten Tips for Test Design

Designing good tests is difficult and requires plenty of practice as well as a willingness to learn from past mistakes. We hope the following tips will help your team avoid some of the more obvious pitfalls while you gain this experience:

1. Let your tables evolve. Start with simple tests and then expand them as your knowledge of the problem grows.

2. Make the tables clear so that business colleagues can understand them without any explanation. It should be obvious what is being tested and why.

3. Refactor your tests on a regular basis to remove duplication and redundant information as well as to make them simpler and easier to understand.

4. Do not combine different tests into the same table. Have each table test just one aspect of a problem.

5. Where possible, compact information spread across different columns. For example, instead of having two columns labeled "start time" and "end time," have just one column labeled "duration."

6. Keep your table short by making sure each row in your table (test scenario) reveals important information when it fails. Include the boundary cases and exceptions, not repetitions of normal values.

7. Action tables will usually involve the sequence of "set up," "change state" (action), and "check." Look carefully for any Action table that has missed any of these steps.

8. Provide a single table that performs any setup required by your tests, instead of including this work at the beginning of each table.

9. Avoid having to frequently change your tests for areas of the code that are constantly changing (such as the user interface) by creating suitable adapters.

10. Frequently review the way your tests are organized and run so that as the numbers grow, they do not become difficult to manage and maintain.

CONCLUSION

In this chapter, we showed how Visual Studio Team System allows you to run tests using third-party (or open source) tools. Although wrapping tests in a generic test so that you can run them during a Team Build does involve some work, we believe that the benefit of introducing storytest-driven development into your development process makes such effort worthwhile.

> **■ TIP**
>
> Use a virtual PC to host the database of the system under test so that you can restore the system state before running your customer tests simply by reloading the server image from a file. This is usually much quicker and easier than attempting to restore the database.

Review of Section 7
Implement Customer Testing

THE OSPACS TEAM quickly embraced the idea of customer testing because it seemed to benefit everyone. Developers would get concrete examples of what the customer wanted in terms of executable tests, and assurance that once these tests passed, the story would be judged complete. Customers would get the features they wanted and the ability to track the team's progress in delivering them. Therefore, they took the following actions to implement customer testing:

- **Created a skeletal test document**—In order to keep all of the customer tests together, the team created a Microsoft Word document and added it to Team Foundation Version Control (TFVC). The customer (Sally) was given "full" access rights to this document because she was considered its owner, but the rest of the team was granted "read" access because they would need to implement the Framework for Integrated Test (FIT) fixtures and stories that corresponded to her tests.

- **Version control**—The team developed a couple of scripts so that Sally could check in and check out the test document without needing to install Visual Studio Team System (VSTS) on her PC.

- **Team Build**—The team updated the project's Team Build types to automate deployment and execution of the customer's tests on the BuildLabPC so that the latest version of the customer tests would run in conjunction with the latest version of the developer's software and fixtures.

- **Access to test results**—The team updated the Team Build types so that the build products would be put into a shared Drop folder on the Team Foundation Server (TFS). In this way, the customer (and the rest of the team) could access the test result files produced by FIT when Team Builds completed.

- **Coaching the customer**—People with testing experience, such as Maggie, agreed to help Sally write her tests. However, everyone clearly understood that the customer would be responsible for producing the tests.

- **Writing FIT fixtures**—The team's developers gained experience developing different types of fixtures to support the customer's tests.

> **■ WARNING**
>
> You should not give defect-laden code to your customer for testing. Therefore, a prerequisite for introducing customer testing is to make sure your team can consistently deliver high-quality software.

The Team's Impressions

The team readily embraced the idea of driving its development with story-tests and was pleased to discover that it could so easily integrate an open source tool such as FIT with VSTS.

CEO: Mike

"I don't need to ask people about their progress. Instead, I just run the customer tests from my office and see what they've achieved."

Developer: Tom

"Storytest-driven development means that we perform User Acceptance Testing throughout the project, not just at the end. However, that's not to say that further testing isn't needed before the software finally goes into production."

"Customer testing shifts power from IT to the business, which means that we're no longer entirely to blame when products aren't ready for shipping with the features our customers are demanding."

Developer: Luke

"The customer's job is to write the tests in a Word document and the developer's job is to write the associated fixtures in C#."

"I found it easy to develop the fixtures needed for Sally's tests, because basically, they are like the Adapter pattern[1] I've been reading about. They just act as a wrapper for our production code."

"It's really cool to use a Word document as a test script. I wouldn't have thought of doing that, but it makes perfect sense to use a tool that businesspeople already know how to use."

Developer: Sarah

"Storytest-driven development sounds a bit like 'design by contract,'[2] except the test becomes the contract. This makes it much clearer what the business wants."

"We'll still use manual tests to check the operation of the user interface, but this involves much less work because Sally's customer tests have already validated its basic function."

Developer: Peter

"The tests give me concrete examples of what is needed, which is much better than having to interpret Sally's wordy descriptions of the underlying business algorithms."

"The customer still needs to perform some manual testing of the user interface, because otherwise, we wouldn't get regular feedback on issues such as performance and usability."

Developer: Maggie

"The team members now view testing as something that helps them deliver software, rather than as a hindrance. There is general enthusiasm for writing tests. Frankly, I'm amazed."

"I like coaching people about writing tests. They respect my skill and experience, which makes me feel much more valued as a professional."

---

1. [DP] Gamma, Erich, et al. *Design Patterns* (Addison-Wesley, 1995).
2. Wikipedia. "Design by contract" (http://en.wikipedia.org/wiki/Design_by_contract).

"For the first time in my career, I feel like I'm part of the team. I'm no longer the bad guy who sits in an office down the corridor, trying to destroy other people's work."

Customer: Sally

"Writing my own tests gives me a measure of progress that I can really believe in. There should be no more surprises just days before a release date about the software not being ready."

"I was a bit skeptical about actually writing executable tests because it all sounded a bit techie. However, after seeing a few sample tables in a Word document, it wasn't really much different from the sorts of specifications I was already writing."

"Maggie has helped me a lot and I'm now writing much better tests, but it's good to have her review my tests from time to time."

Agile Values

Implementing storytest-driven development (STDD) and the Real Customer Involvement practice helped the team apply Agile values in the following ways.

Communication

Real customer involvement means there is direct contact between the people who decide "what" the system should do and the people who decide "how" these needs are best satisfied. Writing customer tests encourages communication among such business and development people by expressing requirement details as specific tests which both parties can readily understand.

Feedback

Giving the customer responsibility for writing these tests means the team's progress can be measured in terms of the value being added to the business. This allows the business to track and understand the project's growth in a way that can never be achieved by reading a periodic progress report. Customer testing also allows developers to learn from functional errors discovered in their software so that they can improve both the product and the development process.

Courage

Customer testing gives the team confidence that it can deliver what is needed, when it is needed. This encourages the team to try out new ideas and more aggressively seek better business value. It also reduces the fear of a small change causing some unforeseen problem, and therefore makes the team less defensive.

Simplicity

Any code not covered by customer tests is likely to be associated with features that add little value to the business and, therefore, represent unnecessary complexity. Customer testing encourages the discipline of developers implementing just enough code to pass the test. It also helps create a system that is easy to test and thereby avoids any tight coupling that otherwise might be introduced inadvertently among components.

Respect

The success of the project is visibly measured in terms of passing customer tests, which makes everyone on the team constantly aware that they are all integral to the success of the project. Without the domain knowledge provided by the business, the developers risk producing software that has no value, and without the skill and dedication of the developers, there would be no product to deliver.

▪ Section 8
Estimate, Prioritize, and Plan

THIS SECTION OF the book is about managing an Agile project so that the team delivers what the business needs, when it needs it. Chapter 25 provides the foundation for Agile planning by explaining the role of story cards in estimating and then prioritizing the team's work. In Chapter 26, we present an Agile approach to planning that involves repeatedly making plans for different time scales throughout the project as well as dynamically controlling it with feedback from both the business and the developers. The section concludes with Chapter 27, which combines an explanation of using the project management facilities provided by Visual Studio Team System

Photograph by Picture Post Hulton Archive (Copyright Getty Images 1953).

Controlling a software project is a bit like navigating a ship, as you constantly need to estimate your position and alter your course to reflect changes in circumstances.

(VSTS) with a walkthrough of the way a small Agile team might plan and execute an iteration.

Story from the Trenches

Most people working in software development will probably experience at least one death-march project[1] during their career. This term is something of a hyperbole, as people are not forced to work under conditions of near starvation and nobody is taken outside and shot for misplacing a curly bracket. However, such projects are distinctly unpleasant to work on and often have a high attrition rate in terms of staff. No one intends to create a death march; it's just something that happens. However, often there are warning signs from the very start of the project.

Several years ago I worked for an avionics company that had embarked upon a project to build a system for aircraft to communicate with ground-based maintenance systems using digital radio. This was a high-profile project that had been won only after an acrimonious battle in which it appeared that politics rather than common sense prevailed. The company was therefore under a lot of pressure to deliver all the features and quality it had promised within the ambitious time scales and budget it had quoted.

When I joined the small team of people charged with implementing this project, they seemed confident that the project would be a success despite their general lack of experience and poor knowledge of its core technology, X.25 data communication. The team leader, Jason, didn't seem too concerned about such issues because he was following a formal process, so he was certain that all the details would slot into place once the team had drawn enough Unified Modeling Language (UML) diagrams. Therefore, the team had been fully occupied for the preceding month developing dozens of class and object drawings which were now neatly bound in the first draft of the project's design document. Meanwhile, the deputy project manager had been busy learning to use Microsoft Project and had papered the walls of his office with Gantt and PERT charts that showed the project

---

1. Yourdon, Edward. *Death March* (Prentice Hall, 2003).

was on course for its target delivery dates. The senior project manager knew very little about software development, but clearly was impressed by all of these visible signs of progress.

After spending a few days familiarizing myself with the project, I felt confident enough to ask Jason some obvious questions, such as why did he think it would take 12 days to develop the data link layer code? On what similar work did the team base its estimate? Did anyone actually know what the data link layer did? Frustrated by his refusal to give me a straight answer, I asked the deputy project manager how he had arrived at this 12-day estimate. The answer was simple: The software had to be delivered in four months, so they had worked backward to allocate the work into the time available. Regardless of the size and complexity of the data link layer coding, it would take 12 days because they didn't have any more time to complete it.

The people on the team I had joined weren't estimating and planning; they were engaged in wishful thinking. Estimating depends upon knowing where you are and where you want to be, and then having some knowledge of the time it takes to travel between such points. Our team didn't know how to implement the software, so how could it identify its path? The team had no experience writing similar code, so how could it judge its speed? Without reliable estimates, the team's plan was no more than a smoke screen hiding the fact that the team was hopelessly lost. When the politics and commercial pressure of this project were added to the mix, there was only one possible outcome: It would become a death-march project.

It was easy for me to foresee that replanning work to correct poor estimates would soon become a regular event and this would inevitably lead to more and more work being demanded from the team. Eventually the developers would find themselves spending 18 hours a day hacking out code in a futile attempt to reach some impossible objective. After missing a few deadlines, the recriminations would start, thereby adding misery to feelings of hopelessness and exhaustion. I would like to be able to say that I stayed with the team, sprinkled some pixie dust, and rescued the project, but actually I left the company within two weeks of joining the team. However, my departure did trigger a radical shake-up and reorganization which allowed the team to eventually reach its target and deliver the system, which I understand was done without exacting too high a price on the individuals involved.

Section 8 presents a way to estimate, prioritize, and plan a software project which allows you to achieve your objectives in a better way than the team managed in this story. However, you should keep in mind that the position of this section in the book reflects the fact that such issues are largely irrelevant until your team has learned how to reliably deliver quality software that provides high value to the customer.

■ 25
Estimating and Prioritizing Stories

A N AGILE TEAM needs to define the software features which have value to the business and then plan their implementation to realize this value without delay. In this chapter, we describe how story cards help teams identify such features and explain how to properly estimate and prioritize the work associated with implementing them. This is important groundwork for Chapter 26, which presents an approach to planning Agile projects.

Working with Customer Stories

Customer stories provide a way to identify the discrete features of a software product that have value to the business. Therefore, the team can use stories to define and plan its work as well as to provide an objective measure of its progress in delivering valuable software to the business. You would normally expect a pair of developers to implement a story within a small number of programming episodes.

> **▪▪ NOTE**
>
> Although customer stories originate from Extreme Programming (XP),[1] they often are used in other types of Agile projects. We prefer the term *customer stories* (or just *stories*) to *user stories* because it avoids any possible confusion with *use cases*.[2]

Overview

We first introduced customer stories in Chapter 3, when we explained that they have three basic parts: card, conversation, and confirmation.[3] Figure 25-1 shows an example of the card part of a story. It contains a summary of the conversation part of the story on its face and describes the confirmation part of the story, a customer test, on its reverse side. Stories arise from brief conversations between developers and customers that happen informally during the life of the project as a result of the Stories practice. Accordingly, most of the information about the feature is not written down, so take care that you don't just look at the card in isolation. For example, the story in Figure 25-1 summarizes a conversation between two members of the OSPACS team: Luke (developer) and Sally (customer). At first glance, the story looks quite simple to implement, but if you could talk to Luke you would quickly discover that it actually represents a significant amount of work, for it involves accessing an external database and then matching the contents of multiple fields which are inconsistently populated in different formats; see Figure 24-4.

> **▪▪ NOTE**
>
> The small size of the card means that it can capture only a small fraction of the issues discussed between the developer and the customer during their conversation. The specific detail is contained in tests which are subsequently written by the customer; see Section 7.

---

1. Beck, Kent. *Extreme Programming Explained, First Edition* (Addison-Wesley, 2000).
2. Jacobson, Ivar. "Object-oriented development in an industrial environment" (OOPSLA, 1987).
3. Jeffries, Ron. "Essential XP: Card, Conversation, Confirmation" (www.xprogramming.com).

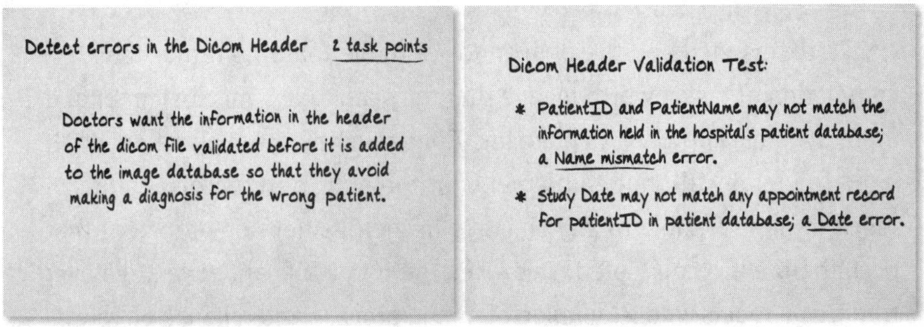

Detect errors in the Dicom Header   2 task points

Doctors want the information in the header
of the dicom file validated before it is added
to the image database so that they avoid
making a diagnosis for the wrong patient.

Dicom Header Validation Test:

* PatientID and PatientName may not match the
  information held in the hospital's patient database;
  a Name mismatch error.

* Study Date may not match any appointment record
  for patientID in patient database; a Date error.

FIGURE 25-1: Story card from the OSPACS project, front and back

Stories Practice

The Stories practice requires the team to plan a project using cards that serve to summarize, estimate, and prioritize the work.

The developer produces a story card during a brief discussion with the customer about something the business wants the software to do. The developer summarizes this conversation on the card in the form of a statement, such as "a <type of user> wants <capability> so that <business value>".[4] He also writes the name of the story on the card, being careful to choose a name that is short and meaningful enough for the team to be able to use it during later discussions.

Soon after the card is written, the team estimates the work required to implement the story. This gives the customer a feel for the cost of implementing the story, which helps decide its priority as indicated by its position in the pile of stories awaiting implementation. At the beginning of each iteration, the team plans its work simply by removing cards from the top of this story pile until the cumulative size reaches the same level delivered in the previous iteration. In this way, the project is regularly replanned to adjust delivery targets according to the team's actual progress and current business priorities.

Continues

---

4. [USA] Cohn, Mike. *User Stories Applied* (Addison-Wesley, 2004).

Agile teams focus on the delivery of valuable features rather than the completion of tasks, which means that they can take a much simpler and more dynamic approach to planning. Consequently, team members don't need to identify all the requirements at the start of the project and can respond more flexibly to any changes in the business environment that occur before it is completed. This gives them a significant advantage over traditional teams whose detailed planning process and reliance on formal documents generally limit them to making a more complex static plan at the start of a project. Such plans tend to be less effective than the simple dynamic plans yielded by the Stories practice in terms of delivering software that satisfies the actual business need.

■ NOTE

Iterations always last for a fixed period. In some projects, they last a week, but in others they may last two or even three weeks.

Generating Stories

When a customer and developer initially sit down to discuss a story, it may take only a few minutes to write out the card and decide on a suitable name. The developer may not ultimately implement the story, so there is little point in getting into specifics at this stage. It's important to consider only those details which are necessary for estimating its size—for example, the number and complexity of business rules, the nature of the user interface, data that needs to be stored, and so forth. Whether the developer summarizes these details on the back of the story card (see Figure 25-1) or puts them in his personal notebook, he needs to put them in general terms, because as we mentioned before, the full details of a story are captured only later, when the customer test is being written.

People become proficient at producing customer stories through practice, so you should look at the examples provided in books such as Mike Cohn's *User Stories Applied*[5] and then try to copy the general style. However, the INVEST acronym, coined by Bill Wake,[6] provides a useful way to remember the attributes of a good customer story and may help you avoid some of the common pitfalls:

- **Independent**—One story should not depend on the implementation of another so that you can prioritize them for business rather than technical reasons.
- **Negotiable**—Neither the customer nor the developer must use his position to dictate the terms of a story.
- **Valuable**—If the feature doesn't offer any direct value or benefit to the business, why would the business want to implement it?
- **Estimate**—Split large stories (epics) into smaller ones and investigate the unknown issues until you can confidently estimate the time they will take to implement.
- **Small**—Split or rework stories until a developer can complete them within a few days. However, don't make them so small that the coding takes minutes rather than hours.
- **Testable**—You must be able to test a story to ensure that there is an agreed-upon criterion for the story's completion. This also guards against you creating stories for nonfunctional requirements such as ease of use, reliability, and so forth.

■ TIP

Do not be tempted to write a program for managing customer stories electronically because this loses the significant value of having physical cards to handle while discussing stories with other people.

---

5. [USA] Cohn, Mike. *User Stories Applied* (Addison-Wesley, 2004).
6. Wake, Bill. "INVEST in Good Stories, and SMART Tasks" (http://xp123.com/xplor/xp0308/index.shtml).

Estimating

Estimates of stories are more reliable when they are produced by people who have some experience doing the work; therefore, estimating is done by developers. There are three common approaches to estimating the size of a story:

- **Gut feel**—After spending a few minutes thinking about the matter, you produce an estimate based on your experience doing similar work. Your gut feelings can be surprisingly accurate if you have the relevant skills and know the team well.
- **Comparison**—You compare the work to similar jobs the team has already completed to produce a relative estimate of its size. This works best when you can size the work as being a little more than job "A," but a little less than job "B."
- **Splitting up the work**—Divide a large task into a set of subtasks that you find easier to estimate by gut feel or comparison, and then sum all the estimates for these subtasks. This is a good way to handle some work that is much larger than the rest, but becomes inaccurate when you split up the work too finely.

Estimates are notoriously difficult to get right, whatever approach you use and regardless of the amount of effort you apply. Indeed, often your initial gut feeling after ten minutes is no worse than an estimate produced after the team has spent hours splitting up the work and deliberating about suitable comparisons to other jobs.

Sizing Stories

Stories describe what features the business requires, not how developers will implement them. Therefore, when estimating the size of a story, start by considering with other developers alternative ways in which you might complete the work. The developer who initially wrote the story card should lead the discussion by describing the sorts of tests the customer envisioned, because this usually reveals a lot about the nature of the work. After five or ten minutes of discussion, the group must then try to reach a consensus about the size of the task that will lead to the most promising solution.

Although you must eventually divide a large story (epic) into smaller stories which you can implement individually within a single iteration, it is not always necessary to split up such epics initially. It is more important to keep discussions about story estimations at a high level and to concentrate on alternatives that have a significant impact on the size of the task being considered. You are not attempting to identify each part of the task, size them individually, and then produce an estimate as the sum of the parts. You are just spending five or ten minutes getting a feel for the size of the job by talking it through with your colleagues, perhaps while standing around the coffee machine. The detailed planning of the task comes much later, just before implementation, as described in Chapter 26.

> **▪ TIP**
>
> When sizing a story, take the opportunity to identify any preparation which would prevent you from completing the story within a single iteration. In this way, the team can make sure it completes this work before attempting to implement it; see the section titled Task Plan, in Chapter 26.

Absolute Values versus Relative Values for Estimation

A common way to state the size of a task is to give a figure for the number of hours it might take, but this can create problems. Consider the following:

> A team of ten developers determines that the tasks comprising a project will require 360 man-weeks' worth of work. Therefore, they predict that they will be able to complete the project in 36 weeks: $36 = 360/10$. Four weeks later, the team is behind schedule: the developers have completed only 20 man-weeks' worth of work instead of the 40 they anticipated they would have been able to complete in this time. Accordingly, they must change every man-week estimate in the project plan to correct for their slow progress, and recalculate their delivery date: $72 = (360 \times 2)/10$.

Putting absolute times into a project plan means that you will need to update each estimate whenever the team's rate of progress changes. Not only does changing all these estimates take a significant amount of time, but also, after a few months, the people involved start to lose confidence in the figures because you've changed them so often, even though the problem is as much about identifying the correct rate of progress as it is about poor initial estimates.

Let's consider how we could improve things by expressing size as a relative quantity instead of an absolute one:

A team of ten developers rates the tasks comprising a project on a scale of 0 to 9, which gives them a total of 2,880 points. They expect to complete 80 points each week, and they anticipate completing the project in 36 weeks: 36 = 2,880/80. Unfortunately, a month later they have completed only 40 points' worth of tasks. However, they don't need to change any estimates in the project plan because their relative size is still correct. Instead, they simply change the number of points they expect to deliver each week to 40 and recalculate the delivery date: 72 = 2,880/40.

Expressing estimates as a relative quantity makes it much easier to keep the project plan up-to-date because the individual figures aren't changing very often. In fact, the only time you need to adjust an individual task estimate is when it becomes obvious that its relative size is wrong. For example, if you estimate the creation of all dialog boxes at 1 point, but later discover that a more realistic size for such a task would be 2 points, it is appropriate to adjust all the other estimates relating to dialog box creation. What really matters is being consistent so that the size of each task is in proportion to all the others.

■ NOTE

The work required to alter absolute estimates makes it difficult to adjust your project plan for changes in the team's rate of progress more than once a month. But using relative estimates you can adjust it frequently, an important consideration when planning dynamically.

Relative Estimate Scales

Most people find it easier to compare the size of things than to produce an absolute value of size. For example, an estimate that your shoes are just a bit bigger than your friend's is likely to be more reliable than an estimate that your shoes are 10.5 inches long. However, it is important to use appropriate scales when making such comparisons. For instance, stating a collection of shoe sizes as 72, 81, 82, 69 on a scale of 1 to 100 is actually less accurate than stating them as 7, 8, 8, 7 on a scale of 1 to 10. Mike Cohn[7] has reported considerable success using the following nonlinear scale for estimating stories:

$$0, 1, 2, 3, 5, 8, 13, 20, 40, 100$$

This scale includes 0 for tasks that are too small to consider for the purposes of planning, but nevertheless need to be completed. Giving such tasks a positive score would result in a false impression of progress when it came to counting how many points had been delivered over a period. However, you can expect to complete only so many of these zero-point tasks during a period before they collectively start to become significant.

Numbers which are larger than 8 in Mike's scale are intended for stories that are much larger than normal, which means that you will estimate most of your stories in terms of being a relative size of 1, 2, 3, 5, or 8. The use of a nonlinear series forces you to be less precise about comparisons as they get bigger so that something that is certainly bigger than 3, but definitely less than 8, becomes a 5. In an ideal world, most of your comparisons would fall as 1, 2, or 3 task points—a range which is small enough for all developers to apply consistently over the course of a project.

Task Points and Story Cost Estimation

The main disadvantage of using a relative quantity for estimating is that it makes the figures more difficult to understand. This is not a problem when developers are discussing estimates among themselves, because everyone very quickly gets a feel for the difference between a 1-, 2-, and 3-point task.

7. [AEP] Cohn, Mike. *Agile Estimating and Planning* (Addison-Wesley, 2006).

However, explaining such differences to people who are not involved in the estimating process can be difficult. For this reason, we suggest you convert task point estimates into story costs with the simple calculation shown in Figure 25-2, where the following terms are used:

- **Task point** is what developers use for estimating. It is the relative size of some work expressed on the nonlinear scale; 0, 1, 2, 3, 5, 8, 13, 20, 40, 100.

- **Velocity** is a measure of the team's progress. It is the sum of the task point values for the stories successfully implemented during an iteration.

- **Iteration burn rate** is the cost of running the project for an iteration.

- **Story cost** is what customers use for budgeting. It expresses the dollar cost of implementing a story. The customer obtains this figure by dividing the sum of the story's task points by the team's velocity, and then multiplying by its iteration burn rate.

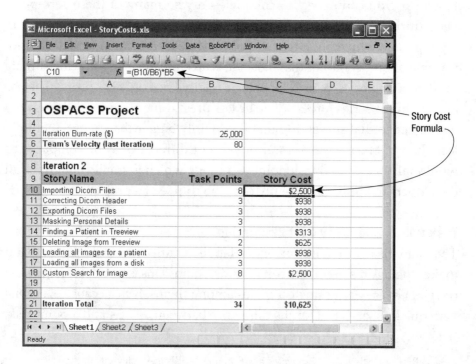

FIGURE 25-2: Spreadsheet showing task points and story cost

> **■ NOTE**
>
> The project's burn rate doesn't have to be the actual cost of running the project for an iteration, but you should make this figure realistic because it helps focus both customers and developers on providing good value for the money being spent.

Budgeting

It is very easy to adjust a project as a result of changes to its budget, because the total number of iterations available for the team to implement its stories depends upon the budget (price) according to the following simple formula:

Total Number of Iterations = Total Project Price / Iteration Burn Rate

Therefore, if you had a budget of $250,000 and an average burn rate of $25,000 per iteration, the team would have ten iterations available to implement the stories, or ten weeks if you assume the iteration length is one week. Reducing this budget by $50,000 takes two iterations away from the team's total, which will cause some of the lowest-priority stories to be canceled and will move the date of the final release forward by two iterations.

> **■ WARNING**
>
> We do not advise that you increase the budget in the hope of increasing your team's velocity, because as Brooks' law[8] states, adding developers to a project that is running late only makes it later. Instead, accept the reality of your velocity and ask the customer to reprioritize.

Prioritizing

The priorities of your stories determine the order in which you should implement them. Deciding priority is primarily a job for customers, because they are ultimately responsible for deciding what should be

---

8. [MMM] Brooks, Frederick P. *The Mythical Man-Month* (Addison-Wesley, 1975).

delivered to the business and when. However, priorities also need to be set in response to technical business issues; therefore, developers must provide some input to the process.

Value

Value starts flowing from the moment the software is released to the business, so it makes sense to prioritize stories that provide the biggest value so that this benefit can accumulate from as early as possible in the project; see Section 10. You can quantify this sort of financial value in terms of discounted cash flow, valued added analysis, and so forth, and then use the figures to set your priorities. However, you also can state value in nonfinancial terms by assessing the relative desirability of a story and the likely level of user satisfaction that might result from its implementation. You can perform this sort of analysis simply by asking a representative selection of customers (and users) to score your stories on some basis, such as the MoSCoW rules of DSDM:[9] Must have, Should have, Could have, and Won't have. Sam Guckenheimer[10] gives a good overview of such techniques in his book, *Software Engineering with Visual Studio Team System*.

> **■ TIP**
>
> Ask an accountant to calculate any financial values; this will lend authority to your analysis and prevent your entire plan from being questioned because of some inappropriate financial assumption.

Business Risk

Risk from a business perspective is about the potential failure of the business to obtain the best possible value from its investment. This may happen because the software is delivered late, so the opportunity cannot be fully exploited; or it may result from the software costing more to develop than

---

9. DSDM: Dynamic Systems Development Method Web site (www.dsdm.org).
10. [SETS] Guckenheimer, Sam, and Juan Perez. *Software Engineering with Microsoft Visual Studio Team System* (Addison-Wesley, 2006).

anticipated, thereby reducing the business's profit margin. However, the most significant business risk is usually that the delivered software doesn't meet the business's current needs.

▪ NOTE

Customers with a business background are usually good at managing the sorts of risks that arise from late delivery or budget overspending, so it makes sense to use these skills by giving them the means to control the project, as described in Chapter 26.

The risk of the delivered software not meeting the current needs of the business arises because of changes in the external environment or because the developers did not properly understand what they must deliver. Therefore, to manage business risks, customers need to reduce the priority of stories that are sensitive to changes in the external environment and increase the priority of stories that are somehow difficult to explain. In this way, the team delivers as late as possible any stories that are likely to be affected by external change, as this gives the environment less time to change between implementation and delivery. It also means that the team delivers any complex stories as soon as possible, so any misunderstandings can be resolved with a minimum of disruption to the flow of business value.

Technical Risk

Risk from a technical perspective concerns the possible failure of the team's developers to fully implement the story by the required delivery date. When technical risk arises due to uncertainty among the team's developers about how they should implement a story, it may be appropriate to increase the priority of the story. This is because the knowledge generated when you start work on a story often reduces the risk by removing some of the uncertainty about the rest of its implementation. It is better to undertake this sort of risk reduction early in the project because it gives you more time to find a technical solution and prevents you from creating a product that cannot be released because it lacks some key feature.

> **▪ NOTE**
>
> The MSF for Agile process template allows you to create work items for any risks you have identified so that you can track and report them. However, on a small team, it is more convenient to write a comment on the story card to remind people about the issue.

Removing Dependencies

Clearly your customer cannot prioritize effectively on the basis of risk and value when dependencies exist between stories; for example, story A can be done only after story B is finished. Therefore, you should avoid creating any dependencies between stories and remove any dependencies that might have been introduced before attempting to set priorities.

Typically, dependences arise when developers are estimating a story rather than when customers are formulating it. This is because during estimation, developers are thinking about implementation, so they may be tempted to split the task for a story into a sequence of subtasks and then declare some of them as being common to other stories in order to optimize the work. When a task relates to more than one story, it creates a dependency between them, so to remove this sort of problem, you simply need to make sure each task relates to just one story and accept the fact that this may result in a certain amount of task duplication. Some of this duplication may be removed when developers start optimizing just before implementation; see the section titled Task Plan, in Chapter 26.

> **▪ NOTE**
>
> Occasionally, the estimate for a story significantly depends upon when it is done. In such cases, you need to bring the issue to the customer's attention when the story is being prioritized, in the same way you would alert the customer of a technical risk.

One of the reasons you should avoid splitting up your work too finely is that you will start to think about optimizing work by sharing tasks among different stories and, as a result, risk creating dependencies. Therefore, the presence of dependencies between stories is often an indication that developers are going into too much detail when estimating their tasks. For this reason, many Agile teams avoid explicitly discussing tasks during estimation and instead write the size of a story directly onto the associated card in units, as "story points." We consider it more natural for people to provide a size for something they will do (task) rather than for something they want (story), and for this reason, we prefer using the term *task points*.

> **■ NOTE**
>
> The traditional Agile measurement for story size is *ideal days*,[11] but you may find other units, such as *story points*,[12] used in some projects. The name of the unit is irrelevant when you are dealing in relative values. What matters is making accurate comparisons between task sizes.

CONCLUSION

In this chapter, we identified the following key points for you to consider when creating, estimating, and prioritizing stories:

- Developers and customers develop stories together in terms of producing a card, having a conversation, and then defining a test as a form of confirmation. The acronym *INVEST* describes the attributes of a good story; it is independent, negotiable, valuable, capable of being estimated, small, and testable.

- Developers estimate a story by writing a value for its relative size on the card in units such as task points. In this way, you can adjust plans for changes in the rate of progress without having to change the estimate of each story. Relative estimates also tend to be more accurate.

---

11. Beck, Kent. *Extreme Programming Explained, First Edition* (Addison-Wesley, 2000).
12. [AEP] Cohn, Mike. *Agile Estimating and Planning* (Addison-Wesley, 2006).

- You should use a nonlinear scale such as 0, 1, 2, 3, 5, 8, 13, 20, 40, 100 to express size; however, most stories will lie within a small range of these values: 1, 2, or 3 task points.

- Customers prioritize stories by arranging the pile of cards awaiting implementation so that the highest-priority ones are put at the top. They set priority according to business value and risk such that the stories that provide the greatest value for the least business risk are done first.

- Developers also play a part in setting the priority of stories because technical risk needs to be addressed sooner rather than later, but technical dependencies between stories must be avoided because they inhibit the setting of business priorities.

■ NOTE

Proper estimates and priorities are a prerequisite for controlling any project, because feeding garbage into a planning process will inevitably result in nothing but garbage coming out.

▪ 26
Agile Planning

I N THIS CHAPTER, we explore the nature of plans and explain the way an Agile team engages in planning at various times throughout the project: daily, weekly, and quarterly. The resulting task, iteration, and release plans are simple to follow as well as easy to produce, which enables a team to control its project more dynamically. In this way, a team can respond effectively to changes in the business environment as well as its own rate of progress, thereby helping the team to satisfy the business it serves through the early and continuous delivery of valuable software.[1]

The Nature of Plans

Plans help us organize a project by creating a schedule of work so that everyone on the team knows what he must do next. Good plans arrange such work so that it provides optimum value for a given set of constraints, such as budget, time, quality, and features. Depending on what you're doing, your plan may operate best when you implement the work according to the schedule with a minimum of variation, or your plan may need frequent adjustment during its execution.

---

1. [ASD] Martin, Robert. *Agile Software Development* (Prentice Hall, 2003).

Plans for Repeated Execution versus One-Time Plans

Plans that are intended for repeated execution should always give the same result. For example, when you follow Mary Berry's recipe for double-chocolate muffins,[2] you get the same sort of muffin each time. The recipe results from much experimentation, but ultimately it consists of a fixed set of instructions for delivering a muffin. Many people's expectations about plans often come from following such recipes.

When you are creating things such as double-chocolate muffins, it is reasonable to look for a plan that has been repeatedly executed because that will minimize variation in what you are attempting to achieve. In this case, at the beginning of the process, you want a plan delivered which contains precise details of the sequence of steps that will lead you to your objective. You should then insist that the steps are followed without variation, as this way you are certain of producing the sort of muffins you want. However, when you are designing things such as software, no existing plan is available for you to follow, for there is seldom any point in producing the same program, in the same way, twice in a row. Therefore, you need to find a plan that is suitable for what Donald Reinertsen calls a one-time process.[3] This type of plan accepts that you cannot precisely define a sequence of tasks at the start of a project, so instead it encourages the team to adapt its schedule regularly in response to its progress toward the current design objective.

Agile Planning

An Agile team understands that it needs a one-time plan, and therefore it does not expect to have a complete plan at the start of a project. Instead, it produces a plan a bit at a time as the project progresses; this is often called **rolling wave planning.** It is accepted that the plan will be wrong, particularly the further you move along in the schedule. However, does it matter whether your plan for next week is wrong? What really matters is having a correct plan for this week and being able to correct next week's plan before the weekend. This is what Mary Poppendieck means when she says, "Do the planning, but throw out the plans." She makes the point that your

---

2. Berry, Mary. *Complete Cookbook* (Dorling Kindersley, 1995).
3. [MTDF] Reinertsen, Donald. *Managing the Design Factory* (Simon and Schuster, 1997).

current plans will rapidly become out-of-date and that you will need to replace them regularly with new ones. Obviously, the further a one-time plan looks into the future, the more likely it is to be wrong, so it is better to concern yourself only with short time scales when creating such plans. Therefore, you achieve long-term goals by following a sequence of small, good plans made on a regular basis to correct for any changes to the objective or variations in the team's rate of progress. An Agile team manages changes to its objective by regularly re-sorting an ordered pile of story cards awaiting implementation (see Chapter 25) as a result of changes to its rate of progress measured in terms of velocity.

■ NOTE

One of the four fundamental statements in the Manifesto of the Agile Alliance[4] is "Responding to change over following a plan." Therefore, you can identify an Agile team by the fact that the team engages in planning throughout the project life cycle rather than just at the start.

Using Velocity to Measure Rate of Progress

Velocity measures the team's progress over a fixed period of time by adding up the task points for the stories which are successfully implemented during an iteration. Therefore, if your iteration length is one week, and during this time your team delivers work that it has estimated to be worth a total of 80 task points, the team's velocity is 80. When the team is able to maintain a constant velocity, it can make projections about the delivery date of the software it is developing. For example, a team with a total of 800 points of work that has an average velocity of 80 points per iteration might be expected to finish in ten iterations (weeks). However, if its velocity fell to 50 points per iteration, it would need 16 iterations to finish (16 = 800 / 50).

At the start of your project, you need to make a rough guess of the team's initial velocity before you can make any projections concerning the likely delivery (release) dates. However, after a couple of iterations, you can

---

4. The Agile Alliance Web site (www.agilealliance.org).

use a rule called "Yesterday's Weather"[5] to determine the team's velocity. This rule states that the best estimate for a team's velocity in the next iteration is the figure that was measured for the previous iteration. It is to be expected that from iteration to iteration, your team's velocity will vary slightly as it delivers work with different task point totals, but after a few iterations, the team ought to be able to establish a fairly constant velocity and therefore present its plans more confidently.

> **■■ NOTE**
>
> You should not attempt to measure the velocity of individual programmers because this leads to members of the team competing against each other, thereby disrupting the cooperation needed for practices such as Pair Programming, Shared Code, and so forth.

Planning at Every Time Scale

The software development life cycle of an Agile project (see Figure 3-2 in Chapter 3) dictates that a project has a number of fixed-length iterations, and that after completing a certain number of iterations, the customer is able to pull the software into the business by calling for a "release." Therefore, the team needs a release plan as well as an iteration plan, both of which are concerned with scheduling the implementation of stories. In addition, developers will create plans to schedule the tasks they need to complete. Consequently, an Agile team regularly makes (and remakes) plans at a time scale of months, weeks, and days, or even hours. In each case, the team follows the same basic approach proposed by Kent Beck:[6]

1. List the items of work that may need to be done.
2. Estimate the size of each item.

---

5. Beck, Kent, and Martin Fowler. *Planning Extreme Programming* (Addison-Wesley, 2001).

6. [XPE2] Beck, Kent, with Cynthia Andres. *Extreme Programming Explained, Second Edition* (Addison-Wesley, 2005).

3. Set a budget for the total size of the work you want to schedule.

4. Negotiate about which items can be added to the schedule, but don't change the budget or the estimates.

> **▪ NOTE**
>
> Iterations serve to time-box the development work, so they each have the same fixed duration for the whole project, typically set at between one and four weeks.

Task Plan

Task plans serve to identify the work that developers must do next. Usually developers agree on a high-level task plan during a meeting at the start of an iteration, and then create their own detailed task plans during the daily team meeting or at the start of a programming episode, as explained in Chapter 27. When creating task plans, you are very much concerned with optimizing the sequence of the work, but the time horizon is short. At most, task plans cover an iteration, and often just the next few hours of work. A developer's detailed task plan is essentially a "to-do" list sequencing the work he is responsible for completing. This includes implementing stories as well as other tasks, such as the following:

- **Spikes**—These are time-boxed investigations into some technical aspect of the project that may be required to reduce risk or improve the accuracy of an estimate.

- **Support**—Developers often need to provide support for software already in the production environment, even for products totally unconnected to the current project. However, as reported by Gerald Weinberg,[7] a significant cost is associated with someone switching among different projects.

---

7. [SQM] Weinberg, Gerald. *Quality Software Management* (Dorset House, 1992).

- **Bugs**—Although the team should identify and correct any defects in its software before declaring it complete, inevitably bugs will be found in stories after the end of the iteration in which they were implemented. Sam Guckenheimer[8] provides good advice about bug reporting in his recent book about VSTS.

Because you make the plan very close to when the work is being performed, it is less sensitive to external events but flexible enough to respond to any last-minute changes in the requirement. However, the short lead time between plan and implementation can be a problem when any advance preparation is needed. For example, if a story requires access to the corporate database, you may need to complete the necessary forms a few days before the work starts. You can handle these sorts of issues by creating the necessary tasks while estimating the story and then flagging them with a suitable sequence in order to remind people that they need to be scheduled separately.

Initially the task of implementing a story is implied by its story card. However, when you identify additional tasks for a story (or a spike, bug, etc.), we suggest that you write a summary of the work on a colored task card such as that shown in Figure 26-1, estimate its size, and then put it in the pile of stories awaiting implementation such that its order sets its priority. These colored task cards provide a visual warning of a problem in the team's planning process, because lots of colored cards indicate either that too much work is unrelated to the stories or that too many dependencies are being created for stories by way of their subtasks.

> **■ NOTE**
>
> You produce a task card for each story during the high-level planning meeting of the iteration in which it is implemented. The card does nothing more than just implement the story and serves only to track the progress of this work during the iteration; see Figure 27-3 in Chapter 27.

---

8. [SETS] Guckenheimer, Sam, and Juan Perez. *Software Engineering with Microsoft Visual System Team System* (Addison-Wesley, 2006).

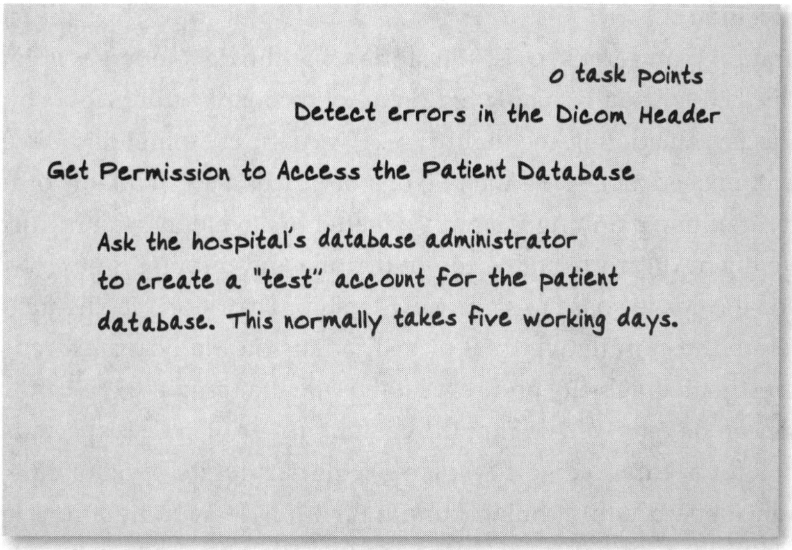

o task points
Detect errors in the Dicom Header

Get Permission to Access the Patient Database

Ask the hospital's database administrator
to create a "test" account for the patient
database. This normally takes five working days.

FIGURE 26-1: Task card: preparing a story for implementation

It should be possible to implement stories in almost any order, because there should not be any dependencies among the stories. But clearly, preparatory tasks may require execution in a certain sequence. Therefore, you may need to add a sequence number to a task card, but this will not create any dependencies among the tasks as long as you do not attempt to share the task among several stories. For this reason, you should state only one "owning" story at the top of each task card. You should give the size of a task in the same units you use to size your stories; however, they do not count toward the team's velocity. Stating the size of a task just helps the team avoid over-committing itself during iteration planning.

> **■ NOTE**
>
> Task cards simply serve as a reminder of some work that needs to be done in some future iteration. In general, you will not create task cards during detailed task planning and should expect only a small percentage of your tasks to have been identified in this way.

Iteration Plan

An iteration plan serves to list the stories that the developers will implement next. It is usually displayed on a notice board with a collection of
story cards pinned to it; see Figure 26-2. Once the customer and developers have finished arranging the pile of story cards into a suitable order of
priority, iteration planning is simply a matter of developers taking turns to
remove the next card from the top of the pile and pinning it next to their
name on the notice board to signify ownership. They stop picking up cards
just before the cumulative total of task points on the board exceeds the
team's estimated velocity and respect the rule that only the top card from
the pile can be removed so that the customer's priority is respected. It is
common for a team to display a plan for the current iteration on one side
of a notice board while constructing a plan for the next iteration on the
other. In this way, iteration planning can take place on a continuous basis.

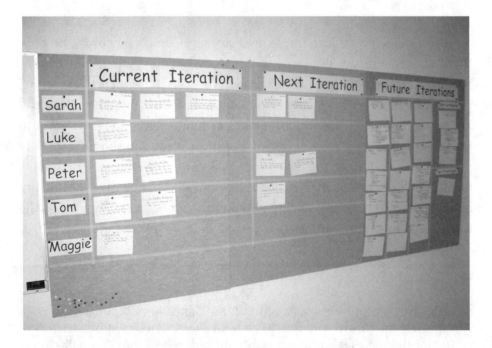

FIGURE 26-2: Iteration board showing stories in successive iterations

> **▪. NOTE**
>
> The developer who owns the story is responsible for making sure it is completed, but during actual implementation, the work is done with help from another developer, as we explained in the Pair Programming practice.

> **▪. NOTE**
>
> Task cards are not displayed on the iteration plan because the iteration plan is concerned with the delivery of features rather than the completion of tasks. People decide for themselves how best to organize their work so that the team can deliver the stories by the end of the iteration.

Developers can expect the customer not to change the iteration plan once the iteration has started so that they are aiming at a fixed target. However, it is usual to have some negotiations during the team's morning meeting on the first day of the iteration when last-minute adjustments are made to make the plan as good as possible. During the iteration, the owner of each story becomes responsible for its completion and will perform the necessary task planning to make sure this happens. The story is judged complete when it passes its customer tests (see Section 7), and only then does it count for the purposes of calculating the team's velocity. Therefore, the story either passes its tests at the end of the iteration and all the task points get credited to the team, or it fails its tests and none of the task points is counted. This may seem a bit harsh, but it provides a powerful incentive for people to finish jobs completely and makes velocity a much more objective measurement.

Weekly Cycle Practice

The Weekly Cycle practice is about synchronizing the achievement of the team's immediate goals with some naturally reoccurring event in the workplace, such as the end of the week (or the end of two weeks). The weekly cycle results in new features being added to the software and therefore is responsible for moving a project forward.

Teams seem to work best when a set of goals are scheduled for completion at the end of a cycle they all share. Most teams finish the week on the same day, so it makes sense to plan for certain goals to be completed by this day. A week is long enough to give flexibility in case some tasks prove more difficult than anticipated, but not so long that people lose sight of their objectives. It also creates an effective planning horizon because it is hard to judge progress when goals are set too far in the future or too close to the present.

Implementing the Weekly Cycle practice means your team must develop software in a series of short, fixed-length iterations. Ideally, an iteration should last a week, though for some teams two weeks may be more appropriate. A short planning meeting will be held before the start of an iteration to decide which stories should be targeted for completion; see the section Iteration Plan, earlier in this chapter. The work typically starts with the development of the customer tests which will show when a story is complete. The developer writes the software needed to make these tests pass and then goes on to refine both code and tests. In this way, the developers and customers work together and create a product which is ready for deployment in the production environment at the end of the iteration.

Release Plan

The software should always be ready for release to the business at the end of each iteration, as explained in Section 9. Therefore, the customer can decide when to deliver the software solely on the basis of the value it contains; this often makes release dates quite irregular. These decisions are contained in the release plan (see Figure 26-3), which is more useful to the business than the team because it allows the business to plan its own activities for the delivery of the new software; for example, training, sales drives, and so forth. Typically, the customer would prepare the release plan in a spreadsheet that lists the new stories together with information such as the following:

- Release date = last release date + (iterations in next release * iteration length)
- Release cost = iterations in next release * iteration burn rate

The release plan may impact an assessment of a story's business value and, therefore, its priority, because it is common for a customer to collect groups of similar stories into themes to give a cohesive set of functionality to each release. For example, the first release might concentrate on all the stories needed to import ultrasound images into the hospital's database so that a particular area of the business can benefit from the software at the earliest possible date.

■ NOTE

Deployment of a team's software may not be instantaneous when organizations have a release process operated by people outside the team which required them to rebuild and retest the software before installing it in the production environment; see Section 9.

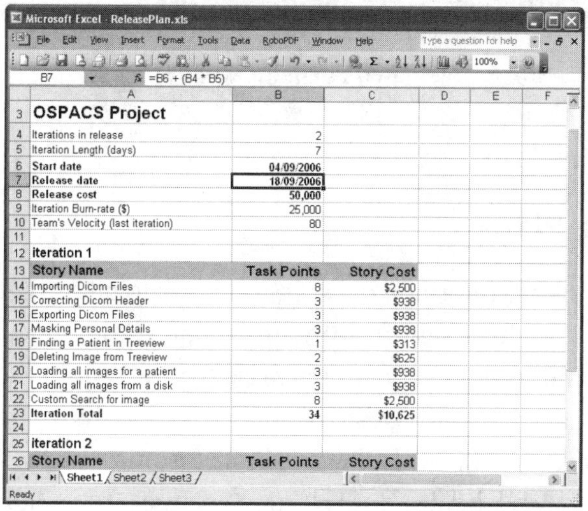

FIGURE 26-3: Excel spreadsheet showing the OSPACS release plan

Quarterly Cycle Practice

The Quarterly Cycle practice promotes the idea of a collection of stories with a common theme being implemented over a number of iterations and then released to the business together so as to satisfy some general strategic goal. Repeating this cycle four (or so) times a year keeps the team in regular synchronization with the business it serves while also aggregating changes to minimize the disruption that inevitably results when new software is put into production.

Introducing a quarterly cycle helps the team view its work in the context of moving toward some longer-term goals without which its software might lose its integrity and become just a collection of disconnected features. The end of the quarterly cycle provides a periodic opportunity for both the business and the developers to realign their objectives. It also provides a time to initiate repairs and correct problems that have accumulated over a number of iterations.

Implementing this practice requires that the team create a release plan at the start of each quarterly cycle; see the section Release Plan, earlier in this chapter. However, this plan may be discarded if the business decides to pull the software into production before the end of the cycle. Therefore, the team always plans for one quarter's worth of iterations in advance and adjusts its quarterly cycle to fit in with the needs of the business. The need for a team to make big adjustments to its quarterly cycle often indicates a more fundamental problem in its development process.

Controlling Plans

The team's plans are reformed on a regular basis to take account of the two types of changes which significantly impact an Agile project. First, variations in the business environment give rise to new requirements as well as the need to change existing ones. This may result in the alteration of budgets or variations in risk or value assessment. Second, the team's actual rate of progress may vary because of resource changes that result from budget adjustments. It can also vary for technical reasons because, for example, the developers have adopted a new tool, or issues such as morale, group cohesion, and energy need to be addressed.

Levers of Control

We previously described a good plan as one that delivers the best value for given feature, budget, date, and quality constraints. Therefore, the people who are ultimately responsible for providing value must react to change by varying these constraints in an attempt to reoptimize the team's delivery of value. For this reason, the customer must be allowed to control an Agile project using the following mechanisms:

- **Features**—Adjusting the priority of stories influences the features that will be made available to the business in the next release. It allows the customer to control a project by changing its scope.
- **Budget and date**—Adjusting the number of iterations affects the total cost of the project and its final delivery date. When the customer reduces the budget, the business gets fewer stories delivered in a shorter time; when the customer increases the budget, the business gets more stories, but they take longer to deliver.
- **Quality**—Adjusting the criterion for passing customer tests influences the team's velocity by changing the way stories are judged to be complete. It allows the customer to control a project by changing the quality of the finished work.

> **▪ NOTE**
>
> Increasing the amount of work a team delivers by reducing the quality threshold is seldom worthwhile because it causes reworking, which reduces morale, often leading to an even steeper decline in velocity. Therefore, in practice, wise customers do not try to control quality.

You can consider the control of an Agile project as a dynamic system (see Figure 26-4), with planning being driven by business changes which are influenced by the results of release plans as well as business events, and velocity changes which arise from the results of iteration plans. Stories lie at the center of the scheme, which emphasizes that the system is more concerned with delivering features than it is with producing plans or tasks. You will note that task plans do not appear on the diagram because they are just mechanisms to help people organize their work and are not concerned with controlling the project.

It is important for any control system to regulate the amount of feedback it generates; otherwise, there is a risk of instability. The control system for an Agile project is no different because too much change causes the system to become chaotic and too little change makes it sluggish. In order to stabilize the system, it is necessary to choose the correct iteration length, indicated by the calendar in Figure 26-3. A week is a convenient scheduling period for most teams, because a day is too short and a month is too long. However, the decision as to whether the iteration length should be one week, two weeks, or even longer needs to be made by each team on the basis of their individual circumstances.

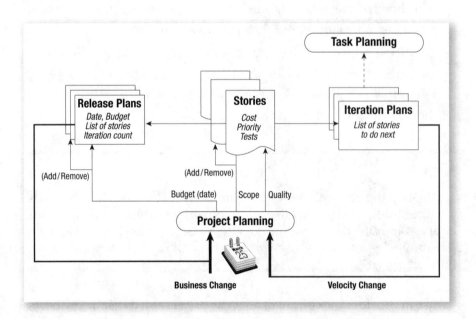

FIGURE 26-4: A dynamic system for controlling an Agile project

> **■ NOTE**
>
> Scope, date, and quality can be considered to form a triangle[9] such that each point is interconnected, so adjusting one parameter affects the others. But Kent Beck[10] adds cost to this list and calls them the "four control variables": cost, time (date), quality, and scope.

Story Life Cycle

Throughout the project, the customer will create new stories as the business thinks of additional requirements (see Figure 26-5). Developers will then estimate these stories during gaps between programming episodes, and the customer will later prioritize them by inserting the corresponding cards at an appropriate location in the pile of stories awaiting implementation. Developers will monitor this pile of stories and perhaps discuss informally among themselves a particular technical risk which may lead to a discussion with the customer and then some reordering of the stories in the pile. There is no need to discuss such matters at a team meeting unless there is a clear difference of opinion about the risk.

> **■ NOTE**
>
> Details of a story, such as the specific business algorithm that must be implemented or the sort of data it concerns, are usually captured from the customer when its tests are written just before the story is actually implemented.

> **■ NOTE**
>
> The implementation of a story is complete when all the related customer tests pass at the end of an iteration. The customer will then remove the story card from the iteration planning board, attribute its size to the team's velocity, and then discard the card.

---

9. Yourdon, Ed. *The Rise and Resurrection of the American Programmer* (Prentice Hall, 1996).
10. Beck, Kent. *Extreme Programming Explained, First Edition* (Addison-Wesley, 2000).

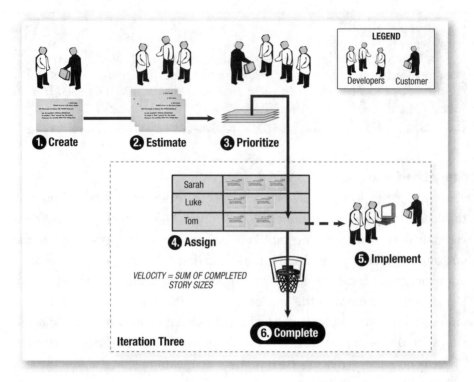

FIGURE 26-5: The life of a story

CONCLUSION

In this chapter, we showed how to plan a software project so that the team can respond rapidly as new business opportunities lead to fresh requirements, and variations in market conditions necessitate adjustments of budgets as well as value and risk assessments. The important aspects of this approach to planning are as follows:

- Goals are based on delivering features (stories) rather than completing tasks so that the team's progress toward them can be measured objectively by the passing of customer tests. To achieve these goals the team follows a sequence of small, good plans which it makes on a regular basis to correct for any changes to the objective or variations in its rate of progress.

- The team's plans are made in a similar way, but at various time scales:
  - **Task plans** allow people to organize their own work and are concerned with optimizing the sequence of tasks in the time scale of hours or days. A high-level task plan may be produced at the start of an iteration, but detailed task plans are no more than people's individual "to-do" lists produced at daily meetings or at the start of programming episodes.
  - **Iteration plans** require individuals to take responsibility for delivering particular stories in the time scale of a week or two. This sort of planning happens continuously as developers take ownership of a story by placing it next to their name on the iteration planning board.
  - **Release plans** are projections of the features a team will deliver in the time scale of months. However, at the end of each iteration, the software is always ready for release, so a customer needs to regularly adjust the release plan so that software is pulled into production when it provides the most value.
- The project is controlled as a dynamic system with feedback being provided by the team's rate of progress (velocity) and by the software delivered to the business. The customer controls the system by adjusting the budget and scope (but not the quality) of this released software to meet the changing demands of the business.

> **■ NOTE**
>
> An Agile team accepts that it cannot create a perfect plan at the start of its project, so it puts considerable effort into planning throughout the project life cycle without any expectation that the resultant plans will survive for more than the briefest periods of time.

■27
Managing Agile Projects

I N THIS CHAPTER, we show you how to use the project management facilities in Visual Studio Team System (VSTS) so that you can import work items into your Team Project from Excel, define iterations, and generate reports to help you manage your project from the information stored about it in Team Foundation Server (TFS). We then describe the way a small Agile team might use these facilities over the course of an iteration, using the approach to estimating, prioritizing, and planning presented in the previous two chapters. The chapter then concludes with ten tips for managing an Agile project.

Using Visual Studio Team System for Project Management

In Section 2, we explained how to create a Team Project for a small Agile team by adapting the MSF for Agile Software Development process template provided with VSTS. We called this process template MSF for XP;[1]

---

1. MSF for Extreme Programming Web site (www.msf4xp.org).

it creates a Team Project with the following project management-related elements:

- **Project Structure**—The team's first three iterations are defined; however, it can add others using the Areas and Iterations dialog box (Team | Team Project Setting | Areas and Iterations).
- **Work item types and queries**—Use Visual Studio's Team menu to add Bug, Story, and Task work items to your project, which you can then list by running a suitable query contained in Team Explorer's Queries folder.
- **Documents**—The Project Portal provides access to documents managed by SharePoint Services, including various Excel workbooks for lists of work items.
- **Reports**—The Team Explorer's Report folder contains a number of standard reports intended to help you manage your project.

We will now look at each element in turn and explain how a small Agile team might use them.

Project Structure

The project structure in VSTS serves to organize the team's work into various time slots called **iterations,** which are equivalent to the sort of iterations that form the columns on an Iteration Plan board; see Figure 26-2. However, within Visual Studio, these iterations are used only for the purposes of classifying work items.

EXERCISE 27-1: Creating a New Iteration for Your Project

In the following exercise, you will add an additional iteration to the three that you defined when you created the Team Project.

1. Log on to the DeveloperPC as Tom (OSPACS Administrator), start Visual Studio, and then connect to the OSPACS Team Project as described in Exercise 5-7 in Chapter 5; see Appendix A for a specification of this machine and details of Tom's security groups.

2. Select the OSPACS project node in Team Explorer and open the Area and Iterations dialog box by choosing Team Project Settings and Areas and Iterations from the Team menu.

3. Select the Iteration tab to display the project's default iterations in a treeview. Add a new iteration by selecting the root item of this tree and choosing New from its context menu. Type the name of your new iteration and then press the Enter key.

4. Close the dialog box and log off, as you have finished this exercise.

Although the Area and Iterations dialog box allows you to create multiple areas and a complex hierarchy of iterations, we do not consider such actions appropriate for a small Agile team. Instead, we suggest you just follow Exercise 27-1 to generate a sequence of iterations with the root node as their common parent. We also suggest you keep the default naming convention (Iteration 0, 1, 2, etc.) because it isolates you from actual dates and conveys the iteration sequence in a clear and unambiguous way.

> **■ NOTE**
>
> You do not need to define any additional areas because Agile teams are not organized into different functional areas, as explained in the Whole Team practice.

Work Item Types and Queries

Each work item type that your process template defines has its own distinct properties as well as those it shares with other work item types; see Table 27-1. The Story and Task work item types correspond to the story cards and task cards presented in the previous chapters; see Figure 25-1 in Chapter 25 and Figure 26-1 in Chapter 26, respectively.

EXERCISE 27-2: Creating a New Story Work Item for Your Project

The following exercise creates a Story work item for your Team Project and then sets its size and priority.

> **■ NOTE**
>
> You may want to repeat this exercise each time anyone in your team starts to implement a new story so that source code changesets, bugs, and so forth can be associated with a particular Story work item. However, agree to such a policy only if you are sure the information gathered in this way will be useful.

1. Log on to the DeveloperPC as Luke (OSPACS Contributor), start Visual Studio, and connect to the OSPACS Team Project.

2. Select the OSPACS project node in Team Explorer and open the form which will define the new story by choosing Add Work Item–Story from the Team menu. Enter into this form the details shown in Figure 27-1 and then save your work (File | Save All).

3. Close the window containing the form for the story you have just created.

> **■ NOTE**
>
> An Agile team should create work items only for the things it is attempting to measure: its metrics. Therefore, don't create a Task work item if you are not measuring and generating reports about tasks.

You can create new Bug and Task work items in the same way described in Exercise 27-2, although in each case, the form is slightly different; see Table 27-1. All these work items are stored in TFS, so you can subsequently open them for editing by executing a suitable query, as explained in the next exercise.

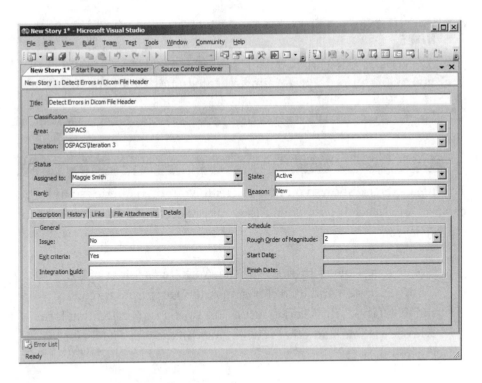

FIGURE 27-1: Creating a new story with VSTS

EXERCISE 27-3: Running a Query to Find an Existing Story Work Item

In the following exercise, you will find the Story work item created in Exercise 27-2, and then assign it to Iteration Three for implementation.

1. Open the Work Items–Team Queries folder of the OSPACS project in Team Explorer and run the All Stories query by double-clicking it. This creates a list of the matching work items in Visual Studio's main window.

2. Open the work item you created in Exercise 27-2 by selecting it from the Query Results window and choosing Open from its context menu. Then specify the iteration in which this story should be implemented by opening the Iteration drop-down list and selecting Iteration Three.

3. Save your changes (File ǀ Save) and close the window containing the form.

> **■ NOTE**
>
> You can associate a work item with a changeset when you are checking in your work prior to performing an Integration Build and Test; see Exercise 12-5 in Chapter 12.

EXERCISE 27-4: Creating a Query to List All Story Work Items for Iteration Three

This next exercise shows you how to create your own queries so that you can find and select the work items for your project stored on its Team Foundation Server.

1. Create a new query by selecting the Work Items folder of the OSPACS project and then choosing Add Query from its context menu (Right-click | Add Query). This opens a query editing form whose first line states that it will return all the work items for the current project:

   ```
   'Team Project' (field) '=' (operator) '@Project' (value)
   ```

2. Qualify the query so that it returns only the story items for Iteration Three by adding the following statements in the next two lines:

   ```
   'And' (and/or) 'Work Item Type' (field) '=' (operator) 'Story' (value)
   'And' (and/or) 'Iteration Path' (field) 'Under' (operator) 'Iteration 3' (value)
   ```

3. Run the query to confirm that it works (Team | Run Query) and then save it as a "My Query" called "All Stories in Iteration 3" using the Save Query dialog box (File | Save Query).

4. Log off, as you have completed the exercise.

> **■ NOTE**
>
> The Save Query dialog box allows you to save a query as a Team Query or as a My Query. In the first case, the query appears in everyone's Team Explorer window in the Work Items–Team Queries folder, but in the second case, it appears only in your My Queries folder.

TABLE 27-1: Main Properties of MSF4XP Process Work Item Types

Property		Story	Bug	Task
Title		X	X	X
Classification	Area	X	X	X
	Iteration	X	X	X
Status	Assigned to	X	X	X
	State (*active, complete, etc.*)	X	X	X
	Priority	X	X	X
Details	Size	X		X
	Integration build (*when completed*)	X	X	X
	Customer test (*document name*)	X		
	Found in build		X	
	Resolved in build		X	
	Test method (`namespace.class.name`)		X	

■ NOTE

Table 27-1 applies only to a Team Project created with the MSF4XP process template. Full details about the properties of work item types defined by any process template should be provided in the Process Guidance section of the Project Portal it creates.

Documents

You can integrate documents into a Team Project using the Project Portal (Web site) and SharePoint Services, although anyone with Visual Studio Team Edition installed on her PC will probably find it easier to access documents from the Documents folder in Team Explorer. The initial folders (and files) that appear within the Documents folder depend upon the process template used to create your Team Project. However, team members can add subfolders and documents to this collection at any time, so it provides a general mechanism for them to collaborate with each other using familiar Microsoft Office applications such as Word and Excel while producing project documentation.

■ NOTE

Team Explorer's Documents folder and the Project Portal's Document Libraries provide different ways of viewing the same collection of folders and files, so changes made with Team Explorer are reflected in the Project Portal and vice versa.

EXERCISE 27-5: Updating an Excel Spreadsheet with Stories from a Team Project

The following exercise adds an Excel spreadsheet to a Team Project's Project Management Document Library and then populates it with a list of the project's Story work items (including the one created in Exercise 27-2).

1. Log on to the DeveloperPC as Luke (OSPACS Contributor), start Visual Studio, and connect to the OSPACS Team Project.

2. Start Excel and create a new workbook (File | New), and then save the file as MyStoryList.xls in a convenient directory on your PC (File | Save). Close Excel.

3. Open the Documents folder for the OSPACS Team Project in your Team Explorer window and then upload the Excel file MyStoryList.xls by selecting the Project Management folder and then choosing Upload Document from its context menu (Right-click | Upload Document).

4. Open the MyStoryList.xls Excel file for editing by selecting this item in the Windows Explorer Project Management folder and selecting Edit from its context menu (Right-click | Edit). This starts Excel and opens the document.

5. Create a new list in the Excel document by clicking the Team toolbar button labeled New List. This causes the New List dialog box to open,

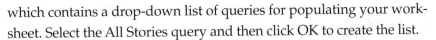

which contains a drop-down list of queries for populating your worksheet. Select the All Stories query and then click OK to create the list.

6. Save the changes you have made to MyStoryList.xls (File | Save) and then close Excel.

> **■ NOTE**
>
> If you created your Team Project from the MSF for XP process template, you can use StoryList.xls instead of having to upload your own Excel spreadsheet to the Project Portal.

EXERCISE 27-6: Updating a Team Project with Stories from an Excel Spreadsheet

In this exercise, you will add some stories to the Excel spreadsheet you created in Exercise 27-5, and then insert these new stories into your Team Project.

1. Open the MyStoryList.xls Excel file for editing by selecting this item in the Team Explorer Project Management folder and selecting Edit from its context menu (Right-click | Edit). This starts Excel and opens the document.

2. Add a new story to MyStoryList.xls by clicking the bottom row of its Story List, selecting Story from the list in the Work Item Type column, and then completing all the remaining columns required for a story (each column marked with a green flag).

3. Save your changes (File | Save) and then publish them to your project's Team Foundation Server by clicking the Publish button in the Team toolbar.

4. Open the Work Items–Team Queries folder of the OSPACS project in Team Explorer and run the query called All Stories to confirm that you have successfully added your new story.

5. Close Excel and log off, as you have finished this exercise.

> **▪ NOTE**
>
> You can synchronize Microsoft Project files to your Team Project in much the same way you would an Excel spreadsheet. This provides an alternative way to manage the work items related to your project for people who like Microsoft Project.

Reports

The reports created by the process template for your Team Project are managed by SQL Server Reporting Services and operate on the work item records held by Team Foundation Server. These reports are contained in your Team Explorer's Report folder and are listed in their own Report Web site (Team | Show Report Site).

> **▪ NOTE**
>
> The Report Web site provides access to a report builder so that you can create custom reports; see Chapter 31.

EXERCISE 27-7: Producing a Bug Rate Report from TFS Work Items

The following exercise creates a chart to describe the total number of active bugs on each day during a given period. It also shows the bugs fixed and the new bugs created each day.

1. Log on to the DeveloperPC as Luke (OSPACS Contributor), start Visual Studio, and connect to the OSPACS Team Project.

2. Open the Report folder for the OSPACS Team Project in Team Explorer and then run the Report item labeled Bug Rates; double-click it. This creates a chart in Visual Studio's main window, like the one shown in Figure 27-2.

3. After reviewing the report, log off, as you have finished the exercises in this chapter.

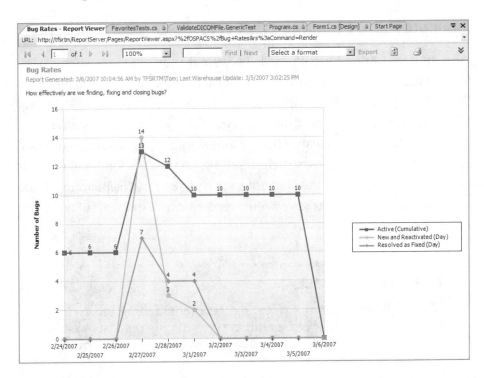

FIGURE 27-2: Bug Rate report

Clearly, the usefulness of these charts depends upon the effort a team puts into collecting the information. If everyone on your team creates a new work item for a bug immediately after it is discovered and then sets its "resolved in build" property (Table 27-1) once the fix has been successfully integrated, your chart will contain meaningful information; if your team doesn't follow such a procedure, it will not.

> **▪. NOTE**
>
> Sam Guckenheimer's recent book[2] about VSTS provides an excellent section, Troubleshooting the Project, which explains how to use some of the most useful standard reports, including Bug Rate reports.

---

2. [SETS] Guckenheimer, Sam, and Juan Perez. *Software Engineering with Visual Studio Team System* (Addison-Wesley, 2006).

Example Agile Planning Life Cycle

We can define a planning life cycle because it is an activity which is performed iteratively throughout the duration of an Agile project. Therefore, the general process of planning changes little from iteration to iteration. The only iteration that is different is the first one, as its objectives are skewed by the need to create a basic framework for the ensuing work (see Section 9) as well as by tasks such as setting up the development, integration, and test environments. Therefore, we will describe the planning of the second iteration in order to give a more representative example of what you should be aiming to do.

■ THIN VERTICAL SLICE

In the first iteration, try to follow the general planning life cycle, but treat this as a learning exercise and set yourself only modest objectives. You might, for example, aim to complete just one story concerned with just saving and restoring an image. This takes a thin vertical slice through the system, thereby allowing your team to encounter the main abstractions of user interface, business logic, and data storage. It results in the team building a basic framework (or skeleton) from which it can hang its future work.

Start of Iteration

The OSPACS team has set its iteration length as one week, so the team members hold a meeting at 8:15 each Monday morning to agree on a high-level task plan for the next five days. At this stage, the developers have already taken ownership of the stories they will each try to deliver before Friday, so the iteration planning board will look much like the one shown in Figure 26-2 in Chapter 26. However, during the course of the meeting, it is not unusual for developers to sign up for some additional stories or put some stories back on the pile if it looks like the team might be overcommitted.

At the start of the meeting, the whole team gathers around its task notice board (which may look like the one shown in Figure 27-3), and the meeting starts with each person taking a couple of minutes to tell everyone else what they intend to work on during the next iteration. This includes not just implementing their stories, but also resolving bugs, conducting spikes, preparing for future stories, and accomplishing any other tasks needed to ensure smooth execution of the project. During these brief presentations, developers remove task cards from the "Pending" area of the notice board and pin them in their row to show the proposed sequence of their work. They also pin in their row the task cards they created for the stories they own, though typically each developer has only one task card per story, with the words "implement story" on it. The emphasis here is directed toward explaining the scope and sequence of the work rather than identifying exactly what must be done, but inevitably people touch on implementation details as well.

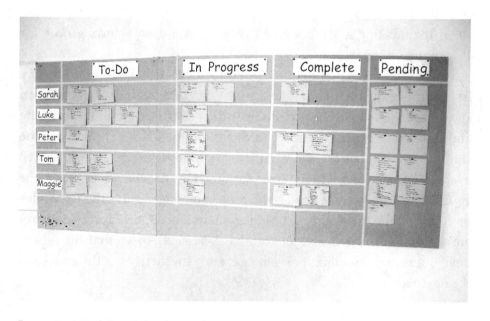

FIGURE 27-3: Task Board showing work in progress during an iteration

> **■ NOTE**
>
> The "Pending" section of the Task Board is a holding area for task cards that the developers will need to complete in some future iteration. It is important to keep such future tasks visible so that they are not forgotten.

After ten minutes or so, everyone has had the opportunity to explain his work, so a more general discussion starts about ways in which the work might be optimized and the conflicts, problems, and risks that are to be addressed. This will cause the team to create some new task cards as well as reorder certain tasks and switch others to different people, until eventually the team has arranged the work into some form of cohesive plan that it feels is realistic, given the time and resources available. It will take less time for the OSPACS team to create such a high-level task plan as it gains more experience organizing its work. However, this is only the second iteration, so there is a general feeling of relief at 9:00 a.m. when the meeting ends, because everyone has been standing now for 45 minutes.

At the end of the planning meeting, the OSPACS team has made any last-minute adjustments to its iteration plan and everyone on the team knows roughly what he has to do over the next five days in terms of the high-level task plan. According to this plan, the team will deliver nine stories by the end of the week, with a cumulative size of 21 task points; in addition, the team will fix three serious bugs as well as complete one spike. Therefore, Tom (who was the project manager) edits the Excel files he added to the team's Project Management Document Library and creates work items for the nine stories (Exercise 27-6) so that his fellow developers can associate their changesets with them over the course of the next week.

Slack Practice

The practice of allowing people enough freedom to effect change is called Slack.[3] The drive for too much efficiency on most teams is counter-productive because it reduces the slack required for the team to do its job properly.

On a software team, you will rarely encounter someone who doesn't work hard enough. You'll often find people working very hard, but going in entirely the wrong direction. You may also find people who lack the skills required for the job. However, most people work too hard, because they don't have enough slack to do the things that might make them more effective, such as automating repetitive tasks, improving their technical knowledge, and learning to use new tools. One of the main reasons people don't have enough slack is that the plan doesn't allow it. All of the people on the team are fully committed to complete tasks that will take 100 percent of their time. This gives rise to a secondary problem: Without slack, people are unable to meet their commitments when something goes wrong. Working on a project without enough slack doesn't just make people less effective; it also makes them losers.

Implementing slack isn't just a matter of accepting that the number of hours in an "ideal" day is less than the hours you actually spend in the office. It also requires a team to factor some slack into its plan. For example, the team might decide to work a 2 x 6 + 1 iteration cycle, thereby allowing one week for developer-chosen tasks after six iterations every two weeks. Alternatively, it might decide to let developers take turns working as the tool builder for an iteration rather than working on the implementation of customer stories.

NOTE

Tom doesn't need to create any work items for the bugs because the team members created them when they first identified them. He will also not create any work items for the spike or for the team's other tasks because it is easier to track them using a Task Board such as the one in Figure 27-3.

---

3. [SLAK] DeMarco, Tom. *Slack* (Broadway Books, 2002).

Sample Programming Episode: Task Planning

A programming episode involves two developers who are pair programming, and it is how all code that is destined for the production environment is written, whether it is stories being implemented or bugs being fixed. Developers on the OSPACS team try to fit two or three programming episodes into their day so that they each complete about 15 of them during each iteration.

> ■ **NOTE**
>
> Teams usually split or combine stories until they can complete them in about three programming episodes. This allows work to "flow"[4] more efficiently because each developer can own two or three stories and still have six episodes per week available to pair with others.

After the team meeting finishes at 9:00 a.m., Sarah quickly asks Luke to help with her first task on the Task Board: the implementation of a particular story. The unwritten rule is that a developer must give help when asked, unless he or she is occupied on another matter. So, because Luke is not yet doing anything, he agrees to help Sarah. Accordingly, Sarah moves the story's task card into her "In Progress" column on the Task Board before sitting down with Luke for ten minutes in order to create a to-do (or test) list; see Chapter 14. The programming episode then proceeds in much the same way as we described in Section 5, as the two of them repeat the micro-cycle of write a test, write the code to pass the test, and then refactor. A few hours later, they have completed each test on their list, so they check in their new code, linking its changeset to the Story work item before running an Integration Build and Test to validate their work; see Exercise 12-5 in Chapter 12. While this is running, they go for coffee together and discuss what they have done.

---

4. [LT] Womack, James P., and Daniel T. Jones. *Lean Thinking* (Simon & Schuster, 2003).

> **■ TIP**
>
> Create a Task work item for "Refactoring" at the start of each iteration so that when people make improvements to the code base (the Share Code practice) which are not related to any story, you can still associate the changeset with a work item to assist with later identification.

Between Programming Episodes

When Sarah returns from coffee at 11:30 the results of the Integration Build and Test show that it was successful, so she judges the programming episode to be complete. There isn't time to start another session before lunch, so she works on her own doing some preparation work for another story which will be implemented in the next iteration. This work has a task card, so she moves it into her "In Progress" column on the Task Board. However, the task doesn't take long to complete, so by noon she moves the card into her "Completed" column.

Sally (the customer) can see that Sarah isn't busy, so she comes over to discuss a new feature with her. The conversation doesn't last more than five minutes, but it results in a new story card appearing in the area of the Iteration Planning Board reserved for stories that have not yet been estimated: the upper-right section of the "Future Iterations" column (see Figure 26-2 in Chapter 26). The Iteration Planning Board is conveniently located in the coffee room, so Sarah immediately manages to engage Tom and Peter in a conversation about the likely size of this new story. They all agree that it seems to be a 2 task point story, so Sarah writes the size on the card and moves it into the area of the Iteration Planning Board reserved for stories that have not yet been prioritized: the lower-right section of the "Future Iterations" column. In this way, the next time Sally is having coffee, she can consider putting the story in her ordered list of stories for future iterations.

■ NOTE

The OSPACS team encourages comments from everyone about priorities by pinning new story cards in priority order to the "Future Iterations" column of the Iteration Planning Board instead of keeping them
out of sight on Sally's desk.

Sarah needs to do a reasonable amount of work between her programming episodes over the next five days, and most of it will never appear on
the Task Board, not to mention in TFS. These are tasks which are not necessarily related to the project, but still need to be done. Therefore, before
breaking for lunch, Sarah spends ten minutes writing her own personal
to-do list for the iteration which includes ordering some books from
Amazon.com and preparing a presentation for the team about a new chart
she wants to introduce.

Planning Customer Tests

After lunch, Sarah and Sally discuss the tests for one of Sarah's stories. They
had first talked about these tests last week when Sarah was considering taking ownership of the story, but now they need to consider the fine details.
Sally has already seen that the story is in Sarah's "In Progress" column, so
during the morning, she created a Word document with some Column Fixture tables containing tests for the business logic she wanted to implement.
It was now clear to Sarah that the business rules were quite simple, and
once they are implemented the story will be complete. Therefore, she goes
back to her desk and starts developing the necessary fixtures so that Sally
can run her tests; see the exercises in Chapter 23.

■ NOTE

The fixtures needed for customer tests just provide the necessary glue
to link the Framework for Integrated Test (FIT) libraries to the component libraries under development. They usually require very little coding, so they can often be produced quite quickly.

Completing a Story

It takes Sarah until 2:30 p.m. to complete the fixtures for Sally's customer tests and make them accessible. However, once Sarah finishes this work, she is confident that she can complete the story with just one more programming episode. This time Sarah asks Peter to be her programming pair, so they work together in the same way she and Luke had done during the morning.

Sarah's prediction that the story would be completed quickly is correct, so by 4:00 p.m., they have checked in and validated their work using an Integration Build and Test. Accordingly, Sarah moves the story's task card into her "Completed" column on the Task Board as a sign to Sally that she should now check that the software passes her tests. If Sally is not satisfied, she has the option of discussing the matter with Sarah and writing some more tests. However, when Sally runs the test, she is satisfied, so the story card is removed from the Iteration Planning Board and its task points are credited to the team's velocity score. Sally also runs a query from her Team Explorer window to find the work item associated with the story (Exercise 27-3) so that she can set its State property to Complete and, therefore, include work in the "Story Burn-down" chart Sarah implemented in the previous iteration. This chart shows after each day the amount of work remaining before the team reaches its iteration targets.

> **■ NOTE**
>
> The completion of spikes, bug fixes, and other work doesn't count toward a team's velocity because it is a measure of the team's rate of progress in the delivery of features valued by the business—in other words, the completion of stories.

Completing a Bug Fix

Although it is 4:00 p.m., Sarah is on a roll having finished her story in two programming episodes rather than the three she had estimated. Therefore, she decides to fit a third programming episode into her day so that she can implement a bug fix before leaving the office. On this occasion, she recruits

Tom to help her, so after moving the corresponding task card on the Task Board into her "In Progress" column, she starts pair programming with her third partner of the day.

Sarah and Tom first run a query to find the work item associated with the bug (see Exercise 27-3). This work item gives them lots of information about the problem, including the steps they need to take in order to reproduce it. Therefore, after ten minutes discussing the issue, they have produced the list of actions they think will lead most swiftly to a fix. Thirty minutes later they have completed the unit test, which takes them directly to the source of the problem. Fixing the bug involves changing a single line of code, but it takes another five minutes for the Integration Build and Test to complete successfully, so it is almost 5:00 p.m. before Sarah is able to move the task card into her "Completed" column on the Task Board. She then updates the work item in TFS, changing its status to Fixed and setting the Integration Build property to the Integration Build she has just run.

> **■ NOTE**
>
> Fixing a bug usually requires some change to the project's code base, and therefore it is a task that the developers who are pair programming should complete. You should approach it in a similar way to implementing a story, except usually there are no customer tests.

Daily Meetings

The OSPACS team holds a stand-up meeting around the Task Board each day at 8:15 a.m. On Mondays, as mentioned earlier, the meeting is mainly about making high-level task plans for the new iteration. However, on other days, people are more concerned with reviewing progress and identifying any actions that might help the team achieve its iteration goals by Friday. Except for the Monday meetings, these meetings seldom last for more than 15 minutes.

At the start of the meeting, each person gives a brief summary of what he did yesterday, what he aims to do today, and what is delaying him, if anything. When you're standing in front of the task planning board, it's difficult to obscure the truth about your progress. However, the meeting isn't about punishing or humiliating people. Instead, anyone who is falling behind with his tasks gets helps from other members of the team. Therefore, throughout the week, the OSPACS team adjusts its task plan by moving cards from one person to another and even reassigning ownership of a story if the circumstances warrant it.

During the course of the week, the OSPACS team doesn't need to set time aside for an iteration planning meeting, because the plan emerges as developers review the pile of stories in the gaps between their programming episodes and pin the next story from the pile next to their name on the notice board. This approach gives the team a significant advantage, because in addition to avoiding the inevitable disruption formal meetings cause to the team's flow of work, they also gain more programming episodes.

> ### ■ NOTE
>
> The OSPACS team doesn't literally have a pile of stories. Instead, the team members pin cards in the pile in priority order to the "Future Iterations" area of their Iteration Planning Board; see Figure 26-2 in Chapter 26.

End of the Iteration

The OSPACS team's iterations end on Friday afternoons at 5:00 p.m. Therefore, toward the end of each week, the team members must consider whether they can add another story to the Task Board, or whether they need to remove one because their progress has been slower than anticipated. It is better to make such plans with the customer in advance rather than discovering that an important story isn't quite complete a few minutes before the deadline.

The developers spend the final hour of the iteration demonstrating their completed stories to the rest of the team using the software generated by the latest Integration Build. These demonstrations show the features operating in real-life scenarios and give everyone an opportunity to spot flaws in the testing. The fact that people know their software will be given such a grilling by the rest of the team at the end of the iteration provides a powerful incentive for them to run proper tests before declaring a story to be complete.

Any significant problems the team finds during the demonstrations may require removal of a story by backing out its changesets from the repository (see Exercise 9-4 in Chapter 9) and then running a new Integration Build and Test. However, this procedure should take less than ten minutes, so before the team members leave on Friday, they should be able to deliver a working Integration Build containing the stories successfully implemented in the iteration. Fortunately, the OSPACS team finds only one largely insignificant bug, which it handles by creating a new Bug work item. Therefore, at 5:00 p.m., all of the team members are able to leave the office for the weekend feeling quite satisfied with their work and looking forward to Monday when iteration three starts.

> **■ NOTE**
>
> The scheduled Daily Build and Test (see Exercise 12-4 in Chapter 12) performs a more thorough check of the software on Friday night so that each Monday morning, the team starts with a solid code base on which to work. If necessary, people come into the office over the weekend to make sure this happens.

Release Planning

The OSPACS developers are not really involved in release planning, because Sally (the customer) does this work while they are working on the code. She prepares the plan on a spreadsheet like the one shown in Figure 26-3 in Chapter 26 and updates it after each iteration to adjust for changes in velocity as well as business need. Primarily the release plan serves to give the business an idea of what it is getting and how long it must wait. This allows the business to adjust the project's budget and resource allocation against financials such as return on investment. However, Sally regularly talks about the release plan during the morning stand-up meetings so that the developers are kept aware of the point to which the iterations must converge. She has also uploaded the release plan spreadsheet to the Project Portal (Exercise 27-5) so that it is available to all members of the team.

> **■ NOTE**
>
> Agile projects generally end when the customer is unable to discover anymore stories whose implementation cost can be justified in terms of the business value they deliver.

Top Ten Tips for Managing Agile Projects

To manage Agile projects you need to create a succession of good plans which allow the team to react dynamically to changes in objectives and rate of progress. We provide the following tips to help you make such plans as well as the accurate estimates and correct priorities upon which they depend:

1. **Plan tasks from the bottom up**—Tasks are the most difficult part of the project to plan, so keep the process simple and let the tasks arise from within the team rather than imposing them from software such as Microsoft Project.

2. **Make good estimates**—Estimate the size of a task (story) rather than the time it will take, and express the size as a comparison using a nonlinear scale. Split and combine work so that you can express most of it as a comparison to something you know, x, in terms of the same size as x, twice the size of x, and three times the size of x.

3. **Set priorities correctly**—Deliver first stories that promise to provide the most value for the least business risk, but also give priority to stories that address technical risk. Remove dependencies between stories so that you can prioritize them separately.

4. **Aim to deliver features rather than complete tasks**—Allow the team to become self-organizing so that people take responsibility for delivering the stories they "own" instead of hiding behind the ambiguity of task definition and completion.

5. **Plan at different time scales**—Produce a sequence of good plans at the time scale of hours and days (task), weeks (iterations), and months (releases). Use the longer-term plans to guide the shorter-term ones and expect to replan frequently.

6. **Provide the team with some slack**—Avoid letting the team become so busy that it doesn't have time to address things that would make it more productive. Allow buffers in the schedule in order to contain tasks that overrun.

7. **Manage the project in iterations**—Set clear goals at the start of each iteration in terms of the stories it will deliver, and make objective measurements of team progress by counting the size of the stories that are actually delivered at the end.

8. **Control the project dynamically**—The customer controls the project with the release budget (price, time) and story priority (scope) using feedback from the business as well as from the team. However, the iteration length and release dates must dictate the amount of feedback so that there is enough to make the team responsive, but not so much that it becomes chaotic.

9. **Communicate**—Involve the whole team in project management by improving communication so that every voice can be heard. It's best to do this via frequent face-to-face interaction rather than through formal meetings and documents posted on the project Web site.

10. **Learn**—You cannot hope to refine a software development plan in the light of its execution because it is a one-time plan. Improvement comes only by gaining knowledge and experience, so make sure that what is done in your current iteration is captured and disseminated to benefit all future ones.

■ NOTE

The OSPACS team occasionally holds meetings over lunch to discuss some technical or educational issue. These are called *brown-bag meetings* for the simple reason that lunch is traditionally provided for the team in brown bags.

CONCLUSION

In this chapter, we showed you how to use the facilities of Visual Studio Team System to manage a small Agile project, and then walked through an iteration so that you could see how you might use them in a real-life Agile project in conjunction with the approach to estimating, prioritizing, and planning that we presented earlier in this section of the book.

Review of Section 8
Estimate, Prioritize, and Plan

THE OSPACS TEAM'S adoption of test-driven development (TDD) and customer testing, combined with the other Agile practices it had introduced over the past few months, at last allowed the developers to deliver consistently high-quality software at the end of each iteration. Consequently, they were much more confident about their ability to plan so that in the future, the business should get more of the software it wants at the time it needs it. Therefore, the team adopted a more Agile approach to estimating, prioritizing, and planning by taking the following actions:

- **Planned around the delivery of stories**—They oriented their planning around the delivery of stories, so the story cards became central to the planning process. Developers were expected to take ownership of a story and assume responsibility for its delivery at the end of a particular iteration.

- **Erected notice boards for iteration and task planning**—They erected notice boards for iteration planning and task planning so that everyone could become involved in the planning process. They also created a spreadsheet for the release plan and added it to the Team Project's Document Library so that everyone could access it.

- **Became self-organizing**—Developers were given the responsibility of producing their own task plans during an iteration, and therefore, they became self-organizing. Everyone agreed on the iteration plans before the iteration started, and release plans became Sally's responsibility.

- **Set relative story size**—The developers started estimating stories in task points rather than man-hours. They compared each story to some work that was rated at 1 task point and used a nonlinear scale of 0, 1, 2, 3, 5, 8, 13, 20, 40, 100.

- **Allowed the customer to set story priority**—Sally based the priority of a story upon its quantifiable value and its associated risk. Sally was also put in charge of controlling the project, which she achieved by setting the number of iterations available to the team as well as the priority of the stories.

- **Tracked bugs**—The developers agreed that they would track bugs by creating a Bug work item for each bug that was discovered.

> **■ TIP**
>
> Improve your ability to estimate and plan by recording in a project notebook the difference between the time you think it will take to do something and the actual time you spend doing it. Make sure your data is meaningful by setting tangible goals for the completion of each task.

The Team's Impressions

Most of the team hadn't really thought too much about estimating, prioritizing, and planning in the past because they relied on Tom to tell them what to do. However, they now realize that on an Agile team, everyone must address these issues.

CEO: Mike

"Finishing weekly iterations on time lets the team practice prioritizing its commitments in order to meet deadlines, which hopefully will allow us to deliver the product's 'must haves' on time, even if this means we lose a few 'nice to haves' along the way."

Developer: Tom

"Giving the customer control of the project seemed like a bad idea, until I realized that the developers would no longer be blamed for exceeding budgets or failing to meet the needs of the business."

"It is easy for a developer to become over-committed by signing up for stories without fully appreciating the number of other tasks that will occupy his (or her) time during the next iteration."

Developer: Luke

"Keeping a personal project notebook has given me a much better understanding about how I spend my time, as well as making me more organized."

"It is hard to improve upon the simplicity of a story card."

Developer: Sarah

"The major benefit we get from the project management facilities of VSTS is bug tracking. It's great to have bug tracking linked directly to our version control system."

"We need to consider carefully how we are going to use the information added to a work item before deciding to collect it."

"People don't spend 100 percent of their time working on the project, so it makes much more sense to reflect this fact in our plans. Allowing people to work on other things also gives us a bit of a buffer in case things go wrong."

Developer: Maggie

"I know that the bug rate has declined rapidly since we starting doing TDD and customer testing. However, the bug tracking features of VSTS promise to make it much easier to manage the few that remain."

"Providing people with a bit of time to work on our tools and utilities is an investment that will pay big dividends. In the past, we've been so busy working on the project that we've not had the time to save time."

Customer: Sally

"Managing the budget by setting the number of iterations available to the team makes my job much easier. I can immediately see the impact of budget changes on what the business will get and when."

Agile Values

The improvement in the way the team estimates, prioritizes, and plans its work, together with the Agile practices of Slack, Stories, Weekly Cycle, and Monthly Cycle, supported the Agile values the team was trying to promote in the following ways.

Communication

The team has pulled the plans from Tom's PC and put them on notice boards that everyone can see. The use of story and task cards also promotes communication during meetings because people can physically handle the cards instead of fighting for control of the keyboard and mouse.

Feedback

The Weekly Cycle practice provides enough feedback to steer the product to the next release, but not so much that the team never manages to finish anything. In a similar way, the Monthly Cycle practice steers the project toward its eventual conclusion.

Courage

The team members feel less defensive about their iteration and task plans because they cover such a small time scale, so they are frequently rewritten. This makes them more willing to undertake challenging work because the impact of any failure is limited to the iteration.

Simplicity

The team has adopted an approach to planning that everyone understands. It requires nothing more complex than a notice board and some index cards. Planning is done regularly, but it mainly addresses short time scales, so the team doesn't need such complex plans.

Respect

The ability of the developers to achieve a constant velocity and to produce estimates that seldom change gives them respect from the businesspeople. The customer's ability to prioritize the work correctly and manage the team's budget gives her the respect of the developers.

The introduction of the Slack practice resulted in developers having the time to meet their commitments and do a proper job, which built up people's trust in the team and its capabilities.

Section 9
Practice for Deployment

I N S ECTION 9, we urge you to practice moving your software products to the production environment from the earliest stages of the project. Chapter 28 describes some of the obstacles you might face achieving this objective within Agile time scales and suggests ways to prepare for the iterative and incremental deployment of your software. Chapter 29 then explains how to develop the sorts of installation programs that will allow you to automate such regular deployments both in the datacenter and on your user's desktop. Finally, Chapter 30 covers the Distributed System Designer tools provided by Visual Studio Team System for Architects and

Photograph by Jo Hale (Copyright Getty Images 2006).

Successful software deployment depends on your team exhaustively practicing a choreographed set of moves before performing them in front of an audience.

explains how you might use them to help you deploy Web services in a distributed system environment.

Story from the Trenches

Some time ago, I accepted a contract from a large insurance company to help it build a call center system so that it could sell its products directly over the telephone. The project was a multimillion-dollar investment for the company and the team comprised more than a hundred people. It had a client-server architecture and was run in a typical Waterfall fashion, with separate phases for analysis, design, code, test, and deployment. Most of the team was concerned with the development of a database to support the new system that would run on the company's mainframe. My job was to provide the glue software that would connect a third-party Windows application to this new database.

Few people on the team knew anything about Windows development, so there was a bit of a cultural divide between us. However, we all got on well enough, and as the months passed, the project finally reached its deployment phase. Our managers viewed this primarily as a data migration exercise, populating the production database with information about real customers and removing all the test data. Nobody had given much thought to the deployment of the desktop software because it didn't seem to involve much more than copying some files onto a bunch of PCs.

The deployment of the database went smoothly enough, but when the components I had written were installed on the production PCs, the desktop application stopped working and even the database connection could not be established. This came as a shock to me because everything had worked perfectly in the system test environment. However, my project manager was more than shocked; he was panic-stricken! Nothing worked, yet a big advertising campaign was already well on the way, promising a launch date in a few days' time. Accordingly, I was dispatched to the call center with clear instructions to sort out the problem or find myself a new job.

When I arrived at the call center the next morning, it quickly became apparent that the production PCs were configured differently than the ones we used during system testing. The deployment team had simply installed the latest versions of all the software without realizing that not all of these versions were compatible with each other. Therefore, I had to start from a production PC that had little more than the operating system installed, and then laboriously install each product, together with its updates, until I had figured out which ones were causing the problem. Eventually, in the early hours of the morning, I completed a list of the allowable updates so that the deployment team could rebuild the 250 production PCs. Later that same day, the business accepted the system so that it could now be launched as planned, which saved my project manager from any further humiliation.

The moral of this story is that software deployment needs to be considered from the start of the project; otherwise, you condemn yourself to discovering problems at a time when you have the least amount of time to fix them. In this section of the book, we discuss the ways in which an Agile team can put such good advice into practice.

28
Moving into Production

THIS CHAPTER INTRODUCES the main issues that a team needs to think about when moving its software into the production environment. It starts by considering the release process and explains the need to remove bottlenecks elsewhere in your organization when your team is not entirely responsible for this work. We then look at how an Agile team can prepare for the iterative and incremental deployment of its software by building up its proficiency in releasing software from the start of a project, while it is still simple to install. Finally, we explore ways in which facilities such as logging and a support Web site can help you monitor the results of your software's deployment so that your team can improve its development process and learn from past mistakes.

Managing Deployment

Developers create software inside their own development environments, but after each programming episode, they check the software into Team Foundation Version Control (TFVC) so that it can be moved into the Build-LabPC for integration with the rest of the team's work. Every night this integrated software is rebuilt from the ground up by the scheduled Daily Build in order to prepare everything required for the possible deployment of the team's work and deposit it into in a shared drop folder; see Figure 11-1 in

Chapter 11. However, before such software can be migrated into the production environment and used by the business, it will typically have to pass through some form of release process.

> **■ NOTE**
>
> Software teams are seldom put in total control of the release process, so they usually hand that control off to a of deployment team, though the point at which that happens varies significantly from organization to organization.

The Release Process

In some organizations, the deployment of a build involves not much more than turning the drop folder into a shared network folder and then inviting your business community to access its contents. However, more typically you will need to follow a process which addresses issues such as the following:

- **Sanity test**—Automated tests often miss things that are immediately obvious to a human tester, so you need to perform some form of manual test of the software's basic functionality. Typically, the team does this as the final part of the Daily Build's Smoke Test, discussed in Chapter 11.

- **System test**—It is often important to predict the performance of the software as a system in your production environment under conditions of normal as well as abnormal load and stress; see Robert Binder's book[1] for more information.

- **System installation**—In order to install your software into its target environment, you may need to arrange for support staff to visit particular machines in order to log on and run some type of installation program.

---

1. Binder, Robert. *Testing Object-Oriented Systems* (Addison-Wesley, 2000).

- **Data migration**—New software often depends on changes to the production database; see the Data Deployment section, later in this chapter. Therefore, such work must be completed before the system can be used.

- **Production of physical material**—A release may require the production of things such as printed manuals and DVDs, so these items need to be prepared in time for the actual release date. This is a particularly important consideration if your team is developing shrink-wrapped software for sale in a store or on an Internet site.

- **Uploading to a Web site**—Someone may need to copy the drop folder to another location so that people can download its contents from a publicly accessible Web site.

- **Provision of support**—Help desk support, user training, bug reporting, and so forth may require updating in regard to the new release. Typically, you need to initiate these sorts of actions well in advance of the scheduled release date.

> **■ NOTE**
>
> The release process is actually a production activity, not a design activity. Therefore, during the deployment of your software, you should seek to minimize variation by following a well-defined procedure, parts of which may be completely prescribed.

In a large organization, it is not unusual for the release process to take months (see Figure 28-1) and, therefore, significantly delay the moment at which the business can get a return on its investment as well as increasing the risk of the software failing to satisfy the real business need. An Agile team addresses such issues by introducing the Daily Deployment practice so that potentially all new software can be installed in the production environment at the start of the next business day. In this way, the business can decide when to use the new software without being constrained by the time delay of actually making the software available to them.

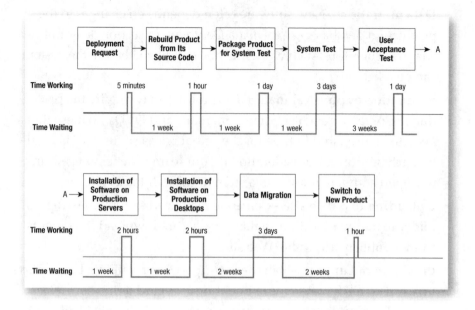

FIGURE 28-1: Timeline showing a five-month deployment schedule

Daily Deployment Practice

Daily deployment requires you to put all new software into the production environment for the start of each business day. In some ways, it is like setting your iteration length to a single day, though clearly you must consider longer periods for the purposes of project planning and control.

The usual reason for implementing daily deployment is when your team is serving a business that needs to respond to daily changes in its market. However, it can also be justified in terms of reducing the time required for your software to transition into production; for the longer this takes, less value is returned, and there is greater risk that the business environment will change and render the software obsolete.

You must face a number of practical issues when you deploy your software into production each day. In particular, you need to consider the impact of even the smallest change to the way people work or use the system. You also need to ensure that the documentation and other related materials are kept in sync with the daily changes you are making to the software. Ultimately, these matters are determined by what the business is prepared to accept, because it is the customer who has to balance the disruption caused by a new release against the value it provides.

Implementing the Daily Deployment practice is a challenge because it requires your team to reduce its bug rates to very low levels as well to set up a release process that delivers software into production with minimal manual intervention. The difficulties of achieving such levels of quality and automation mean that daily deployment often remains more of an objective than something a team actually manages to achieve.

■ TIP

Set the more realistic goal of your team releasing its software each day into some form of preproduction environment by way of a handoff to another team, which will then take responsibility for selecting a build and completing the rest of the release process.

Removing Bottlenecks

If your organization's release process involves transitioning through stages such as system testing, quality control, auditing, and beta testing, you should press for the reengineering of these processes along Agile lines to remove any bottlenecks that might delay deployment. There may be good reasons why you cannot move your software into production right away; for example, it might be a safety-critical system that requires external validation of code changes. However, aiming for daily deployment can only help improve the flow of your organization's value stream[2] and

---

2. [LSD] Poppendieck, Mary, and Tom Poppendieck. *Lean Software Development* (Addison-Wesley, 2003).

reduce its cost through the automation of its processes, so it remains a good goal to aim for, even when there are insurmountable barriers to its actual introduction.

> **■ NOTE**
>
> A software team never works in total isolation, so the benefits of an Agile approach to development cannot be fully realized until the concept of lean thinking[3] has become well established across the whole organization.

Handing Over the Release to a Deployment Team

Companies with large IT infrastructures more often than not have rigorous standards for deploying software and employ specialist deployment teams to ensure that they are correctly implemented. This work is essentially a configuration management exercise requiring strict control of any changes to the baselines carefully established for each type of platform the organization uses. Therefore, such teams are not only concerned with the deployment of software that originates from within their organizations, but also must handle software from external sources such as third-party applications, updates, and operating system service packs.

You can get a general idea of what a deployment team does from such literature as "The 20 Commandments of Software Packaging."[4] However, when it comes to handling the release of software from an internal development team, it is normally a matter of the following:

- The deployment team rebuilds the software in its own Build Lab as a test of the developer's configuration management process.

---

3. [LT] Womack, James P., and Daniel T. Jones. *Lean Thinking* (Simon & Schuster, 2003).
4. Ruest, Nelson, and Danielle Ruest. "The 20 Commandments of Software Packaging" (www.sms-alliance.com).

- The team checks the software's compatibility with the target environment.
- The team packages the software for automated deployment using tools such as the following:
  - Macrovision's FLEXnet AdminStudio,[5] which allows you to implement a standard process for preparing and testing software packages
  - Microsoft's Systems Management Server (SMS),[6] a change and configuration management solution for deploying software packages and updates across an enterprise

> **■ NOTE**
>
> When an organization has a dedicated team responsible for deploying all its software, there may be a delay of several weeks (or even months) before the team's release becomes available to the business, which significantly reduces the benefits of its Agile approach.

Preparing for Deployment

It is best for a team to consider deployment problems from the start of a project when the software products are still simple. You can then build up your expertise so that deployment becomes a polished and well-practiced process. Therefore, we suggest that you aim to have a functional installation program by the end of your first iteration, if not before. In this way, you start with the simplest possible installation program and then slowly add the necessary support as your software becomes more complex.

---

5. FLEXnet Admin Studio Web site (www.macrovision.com/products/flexnet_adminstudio).
6. Microsoft SMS Web site (www.microsoft.com/smserver).

The Installation Program

The most obvious sign of your team's commitment to reducing delays in deployment is the development of an installation program which, with not much more than a single mouse-click, allows a release to be deployed or rolled back. In a simple project, you might be able to satisfy this requirement by creating a batch file,[7] but in most cases, a team will use a tool such as InstallShield[8] (or WiX[9]) to develop its installation program(s). These sorts of programs generally handle all aspects of deployment to the desktop or data-center, including the following:

- Detecting any installation prerequisites on the target platform, such as operating system type, service packs, and components

- Providing guidance for the person deploying your system, and collecting any information such as the target directory location, license acceptance statements, and so forth

- Installing the executable files (.exe, .dll) generated by your build, together with all the redistributable software components upon which they depend

- Configuring the Windows environment through environment variables, configuration files, and Registry settings, as well as configuring server components such as Internet Information Services (IIS), COM+ servers, and applications

- Copying help, release notes, license, and other forms of documentation for your product into the appropriate directories

- Executing SQL scripts and installing any data files that your software may require

- Creating shortcuts to your program on the target platform desktop, handling localization issues, and so forth

---

7. Advice on creating DOS batch files is available at www.computerhope.com/batch.htm.
8. InstallShield Web site (www.macrovision.com/products/flexnet_installshield).
9. Windows Installer XML (http://wix.sourceforge.net).

> **▪ NOTE**
>
> We will address some of these issues in the next chapter, when we explain how to create a basic desktop installation program with Install-Shield. The issues associated with deploying Web services to a data-center are covered in Chapter 30.

Deploying the First Iteration

It is the customer who ultimately decides which stories the developers should address in each iteration, a decision the customer normally bases on the value the stories offer to the business. However, in the first iteration, this decision is influenced by the team's need to create a framework (or skeleton) upon which it can hang its subsequent work. Such a framework takes a thin vertical slice through the system and usually implements elements of its most important layers. For example, the OSPACS team aimed to complete just one story in its first iteration, which required its developers to build components for the user interface, business logic, and data storage so that a user of the system could simply save and restore an image.

It is unlikely that the software the team produces during the first iteration will have sufficient business value to warrant its immediate deployment. However, you should still prepare an installation program because, like your software framework, it provides a thin vertical slice through the issues you must face. Therefore, at the end of the first iteration, your team should not only be able to demonstrate a functioning program that does something the business wants, but also show that you have the means to deploy it into the production environment. It doesn't matter whether the stories you have implemented are low on the list of business priorities, for this is justified by them addressing the technical risk of building a suitable initial architecture. What is important is the proof you have provided to the business of your team's ability to deliver working software. Each new bit of the product which is deployed will act to reinforce this trust and confidence in your team and its work.

Incremental Deployment Practice

Incremental deployment means releasing a product a bit at a time rather than attempting to release it all at once. This practice is particularly important when you are replacing a legacy system because it avoids having to make an abrupt transition to the new system, the big-bang approach.

Taking an all-or-nothing approach to deploying a new system is risky because in the event of a serious problem, you must roll back everything and restore the old system. In such circumstances, management support for the new system may evaporate, especially when a significant amount of time and money was lost preparing for the ill-fated transition. Incremental deployment addresses this risk by delivering the system in parts. Therefore, even if it is necessary to roll back the deployment of one part, its predecessors remain in place and continue to provide value. It also limits the cost of such failure to just the preparation of the part whose deployment was aborted. Anyone who has participated in a big-bang deployment will appreciate the toll it takes on the team in terms of the stress and workload of preparing for the big day. Incremental deployment prevents teams from having to enter such long and arduous deployment phases, which allows them to keep their work flowing at a steady rate, consistent with good Agile practice.[10]

In order to practice incremental deployment, it must be possible to gradually switch off parts of the old system so that you can replace them with parts of the new system. Accordingly, both systems must run as one in the production environment, and this may require the team to undertake additional work, such as the construction of scaffolding[11] for the temporary integration of the two systems. Working in this way, you can gradually replace the old system with the new one through a series of small, reversible deployments. Eventually, when the new system is doing all the

---

10. [LSD] Poppendieck, Mary, and Tom Poppendieck. *Lean Software Development* (Addison-Wesley, 2003).

11. *Scaffolding* usually refers to the temporary code, files, and data that support the operation of an incomplete system. However, in this case, scaffolding serves to integrate the different parts of the old and new system so that they can work together.

work, you complete its deployment by removing the scaffolding as well as all remnants of the old system. Although the accumulated cost of incremental deployment might exceed the cost of deploying in a single big bang, this is justified by the reduction in risk as well as the savings made by terminating failing projects much earlier in their life cycles—in other words, you discover at the start of your project that the system can't be deployed, not at the end.

Stubs and Scaffolding

When creating a thin vertical slice through your system, you often need to write some temporary code in order to support the story you are implementing. This sort of code is called **scaffolding** when it calls your story (production) code and a **stub** when it is called by your story code. For example, your story code may require some scaffolding to implement the program's `main()` entry point and a stub that acts as a placeholder for the `PatientName()` method in some database object that you will implement later. In this way, you can create a working system from the outset and slowly bring the production code into service by displacing scaffolding and stub code piece by piece.

> ### ■ TIP
>
> Put your scaffolding and stub code in a separate namespace (and library) so that as you implement the equivalent production code, you can discard it easily and so that during deployment, there is a clear separation between production and nonproduction components.

Data Deployment

One of the biggest challenges of incremental deployment is keeping the data synchronized with your code changes, particularly in regard to data held in databases. At the very least, you should have a data deprecation mechanism in place so that it is possible for old and new data to exist side by side for a time until you can safely remove the old data. For example, you might take the following steps when implementing separate first name and last name fields in a database table that currently has a single name field:

1. Add two new fields to the table for first name and last name, and create a script to populate them with appropriate data from the current name field.

2. Develop a database trigger to keep the new field contents synchronized with contents of the old field. Therefore, a change to the name field propagates to the first name and last name fields and vice versa.

3. Declare the old name field as deprecated and announce the date when it will be removed. In the case of a production database that is shared by several teams, this date may be months (or years) in the future.

4. Write all new code to use the new fields, and gradually refactor all existing code to use them too.

5. Remove the old name field from the table after the deprecation date has expired, but be prepared to roll back this change if necessary.

> **■ NOTE**
>
> Data deployment is a big topic which we have barely introduced. People who want to know more about this subject should read Scott Ambler's book, *Refactoring Databases*.[12]

Monitoring the Production Environment

By carefully monitoring deployed systems, you often avoid the need to provide an emergency response to a problem and can perform preventive maintenance instead. For example, your system might require a certain amount of free disk space, so by monitoring the hard drives of the machines

---

12. [RDB] Ambler, Scott, and Pramod Sadalage. *Refactoring Databases* (Addison-Wesley, 2006).

on which it is deployed, you can ensure that appropriate maintenance action is scheduled after a defined space threshold is reached. In the same way, you might monitor the amount of CPU usage so that you can alter the priority of certain threads in your program to keep it within acceptable bounds. Products that allow sophisticated monitoring of systems are available from vendors such as AVIcode,[13] but even without this sort of budget, you can easily monitor your product by implementing simple logging facilities and a support Web site.

> **■ NOTE**
>
> The monitoring of deployed systems provides an Agile team with useful feedback about its work, so it is important to provide mechanisms that encourage the communication of this sort of information.

Logging

Programmers traditionally created a log file by adding statements to their code which caused information about its runtime behavior to be recorded in a simple ASCII text file. However, thanks to the provision of .NET library classes such as EventLog, you no longer need to be concerned with the mechanics of creating and maintaining such log files. Instead, you can use the event management facilities the operating system provides and just write the information you want captured to an easily accessible object. In this way, you can manage the logs of all programs consistently, often from a remote computer.

> **■ TIP**
>
> Microsoft's Patterns & Practices initiative[14] has produced a reusable application block that allows you to add very sophisticated logging facilities to your programs, as we mentioned in Chapter 21.

---

13. AVIcode Web site for Intercept Studio 3 (www.avicode.com).
14. Microsoft's Patterns & Practices Web site area (http://msdn.microsoft.com/practices).

Creating a Support Web Site

A support Web site provides an excellent platform from which you can distribute new versions of your software, updates, and so forth, particularly if it can be accessed directly from your application (Help | Support | Website). The Web site at www.ospacs.org/support gives an example of what you can achieve and includes the following features which are integrated via Web services into the OSPACS product:

- **Bug reporting**—You can report bugs in the product by completing a form on the Web site or a dialog box in the application.
- **Health monitoring**—Information in the application's event log can be automatically uploaded to the Web site to help identify problems.
- **Usage statistics**—Usage and performance statistics that the application gathers can be automatically uploaded to the Web site to provide the developer with information about the popularity of particular features.

■ TIP

Consider providing a facility so that members of your team can create a Bug work item directly from the information in your product's support Web site about a particular bug, as submitted by one of your users.

CONCLUSION

Try to automate your release process so that your Daily Build becomes a dress rehearsal for the actual deployment of your software. Practicing for a release in this way will make the actual event much less problematic and prepares your team for putting its software into production at the start of each business day (the Daily Deployment practice). However, we recognize that in most organizations, software deployment is a complex matter which is taken out of the hands of a development team, so it is not always possible to deploy with such regularity. Nevertheless, you should work to establish the ideas of lean thinking across your organization and seek to implement the Incremental Deployment practice so that you are able to release your product a bit at a time rather than all at once.

> **■ NOTE**
>
> Incremental deployment gives the team regular feedback from the business about the actual value being delivered by its software, so it is essential for effective management and control of an Agile project.

■ 29
Developing Installation Programs

T HIS CHAPTER DESCRIBES how Windows Installer and ClickOnce provide two different ways of automating deployment software into its
target environment. We start by introducing you to Windows Installer
because this is the most common mechanism for installing software on
most modern Microsoft platforms. We briefly explain how it works and
take you step by step through the creation of an installation program using
the well-known InstallShield tool as well as its team-based counterpart,
InstallShield Collaboration. The chapter concludes with a description of the
new ClickOnce technology provided by .NET 2.0 for Windows Forms client
applications and shows you just how much it simplifies the processes of
publishing, deploying, and updating such software.

Introduction to Windows Installer

The Microsoft Office 2000 development team developed Windows Installer
to address the problems people faced when installing its product. At the
time, there was no common way to install software on a Windows platform,
so machines would often be left in an unstable state because of things such
as .dll file version conflicts and partially completed installs. Large organizations were also finding it difficult to manage applications such as
Microsoft Office because the installation programs were not standardized,
which made them difficult to administer and control.

The Office team's Installer didn't immediately solve all these problems, but it did enough to convince Microsoft to develop the technology further. Accordingly, Microsoft decided to make the Windows Installer service part of the operating system so that people might have a uniform way to deploy software on their PCs.

> ■ **NOTE**
>
> Windows Installer first appeared with Windows 2000, but it is now present on all the main Microsoft platforms: Windows XP, Windows Server 2003, and Windows Vista.

Basic Concepts

From a user's perspective, a software product is composed of a collection of features, whereas from the developer's point of view, it is simply a collection of components. Therefore, Windows Installer maps the components the developers have produced onto the features a user wants to install by introducing the following concepts:

- Products are what you might create in a Visual Studio Solution. Products are formed from components which implement a product's features. You can sometimes get more features for a product by buying and installing additional components.
- Features are the sorts of things a story describes. Each feature relates to a particular product, and they are made available to the user through menus and other elements of the user interface, but otherwise they have no physical meaning.
- Components are what you might create in a Visual Studio Project. They are executable files (.exe, .dll) as well as other resources such as Registry entries, shortcuts on the desktop, typelibs, and so on. One component may provide one or more features and may serve more than one product.

Therefore, during the construction of your installation program, you define the components of a product and then map them to the features they provide. For example, Figure 29-1 shows how you might create a hierarchy for the components and features that belong to two products built by the OSPACS team: osImageManager and MxScreenMap.

A product has a core set of features implemented within key components, such as its main executable file, and these will always be installed. However, the product may also have optional features which you can select when the installation program is run to put additional components on your PC; see Figure 29-2. Furthermore, as you're doubtless aware, you don't need to make all of these selections initially, because the Windows Installer service also has a maintenance function which permits the product's installation program to be run again so that you can install more features or remove ones previously installed as well as reinstall the product, repair it, or remove it from your computer.

▪ TIP

Test your installation program by deploying your software in a Virtual PC[1] environment. In this way, before running the test, you can restore the system to a known state simply by reloading the hard disk image.

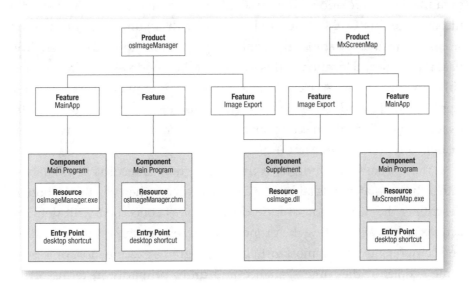

FIGURE 29-1: Two products sharing common components

---

1. Microsoft Web site for Virtual PC 2004 (www.microsoft.com/windows/virtualpc).

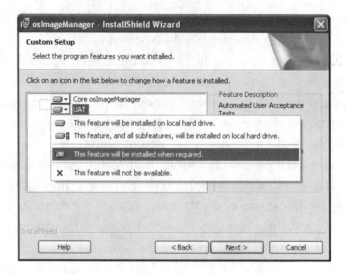

FIGURE 29-2: Selecting features to install via the Add or Remove
Programs applet

Principles of Operation

Your product's installation program is actually formed by a set of data
organized into a relational database. This database is packed into an MSI
file arranged as COM structured storage with a summary information
stream as well as a cabinet file containing the items to be deployed. You
pass the name and location of this MSI file to the Windows Installer service,
either by running msiexec.exe from a command prompt or by executing the
Control Panel's Add or Remove Programs applet. This results in the database being loaded into memory so that its contents can be used to drive the
installation process; see Figure 29-3.

It may strike you as odd to express a program as records in a database
rather than as statements laid out in a file. However, when you think about it,
describing the installation of a product is not as concerned with defining
actions as it is with setting the properties and relationships among features
and components. In fact, most installation programs execute more or less the
same actions in the same sequence and differ primarily in terms of the
parameters passed to standard functions that copy files, write to the Registry,

and so forth. Therefore, developing an installation program becomes just a matter of creating a sequence of records in an Installation Procedure table such that each record invokes a particular function from a library and sets its parameters according to the data read from rows in other tables. You can get some idea as to how this might work by considering the following tables:

- **Feature**—Each row refers to a particular feature of a product and defines its name, description, and other properties. It has relationships with numerous other tables, including the Component and Directory tables.

- **Component**—Each row refers to a resource that implements one or many features (or some part of them). It too has relationships with numerous other tables, including the Feature, Directory, File, Registry, Typelib, and Shortcut tables.

- **Directory**—Its rows identify the sources and targets for files copied or created during the installation process. The table may be modified by the end user's choice of directory settings, but ultimately it defines the directory structure of the installed product.

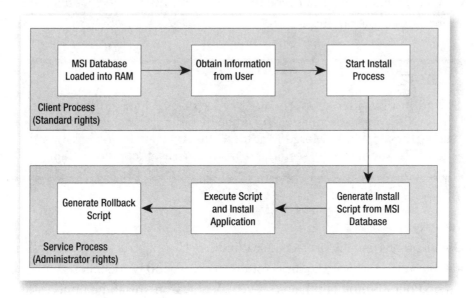

FIGURE 29-3: Operation of Windows Installer

You can categorize a number of other tables in the MSI database into groups, such as Files, Registry, and User Interface (tables that describe the properties of dialog boxes and their controls).

> **■ NOTE**
>
> Depending on the parameters passed to Windows Installer, the user interface can be full, reduced, basic, or silent, which allows installation programs to be run with or without user supervision. A reduced or basic user interface displays only modeless dialog boxes to show progress.

The huge advantage of using a database to express your installation program is that any subsequent maintenance and modification becomes a matter of editing data in tables rather than changing statements in a program or script. This means that once you understand how these tables work, you can alter any installation program developed for Windows Installer without necessarily needing to know how it was constructed. When you put yourself in the shoes of someone working on a specialist deployment team who has to customize hundreds of different products, the benefits of this approach become obvious.

> **■ NOTE**
>
> Windows Installer supports other types of COM structured storage files which are sometimes useful when installing or maintaining products. These include Merge Modules (.msm), Transforms (.mst), and Patch Packages (.msp); see http://msdn.microsoft.com for details.

Security

Organizations usually protect their Windows IT infrastructure by establishing centralized security controls for their servers and workstations with the Group Policy Editor. This helps prevent people from installing unnecessary, harmful, or unlicensed programs on their computers, by allowing only users who are logged on as Administrators to have unrestricted access to the Registry, filesystem, and so forth. However, this has the less desirable effect of stopping users from installing authorized programs on their PCs as well.

Fortunately, Windows Installer runs the install execution script (created by Windows Installer from the MSI database) with the elevated privileges of the Windows Installer service process; see Figure 29-3. Therefore, even if the logged-on user doesn't have the necessary Administrator rights needed to install all programs, these rights can be granted to the Windows Installer service in such a way that his (or her) membership of a particular security group is enough to allow the installation of specific programs to proceed. Indeed, this makes it possible to automate the remote deployment of programs in the following ways:

- **Assign to a computer**—There is no need for anyone to log on to the computer, because the program is automatically installed the next time it is rebooted (by the user or remotely).
- **Assign to a user**—The programs that members of a particular security group need are made available for installation through the Control Panel's Add or Remove Programs applet whenever the user logs on to a computer or when he attempts to open particular types of files.
- **Publish**—The program is made available to all users on all computers through the Control Panel's Add or Remove Programs applet. The installation may also be triggered when a user tries to open a file associated with the program. For example, attempting to open a PDF file might start the installation of Adobe Acrobat.

■ NOTE

The IntelliMirror technology allows users to roam between different machines by mirroring their desktop data, settings, and programs on a Windows 2003 (or 2000) server.

Remote product deployment depends upon a Windows Installer facility called Advertising, which creates the entry points for a program, such as an item in the Add or Remove Programs applet or an association with a particular file type, without actually installing it. You can install a product in this way by setting the top-level action parameter of msiexec.exe to ADVERTISE (/j) in place of INSTALL (/i) or ADMIN (/a). Run `msiexec.exe /?` from the command prompt to display a list of its options and parameters.

Creating an Installation Project with InstallShield

Although you should be aware of the facilities that Windows Installer provides and have some idea about how it works, you'll be happy to know that there is no need for you to delve into the specifics of COM structured storage and MSI databases. This is because tools such as InstallShield are available to guide you through the process.

> **■ NOTE**
>
> Visual Studio 2005 provides a template for creating a Setup Project in the Other Project Types category which produces a simple installation program, but as your team's deployment requirements become more sophisticated, you will probably outgrow this facility.

Using InstallShield with Visual Studio

You can integrate InstallShield directly into Visual Studio 2005 so that you can develop an install project in the same environment as the other projects that compose your Solution. However, InstallShield also comes with its own Integrated Development Environment (IDE) and some teams prefer this option because it helps create a clear boundary between software development and software deployment. Regardless of which IDE you decide to use, InstallShield provides two different views of your installation project: the Project Assistant view and the Installation Designer view.

▪■ WARNING

Knowledge Base article 922989 relates to problems in the support provided by Visual Studio Team Suite for add-ins such as InstallShield version 12. Until these problems are resolved, you should disable the Visual Studio .NET integration when installing InstallShield.

Using the InstallShield IDE

The Project Assistant takes you through the main steps of defining your installation project, which provides a useful introduction to the process, but it doesn't give you much more than you could achieve using a Visual Studio Setup project. Therefore, we suggest you create a test install project (spike) using the Project Assistant (see Figure 29-4) and then follow Exercise 29-1 to see how the Installation Designer gives you complete control over the process.

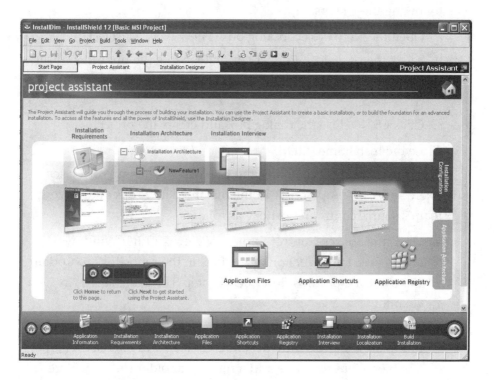

FIGURE 29-4: InstallShield Project Assistant workflow

> **■ NOTE**
>
> The first time you start InstallShield it performs some initialization which requires you to be logged on with an account that has local Administrator rights. Members of the OSPACS team, such as Luke, should have been granted these rights; see Appendix A.

EXERCISE 29-1: Creating an InstallShield Project

This exercise uses the InstallShield IDE to create a Basic MSI Project called osImageManagerInstall and adds its file to the OSPACS team's repository.

1. Log on to the TesterPC as Luke (OSPACS Contributor) and start the InstallShield IDE; see Appendix A for a specification of this machine and details of Luke's security groups.

2. Create a new Basic MSI Project called osImageManagerInstall by following these steps:

   a. Open the New Project dialog box (File | New | Project).

   b. Select the Basic MSI Project template, name the project, and set its location to the osImageManager\Install directory in Luke's workspace.

   c. Click OK to close the dialog box and create the project.

3. Close the InstallShield IDE.

4. Start Visual Studio and connect to the OSPACS Team Project; see Exercise 5-7 in Chapter 5. Add the InstallShield Project file to your team's source control repository as follows:

   a. Open the Source Control Explorer (View | Other Windows) and get the latest version of the files in the repository to update Luke's workspace, as described in step 3 of Exercise 9-1, in Chapter 9.

   b. Add the osImageManagerInstall.ism file to version control by following the procedure described in step 2 of Exercise 8-3, in Chapter 8, but this time add a file, not a folder (File | Source Control | Add to Source Control).

5. Check in your changes by clicking the Check In button in Visual Studio's Pending Changes window; see step 9 of Exercise 9-1, in Chapter 9.

■ NOTE

If you were creating your InstallShield project from the Visual Studio IDE, you could add it to source control just by checking a box in the New Project dialog box.

EXERCISE 29-2: Creating a Windows Forms Application for Your Install Project

This exercise adds an HTML file to the simple Windows Forms application we created in Exercise 8-4 in Chapter 8, and then rebuilds its Visual Studio Solution using the standard Release configuration settings.

1. Open the osImageManager Visual Studio Solution, as described in step 5 of Exercise 9-1, in Chapter 9.

2. Add a Help file called osImageManagerApp.htm to your osImageManagerApp Visual Studio Project by following these steps:

   a. Select the osImageManagerApp project in the Solution Explorer window and open the New Item dialog by choosing Add and then New Item from its context menu.

   b. Select HTML Page from the list of templates, name it osImageManagerApp.htm, and then click the Add button to both close the dialog box and add the file to your project.

3. Build a release version of the osImageManager Visual Studio Solution as follows:

   a. Select osImageManager in your Solution Explorer window and use the Properties window (View | Properties) to change its Active config property to Release | Any CPU.

   b. Rebuild the Solution and all of its Visual Studio Projects (Build | Build Solution).

EXERCISE 29-3: Using the Installation Designer to Define the Installation

The following exercise defines the features and components of your installation product and sets up the shortcuts that will be installed on the target PC's Program menu.

1. Use the Source Control Explorer window to check out osImageManagerInstall.ism for editing as follows:

   a. Select the file in the Install folder and open the Check Out dialog box (File | Source Control | Check out for Edit).

   b. Select "allow shared checkout" in the dialog box and click Check Out.

2. Start the InstallShield IDE, open the Install project file you created in Exercise 29-1 (File | Open), and switch to the designer view of your MSI project by clicking the Installation Designer tab at the top of InstallShield's main window; see Figure 29-5.

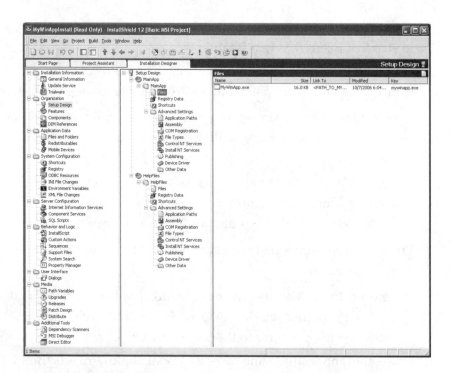

FIGURE 29-5: Installation Designer view

3. Open the designer view's list window (View | View List) so that you can see the various categories of information in the MSI database. Make changes to the following sections:

a. **Installation Information, General Information**—Select Product Properties in the middle window and set INSTALLDIR as:

```
{OSIMAGEMANAGER}[ProgramFilesFolder]OSPACS\osImageManager
```

b. **Organization, Features**—Add an item called MainApp and another called HelpFiles as follows:

   i. Select Features in the Organization folder (left window).

   ii. Select Features in the middle window and choose New Feature from its context menu (Right-click | New Feature).

   iii. Rename both your new Feature item and its Display Name property appropriately.

c. **Organization, Components**—Set up your Product's HelpFiles features as follows:

   i. **Add a component for your Help file**—Select Components in the Organization folder at the left of the window; select Components in the middle window, and choose New Component from its context menu (Right-click | New Component). Finally, type "HelpFiles" to name it.

   ii. **Define the resources for the HelpFiles component**—Click the + icon next to the HelpFiles folder in the middle window and then click its Files item; move your mouse over the right window and choose Add from its context menu (Right-click | Add). This opens a standard File Open dialog box so that you can select the osImageManageApp.htm file you created in step 2 of Exercise 29-2.

   iii. **Add a shortcut for the HelpFile to the Programs menu**—Select the Shortcuts item in the middle window, then select Programs Menu in the next window before choosing New Shortcut from its context menu (Right-click | New Shortcut). This opens a dialog box that will allow you to select the osImageManageApp.htm file in INSTALLDIR. Name this shortcut "Help."

iv. **Associate the component with the feature**—Select Setup Design in the Organization folder at the left of the window, then select HelpFiles in the middle of the window, apply Right-click | Associate Components, and select the HelpFile component in the dialog box before clicking OK.

d. **Organization, Components**—Set up your Product's MainApp feature in the same way as you did in step 3c, but this time do the following:

i. Add a component for your executable files and call it "Binaries."

ii. Define the files for the Binaries component as the executable files in your project's Release folder (e.g., osImageManagerApp.exe).

iii. Add a shortcut called Start osImageManagerApp and select the osImageManagerApp.exe file in INSTALLDIR.

iv. Associate the Binaries component with the MainApp feature.

4. Check for any components that osImageManagerApp depends upon by performing a dynamic scan as follows:

a. Start the Dynamic Scan tool (Project | Perform Dynamic Scan), which then runs your Windows Forms application so that you can exercise its various features.

b. Add any dependencies the tool finds to the Binaries component, as described in step 3b (ii). For example, if you completed Exercise 17-1 in Chapter 17, you will need to add the class library executable LocalFavorites.dll.

5. Close the InstallShield IDE and then check in your changes by clicking the Check In button in Visual Studio's Pending Changes window. Then check out osImageManagerInstall.ism for editing; see step 1.

6. Log off, as you have finished the exercise.

> **■ NOTE**
>
> You can customize the install user interface by editing the layout and behavior of the dialogs listed under Sequences-Installation-User Interface in the Behavior and Logic section of the Installation Designer's list view.

> **■ TIP**
>
> Set one of your component files as a Key File (Right-click | Set Key File) so that the component will be judged correctly installed if Windows Installer detects its presence in the right location in the target machine.

EXERCISE 29-4: Using the Release Wizard to Create Your Install Files

This exercise gathers the settings that will be used to shape the creation of your installation program and produces the collection of files needed for people to download and install the osImageManagerApp program from your Web site with just one click.

1. Start the InstallShield IDE, and open the Install project file created in Exercise 29-1 (File | Open).

2. Start the Release Wizard (Build | Release Wizard) and then use the information in Table 29-1 to supply the necessary responses. The last page of the wizard gives you the option of building the install, but you can build the release at a later date by choosing Build Beta from its Build menu.

3. Test the Install on your TestPC by choosing Run Beta from the Build menu (Build | Run Beta).

4. Remove the osImageManagerApp from your PC using the Control Panel's Add or Remove Programs applet (Start | Settings | Control Panel) and close the InstallShield IDE.

5. Check in your changes by clicking the Check In button in Visual Studio's Pending Changes window; see step 9 of Exercise 9-1, in Chapter 9.

> ## ■. NOTE
>
> InstallShield allows you to validate your install program to check that it compiles with various Microsoft Logo certification requirements (Build | Validate).

TABLE 29-1: Example Settings for InstallShield's Release Wizard

Wizard Step	Settings to Apply	Comment
Product Configuration	New Product named Std Product	Creates various configurations, each with a different collection of wizard settings.
Specify a Release	New Release named Beta	Creates variants of a particular configuration.
Filter Settings	(none)	Sets flags to include special features or resources for a specific language.
Setup Languages	English	Creates installations with user interfaces for different languages.
Media Type	Network Image	Creates install files suitable for distribution from a network server.
Release Configuration	Compress all files	Creates a single installation file.
Setup Launcher	Version 3.1 or 2.0 (best fit for system)	Setup.exe installs the Windows Installer (if necessary) and then passes it the MSI file as a parameter.
Windows Installer Location	Download from the Web	Freely available from Microsoft.
Local Machine	Cache installation on local machine	Saves download on target machine.

Wizard Step	Settings to Apply	Comment
Digital Signature	(none)	Signs your files to prevent them from being modified.
Password and Copyright	(none)	Protects your install program.
.NET Framework	Include .NET 2.0 by downloading from the Web	Installs .NET 2.0 on the target machine, if required.
.NET Run-Time Options	(none)	Parameters to pass to Dotnetfx.exe (its install program) and language support.
.NET Language Pack Run-Time Options	(none)	Parameters to pass to LangPack.exe.
Visual J# Run-Time Options	(none)	
Advanced Settings	(default)	
Summary	Select "Build the release"	Checks that your options are correct.

■ NOTE

InstallShield allows you to create a setup.exe file which handles any required updates on your PC and then automatically starts the execution of your installation program file (.msi). However, not all installation tools offer this facility.

Developing Installation Programs on an Agile Team

In many organizations, installation program development is considered a specialist task which is best done by an expert "installation developer" (or team). However, we believe that Agile teams should undertake this work, because otherwise they are not applying the Whole Team practice. It also helps your team avoid the problems that often arise when deployment requirements are passed between the group of people writing the software and the group of people producing the installation program.

■ NOTE

When your installation program has developed beyond the sort of simple affair we described in previous exercises, consider employing an installation developer consultant for a few days to train the team and suggest ways in which your installation program might be improved.

InstallShield Collaboration

Recognizing the need for software development teams to become more involved in the gathering of deployment requirements, Macrovision[2] has produced a tool called InstallShield Collaboration which allows developers to record deployment details in a type of XML file termed a *Dim* file. In this way, the team can gather its various Dim files and import them into Install-Shield to define the components of its software product's Windows Installer MSI database.

EXERCISE 29-5: Creating DIM Projects to Gather Installation Requirements

The first part of this exercise creates a Dim project called InstallMainExeReq for the osImageManager Solution you created in Exercise 8-2 in Chapter 8 so that your team can gather the installation requirements for osImageManagerApp during development.

1. Log on to the DeveloperPC as Luke (OSPACS Contributor), start Visual Studio, and then connect to the OSPACS Team Project, as described in Exercise 5-7 in Chapter 5. Note that the specification for this machine includes the installation of InstallShield Collaboration; see Appendix A.

---

2. InstallShield Collaboration Web site (www.macrovision.com/products/flexnet_installshield/collaboration).

2. Update Luke's workspace with the latest version of the files in the repository and open the osImageManager Visual Studio Solution as described in steps 3 and 5 of Exercise 9-1, in Chapter 9.

> **■ NOTE**
>
> Although the InstallShield IDE is not installed on the DeveloperPC, you can still edit the InstallShield Project created in Exercise 29-1 from your Visual Studio IDE, but it doesn't offer the same rich features and isn't intended for gathering installation requirements.

3. Create a new Visual Studio Project called InstallMainExeReq using the InstallShield Collaboration Project template and add it to your osImageManager Solution, as explained in Exercise 8-4 in Chapter 8.

4. Rename the Dim file created for your project as MainAsmby.dim by selecting Dim1.dim in Solution Explorer's InstallMainExeReq folder and then choosing "rename" from its context menu (Right-click | Rename).

5. Set the General properties of MainAsmby.dim, such as Name, Version, Description, and so on, using the form that appears when you select the General tab at the bottom of the editor window.

6. Add a description for the Prerequisites Meta Information; double-click the Description column of the Prerequisites row at the bottom of the form and type "Install .NET 2.0".

7. Add the osImageManagerApp.exe file to the Contents page of your Dim file by taking the following steps:

   a. Select the Contents tab at the bottom of the editor window and then select the File System folder that appears in the editor's left window; see Figure 29-6.

   b. Open a form in your editor window by choosing Add File Set from the File System folder's context menu (Right-click | Add File Set).

   c. Click the Add button in the form and then select the executable files osImageManagerApp.exe and LocalFavorites.dll belonging to the release version of your osImageManagerApp project.

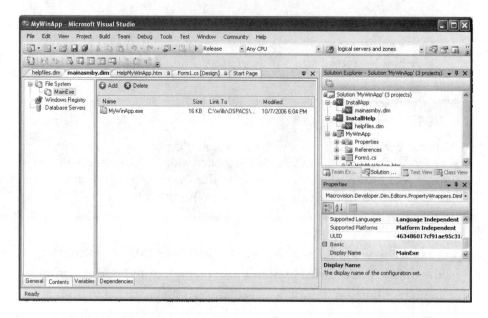

FIGURE 29-6: InstallShield Collaboration project

8. Rename the item you just added to the File System folder as Main Exe. Just select New File Set, and choose Rename from its context menu (Right-click | Rename).

The second part of the exercise takes you through an InstallShield Collaboration's unit test procedure to check that your Dim file can generate a valid installation program.

9. Set your InstallMainExeReq project as the osImageManager Visual Studio Solution's start-up project (select the InstallMainExeReq project, Right-click | Set as Startup Project).

10. Check that your Dim file can generate a valid install file by following these steps to run a unit test:

   a. Build the project (Build | Build InstallMainExeReq).

b. Start the install program using the Unit Test tool (Debug | Start without Debugging), and then follow the instructions to install osImageManagerApp on your PC.

c. Start osImageManagerApp.exe from the Main Assembly DIM directory which has been created in c:\Program Files\OSPACS.

d. Close osImageManagerApp.exe and remove it from your PC using the Control Panel's Add or Remove Programs applet.

The final part of the exercise creates another DIM project called InstallHelpReq for the osImageManager Solution so that your team can gather the installation requirements for its Help files during development.

11. Create another InstallShield Collaboration Project called InstallHelpReq by repeating steps 3 through 10, but this time enter values that are appropriate for the Help file you created in step 2 of Exercise 29-2; specifically:

a. Rename the Dim file HelpFiles.dim.

b. Add HelpMyWinApp.htm in the File System folder to the Contents page of your Dim file (step 7 of this exercise).

c. Rename the item in the File System folder as "Help File Set".

12. Check in your changes by clicking the Check In button in Visual Studio's Pending Changes window; see step 9 of Exercise 9-1, in Chapter 9.

■ NOTE

Typically a Dim file will be created for each Visual Studio Project in your Solution. However, developer pairs who are working simultaneously on the same project will still need to avoid conflicts by regularly checking in any changes to the Dim file they are sharing.

EXERCISE 29-6: Creating an Install Program from DIM Files

This exercise uses the Dim files you prepared in Exercise 29-4 to create a new installation program called osImageManagerInstallDim.

1. Use the InstallShield IDE to create a new install project in Luke's workspace by following the instructions in Exercise 29-1. However, this time call your new Basic MSI Project "osImageManagerInstallDim".

2. Define your new installation project in the same way you did in Exercise 29-3, but instead of defining the components yourself (steps 3c and 3d), import the settings from your Dim files as follows:

   a. Select Setup Design in the Organization folder at the left of the window, and then select MainApp in the middle of the window so that you can open the New Dim Reference dialog and select the MainAsmby.dim file created in step 4 of Exercise 29-5.

   b. Select HelpFiles in the middle of the window, apply Right-click | New Dim Reference, and select the HelpFiles.dim file created in step 11 of Exercise 29-5.

   c. Select Shortcuts in the System Configuration folder at the left of the window, and select Programs Menu in the next window before opening the New Shortcut dialog box so that you can select the osImageManagerApp.exe file.

   d. Repeat the preceding step to create a shortcut for the Help file in HelpFiles.dim.

   e. Name your shortcuts "Launch osImageManager" and "Help".

   f. Create the Install files for your new Installation project in the same way you did in Exercise 29-4, and confirm that your installation program works as you expect. When you have finished, remove it from your PC using the Control Panel's Add or Remove Programs applet.

3. Add osImageManagerInstallDim.ism to version control (see Exercise 8-3 in Chapter 8) and then check in your changes by clicking the Check In button in Visual Studio's Pending Changes window (see step 9 of Exercise 9-1, in Chapter 9). Finally, log off, as you have completed this exercise.

> **TIP**
>
> Create collaboration projects for gathering your installation requirements at the start of the project, when things are relatively simple, because these requirements will only become more complex as time goes by.

Automating the Creation of Your Installation Program

When an Agile team has responsibility for producing an installation program, it makes sense to automate the task so that the team can perform it each day during the Daily Build. In this way, the team can deploy the product at the start of any day just by granting people access to the Web site that holds its installation files. Fortunately, a stand-alone version of the InstallShield product is available that can use a file such as osImageManagerInstall.ism to generate the necessary installation files from the command line. Therefore, after installing this product on your BuildLabPC, you should add some custom build steps to your Daily Team Build in order to automate the production of your installation program at the end of the build process and then copy its files to a suitable Web server directory.

> **TIP**
>
> Select settings in InstallShield's Release Wizard to generate a "one-click install" Web page, and then provide a link to this page from your Team Project's Portal to make it simple for people to install the latest software on their PC.

> **NOTE**
>
> Developers often have the Administrator rights they need to install software on their PCs, but this is seldom true in the case of business-people. Therefore, you may have to consider other ways to actually deploy your software to production, such as by using Systems Management Server (SMS).[3]

---

3. Microsoft: SMS Web site (www.microsoft.com/smserver).

ClickOnce Technology

ClickOnce[4] technology provides a much simpler alternative to Windows Installer and the MSI database for certain classes of applications. In some respects, these applications give you the best of all worlds because you can deploy them like thin clients, yet they support the sort of rich user experience that only a desktop application can provide. Furthermore, they execute in a security sandbox, which prevents them from harming other applications (or data), and they can be automatically updated whenever a new version is loaded on the source server, typically a file share or basic Web server.

> **■ NOTE**
>
> Users do not need Administrator rights to install a ClickOnce application, so you can just publish its program files to a source server and then send people a link to this location so that they can deploy the application themselves.

Suitable Applications

You can use ClickOnce technology only for Windows Forms applications using .NET 2.0[5] (or greater) and similar modern technologies which are operating on the target PC in one of two modes:

- **Installed**—Clicking on this link to the source server deploys the application by creating entries in the target computer's Start menu as well as its Add or Remove Programs database. It also copies all the program files into a cache so that the application can be run in the future without any connection to its source server, but obviously it will not be updated until the connection is restored.

- **Online-Only**—Clicking on this link copies all the program files into a cache from which the application is run. However, the cache is refreshed each time you click on the link, so you cannot run the application without a link to its source server.

---

4. Microsoft: ClickOnce Web site (http://msdn.microsoft.com/clickonce).
5. "No-touch" deployment is a predecessor of this technology, which supports .NET 1.*x*.

ClickOnce is not suitable for Windows Forms applications that need to operate outside the sandbox provided by .NET Code Access Security, perhaps because they need unrestricted access to the filesystem, Registry, or other privileged aspects of the target machine. You also cannot use it to install services, shared assemblies in the Global Assembly Cache (GAC), device drivers, and similar system-level software. For these sorts of installation jobs, you require Windows Installer or some form of bootstrapper. However, for deploying something such as the client part of a distributed system, ClickOnce is often an ideal solution, particularly if your client needs to provide some type of sophisticated user interaction which is going to be difficult to implement on a Web page (thin client).

Basic Concepts

You develop a ClickOnce application as you would any other Windows Forms application and it requires no special classes, though you can programmatically control when updates are obtained by using classes in the `System.Deployment` namespace. The deployment mechanism is contained in the .NET 2.0 Framework and simply requires that you provide a couple of XML files called the *application and deployment manifests*. Fortunately, Visual Studio 2005 generates these files for you, so all you need to do is supply the appropriate settings in your project's properties; see Exercise 29-7.

The application and deployment manifests act like the MSI database in terms of describing the application and its settings, though they contain information that is specific to ClickOnce deployment, such as the way it should be updated from the source server, its security settings, and so forth. In general, you should set the security settings of your application so that they are no greater than the security policy expected on the target PC, although you can allow users the option of granting one-click applications elevated permissions when prompted from the .NET runtime.

> ### ■ NOTE
>
> Visual Studio generates setup.exe as part of the publishing process which can install .NET 2.0 (and other dependencies) on the target machine, but for this to work the user must have Administrator rights, so you may need to distribute it with a tool such as Microsoft SMS.

Publishing and Deploying

Anyone who has deployed any software in a corporate environment using Windows Installer will be heartened by how easy it is to achieve the same sort of result with ClickOnce technology. It really is very simple, and although in the following example your application is published from Visual Studio 2005, you will probably want to automate the process by making it a task for Team Build to perform at the end of your Daily Build.

■ NOTE

Brain Noyes' book, *Smart Client Deployment with ClickOnce*,[6] provides a lot of information that might be useful to anyone considering using ClickOnce technology in her project.

EXERCISE 29-7: Creating, Publishing, and Deploying a ClickOnce Application

You do not need to use Team Project to complete the following exercise, for it just creates a simple Windows Forms application and then publishes it to your local Internet Information Services (IIS) Web server from where it is deployed.

1. Log on to the DeveloperPC as Luke and start Visual Studio.

2. Create a new C# Windows Forms application in its own Visual Studio Solution using the template in your New Project dialog box (File | New Project). Name this project "ClickOnce" and locate its files in a convenient local directory (e.g., c:\Luke\OSPACS\Spike). Do not add this project to version control.

3. Set the following publishing properties for ClickOnce by choosing Properties from Visual Studio's Project menu and then selecting the Publish page:

   a. Publishing location: c:\Luke\OSPACS\Spike\ClickOnce\

   b. Installation URL: \\localhost\Drops\

---

6. [SCD] Noyes, Brian. *Smart Client Deployment with ClickOnce* (Addison-Wesley, 2007).

    c. Install mode: Application is available offline as well.

4. Build and publish the application by clicking the Publish Now button on the Publish page shown in Figure 29-7, and then manually copy the files from the publishing location to the installation URL.

5. Deploy the application on your own PC by following these steps:

    a. Open in your browser the Web page publish.htm in the location defined in step 3b.

    b. Click the Install button on this page and follow the instructions.

6. Confirm that your program works as you expect and then remove it from your PC using the Control Panel's Add or Remove Programs applet.

7. Log off, as you have finished the exercises in this chapter.

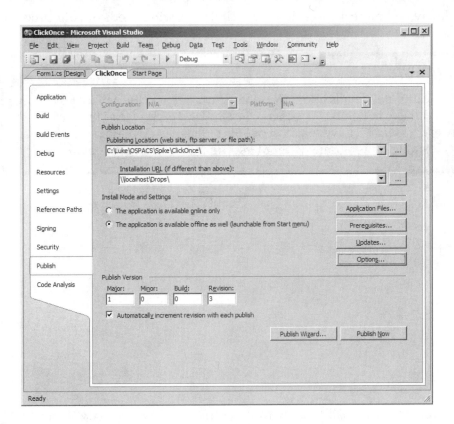

FIGURE 29-7: ClickOnce publishing from Visual Studio

> **■ NOTE**
>
> You would not deploy the server components of a distributed system using ClickOnce, but instead might prepare a Windows Installer MSI database using information generated by tools such as the Visual Studio Team System (VSTS) Deployment Designer; see Chapter 30.

CONCLUSION

This chapter introduced the basic information an Agile team needs to build the sorts of installation programs that will deploy its software into the production environment, whether on a user's desktop or on a server in some datacenter. Although the exercises are not comprehensive, they are enough to get you started, and from these simple projects you should be able to slowly add more complexity to match the growing needs of your product.

> **■ NOTE**
>
> Additional details about Windows Installer and the MSI database are available in Bob Baker's classic *InstallShield for Windows Installer Developer's Guide*.[7] However, most people manage to develop perfectly good installation programs without getting into this level of detail.

---

7. [OIW] Baker, Bob. *InstallShield for Windows Installer Developer's Guide* (M&T Books, 2001).

■ 30
Deployment of Distributed Systems

THIS CHAPTER EXPLAINS how the Distributed System Designer (DSD) tools provided with Visual Studio Team Edition for Architects allow you to model the deployment of a Web service-based distributed system into a variety of different datacenters. We start by explaining why advances in computer hardware have made distributed systems so important to developers working with Microsoft technology and how the System Definition Model (SDM) helps you describe them. We then introduce each DSD tool in turn and take you through the process of creating the diagrams that allow you to model the deployment of your application.

Distributed System Architecture

A succession of technological advances have allowed each generation of PC hardware to replace its predecessor with better processors, larger amounts of memory, and more sophisticated communication facilities. Therefore, we are now at a stage when extremely powerful computing resources can be created simply by connecting relatively cheap PC boxes into some form of distributed system. This has caused many organizations to fundamentally rethink the way their computing resources are provisioned.

> **■ NOTE**
>
> In 1990, a Cray supercomputer cost $40 million and had a performance of 10 gigaflops. Today you get the same performance from a four-processor PC costing less than $3,000, which is why racks of PCs are displacing mainframe computers in many datacenters.

Distributed Components

In client-server architectures, the system's data layer is located on a single (database) server, so it can be shared by a collection of desktop PCs running its client part. This idea is extended for systems that have a distributed component architecture so that not only can the business layer execute on its own server (host), separately from the data layer and the user interface layer, but also the workload can be dynamically moved between machines to avoid bottlenecks forming at particular servers. This allows you to build systems from PC boxes with transaction rates that can surpass those found on most mainframe architectures. However, successful deployment of such systems requires a high level of specialist skills as well as close cooperation between developers and the operations staff who are responsible for maintaining these systems.

Service-Oriented Architecture (SOA)

The difficulty of building systems based on a distributed component architecture combined with the need to make best use of legacy systems based on a range of different platforms has made Service-Oriented Architecture (SOA) an attractive proposition for many organizations. It is based on the idea of providing a relatively simple interface which provides a rich and coherent business service to collections of disparate systems. Therefore, when building a new system in an SOA environment, you become more concerned with combining such services in novel ways than implementing entirely new sets of (distributed) components. This isn't to say that you can't create your own hosted applications, but that your aim in doing so is to supply useful business services for others to use through the interfaces you supply. Typically, to provide such a service you would need several components as well as some form of back-end database.

> **▪ NOTE**
>
> Services are usually supplied as Web services and described in terms of an interface contract using Web Services Description Language (WSDL). In this way, they can be consumed by distributed systems regardless of their geographic location or technical platform.

System Definition Model (SDM)

In the SOA world, a Web service could just as easily be supplied by a business partner in Bangalore as it could be provided by the machines in your basement, so when it comes to deploying and managing these sorts of systems, you can't simply rely on getting things done by building personal relationships with your datacenter staff. For this reason, Microsoft and its partners are encouraging the formation of standards to automate the management of distributed systems through the Dynamic Systems Initiative (DSI).[1]

The System Definition Model (SDM) is the part of the DSI that is concerned with creating a schema for distributed systems that allows their logical and physical organization to be separated in much the same way as a database schema isolates us from the arrangement of data sectors on a disk drive. These models are already supported by tools such as the Visual Studio Team System (VSTS) Distributed System Designers, but with the release of Windows Longhorn, they will start to take an active role in the live management of the server. Therefore, in the future, people will no longer have to work at the level of physical components and their configuration files, for they will be able to use an application's SDM in conjunction with an automated deployment mechanism such as SMS[2] to affect its installation and subsequent management.

---

1. DSI home page (www.microsoft.com/windowsserversystems/dsi).
2. Microsoft: SMS Web site (www.microsoft.com/smserver).

> **■ NOTE**
>
> SDM models are actually created using the sort of XML-based Domain-Specific Language (DSL) described in Chapter 21, so you can present the information they contain in different ways and easily transfer it among the management tools on different systems.

VSTS Distributed System Designers

Visual Studio Team System for Architects provides the following four tools which are collectively known as the Distributed System Designers (DSDs). These tools allow you to create a set of editable diagrams which define the SDM for your Web service-based distributed systems:

- **Logical Datacenter Designer (LDD)**—Models a particular datacenter in terms of its security zones and the different types of servers found within them

- **Application Designer (AD)**—Models the components your team is developing to provide and consume Web services

- **System Designer (SD)**—Models the assembly and configuration of components from an AD model into reusable applications as well as complete systems

- **Deployment Designer (DD)**—Creates a validated model for the deployment of SD (and AD) models into the LDD model, which can then be used to generate an XML report of your actual deployment requirements

The XML-based language of the SDM is suitable for any system that needs to be managed, from large distributed systems to small systems on a single machine. Therefore, Microsoft envisions that within the next few years, this language and its associated tools will let you manage your systems just as easily as you can now manage your databases using SQL and Enterprise Manager.

> **■ NOTE**
>
> Although the DSD tools allow you to model at the separate levels of Application, System, Datacenter, and Deployment, what you are actually creating is a set of diagrams that combine to form a unified System Definition Model.

Logical Datacenter Designer

The computers in a datacenter are usually connected together into some form of network which is split by various communication boundaries into a collection of different zones, each with their own level of security. Therefore, your organization might create a secure inner zone for the server hosting its private customer database and then establish a less secure outer zone for the server hosting its public Web site in such a way that all communication between the two zones goes through a boundary controlled by a firewall. The Logical Datacenter Designer (LDD) allows you to create models of such datacenters in terms of the servers in their various security zones as well as the settings and constraints that apply to them.

> **■ NOTE**
>
> The models that the LDD creates cannot (yet) represent the physical servers in a zone, so although your model might represent a Web site server and a database server as separate entities, in reality they could conceivably be hosted on the same machine.

Creating a Logical Model of a Datacenter

In the following exercises, you will model a hypothetical datacenter with just two zones and two servers. However, you should subsequently create models that accurately reflect the servers and zones in your actual production datacenters as well as the test machines in your Build and Test Environment (see Chapter 11), something that future versions of the tools will doubtless do automatically.

EXERCISE 30-1: Making a Visual Studio Solution for Your Logical Datacenter Diagrams (.ldd)

This exercise creates a Logical Datacenter Solution called CommonData-centers for your organization's Logical Datacenter Diagrams and adds it to the OSPACS repository.

1. Log on to the ArchitectPC as Luke (OSPACS Contributor), start Visual Studio, and then connect to the OSPACS Team Project, as described in Exercise 5-7 in Chapter 5; see Appendix A for a specification of this machine and details of Luke's security groups.

2. Update Luke's workspace with the latest version of the files in the repository, as described in step 3 of Exercise 9-1, in Chapter 9.

3. Create a new Visual Studio Logical Datacenter Solution called CommonDatacenters using the New Project dialog as follows:

   a. Open the New Project dialog box (File | New | Project) and select the Distributed System Solutions–Logical Datacenter template.

   b. Name the Solution, set its location to the Production directory in Luke's workspace and then check the Add to Source Control box.

   c. Click OK to close the New Project Dialog box and, when prompted, select the $/OSPACS/Production folder as the location for storing your Solution in the repository.

4. A default LDD file is automatically opened in the Visual Studio editor window after you create your Solution, but you should close this file (File | Close) and then remove it from the Solution Items folder in your Solution Explorer window (Right-click | Remove).

5. Check in your changes by clicking the Check In button in Visual Studio's Pending Changes window; see step 9 of Exercise 9-1, in Chapter 9.

■ TIP

Create just one Visual Studio Solution to contain all your organization's Logical Datacenter Diagrams so that multiple (team) projects can share them and the people responsible for maintaining the machines to which they relate can keep them up-to-date.

EXERCISE 30-2: Creating a Logical Datacenter Diagram (.ldd) with Zones and Servers

We continue the preceding exercise by adding an LDD to the Visual Studio Solution and then adding various zones and servers to reflect the layout of our hypothetical datacenter.

1. Add a new LDD file to the CommonDatacenters Solution and call it BartsDatacenter by taking the following steps:

   a. Select the Solution Items folder in your Solution Explorer window and choose Add | New Distributed System Diagram from its context menu in order to open the Add New Item dialog box.

   b. Select the Logical Datacenter Diagram, type its new name, and click OK to close the dialog box and create the new diagram.

2. Add the first zone to your diagram by opening the toolbox (View | Toolbox) and drag-dropping its Zone icon into the middle of the LDD editor window. Rename the zone and its endpoint to "Public" and "Public_EP", respectively; double-click the default names and then type the new names.

3. Add the second zone to your diagram by repeating step 1, but this time name the zone and its endpoint, respectively, "Private" and "Private_EP".

■ TIP

You can drag-drop the various endpoint icons around the perimeters of their zones and servers to make the diagram look neat. You can also display or hide their associated labels from their context menus by selecting each one and applying Right-click | Show Label.

---

4. Add an IISWebServer to the Public zone by drag-dropping its icon from the toolbox into the middle of the Public zone in the LDD editor window.

5. Rename this IISWebServer server to "IISPublic" in order to reflect its role rather than its physical presence. You should also rename the Web site endpoint of this IISPublic server to "IISPublic_EP".

6. Add a DatabaseServer to the Private zone by drag-dropping its icon from the toolbox, as you did in step 4. Rename this server and its endpoint, respectively, to "DbPrivate" and "DbPrivate EP".

7. Join the servers to their zones by selecting each server's endpoint in turn and delegating it to the endpoint of its corresponding zone. For example, select the icon labeled IISPublic_EP, open the Delegate to Endpoint dialog box (Right-click | Delegate), and then select Public as the zone and Public_EP as the endpoint.

8. Form a communication pathway between the Public zone and the Private zone by following these steps:

   a. Select the Public zone's outbound endpoint and choose Connection from its context menu to open the Create Connection dialog box.

   b. Set the Connect To zone as Private and the endpoint as Private_EP, as shown in Figure 30-1.

9. Check in all the files you have created by clicking the Check In button in the Pending Changes window; see step 9 of Exercise 9-1, in Chapter 9.

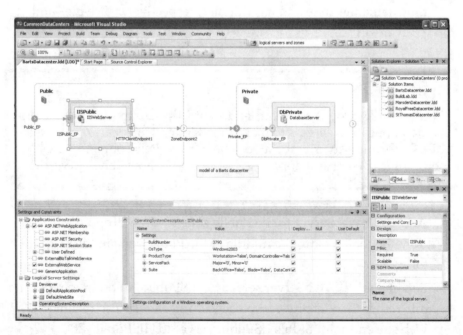

FIGURE 30-1: LDD diagram

> ■ **NOTE**
>
> It is sometimes better to think of communication pathways between servers being formed through "boundary points" because "endpoints" do not always refer to things that are actually at the end of a communication pathway.

Endpoints and Servers in Your Toolbox

You use endpoints to define communication pathways between logical servers as well as between zones. However, you can create these pathways only between endpoints that are compatible in terms of their type and properties. For example, a zone endpoint whose communication flow property is set to outbound might be connected to another inbound (or bidirectional) zone endpoint, but not to another outbound one.

The most important thing to remember about endpoints is that you cannot directly connect a server endpoint in one zone to a server endpoint in another zone; instead, you must delegate each server's endpoint to a zone endpoint so that a connection can then be formed between the two zone endpoints. Visual Studio's toolbox (View | Toolbox) contains a variety of endpoints which you can add to following logical servers:

- **IISWebServer**—Models a Microsoft Internet Information Services (IIS) Web server that hosts ASP.NET Web applications, generic applications, and external Web services as well as BizTalk.[3] It provides all types of endpoints, including `WebSiteEndPoint`, so it can render Web pages to any server (or Windows client) having an `HTTPClientEndpoint`.

- **DatabaseServer**—Hosts all types of external databases as well as generic applications and can provide the endpoint of communication pathways to most types of servers. However, it normally acts as a database server endpoint.

---

3. Microsoft: BizTalk Web site (www.microsoft.com/biztalk).

- **GenericServer**—Hosts all types of external Web services as well as generic applications, and provides all types of endpoints. Therefore, in addition to acting as a generic server, it can supply and consume Web pages, form a database client, and act as a client of its own (or another) generic server.

In due course, you should expect Microsoft and third-party vendors to add other server types to the toolbox that model specific products more closely than the current generic or database servers. However, in the meantime, you must make do with these general server templates and mostly set up each server in your model manually.

■ TIP

After adding a server to your LDD diagram and manually entering its settings, you should add the server to your toolbox so that you can use it to define the next server of that type without having to reenter all the settings. You can do this by selecting the server in the diagram and choosing Add to Toolbox from its context menu.

Properties, Settings, and Constraints

When you select an element in your LDD diagram you can set its properties from Visual Studio's Properties window (View | Properties Window), and this usually gives you a good idea of what it does. For example, an endpoint's direction property might indicate that it is a consumer, so you know it must connect to a provider endpoint. However, the most interesting part of these properties is the section for settings and constraints, which are displayed in their own window; click Setting and Constraints in the Properties window and then click its "…" button.

Constraints act to limit the way you can use an endpoint—either as a server or as a zone. For example, you can set a constraint for the Public zone in Figure 30-1 to prohibit anyone from adding a database server to this part of the model. You can also add constraints to a zone so that only

IISWebServers with settings for a particular version of the Common Language Runtime (CLR) are valid within the zone (see Figure 30-2). In this way, you can model your datacenter in terms of the settings of its various zones, servers, and endpoints and the constraints that apply to the way each of these elements may interact.

Some constraints are implicit, so you cannot alter them; others you can set explicitly, such as requiring a particular version of the CLR. A third type of constraint is user-defined, which means that you can add your own requirements for the way something must be used. Similarly, settings can also be implicit, explicit, or user-defined. You should think of explicit settings as the things you would find in your server's configuration file, or the things you might set from its Options dialog box, and the process of validating the model as confirming that these settings are compatible with the components you intend to deploy and the environment in which they must operate.

> **■ NOTE**
>
> Properties, settings, and constraints are associated with almost every element in the diagrams produced by the DSD tools and form an important part of the modeling mechanism.

FIGURE 30-2: Settings and constraints for IISWebServer

Importing Settings from Your Existing IIS

IISWebServer is an example of the sort of server you would hope to find in your toolbox because it represents a specific product commonly found in datacenters. Therefore, its properties, settings, and constraints are closely allied to those actually found in a real server of this type. Indeed, rather than modeling a server by entering these properties by hand, you can import them directly from the corresponding device in your datacenter.

EXERCISE 30-3: Importing Settings from the IIS in Your Datacenter

We continue the preceding exercise by adding a new server type to your toolbox that contains the settings which apply to the IIS in your organization.

1. Initiate the process of importing the settings of an IIS located in your datacenter into your model's IISWebServer by starting the Import IIS Settings Wizard as follows:

   a. To start the wizard, select IISWebServer in the Public zone and choose Import Settings from its context menu (Right-click | Import Settings).

   b. Move to the wizard's second page (click Next) and select the physical server hosting IIS in your datacenter by clicking the Browse button and navigating to your physical server (or type "localhost"). Enter an Administrator's username and password for this server and then click Next.

   c. Set the endpoint in your model that will be bound to the Default Web Site on the physical IIS server by selecting IISPublic_EP from the drop-down list and then click Next.

   d. Import the settings into your model by clicking Next on the wizard's Summary page.

   e. Click Finish to close the wizard.

2. Make any further adjustments to the IISWebServer's properties, settings, or constraints as follows:

   a. Select IISWebServer in the Public zone and change its values in the Properties window (View | Properties).

b. Adjust the contents of the Settings and Constraints window (Right-click | Settings and Constraints).

3. Add a new server type to your toolbox that reflects this IISWebServer's properties, settings, and constraints as follows:

    a. Open the Add to Toolbox dialog box so that you can name the new server by typing "MyIIS" into the appropriate edit box; select IISWebServer, right-click, and then select Add to Toolbox.

    b. After you click OK, you are prompted to save your server prototype, so accept the suggested filename and click the Save button to complete this action.

4. Check in all the files you have created by clicking the Check In button in the Pending Changes window; see step 9 of Exercise 9-1, in Chapter 9.

5. Log off, as you have completed this exercise.

■. NOTE

Future versions of the DSD tools might provide additional wizards to allow the automatic discovery of servers in a datacenter and support the modeling of physical servers as well as logical ones.

Application of LDD Models

In a large organization, an Agile team might not use the LDD tool, but simply use the diagrams produced by other people to validate the deployment of the components they are developing. In such a situation, the people responsible for maintaining the datacenter are often the best placed to create and preserve its LDD diagram(s) because they are managing the configuration of the servers on a day-to-day basis. However, in smaller organizations (or when the components under development are intended for external deployment), an Agile team may have responsibility for this work. In such cases, it is more of a challenge to keep the model up-to-date, particularly if the team does not also control the datacenter. However, even an imperfect model serves to remind the team about deployment issues and provides a more accessible alternative than looking at IIS config files or the management console.

> ■ **NOTE**
>
> A datacenter is not always a massive air-conditioned room in some secret bunker. It may be just a couple of servers underneath someone's desk.

Application Designer

The construction of distributed systems based on an SOA depends upon components located on different machines that are able to communicate with each other. In practice, this usually means that they must consume and expose Web services. The Application Designer (AD) allows you to model the components that implement these Web services as well as the services and applications with which they interact. The AD model is implicitly associated with a corresponding Visual Studio Solution, so you can both create the model from your existing code and generate the code from your model.

> ■ **NOTE**
>
> The components which provide and consume the Web services defined by the AD diagram must be implemented by Visual Studio Projects which share the same Visual Studio Solution. For this reason, you can add only one AD diagram to each Visual Studio Solution.

Creating an AD Diagram

Some teams will create an AD diagram while preparing for the deployment of their completed components, in which case they will probably reverse-engineer it from an existing Visual Studio Solution. However, other teams will create an AD diagram to help them define the structure of their solution, so they will draw it while group modeling at the start of the project.

We will start by taking this second approach because the process is more transparent, but we'll focus on the mechanics of creating the diagram because we already covered group modeling in Chapter 18.

EXERCISE 30-4: Making a Visual Studio Solution for Your Application Designer (.ad) Diagram

This exercise creates a Visual Studio Solution for your AD diagram and adds it to source control.

1. Log on to the ArchitectPC as Luke (OSPACS Contributor), start Visual Studio, and then connect to the OSPACS Team Project, as described in Exercise 5-7 in Chapter 5.

2. Create a new Distributed System Solution called DistibOspacs and add it to the OSPACS repository in the same way as you did in step 3 of Exercise 30-1.

3. A default AD file is automatically opened in a Visual Studio editor window, but you should close this file (File | Close) and then remove it from the Solution Items folder in your Solution Explorer window (Right-click | Remove).

4. Check in all the files you have created by clicking the Check In button in the Pending Changes window; see step 9 of Exercise 9-1, in Chapter 9.

EXERCISE 30-5: Drawing an Application Designer Diagram

You now will add an AD diagram to the Visual Studio Solution created in the preceding exercise, and you will add the various components required for your distributed system as identified from your group modeling session; a database component, a Web service component, and a Web application for the user interface.

1. Add a new AD file to the DistibOspacs Solution and call it DistribAppDiagram; see Figure 30-3.

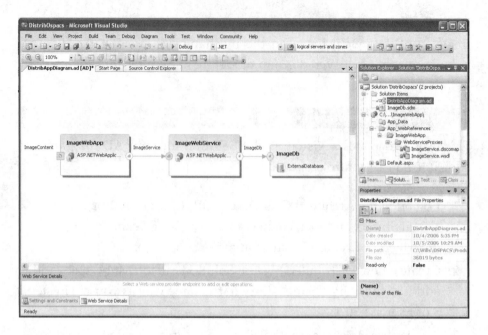

FIGURE 30-3: AD diagram

    a. Select your Solution Items folder, and then choose Add and then New Distributed System Diagram from its context menu to open the Add New Item dialog box.

    b. Select Application Diagram and then click the Add button to close the dialog box.

2. Add a database component to your diagram by opening the Toolbox (View | Toolbox) and drag-dropping its ExternalDatabase icon into the middle of the AD editor window; then take the following steps:

    a. Rename the database to "ImageDb"; double-click the default names and type the new name (the database component's end-point is renamed at the same time).

    b. Rename the file that now appears in your Solution Items folder to "ImageDb.sdm".

3. Add an ASP.NETWebService component and an ASP.NETWebApplication to your drawing in the same way you

added the database component, but rename them "ImageWebService" and "ImageWebApp" before changing their endpoint names to "ImageService" and "ImageContent".

4. Define the communication pathway between these components, starting with ImageWebApp and proceeding through the ImageWebService component to ImageDb as follows:

   a. Select the component and choose Connect from its context menu (Right-click | Connect).

   b. The Choose Datasource dialog opens automatically when you connect the ImageWebService to the ImageDb endpoint, but click Cancel as you will set these properties later.

5. Check in all the files you have created by clicking the Check In button in the Pending Changes window.

■ NOTE

Use the "connection" tool in the toolbox to create connections by positioning the tool over a component (or endpoint), and then clicking to start the connection, dragging the connection to the target element, and then clicking once more to complete the action.

The toolbox's ASP.NetWebApplication and ASP.NetWebService differ only in terms of the default endpoint created when they are dropped onto a diagram. ImageWebApp is created with a "Web content" endpoint whereas ImageWebService is created with a "Web service" endpoint. However, both of these endpoints are "providers," so a new "consumer" endpoint is automatically created in ImageWebApp when they are connected. This is because communication between components is always through compatible endpoints (consider them as boundary points), so a "provider" can connect only to a "consumer" and not to another "provider."

The purpose of consumer and provider endpoints is simple: A consumer needs something that a provider supplies and their endpoints form the conduit for this transfer of information. You can add consumer endpoints to a component using the Create Connection dialog[4] either when you have selected the component and are connecting to a provider endpoint, or when you have selected the provider endpoint and are connecting to a component. However, you can add provider endpoints directly to a component from the component's context menu (Right-click | Add New | Endpoint).

> **■. NOTE**
>
> A consumer endpoint connects to only one provider endpoint, but a single provider endpoint may have multiple consumers connected to it. However, remember that only endpoints of a compatible type can be connected together.

EXERCISE 30-6: Defining Operations for a Component's Provider Endpoint

This next exercise walks you through the steps required to expose an operation provided by one of your components (also known as an *Application*). This could be consumed by another one of your components or by some external component seeking to use the Web service you are providing.

1. Open Visual Studio's Web Service Details window by selecting the ImageService endpoint in your AD diagram and choosing Define Operations from its context menu (Right-click | Define Operations).

2. Add an operation to ImageService by following these steps:

   a. Click on the <add operation> line and type its name: "FindPatientImageCount".

   b. Qualify the properties of this operation by setting its type as String and then entering some suitable text in the summary field; for example, "return the number of images stored for the given patient".

3. Add a parameter for FindPatientImage by expanding its node and typing its name: "PatientID". Qualify the properties of this parameter

---

4. The Create Connection dialog refers to the components in your AD diagram as *Applications*.

by setting its type as Integer and its summary as "unique patient identifier".

4. Check in the file you have created by clicking the Check In button in the Pending Changes window.

EXERCISE 30-7: Defining a Connection String to a Database

Typically, you define the physical connection between your program and an external database via a connection string contained in some form of configuration file. The following exercise adds this connection string to your model and assumes that you have already created a SQL Server database called osImage on a server called TFSRTM\SQLEXPRESS that you can access using Windows authentication.

1. Set the database connection string for the ImageWebService consumer endpoint in the Connection Properties dialog as follows:

   a. Open the Connection Properties dialog by selecting the endpoint and choosing Define Connection String from its context menu (Right-click | Define Connection String).

   b. Define the name of your database server by typing "TFSRTM\SQLEXPRESS" and then select Use Windows Authentication before selecting osImage from the list of database names.

   c. Check the connection by clicking Test Connection.

   d. Click OK to close the dialog box and save your settings.

2. Check in all the files you have created by clicking the Check In button in the Pending Changes window.

■ NOTE

The shaded boarder of the ImageDb in your diagram signifies that it has been implemented, which is a reasonable assumption for an external database. However, the other elements in your diagram have not yet been implemented, so their borders are unshaded.

In the next exercise, you will forward-engineer the applications (components) in the AD diagram into a collection of Visual Studio Projects that are part of your Visual Studio Solution. You will then build this Solution to provide an implementation of your model.

1. Set the Language property for ImageWebApp and ImageWebService to Visual C# by selecting them in turn and choosing Properties and Language from their context menus.

2. Create Visual Studio Projects for ImageWebApp and ImageWebService as follows:

   a. Select a blank area of the diagram and choose Implement All Applications from its context menu (Right-click | Implement All Applications).

   b. When a dialog box appears with a summary of the Project that will be created, click OK to confirm this operation.

3. Close any Security Warning messages that might appear and then rebuild your Visual Studio Solution (Build | Build Solution).

4. Check in all the files you have created by clicking the Check In button in the Pending Changes window.

■ NOTE

All the boxes in your AD diagram have a shaded border because there is now an implementation for each of them. You can also find the database connection string you defined in Exercise 30-7 in the web.config file of the ImageWebService project.

The Visual Studio Project that implements your Web service includes a Web page which provides access to its operations from a browser. In the following exercise, you will use such a page to test the operations you defined for your Web service in Exercise 30-6.

1. Set ImageWebService as the Startup project by selecting it in Solution Explorer and choosing Set as Startup Project from its context menu.

2. Open the Web page that has been generated to facilitate the testing of your ImageWebService:

   a. Open the project's directory listing (Debug | Start without Debugging) and then open the ImageService.asmx file in your browser by double-clicking it.

   b. Click the hyperlink to open another Web page containing details of the FindPatientImage operation.

   c. Enter "999" into the PatientID field and click the Invoke button; see Figure 30-4. This causes an HTTP 500 Internal Server Error because the underlying code has thrown an exception, so close all the browser pages and return your attention to Visual Studio.

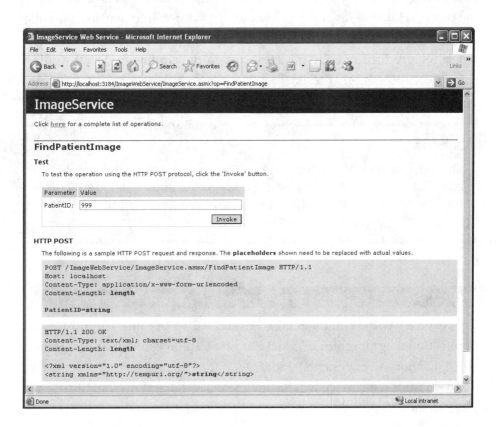

FIGURE 30-4: Web page for testing ImageService

3. Correct the problem in the ImageWebService code by opening ImageService.cs in Visual Studio and replacing the throw statement in the FindPatientImage method with the following:

```
return "4";
```

4. Rebuild your Visual Studio Solution and repeat step 2; this time you should get the correct result.

5. Check in all the files you have created by clicking the Check In button in the Pending Changes window.

Ultimately, you will want to create a connection to the osImage database and execute a SQL query so that you can return the correct number of rows in the image table for the given patient, but we leave this as an exercise for the reader. However, everything is now ready for you to develop the code for your Web service using the practices and policies your team has mandated for production code (i.e., test-driven development [TDD], coding standards, and customer tests).

> **■ NOTE**
>
> The model and the Visual Studio Projects are now based on the same SDM language, so if you alter ImageService.cs so that the FindPatientImage method's return type is String, your AD diagram will immediately reflect this change and vice versa.

EXERCISE 30-10: Reverse-Engineering an AD Diagram from a Visual Studio Solution

This exercise is the complement to Exercise 30-8 because it produces an application diagram from a Visual Studio Solution containing a collection of applications (components). However, rather than ask you to create this Solution from scratch, we will just delete the AD diagram from the one we have already implemented and then regenerate it.

1. Close all the documents in Visual Studio (Window | Close all Documents) and then use Solution Explorer to remove the DistribAppDiagram.ad file from your Solution (Right-click | Remove).

2. Add a new AD diagram to your Visual Studio Solution as follows:

   a. Open the Add New Item dialog by selecting the Solution Items folder and choosing Add and then New Distributed System Diagram from its context menu.

   b. Select the Application Diagram, name it "DistribApp2Diagram.ad", and click Add.

   c. Click OK to close the dialog and create the diagram.

3. You may need to reposition the elements in your new AD diagram to make it look neat and tidy, but otherwise it is the same as the one you removed in step 1.

4. Check in all the files you have created by clicking the Check In button in the Pending Changes window.

5. Log off, as you have finished this exercise.

Terms such as *reverse-engineer* and *forward-engineer* are usually associated with the round-trip facilities of certain CASE tools, such as Rational Rose;[5] in other words, they can generate code from a model and a model from the code. However, in this case, the models that the DSD tools display and the implementation that Visual Studio displays are really just different views of the same SDM language; see the section Emergence of Domain Specific Languages, in Chapter 21. Therefore, because VSTS has no "round-trip" step, the model and its implementation are always synchronized.

> ■ **NOTE**
>
> The AD diagram shows ImageService as an endpoint of the ImageWebService application, but in a Class Designer diagram, it is shown in terms of the interface that it supplies (select the endpoint, right-click, and then select View in Class Diagram).

---

5. IBM: Rational Rose Web site (www.ibm.com/software/rational).

Defining Settings and Constraints

Elements in an AD diagram have properties that include settings and constraints such as those described earlier; see the section Logical Datacenter Designer, earlier in this chapter. However, in this case, the settings and constraints are primarily concerned with specifying how components should be deployed. For example, you can apply a constraint to your ImageWebService application (component) that limits its deployment to an IISWebServer running on Windows 2003 with a particular service pack and/or build number. You can also stipulate settings for the way in which your component should be installed—for instance, whether it should be run as an InProcess or as a PooledProcess.

> **■ NOTE**
>
> An AD diagram can serve a similar purpose to the InstallShield Collaboration product (described in Chapter 29) in terms of gathering deployment requirements from the development team.

Application of AD Models

An Agile team might find an AD diagram helpful in terms of implementing the sort of thin vertical slice through the system discussed in Chapter 27. Alternatively, the team may reverse-engineer the diagram from a Visual Studio Solution which already contains such an architectural vision. Either way, the team needs to produce this type of diagram during the early stages of the project so that it can properly explore distributed Web services deployment before making implementation decisions which may prove difficult to change later on.

The AD diagram becomes useful to your team in other ways which become evident as the project progresses. For example, it allows the team to regularly validate the deployment of its work against a range of different datacenters (as described shortly), and it helps the team manage its deployment requirements (as mentioned earlier). Indeed, when it comes to packaging distributed Web service components for deployment, the AD diagram serves a similar purpose to the MSI database (see Chapter 29), so it may warrant being distributed along with your team's other project outputs.

System Designer

The System Designer (SD) allows you to model systems as units of deployment created by aggregating the sorts of applications defined in an AD diagram or by combining systems that have already been created in this way. Therefore, armed with a suitable collection of AD and SD diagrams, you might be able to satisfy some new business requirement just by recombining existing implementations into a new (and possibly very large) system. This makes the job of building distributed systems into an exercise of defining new collections of deployable units that can be mapped onto logical models of one or more physical datacenters using the reports generated by the Deployment Designer (DD), described shortly.

Creating SD Diagrams

An SD diagram can be a simple representation of some or all of the applications in your Visual Studio Solution. It can also provide a composite representation of a collection of SD diagrams gathered from the same (or different) Visual Studio Solution(s). Therefore, you might produce a simple SD diagram to help you deploy all your applications (components) into the team's test environment and produce a number of other simple SD diagrams to define how various subsets of these applications (components) could provide certain useful services to the business. You could then create a composite SD diagram from some of these simple SD diagrams to define a collection of services for a particular client.

EXERCISE 30-11: Creating System Designer Diagrams from an AD Diagram

The following exercise creates an SD diagram from the applications created in the previous exercises.

1. Log on to the ArchitectPC as Luke (OSPACS Contributor), start Visual Studio, and then connect to the OSPACS Team Project, as described in Exercise 5-7 in Chapter 5.

2. Open DistibOspacs, the Visual Studio Solution created in the previous exercises, or complete Exercises 30-4 through 30-7 to create an AD diagram with some components and a Web service. Open the

DistribAppDiagram.ad file from your Solution Explorer; double-click it.

3. Create an SD diagram from the AD diagram to describe the system which you will deploy in your Build Lab by following these steps:

   a. Open the Design Application System dialog box by choosing Design Application System from the Diagram menu (Diagram | Design Application System).

   b. Enter "TestImageSystem" in the dialog box to name your new diagram.

   c. Click OK to close the dialog box and create your diagram; see Figure 30-5.

4. Create another SD diagram from the AD diagram to describe the system which you will deploy to your client by following these steps:

   a. Select the ImageWebService and the ImageDb applications.

   b. Open the Design Application System dialog box as you did before, but this time, name your new diagram "BasicImageSystem".

   c. Click OK to close the dialog box and create your diagram.

5. Create a proxy for the `ImageService` endpoint belonging to the ImageWebService application (component) as follows:

   a. Select the ImageService endpoint in the BasicImageSystem diagram and choose Add Proxy Endpoint from its context menu (Right-click | Add Proxy Endpoint).

   b. Rename this new proxy endpoint to "ImageServiceProxy".

6. Check in the file(s) you have created by clicking the Check In button in the Pending Changes window.

■ NOTE

An SD diagram is always associated with an AD diagram whose contents are shown in the System View window as a collection of applications. Other SD diagrams in your Visual Studio Solution are also shown in this window as a collection of systems.

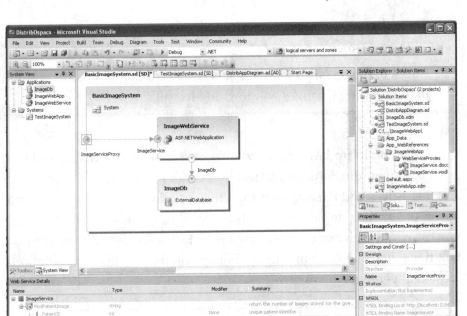

FIGURE 30-5: SD diagram

EXERCISE 30-12: Creating Composite System Designer Diagrams

In this exercise, you will create an SD diagram which contains another SD diagram as well as an application.

1. Create a new SD diagram called BartsHospital.sd and add the BasicImageSystem to it together with the ImageWebApp application by selecting the Solution Items folder and choosing Add New Distributed System Diagram from its context menu before dragging the item from your System View window.

2. Connect the ImageWebApp application to the BasicImageSystem (subsystem) as follows:

    a. Use the Toolbox connection pointer to click BasicImageSystem's ImageServiceProxy endpoint.

   b. Drag-drop a connection to the ImageWebApp Application's
      ImageContent endpoint.

3. Check in the file(s) you have created by clicking the Check In button
   in the Pending Changes window, and log off.

You can build up large-scale systems by importing SD diagrams from
other Visual Studio Solutions (select the Solution Items folder, right-click,
and then select Add Existing Item), but their applications will appear in red
(error) unless their implementation is accessible to your Solution. However,
you can avoid such errors by organizing the locations of your Visual Studio
Solutions such that you build up the Solution at the root from the Solutions
located lower in the hierarchy.

Defining Settings and Constraints

The various settings and constraints applied in your AD diagram are aggre-
gated together in the SD diagrams to form the settings and constraints for
the system you will deploy. Therefore, if you've applied a constraint to your
ImageWebService application that limits its deployment to an IISWebServer
running on Windows 2003 Service Pack 2, this becomes a constraint for any
SD diagram that contains this application (or any subsystem in which it is
included). However, you can override in the SD diagram some of the settings applied in your AD diagram so that you can configure your applications for a particular deployment environment. One of the main benefits of
the SD tool is this facility to develop a set of applications that you can deploy
in a variety of different ways.

Application of SD Models

An Agile team might use a simple SD diagram to define how its Visual Studio Solution should be deployed in its Build Lab (e.g., BuildLabPC). This
deployment would probably include various applications that are not destined for the production environment, but serve just to provide a convenient way to exercise the system; an ASP.NetWebApplication test, for

example. The team might also use composite SD diagrams to build useful collections of Web services for other teams to use in the construction of their systems as an alternative to sharing a common set of Web services in the production datacenter. In this way, each client could have completely independent distributed systems that didn't need to share services outsourced to some datacenter.

Deployment Designer

The Deployment Designer (DD) produces a diagram that models the deployment of a given collection of software components into a particular datacenter. This model is first validated against the constraints and settings defined in the SD diagram as well as those defined in the LDD diagram and then used to create a report which specifies the deployment requirements. In this way, you can identify deployment problems from the start of a project at a time when you don't necessarily have any physical components to deploy or even a finished datacenter in which to put them.

> **■ NOTE**
>
> The DD does not go so far as to create any form of installation program or Unified Modeling Language (UML) deployment diagram because this would require information about the datacenter's physical representation that isn't (yet) present in the deployment model.

Creating a DD Diagram

Although you can create any number of DD diagrams for the various SD diagrams in your Visual Studio Solution, it is more likely that there will be a one-to-one correspondence between an SD diagram and the DD diagram that defines how such a system could be deployed.

EXERCISE 30-13: Creating Deployment Designer Diagrams from an SD Diagram

This exercise models the deployment of a system defined by its SD diagram into a datacenter modeled by an LDD diagram.

1. Log on to the ArchitectPC as Luke (OSPACS Contributor), start Visual Studio, and then connect to the OSPACS Team Project, as described in Exercise 5-7 in Chapter 5.

2. Open DistibOspacs, the Visual Studio Solution for which you created an SD diagram in Exercise 30-12. Open the BartsHospital.sd file from your Solution Explorer; double-click it.

3. Create a DD diagram for this SD diagram by opening the Define Deployment dialog box (Diagram | Define Deployment), selecting the BartsDatacenter.ldd file created in Exercise 30-2 (Browse), and clicking the Open button. Your diagram should now look like Figure 30-6.

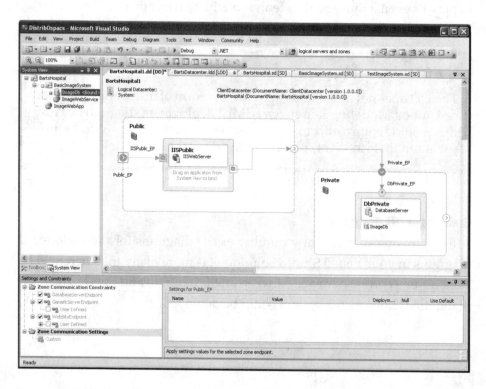

FIGURE 30-6: DD diagram

4. Bind the applications from the BartsHospital SD diagram to the appropriate logical servers in the BartsDatacenter LDD diagram by using the System View window to select each application in turn so that you can do the following:

   a. Open the Bind Application dialog (Right-click | Bind Application).

   b. Select a compatible logical server in the dialog box.

   c. Click OK to close the dialog box and bind the application.

■ NOTE

You can generate a deployment model directly from your AD diagram, but it is intended that actual deployments will be defined by a model created explicitly from an SD diagram so that you can configure them for different production environments.

Deployment Properties

The properties of a DD diagram are displayed in Visual Studio's Properties window (View | Properties Window) in the same way as other elements in your Solution. The properties you are most likely to alter are contained in the Project Files and Report sections because they determine the location of your deployment report, the files that will be included with it, the various settings relating to errors, and so on.

EXERCISE 30-14: Setting the Properties of Your Deployment Designer Diagram

In the following exercise, you will set the properties of the DD diagram created in Exercise 30-13 so that any deployment report generated from it will be created in a suitable directory.

1. Set the Destination Path property of your DD diagram as follows:

   a. Open Visual Studio's Properties window (View | Properties Window).

b. Click on the surface of the diagram and set the Directory Path property to a suitable directory in Luke's workspace (e.g., c:\Luke\OSPACS\Production\Docs).

2. Check in the file(s) you have created by clicking the Check In button in the Pending Changes window.

■ TIP

Set properties to include binary and content files along with your deployment report so that everything needed for deployment is put into your Destination Path. The types of files copied into this directory depend upon the project, but may include .dll, .exe, .config, and .wsdl files.

Validating Deployment

The key facility of the DD tool is its capability to validate the model of your system in terms of its SD diagram against the model of your datacenter in terms of its LDD diagram. This allows you to identify potential deployment issues from the earliest stages of your project.

EXERCISE 30-15: Validating a Deployment Designer Diagram

This exercise validates the DD diagram and generates a list of errors or warnings in regard to any incompatibility between the constraints and settings of the system and the datacenter where it will be deployed.

1. List any errors or warnings about your intended deployment by validating the DD diagram (Diagram | Validate Diagram). Review the error messages that are generated.

2. Check in the file(s) you have altered by clicking the Check In button in the Pending Changes window.

> **■ NOTE**
>
> It is easy to identify the source of errors generated during validation because they are listed in Visual Studio's Error List window, and double-clicking an error (or warning) opens the Settings and Constraints window, taking you straight to the source of the problem.

Creating a Deployment Report

The actual deployment report is XML-based so that it is machine-readable, but a human-readable form is also rendered into an HTML page that may include a list of errors and warnings as well as the related DSD. Typically, you would pass this report to your deployment team or use it yourself to help you complete the physical installation of your components into the selected datacenter.

EXERCISE 30-16: Creating a Deployment Report

In this exercise, you will generate a report in order to help you deploy the components your team has developed into a specific datacenter.

1. Prepare for the deployment of your components by producing a deployment report, which you do by choosing Generate Deployment Report from the Diagram menu.
2. Check in the file(s) you have altered by clicking the Check In button in the Pending Changes window.
3. Log off, as you have finished the exercises in this chapter.

> **■ NOTE**
>
> The deployment report's original HTML and XML files are stored in the main directory of your Visual Studio Solution. However, the equivalent .sdm document files are created in the directory you set as your DD diagram's Destination Path property.

Application of DD Models

An Agile team should create a DD diagram for its Integration and Build environment (Build Lab) as well as for its target production environment(s) so that it can include in its automated Team Build process the validation of these diagrams against the current settings and constraints in its AD diagram. In this way, any small deployment issues will not be allowed to accumulate in the project because they will be regularly identified and corrected during the Integration (or Daily) Build.

Ideally your Team Build would also generate a deployment report for the DD diagram associated with your Build Lab and then use it to automate the actual deployment of the build products into this environment. However, this would require an additional tool capable of translating a deployment report into a form of installation program that you could automatically apply to your physical datacenter (Build Lab). At present, the Microsoft tools go only as far as a logical datacenter, but doubtless this is a limitation that will soon be addressed.

> ### ■ NOTE
>
> Macrovision[6] is developing a product which uses the VSTS deployment report to generate an install package that you can distribute with the Microsoft Systems Management Server (SMS), thereby opening the way for automated deployment from your Team Build.

CONCLUSION

The models that the DSD tools generate certainly make it much easier for teams to design, develop, and deploy distributed systems based on Web services. However, at present the automated deployment of their components into a datacenter is still dependant upon someone developing some form of installation program. Clearly, before too long, tools will be released

---

6. Macrovision: SDM Web site (www.macrovision.com/sdm).

to automate even this step so that in a matter of days, organizations can go from initial business requirement to production system.

> **▪ NOTE**
>
> Undoubtedly, not everyone will want to implement the Daily Deployment practice (see Chapter 28), but in the future, this will be for business reasons rather than because of any technical constraints in the development and release process.

Review of Section 9
Practice for Deployment

I N THE PAST, the OSPACS team didn't do a great job deploying its products. This was because by the time it came to writing the installation program, the developers had forgotten some of the important presumptions they had made during coding about the presence on the target platform of things such as Registry values, data files, service pack updates, and security settings. Therefore, after running the installation program, there was always some additional tweaking to be done before their system could be considered successfully deployed in the production environment. To improve matters, the team had already taken the following actions at the start of its project:

- Made its installation program a mandatory product of the iteration in the same way as its executable files
- Engaged an expert for three days to teach the developers about installation programs and help them create a basic installation program using InstallShield,[1] which they could then extend as the project progressed
- Installed InstallShield Collaboration on the PCs in the team's development environment to encourage the gathering of deployment requirements at the time the code was being written

---

1. Macrovision: InstallShield Web site (www.macrovision.com/products/flexnet_installshield).

However, they now built upon this work by completing the following work:

- Implemented logging in their applications so that they could monitor their software once it was in the production environment
- Created a simple Web site to support their products and gain feedback from users about their problems and suggestions
- Worked with people in other departments to remove some of the technical bottlenecks that were stopping the team from deploying its software quickly
- Undertook a spike to investigate how the Distributed System Designer (DSD) tools might help them better understand their clients' datacenter environments

The Team's Impressions

The team learned a lot about writing installation programs from the expert it had engaged and therefore felt more confident about including this task in its Daily Build process. The team members realized that instead of attempting to build a large and intricate installation program at the end of their project, they should start with a small and simple one and then slowly add complexity as the work progressed.

CEO: Mike

"Practicing the deployment of a system from the earliest stages of the project helps us identify issues that might have an impact on the project's business case. For example, if we know that we cannot install a certain component in a client's datacenter, why waste time and money building something that can't actually be deployed?"

Developer: Tom

"I can't imagine any commercial team really doing daily deployment, but there's nothing wrong with people trying to automate the deployment process and remove those bottlenecks in our organization that add no value."

"Clearly, future versions of the DSD tools will give us accurate data-center models by actively probing our client's production servers. It's a shame that these facilities aren't available to us yet."

Developer: Luke

"I'm trying to improve my skill at writing installation programs because I like the idea of seeing the whole project through from beginning to end."

"Regular deployment helps the team members build expertise in this area so that when they deploy at a client's site, it is a case of executing a well-polished procedure."

Developer: Sarah

"It is exciting to envision people building systems simply by integrating our different services into some form of Web site."

"We should always apply the Incremental Deployment practice when upgrading a legacy system."

Developer: Peter

"We should continue to develop client-server solutions and stand-alone applications in those situations when this sort of architecture provides the simplest and most appropriate way of meeting the business needs."

"Daily deployment is something for very small user groups, not for a larger organization. The last place I worked had monthly production releases, and many people thought that was too fast because each deployment cost the business so much time in terms of changing procedures, training, and so on."

Developer: Maggie

"It is much easier to system-test the team's software when there is an installation program that deploys it automatically. In the past, it was never clear whether problems were due to a bug or the way a program was set up."

Agile Values

The Daily Deployment and Incremental Deployment practices reinforced the team's Agile values in the following ways.

Communication

Capturing deployment requirements at the time the code is written ensures that this information is accurately transferred from development to operations. Frequent deployment also encourages development staff and operations staff to talk with each other on a more regular basis.

Feedback

Early deployment allows a team to learn from its mistakes and therefore improve the future releases of its product. It also gives the team earlier feedback from real users, particularly when it is monitoring the production environment.

Courage

Teams feel less apprehensive about their system when they deploy it incrementally because they can start with something simple and then add sophistication as it is required. This makes them willing to undertake more challenging work because the impact of any failure is limited to the next deployment.

Simplicity

The team's objective is to totally automate deployment so that it can be completed with little more than a single mouse-click. The team will handle the increasing complexity of its production environment by developing models that allow the team to view them in a simpler way.

Respect

Regular deployment encourages respect between the people in development, operations, and the business because the value of their respective work is visible from the early stages of a project.

■ Section 10
Provide and Reveal Value

I N THIS FINAL section of the book, we consider the importance of a team providing and revealing the value that exists in its work from the earliest stages of a project. Chapter 31 addresses the value that a team can obtain from the technical information gathered about its activities by Team Foundation Server (TFS), and in particular, it looks at how a team might produce reports from this data to help improve performance. Chapter 32 then discusses the value the business can obtain by exploiting the team's software earlier in the development cycle as a result of the team revealing its features iteratively and incrementally. Ultimately, it is this ability to provide and

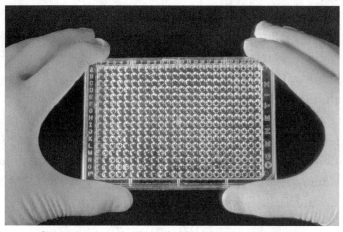

Photograph by James King-Holmes (Copyright Science Photo Library, 2006).

In the same way biologists can identify the genetic traits of an organism before it matures, your customers should be able to discover the value in your software from the earliest stages of its development.

reveal value which defines an Agile team and leads the team to better software development.

Story from the Trenches

A few years ago, I joined a team that was developing a capital markets trading system for large banks and other financial institutions. A number of very talented developers were working on the project and they had already produced a good product. Although this system wasn't perfect, it did have a number of significant advantages over its competitors and the bank that had been our initial development partner was actually using it. The team's next objective was to rewrite the system so that it could be easily customized to meet the needs of other customers. However, it was a race against time because the cost of running the project was crippling the company and no income was being generated.

Shortly after starting the job, I attended a meeting to discuss our priorities for the next few months. The businesspeople sat at one end of the table and the developers sat at the other. Each side quickly established its position. The business was adamant that it must have something to show to its customers, and we were equally insistent that we needed to restructure the code before working on any form of demonstration. Given that nobody knew whether he or she would be paid at the end of the month, the atmosphere became highly charged as both sides struggled to dominate the meeting.

The matter came to a head when the sales director, Charles, declared that without anything to show his customers, he couldn't close a single sale. This resulted in my boss, James, telling him flatly that nobody would be giving demonstrations until we had sorted out the code structure. The two men then stared at each other across the table, in stony silence. It was clear that James would walk out of the meeting and probably out of the company if pressed any further on this question of a demonstration. It was equally clear that unless Charles could make these sales, everyone's future was in jeopardy. The meeting broke up without this impasse being breached. We had not really understood the problems the business faced and the business had clearly not understood our need to address the technical issues that were worrying James. Both groups might as well have been speaking a different language which, indeed, in some ways they were.

Over the next three months, the company somehow managed to fund our team, so eventually we were able to restructure the code and deliver a demonstration version of the product. When Charles demonstrated this system to his potential customers, they were clearly impressed, so it seemed he was only a few weeks away from getting the sales that would secure our future. Unfortunately, though, before they materialized, the entire business was sold to a competitor. It transpired that our parent company was fighting a takeover battle and had already taken the decision to dump us for a knockdown price. The company probably would not have taken this action had it realized the true value that existed in our software. The problem was that we could see the value in our software, but we hadn't revealed it in time to save the business.

■ 31
Producing Technical Reports

THIS CHAPTER STARTS by reviewing some of the standard queries and reports generated from the template selected when you created your Team Project. We briefly explain what they do and how they might be useful to you. However, the real message of the chapter is that each team is different in terms of the information it needs, so each team must take responsibility for creating and presenting its own reports. Therefore, we explain how you can develop your own queries and reports from the information about your project which is gathered in the relational and On Line Analytical Processing databases of Team Foundation Server.

Revealing Valuable Information

Team Foundation Server (TFS) stores a huge amount of information about your team's software development activities, but in practice, only a small subset of this data will be useful for managing and controlling your project. Indeed, some of the most important information about your project isn't stored in TFS at all; it's in the working software you deliver to your customer, on the Task Boards on your office walls, and in the story cards people have written. This isn't to say that you can learn much from the data gathered in TFS, but rather that you need to be selective in terms of how it is used. For this reason, we will concentrate on covering only a few of the standard queries and reports created for your Team Project, and then we'll discuss ways in which you can maximize the value of this information by presenting it effectively.

■ NOTE

Teams that regularly deliver working software do not need to spend a lot of time producing traditional project reports. Instead, they can simply invite customers to run their tests to see what has been achieved and what remains to be done; see Section 7.

Standard Queries and Reports

Queries typically create simple lists of information, as they involve just running a SQL query statement against a collection of tables in a relational database. Reports, on the other hand, can generate much more sophisticated sets of information because they operate on data provided from an On Line Analytical Processing (OLAP) database. The standard queries and reports listed in Team Explorer are determined by the template you selected when creating your Team Project. For example, the following queries and reports are among those created by MSF for Agile Software Development:

- **Active Bugs**—A query that lists all work items of type Bug whose state is set as Active. This allows you to display all the known bugs in your system ordered by their priority or by the person to whom they are assigned. When a particular bug is selected, its properties appear at the bottom of the window; these include its history, links to other work items (e.g., bugs), and details of the build in which it was first detected.
- **All Work Items**—A query that lists all work items of any type. This summarizes all the work about which the team is gathering metrics (see Figure 31-1).
- **Bug Rates**—A report that charts the number of bugs being found and resolved each day against the total number of active bugs that

have been identified in your code. Preferably you would like to see more bugs being resolved than are being found each day until your team has cleared its bug backlog, but a low rate of bug discovery might actually reflect problems with your testing practices.

- **Quality Indicators**—A report that charts the number of passing and failing (or inconclusive) tests each day against the percentage of code coverage, active bugs, and the lines of code that have been added or changed (code churn). Any lag between the bug total and code churn curves indicates a delay in finding bugs, which might mean you need to increase the code coverage achieved during your unit testing. An Agile team should not keep code checked in that causes a test to fail, and should maintain a high percentage of code coverage even when there is a large amount of code churn.

- **Builds**—A report that lists your Team Builds showing the percentage of tests passed, code coverage, and code churn. You can drill down into the details of each build to discover more about the composition of this data; see Figure 12-5 in Chapter 12.

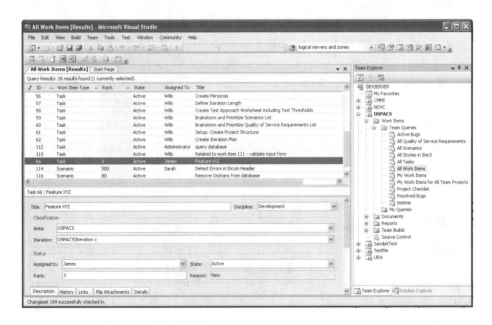

FIGURE 31-1: Results of an All Work Items query

> **■ NOTE**
>
> You run the queries and reports belonging to a Team Project simply by double-clicking the item in the Team Explorer window; see Exercises 27-3 and 27-7 in Chapter 27. You can also add new queries and reports to your Team Project, as described shortly and as discussed in Exercise 27-4 in Chapter 27.

Gathering and Presenting Information

Visual Studio Team System (VSTS) takes a lot of the hard work out of gathering the data needed to produce your Team Project's queries and reports because most of the information is collected automatically as people perform day-to-day tasks such as creating bug reports, checking in their code, running builds, and so forth. In theory, this means that team members should be able to spend more time analyzing and acting upon the information, but unless you're careful, the shear amount of data may prove overwhelming and result in people disengaging from the entire process. Therefore, we suggest you start with a small number of standard queries and reports, selected because they have a clear purpose in terms of revealing information that might help a team improve its performance. You should then discuss how the data is gathered and its relevance to the team before encouraging people to consider how the information might be presented in a more meaningful way. This isn't just a case of asking for some suggestions to adapt existing reports, but it might go so far as to rig up a dot-matrix moving message sign to broadcast the percentage of code coverage achieved in the last Team Build.

> **■ NOTE**
>
> You need to generate enthusiasm for finding and resolving the issues that are preventing the team from performing better. This won't happen while people are still looking at reports developed by other teams that are based on metrics which they don't really understand.

Informative Workspace Practice

The Informative Workspace practice is about the team taking control of its environment and making it support the work it is doing. It is an antidote to the institutionalization that exists in many workplaces.

The artifacts of an informative workspace are usually practical as well as symbolic. A large sign placed very visibly on a wall showing the results of the latest Team Build, for example, tells people whether their work has been successfully integrated into the product, something they really need to know. However, the sign also acts like a flag because it tells the world that the team has created working software! Such symbolism helps create a team identity and is the sort of thing that inspires people to go beyond the usual boundaries of their jobs. It signifies that people are part of a team and that they care about what they do. This is not about window dressing; it's about creating an environment that encourages the behavior and actions of a successful team.

You know when you've joined a team that is applying the Informative Workspace practice because from the first time you enter the team's space, you immediately know the sort of people you'll be working with and the nature of their project. You can sense the enthusiasm and passion; notice boards inform you about the tasks they're doing; and Big Visible Charts (BVCs; discussed shortly) on the walls tell you what's really important to the team and the progress they're making on these issues. When you wander into the kitchen, you see that there's space for people to sit and talk, and the smell of fresh coffee percolates through the air. To apply the Informative Workspace practice, start by asking what message your current environment gives people and then consider how changing that message might help your team produce better work.

Big Visible Charts

You might put a lot of effort into selecting your metrics and then presenting them in a thoughtful manner, but unless this information is communicated properly, its value may be completely lost. For this reason, Agile teams often put their most important information on big charts which they pin to the walls of their offices. When is comes to attracting attention, it's hard to beat these Big Visible Charts (BVCs).[1] However, you shouldn't spend too much time making them look like they've come out of a graphic design studio because part of their appeal is that you can draw them quickly and then discard them once they've served their purpose. Indeed, this casual look emphasizes their immediacy and relevance to the team's current problems.

> **■ WARNING**
>
> The power of a BVC is diminished when there are too many charts on the wall or when you do not update them regularly. Therefore, decide what information is really important, and then apply the resources needed to present it reliably and effectively to the whole team.

Extracting Data from Team Foundation Server

Team Foundation Server (TFS) acts as a central repository for all the data associated with your Team Project, such as its source code, work items, build products, and so forth. Most of the time you access this data through Visual Studio, but occasionally you may need to get at the information directly. Therefore, we will give you a brief overview of the structure of the TFS Data Warehouse before describing how you can access it both as a traditional On Line Transaction Processing (OLTP) database and as an On Line Analytical Processing (OLAP) database.

> **■ NOTE**
>
> The Bibliography contains references to a number of good books about relational databases, SQL, and data mining. We recommend you obtain a basic knowledge of these subjects before attempting to do any serious work with the TFS Data Warehouse.

---

1. Jeffries, Ron. "Big Visible Charts" (www.xprogramming.com/xpmag/BigVisibleCharts.htm).

Introduction to the TFS Data Warehouse

Relational databases are based on the idea of collections of tables containing rows (records) and columns (fields) which have certain relationships to each other. This arrangement is fine for applications that are largely transactional in their nature, but it's less good when you need to pull together information from different sources so that you can perform complex analysis on large data sets. For this sort of data mining work you really need an OLAP database. You build this type of database by automatically *extracting* data from different sources (such as relational databases), performing any *translation* of the data that may be required to put it in a common form, and then *loading* the resulting data into the cube structures that characterize the OLAP database. Once you've created these cubes, it's a quick and easy matter for people to drill down into the data and find all the information they want.

The TFS Data Warehouse is composed of both a relational database and an OLAP database which are both provided by SQL Server 2005. You can access the relational database using the SQL Server Management Studio tool (see Exercise 31-1). The following tools are concerned with the OLAP database (see Exercise 31-2):

- **SQL Server Integration Services (SSIS)**—Performs the extracting, translation, and loading (ETL) of the OLAP database.

- **SQL Server Analysis Services (SSAS)**—Unifies the information held in the relational database with the information held in the OLAP database so that reports are always generated using the latest information.

- **SQL Server Reporting Services (SSRS)**—Creates and manages report definitions authored in Report Definition Language (RDL). It also publishes and manages reports on the report server.

■ WARNING

The preceding tools are not installed with VSTS, so you must use the SQL Server 2005 installation disk supplied with your MSDN subscription to install them on your PC and then set up the necessary user rights before starting the exercises in this chapter.

Accessing Data in the TFS Relational Database

You should spend some time exploring the data stored in the various TFS databases so that you gain a basic understanding of what data is available to you and how it is organized. Fortunately, the SQL Server Management Studio tool makes this easy to do, as you can see from the following exercise.

■. NOTE

SQL Server Management Studio replaces the Enterprise Manager and Query Analyzer tools found in previous versions of Microsoft SQL Server.

EXERCISE 31-1: Running a SQL Query on the TFSWarehouse Relational Database

This exercise shows you how easy it is to obtain information about your builds from TFS's TFSWarehouse database. It's a good idea to complete this exercise to check that you have the necessary rights to access the TFS databases.

1. Log on to the ArchitectPC as Luke (OSPACS Contributor) and start SQL Server Management Studio; see Appendix A for a specification of this machine and details of Luke's security groups.

2. Connect to the database engine on the server that hosts your TFS (e.g., DEVSERVER) using Windows Authentication by making the appropriate selections from the drop-down list controls in the Connect to Server dialog box.

3. Prepare a SQL Query on the TFSWarehouse database as follows:

   a. Open the Databases folder.

   b. Open the Tables folder in the TFSWarehouse database.

   c. Select the Build table, and then right-click and select Script Table As | SELECT To | New Query Editor Window. This creates a SQL Query in the Query Editor.

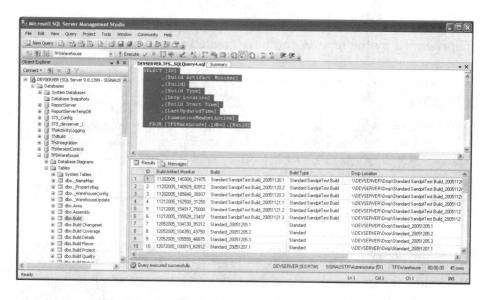

FIGURE 31-2: SQL Server Management Studio running a query

4. Run the SQL Query to list all the records in the Build table by select-
   ing all the text in the Query Editor window (Edit | Select All) and
   then applying Query | Execute; see Figure 31-2.
5. Log off, as you have completed this exercise.

■ WARNING

Altering data in the TFSWarehouse database directly using SQL statements may have unforeseen consequences, so we suggest you use the
TFS API to make any changes you might require.

Creating a Custom Report from the TFS OLAP Database

Microsoft uses the term *business intelligence* to describe the way its tools
allow valuable business information to be obtained from a central data
warehouse. The business information in which you are interested relates

to the metrics gathered during the operation of your Team Project and will be presented by the reports you have created using the Report Designer.

> **■ NOTE**
>
> Your Team Project's Report Site contains a button labeled Report Builder, which starts a tool that also allows you to generate reports from an OLAP database. However, you should use the Report Designer when working with the TFSWarehouse.

EXERCISE 31-2: Using the Report Designer to Create a Custom Report

The following exercise takes you through the process of adding a report to your team's Report Site. In practice, though, you will probably want to construct more sophisticated reports than the simple one we describe here.

1. Log on to the ArchitectPC as Luke (OSPACS Contributor), start SQL Server Business Intelligence Development Studio (Visual Studio), and then connect to the OSPACS Team Project, as described in Exercise 5-7 in Chapter 5; see Appendix A for a specification of this machine and details of Luke's security groups.

2. Create a Business Intelligence Project using the Report Server Project Wizard, call it "WICountReport", and call its solution "Reports" (File | New | Project, Business Intelligence Project | Report Server Project Wizard). You do not need to add this project to version control.

3. Read the comments on the Welcome page of the Report Wizard and then click Next.

4. Select a new data source for your report, name it "reportsTFS", and set its type as Microsoft SQL Server Analysis Services. Then click the Edit button to open the Connection Properties dialog box so that you can do the following:

   a. Type "DEVSERVER" as the server name and "TFSWarehouse" as the database name.

   b. Click the Test Connection button to confirm your connection and then click OK to close the dialog box.

5. Confirm that the connection string appears in the Select Data Source page of the wizard, and then click Next.

6. Design your query by clicking the Query Builder button in the Design the Query page of the wizard, and then do the following (see Figure 31-3):

   a. Select Team System in the drop-down box at the top of the left-hand window.

   b. Add the Assigned To dimension to your report by expanding the Assigned To item in the left side of the window, selecting Person, and then right-clicking and selecting Add to Query.

   c. Add the Team Project dimension to your report by expanding the Team Project item in the left side of the window, selecting Team Project, and then right-clicking and selecting Add to Query.

   d. Add the Cumulative Count measure to your query by opening the Measures folder and then opening the Work Item History folder before selecting Cumulative Count, right-clicking, and selecting Add to Query.

   e. Close the Query Builder by clicking OK.

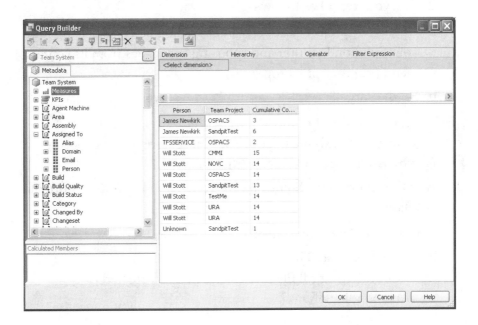

FIGURE 31-3: The Query Builder

7. Confirm that the query string appears in the Design the Query page of the wizard and then click Next.

8. Select the Report Type as Tabular and click Next.

9. Group the data in your table by setting Team_Project as Page, Person as Group, and Cumulative Count as Details. You can do this by selecting the item in the Available Fields list and then clicking the appropriate buttons. After completing the Design the Table page of the wizard, click Next.

10. Leave the default values in the Choose the Table Layout page and click Next.

11. Select the style as Corporate on the Choose the Table Style page and click Next.

12. On the Choose the Deployment Location page, set the URL of the Report Server as http://devserver/ReportServer and the deployment folder as WICountReport, and then click Next.

13. Name the report "WICountReport" on the Completing the Wizard page and click Finish.

14. Set the properties of your WICountReport project so that you can deploy your report as follows:

    a. Open your project's Property Pages dialog box by selecting it in your Solution Explorer and choosing Properties from its context menu (Right-click | Properties).

    b. Set the TargetServerURL as http://devserver/ReportServer.

15. Deploy your report to the Report Server by selecting the WICountReport.rdl file in your Solution Explorer and choosing Deploy from its context menu (Right-click | Deploy).

16. Add the report to the home page of your Team Project's Report Site as follows:

    a. Open the Report Site (Team | Show Report Site).

    b. Click the Upload File button and then select the WICountReport.rdl file in the directory you created for your Visual Studio Solution.

17. Confirm that this new report works correctly by running it from the Report Site (click on its link) as well as from the Team Explorer window (refresh the OSPACS Reports folder and then double-click the WICountReport item).

18. Log off, as you have finished the last exercise in this book.

You should investigate how the standard reports supplied with your Team Project template are written by downloading their RDL files from the Report Site and adding them to your Visual Studio Solution. You can download a report's RDL file by clicking the Edit link in the Report Definition section of its Properties page and then saving the file on your PC. You then can add this file to the Reports folder in your WICountReport Visual Studio Project (Right-click | Add Existing Item) so that you can edit it, as shown in Figure 31-4, and later redeploy it, as described in the preceding exercise.

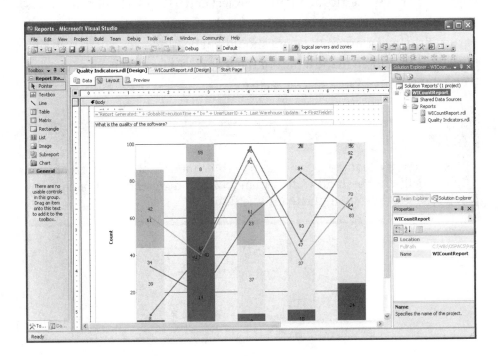

FIGURE 31-4: The Report Design Language Editor

> **⬛ NOTE**
>
> The bibliography on the book's Web site lists a number of books that explain how to use and interpret the standard reports supplied with the MSF Agile process template. However, we particularly recommend the one by Sam Guckenheimer and Juan Perez.[2]

CONCLUSION

People gain a far deeper understanding of what some information means when they have been involved in gathering, analyzing, and presenting the underlying data. When using VSTS, you must take care that the automation of these processes doesn't inhibit the ability of your team to improve its performance by learning from the information provided in its queries and reports. For this reason, you should encourage people to consider how they might gather new metrics about their project and to think about better ways in which the data might be combined and presented. Information that is particularly important to the team should not be hidden on some Web site, but rather should be made a part of the team's environment, as suggested by the Informative Workspace practice.

> **⬛ TIP**
>
> It is better for a team to monitor two or three metrics of its performance that it really understands rather than look at a dozen charts which are not really connected to the team's activities.

---

2. [SETS] Guckenheimer, Sam, and Juan Perez. *Software Engineering with Microsoft Visual Studio Team System* (Addison-Wesley, 2006).

■ 32
Generating Business Value

IN THIS CHAPTER, we will look at the potential of lean thinking to change the economics of software development so that we can identify value and make it flow, thereby allowing customers to pull products into production at a time when they can generate the most business value from them. The chapter concludes with a brief discussion about how Agile software development complements process improvement initiatives such as Six Sigma, which other areas of your organization may already be promoting.

Lean Thinking

When people talk about generating value, they usually mean *doing more with less,* and when researching this subject you can't go very far without encountering the Toyota Production System. Indeed, most books about Agile software development refer directly or indirectly to automobile-making ideas first pioneered at Toyota. At first, it may seem strange to connect software development with this sort of manufacturing process. However, the classic book, *Lean Thinking,* by James Womack and Daniel Jones,[1] identifies five basic principles at work in the Toyota Production System that you can apply to almost any type of production or design process.

---

1. [LT] Womack, James P., and Daniel T. Jones. *Lean Thinking* (Simon & Schuster, 2003).

Therefore, let's start our discussion about generating value by looking at how each principle might apply to an Agile team.

Specifying Value

The value that software provides, from a customer's perspective, lies in its capability to meet a current business need as well as its potential for future adaptation, which allows the exploitation of any new opportunities that might arise. Customers are seldom interested in how the solution works as long as it provides a good return on their investment and does what they want. Unfortunately, though, customers often don't know what they want until they start using the software and discover its shortcomings. Even then the business can move faster than traditional software development is able to deliver, so the opportunity may have gone by the time the software the business needs is finally released. In this sort of environment, it is not surprising that many customers value their spreadsheets more than the products of the IT department.

An Agile team rapidly and regularly delivers working software to the business, which helps the business to identify its real needs and more precisely specify the value it requires.

Identifying the Value Stream

The identification of a value stream requires you to look at each step in a process and then discover what actions create value to the customer, what actions create no value but are unavoidable, and what actions are both avoidable and create no value. The objective is to eliminate the waste caused by doing things that don't add value to the customer. For example, Table 32-1 identifies "gold-plating" (code that implements a feature with no obvious business value) as something that adds no value and is entirely avoidable, but identifies "implementing a feature needed by the business" as something that creates value. Performing this sort of analysis on the team's activities can be highly beneficial and is easy to do; you just need to identify what artifacts a team produces and then ask, *if we didn't do that would the customer notice?* It may surprise you how much of what you do adds no value and is entirely avoidable.

TABLE 32-1: Classifying Actions That Occur in a Value Stream

Process Step	Creates Value	Creates No Value, but Is Unavoidable	Creates No Value, and Is Avoidable
Planning and communicating	Specifications used to identify business need	Specifications used to identify nonfunctional requirements	Specifications nobody reads
Analysis and design	Spikes that help you explore the problem	Documents used only to satisfy a company policy	Models that don't reveal anything about the problem
Writing the source code	Implementing a feature needed by the business	Code thrown away because the business need changed	Gold-plating
Build	Successfully translating the code into a product	Maintaining the build machine	Builds that fail
Testing	Writing a test that identifies a new bug	Running regression tests that pass	Writing a test that doesn't fail
Release	Deploying a product into the production environment	Passing the user acceptance test	Release that nobody uses

Making Value Flow

We often tend to view efficiency in terms of utilization. For example, a testing department may be judged in terms of the lines of code tested in a month and therefore holds a large stock of code to ensure that its people are always kept busy and throughput is maximized. However, such high levels of utilization often come at a price, because your test department's need to hold large stocks of code results in the business losing opportunities and potential profits while the software sits waiting to be tested. The cumulative effect of such queues at different stages of the process might add months to the time taken to deploy your software into the business environment; see Figure 28-1 in Chapter 28.

The Agile alternative to this sort of batch and queue is a continuous flow of work achieved by having a team of people who are able to perform all the tasks involved in releasing software to the business. To make this work the team needs to be trained across a range of disciplines and have access to tools that reduce the need for specialists; see the Whole Team practice in Chapter 4. In this regard, making the value flow might mean eliminating the testing department bottleneck by getting the customer to write and execute tests.

Allowing the Customer to Pull Value

Traditional projects deliver software to the business on a release cycle decided by the IT department. That is to say, perhaps twice a year, the development team *pushes* its products into the business. Accordingly, many months may pass between when the code is written and when it starts providing the business with any value simply because the development team has decided to include other, less valuable features in the same release.

In an Agile project, the customer knows the value that exists in the software, because at any time he can just click a button to execute the customer tests. Therefore, it becomes a business decision as to whether this value should be released immediately or held over until the next scheduled release. Indeed, the customer might then decide that this scheduled release doesn't contain enough value to justify the disruption to the business and, therefore, further delay the deployment of the feature. In this way, the business is said to *pull* the product from the development environment to maximize the return on its investment.

Seeking Perfection

Jack Reeves[2] points out that software is almost free to manufacture because it is a job that you can automate with tools such as compilers and linkers. The cost lays in the development of the design documents that provide the

---

2. Reeves, Jack. "What is Software Design?" (Publications, www.bleading-edge.com).

input to these tools—in other words, the program's source code written in a computer language such as Visual Basic or C#. Accordingly, most types of software development involve iterating through a cycle of design, build, and test until the software meets the customer's requirements. This is because the design doesn't need to be perfected before it is manufactured, as there are no production lines to build, no tooling costs, and no raw materials to buy.

An Agile project is characterized by its many short iterations during which design, build, and test are continuously repeated. The design is therefore more frequently improved as a result of testing than it is in non-Agile projects. This improvement takes place at a structural level in the design of the code as a result of programmer tests. It also takes place at a function level in the design of the system as a result of customer tests. However, it is not only the program that an Agile team seeks to perfect, for each iteration provides an opportunity for the team to improve upon what it did before by finding and correcting the problems associated with its development process. This is how an Agile team continuously improves its process.

Root Cause Analysis Practice

Root cause analysis requires you to identify and correct the real cause of a problem rather than addressing just its symptoms. The practice originates from the Toyota Production System[3] and entails asking *why* a problem arose five times so that with each answer you come closer to its real cause.

The importance of root cause analysis is best illustrated with an example, so let's suppose that after your Team Build fails, you ask the following questions and answer them accordingly:

- *Why* did the build break? Because a file hadn't been checked in.

- *Why* wasn't the file checked in? Because it wasn't in the pending changes list.

- *Why* wasn't the file in this list? Because it wasn't created by Visual Studio.

Continues

---

3. [TPS] Ohno, Taiichi. *Toyota Production System* (Productivity Press, 1988).

- *Why* wasn't it created by Visual Studio? Because we haven't created an item template for test data files.

- *Why* haven't we got this template? Because we don't spend enough time automating things.

Without asking *why* five times, your analysis of the problem might go no further than identifying that a file hadn't been added to source control, therefore allowing the real problem to reappear in a different guise over and over again. The Root Cause Analysis practice helps a team seek perfection by revealing such fundamental defects in its development process.

The main difficulty you face when implementing root cause analysis is deciding when to apply it, because a design process is about generating problems and it's just not feasible to get to the root cause of them all. For this reason, we suggest you start by applying the practice to activities that are somewhat production-like, such as your Team Build and Deployment process, and then gradually introduce it into your design activities as well. For example, your team can learn from every bug it fixes by writing a set of customer and unit tests that will reveal similar problems at a much earlier stage of the development cycle. In this way, you don't repeat *why* five times, but instead repeatedly write tests that probe the problem at five different levels. This not only helps you fix the bug properly, but also may prevent dozens more from arising in the future.

> **■ NOTE**
> Writing tests that probe a problem at five different levels is much harder than asking *why* five times, so you might start by writing just one or two extra tests that go beyond the immediate scope of the bug to explore its context more thoroughly.

Changing the Economics of Software Development

There is a strong economic argument for taking an Agile approach to your software development, because it allows you to generate business value much earlier in the project life cycle and this is value that would otherwise be lost. To illustrate the point, let's compare the anticipated return for an Agile project against that of a traditional project. In both projects, it is assumed that the team has identical costs and works for 24 weeks, so costs start at zero and rise at a constant rate to $160,000 when funding stops at the end of the project.

> ## ■ NOTE
>
> These two teams are fictitious; you wouldn't waste money getting two equally matched teams to develop the same product using different methodologies. However, we feel that Figure 32-1 provides a reasonable model of what might happen in such a scenario.

Value Generated by an Agile Project

The value in the software developed by the Agile team is visible to the business from the start of the project due to its customer tests; therefore, the team decides to release a version of the software into production after the third two-week iteration (six weeks into the project). The business, therefore, starts getting a return on its investment from week six of the project and this benefit accumulates as the development continues and later versions of the software are released. However, let's take a conservative position over the value of these later versions and assume that they don't make any further contribution to the rate of return. Therefore, eight weeks later the break-even point is reached when the accumulated returns equal the accumulated investment. After this date, the returns continue at the same rate, past the end of the project when investment stops, until some point in the distant future when benefits start to erode due to some external factor such as a change in the business.

Value Generated by a Waterfall Project

In a traditional project, the business becomes aware of the value in the software only when it is finally released, so it must wait until week 24 before discovering its value. At this time, the Agile team has already provided a return of $225,000 to the business. So in order to recover this ground, the software produced by the traditional team must supply a greater rate of return.

However, there is no reason to suppose this might happen, because the two teams are equally matched in terms of their skills and they have both spent the same amount of time writing the code. Therefore, the gap between their respective returns remains constant at $225,000 through the lifetime of the software, which is the projected cost advantage of the Agile project.

> ### ■ NOTE
>
> Figure 32-1 is reproduced from the paper "Driving Development with Customer Tests," by Will Stott and David Putman, which they presented at the EuroSTAR 2004 Conference in December 2004. It is reproduced with kind permission of QualTech Conferences.

It could be argued that the value of the software delivered by the Agile project at week six is considerably less than the value of the final software delivered at the end of the project, and therefore the rate of return will not be constant. However, there is a counter-argument that 80 percent of the value is delivered by 20 percent of the code, and because the stories are ordered so that the ones with the most value to the business are done first, a release after 25 percent of the code has been written (week six) will contain 80 percent of the value. There is merit in both positions, but what seems clear is that no matter how you might reasonably adjust the figures, the Agile project will always have a lead in the gap between the anticipated returns for the two projects and will always break even earlier, therefore reducing its risk.

Linking Agile to Other Process Improvement Initiatives

Agile software development seeks to drive efficiency in the software industry in much the same way that initiatives such as the Toyota Production System have served other industries. Indeed, if you work for a company whose core business is not software development, you may find that other departments are already engaged in forms of process improvement inspired by the Toyota Production System. Therefore, you might gain their support by expressing the concepts of Agile software development in terms that they already understand.

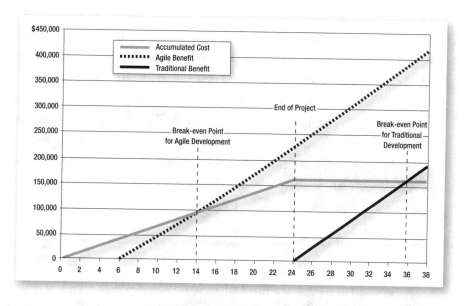

FIGURE 32-1: Cost-benefit comparison for Agile and non-Agile projects

Agile Development in the Context of Design for Six Sigma

Design for Six Sigma[4] promotes values and practices that allow software teams to work quickly and respond to change, producing work in a way that minimizes mistakes, waste, and rework. Accordingly, you might describe the Agile manifesto to Six Sigma teams in terms of the following:

- **Customer collaboration**—Applying resources to finding out what customers really want and then devoting the entire project to meeting the needs and desires of these customers.

- **Working software**—The customer *defines* some tests, developers create software that can be *measured* against these tests, *analysis* of the test results determines progress, *improvement* is made by generating new tests and better software, and *control* is provided by allowing the team to learn each time it delivers its software.

---

4. [DF6S] Chowdhury, Subir. *Design for Six Sigma* (Dearborn Trade Pub., 2002).

- **Individuals and interactions**—Typically, between six and 18 people with cross-functional skills work together to produce a piece of software that can be delivered to the business to give demonstrable value. The team is self-organizing, taking responsibility for things such as setting priorities and scheduling work.

- **Responding to change**—Waste and rework arising from changes in requirements or business priorities is minimized by delivering software through a succession of short iterations, each of which provides working software ready for pulling into production should the business decide it provides sufficient value.

> **■ NOTE**
>
> The Bibliography lists a number of books that provide much more detailed coverage of introducing Agile software development ideas into an organization. In this book, we concentrated on just explaining the technical aspects of this task.

CONCLUSION

The need for organizations to become more Agile in their approach to software development is driven by the plain economics of doing more with less. Ultimately, it is not Visual Studio Team System that will deliver this objective, but the people in your organization. Therefore, we have completed this book by giving you some ideas about the issues you face and hope this stimulates your interest in the wider issues of lean thinking and agility.

Review of Section 10
Provide and Reveal Value

A T THIS STAGE, the OSPACS team had implemented all the basic practices and therefore concentrated on delivering increased value to the business by improving its performance. The team did this by taking the following actions:

- At the start of each iteration, the team discussed whether it could improve the metrics it was monitoring. Each group of metrics was allocated to a member of the team who took responsibility for checking the data and presenting it to the team.
- Team members were asked to suggest ways in which the metrics they gathered could be better presented. Developers were then allowed some time to put the best of these ideas into practice.
- The team took a critical look at its workspace and found ways to make it more informative by arranging for some more notice boards to be put in the coffee area and generally taking more of an interest in its working environment.
- It was decided that the team should write at least two different tests to illustrate each new bug as part of the process of fixing it. These tests should attempt to test the same issue orthogonally.

The Team's Impressions

The team is now starting to experience the benefits of working in a more Agile way, but in order to improve further, it needs to analyze why things have gone wrong and learn from the information it reveals.

CEO: Mike

"I certainly agree that 80 percent of the value lies in 20 percent of the features, so clearly we need to identify and develop this 20 percent before anything else. Isn't this what we are doing with storytest-driven development?"

Developer: Tom

"Teams are more likely to improve their performance when they are involved in deciding what metrics to monitor and have themselves designed the reports which present this information."

"It was highly instructive to identify the things we did that actually added value to the customer. It showed us just how much waste we needed to eliminate."

Developer: Luke

"The charts on the walls are ours. We own them. They're not a management gimmick."

"I'm glad to hear that everyone will take part in updating those charts we've put on the walls. I feared that would become yet another job for me."

Developer: Peter

"There's more to the Informative Workspace practice than just putting Big Visible Charts on the wall. It's an expression of the culture on our team."

"The route-cause analysis should help us address our fundamental problems so that we don't spend all our time fighting fires."

Developer: Maggie

"I was impressed when I saw the chart showing the team's bug count displayed above Tom's desk. It shows he really does care about this issue."

"We always knew the old test department was a bottleneck, but nobody could suggest how to get rid of it. Part of the problem was that I wanted to appear busy, so I would always make sure there was plenty of work stacked up."

Agile Values

The work the OSPACS team did in making its workspace more informative has built a lot of team spirit and there is now a genuine interest in the metrics gathered by Visual Studio Team System (VSTS). The other improvements the team made to the way it worked promoted Agile values in the following ways.

Communication

The Big Visible Charts (BVCs) on the wall of the office make clear the metrics that the team considers to be most important and its progress toward resolving the issues that they underline.

Feedback

The data automatically gathered by VSTS as the team carries out its daily tasks provides a great source of information for the present projects as well as future ones. It allows the team to learn from its mistakes.

Courage

In the past, the business avoided undertaking ambitious work because it feared that the developers would hide the real problems until the very last minute. The transparency provided by things such as customer tests means the business is now less afraid of risk because it feels better able to manage the risk.

Simplicity

The informal way of hand-drawing the charts the team has fixed to the walls reinforces the team's belief that simple ideas are often best. These charts take so little time to produce that people are quite happy to throw them away once they've served their purpose.

Route cause analysis helps the team strip away all the layers that obscure the fundamental problem. These layers contain the complexity, but often the problem itself is something quite simple.

Respect

The transparent way in which the development team and the business now operate does a lot to build trust and respect among people.

Retrospective
Fixing the Process

I T IS NINE MONTHS since the OSPACS team installed Visual Studio Team System (VSTS) and started its journey toward becoming an Agile team. The team members have worked on the issues in the road map they created in the Introduction (Table I-1), but more important, they've just delivered the new generic version of their system to one of their new customers. Accordingly, it is a good time for them to conduct a retrospective.

> ### ■ NOTE
>
> Before arranging a retrospective for your own team, we recommend that you read *Agile Retrospectives*, by Esther Derby and Diana Larsen,[1] as well as *Project Retrospectives*, by Norman Kerth.[2] These books describe many useful exercises, including those mentioned in this retrospective.

About Retrospectives

Agile teams commonly hold retrospectives at various points in their projects in order to promote the sort of learning that leads to further improvements in the way they develop software. Some teams hold short retrospectives at the end of every iteration, whereas others may hold longer retrospectives at significant milestones, such as after a major release or at the end of a project. There are advantages to both approaches, so you

---

1. [AR] Derby, Esther, and Diane Larsen. *Agile Retrospectives* (Pragmatic Bookshelf, 2006).
2. [PR] Kerth, Norman. *Project Retrospectives* (Dorset House, 2001).

should decide what works best for your team, perhaps even combining regular short retrospectives with the occasional longer one.

> ### ■ WARNING
>
> Engage an experienced external facilitator when holding a retrospective, even if it is just a manager from another part of your organization. This person must be able to lead the group, handle conflicts, and create a safe environment that ensures that everyone's voice is heard.

Preparation

The OSPACS team exceeded all expectations by releasing a generic version of the system to its first client by the start of the fourth quarter, so Mike (the CEO) decided to reward the team by funding a team-building weekend. However, after some discussion, he was persuaded to extend the weekend by one day so that the team could combine its team building with a formal retrospective because everyone felt there was a need to consolidate what they had learned over the past nine months. He was also persuaded to pay for a qualified retrospective facilitator[3] to ensure that the team arrived at a proper set of conclusions, which the team could then form into an action plan for the next stage of its project. Accordingly, the OSPACS team employed a freelance facilitator, named Mary, who then set about preparing and organizing the retrospective in the following way:

- She booked a ski lodge in Colorado, because it was only a two-hour drive from the office (and she got a good price because it was out of season).
- Two weeks before the event she sent everyone an information pack containing the following:
  - Details of the accommodation
  - A brief description of the format of the retrospective, which includes a statement of its purpose and general objectives

---

3. Retrospective Facilitators (http://finance.groups.yahoo.com/group/retrospectives).

- A copy of her biography so that the team would know about her previous experience and background as a contract IT developer
- A list of things for them to do prior to arriving in Colorado

The most important thing Mary asked the team to do before the retrospective was to answer a questionnaire so that she could gauge the developers' feelings about the project and the forthcoming retrospective.

Creating a Plan

A few days before the retrospective, Mary created a plan guided by the feedback she obtained from the questionnaire as well as from some meetings she had arranged with Mike and a few of the team members. This plan included the following:

- Setting the objectives:
  - Identifying the importance of Agile values and practices to the team's work
  - Finding ways to improve the team's performance for the next project
  - Creating a report after the retrospective had been completed containing a summary of the actions the team wanted to take during the next project
- Structuring the activities:
  - **Friday**—"Create Safety" exercise, white-water rafting, "Developing a Timeline" exercise (Parts A and B)
  - **Saturday**—"Developing a Timeline" exercise (Part C), fly-fishing, "Passive Analogy" exercise, "Retrospective Meal"
  - **Sunday**—"Making the Magic Happen" exercise, lunch, "Closing the Retrospective" exercise

> **TIP**
>
> Create an archive for your retrospective reports because they contain a lot of valuable information and often help organizations improve their whole approach to running projects.

The OSPACS Team's Retrospective

Mary started the retrospective with the usual sort of introductory speech and then spent some time helping the team to define its objectives and ensuring that people felt comfortable about speaking out without fear of looking stupid or saying something out of turn. That is to say, she created a feeling of safety and established "Kerth's Prime Directive," which is as follows:

> Regardless of what we discover, we must understand and truly believe that everyone did the best job he or she could, given what was known at the time, his or her skills and abilities, the resources available, and the situation at hand.

After the team members discussed their mutual concerns over coffee, they left for the white-water rafting event, which included lunch. Therefore, it was late afternoon before the team returned to the ski lodge and started the serious work of the day, which was the "Developing a Timeline" exercise.

Developing a Timeline

This exercise aims to provide everyone with the big picture of the project. It is a period-by-period review of all the main events that actually happened as seen from different people's points of view. The objective of the exercise is to find out what worked well in the past and what needs to be done differently in the future.

■ NOTE

During a project, people often become focused on a particular task and can easily forget the issues they had to address a month or even a week ago. The timeline exercise helps the team collectively refresh its memory of such issues and then put them into a proper context.

Typically, the exercise takes between three and five hours, split over two days. It is divided into three parts. First, the team creates the timeline, which may take a couple of hours. Second, the team gathers particular sorts of information from it, a process called *mining for gold*. Third, the team uses the information it gathered to stimulate further discussion, which might last for another few hours. At the end of the exercise, the team summarizes the information it generated and records it as a series of bullet points which form an important part of the Retrospect Report.

Creating the Timeline

In order to create the timeline, the OSPACS team split into groups of natural affinity so that people who would naturally work together on the project were put in the same group. Each group then received a different color pen and three pads of self-adhesive Post-it Notes.[4] People in the group used these self-adhesive notes to identify the main events that happened during the project from their own perspectives. For example, Sally thought that the moment when she was able to run her own customer tests was the most important event of the entire project, but Luke only remembered the tedious work that he had to do writing all her test fixtures. Each team member wrote each type of event on different color paper, based on the following:

- **Green**—Significant events: strengths, opportunities, achievements (praise). These are the events people thought were particularly significant in terms of creating opportunities or achieving something worthwhile.
- **Red**—Difficult events: weaknesses, threats, hard or risky work (action needed). These are the events that the exercise was really trying to find because these would lead to discussions about how the team might improve its performance for the next project.
- **Yellow**—Other noteworthy events, such as people joining or leaving the team, significant external decisions that influenced the team (the first sale of the system), or just when the team did something particularly memorable.

---

4. Post-it Notes are produced by 3M (www.3m.com/us/office/postit).

> ■ **NOTE**
>
> The significant events that the OSPACS team identified have a black border around them in Figure R-2 to help differentiate them from the lighter "yellow" self-adhesive notes and the darker "red" ones which relate to difficult events.

While the team was discussing the events of the past nine months, Mary drew a timeline on a whiteboard to divide it into segments according to the iterations the team had completed during this time; see Figure R-1. She then wandered among the groups helping them to arrive at a consensus about what events they needed to record.

After a couple of hours, each group had independently written up their events on these self-adhesive notes, so they placed them on the whiteboard at a horizontal position corresponding to the approximate date the event happened; see Figure R-2. After they did this, they gathered around the whiteboard and used their colored pens to indicate how they felt at various points in the project. Were they happy about the way things were going, or were they concerned? In this way, they created a scattergram of their morale over the course of the project.

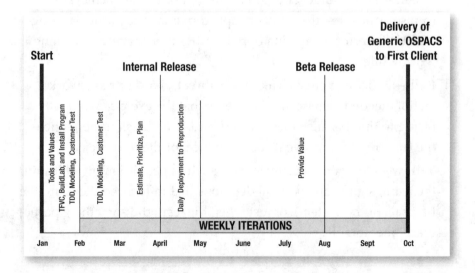

FIGURE R-1: The OSPACS project timeline

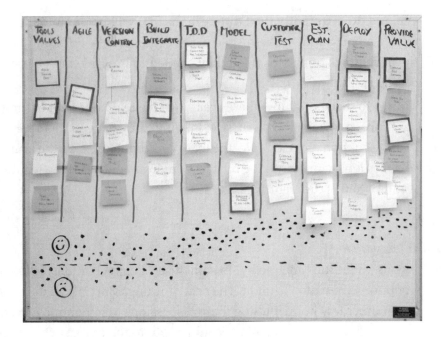

FIGURE R-2: The completed Retrospective timeline

Mining for Gold

The timeline that the OSPACS team created helped the team view through other people's eyes the events they had all shared during the project. The information this yielded provided a valuable context for the team's future exercises and discussions, so Mary had asked them to discuss the timeline as a team and then classify the various Post-it Notes onto four flip charts (based on the following four categories), which she placed around the room:

- **What worked well (and must not be forgotten)**—Items on the timeline that point to matters which might easily be overlooked in a subsequent project. For example, installing VSTS is unlikely to be forgotten, but checking that it has been set up properly with all the necessary permissions might be.

- **What the team learned**—These are the most important ways in which the project has influenced the team's future behavior. For example, the team learned how to handle changing and unknown requirements.

- **What to do differently next time**—Items that will be put into the team's report about the retrospective as action points. For example, the developers on the team felt they needed to improve their basic coding skills.

- **Things to discuss later**—These are things the team does not entirely agree on, so to keep the discussion moving, they flagged them for later discussion. For example, the team could not agree on the issue of daily deployment into the business environment—did the team want to do this differently next time?

Further Discussion

Discussions about the timeline led to some useful conversations; some of them continued well into the night. The next morning, Mary asked the team to spend another few hours pulling these discussions together into a list of action points that the team members could apply to their work when they returned to the office. In particular, she asked them to try to identify trends as well as explanations for certain anomalies—for instance, the fact that the scattergram at the bottom of the timeline didn't correspond to the aggregate color of the sticky notes above it.

> ■ **NOTE**
>
> In general, when you are doing hard or risky work that results in weaknesses and threats, morale will be lower than when you're doing work that results in a sense of achievement which gives rise to strengths and opportunities for the team.

Other Exercises

Mary led the team on a number of other exercises over the next day and a half which helped the team explore how its road map to Agility had changed its ideas about software development. The exercises were informal and included a number of fun activities. However, by the end of the weekend, nobody was left with any doubt about the value of the three days spent in Colorado.

Analysis of the Project Timeline

The OSPACS team's timeline corresponding to its iterations is shown in Figure R-1. This may help you understand the structure of the project and how it related to the steps on the team's road map to Agility; see Table I-1 in the Introduction.

Structure of the Project

The project started the first week of January, and after nine months, the team had delivered the new OSPACS product to its first paying client. After the first month, the team decided to work in weekly iterations. Here is a summary of the team's work:

- **Iteration zero**—Setting up the project and learning key skills, such as test-driven development (TDD) and modeling. During this time, the team also familiarized itself with VSTS and its new tools by conducting various spikes which had the added benefit of helping the team to explore its problem domain with the customer. This resulted in an initial set of stories for the team to implement.

- **Iterations 1 to 4**—The team focused on implementing the customer's stories using the practices it had learned: TDD, modeling, and customer testing. After the end of the first iteration, the team had created a thin vertical slice through the system to establish a basic architecture which included the user interface, business, and data layers.

- **Iterations 5 to 8**—During these iterations, the team focused on activities that would help it estimate, prioritize, and plan, with the aim of satisfying the business with the regular release of valuable software. At the end of iteration eight, the team released the initial version of the product in the company's preproduction environment for evaluation by the sales team.

- **Iterations 9 to 12**—At this stage of the project, the team was becoming good at delivering high-quality software according to a plan, so it switched its attention to the problem of deploying its software each day into the company's preproduction environment.

- **Iterations 13 to 35**—The team now got into its stride and started to really apply the Extreme Programming (XP) practices it had accumulated in order to provide to the business the best possible return on its investment. After the end of iteration 35, the business decided the system was ready for final deployment at the customer site.

The developers did not undertake much serious planning until the second month of the project. This was because they first needed to prove to themselves that they could reliably deliver high-quality software. Upon reflection, they decide this approach was no worse than the two months they had spent in their previous project doing analysis and design work, most of which they threw away a month after they started to write the code.

■ NOTE

The OSPACS team didn't start doing weekly iterations until a month into the project because it had to acquire the basic skills needed to use VSTS and develop in an Agile way. A more experienced team would start doing iterations from the start of the project.

Things They Discovered

The OSPACS team's road map to Agility (Table I-1 in the Introduction) had taken the team on a journey which it now agreed had been extremely beneficial. The green and red self-adhesive notes it had added to its timeline told their own story.

Green: Significant Events, Strengths, Opportunities

- **Installing VSTS**—A memorable party was held after Tom got VSTS to pass his tests so that the team could finally connect Team Explorer to the OSPACS Team Project and start using its new tools.
- **Agile training days**—The day the people from the local Agile User Group started their training will be remembered for some time. It was when the team first began to believe that it could learn to operate like a top-performing team.

- **Office reorganization**—The act of removing the office partitions was a very visible commitment to change. It was also the point at which people first acted collectively to organize their own work, which brought them together as a team.

- **Ten-Minute Build practice**—Everyone remembers when a pair of programmers first managed to complete a programming episode by checking their code changes and running the Integration Build and Test.

- **TDD**—The day after the training stopped and the developers decided that from then on they would develop all new production code using Test-First Programming was a significant day for most people.

- **Customer runs own tests**—Nobody will forget the smile on Sally's face when she announced to the team at the morning meeting that she had run her first test without help from the developers.

- **Identified value stream**—The team was shocked when it first looked at all the things it did which had no real value to the business.

Red: Difficult Events, Weakness, Threats

- **Preaching about Agile values**—Tom realized that he was starting to sound evangelical about Agile values when someone put a priest's collar on his desk with the words *communicate* and *feedback* written on it.

- **Overkill on creating work items**—People recalled the day when the team's All Tasks report doubled in size because Luke had created a work item for each step he intended to undertake when completing a story. At the next team meeting, he agreed to put his personal to-do list on an index card like everyone else.

- **Introduction of coding standards**—Early discussions about coding standards revealed some shocking gaps in people's knowledge of basic C# coding matters.

- **Group modeling with electronic tools**—The memory of the team huddled around a PC as Tom attempted to walk through the class hierarchy made the point that it was best to do group modeling on a whiteboard.

Has the OSPACS Team Fixed Its Process?

Table R-1 shows the results of the OSPACS team's attempt to mine its development timeline for gold. It shows that the team is well on its way to being an Agile team, though there was some discussion about what this actually meant.

TABLE R-1: Results of the OSPACS Team Mining for Gold

Area	Analysis
What worked well (and must not be forgotten)	• Let people's values develop through what they do rather than what they're told. • Training is best done little and often, so arrange regular brown-bag technical sessions for the team to learn about things such as design patterns, and organize external training to occur during short sessions throughout the project. • Get an InstallShield expert to set up a skeletal installation program at the start of the project and then train the team to develop it as the project proceeds. • Set up a Team Build so that it initiates the sending of a text message to the team when the build fails; the noise of five cell phones ringing in unison makes a point!
What the team learned	• Ways to identify and then deliver what the business wants within agreed-upon time scales • How to handle changing and unknown requirements • The importance of migrating code among different environments (development, build and test, production) • How to write quality code (TDD, pairing, etc.) • The benefits of drawing free-form model diagrams • How version control allows a team to share code effectively • How to identify the things the team produced that add real value to the business

Area	Analysis
What to do differently next time	• Hold more retrospectives so that the team can regularly reflect upon how it might become more effective, and then adjust its activities accordingly
	• Create a set of tests to validate the setup of VSTS before starting any development work
	• Remove more bottlenecks that are delaying deployment
	• Create work items only for the things they want to measure
What still troubles the team	• The need for developers to improve their basic coding skills and learn more patterns
	• The tendency for people to create work items that don't measure anything useful
Things to discuss later	• Should the team attempt to deploy into production on a daily basis?
	• Are developers willing to write two tests for each bug rather than just one?

■ NOTE

In the Introduction to this book, we said we wrote the book for people who wanted to change their process because it was broken in some way. Therefore, if the OSPACS team read a similar statement in a book today, we hope the team would put the book right back on the shelf.

Is the OSPACS Team Extreme?

There is no form of certification for Extreme Programming, so how does a team know when it has finally made the transition to this software development approach? When can the team members proudly say, "We do XP"? Such a question is hard to answer because there is no golden moment when a team "becomes XP" because, for instance, it has implemented 90 percent of the practices and has managed to condition everyone into valuing communication, feedback, courage, simplicity, and respect. It is more a question of a team calling itself "Extreme," because that is what best describes how it regularly delivers valuable software to its business.

How the OSPACS Team Became Agile

Nine months after the OSPACS team first decided to fix its process by applying the practices and values of XP to its work, it can reasonably claim to be "doing XP" because of the following:

- It cares about doing most of the XP practices, though it does some more rigorously than others. For example, all production code is developed by pairs of developers using Test-First Programming, but they deploy daily only into a production environment rather than the business itself.

- Adopting the XP practices has helped the team improve its communication and feedback while also fostering a spirit of courage and respect. However, a few people on the team don't quite get the idea of simplicity because they still tend to expect that tools such as VSTS will play an important part of the solution to every problem.

- The team has replaced its old, broken process with something that helps it successfully deliver high-quality software on time, within budget, and with the features that the business needs most. Its new process has also resulted in the team binding together as a group so that people no longer wanted to leave. Indeed, most people reported the previous nine months as being the most satisfying of their career.

However, the team realizes that it is not yet at the sweet spot of Agile development and that it needs to make additional improvements to the way it does things. In fact, it is clear to the team that even years down the line, it will still be holding retrospectives in order to learn from what it has done to improve upon its performance in the future.

Personal Agility

Helping your team to become Agile may seem like a daunting task, because as you should now understand, it involves more than just putting a new tool on the team's computers or presenting the team with some form of prescriptive process. It is really about changing the way people look at their world by leading them on a sort of journey during which they will learn to do various things that, given time, will influence their values, hopefully in a way that proves beneficial to everyone on the team. However, you must respect the fact that this is a personal journey, and therefore, to some degree people need to find their own way, albeit guided by others who have made similar journeys themselves. In this respect, perhaps the first step on your personal road map to Agility should be to consider advice given by Kent Beck and Cynthia Andres in the preface of their book.[5] They simply state:

- "No matter the circumstance you can always improve."
- "You can always start improving with yourself."
- "You can always start improving today."

> **■ TIP**
>
> The following joke was found in a Christmas cracker, but it is actually quite profound: Q. How do you eat an elephant? A. One bite at a time!

---

5. [XPE2] Beck, Kent, with Cynthia Andres. *Extreme Programming Explained, Second Edition* (Addison-Wesley, 2005).

Appendixes

A
Setting Up VSTS for the Exercises

WE WROTE THE exercises in this book from the perspective of the five-developer OSPACS team described at the beginning of the book; see the Introduction and Figure 1-1 in Chapter 1. However, if you apply the instructions in this appendix, you should be able to set up Visual Studio Team System (VSTS) in such a way that you can use your own PC(s) to perform these same exercises.

> **TIP**
>
> Photocopy the pages at the end of this appendix that contains Tables A-4 and A-5 so that you can create a record of how the names of the computers and user accounts in the book are mapped to the computer(s) and user accounts in your own environment.

We imagine most readers will take one of three options when setting up a Software Project Environment to follow the exercises in this book:

- **Set up a single evaluation server**—You might take this option when reading the book on your own and working with a single PC in conjunction with one of following products:

- **Team System Virtual PC (VPC)**—This requires that you install the Microsoft Virtual PC[1] on your desktop PC; see Figure A-1. In this way, you can load and run the Visual Studio 2005 Team System VPC Evaluation image which is supplied by Microsoft as a virtual machine file (.vmc).

- **Team Foundation Server (TFS) Trial Edition**—This involves installing the Visual Studio 2005 TFS Trial Edition on a PC that is running Windows Server 2003 Service Pack 2 (or R2).

• **Set up TFS and Team Suite on a network**—You might take this option if you are reading the book in preparation for starting an actual project and are working with a collection of PCs in conjunction with one of the following products:

- Visual Studio Team Suite with MSDN Premium Subscription
- Visual Studio Team Edition(s) with MSDN Premium Subscription
- TFS Trial Edition

• **Use an existing installation**—You would take this option if you have access to a Team Foundation Server (TFS) and Visual Studio Team Suite (or Team Edition[2]) that has already been installed. In this case, you just need to follow the instructions in the section Actions for All Set-Up Options, later in this appendix.

■ NOTE

You can download the Team System VPC or the TFS Trial Edition product from the VSTS Web site,[3] or copy them to your target PC from a Microsoft DVD.

---

1. Microsoft: Virtual PC 2004 Web site (www.microsoft.com/windows/virtualpc).
2. The List of Exercises section of this book identifies restrictions that apply to people using just a single Team Edition.
3. Microsoft: Team System Web site (http://msdn.microsoft.com/teamsystem).

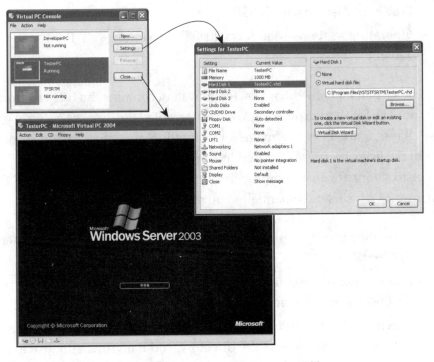

FIGURE A-1: Microsoft Virtual PC console, settings, and machine

Set Up a Single Evaluation Server

People who decide to set up a single evaluation server should first set up Team System VPC or TFS Trial Edition as described in the following section, and then follow the instructions in the Actions for All Set-Up Options section.

Setting Up Team System VPC

You must have a PC capable of running Microsoft Virtual PC 2004 when hosting TFS and Visual Studio Team Suite. The full system requirements are provided on their respective product Web sites, but essentially this means your PC should have the following:

- **Processor**—2.0 GHz Athlon, Duron, Celeron, or Pentium II, III, or 4 (or greater)
- **RAM**—2 GB, level-2 cache

- **Free hard disk space**—50 GB
- **Operating system**—Windows 2000 Pro, Windows XP Pro (or Tablet PC)

The virtual machine image of Team System contains the full TFS product (not TFS for Workgroups). You are also granted the licenses necessary to use all the products in the image for evaluation purposes, so don't worry about the license issues discussed in Appendix B.

Instructions for installing the Team System VPC are available on the Microsoft Web site, but essentially you must do the following:

1. Copy the self-extracting executable files containing the Team System VPC onto your PC.
2. Run the .exe file to extract the Virtual Machine file (.vmc) and some documentation to a temporary directory.
3. Download the Microsoft Virtual PC application, extract its installation program to a temporary directory, and then run Setup.exe to install it on your PC.
4. Start the Virtual PC Console and use its New Virtual Machine Wizard to add an existing virtual machine (i.e., the TFS Virtual Machine file you extracted in step 2).
5. Start the TFS Virtual Machine from the Virtual PC Console and then log on (Action | Ctrl-Alt-Del) using the user account and password supplied; see the note following this list of steps.
6. Follow the instructions in the Actions for All Set-Up Options section.

■. NOTE

Type the password into the username box to check that your keyboard is correctly mapped to the virtual machine; otherwise, you might enter a different character than you intended. For example, pressing the @ key may result in you entering " (and vice versa).

Setting Up TFS Trial Edition

Your server PC must run Windows Server 2003 SP2 (or R2) and would typically have a 2.0 GHz processor, 2 GB of RAM, and a 100 GB hard disk. The TFS Trial Edition is the full TFS product, but it expires 180 days after you install it. You are also granted the licenses necessary to use all the products in the trial package for evaluation purposes, so you do not need to worry about the license issues discussed in Appendix B.

Instructions for installing the TFS Trial Edition are available on the Microsoft Web site, but essentially you must do the following:

1. Copy the .iso disk image file containing the TFS Trial Edition onto your PC.

2. Use a program such as Roxio Easy CD and DVD Creator[4] to burn a DVD from this image file.

3. Download the TFS Installation Guide[5] from the Microsoft Technical Web site and follow the instructions relating to single-server deployment to install TFS on your server PC (i.e., DevServer in Figure B-1 in Appendix B). This involves installing the following:

   a. Internet Information Services (IIS) (if not already installed)

   b. Microsoft SQL Server 2005 Standard Edition (supplied with TFS)

   c. SharePoint Services 2.0 with SP2 (which you can download from the Microsoft Web site)[6]

   d. TFS

4. Follow the instructions in the Actions for All Set-Up Options section, but install all programs on the same PC.

■ WARNING

You must use the 32-bit version of Microsoft Server 2003 when installing TFS on a single server because the Application Tier doesn't support WOW64.

---

4. Roxio Web site: (www.roxio.com).
5. Microsoft: TFS Installation Guide (http://go.microsoft.com/fwlink/?LinkId=40042).
6. Microsoft: SharePoint Services 2.0 download (http://go.microsoft.com/fwlink/?LinkID=55087).

Set Up TFS and Team Suite on a Network

People who decide to set up TFS and Team Suite on a network should first read the following information and then follow the instructions in the Actions for All Set-Up Options section.

Hardware Overview

The TFS Data and Application Tiers are located on one physical PC with a specification similar to the TFS specified in Table B-1 in Appendix B. The TFS Client Tier and Visual Studio Integrated Development Environment (IDE) are installed on another PC with a specification similar to the Developer PC specified in Table B-1. Therefore, your hardware configuration would be as follows:

- One DevServer for the TFS Data and Application Tiers
- One PDC for the Primary Domain Controller (not required for Windows Workgroups)
- One BuildLabPC for TF Build (optionally, you can install this on DevServer)
- Between one and five DeveloperPCs for your Visual Studio IDE with TFS Client Tier

> **■ WARNING**
>
> When using the TFS Workgroup Edition, you have to install TFS on a single physical server, which means you must use the 32-bit version of Microsoft Server 2003 because the TFS Application Tier doesn't support WOW64.

Team Foundation Server for Workgroups

Teams of five people or less will normally start using VSTS with the TFS for Workgroups product that is available when team members buy Visual Studio Team Suite, or Editions for Developers, Testers, or Architects; see

Appendix B. TFS for Workgroups has the same functionality as the full TFS product, except for the following:

- It is limited to five users.
- It doesn't need TFS Client Access licenses.
- You can set it up in either a domain or with Windows Workgroups.

▪ TIP

You must operate the full TFS product in a domain, so using Windows Workgroups will require you to take a far more difficult upgrade path should your team ever expand beyond five developers.

Setting Up a Software Project Environment

You install the TFS Data and Application Tiers in the same way you set up the TFS Trial Edition, except, of course, you install the products on different PCs. After completing these steps, you should follow the instructions in the Actions for All Set-Up Options section.

Actions for All Set-Up Options

You should now have access to the basic infrastructure you need to operate VSTS. Therefore, you only need to take the following steps before you are ready to start the exercises in the book:

1. Confirm that the software packages in Table A-1 are installed on the appropriate PCs and then complete Table A-4 so that you have a record of how the names of your machines map to the names of the computers in the book.
2. Add the system environment variable settings in Table A-2 to each PC.
3. Set up on your PCs the security groups and user accounts in Table A-3 and complete Table A-5 to record how you have mapped their names to the names of the accounts in the book.

Depending on the machines available to you, you may be able to combine some of the software packages in Table A-1 onto fewer machines. For example, if you are setting up a single evaluation server, you would just install everything onto one PC and then write its name in the right-hand column of each row in Table A-4.

Software Installation

The exercises in the book assume you have installed the software in Table A-1 on the machines in your Software Project Environment. The full product name, current version, license type, and vendor Web site for these products are specified in Appendix B, Tables B-3, B-4, and B-6.

TABLE A-1: Software Installation Needed for Exercises in This Book

Book Machine Name	PC Specification	Packages to Install
DevServer	Team Foundation Server	• IIS v6.0 • SQL Server 2005 • SharePoint Services 2.0 SP2 • TFS Data and Application Tiers
DeveloperPC DeveloperPC2 DeveloperPC3	Desktop PC	• Visual Studio 2005 Team Suite (or Developer Edition) • InstallShield Collaboration for Visual Studio • Software Development Kits (SDKs): Microsoft Solutions Framework (MSF) and Process Customization, .NET Framework 2.0
ArchitectPC	Desktop PC	• Visual Studio 2005 Team Suite (or Architect Edition) • Microsoft SQL Server 2005 Standard Edition Client Components

Book Machine Name	PC Specification	Packages to Install
TesterPC	Desktop PC	• Visual Studio 2005 Team Suite (or Testers Edition) • InstallShield v12 (or later)
BuildLabPC	Desktop PC	• Visual Studio 2005 Team Suite (or Developer Edition) • TFS Build
(all)	Desktop PC	• Microsoft Office Software: Word, Excel, Project, Visio • Testing Automation: Framework for Integrated Test (FIT)

System Settings

The exercises in the book assume you have applied the system environment variable settings shown in Table A-2 to all machines that are used to run programs from the command prompt or customer tests.

> **■ NOTE**
>
> Open the Environment Variables dialog box by clicking the button in the Advanced page of your System Properties applet (Control Panel | System).

TABLE A-2: System Environment Variable Settings

Setting	Value
PATH	Append the following directory paths to the end of the existing value for the PATH variable:

	`;c:\Program Files\Microsoft Visual Studio 8\Common7\IDE`
	`;c:\Program Files\Microsoft Visual Studio 2005 Team`
	`Foundation Server\Tools;`

Setting Up User Accounts and Security Groups

The exercises in the book assume you have created the user accounts and security groups listed in Table A-3. Consult your operating system's Help manual for specific instructions about creating such user accounts and security groups

TABLE A-3: Security Group Membership Needed for Exercises

Book Group	Security Group Membership or Settings
OSPACSAdmins	• [SERVER]\Team Foundation Administrators *(see Notes 1 and 2)* • [OSPACS]\Administrators *(see Notes 5 and 6)* • SQL Server Reporting Services: Browser, Content Manager, My Reports, Publisher, Report Builder *(see Notes 1 and 3)* • SharePoint Administration Group Account *(see Notes 1 and 4)* • Domain Admins
OSPACSDevs	• [OSPACS]\Contributors *(see Notes 5 and 7)* • SQL Server Reporting Services: Browser, My Reports, Publisher, Report Builder *(see Notes 5 and 8)* • SharePoint OSPACS Site Contributor *(see Notes 5 and 8)* • (Local) Administrators, Domain Users, Users
Book User	**Security Group Membership**
Tom	• OSPACSAdmins, OSPACSDevs
Luke	• OSPACSDevs
Peter	• OSPACSDevs
Sarah	• OSPACSDevs
Maggie	• OSPACSDevs

TABLE A-3: Notes

1. Log on using the same account used to install TFS[7] (e.g., TFSSETUP) to ensure that you have the rights and permissions needed to make OSPACSAdmins a member of [SERVER]\Team Foundation Administrators as well as giving it the required security permissions for SQL Server Reporting Services and SharePoint Services; see Notes 2, 4, and 5.

2. In order to make OSPACSAdmins a member of [SERVER]\Team Foundation Administrators, follow the instructions in Exercise 5-3 in Chapter 5, but at step 3, type the following at the command prompt: TFSSecurity /server:DevServer /g+ "[SERVER]\Team Foundation Administrators" n:OurDomain\OSPACSAdmins.

   (In the preceding command, replace DevServer with the name of the PC hosting your TFS and OurDomain with the name of the domain containing your OSPACSAdmins group account. However, if OSPACSAdmins is a local group on your TFS, replace OurDomain with the name of the TFS PC—for example, DevServer.)

3. In order to grant OSPACSAdmins the necessary security permissions for SQL Server Reporting Services, follow the instructions in step 4 of Exercise 5-4, in Chapter 5, but open the following page in your browser: http://DevServer/Reports/Pages/Folder.aspx.

   (In the preceding command, replace DevServer with the name of the PC hosting your TFS.)

4. In order to grant OSPACSAdmins the security permissions for SharePoint Services, open the SharePoint Central Administration Web page (All Programs | Administrative Tools) and use the group account name OurDomain\OSPACSAdmins as the SharePoint administration group. However, if OSPACAdmins is a local group on your TFS, use a suitable user account name, such as DevServer\Tom.

5. After creating the OSPACS Team Project (Exercise 5-1 in Chapter 5), you need to add OSPACSAdmins and OSPACSDevs to its security groups as well as grant them access to its Project Portal and Report Site; see Notes 6, 7, and 8.

6. Follow the instructions in Exercise 5-3 in Chapter 5 to make OSPACSAdmins a member of [OSPACS]\Administrators, but at step 3, type the following at the command prompt: TFSSecurity /server:DevServer /g+ "[OSPACS]\Project Administrators" n:OurDomain\OSPACSAdmins.

7. Exercise 5-3 in Chapter 5 explains how to make someone a Team Project Contributor.

8. The instructions in Exercise 5-4 in Chapter 5 explain how to grant people access to the OSPACS Team Project Portal and Report Site.

■ **NOTE**

If you are using the TFS for Workgroups product, you must also make each developer's user account a member of the special Team Foundation Licensed Users security group created during installation of the Workgroup Edition; see Appendix B.

---

7. Microsoft: TFS Installation Guide (http://go.microsoft.com/fwlink/?LinkId=40042).

Machines and Users Named in the Exercises

We suggest you photocopy Tables A-4 and A-5 and then enter the names of the machines and security groups in your environment that correspond to ones to which we refer in the exercises.

TABLE A-4: Mapping of Machines Named in the Exercises

Book Machine Name	Your Machine Name
DeveloperPC	
DeveloperPC2	
DeveloperPC3	
ArchitectPC	
TesterPC	
ExecutivePC	
BuildLabPC	
DevServer (TFS)	
PDC	

■ NOTE

We do not refer to the Primary Domain Controller (PDC) in any of the exercises. However, it is recommended that you have a separate machine for this function when setting up a commercial Software Project Environment; see Appendix B.

TABLE A-5: Mapping of Usernames and Security Groups Named in the Exercises

Book Username or Security Group	Your Username or Security Group
OSPACSDevs	
Luke	
Peter	
Sarah	
Tom	
Maggie	

◼ B

Software Project Environment for a Small Team

I N THIS APPENDIX, we will specify the hardware and software products that a five-developer team would need. This corresponds to the Software Project Environment for the OSPACS team, as shown in Figure B-1. We will also explore some of the licensing issues you may need to address when such a team uses Visual Studio Team System (VSTS) in this environment.

Legal Disclaimer: Readers should verify for themselves that their use of any software product is consistent with the actual license agreements they (or their organization) have made. The information in this appendix and elsewhere in the book is intended only to help people understand the general issues rather than providing any form of specific legal advice.

Hardware Requirements

Some teams spend a lot of time researching the hardware they need before making their purchasing decision, and others just buy from well-known suppliers. For the benefit of people in this latter category, we provide a list of the computers and other equipment you need in order to create the sort of Software Project Environment shown in Figure B-1.

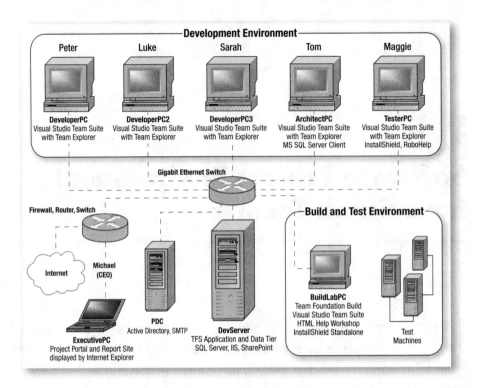

FIGURE B-1: The OSPACS team's Software Project Environment

■ NOTE

The lists of hardware in Tables B-1 and B-2 are available on this book's Web site. We intend to update these lists from time to time as a result of reader feedback, so if you have some alternative hardware suggestions, please send them to us.

Computers

Agile development teams should not constrain themselves by buying computers that do not provide adequate performance. It is always better to over-specify a development PC, particularly given the relatively low cost of today's machines.

TABLE B-1: Hardware Shopping List for the OSPACS Team

Item	Typical Specification	Quantity
Team Foundation Server (TFS) (DevServer)	Dell PowerEdge 2900 with Xeon 3.0 GHz dual core processor, 4 GB of RAM, two 320 GB SATA drives, two RAID cards, 19-inch monitor, keyboard, mouse, 16x DVD±RW Preinstalled with 32-bit Windows Server 2003 R2	1
Primary domain controller (PDC)	Dell PowerEdge SC440 with Pentium D 2.8 GHz processor, 1 GB of RAM, two 250 GB SATA drives, one RAID card, 16x DVD±RW Preinstalled with 32-bit Windows Server 2003 R2	1
Desktop PC (five DeveloperPCs and one BuildLabPC)	Dell Precision 690 with Xeon 2.0 GHz processor, 2 GB of RAM, 250 GB SATA drive, two 19-inch monitors, keyboard, mouse, 16x DVD±RW Preinstalled with Windows XP Pro SP2 *(see note 3)*	6

1. The PCs in Table B-1 far exceed the system requirements in the Visual Studio Team Foundation Installation Guide, but they are more like the machines that a small team might sensibly buy.

2. Microsoft claims that in a small team environment, Team Foundation Build will run satisfactorily on a machine with just a 1.5 GHz processor and 512 MB of RAM. However, we suggest that you give your BuildLabPC the same sort of specification as the other desktop PCs because this will allow you to install Visual Studio Team Suite so that you can run customer and unit tests as part of your Team Builds.

3. Any desktop PC that needs to run a Virtual PC in order to emulate the production environment during testing must allow between 50 MB and 2 GB of hard disk space for each virtual hard disk that will be created. This is just for the operating system; more space will be required for your database, system under test, and so on.

4. If you are developing only 32-bit software products, consider specifying a faster Pentium 4 or Athlon in place of the Xeon processor for your desktop PCs. Visual Studio 2005 is a 32-bit application and you should not expect any performance improvement when you run it on a multicore or multiprocessor PC.

5. You will experience performance gains when you run SQL Server 2005 on a multicore or multiprocessor PC. Therefore, you might consider specifying an additional processor for the TFS to improve the performance of your TFS Data Tier.

Continues

TABLE B-1: Notes, *Continued*

6. Do not be tempted to save money by buying your desktop PCs with a Linux or MS-DOS operating system and then installing Windows XP using the disk provided with your team's MSDN Premium Subscriptions, because if these machine break down, you will want the PC vendor to repair them without having to restore the original operating system. This would also constitute a "production" use of Windows XP and therefore would violate your MSDN license.

7. You might save some money by not buying a desktop PC for each developer on your team because they can be expected to spend most of their time sharing a machine while pair programming. However, it is likely that a team of five developers would simultaneously use five machines often enough to justify the expense. You should also remember that the Team System licenses specified in Table B-2 are granted per user, not per machine.

8. You should not use the disks provided with your MSDN Premium Subscriptions to install Windows Server 2003 on TFS or the PDC because again, this constitutes a *production* use of the product. Therefore, you should buy these servers with preinstalled operating systems, but make sure you obtain the five Windows client access licenses (CALs) for devices rather than users.

9. If you are developing software to support 64-bit processors, you should install Windows XP Professional for 64-bit on your desktop PCs. However, Visual Studio 2005 is a 32-bit application, so do not expect any performance gain when using it with a 64-bit operating system.[1]

Other Equipment

You must not forget the other sorts of hardware equipment your team needs in order to do a good job; see Table B-2.

TABLE B-2: Other Equipment for the OSPACS Team

Item	Typical Specification	Quantity
Printer	Brother Laser Printer HL-2070N	1
Scanner	HP Scanjet N6010 Document Sheetfeed Scanner	1
Switch	Blackbox 16 Port 10/100/1000 Mbps switch	1
Internet connection, firewall, router	Netgear DG834 ADSL firewall, router, and switch	1

---

1. Sutter, Herb. "The Free Lunch Is Over: A Fundamental Turn Toward Concurrency in Software" (www.gotw.ca/publications/concurrency-ddj.htm).

Item	Typical Specification	Quantity
Backup device[1]	Maxtor 300 GB external hard drive with USB 2.0	2
UPS for servers	APC Smart-UPS 1500VA with serial connection	2
Server KVM switch	Blackbox Personal KVM ServSwitch with two cabling kits to switch monitor, mouse, and keyboard between the DevServer and PDC	1
Network cables	Ethernet CAT6 cables terminated with RJ45 plugs	12
Power strips	Six-outlet power strip with surge protection	2
Server trolley	Two shelves approximately 3-by-2 feet and four uprights with wheels approximately 3 feet long	1

1. Keep one backup device off-site and swap it with the on-site backup device on a regular basis. If your servers are stolen, you should lose only a few days' worth of development work.

Software Requirements

The software you need to install in your Software Project Environment can be categorized as the tools you need to buy, the software that is supplied with other products, and the software which is freely available.

Software Tools to Buy and Install on the OSPACS Developer PCs

The basic tools that your team needs to buy are listed in Table B-3. However, you should also consult the book's Web site for details of various other tools that you might consider buying in order to help your development effort.

TABLE B-3: Software Shopping List for the OSPACS Developer PCs

Product Name for Purchase Order	Buy From	License Type	Quantity to Buy
Visual Studio 2005 Team Suite with MSDN Premium Subscription *(alternative to Team Editions)*	http://msdn.microsoft.com	New licence or renewal	5
Visual Studio 2005 Team Edition for Developers with MSDN Premium Subscription *(alternative to Team Suite)*	http://msdn.microsoft.com	Free upgrade from MSDN Universal, renewal, or new licence *(see notes 1 and 2)*	3
Visual Studio 2005 Team Edition for Architects with MSDN Premium Subscription *(alternative to Team Suite)*	http://msdn.microsoft.com	Free upgrade from MSDN Universal, renewal, or new licence *(see notes 1 and 2)*	1
Visual Studio 2005 Team Edition for Testers with MSDN Premium Subscription *(alternative to Team Suite)*	http://msdn.microsoft.com	Free upgrade from MSDN Universal, renewal, or new licence *(see notes 1 and 2)*	1
FLEXnet InstallShield 12 Windows Premier Edition	www.macrovision.com	Upgrade or new	1
Macromedia RoboHelp Office X5	www.adobe.com	Upgrade or new	1

TABLE B-3: Notes

1. We specified the separate Visual Studio Team Editions for Developers, Architects, and Testers in Table B-3 because on many small teams, people will be obtaining a free upgrade from their MSDN Universal Subscriptions.

2. If you must buy separate Visual Studio Team Editions and are not doing Web service development, consider purchasing another Developer Edition rather than the Architect Edition. Alternatively, you might want to buy just five copies of the Tester Edition; see the Tester PC subsection of the Licensing Issues section, later in this appendix.

3. Table B-2 does not include any operating systems and software products required to emulate your production environment during testing.

4. We expect developers to create individual help topics as Word documents and store them in the repository so that the team's documentation expert can subsequently assemble them into a cohesive document using RoboHelp on the TesterPC. The resulting project file and HTML files would then be built into a Microsoft HTML Help file (.chm) using the freely available HTML Help Workshop command-line tools installed on your BuildLabPC; see the book's Web site for further details. For this reason, we specify just one RoboHelp license.

5. We assume InstallShield (full product) and RoboHelp will be installed on the Tester PC because on the OSPACS team, Maggie has responsibility for creating the installation program and writing Help documentation. However, you could also install it on one of the Developer PCs or the Architect PC.

■ TIP

Due to the licensing issues raised later in this appendix, we suggest you purchase Visual Studio Team Suite for each developer on your team rather than installing separate Team Editions for people with specific roles (developer, tester, and architect).

Software Products to Buy and Install on Server PCs

The software products listed in Table B-4 are not strictly needed for software development, but they will protect your TFS and PDC in case of power failure or other disasters.

Table B-4: Software Shopping List for the OSPACS Team's Servers

Product Name for Purchase Order	Buy From	License Type	Quantity to Buy
APC PowerChute v7.0.2 Business Basic Edition	www.apc.com	Discounted or new	2
Symantec Backup Exec for Windows Small Business Server v11d	www.symantec.com	Single-server license	2

Software Supplied with Other Products

Some of the software your team needs for its Software Project Environment will probably be bundled with other products; see Table B-5. For example, when you buy a PC the operating system is generally included in the price.

Table B-5: Software Provided with Other Products on the OSPACS Team Shopping List

Product Name	Supplied With	Machine for Install	Quantity to Install
Windows XP Professional SP2	Desktop PC	Desktop PCs	5
Windows XP Professional SP2	BuildLab PC	BuildLabPC	1
Windows Server 2003 SP1 or R2 with five CALs for devices	DevServer PC	DevServer	1
Windows Server 2003 SP1 or R2 with five CALs for devices	PDC PC	PDC	1
TFS Workgroup Edition	Visual Studio Team Suite (or Editions) with MSDN Premium Subscription	DevServer	1

Product Name	Supplied With	Machine for Install	Quantity to Install
Team Foundation Build	TFS Workgroup Edition	BuildLabPC	1
Microsoft SQL Server 2005 Standard Edition	TFS Workgroup Edition	DevServer	1
IIS v6.0	Windows Server	DevServer	1
MS Office Software	MSDN Premium Subscription	Desktop PC	5
Microsoft SQL Server 2005 Client Components	Packaged with PC	ArchitectPC	1
InstallShield Standalone Build Engine	FLEXnet InstallShield Windows Premier Edition	TesterPC	1
InstallShield Collaboration for Visual Studio	FLEXnet InstallShield Windows Premier Edition	Desktop PCs	5

1. You can use single-server TFS installations to support project teams with as many as 400 users. Bigger teams or teams with requirements for better performance and reliability should consider dual-server TFS installations, running the Data Tier on clusters of machines, or using a caching proxy server; see the VSTS Installation Guide.

2. Windows Server 2003 is available as Datacenter, Enterprise, and Standard editions for both 32-bit and 64-bit processors. In a small team environment, there is no advantage to installing anything other than the Standard Edition with SP1.

3. The TFS Data Tier and Microsoft SQL Server 2005 support both 32-bit and 64-bit platforms, but the TFS Application Tier runs only in a native 32-bit environment. Therefore, in a single-server TFS installation, you must use a 32-bit operating system.

4. You should not use the PDC for much more than running the Active Directory for your domain and hosting a SMTP mail server. In particular, you should not install TFS on this machine.

5. Using SQL Server as the Data Tier of TFS is considered to be a production use of the product, so you cannot use it under the terms of your MSDN license. Accordingly, you must either buy normal end-user licenses, or use the license provided by TFS Workgroup Edition.

6. InstallShield Collaboration is installed on each developer's PC to facilitate the gathering of deployment requirements. These requirements are stored in DIM files for subsequent incorporation into an InstallShield setup project which can then be built into an install program by the Standalone InstallShield Build Engine installed on the BuildLab PC; see Chapter 29.

> **■ WARNING**
>
> You must use the 32-bit version of Microsoft Server 2003 when installing TFS on a single server because the Application Tier doesn't support WOW64.

Open Source or Freely Available Software

You should take advantage of the software listed in Table B-6 as it can be installed on your PC for no cost and yet provides important functionality. The book's Web site lists other types of open source or freely available software that might be of interest to an Agile software development team.

TABLE B-6: Freely Available Software Needed by the OSPACS Team

Product Name	Machine for Install	Quantity to Install	Obtain From
.NET Framework 2.0 Redistributable pack	All PCs	1	http://msdn.microsoft.com (.NET framework, downloads)
.NET Framework 2.0 SDK	DeveloperPCs	1	
Domain-Specific Languages (DSLs)	DeveloperPCs	5	http://msdn.microsoft.com/ vstudio/teamsystem/downloads
MSF and Process Customization	ArchitectPC	1	
TFS Power Toy	Desktop PCs	6	
SharePoint Services 2.0 SP2	DevServer	1	http://go.microsoft.com/fwlink/ ?linkid=55087
HTML Help Workshop v1.4	BuildLabPC	1	http://msdn.microsoft.com (Win32 Development, Tools, HTML Help, 1.4 SDK, downloads)
FIT v1.1 for .NET	Desktop PCs	6	http://fit.c2.com (downloads)
PsExec	Desktop PCs	6	www.microsoft.com/technet/ sysinternals/utilities/psexec.mspx

> **▪ NOTE**
>
> PsExec is a lightweight Telnet replacement that lets you execute processes on other systems, complete with full interactivity for console applications, without having to manually install client software.

Licensing Issues for a Five-Person Team

In order to start work on a five-person project team, such as the OSPACS team, you need to buy the software listed in Tables B-3 and B-4. Essentially, this involves buying the following:

- Visual Studio 2005 Team Suite Edition with MSDN Premium Subscription for each person
- RoboHelp and InstallShield for the TesterPC
- Backup Exec and Powerchute for the DevServer and PDC

Given that all the PCs are bought with preinstalled operating systems, the license implications for the team in this scenario are explained in the following sections.

Primary Domain Controller

The machine that acts as your PDC should be supplied with the Windows Server 2003 operating system already installed. Therefore, you should consider the following in regard to the five Windows CALs that are typically supplied with such a machine:

- You can assign CALs to a device such as a DeveloperPC (device mode), but you can also assign them to a user (per-user mode). Alternatively, you can assign a CAL to a particular server (per-server mode). We suggest you buy CALs for assigning to a device because this allows the customer (or other nonteam member) to occasionally access files and so forth on the PDC or the DevServer using one of the team's desktop PCs.

- You do not need a CAL to log on directly to the DevServer in order to carry out administrative tasks such as backing up data, cleaning up the hard disk, and so forth. However, any other device (or user) that wants to access the domain hosted by the PDC or its services needs a CAL. If you have bought two servers with operating systems preinstalled, you should have five spare CALs, so you will not need to buy additional CALs until you want to access your PDC and DevServer from more than ten PCs.

TFS (DevServer)

DevServer, like the PDC, should be supplied with Windows Server 2003 preinstalled. The OSPACS team assigned one of the CALs provided with this operating system to Michael's PC and kept the remaining four licenses as spares. This is because the team's five desktop PCs have been assigned the per-device-mode CALs that came with the PDC and therefore are licensed to access any Windows server.

> **■. NOTE**
>
> The VSTS Licensing White Paper[2] states "non-licensed users may access the [TFS] operating system and server software solely for the purpose of user acceptance testing." We interpret this as meaning that people do require a specific license for VSTS if they are just creating and running the sort of customer acceptance tests described in Section 7.

TFS Workgroup Edition

TFS Workgroup Edition should be installed on the DevServer because its license is included with any MSDN Premium Subscription that is bought

---

2. "Microsoft Visual Studio 2005 Team System Licensing White Paper," Nov. 2005 (http://go.microsoft.com/fwlink/?LinkId=55164).

with Visual Studio 2005 Team Edition (or Suite). However, you should be aware of the following:

- TFS Workgroup Edition is functionally identical to the full TFS product except that it is limited to five users and doesn't require any TFS CALs.

- Despite its name, you can use the TFS Workgroup Edition within a domain as well as within a workgroup. Indeed, we suggest that you make your development, build, and test environments part of a domain.

- All five members of the OSPACS team have purchased MSDN Premium Subscriptions with Visual Studio Team Edition and therefore are licensed to access the TFS Workgroup Edition installed on the DevServer. This license is per-user, not per-device. These users must be added to the special Team Foundation Licensed Users security group created during the installation of the Workgroup Edition in order for them to connect to the server. This security group is limited to five members and is not created during the installation of the full (or trial) edition of TFS.

- TFS is normally accessed from desktop PCs using Team Explorer. There is no restriction on the number of PCs upon which an OSPACS team member can install Team Explorer as the license is per-person and not per-device. However, this means that non-team members (such as Michael) cannot use a team member's desktop PC to access his TFS, though a TFS CAL can be purchased for a particular user (or device) if such access is required.

- An exception is provided so that non-team members can use a team member's desktop PC to access his TFS solely for the purposes of user acceptance testing.

- Members of a team who are sharing TFS Workgroup Edition do not need to be employees of the same company, but in general, they must all work together in the same place. Although team members are allowed to make occasional remote connections to the DevServer— for example, when working from home—such permissions do not extend to people who are normally working off-site.

Microsoft SQL Server 2005

Microsoft SQL Server 2005 must be installed on the DevServer prior to the installation of TFS Workgroup Edition (or full TFS); see Appendix A. TFS Workgroup Edition includes a license for Microsoft SQL Server 2005 Standard Edition with the following restrictions:

- SQL Server software must be used only with TFS and not for other purposes. However, the MSDN Premium Subscription gives you the right to install SQL Server 2005 (any edition) on a machine for development purposes.
- The SQL Server that provides the VSTS Data Tier must be installed on the same physical machine as the Application Tier, so you have to install TFS on a single physical server.
- Only the five members of the OSPACS team can view reports generated by SQL Server 2005 Reporting Services. However, a TFS CAL can be purchased for a particular user (or device) so that non-team members such as Michael can view these reports.

Internet Information Server and SharePoint Services

Internet Information Server (IIS) and SharePoint Services must be installed on the DevServer PC prior to the installation of TFS Workgroup Edition (or full TFS). Use of IIS and SharePoint services is subject to the Windows Server 2003 license supplied with the DevServer PC. However, you should note the following:

- There is no restriction on people distributing information using the Team Web site (Project Portal) beyond the need for a CAL in regard to the DevServer.
- Team members can manually distribute information they have gathered from their TFS to third parties. Therefore, a team member could run a query to list the project's active bugs and save the results in an Excel file which could then be attached to an e-mail and sent to someone in, say, London.

- You can automate the periodic distribution of information gathered from TFS to third parties, but non-team members (such as Michael) cannot initiate the gathering and distribution of this information. Therefore, the OSPACS team could add a Web Part to its Project Portal which lists the ten most important bugs at the start of each day, but the team could not allow Michael to update the list by pressing a button.

- Team members can manually input information into TFS from third parties. For example, Michael can use his Executive PC to change a project plan and then upload the file to the OSPACS team Web site so that a team member can update the project plan held in TFS. However, you cannot automate this process so that Michael can make changes to the project plan that result in the information held by TFS being updated without the involvement of a team member.

- A link can be provided on the OSPACS team Web site to a file in the Team Build drop folder so that non-team members can access the products of a Team Build. However, the drop folder would need to be located on a machine for which the non-team member had a CAL, unless the build is being accessed for the purposes of customer testing.

> **■ NOTE**
>
> The various licenses for Microsoft products installed on the DevServer seek to prevent people from using third-party products with the aim of reducing the number of licenses required by a project team.

Developer PCs

The Developer PCs should be supplied with Windows XP preinstalled. They should also have a per-device CAL for the DevServer and PDC. Therefore, anyone is licensed to use these machines as well as the basic facilities of the team's servers. However, as described earlier, only the five team members can access the facilities provided by their TFS.

Given that the three developers on the OSPACS team who are responsible for writing code (Sarah, Peter, and Luke) buy a Visual Studio 2005 Team Edition for Developers with an MSDN Premium Subscription, you need to consider the following issues:

- The license is per-user, not per-device. Therefore, Sarah, Peter, and Luke can use each other's PCs, but not the Architect PC or the Tester PC. This conflicts with the Whole Team practice because it encourages people to have particular roles, and for this reason, you may want to buy the more expensive Visual Studio 2005 Team Suite for all five team members.

- Sarah, Peter, and Luke can pair-program together in any combination. There is no restriction on two people using the same Developer PC at the same time as long as they both have a license to use the machine individually. However, Tom and Maggie would be unable to pair-program with anyone.

- Sarah, Peter, and Luke cannot create, manage, or run generic, manual, or Web tests on their Developer PCs because this requires Team Edition for Testers. They are also not able to use the Distributed Application Designer tools because this requires Team Edition for Architects.

- Any team member can use InstallShield Collaboration for Visual Studio on the Developer PCs to gather installation requirements; see Chapter 29. The license for this product is per-device. A five-pack license is included with the Premier Edition of FLEXNet InstallShield 12.

- Non-team members can use a Developer PC to access TFS solely for the purposes of user acceptance testing.

- The license and MSDN Premium Subscription can be reassigned if one person leaves the team and another person joins. However, licenses cannot be regularly reassigned within the team. For example, Tom (Architect PC) and Luke (Developer PC) cannot swap licenses in the morning and then swap them back again in the afternoon.

- The MSDN Premium Subscription gives all five team members the right to install most of the Microsoft products on multiple devices for development purposes. However, certain products are subject to restrictions—for instance, Microsoft SQL Server 2005 and VSTS.

■ DOES YOUR LICENSE PERMIT PAIR PROGRAMMING?

There may be clauses in your Microsoft license agreements that seem to prohibit more than one person at a time from using a single PC. However, as Microsoft encourages pair programming, it could be argued that you are not breaking the intention of your agreement. It is just that the license was written before pair programming became popular. In practice, it seems unlikely that Microsoft would enforce such clauses if both people are licensed to use the PC individually.

Architect PC

The Architect PC should be supplied with Windows XP preinstalled, so our comments about basic access to the Developer PCs also apply to this PC. Given that the architect on the OSPACS team (Tom) buys a Visual Studio 2005 Team Edition for Architects with an MSDN Premium Subscription, consider the following:

- The license is per-user, not per-device. Therefore, Tom can use only the Architect PC; he cannot use the Tester PC or any of the Developer PCs. This conflicts with the Whole Team practice, as described earlier. It also means that Tom cannot take part in pair programming with the rest of the OSPACS team.
- Tom cannot create, manage, or run generic, manual, or Web tests on his Architect PC because this requires Team Edition for Testers. He is also not able to use the unit testing, code coverage, or code analyzer/code profiler tools because this requires Team Edition for Developers. However, unless the OSPACS team is developing distributed Web services, there is no justification for Tom buying Team

Edition for Architects, so he should buy one of the other editions instead.

- Non-team members can use the Architect PC to access TFS solely for the purposes of user acceptance testing.

- Microsoft SQL Server 2005 Standard Edition Client Components may also be installed on any Desktop PC (or server) and used by anyone with an MSDN Premium Subscription. However, on the OSPACS team, only Tom wants to use these tools, so they are installed on the Architect PC.

- The license for the Architect Edition can be reassigned if Tom leaves the team in the same way as the license for the Developer Edition can be reassigned, as noted earlier. Tom also has the same rights as other team members to install Microsoft software products for development purposes as a result of his MSDN Premium Subscription (as noted earlier).

Tester PC

The Architect PC should be supplied with Windows XP preinstalled, so our comments about basic access to the Developer PCs also apply to this PC. Given that the tester on the OSPACS team (Maggie) buys a Visual Studio 2005 Team Edition for Testers PC with an MSDN Premium Subscription, reflect on the following issues:

- The license is per-user, not per-device. Therefore, Maggie can use only the Tester PC; she cannot use the Architect PC or any of the Developer PCs. This conflicts with the Whole Team practice, as described earlier, and means that Maggie cannot take part in pair programming with the rest of the OSPACS team.

- Maggie cannot use the code analyzer or code profiler tools because this requires Team Edition for Developers. She also cannot use the Distributed Application Designer tools because this requires Team Edition for Architects. However, if these tools are not usually used by the OSPACS team, there is a case for all five team members buying

Team Edition for Testers because this would allow them to implement the Whole Team practice and pair-program with each other.

- Non-team members can use the Tester PC to access TFS solely for the purposes of user acceptance testing.
- The license for the Tester Edition can be reassigned if Maggie leaves the team in the same way as the license for the Developer Edition can be reassigned, as described earlier. Maggie also has the same rights as other team members to install Microsoft software products for development purposes as a result of her MSDN Premium Subscription (as noted earlier).

BuildLab PC

The BuildLab PC should be supplied with Windows XP preinstalled, so our comments about basic access to the Developer PCs also apply to this PC. The following issues should be considered:

- Team Build is provided as part of the .NET SDK, so it can be installed on any suitable PC (or collection of PCs) and anyone can script, schedule, or start a Team Build as long as it does not need access to a TFS.
- Only the five OSPACS team members can create, schedule, or start a Team Build that requires access to their TFS Workgroup Edition. There also certain restrictions:
  - OSPACS team members who do not have a license to use Team Edition for Developers cannot script a build that includes code coverage or code analysis.
  - OSPACS team members who do not have a license to use Team Edition for Developers or Team Edition for Testers cannot script a build that includes unit tests.
  - OSPACS team members who do not have a license to use Team Edition for Testers cannot script a build that includes generic, manual, load, or Web tests.

- InstallShield provides a license that allows the Standalone Build Engine to be used by an automated build process such as Team Build. In this way, the InstallShield set-up project prepared by the full InstallShield product (see the Tester PC section) can be built into an install program as part of a Team Build.

■ NOTE

The BuildLabPC must have Visual Studio Team Suite installed in order for Team Foundation Build to run tests that use the tools listed earlier.

Standby TFS

It is a good idea for a team to keep a spare server on standby in case its main DevServer fails for whatever reason. Ideally, this machine should be an exact replica of the main DevServer in terms of hardware, but you might also make do with a PC that has a lesser specification. There are a number of issues to consider:

- If you intend to have both machines switched on at the same time (warm standby), you need to buy the same set of licenses for the standby machine as for the main DevServer. However, if you have purchased Microsoft's Software Assurance with your licenses, you can install them on the standby machine without needing to buy a duplicate set of licenses as long as both machines are not switched on at the same time.
- It is advisable to validate your backup process by regularly restoring the latest backup to the standby DevServer. You should restore the standby DevServer from bare metal so that the machine should not even have its operating system installed at the start of the restore process.
- Occasionally using the standby DevServer in place of the main server for a day helps identify any subtle problems with your backup and restore process.

> **■ NOTE**
> Consult the "Visual Studio Team Foundation Administrator Guide"
> for specific details about backing up and restoring TFS.

Multiprocessor PCs and Multicore Processors

There are no license limitations in terms of TFS Workgroup Edition (or any of the Visual Studio Team Editions) being used on machines with multiple processors or single multicore processors. However, before buying multiple-processor machines, we recommend that you read the notes in Table B-1 that explain the performance gains you might expect to achieve:

- The Test Load Agent (not covered in this book) is licensed per processor.
- The Data and Application Tiers of the TFS Workgroup Edition must be installed on the same physical machine. However, you can install the Data and Application Tiers on different machines when using the full TFS product and the Data Tier can then be further distributed into a server cluster.
- Software products such as RoboHelp and InstallShield do not take advantage of multiple processors, so you should not expect any performance gains when using them on multicore or multiprocessor machines.

Increasing Your Team beyond Five People

In addition to buying an additional Desktop PC (with the Windows XP operating system preinstalled), you will need to buy the licenses shown in Tables B-7 and B-8 when your team size exceeds five.

TABLE B-7: License Requirements for Sixth Team Member

Product Name	License For	Buy Because
Visual Studio 2005 Team Suite (or Edition for Developer, Tester, Architect)	User	Someone new has joined the team.
TFS CAL	User	More than five people are working on the team, so you can no longer use TFS for Workgroups.
TFS Server License (sold per server)	DevServer	
Windows Server 2003 CAL (typically sold as pack of five)	Desktop PCs	
Windows SQL Server	DevServer	

TABLE B-8: Per-Member License Requirements for Seven or More Team Members

Product Name	License For	Buy Whenever
Visual Studio 2005 Team Suite (or Edition for Developer, Tester, Architect)	User	Someone new joins the team
TFS CAL	User	Someone new joins the team
Windows Server 2003 CAL (typically sold as pack of five)	Desktop PCs	The number of PCs exceeds ten, 15, etc.

1. In order to put the Data and Application Tiers of VSTS on different servers (dual-server installation), you must buy a TFS license for each physical server. Furthermore, if you then want to cluster the Data Tier on a number of servers, you must again buy additional TFS licenses for each machine.

2. A geographically dispersed team needs to buy a TFS license for any machine which is used as a TFS proxy.

3. People who do not normally work in the same location as the team and are not employed by the same organization are usually considered *external* users. Such people require an external connector license to connect with the team's TFS, whether this is via a TFS proxy or some direct network connection such as a VPN.

4. When your team has more than five Developer PCs you will need to buy additional FLEXnet InstallShield Collaboration licenses for each machine.

> ■ **NOTE**
>
> Teams that are operating in a domain can move from TFS for Work-groups to the full TFS product simply by updating their DevServer. There is no need for them to create a new Team Project, apply new security settings, or take any other sort of action.

▪ C
Agile Workspace

THIS APPENDIX PRESENTS some ideas for creating the sort of space that helps a small Agile team work together more effectively. It also lists some of the things you might find in such a workspace. However, we recognize that each Agile team has its own unique needs and constraints, so what we propose might not work as well in every case. Therefore, you should read this appendix simply with the aim of changing your environment so that it works for your team rather than against it.

Basic Office Layout

A team seldom has much choice about the basic floor plan of its workspace, particularly in regard to window and kitchen locations. However, this should not discourage you from seeking to rearrange your allocated office space to create the various areas you need, such as those shown in Figure C-1.

> ▪ **TIP**
>
> Plan for your team size to increase, and always try to exceed the minimum floor space requirements for employees in your organization. The total floor area in Figure C-1 is about 1,000 square feet, which corresponds to 125 square feet per person for a team of eight.

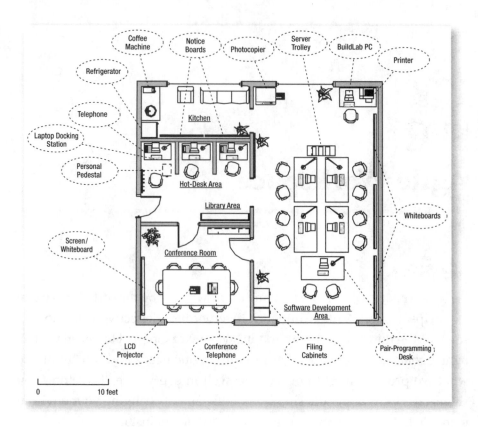

FIGURE C-1: Floor plan for a small Agile team

Software Development Area

The essential requirement for the software development area is that it must be an open space which is large enough for the entire team to sit together for most of the day; see the Sit Together practice in Chapter 4. In particular, you must avoid having separate offices, cubicles, or desks separated by any sort of partition. Most Agile teams arrange themselves in a cluster of desks such as those shown in Figure C-1, but other elements of your software development area that you should consider include the following:

- **Space to hold impromptu group discussions**—Your team needs somewhere to explore ideas without moving out of its immediate working space. This is why the desks in Figure C-1 leave space next to the kitchen.

- **Pair-programming desks**—It must be possible for two people to share the same desk. Therefore, don't waste money buying desks with fitted cabinets or drawers that might restrict leg room. Instead, spend your money on comfortable chairs, good-quality desk lamps, and decent keyboards/mice. You should also provide each desk with plenty of pens and index cards, as well as a desk organizer in which to keep them and a waste basket for trash.

- **Server trolley**—Put the team's servers (see Appendix B) on a trolley together with equipment such as the Ethernet switch and UPS devices. This gives you easy access to the back of these machines and provides a central point from which to run power and network cables to the PC on each pair-programming desk.

- **BuildLab PC**—The build and test environment should be separated from the development environment, but still easily accessible. In Figure C-1, the test machines are kept under the desk, but your team might require more space for them.

- **Whiteboards, flip charts, and notice boards**—Provide plenty of space for people to present information. It is useful to have some whiteboards on a movable frame so that you can position them as required.

- **Storage**—Provide lots of space for your team's paperwork as well as for supplies such as disks, toner cartridges, and other stationery items. You should also keep a supply of spare equipment cords, power strips, and so on.

> **■ NOTE**
>
> Make your software development area a pleasant place in which to work by utilizing natural light, growing plants, and having well-coordinated wall colors. You also need effective air conditioning, or better still, windows that open as well as blinds and fans.

Kitchen Area

The kitchen area provides a place for people to rest between the sort of programming episodes we described in Chapter 12 (and elsewhere). However, it also serves to promote the exchange of information and ideas among team members. Therefore, insist on your team having its own private kitchen area, or alternatively, make an area that serves as such, even if it lacks a sink or water supply. In addition to a coffee maker and refrigerator, your kitchen should have the following:

- Whiteboards for sketching ideas and notice boards for things such as story cards that have not been estimated or assigned (see Chapter 27).
- The latest technical magazines, books, and other material to keep people aware of what is going on outside their immediate team; see the Library Area section, later in this appendix.
- Fruit, cookies, and other sources of sustenance to keep people going. You might also consider providing a microwave as well as cutlery and tableware for instant meals.

■ TIP

A well-organized kitchen is often an indicator of a well-organized team, so let the team decide how best to stock its kitchen. However, don't forget things such as cleaning materials as well as a large trash bin so that you can keep the area tidy.

Hot-Desk Area

People sometimes need to work on their own, away from the rest of the team, whether this is to develop an idea (spike) or simply to do personal things such as answer e-mail and make dentist appointments. A hot-desk area is an efficient way to meet such needs because instead of allocating a particular desk to each person, a collection of desks are provided which are used only for as long as people require them. Therefore, a team of eight people might share three hot desks because, most of the time, they will be pair programming in the software development area. Each hot desk should be equipped with the following:

- **Desk telephone**—Although most people have a cell phone, it is better to provide a desk telephone away from the software development area because this reduces the disruption caused by telephone calls. Replacing the bell on these telephones with a flashing light will further improve the team's working environment.
- **Space for a personal pedestal**—Each person should have his own set of drawers on wheels that so it can be easily moved to any desk. Such pedestals enable people to have their own personal things around them, and each should have at least one lockable drawer.
- **Laptop docking station with monitor, keyboard, and mouse**—You gain more flexibility by supplying quick-fitting connectors to the monitor, keyboard, and mouse (together with network and power connections) rather than having a plug-in docking station for a specific type of laptop.

■ TIP

Put people's desktop PCs on low trolleys so that they can easily move them to wherever they are working. The use of quick-fit connectors further encourages the mobility of machines between different desks.

The use of hot desks is a contentious issue because most software developers expect to have their own personal space, complete with a desk and PC. Therefore, you should address these issues by letting the team decide whether to use hot desks. For example, if initially five developers and a customer were sharing the workspace in Figure C-1, the developers might each "own" a pair-programming desk and the customer might "own" a particular hot desk, leaving two hot desks as spares. However, once another developer joins this team and takes ownership of another hot desk, the demand for the remaining hot desk is likely to be such that people would become less proprietary about their desks. Certainly, by the time this team had grown to nine developers, it is reasonable to expect that it should have established the basic principle that people didn't "own" a particular desk, but shared them as they were needed.

> **■ NOTE**
>
> Hot-desking is really about the provision of personal space, and the team must decide whether the occasional privacy provided by a hot desk is worth sacrificing ownership of a specific desk in the software development area.

Library Area

The team needs an area to store technical books and magazines. This area should not be hidden away, but carefully positioned so that it catches people's eyes. For example, the location of the library in Figure C-1 is such that it is the first thing people see when they walk into the team's environment. The team needs to take responsibility for stocking the library as well as its administration, because otherwise it will quickly become out-of-date and disorganized. In particular, you must track your books and magazines so that you can always find them easily.

> **■ TIP**
>
> The Bibliography identifies some of the books you might want to buy when establishing your library, but you should organize your own review process to ensure that new books are bought each month and are read by at least one team member.

Conference Room

The conference room provides a place for people to hold private conversations in addition to serving as a location for the team's formal presentations. It does not need to be contained within the rest of the team's workspace, as shown in Figure C-1, but it does need to be readily accessible. You should consider the following aspects when setting up your conference room:

- Provide a large table so that people can spread out index cards and so forth during group modeling sessions, or when trying to resolve planning issues.
- Ensure that the room projects the desired image of the team to visitors such as potential recruits, clients, business sponsors, and so on.
- Provide adequate power and network connections and floor space so that you can move computers into the room when you need them.
- An LCD projector and screen allow you to give PowerPoint presentations and demonstrate the team's software.
- Arrange for the room to be acoustically insulated so that conversations cannot be overheard when the door is closed.
- Organize a booking system to discourage your customer (and others) from taking it over as a private office. You should also keep this information because it may help you substantiate future discussions about the room's value to your team.

When you are negotiating for your team's own conference room, make the point that it replaces the traditional project manager's office and provides somewhere for your customer to hold confidential business discussions. However, you may ultimately need to concede that it will be shared with other teams.

Supplies and Equipment

It goes without saying that to function efficiently as a team, you need to have adequate supplies of stationery as well as miscellaneous other small items of equipment which all help to make life easy for everyone. The following items were collated from various suggestions made by people in the

Extreme Programming Yahoo! Group[1] about the typical supplies and low-tech tools required by Agile teams:

- Small items of equipment:
  - Digital camera to capture whiteboard contents
  - Scanner to capture index cards
  - Paper and disk shredder
  - Staplers, hole punches, scissors, paper trimmer
  - Kitchen timers for timing box meetings, etc.
  - Toolbox, cable ties, duct tape
  - Magazine boxes, plastic storage bins (for spare cords), etc.
- Miscellaneous office items:
  - Wall clock
  - Place to hang coats, etc.
  - Movable uplighters to control ambient light
  - First-aid kit

Imposing the Team's Individuality

If you accept the idea that an Agile team knows best how to organize its own work, it follows that the team must be given control of its environment so that it can optimize it for its specific way of working. Unfortunately, though, attempts by people to establish their own environment often create conflict with other people in the organization who are seeking to impose their own ideas of order and uniformity. However, these battles need to be fought because they sometimes provide the catalyst that people need to start working together as a cohesive, self-organizing team.

---

1. Extreme Programming Group (http://tech.groups.yahoo.com/group/extremeprogramming).

> **■ NOTE**
>
> An old Bank of America advertisement about investing in disadvantaged neighborhoods makes the point that the bank knew it had succeeded when flowerboxes started showing up on front porches. What flowerboxes does your team display?

List of Exercises

We have listed here all the exercises in the book in order to help people who just want to find out how to complete a specific task using Visual Studio Team System (VSTS). The "Depends On" column in each table identifies any exercises upon which the given exercise depends. For people who are using a PC that does not have the full Team Suite installed, this column also identifies any exercise which requires a specific Visual Studio Team Edition as follows:

D—Visual Studio Team Edition for Developers

T—Visual Studio Team Edition for Testers

A—Visual Studio Team Edition for Architects

> **■. NOTE**
>
> Framework for Integrated Test (FIT) is required for Section 7, but it is freely available from the C2 Web site.[1] InstallShield and Installation Collaboration are needed for the exercises in Chapter 29, but free evaluation editions are provided on the Microvison Web site.[2]

---

1. Ward Cunningham's C2 Web site for FIT (http://fit.c2.com).
2. Macrovision's Web site for InstallShield (www.macrovision.com/downloads).

Setting Up a Team Project	Depends On	Page
Exercise 5-1: Creating a Team Project		85
Exercise 5-2: Deleting a Team Project	Exercise 5-1	87
Exercise 5-3: Making a User into a Team Project Contributor	Exercise 5-1	89
Exercise 5-4: Gaining Access to Your Team Project Portal and Report Site	Exercise 5-3	90
Exercise 5-5: Granting Permission to Administer a Build	Exercise 5-1	92
Exercise 5-6: Allowing All Valid Users to Create a Workspace	Exercise 5-1	92
Exercise 5-7: Connecting to Your Team Project	Exercise 5-4	94

Process Templates	Depends On	Page
Exercise 6-1: Adding a New Work Item Type to a Team Project	Exercise 5-7	108
Exercise 6-2: Adding a New Query to a Team Project	Exercise 5-7	109
Exercise 6-3: Exporting a Process Template to Your Hard Disk As XML	Exercise 5-7	113
Exercise 6-4: Importing a Process Template from Your Hard Disk	Exercise 6-3	114
Exercise 6-5: Changing Work Item Types in Your Process Template	Exercise 6-3	115

Version Control	Depends On	Page
Exercise 8-1: Creating Folders in Your Repository	Exercise 5-7	150
Exercise 8-2: Adding a Visual Studio Solution into a Directory Structure	Exercise 8-1	153
Exercise 8-3: Adding Existing Files and Directories to Version Control	Exercise 8-2	160
Exercise 8-4: Adding a Visual Studio Project into a Directory Structure	Exercise 8-3	163
Exercise 8-5: Checking In Pending Changes and Creating a Baseline Label	Exercise 8-4	164
Exercise 9-1: Using Version Control to Share Code Changes among Your Team	Exercise 8-5	174
Exercise 9-2: Creating an Additional Workspace	Exercise 5-7	178
Exercise 9-3: Merging Changes Made by Two Developers to the Same File	Exercise 9-1	180
Exercise 9-4: Rolling Back to a Previous Version	Exercise 9-3	184
Exercise 9-5: Creating a Code Branch	Exercise 8-4	186
Exercise 9-6: Saving and Restoring a Shelveset	Exercise 9-4	188
Exercise 10-1: Making a File Check Out Only for Project Administrators	Exercise 8-4	192
Exercise 10-2: Using Static Code Analysis on Your Own PC	Exercise 8-4 (D)	196
Exercise 10-3: Setting a Static Code Analysis Check-in Policy	Exercise 8-4 (D)	199
Exercise 10-4: Overriding a Static Code Analysis Check-in Policy	Exercise 10-3 (D)	202

Build and Integration	Depends On	Page
Exercise 12-1: Creating a Build Validation Test	Exercise 8-2 (T)	233
Exercise 12-2: Allowing Developers to Create and Run Team Builds	Exercise 5-7	236
Exercise 12-3: Creating a Team Build Type for Integration	Exercise 12-2	237
Exercise 12-4: Scheduling a Daily Team Build	Exercise 12-3	239
Exercise 12-5: Programming Episode Walkthrough and Integration Build	Exercise 12-3	240
Exercise 12-6: Deleting Build Products	Exercise 12-3	244
Exercise 12-7: Creating an Incremental Team Build Type	Exercise 12-3	250

TDD	Depends On	Page
Exercise 13-1: Implementing a Simple Test Harness		270
Exercise 13-2: Writing a Failing Test	Exercise 13-1	272
Exercise 13-3: Fixing the Code to Pass the Test	Exercise 13-2	273
Exercise 13-4: Writing Another Failing Test	Exercise 13-3	273
Exercise 13-5: Fixing the Code Again	Exercise 13-4	274
Exercise 13-6: Refactoring (To Make the Code Easier to Maintain)	Exercise 13-5	274
Exercise 14-1: Creating Visual Studio Projects for Tests and Production Code	Exercise 8-2	286
Exercise 14-2: Implementing a Test List	Exercise 14-1	292
Exercise 14-3: Implementing the First Test	Exercise 14-2	294
Exercise 14-4: Fixing a Failing Test	Exercise 14-3	297

TDD	Depends On	Page
Exercise 15-1: Implementing the ICollection Interface	Exercise 14-4	304
Exercise 15-2: Implementing the SetUp Refactoring Pattern	Exercise 15-1	307
Exercise 15-3: Adding a New Test: AddRemoveReturnsTrue	Exercise 15-2	308
Exercise 15-4: Storing Favorite Items in a Collection	Exercise 15-3	309
Exercise 15-5: Implementing a Linked List	Exercise 15-4	311
Exercise 15-6: Removing Items from an Empty Collection	Exercise 15-5	313
Exercise 15-7: Finding a Favorite from Its Label	Exercise 15-6	315
Exercise 15-8: Testing for an ArgumentNullException	Exercise 15-7	316
Exercise 15-9: Significant Refactoring of the Implementation under Test	Exercise 15-8	320
Exercise 16-1: Generating Code Coverage Information	Exercise 15-9 (D)	326
Exercise 16-2: Performance Session for a Unit Test	Exercise 15-9 (D)	333
Exercise 17-1: Providing a User Interface for LocalFavorites	Exercise 15-9	342

Modeling	Depends On	Page
Exercise 19-1: Editing a Source File Using Class Designer and Text Editor		387

Customer Test	Depends On	Page
Exercise 22-1: Installing FIT on a Developer PC		448
Exercise 22-2: Setting Up FIT for Customer Testing on a Developer PC	Exercise 8-4	449
Exercise 22-3: Running Customer Tests on Your Developer PC	Exercise 22-2	451
Exercise 23-1: Using a Column Fixture in a Customer Test	Exercise 22-3	461
Exercise 23-2: Using a Row Fixture in a Customer Test	Exercise 22-3	466
Exercise 23-3: Using an Action Fixture in a Customer Test	Exercise 22-3	472
Exercise 24-1: Setting Up FIT for Customer Testing in Your Build Lab	Exercise 22-3 (T)	483
Exercise 24-2: Running a Generic Test with MSTest	Exercise 24-1 (T)	486
Exercise 24-3: Running Customer Tests As Part of a Team Build	Exercise 24-1	487

Planning	Depends On	Page
Exercise 27-1: Creating a New Iteration for Your Project	Exercise 5-7	546
Exercise 27-2: Creating a New Story Work Item for Your Project	Exercise 5-7	548
Exercise 27-3: Running a Query to Find an Existing Story Work Item	Exercise 27-2	549
Exercise 27-4: Creating a Query to List All Story Work Items for Iteration Three	Exercise 27-3	550
Exercise 27-5: Updating an Excel Spreadsheet with Stories from a Team Project	Exercise 27-3	552

Planning	Depends On	Page
Exercise 27-6: Updating a Team Project with Stories from an Excel Spreadsheet	Exercise 27-5	553
Exercise 27-7: Producing a Bug Rate Report from TFS Work Items	Exercise 5-7	554

Deployment	Depends On	Page
Exercise 29-1: Creating an InstallShield Project	Exercise 8-4	606
Exercise 29-2: Creating a Windows Forms Application for Your Install Project	Exercise 29-1	607
Exercise 29-3: Using the Installation Designer to Define the Installation	Exercise 29-2	608
Exercise 29-4: Using the Release Wizard to Create Your Install Files	Exercise 29-3	611
Exercise 29-5: Creating DIM Projects to Gather Installation Requirements	Exercise 29-4	614
Exercise 29-6: Creating an Install Program from DIM Files	Exercise 29-5	618
Exercise 29-7: Creating, Publishing, and Deploying a ClickOnce Application		622
Exercise 30-1: Making a Visual Studio Solution for Your Logical Datacenter Diagrams (.ldd)	(A)	630
Exercise 30-2: Creating a Logical Datacenter Diagram (.ldd) with Zones and Servers	Exercise 30-1 (A)	631
Exercise 30-3: Importing Settings from the IIS in Your Datacenter	Exercise 30-2 (A)	636
Exercise 30-4: Making a Visual Studio Solution for Your Application Designer (.ad) Diagram	(A)	639
Exercise 30-5: Drawing an Application Designer Diagram	Exercise 30-4 (A)	639

Continues

Deployment	Depends On	Page
Exercise 30-6: Defining Operations for a Component's Provider Endpoint	Exercise 30-5 (A)	642
Exercise 30-7: Defining a Connection String to a Database	Exercise 30-6 (A)	643
Exercise 30-8: Implementing Your AD Diagram As a Collection of Visual Studio Projects	Exercise 30-7 (A)	644
Exercise 30-9: Testing a Web Service from Visual Studio	Exercise 30-8 (A)	644
Exercise 30-10: Reverse-Engineering an AD Diagram from a Visual Studio Solution	Exercise 30-9 A	646
Exercise 30-11: Creating System Designer Diagrams from an AD Diagram	Exercise 30-7 (A)	649
Exercise 30-12: Creating Composite System Designer Diagrams	Exercise 30-11 (A)	651
Exercise 30-13: Creating Deployment Designer Diagrams from an SD Diagram	Exercise 30-12 (A)	654
Exercise 30-14: Setting the Properties of Your Deployment Designer Diagram	Exercise 30-13 (A)	655
Exercise 30-15: Validating a Deployment Designer Diagram	Exercise 30-14 (A)	656
Exercise 30-16: Creating a Deployment Report	Exercise 30-15 (A)	657

Reveal Value	Depends On	Page
Exercise 31-1: Running a SQL Query on the TFSWarehouse Relational Database		676
Exercise 31-2: Using the Report Designer to Create a Custom Report		678

List of Extreme Programming Practices

The second edition of Kent Beck's book, *Extreme Programming Explained*,[1] defines 24 practices that an Agile team should apply to its work. You can read our interpretation of these practices in this book, as outlined in the following table:

Practice	Chapter	Page
Pair Programming	2	38
Whole Team	4	67
Sit Together	4	73
Team Continuity	4	77
Shared Code	7	131
Single Code Base	7	140
Code and Tests	8	155
Ten Minute Build	11	218

Continues

---

1. [XPE2] Beck, Kent, with Cynthia Andres. *Extreme Programming Explained, Second Edition* (Addison-Wesley, 2005).

Practice	Chapter	Page
Continuous Integration	11	224
Test-First Programming	13	266
Energized Work	15	323
Incremental Design	18	372
Real Customer Involvement	22	456
Stories	25	513
Weekly Cycle	26	536
Quarterly Cycle	26	538
Slack	27	559
Daily Deployment	28	584
Incremental Deployment	28	590
Informative Workspace	31	673
Root Cause Analysis	32	687

■ **NOTE**

We do not cover the Negotiated Scope Contract, Pay-per-Use, and Shrinking Teams practices in this book, but you can find information about them on the book's Web site.

Glossary

At the start of a project, there are often subtle differences between people's understanding of the same terms. However, in time, a common language develops so that everyone is able to communicate more effectively. This process of acquiring the team's language includes learning terms that are specific to the business solution being developed (domain language) as well as those specific to the technologies being used in the project. We hope the following glossary helps your team in this process of adopting its own language.

Key

A Term with meaning in the Agile community. For example, *customer* has a specific meaning when used in regard to an Agile team.

V Term with meaning in the context of Visual Studio Team System (VSTS). For example, you might create a *test list* to run a collection of unit tests in a Visual Studio Test Project.

M Term with meaning in the Microsoft community. For example, *Visual Studio* is Microsoft's Integrated Development Environment (IDE).

X Term that we have defined or something that is not in common use.

▪▪ NOTE

Words put in an italic font are defined elsewhere in the glossary. The acronym *a.k.a.* stands for *also known as* and is used to indicate other terms that share a similar meaning.

BIG DESIGN UP FRONT   A   Approach to software development that requires a team to produce a complete design before writing any code (see Chapter 17); a.k.a. BDUF. Contrast with *simple design*.

BIG VISIBLE CHARTS   A   Display of the team's *metrics* on charts drawn on large sheets of paper attached to office walls and windows (see Chapter 31).

BUILD DROP FOLDER   V   Directory used for storing *build products* (see Figure 12-1 in Chapter 12); a.k.a. drop folder.

BUILD ENVIRONMENT   Common place for a team to build and test its software that is separate from the team's individual *development environments* and the eventual *production environment* (see Figure 11-1 in Chapter 11); a.k.a. Build Lab, integration environment.

BUILD PROCESS   Steps taken to create *build products.* An Agile team will usually define a number of different build processes, such as its *Integration Build* and its *Daily Build* (see Chapter 11).

BUILD PRODUCTS   Files generated during the execution of a particular *build process*. In VSTS, the build products of a given *Team Foundation Build type* are deposited in its *build drop folder* and may include such things as the executable binary files (.exe, .dll), help system file (.chm), installation program, a build log, and *Build Validation Test* (BVT) results (see Chapter 12).

BUILD VALIDATION TEST   V   Run at the end of the *build process* to confirm that the latest changes to the software work as intended and do not have any undesirable side effects on the existing code (see Chapter 12); a.k.a. BVT.

CASE TOOLS   Computer-aided software engineering tools are usually concerned with helping people to produce Unified Modeling Language (UML) diagrams from which source code can be automatically generated (forward engineering). However, the more sophisticated of these tools may also allow you to generate UML diagrams from the code (reverse engineering) and so are termed *round-trip tools*.

CHANGESET	V	Collection of files in a *developer's* workspace that have been altered since they were last synchronized with the *repository*. A changeset is eventually checked in as a single atomic change to the team's shared code base (see Chapter 9).
CHECK-IN POLICIES	V	Validation performed before a *changeset* is applied to the *repository*. For example, you might not be able to check in your changeset without first adding some notes and linking it to a *work item* (see Chapter 10).
CLOAKED	V	Projects (and directories) in your workspace marked as *cloaked* are effectively ignored when version control commands such as Check-in and Get Latest Version are applied to parent directories (see Figure 9-2 in Chapter 9).
CODE CHURN	V	Metric that reflects the number of lines added, modified, or deleted between one version of a file and another. Code churn data is automatically gathered when people check in their *changesets* and this information is used with other *metrics* to help identify problems.
CODE COVERAGE		Metric that reflects the number of lines of code executed when a test suite is run against the number of lines of code that are not executed, usually expressed as a percentage (see Chapter 16).
CODE SMELL	A	Unquantifiable indication that something is wrong with the organization of some code (see Chapter 15); a.k.a. hunch, smell.
CONTEXT MENU		Menu that opens when you click your right mouse button after selecting an object in a window.
CROSS-FUNCTIONAL TEAM		Group of people with different types of expertise, but who share a common goal so that their objectives align to their team rather than to their department (see the Whole Team practice and Chapter 4).

CUSTOMER	A	Representative of the business who gets to say "what" the product must do. This may be someone who is considered a full-time member of the team or it may be treated simply as a role which is then split among a customer group (see Chapter 4).
CUSTOMER ACCEPTANCE TEST	A	*Functional test* to verify that the software meets a particular business requirement (see Section 7); a.k.a. user acceptance test, acceptance test, customer test.
CUSTOMER STORY	A	Defines a particular feature that has value to the business funding the project. It mainly takes the form of a conversation between the team's *customer* and a *developer,* but it is also summarized on an index card and confirmed by a *customer acceptance test* (see the Stories practice and Chapters 3 and 25); a.k.a. *user story, story.*
DAILY BUILD		*Build process* that runs overnight in order to generate the *build products* required for creating a release of the team's software (see Chapter 11).
DECLARATIVE PROGRAMMING		Style of programming characterized by setting the properties and events associated with objects using a visual editor (see Exercise 17-1 in Chapter 17).
DELTA ENCODING		Records different versions of the same file in terms of their differences rather than as separate files. Therefore, you can recover any version of a file by starting from the original file and then successively applying the required number of deltas (see Chapter 7); a.k.a. delta.
DEPLOYMENT		Activities associated with preparing a *build product* for use in its *production environment,* often expressed in terms of a formal *release process* (see Chapter 28).
DEVELOPER		Technical person who gets to say "how" the needs of the business will be implemented, usually combining the roles of analyst, designer, programmer, and tester.

| DEVELOPMENT ENVIRONMENT | Place for individuals (or pair programmers) to write and test their code that is separate from the team's common *build environment* and the eventual *production environment* (see Figure 11-1 in Chapter 11). |

| DOMAIN EXPERT | Someone with knowledge, skills, and experience in some particular area, usually related to the business funding the project. |

| DOMAIN-SPECIFIC LANGUAGE | Language and terms used by a *domain expert*. Domain-Specific Languages allow domain experts to produce programs expressed in their own domain language rather than having to write them in a computer language such as C# (see Chapter 21); a.k.a. DSL. |

| ELECTIVE PROCESS | Requires people to decide for themselves how best to complete their work. For example, *Extreme Programming* (XP) is an elective process because the team can decide whether it should adopt a particular practice (see Chapter 5). |

| EXTREME PROGRAMMING | A | Practices and values for an Agile team, as described in Kent Beck's book.[1] This approach to software development forms the basis for our book. |

| FUNCTIONAL TEST | Treats the software under test as a black box which exists in a number of defined states, such that for each state, the application of certain inputs should result in particular measurable outputs. In other words, the test seeks to prove that the software conforms to its external specification, that it does what the *customer* intended (see Chapter 22). Contrast with *structural test*. |

| GROUP SECURITY ACCOUNT | M | Grants access rights and privileges to someone performing a particular role. Typically, *user accounts* are made members of the various group security accounts which correspond to their roles in an organization. |

---

1. [XPE2] Beck, Kent, with Cynthia Andres. *Extreme Programming Explained, Second Edition* (Addison-Wesley, 2005).

IDEAL DAY	A	Time available to a *developer* during a normal office day for working on the implementation of *customer stories*, assuming there are no interruptions and everything needed is readily available. Stories are often estimated in ideal days (see Chapter 25).
INCREMENTAL		Reaching some objective by taking a series of small steps rather than taking the big-bang approach of trying to achieve everything in one try. Agile teams usually take an incremental approach to things such as development, *deployment*, and *integration*. See *iterative*, later in this glossary.
INTEGRATED DEVELOPMENT ENVIRONMENT		Collection of tools typically used in the *development environment* that interoperate in such a way that a *developer* can work from a single user interface. For example, Visual Studio integrates a set of tools from various sources so that you can edit files, build programs, and debug programs (see Chapter 1); a.k.a. IDE.
INTEGRATION		Process of adding different people's code changes to the team's shared code base in order to create a tested *build product* that contains everyone's work (see Chapter 11). See *single code base*, later in this glossary.
INTEGRATION BUILD	A	*Build process* run frequently during the day to *integrate* the changes made by different *developers* to the team's shared source code files (see the Ten Minute Build and Continuous Integration practices, and Chapter 11).
ITERATION	A	Fixed period during which the team will completely implement a given collection of *stories* and prepare its software for *deployment*. It typically lasts one or two weeks (see Chapters 3 and 26).

ITERATION BURN RATE	X	Cost of running the project for an *iteration*. Essentially, it is the sum of a project's fixed costs (salary, office rent, etc.) apportioned over the time scale of an iteration (see Chapter 25).
ITERATION PLAN	A	Collection of *stories* that a team intends to complete during the *iteration*. It is often created by pinning *customer story* index cards against specific *developers'* names on an iteration planning board (see Figure 26-2 in Chapter 26).
ITERATION ZERO	A	Preparation work done before a team starts performing fixed-length *iterations*; in other words, setup of the *version control* system, *development environments*, and *build environment* (see *retrospective*, later in this glossary).
ITERATIVE		Repeating a given sequence of steps in order to complete an *incremental* move toward some objective. Agile teams usually take an iterative approach to things such as development and *deployment* (see the Weekly Cycle practice).
MANAGED TEAM		Gives people little responsibility for deciding how or when their work should be done because their activities are controlled by someone in a supervisory role, such as a project manager (see Chapter 4). Contrast with a *self-organizing team*.
METAMODEL		*Meta* comes from the Greek verb *to build,* so a metamodel is a model that allows you to build other models (see Chapter 5).
METHODOLOGY		Common set of methods, practices, and rationale that form the basis of the *processes* adopted by teams in an organization. This provides a general strategic approach for undertaking software projects.

METRICS	A	Measurements made by a team in order to better understand the problems associated with its work. In VSTS, metrics are specifically gathered by a team through the creation of *work items,* but they are also implicitly gathered during activities such as checking files into *version control* (see Chapter 31).
MOTHBALL	A	Process of archiving a project prior to its closure so that it can be restarted at some future date without too much difficulty (see Chapter 3).
MULTIPLE CHECKOUT		Synchronizes updates made by different people to a file held in the team's *repository* so that you are prevented from checking in your changes only when someone else has already checked in a new version of the file before you (see Chapter 7); a.k.a. optimistic locking. Contrast with *single checkout.*
NONFUNCTIONAL REQUIREMENT		Requirement that relates to the operation of the software product rather than to the implementation of some specific feature. Nonfunctional requirements are concerned with matters such as performance, availability, reliability, and so forth; a.k.a. *Quality of Service* (QoS).
PERSONAS		Fictitious characters created to help personify a role that has a need for some particular feature under development. It is often helpful to link a persona to a photograph, as we did when describing the OSPACS team in the Introduction.
PHASED DEVELOPMENT		Divides the work of software development into distinct phases which are completed in a set sequence. For example, the analysis phase leads to the design phase, which leads to the coding phase, and so on.
PREPRODUCTION ENVIRONMENT		Place where the team's *build products* are *deployed* so that they can be subjected to further testing before being moved into the production environment (see Chapter 28).

PRESCRIPTIVE PROCESS		Sequence of activities required to transform a work product from one state into another, described in such detail that there is little possibility for variance from the plan (see Chapter 5). Contrast with an *elective process*.
PROCESS		Common set of methods, practices, and rationale which guide a team during the execution of a project. Typically, a team's process is based on its organization's *methodology*, but is adapted to meet the specific needs of the team and the project. This provides a specific tactical approach for undertaking a particular software project. Contrast with *methodology*.
PROCESS FRAMEWORK	V	Defines the *work item types, Process Guidance,* and so forth for a *Team Project* that is intended to support a particular type of software development *process*. VSTS provides a Process Framework for MSF for Agile and MSF for CMMI, but other frameworks are available from third parties (see Chapter 5); a.k.a. Process Template.
PROCESS GUIDANCE	V	Explains to team members the basic concepts of the *process* they are following as well as giving specific guidance about how they should perform the roles assigned to them. It is provided as a Web site which is part of the *Project Portal* created for a specific *Team Project*.
PROCESS TECHNICIAN	M	Person responsible for ensuring the success of the team's various *build processes* (see Chapter 12); a.k.a. build coordinator, build master, integration coordinator.
PRODUCTION CODE		Code that is intended for eventual *deployment* into the *production environment* as opposed to code that is written to support testing or other aspects of development. Typically, production code is subjected to certain policies and standards set by the team (see Chapter 10).

PRODUCTION ENVIRONMENT		Place where the team's *build products* will eventually be *deployed* and used for business purposes. This environment usually is separate from the team's *development environments* and *build environment* (see Figure 11-1 in Chapter 11).
PROGRAMMER TESTS	A	Structural tests written by a *developer* during test-driven development. In VSTS, these are formed by adding *unit tests* to a Visual Studio Test Project (see Exercise 14-1 in Chapter 14); a.k.a. unit tests.
PROGRAMMING EPISODE	X	Period lasting a couple of hours during which a pair of *developers* will implement some part of a story. Typically, it ends when the developers check in their *changeset* and complete a successful Integration Build (see Chapters 9, 12, and 27).
PROJECT PORTAL	X	Helps a team communicate during the completion of its project by providing the team with an editable Web site. The Project Portal created by VSTS contains areas for people to make announcements and share documents, and it has links to other sites such as the team's *Process Guidance* site (see Chapter 1); a.k.a. project Web site.
QUALITY OF SERVICE	M	A.k.a. QoS. See *nonfunctional requirement*, earlier in this glossary.
REFACTORING	A	Aims to improve the design of existing code without changing its behavior. Refactored code is simpler, easier to understand, and not duplicated elsewhere in the code base (see Chapter 15).
RELEASE PLAN	A	High-level plan showing the number of *iterations* available to the team (as calculated from its *iteration burn rate*) and the individual *stories* scheduled for completion by the end of specific iterations during this period (see Chapter 26).
RELEASE PROCESS		A defined sequence of actions that are taken when *deploying* the team's *build products* into the *production environment* (see Chapter 28).

REPORT SITE	X	Provides reports that analyze the *metrics* generated by the team as it completes its project (see Chapter 31).
REPOSITORY		Central place for holding files. In VSTS it is located in the *Team Foundation Server* Data Tier and is accessed using the *Team Foundation Version Control* system (see Chapter 7).
RETROSPECTIVE	A	Time set aside for the team to reflect so that it might find ways to improve upon its performance. Retrospectives are usually held after the team has reached a significant milestone.
SECURITY GROUP	M	See *group security account,* earlier in this glossary.
SELF-ORGANIZING TEAM		Gives its members full responsibility for deciding how or when their work should be done (see Chapter 4). Contrast with *managed teams.*
SHELVESET	V	Allows people to save their work in the *repository* without it being integrated or shared with others on their team (see Chapter 9); a.k.a. shelve.
SIMPLE DESIGN	A	An approach to software development that defers making many design decisions until after the team has gained a better understanding of the problem by implementing parts of the solution. It aims to provide simple solutions by just solving today's problems without making tomorrow's any worse (see Chapter 17). Contrast with *Big Up Front Design.*
SINGLE CHECKOUT		Synchronizes updates made by different people to a file held in the team's *repository* so that only one person at a time is allowed to check out a file for editing (see Chapter 7); a.k.a. pessimistic locking, strict locking. Contrast with *multiple checkout.*
SMOKE TEST		Collection of tests applied to new *build products* that aim to identify any obvious problems before conducting further testing. Typically, a Smoke Test is performed part automatically and part manually (see Chapter 11).

SOFTWARE PROJECT ENVIRONMENT	X	Provides a set of tools that are controlled from a common interface to help a group of people work together. For example, VSTS integrates version control, team build, planning, metric gathering, reporting, and so on (see Chapter 1); a.k.a. SPE.
SOURCE CONTROL		A.k.a. *version control*, revision control.
SPIKE	A	Time-limited exploration of a particular aspect of the software under development in order to solve a perceived problem or quantify some identified risk; a.k.a. prototype.
STORY	A	A.k.a. *customer story.*
STRUCTURAL TEST		Approach to testing that relies on measuring the response of the software to certain inputs applied at specific points in the code (see Chapter 13). That is to say, the test seeks to prove that the software conforms to its internal specification; it does what the programmer intended.
SYSTEM METAPHOR	A	Unifying concept applied to the software under development in order to help people understand how its parts come together as a whole. For example, a shopping cart may be a good metaphor for a Web site that sells consumer goods (see Chapter 20).
TASK CARD	A	Summary of the work required to implement a *story* produced to help a team plan the *iteration.* These cards are typically written on an index card and then pinned to a task board (see Figure 27-3 in Chapter 27).
TASK POINT	X	Relative measure of the work required to implement a story expressed in terms of a nonlinear scale. Similar measures used by Agile teams for sizing a story include *ideal days* and story points (see Chapter 25).

TEAM FOUNDATION BUILD	V	Components of VSTS concerned with the execution of a *Team Foundation Build type* in order to generate a set of *build products* (see Figure 12-1 in Chapter 12); a.k.a. TFB.
TEAM FOUNDATION BUILD TYPE	V	Special XML file defining the steps of a particular *build process* which is listed in the Team Builds folder of your *Team Project*. Teams usually create a number of build types for different purposes, such as their *Integration Build* and their *Daily Build* (see Chapter 12).
TEAM FOUNDATION SERVER	V	Components of VSTS that form its Application and Data Tiers are installed on one or more physical servers (see Chapter 1); a.k.a. TFS.
TEAM FOUNDATION VERSION CONTROL	V	Components of VSTS which provide a *repository* on the TFS Data Tier as well as the various tools needed to provide *version control* for the files it stores (see Chapter 8); a.k.a. TFVC.
TEAM PROJECT	V	Organizes a collection of people who are collaborating in the development of some software and who share a common schedule. A team will usually create a Team Project at the start of its software project (see Chapter 5).
TEST ENVIRONMENT		Environment that emulates the *production environment* for the purposes of testing a set of *build products*. Typically, the test environment is made part of the *build environment* and is separate from the team's *development environments* and the production environment (see Figure 11-1 in Chapter 11).
TEST LIST	V	Collection of tests that are executed together during a *Build Validation Test* as well as during other forms of testing (see Chapter 12); a.k.a. test suite.
TEST LIST	A	Collection of tests written down as a to-do list which drives the development during TDD (see Table 14-1 in Chapter 14).

TREEVIEW	M	Windows control that displays a collection of items in a treelike structure, such as the list of directories displayed by Windows Explorer.
UNIT TEST		A.k.a. *programmer test.*
USE CASE		Collection of one or more scenarios relating to a particular form of interaction between a user (actor) and the system under development (see Chapter 20). Contrast with *customer stories.*
USER STORY	A	A.k.a. *customer story.*
VELOCITY	A	Measure of the team's progress in terms of the sum of story sizes for stories that were completed during the previous *iteration*. We recommend stories be sized as *task points.*
VERSION CONTROL SYSTEM		Controls changes to a collection of files stored in a *repository* and shared by a team of people. In particular, it resolves any conflicts that arise due to several people altering the same file at the same time (see Chapter 7); a.k.a. *Source Control,* revision control.
VISUAL STUDIO	M	Microsoft's *Integrated Development Environment* (IDE).
VISUAL STUDIO TEAM SYSTEM	V	Microsoft's *Software Project Environment* that is composed of *Team Foundation Server* (Data and Application Tiers), Visual Studio Professional with Team Explorer (Client Tier), *Project Portal* and *Report Sites,* and *Team Foundation Build* (see Chapter 1); a.k.a. VSTS.
WORK ITEM	V	Instance of some metric that the team wants to measure. It is in the *Team Foundation Server* Data Tier.
WORK ITEM TYPE	V	*Work items* are categorized by types such as Task or Bug. The types available to you depend upon the *Process Framework* selected when you start your *Team Project* as well as any additional types added during the course of the project (see Chapters 5 and 6).

WORKSPACE

Set of directories in a *development environment* which are mapped to folders in a *repository* such that a version control command such as Get Latest Version will update the *developer's* workspace with the latest versions of the files in the repository, and a command such as Check-in will update the repository with the changes the developer has made to the files in his or her workspace (see Chapter 9).

Bibliography

The books referenced in the text are listed below under a collection of different headings to help you find other books in the same category. We also include some books that are not referenced in the text but nevertheless may be of interest to you. All these books are on our bookshelves and are heavily marked up with highlighter pen.

> **⬛ NOTE**
>
> You'll find more details about these books on our Web site,[1] as well as other titles that we come across which we think might be of interest to our readers.

Books about Agile Software Development

[AEP] Cohn, Mike. *Agile Estimating and Planning* (Prentice Hall, 2006).

[APM] Schwaber, Ken. *Agile Project Management with Scrum* (Microsoft Press, 2004).

[ASD] Martin, Robert. *Agile Software Development, Principles, Patterns, and Practices* (Prentice Hall, 2003).

[FIT] Mugridge, Rick, and Ward Cunningham. *Fit for Developing Software: Framework for Integrated Tests* (Prentice Hall, 2005).

---

1. This book's Web site (www.BetterSoftwareDevelopment.org).

[LSD] Poppendieck, Mary, and Tom Poppendieck. *Lean Software Development: An Agile Toolkit* (Addison-Wesley, 2003).

[QXP] McBreen, Pete. *Questioning Extreme Programming* (Addison-Wesley, 2003).

[USA] Cohn, Mike. *User Stories Applied: For Agile Software Development* (Addison-Wesley, 2004).

[XC] Cockburn, Alistair. *Crystal Clear: A Human-Powered Methodology for Small Teams* (Addison-Wesley, 2005).

[XPE2] Beck, Kent, with Cynthia Andres. *Extreme Programming Explained: Embrace Change, Second Edition* (Addison-Wesley, 2005).

Coplien, James O., and Neil B. Harrison. *Organizational Patterns of Agile Software Development* (Prentice Hall, 2005).

Succi, Giancarlo, and Michele Marchesi. *Extreme Programming Examined* (Addison-Wesley, 2001).

General Books about Software Development

[AR] Derby, Esther, and Diana Larsen. *Agile Retrospectives: Making Good Teams Great* (Pragmatic Bookshelf, 2006).

[CC] McConnell, Steve. *Code Complete: A Practical Handbook of Software Construction* (Microsoft Press, 1993).

[DM] Yourdon, Edward. *Death March, Second Edition* (Prentice Hall, 2004).

[MMM] Brooks, Frederick P. *The Mythical Man-Month: Essays on Software Engineering, First Edition* (Addison-Wesley, 1975).

[PR] Kerth, Norman. *Project Retrospectives: A Handbook for Team Reviews* (Dorset House, 2001).

[PSP] Humphrey, Watts. *Introduction to the Personal Software Process* (Addison-Wesley, 1997).

[RD] McConnell, Steve. *Rapid Development: Taming Wild Software Schedules, First Edition* (Microsoft Press, 1996).

[SQM] Weinberg, Gerald. *Quality Software Management: Systems Thinking* (Dorset House, 1992).

[UCA] Jacobson, Ivar, et al. *Object-Oriented Software Engineering: A Use Case Driven Approach* (Addison-Wesley, 1992).

[UDP] Jacobson, Ivar, et al. *The Unified Software Development Process* (Addison-Wesley, 1999).

DeMarco, Tom, and Timothy Lister. *Peopleware: Productive Projects and Teams, Second Edition* (Dorset House, 1999).

Hunt, Andrew, and David Thomas. *The Pragmatic Programmer: From Journeyman to Master* (Addison-Wesley, 2000).

Yourdon, Edward. *Rise & Resurrection of the American Programmer* (Prentice Hall, 1996).

Weinberg, Gerald. *The Psychology of Computer Programming* (Van Nostrand Reinhold, 1971).

Books about Software Patterns, Analysis, Design, and Modeling

[AP] Fowler, Martin. *Analysis Patterns: Reusable Object Models* (Addison-Wesley, 1997).

[DOOS] Wirfs-Brock, Rebecca, et al. *Designing Object-Oriented Software* (Prentice Hall, 1990).

[DP] Gamma, Erich, et al. *Design Patterns: Elements of Reusable Object-Oriented Software* (Addison-Wesley, 1995).

[DPE] Shalloway, Alan, and James R. Trott. *Design Patterns Explained: A New Perspective on Object-Oriented Design* (Addison-Wesley, 2002).

[EUML] Ambler, Scott. *Elements of UML 2.0 Style* (Cambridge University Press, 2005).

[OD] Wirfs-Brock, Rebecca, and Alan McKean. *Object Design—Roles, Responsibilities, and Collaborations* (Addison-Wesley, 2003)

[OOSE] Jacobson, Ivar, et al. *Object-Oriented Software Engineering: A Use Case Driven Approach* (Addison-Wesley, 1992).

[SCM] Berczuk, Stephen P., with Brad Appleton. *Software Configuration Management Patterns: Effective Teamwork, Practical Integration* (Addison-Wesley, 2003).

[TOP] Ambler, Scott. *The Object Primer: Agile Model-Driven Development with UML 2.0, Third Edition* (Cambridge University Press, 2004).

[UMLD] Fowler, Martin, and Kendall Scott. *UML Distilled: A Brief Guide to the Standard Object Modeling Language, Third Edition* (Addison-Wesley, 2004).

Greenfield, Jack, et al. *Software Factories: Assembling Applications with Patterns, Models, Frameworks, and Tools* (Wiley, 2004).

Books about Testing

[AST] Myers, Glenford J., et al. *The Art of Software Testing, Second Edition* (John Wiley & Sons, 2004).

[BBT] Beizer, Boris. *Black-Box Testing* (John Wiley & Sons, 1995).

[TOOS] Binder, Robert. *Testing Object-Oriented Systems: Models, Patterns and Tools* (Addison-Wesley, 2000).

Books about Refactoring and Test-Driven Development

[PUT] Hunt, Andy, and Dave Thomas. *Pragmatic Unit Testing with NUnit* (Pragmatic Programmers, 2004).

[R2P] Kerievsky, Joshua. *Refactoring to Patterns* (Addison-Wesley, 2005).

[RDB] Ambler, Scott W., and Pramod J. Sadalage. *Refactoring Databases: Evolutionary Database Design* (Addison-Wesley, 2006).

[RIDEC] Fowler, Martin, et al. *Refactoring: Improving the Design of Existing Code* (Addison-Wesley, 1999).

[TDDE] Beck, Kent. *Test-Driven Development by Example* (Addison-Wesley, 2003).

[TDDM] Newkirk, James W., and Alexei A. Vorontsov. *Test-Driven Development in Microsoft .NET* (Microsoft Press, 2004).

[TDPG] Astels, David. *Test-Driven Development: A Practical Guide* (Prentice Hall, 2004).

[XNET] Roodyn, Neil. *Extreme .NET: Introducing Extreme Programming Techniques to .NET Developers* (Addison-Wesley, 2005).

[XPAC] Jeffries, Ron. *Extreme Programming Adventures in C#* (Microsoft Press, 2004).

Wake, William. *Refactoring Workbook* (Addison-Wesley, 2004).

Books about C# Programming and .NET

Thai, Thuan, and Hoang Q. Lam. *.NET Framework Essentials: Introducing the .NET Framework* (O'Reilly, 2001).

[ADO2] Johnson, Glenn. *ADO.NET 2.0 Applications* (Microsoft Press, 2006).

[CCB] Hilyard, Jay, and Stephen Tielhet. *C# Cookbook* (O'Reilly, 2004).

[CPC] Jones, Allen. *C# Programmer's Cookbook* (Microsoft Press, 2004).

[EC#] Wagner, Bill. *Effective C#* (Addison-Wesley, 2005).

[PWF] Petzold, Charles. *Programming Microsoft Windows Forms* (Microsoft Press, 2005).

Albahari, Ben, et al. *C# Essentials: Programming the .NET Framework, Second Edition* (O'Reilly, 2002).

Sestoft, Peter, and Henrik I. Hansen. *C# Precisely* (MIT Press, 2004).

Hejlsberg, Anders, et al. *The C# Programming Language, Second Edition* (Addison-Wesley, 2006).

Roodyn, Neil. *Extreme .NET: Introducing Extreme Programming Techniques to .NET Developers* (Addison-Wesley, 2005).

Liberty, Jesse. *Programming in C#: Building .NET Applications* (O'Reilly, 2001).

Liberty, Jesse. *Visual C# 2005: A Developer's Notebook* (O'Reilly, 2005).

Sells, Chris. *Windows Forms Programming in C#* (Addison-Wesley, 2004).

Books about Visual Studio and VSTS

[SETS] Guckenheimer, Sam, and Juan Perez. *Software Engineering with Microsoft Visual Studio Team System* (Addison-Wesley, 2006).

[VSTS] Hundhausen, Richard. *Working with Microsoft Visual Studio Team System* (Microsoft Press, 2005).

Grimes, Richard. *Developing Applications with Visual Studio .NET* (Addison-Wesley, 2002).

Skibo, Craig, et al. *Working with Visual Studio 2005* (Microsoft Press, 2006).

Books about Other Specific Products

[OIW] Baker, Bob. *The Official InstallShield for Windows Installer Developer's Guide* (M&T Books, 2001).

[ECOM] Box, Don. *Essential COM* (Addison-Wesley, 1998).

[SCD] Noyes, Brian. *Smart Client Deployment with ClickOnce* (Addison-Wesley, 2007).

[SQLRS] Larson, Brian. *Microsoft SQL Server 2005 Reporting Services 2005* (McGraw-Hill Osborne, 2005).

[TYSP] Spence, Colin, and Michael Noel. *Teach Yourself Microsoft SharePoint 2003 in 10 Minutes* (SAMS, 2004).

Hillier, Scot P. *Microsoft SharePoint: Building Office 2003 Solutions* (Apress, 2004).

Landrum, Rodney, and Walter J. Voytek II. *Pro SQL Server 2005 Reporting Services* (Apress, 2006).

[PPA] Clark, Mike. *Pragmatic Project Automation: How to Build, Deploy and Monitor Java Applications* (The Pragmatic Bookshelf, 2004).

Petzold, Charles. *Programming Windows Version 3, Second Edition* (Microsoft Press, 1990).

General Books about Agile Concepts

[DF6S] Chowdhury, Subir. *Design for Six Sigma* (Dearborn Trade Pub., 2002).

[FT] Manns, Mary Lynn, and Linda Rising. *Fearless Change: Patterns for Introducing New Ideas* (Addison-Wesley, 2005).

[LEANT] Womack, James, and Daniel Jones. *Lean Thinking: Banish Waste and Create Wealth in Your Corporation* (Simon & Schuster, 2003).

[MTDF] Reinertsen, Donald. *Managing the Design Factory: A Product Developer's Toolkit* (Simon & Schuster, 1997).

[SLAK] DeMarco, Tom. *Slack: Getting Past Burnout, Busywork, and the Myth of Total Efficiency* (Broadway Books, 2002).

[TPS] Ohno, Taiichi. *Toyota Production System: Beyond Large-Scale Production* (Productivity Press, 1988).

[WWB] DeMarco, Tom, and Timothy Lister. *Waltzing with Bears: Managing Risk on Software Projects, First Edition* (Dorset House, 2003).

> **▪ TIP**
>
> When joining a new team, take a look at the team's bookshelves. What sorts of books and magazines does the team have? Are they up-to-date and obviously well read, or are they old but still pristine? A team's books will tell you a lot about the people you're going to work with.

Resources

We have organized the Web site addresses we provided throughout the book into the following two tables. Table R-1 lists product Web sites and Table R-2 lists information Web sites. The book's Web site, www.BetterSoftwareDevelopment.org, lists additional resources which we will update from time to time.

TABLE R-1: Product Web Sites

Description	URL	Chapter(s)
AVIcode: Intercept Studio 3	www.avicode.com	28
IBM: Rational Rose	www.ibm.com/software/rational	19, 30
Macrovision: Admin Studio	www.macrovision.com/products/flexnet_adminstudio	28
Macrovision: InstallShield	www.macrovision.com/products/flexnet_installshield	28
Macrovision: InstallShield Collaboration	www.macrovision.com/products/flexnet_installshield/collaboration	29
Macrovision: InstallShield evaluation	www.macrovision.com/downloads	Preface
Macrovision: SDM	www.macrovision.com/sdm	30
Microsoft: .NET Framework	http://msdn.microsoft.com/netframework	1
Microsoft: BizTalk	www.microsoft.com/biztalk	30
Microsoft: ClickOnce	http://msdn.microsoft.com/clickonce	29
Microsoft: DSI	www.microsoft.com/windowsserversystems/dsi	30
Microsoft: SMS	www.microsoft.com/smserver	28, 29, 30

Description	URL	Chapter(s)
Microsoft: SysInternals PsExec	www.microsoft.com/technet/sysinternals/utilities/psexec.mspx	24
Microsoft: TFS Administrators Guide	http://go.microsoft.com/fwlink/?LinkID=52459	5, 7
Microsoft: TFS Installation Guide	http://go.microsoft.com/fwlink/?LinkId=40042	1, 12, Appendix A
Microsoft: Virtual PC 2004	www.microsoft.com/windows/virtualpc	12, 28, Appendix A
Microsoft: Visual SourceSafe 2005	http://msdn.microsoft.com/vstudio/products	7
Microsoft: Visual Studio	http://msdn.microsoft.com/vstudio	1
Microsoft: Visual Studio 2005 SDK	http://msdn.microsoft.com/vstudio/extend/	21
Microsoft: VSTS evaluation	http://msdn.microsoft.com/teamsystem	Preface, Appendix A
Microsoft: Windows SharePoint Services 2.0 with SP2	http://go.microsoft.com/fwlink/?LinkID=55087	Appendix A
Open source: CVS source control tool	http://sourceforge.net/docs/E04/	7
Open source: Eclipse project	www.eclipse.org	7

Continues

TABLE R-1: *Continued*

Description	URL	Chapter(s)
Open source: FIT	http://fit.c2.com	Preface, 22
Open source: FitNesse	www.fitnesse.org	22, 23
Open source: MSF4XP	www.msf4xp.org	5, 31
Open source: NUnit Web site	www.nunit.org	1, 13, 15
Open source: OSPACS	www.ospacs.org	(all)
Open source: Subversion source control tool	http://subversion.tigris.org	7
Open source: WiX (Windows Installer XML)	http://wix.sourceforge.net	28
Roxio: DVD Creator	www.roxio.com	Appendix A
Sun Microsystems: Java	http://java.sun.com	20
Teamprise: SourceGear access to TFS from Eclipse	www.teamprise.com	7

TABLE R-2: Information Web Sites

Description	URL	Chapter(s)
Agile Alliance	www.agilealliance.org	2
Agile Alliance—user groups listed under Resources	www.agilealliance.com	Introduction
Agile communication	www.agilemodeling.com/essays/communication.htm	2
Agile Manifesto	www.agilemanifesto.org	2
Agile Modeling Web site	www.agilemodeling.com	18
Big design upfront	http://xp.c2.com/BigDesignUpFront.html	3
Big Visible Charts	www.xprogramming.com/xpmag/BigVisibleCharts.htm	31
C# Language reference: ICollection	http://msdn.microsoft.com	15
Card, Conversation, Confirmation	www.xprogramming.com	3, 25
Coding Style Guidelines	www.ambysoft.com/essays/codingGuidelines.html	7
Cost of Change	www.agilemodeling.com/essays/costOfChange.htm	3
Extreme Programming Group	http://tech.groups.yahoo.com/group/extremeprogramming	Appendix C

Continues

TABLE R-2: *Continued*

Description	URL	Chapter(s)
Full Life Cycle Object-Oriented Testing	www.ambysoft.com/essays/floot.html	11
FxCop Rules Bug Slayer (*MSDN Magazine*, Sept. 2004)	http://msdn.microsoft.com/msdnmag	10
Generalizing Specialists	www.agilemodeling.com/essays	4
Get Your Customers Involved in the Testing Process (*MSDN Magazine*, Feb. 2005)	http://msdn.microsoft.com/msdnmag	22
Group Size	www.dmu.ac.uk/~jamesa/teaching/group_size.htm	4
INVEST in Good Stories	http://xp123.com/xplor/xp0308/index.shtml	25
Laboratory for Teaching Object-Oriented Thinking	http://c2.com/doc/oopsla89/paper.html	20
Language Workbenches: The Killer-App for DSL	www.martinfowler.com	21
MDA: Object Management Group	www.omg.org/mda	18
Microsoft Solution Framework	www.microsoft.com/technet/itsolutions/msf	5

Description	URL	Chapter(s)
Microsoft: C# Programmer Reference	http://msdn.microsoft.com	14
Microsoft: Patterns & Practices Initiative	http://msdn.microsoft.com/practices	21, 28
Migrating from Visual SourceSafe	http://msdn.microsoft.com/teamsystem	8
MSDN Magazine Web site	http://msdn.microsoft.com/msdnmag	Introduction
MSF for XP	www.msf4xp.org	5
Object Management Group	www.omg.org	19
Open source Microsoft projects and code examples	www.codeproject.com	1
PACS: general information	www.auntminnie.com	Introduction
Patterns	http://c2.com/cgi/wiki?search=patterns; www.dofactory.com	21
Program Customized Testing Environments (*MSDN Magazine*, Aug. 2004)	http://msdn.microsoft.com/msdnmag	11
Rapid Abstract Prototyping	www.foruse.com	20

Continues

TABLE R-2: *Continued*

Description	URL	Chapter(s)
Retrospective Facilitators	http://finance.groups.yahoo.com/group/retrospectives	Retrospective
Roadmap to Agility	www.agilealliance.org/resources	2
The Free Lunch Is Over	www.gotw.ca/publications/concurrency-ddj.htm	Appendix B
UML Specification	www.uml.org	19
Visual Studio Team System Licensing White Paper	http://msdn.microsoft.com/teamsystem, Nov. 2005	Appendix B
VSTS Licensing White Paper (Nov. 2005)	www.microsoft.com/teamsystem	24
What is CMMI?	www.sei.cmu.edu/cmmi/general/general.html	5
What is Software Design?	www.bleading-edge.com	4, 32

Index

A

Account setup, 724–725
Action fixtures, 470–476
Action tables, 498
Active Bugs queries, 670
Activity diagrams, 414
Administrator rights
  ClickOnce, 620
  InstallShield, 606
  Software installation, 619
  Windows Installer, 603
Agile Alliance, 36–37
Agile Model-Driven Development (AMDD),
  361, 372–374
Agile Modeling, 357, 361
  practices, 364–365
  principles, 363–364
  values, 363
Agile teams, 65
  building and integrating by, 214
  inappropriate work for, 69–70
  nature of, 65–66
  roles
    associated, 75–76
    customer, 70–72
    developer, 72–73
  self-organizing, 68
  size, 68–69
Agile values
  Agile Alliance, 36–37
  tools and values, 33–35

Alexander, Christopher, 416
Ambler, Scott
  Agile Modeling, 363, 366
  AMDD, 372
  Coding Guidelines, 132, 195
  Refactoring Databases, 592
  UML, 392
AMDD (Agile Model-Driven Development),
  361, 372–374
Analysis Class diagrams, 399–401
Analysis Patterns, 419–420
Appleton, Brad, 144
Application Designer (AD) tool, 408, 628, 638
  application of, 648
  description, 26
  diagrams
    creating, 638–647
    System Designer diagrams from,
      649–651
  settings and constraints, 648
Applications architect role, 75
Apply Modeling Standards practice, 366
Apply Patterns Gently practice, 366, 422
Architects
  on Agile teams, 406
  developers as, 72–73
  PC licensing issues, 745–746
Architectural models, 368, 405–406
  evolving, 408–410
  skeletal, 406–407
  system metaphor for, 411
Associated roles, 75–76

Atherton, James, 69
Atomic check-in, 134

B

Backups
 shared folders for, 128
 Team Foundation Server version control, 170–171
Bad smells in code, 422
Baselines, 160
 checking in and labeling, 164–166
 configuration management, 142–143
BDUF. See Big Design Up Front
Beck, Kent, 37, 64
 on code duplication, 267
 on code problems, 422
 on costs, 541
 on Domain Modeling, 396
 on pattern languages, 416
 on planning, 530
 on software design, 348
Berczuk, Stephen P., 144
Big-bang deployment, 590
Big Design Up Front (BDUF) thinking, 63, 348, 369, 372
Big Visible Charts (BVCs), 673–674
Binder, Robert
 on test cases, 270, 279
 on Testing Object-Oriented Systems, 221
BisSubscribe tool, 246
Black-box testing, 219–220
Booch, Grady, 285, 377
Bottom up approach
 tasks planning, 567
 test-driven development, 268
Box, Don, 160
Branching in version control, 138–139, 146, 185–187
Brooks, Frederick, 34, 521
Brown-bag sessions, 568
Budgets
 in plan control, 539
 in project life cycle, 58
 in story estimates, 520–521
Bugs
 queries, 670–671
 reports, 554–555, 594
 tasks, 532
 work items, 96, 548

Build Labs, 213
 customer tests in, 482–486
 licensing issues, 747–748
Build Validation Tests (BVTs), 227, 233–235, 465, 481
Builds
 managing, 245
  identification, names, 247–248
  notifications, 246
  reports, 248–249, 671
 notes for, 158
 daily builds, 227–228
 integration builds, 225–227
 local builds, 222–223
 test cycles, 222–228
Build Drop folder, 215
Business analysts role, 71
Buy or build decisions for tools, 34
BVCs. See Big Visible Charts
BVTs. See Build Validation Tests

C

Capability Maturity Model Integration (CMMI), 100–101, 103–104
Changesets, 134–135
Check in, 130
 constraints, 193–194
 policies
  overriding, 201–203
  static code analysis as, 198–200
 in version control systems, 134
 for work items and builds, 146
 Items settings, 169
Check-out, 129
 in version control systems, 129
 only files, 192–193
Class Designer tool, 23
 language workbenches, 428
 for modeling, 370, 385–389
Class diagrams, 156
 Class Designer for, 388
 for structural models, 412
 UML, 377–382
 Visio for Enterprise Architects for, 389
Classes
 in CRC, 397
 dependencies, 251–253
 names, 198, 400–401
 testing, 222
 for user interface design, 347

ClickOnce technology, 620
    basic concepts, 621
    publishing and deploying, 622–624
    suitable applications for, 620–621
Client parts of VSTS, 17
    Team Explorer window, 20–22
    Visual Studio Professional, 18–19
Coaching
    in Agile teams, 75
    in storytest-driven development, 457
Cockburn, Alistair, 404
Code
    branching, 138–139, 146, 185–187
    coverage, 325–330
    duplication, 140
    patterns in, 420
    standards, 132, 195, 200–201
Code Analyzer tool, 331
Code and Tests practice, 155–156
Code Coverage tool, 24–25, 326–330
Coding Guidelines, 132, 195
Cohn, Mike, 515, 519
Collaborations
    CRC, 398–399
    pair programming, 38
    requirements gathering, 619
Column fixtures, 460–464
Communication
    as Agile value
        Agile development, 121
        Extreme Programming, 39–40
Component-based development, 425
Component diagrams
    in architectural models, 409
    in structural models, 412
Components
    distributed, 626
    factories for, 429–430
    Installation Designer view settings,
        609–610
    Reusable, 425, 429–430
    in Windows Installer, 598–599, 601
Conflicts in version control, 182–183
Connecting to team projects, 93–94
Constantine, Larry, 39, 402
Constraints
    Application Designer, 648
    check-in, 193–194

Logical Datacenter Designer, 634–635
    System Designer, 652
Consultant role, 75
Consumer endpoints, 641–642
Continuous integration, 134, 356
Continuous Integration practice, 132, 224
Contributors, 82
Cost estimation for customer stories, 519–521
Courage as Agile value
    Agile development, 122
    Extreme Programming, 41
CRC (Class, Responsibilities, and
        Collaborations), 396
Create Several Models in Parallel practice,
        412
Cross-functional teams, 67
CruiseControl.NET tool, 224
Crystal Clear, 404
Cunningham, Ward
    and CRC, 396
    and Extreme Programming, 37
    and FIT, 445, 478
    on pattern languages, 416
Customer stories, 404–405, 511–512
    completing, 563
    estimating, 516–521
    in Extreme Programming, 59–61, 63
    generating, 514–515
    life cycle, 541–542
    overview, 512
    prioritizing, 521–525
    for specifying requirements, 55–57
    Stories practice, 513–514
    tasks in, 288–289
    for Test-First Programming, 287–289
Customer Acceptance tests, 439–440
    automated, 487–491
    in Build Lab, 482–486
    FIT. *See* Framework for Integrated Test
        (FIT)
    fixtures in
        action, 472–476
        column, 461–464
        row, 466–470
    introducing to teams, 491–498
    overview, 443
    planning, 562
    storytest-driven development, 454–458

Customers
   in Agile teams, 70–72
   in Agile software development, 36
   in Six Sigma, 691
   identifying, 76
   pulling value, 686
CVS version control systems, 133

D

Daily Builds, 224, 227–228
   in customer testing, 457
   in project management, 566
   Team Foundation Builds, 239–240
Daily Deployment practice, 583–585
Data Definition Language (DDL) scripts, 390
Data deployment, 591–592
Data migration, 583
Databases
   connection strings to, 643
   Model diagrams, 390
   with Windows Installer, 600–602
Death-march projects, 508
Deleting
   build products, 243–244
   team projects, 87
Deltas, 135
DeMarco, Tom, 41, 73
Dependencies
   in building, 251–253
   in class diagrams, 379
   in prioritizing stories, 524–525
Depict Models Simply practice, 367
Deployment, 577–578
   with ClickOnce technology, 622–624
   data, 591–592
   first iteration, 589
   Incremental Deployment practice, 590–591
   Installation programs. *See* Installation
      programs
   bottlenecks in, 585–586
   Daily Deployment practice, 583–585
   deployment teams in, 586–587
   release process, 582–584
   monitoring, 592–594
   preparing for, 587–592
   stubs and scaffolding in, 590–591
Deployment Designer (DD) tool, 628, 653
   application of, 658
   description, 26

   diagrams, 653–657
   properties, 655
Derby, Esther, 697
Design
   Agile teams for, 66–68
   for building and integrating, 214
   for patterns, 420
   for Six Sigma, 691–692
   Patterns, 416–417, 420, 423
Developers
   in Agile teams, 72–73
   identifying, 76
   licensing issues, 743–745
Development phases, 54–55
Development environment, 215
Diagrams
   Analysis Class, 399–401
   Application Designer, 638–647
   class, 156
      Class Designer for, 388
      for structural models, 412
      UML, 377–382
      Visio for Enterprise Architects for, 389
   class package, 409
   Deployment Designer, 653–657
   for models
      dynamic, 413–414
      free-form, 375–376, 407–410
      structural, 412–413
      tips, 391–392
      UML, 377–385
   System Designer, 649–652
Dim files
   preparing, 614–617
   working with, 618
Directories
   adding to version control, 160–164
   mapping, 154, 177–178, 180
   in Windows Installer, 601
Discard Temporary Models practice, 366, 368
Distributed System Designers (DSDs), 628–629
Distributed systems, 625
   architecture, 625–629
   Deployment Designer, 653–658
DLL Hell, 160
Documents
   in project management, 551–554
   in Team Explorer window, 20
   version control for, 156–158

Documents folder, 156–158, 552
Domain Modeling, 396–401
Domain-Specific Languages (DSLs), 66, 192
    language workbenches for, 427–429
    software factories, 429–430
Drop Site folder, 216, 243
DSDM (Dynamic Systems Development
    Method), 522
DSDs (Distributed System Designers),
    628–629
DSI (Dynamic Systems Initiative), 627
Dynamic Code Analyzer tool, 24, 331,
    334–337
Dynamic models, 413–414
Dynamic Scan tool, 610

E

Eclipse support, 147
Economics of software development,
    688–690
Elective process, 102
End user role, 71
Energized Work practice, 323–324
Enterprise architect role, 75
Estimating, 507–508
    in project management, 567
    stories, 515–516
        absolute vs. relative values, 517–518
        budgeting in, 521
        relative estimate scales, 519
        size, 516–517
        task points for, 519–520
Evolving
    architectural models, 408–410
    legacy code, 422–424
Executive role in Agile teams, 75
Exporting process templates, 112–113
Extending VSTS, 30–31
Extracting data from Team Foundation
    Server, 674–682
Extreme Programming (XP), 37, 57–58
    Agile values in
        communication, 39–40
        courage, 41
        feedback, 40–41
        respect, 43
        simplicity, 42–43
    project life cycle in, 58
    transition to, 709–711

Facade Pattern
    evolving legacy code with, 422–424
    information for, 417–419
Facilitators for retrospectives, 698
Failing tests
    fixing, 296–299
    writing, 272–273
Features
    vs. tasks, 514, 539, 567
    Windows Installer, 598–601
Feedback
    in Agile, 55
    as Agile value
        Agile development, 121
        Extreme Programming, 40–41
Files
    access to, 192–193
    adding to version control, 160–164
First iteration, 589
FIT. *See* Framework for Integrated Test (FIT)
FitNesse IDE, 454
FLEXnet AdminStudio, 587
Folders
    access to, 192–193
    for repositories, 150–151
    shared, 128–129
Forward-engineering, 647
Fowler, Martin
    and Extreme Programming, 37
    on language workbenches, 427–428
    on patterns, 415, 419–420, 422
    on refactoring, 280–281, 312, 424
    Remove the Middle Man pattern, 318
    UML Distilled, 377, 392
Framework for Integrated Test (FIT)
    fixtures, 459
        action, 470–476
        column, 460–464
        custom, 476–479
        row, 465–470
        standard, 459–460
    installing and running, 447–453
    overview, 445–447
    with storytest-driven development, 454–458
    with Team Foundation Build, 481
        automated customer tests, 487–491
        customer test introduction, 491–498
        customer tests in Build Lab, 482–486
    test organization, 453–454

Free-form diagrams
    for models, 375–376
    for skeletal architectural models, 407–410
Friendly Assemblies, 285
Functional components, 16
Functional tests, 219–220, 447
FxCop program, 196, 200

G

Gamma, Erich, 37, 416
Generalizing specialists, 68
Generating business value, 683
    lean thinking in, 683–688
    linking to other process improvement
        initiatives, 690–692
    software development economics, 688–690
Generic tests
    Adapter tool, 25
    with MSTest, 486
    wrapping FIT in, 482–485
Glass box testing, 220
Gold-plating code, 684–685
Groups
    for modeling, 366–369
    for projects, 82
Guckenheimer, Sam
    on bugs, 532, 555
    and Extreme Programming, 58
    on release process, 458
    on reports, 682
    on value, 522

H

Hacking vs. Extreme Programming, 62–63
Helm, Richard, 416
Hierarchy of iterations, 547
Horizontal markets, 426–427
Hot-desk area, 756–758
Humility, 363

I

Ideal days, 525
Identification of builds, 247–248
IDEs (Integrated Development
    Environments), 16
    Visual Studio, 18
    InstallShield, 605–613

Idioms, 420
Implementation models, 411–412
    dynamic, 413–414
    sequence diagrams in, 382
    structural, 412–413
Importing
    datacenter settings, 636–637
    process templates, 114
    source files, 166
Incremental builds, 245, 250–251
Incremental Deployment practice, 590–591
Incremental Design practice, 371–372
Individuals
    in Agile software development, 36
    with Six Sigma, 692
    Individuality, 760
Informative Workspace practice, 673
Infrastructure architect role, 75
Installation Designer view, 604, 608–611
Installation programs, 597
    ClickOnce technology, 620
        basic concepts, 621
        publishing and deploying, 622–624
        suitable applications for, 620–621
    developing, 613–614
    Dim files for, 617–618
    InstallShield, 604–613
    Windows Installer, 597–598
        basic concepts, 598–600
        operation, 600–602
        security for, 602–604
Installer role, 71
Installing third-party libraries, 158–159
InstallShield, 605–613
InstallShield Collaboration tool, 614–617
Instrumentation for performance, 331–332
Integration. *See also* Building and
    integrating
Interaction designer role, 71
INVEST acronym, 515
Iterate to Another Artifact practice, 412
Iteration Burn rate, 520–521
Iteration Planning Boards, 561
Iteration zero
    AMDD in, 373
    on timelines, 705
    version control in, 171

Iterations
   in Agile Modeling, 365
   in Extreme Programming
      and increments, 58–59
      productional-quality code from, 60–61
      and release cycles, 59–60
   fixed periods for, 514
   planning life cycle, 556–558, 565–566
   plans, 534–535
   in project management, 568
   in project structure, 546–547

J

Jacobson, Ivar, 57, 404
Jeffries, Ron
   on customer stories, 56
   and Extreme Programming, 37
Johnson, Ralph, 416
Jones, Allen, 420
Jones, Daniel, 683

K

Kerievsky, Joshua, 281, 420, 423
Kerth, Norman, 697

L

Labels
   baselines, 164–166
   favorites, 315
   version control, 138–139, 146, 184–185
Language workbenches, 427–429
Languages, pattern, 416–417
Larsen, Diana, 697
Lean thinking, 36, 683–684
   customs in, 686
   perfection seeking in, 686–687
   specifying value in, 684
   value flow in, 685–686
   value stream in, 684–685
Legacy code, evolving, 422–424
Libraries
   installing, 158–159
   performance analysis, 335–337
Licensing issues
   architect PC, 745–746
   BuildLab PC, 747–748
   developer PCs, 743–745
   multiprocessor PCs and multicore
      processors, 749

pair programming, 745
Primary Domain Controller, 739–740
standby TFS, 748
Team Foundation Server, 740–742
team size, 749–750
tester PC, 746–747
Life cycles
   customer stories, 541–542
   planning. *See* Planning life cycle
Lists
   for modeling in pairs, 371
   of tests, 454
      in test-driven development, 269
      in Test-First Programming, 278
Load Testing tool, 25
Local builds, 185, 222–223, 232
Lock and Merge feature, 136–138, 146
Locking graphics files, 183
Lockwood, Lucy, 402
Logical Data Model (LDM) diagrams, 413
Logical Datacenter Designer (LDD) tool,
      628–629
   applications of, 637–638
   description, 26
   diagrams, 633
   properties, settings, and constraints for,
      634–637
   working with, 629–632

M

Manifesto of the Agile Alliance, 529
Manual Testing tool, 25
Mapping directories, 154, 177–178, 180
MDA (Model-Driven Architecture), 372
Mentor role, 73
Merging in version control, 136–138, 167,
      180–183
Metaphors for architectural models, 411
Metrics for process frameworks, 107–110
Microsoft Solutions Framework (MSF), 95
   activities in, 97
   MSF for Agile, 85–86, 95, 102–104
   MSF for CMMI, 95, 100–101, 103–104
   MSF for XP, 102–104
   roles in, 97
   tracks and governance checkpoints in,
      98–100
   work items in, 96–97
Mining for gold, 701, 703–704, 708–709

Model-Driven Architecture (MDA), 372
Models, 357
  Agile. *See* Agile Modeling (AG)
  architectural, 368, 405–406
    evolving, 408–410
    skeletal, 406–407
    system metaphor for, 411
  Class Designer for, 385–389
  Domain Modeling, 396–401
  free-form diagrams for, 375–376
  implementation, 411–412
    dynamic, 413–414
    sequence diagrams, 382
    structural, 412–413
  introduction, 361–362
  UML diagrams, 377
    class, 377–382
    sequence, 382–385
  use case, 403–404
  user interface, 401–403
  Visio for Enterprise Architects for,
    389–390
Moore, Geoffrey, 14
MoSCoW rules, 522
Mothballing projects, 61
MSBuild engine, 229–232
MSF. *See* Microsoft Solutions Framework
  (MSF)
MSF4XP process template, 551
MSTest, 486
Mugridge, Rick, 478
Multiple-checkout approach, 136–138, 167
Multiplicity indicators, 380
Myers, Glen, 279

N

Namespaces for stubs and scaffolding, 591
Naming Rules list, 199
Network diagrams, 409–410
Notes
  for builds, 158
  in class diagrams, 380
  in Document folder, 157
Notifications, build, 246
Non-functional requirement, 220
Nouns
  for class names, 401
  in CRC, 397
Noyes, Brain, 622
NUnit tool, 24, 267

O

Object diagrams, 412
Object Management Group, 377
Object Modeling Technique (OMT), 377
Object Test Bench tool, 388
Objects in sequence diagrams, 383–384
Office space and layout, 753
OLAP database, 675, 677–678
OMT (Object Modeling Technique), 377
One-click installs, 619–624
One-time plans, 528
Open and Honest Communication principle,
  366
Optimistic locking, 136–138
Ordered Test Adapter tool, 25
OSPACS team, 1
  background, 1–2
  organizational structure and personas,
    2–5
  road map for, 6–8
Overriding check-in policies, 201–203

P

Package dependencies, 251–253
Package diagrams, 413
Pair programming practice, 38
Pair programming, 37–39, 43
  in Agile Modeling, 370–371
  desks for, 755
  for implementation models, 411–412
  licensing issues, 745
  in Shared Code practice, 132
  in Test-Driven Development, 356
Parallel models, 365
Pascal, Blaise, 348
Patch Packages (.msp), 602
PATH environment variable, 449, 723
Pattern-happy condition, 421
Patterns, 415
  Domain-Specific Languages for, 426–430
  example, 417–419
  implementation, 424–426
  languages, 416–417
  sources, 419–421
  working with, 421–424
Patterns & Practices initiative, 593
Performance analysis, 331
  build configuration for, 335
  example profiling session, 332–334
  instrumentation for, 332

sampling for, 332
system performance, 337
Permissions
build, 92
files and folders, 192–193
projects, 82
Team Foundation Build, 235–236
workspaces, 92–93
Phased development processes, 54–55
Plans and planning, 507–508, 527
controlling, 538–542
customer tests, 562
planning life cycle, 556
nature of, 527–530
rate of progress measures, 529–530
repeated execution vs. one-time, 528
time scales in, 530–538
Plug-ins
process templates, 111–112
Visual Studio source control selections,
168
Policies for source code
coding standards in, 195
overriding, 201–203
rules updating for, 201
static code analysis for, 196–200
Poppendieck, Mary, 528–529
Practices in Agile Modeling, 364–365
Preproduction Environment, 585
Principles in Agile Modeling, 363–364
Prioritizing, 507–508
stories, 521–522, 567
business risk in, 522–523
dependencies in, 524–525
technical risk in, 523
value in, 522
Problem analysis, 687–688
Process frameworks, 107
description, 23
metrics for, 107–110
process improvement, 110–116
Process Guidance, 23, 84–85
Process technician role
build management, 245
for developers, 72
Process templates, 86
changing, 115
importing and exporting, 112–114
Product manager role, 71

Production environment, 592–594
Programmer role for developers, 72
Programmer tests, 352
Programming episodes, 60, 222, 560
Project Administrators, 82, 88
Project managers
responsibilities, 77
roles, 75
Project Portal, 27–28, 546, 551–552
for projects, 83–84, 90–91
for version control, 157
templates for, 112
Projects and project management, 545–546
documents in, 551–554
planning life cycle. See Planning life cycle
reports in, 554–555
structure, 82, 546–547
Prove It with Code practice, 373
Provider endpoints, 641–643
Proxy endpoints, 650–651
Publishing
with ClickOnce technology, 622–624
in remote deployment, 603
Purchaser role, 71
Putman, David, 690

Q
Quality
from Extreme Programming, 60–61
for models, 364
in plan control, 539, 541
Quality Indicators queries, 671
Quality of Service (QoS) tests, 220–221
Quarterly Cycle practice, 538
Queries
adding, 109–110
in project management, 547–551
for projects, 83
standard, 670–672
Queries folder, 546
Query Builder, 679

R
Rational Unified Process (RUP), 54, 377
RDL (Report Definition Language), 675, 681
Readers, 82, 88
Real Customer Involvement practice, 43, 456
Reeves, Jack, 66, 347, 686

Refactoring, 127, 281, 303, 312, 318, 420, 422, 424
    collection types in, 319–322
    Remove the Middle Man pattern, 318–319
    work breaks in, 322–323
    opportunities, 316–317
    for patterns, 420
    tasks for, 561
    in Test-First Programming, 280–281, 299–300
Refactoring Databases, 592
Refactoring to Patterns, 420
Regression testing, 219
Reinertsen, Donald, 66, 528
Relationships in class diagrams, 379, 382
Release manager role, 72
Releases and release process, 582–584
    customer testing in, 457–458
    to deployment teams, 586–587
    in Extreme Programming, 59–60
    notes for, 157
    plans, 536–537, 566–567
    in value stream, 685
    in version control systems, 141
Remote access
    Team Foundation Server, 489–490
    Team Foundation Version Control, 146
Remote deployment, 603–604
Repeated execution plans, 528
Report Builder, 678
Report Definition Language (RDL), 675, 681
Report Designer, 678–681
Reports, 83
    builds, 248–249
    deployment, 657
    in project management, 554–555
    in Team Explorer window, 20
    templates for, 112
Report Site, 16, 678
Repositories
    folders for, 150–151
    for sharing information, 129–131
    in version control system. See Version control
Requirement models, 368, 395–396
    customer stories, 404–405
    Domain Modeling and CRC cards, 396–401
    use case models, 403–404
    user interface models, 401–403

Requirements gathering, 614–617
Respect as Agile value
    Agile development, 122
    Extreme Programming, 43
Responding to change, 36
Responsibilities in CRC, 397–398
Retrospectives, 697
    overview, 697–698
    planning, 699
    preparation for, 698–699
Reusable application blocks, patterns in, 421
Reuse-Release Equivalence Principle, 425
Reverse-engineering AD diagrams, 646–647
Roles
    associated, 75–76
    customer, 70–72
    developer, 72–73
Rolling back versions
    deltas in, 135
    shared folders for, 128
    in version control systems, 134–135, 183–184
Rolling wave planning, 528
Root Cause Analysis practice, 687–688
Round-trip facilities, 647
Row fixtures, 465–470
RUP (Rational Unified Process), 54, 377

S

Sampling for performance, 331–332
Sanity tests, 582
Scaffolding in deployment, 590–591
Scenarios
    in MSF 4.0, 96
    in sequence diagrams, 382
    in use case models, 403
Scheduling daily builds, 239–240
SCM (Software Configuration Management), 142–144
Scope in plan control, 541
SDLC (software development life cycle), 58–59
SDM (System Definition Model), 627–628
Securities page, 169
Security
    groups
        membership, 88–89
        setting up, 724–725
    repository, 143
    team project settings, 91–94

version control, 133, 169–170
Windows Installer, 602–604
Self-organizing teams, 68
Sequence diagrams
for dynamic models, 413
UML, 382–385
Server parts of VSTS, 27
Project Portal, 27–29
Team Foundation Build, 29
Team Foundation Server, 27
Service-Oriented Architecture (SOA),
626–627
Setup, 715–716
machine and user identification, 726–727
network, 720–721
single evaluation servers, 717–719
software installation, 722–723
system settings, 723
user accounts and security groups,
724–725
Shared Code practice, 131–132, 356
SharePoint Services, 742–743
Sharing information, 127–128
repositories for, 129–131
Shared Code practice, 131–132
shared folders for, 128–129
Sharp Tools, 34
Shelveset (TFVC), 146, 187–190
Simple Design, 346
Simplicity
as Agile value
Agile development, 122
Extreme Programming, 42–43
Single-checkout approach, 136
Single Code Base practice, 140–141, 356
Sit Together practice, 73–74
Six Sigma, 691–692
Size
Agile teams, 68–69
stories, 516–517
Skeletal architectural models, 406–407
Slack practice, 568, 559
Smoke tests, 219, 221
SMS (Systems Management Server), 246,
587, 619
SOA (Service-Oriented Architecture),
626–627
Software
automated testing, 217–221
development economics of, 688–690

small team requirements, 733–739
software factories for, 429–430
values and traditions, 35
Software Configuration Management (SCM),
142–144
Software development area, 754–755
Software development life cycle (SDLC),
58–59
Software factories, 429–430
Software Project Environment (SPE), 14-15
Source code.
Class Designer for, 385–389
importing, 166
policies
coding standards in, 195, 200–201
overriding, 201–203
rules updating for, 201
static code analysis for, 196–200
protecting, 191–194
repositories for, 129–131
in Team Explorer window, 20
SourceSafe tool, 144
Spike folder, 149–151
Spike tasks, 531
SQL Server Analysis Services (SSAS), 675
SQL Server Business Intelligence
Development Studio, 678
SQL Server Integration Services (SSIS), 675
SQL Server Reporting Services (SSRS), 554,
675
Standard queries and reports, 670–672
State diagrams, 413–414
Static Code Analysis tool, 23
rules updating for, 201
for source code policies, 196–200
STDD (storytest-driven development),
454–455
costs and benefits, 455
testers, 457
Stereotypes in class diagrams, 380
Storage space, 755
Stories. See Customer stories
Stories practice, 513–514
Story points, 525
Storytest-driven development (STDD),
454–455
costs and benefits, 455
testers, 457
Strict locking, 136, 183
Structural models, 412–413

Structural tests, 220
Stubs in deployment, 590–591
Subversion version control systems, 133
Support role
    in Agile teams, 75
    for customers, 71
Support sites, 594
Support tasks, 531
Synchronizing
    Daily Builds, 227, 239
    deployment, 591–592
    libraries, 159
    repositories, 129, 140, 151
    shared data, 27
System Definition Model (SDM), 627–628
System Designer (SD) tool, 628, 649
    applications of, 652–653
    description, 26
    diagrams
        creating, 649–652
        Deployment Designer diagrams from,
            654–655
    settings and constraints, 652
System metaphor, 411
System performance, 337
System settings, 723
System tests, 582
Systems Management Server (SMS), 246,
    587, 619

T

TableFixture class, 477, 479
Tables
    for customer tests
        information, 493–495
        sequences of, 496–497
    for modeling in pairs, 371
Task boards, 557–558, 560
Task cards, 532–535
Task points, 519–520
Task work item, 96, 548
Tasks
    vs. features, 514, 567
    plans, 531–533
    in stories, 288–289
TDD. *See* Test-driven development (TDD)
Team Builds, 29–30. *See also* Team
    Foundation Build (TFB)

Team Continuity practice, 77–78
Team Foundation Build (TFB), 16, 29,
    229–230
    build management, 245–249
    Build Validation Test for, 233–235
    Daily Builds, 239–240
    deleting build products, 243–244
    FIT with, 481
        automated customer tests, 487–491
        customer test introduction, 491–498
        customer tests in Build Lab, 482–486
    integration builds, 240–243
    MSBuild engine role in, 231–232
    operation of, 230–231
    permissions for, 235–236
    scaling up team integration builds,
        249–253
    setting up, 230
    types, 237–238
Team Foundation Server (TFS), 16, 27, 81,
    149
    backup and restore, 170–171
    Client Tier, 16
    extracting data from, 674–682
    folders for, 149–151
    importing source files, 166
    licensing issues, 740–742
    remote access to, 489–490
    reports from. *See* Technical reports
    repositories in, 174
    security settings, 92–93, 169–170
    source control options, 168–169
    structure for, 149–160
    Team Project options, 167–168
    Visual Studio options, 168–169
    for workgroups, 720–721, 740–741, 751
Team Foundation Version Control (TFVC),
    127, 173, 581
    branching in, 185–187
    in coding, 173–176
    features, 145–147
    merging changes in, 180–183
    rolling back to previous versions,
        183–184
    shelves in, 187–190
    source code policies in, 195–203
    source code protection in, 191–194
    workspaces, 177–180

Team Projects, 21, 81–82
  artifacts from, 82–85
  deleting, 87
  documents, 152, 156–158
  membership, 88–89
  MSF for, 85–86
  policy settings migration, 201
  portal and report site access, 90–91
  security settings, 91–94
  service access, 89–90
  version control options, 167–168
Teams. *See* Agile teams
Technical risk in prioritizing stories, 523
Technical writer role, 71
Templates
  changing, 115
  importing and exporting, 112–114
  for processes, 86, 111–116
  for Setup Project, 604
  projects, 421
Ten Minute Build practice, 218, 224–225, 227, 356
Test adapters, 284
Test Case Management tool, 25
Test cases, 270
Test cycles, 222
  daily builds, 227–228
  integration builds, 225–227
  local builds, 222–223
Test-driven development (TDD), 53, 60, 63, 261–262, 265
  class diagrams for, 378
  code coverage, 325–330
  cycles in, 271–277
  list of tests in, 269
  nature of, 265
  operating system development team story, 262–263
  performance. *See* Performance analysis
  refactoring. *See* Refactoring
  rhythm of, 265–266
  in Shared Code practice, 132
  Test-First Programming. *See* Test-First Programming (TFP)
  test harness for, 269–271
  top down vs. bottom up approach, 268
  in version control, 174

Test-First Programming (TFP)
  applying, 277
  code coverage, 330
  conclusion, 301
  cycles in, 271–277
  finding tests for, 278–279
  implementing, 294–300
  list of tests in, 278
  for modeling in pairs, 371
  for performance, 336
  refactoring in, 280–281, 299–300
  stories for, 287–289
  test lists for, 289–293
  with user interface. *See* User interface
  Visual Studio Projects for, 283–287
Test-First Programming (TFP) practice, 266–267
Test fixtures, 445
Test harnesses
  in test-driven development, 269–271
  in Test-First Programming, 284–285
  vs. test runners, 483
Test lists, 278, 289–293, 454
Test Load Agent, 749
Test Manager window
  for Build Validation Tests, 234
  Visual Studio Professional, 19
Test managers
  OSPACS team, 3
Test runners, 483
Testable attribute, 515
Testers
  for developers, 72
  PC licensing issues, 746–747
  in storytest-driven development, 457
Testing Object-Oriented Systems, 221
Testing policy, 194
Tests
  customer. *See* Customer tests
  FIT. *See* Framework for Integrated Test (FIT)
  for integration, 216–217
  for interface design, 347
  TDD. *See* Test-driven development (TDD)
  TFP. *See* Test-First Programming (TFP)
  in value stream, 685
  in Waterfall process, 54
  Web services, 644–646

TFB. *See* Team Foundation Build (TFB)
TFP. *See* Test-First Programming (TFP)
TFS. *See* Team Foundation Server (TFS)
TFS Data Warehouse, 675–678
TFS Installation Guide, 16
TFS Trial Edition setup, 719
TFVC. *See* Team Foundation Version Control (TFVC)
Thin user interface layers, 344–346
Thin vertical slices, 556
Third-party libraries, 158–159
Time scales
    in planning, 530–538
    in project management, 568
Timelines, 700–701
    creating, 701–703
    discoveries from, 706–707
    mining for gold process, 703–704
    for project structure, 705–706
    results from, 708–709
Tools
    buy or build decisions, 34
    OSPACS team impressions, 45–46
    VSTS, 22
        all editions, 22–23
        Visual Studio Architect Edition, 26–27
        Visual Studio Developer Edition, 22–24
        Visual Studio Tester Edition, 24–25
Top down approach, 268
Toyota Production System, 683, 687
Tracker role, 73
Traditional projects vs. agile development, 53–57
Trainer role
    in Agile teams, 75
    for customers, 71
Translation of TFS data, 675
Twain, Mark, 289

U

UML Distilled, 377, 392
UML Modeling tool, 23
Unified Modeling Language (UML)
    diagrams, 358–359, 377
    class, 377–382
    Class Designer for, 388
    sequence, 382–385
Unit Test tool, 24–25

Unit tests, 220
    performance session for, 333–334
    setting up, 285–287
    support for, 283–285
Update Only When It Hurts practice, 366
Usage statistics, support for, 594
Use cases, 57, 382, 403–404
User interface, 339
    action fixtures, 470–476
    Big Design Up Front, 348
    defining, 340
    modeling, 401–403
    sample design, 346–348
    task lists for, 341
    thin layers, 344–346
    Windows Forms for, 342–344
User stories. *See* Customer stories

V

Validation
    Build Validation Tests, 233–235
    Deployment Designer diagrams, 656–657
Value, 665–666
    in Agile Modeling, 363
    generating. *See* Generating business value
    in prioritizing stories, 522
    technical reports. *See* Technical reports
Values. *See* Agile values
Velocity
    as rate of progress measure, 529–530
    in story cost estimation, 520
Version control, 123–124, 133
    atomic check-in, 134
    conclusion, 147–148
    integration in, 134
    labeling and branching, 138–139, 146
    locking and merging, 136–138
    rolling back versions, 134–135
    security, 133
    Single Code Base practice, 140–141
    Software Configuration Management, 142–144
    support for, 144–147
    for Team Documents, 156–158
    templates for, 112
    TFS. *See* Team Foundation Server (TFS)
    TFVC. *See* Team Foundation Version Control (TFVC)
Virtual PC environment, 217, 599, 717–718

Visibility symbols, 380
Visio for Enterprise Architects tool, 23,
    389–390
Vision statement, 157–158
Visual Studio
    solutions, projects, and directories in,
        151–154
    source control options, 168–169
    version control system integration in,
        144–145
Visual Studio Industry Partner (VSIP)
    program, 30
Visual Studio Professional, 18–19
Visual Studio SDK, 30–31
Visual Studio Team Edition for Architects,
    17, 26–27, 410
Visual Studio Team Edition for Database
    Professionals, 17
Visual Studio Team Edition for Developers,
    17, 22–24
Visual Studio Team Edition for Testers, 17
Visual Studio Tester Edition, 24–25
Vlissides, John, 416
VSIP (Visual Studio Industry Partner)
    program, 30

W

Wake, William, 281, 515
Waterfall projects
    phases in, 54–55
    value generated by, 689–690
Web services, 644–646
Web Services Description Language (WSDL),
    627
Web Test tool, 25
Weekly Cycle practice, 536
White box testing, 220
Whiteboards
    for customer tests, 492–493
    in office space, 755–756
Whole Team practice, 67–68
Williams, Laurie, 39
Window Scheduled Task Wizard, 239
Windows
    Code Coverage Results, 326–328
    Error List, 196–198, 657
    Pending Changes, 181-182
    Performance Explorer, 333–334
    Query Editor, 676–677

Query Results, 549
Solution Explorer, 18
Source Control Explorer, 184
Team Build Report, 242
Team Explorer window, 20–22, 86
Test Results, 241, 295–296
Test View, 19, 298–300
Windows Forms applications
    creating, 607
    for user interface, 342–344, 475
Windows Installer, 597–598
    basic concepts, 598–600
    operation, 600–602
    security for, 602–604
Windows SharePoint Services (WSS), 112,
    156–157
WinFITRunner, 454
Wirfs-Brock, Rebecca, 396–397
Wizards
    Import IIS Settings, 636–637
    Performance, 333
    Release, 611–613
    Report Server Project, 678
    Team Build Type, 237
    Team Project, 85–86, 129
    Virtual Machine, 718
Womack, James, 683
Work items
    adding, 108–109
    Check-in Policy constraint, 194
    for projects, 83, 547–551
    templates for, 112
Work products, 83
Workgroups, TFS, 720–721, 740–741, 751
Workspace
    permissions, 92–93
    for TFVC, 177–180
WSDL (Web Services Description Language),
    627
WSS (Windows SharePoint Services), 112,
    156–157

X–Z

XP. *See* Extreme Programming (XP)

Yesterday's Weather rule, 530

Zones in Logical Datacenter Designer,
    631–633

THIS BOOK IS SAFARI ENABLED

INCLUDES FREE 45-DAY ACCESS TO THE ONLINE EDITION

The Safari® Enabled icon on the cover of your favorite technology book means the book is available through Safari Bookshelf. When you buy this book, you get free access to the online edition for 45 days.

Safari Bookshelf is an electronic reference library that lets you easily search thousands of technical books, find code samples, download chapters, and access technical information whenever and wherever you need it.

TO GAIN 45-DAY SAFARI ENABLED ACCESS TO THIS BOOK:

- Go to **http://www.awprofessional.com/safarienabled**
- Complete the brief registration form
- Enter the coupon code found in the front of this book on the "Copyright" page

Addison
Wesley

Microsoft .NET Development Series

0321154894

0321194454

0321374479

0321113594

0321334884

0321411757

0321160770

0321246756

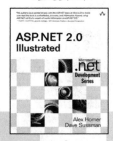

0321418344

0321350170

0321150775

0321154932

0201760401

0201760398

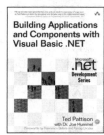

0201734958

0321341384

0321169514

A Developer's Guide to SQL Server 2005

Bob Beauchemin
Dan Sullivan

0321382188

Essential .NET Volume 1
The Common Language Runtime

Don Box
with Chris Sells

0201734117

The .NET Developer's Guide to Windows Security

Keith Brown

0321228359

Effective Use of Microsoft Enterprise Library
Building Blocks for Creating Enterprise Applications and Services

Len Fenster

0321334213

Software Engineering with Microsoft Visual Studio Team System

Sam Guckenheimer
with Juan J. Perez

0321278720

The C# Programming Language
Second Edition

Anders Hejlsberg
Scott Wiltamuth
Peter Golde

0321334434

Enterprise Services with the .NET Framework
Developing Distributed Business Solutions with .NET Enterprise Services

Christian Nagel

032124673X

Data Binding with Windows Forms 2.0
Programming Smart Client Data Applications with .NET

Brian Noyes

032126892X

Smart Client Deployment with ClickOnce
Deploying Windows Forms Applications with ClickOnce

Brian Noyes

0321197690

Essential ASP.NET 2.0

Fritz Onion
with Keith Brown

0321237706

Designing Forms for Microsoft Office InfoPath and Forms Services 2007

Scott Roberts
Hagen Green

0321410599

eXtreme .NET
Introducing eXtreme Programming Techniques to .NET Developers

Dr. Neil Roodyn

0321303636

Windows Forms 2.0 Programming

Chris Sells
Michael Weinhardt

0321267966

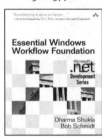

Essential Windows Workflow Foundation

Dharma Shukla
Bob Schmidt

0321399838

Programming in the .NET Environment

Damien Watkins
Mark Hammond
Brad Abrams

0201770180

Pragmatic ADO.NET
Data Access for the Internet World

Shawn Wildermuth

0201745682

.NET Compact Framework Programming with C#

Paul Yao
David Durant

0321174038

.NET Compact Framework Programming with Visual Basic .NET

Paul Yao
David Durant

0321174046